The industrial urban community

The industrial
urban community
historical and
comparative perspectives

nels anderson
university of new brunswick

APPLETON-CENTURY-CROFTS
Educational Division
New York   MEREDITH CORPORATION

To helen my wife

Contents

Preface *ix*

1 Modern society and the urban culture *1*

2 Urban communities and their functions *24*

3 Evolution of the urban community *44*

4 Rural ways of life and the confrontation with urbanism *68*

5 Ecology and the human community *88*

6 Industrial urbanism and population *110*

7 Urbanism and mobility phenomena *133*

8 Urbanism and its incongruities *157*

9 The behavior of urban agglomerates *178*

10 Social groups and classes in cities *202*

11 The family and industrial urbanism *222*

12 Communities and their collective work *244*

13 Work in the industrial urban life *265*

14 Industrial urbanism and leisure *293*

15 Urban people and their livelihood *318*

16 Industrial urbanism and welfare *344*

17 Social control in urban society *370*

18 The urban habitat and urban planning *396*

Index *423*

Preface

What subject matter should be included in an urban sociology text could hardly be determined by reading existing works, which is not said in depreciation. Existing works differ widely, and there is no reason why they should not. One approaches the subject with his own views and he uses the method that serves him. There are many perspectives which may fruitfully be used in the study of cities.

Were the question put to me, I would be hard hit to describe my own approach, which I must now do. In a not too systematic way, I have tried to carry five major themes through these chapters. These are:

POPULATION AND URBANISM

World population in every major region is making for urban growth. If half the population of this globe will be living in cities of 100,000 or more by 1990, we can be sure that half that number will be living in cities of smaller size. The prospect of urbanizing and industrializing thousands of millions is staggering. The more people crowd into cities, the more jobs must be provided, the shorter the water supply, and the more air and water will be polluted. Mankind will one day meet these problems as well as the challenge of underemployment, poverty, and slums; until then we can expect the pressures to continue, if not increase.

POLLUTION AND SANITATION

We can expect the shortage of housing to worsen before it betters. Too few economies are able to meet these demands. Funds must first be used to provide jobs and to keep the urban habitat clean. In many re-

gions pollution has passed the danger point, destroying animal and vege-
table life, and is threatening the health of humans. The cities of highest
culture and greatest affluence are the most threatened. Says Abel Wolman, for each urbanite there is produced 120 gallons of sewage and four
pounds of refuse, and nearly two pounds of pollutants are blown into
the air. Multiply that by the millions of urbanites in any industrial
country.

OUR CIVILIZATION'S GLOBAL ARENA

An oil syndicate has a hundred affiliates around the world, an auto
manufacturing company of worldwide reach has a greater income than
the national budget of Holland. A single firm, located in a city of a half-
million, sends its products to cities on every continent. No corner of the
earth is out of reach of the global news networks. Every major sport
becomes an international sport. Whether we think of urbanism or industrialism, neither is held by political bounds or restrained by traditional deterrent. This spread from city to city radiates out of every city.

TECHNOLOGY, SCIENCE, AND CITIES

Probably since they first appeared cities have been seedbeds for invention and innovation. They needed to be for their survival. They
have become, for the same reason, the habitat of technology and science.
They sustain themselves by making merchandise of knowledge and
know-how. As this influence spreads they prosper by it, and attract to
themselves talent from their hinterlands. In this wise, ways of work and
life in rural areas are transformed, and in the process people are increasingly drawn to the cities until the peasant is a vanished species.

THE SOCIAL PERTINENCE OF WORK

Sociologists, and other social scientists no less, so it seems to me, tend
to avoid any but a token discussion of work, perhaps the most vital factor in the development of cultures. Change the ways of work of a people
and their culture must change. It is only as cities can find more work and
new types of work that they are able to receive more income. Mainly
in terms of types of work they do, these urban masses come to be structured into those social layers we call classes. They strive for education
that they may be identified with higher-level occupations. Work is a
good word, and it is time to cease handling it gingerly.

There is a bias which I must confess (but which I enjoy somewhat) against those who write or declaim against cities as they are. These critics have been around for generations, since before Shelley described Hell as a "city much like London." Cities have always been ugly because they have always been work places, from grubby little shops to smoky, noisy factories filled with ordinary people in dirty clothes, whose poor abodes often irritate the aesthetic critic. Whether philosopher, poet, or professional journalist, the critic often fails to understand that growing cities must and do change, building and rebuilding. More people pour in and move about, competing for advantage. In many world regions those who pour in have no other alternative. This is not to underrate beauty, but there are times when beauty must wait on bed, board, and jobs. I am optimist enough to believe that these urgencies will one day be met.

A century ago John Ruskin wrote *Fors Clavigera*, his long argument against the chaotic growth of grimy cities in which men were degraded and increasingly enslaved by machines. He wished all to return to the land. And a century ago Samuel Butler wrote *Erewhon*, his utopian report on a mythical people who centuries ago had attained great technical efficiency. When these people discovered that machines were withering the mental faculties and physical capacities of men, they destroyed all machines and even wiped out all technical vocabulary. They found heaven on earth by returning to the simple rural way of life.

The same arguments are with us still, advanced by thinkers who fail to recognize that since the 1870's the world population has increased fourfold and urban population by twelve times.

I cannot run with those who speak of "cities in final decay," and who nostalgically wish for the creative craftsmanship of medieval times. I prefer to believe that only in the city, man's most ingenious invention, will he be able to meet the challenges that threaten. It is only in the city where the problems of population pressure will be met. The urban way of lowering birth rates as affluence goes up is very old, although there may be a generation delay before newcomers acquire those urban attitudes. In the meanwhile underemployment, poverty, and slums may encourage the notion that cities are in "final decay."

Industrial work, a revolutionary urban invention, is responsible for separating leisure from work Many thinkers view this transition with concern, believing that the wholesome life is realized only as one centers his major interests in work. Instead, people increasingly view work as a way to earn the money to sustain their interests in living. It seems at present difficult to think of the good citizen as one who can perform his work well but who keeps his job interests separate from his nonwork interests, who regards leisure as his own time, while work is the time he sells, along with skills and talent, to the impersonal employer. This is called unnatural and the attending attitudes are called alienation.

Not unlikely, our thinking on this matter will change. We certainly need to regard work as a necessity, but of the two leisure is more a blessing

It must be recognized that cities, to the point of pain for some critics, are inefficient and wasteful. Facing urgent problems (pollution, for example) is usually delayed until almost too late. Or the proffered remedy is less than enough for the ailment. The obvious is often too long debated by those of clashing views and interests. That in the long run may be a virtue; the city can never be brought under the control of some single wise authority whose thinking for 1970 may be called a great mistake in 1990. Warren G. Bennis and Philip E. Slater, in *The Temporary Society,* touch this point. They see the city as ever exceeding itself and, in our time, it cannot do otherwise. It must grow and it must change. It must be planned and planning must be continuous. There can be no final plan; that of yesterday may have to be altered this way or that for tomorrow. The direction, the rate, and the nature of changes are predictable only to a minor degree.

Planning, then, must be flexible, and efforts to control must be equally flexible. This society is both industrial and urban; therefore, as Bennis and Slater hold, it must also be democratic. A democratic society can face its problems, but only in its own way. If this kind of industrial society ceases to be dynamic and democratic, we can expect it to stagnate. The prospect of such a turn of events seems at present remote.

I must acknowledge my debt to John N. Edwards who read this manuscript as he would his own. I am also grateful to Andrew K. Morrow and Marilyn S. Sutherland for help with bibliography and the index.

N. A.

The industrial urban community

Modern society and the urban culture | 1

THE CITY AND URBAN LIFE

Our attention in this study is on the urban community, primarily the urban community in the more industrial countries. This kind of urban community is sustained by an industrial system of work, even if it is in a country in the industrialized West but is not itself industrial. It is identified with an industrial economy and its urbanism is industry-based.

We recognize that not all countries are equally industrial, but to the extent to which they are, their industrialism resides in cities, or its regulation radiates from cities. We know, too, less industrial countries everywhere are striving, even if awkwardly, to become more industrial. And the model being imitated is the industrialism of the West.

Moreover, we can speak of cities as having a way of life, which is very different from the rural way of life. In this chapter we will consider some of the salient features of urban life, sometimes referred to as style of life. As we shall see, this way of life, centering in cities, radiates its influence outward. This has always been true of cities, but in our day, the means being more effective, urbanism as a way of life spreads its influence outward in a more rapid and compelling fashion than ever before.

When we speak of urbanism as a way of life we think of people earning their livelihood at industrial types of work. Normally ruralism as a way of life is associated with people earning their livelihood from agriculture, fishing, or herding. As between the two ways of life, urbanism is more dynamic and responsive in accepting change, ruralism is more tradition-oriented and resistant to change. In general, urbanism is associated with living in cities or towns, while ruralism is associated with village life. In the more industrial countries, however, people may be quite urbanized although they live in villages and not in cities. They may become quite urbanized and continue to engage in agricultural work.

To understand the city and its life, we need to see more than the urban place as a spot on a map. Its life is not confined by political boundaries; it is influenced by, as it also influences, all surrounding places. Its population is rarely composed of one homogeneous people, but may be a mixture of races, nationality groups, social classes, and other groupings, all tied together by certain common interests. Nor do we understand such an urban community in "still picture" terms, however well it may be described for any particular year. It changes through time, and every aspect of it has its own unique antecedents, and is changing in terms of its present, its past, and its prospects.

Precisely because each urban community has its own unique antecedents, economically, politically, socially, culturally, it may be seen as being "different" in many ways from another city in the same country, yet in many ways quite like that other city. As we shall note in another chapter, each city in its development may be subject to different geographical and ecological influences. All these unique features figure in its traditions. The people of a city constitute a society, and it will be different in some ways from the society of the people of another city. Also, the same people in each city comprise a community. Here let us note Wirth's distinction between a society and a community.

1. A territorial base distributed in space of men, institutions, and activities, close living together on the basis of kinship and organic interdependence, and a common life based on mutual correspondence of interests tend to characterize a community.
2. Society, on the other hand, has come more to refer to the willed and contractural relationships between men which, it has been assumed, are less directly affected than their organic relationships by their distribution in space. . . .
3. Of social groups there may be distinguished two general orders; those that are best conceived as communities and those that can best be understood if regarded as societies. These may indeed be the same groups. Every social group may be said to be distributed in space, although in some this territorial distribution may be of minor significance when compared with other aspects of group life.[1]

To look at an aggregate of people behaving collectively as members of families, churches, political parties, patriotic societies, labor unions, and social clubs—as having agreements and mutual obligations—is to see them as a society. To look at the same aggregate in terms of their distribution and activities with respect to an area, which may be a village,

[1] Louis Wirth, "Scope and Problems of Community," in Albert J. Reiss, Jr. (Ed.), *On Cities and Social Life,* Chicago, University of Chicago Press, 1964, pp. 166–167.

town, or city, as having work places here, homes there, recreation places elsewhere, and as being affected by the distribution, is to see them as a community. Obviously, the concepts of society and community interpenetrate.

An important characteristic of urbanism, to which reference will be made often in the pages ahead, is its increasing universality. Cities are places of different sizes, having particular physical characteristics, all of which need to be considered. They are also human collectivities, people behaving in ways that reflect the needs and features of urban living. That way of life, with pertinent variations, tends to be characteristic of all cities in the world. Thus we can speak of urbanism as global. It becomes increasingly global as commerce and industry become increasingly intermeshed in global networks.

Let us, then, list some of the more obvious manifestations of modern urbanism as global phenomena. Each of these represents a cluster of industries which are tied into world networks.

1. *News and communication.* A businessman or socialite in any city or village, in a very short time can speak with another in almost any part of the world. And the news-gathering network touches every section of the earth. So penetrating is the news network that no government can prevent news from getting out.
2. *Fads and fashions.* The mode in dress, hair style, latest song hits, and new fads, whether from New York, Hollywood, Paris, or London, are known about the same moment in cities around the world and quickly imitated. They later are copied by rural areas surrounding great cities.
3. *Entertainment and sport.* The movie industry deliberately produces films for the world market, more so than two or three decades ago. International competition in all forms of sport and international interest in these sports increases. More than ever tourism becomes a globe-trotting form of leisure activity, an industry supported by governments everywhere.
4. *Transportation and amenities.* Means of transport (railway, airplane, ship, automobile) come to be technically similar in all countries, and their use increases. They tend to stimulate globally a highly uniform "culture of mobility."

As any international traveler knows, it matters little to which city he comes, he will find great similarities in hotel services, restaurants, and other services. He will find goods of the standard brands in the stores. Indeed, the downtown in any world city, despite some unique features, has much in common with the downtown of any other world city.

Generally it is the metropolis that becomes a world city. More effort is expended in the metropolis to discover and develop faraway markets. Small cities may become known only for some special product produced there, e.g., movies from Hollywood, silverware from Solingen, Germany.

The urbanism that spreads through the distribution of things and services, assumes the aspect of a civilization, compared with which the
civilizations of Babylon or Greece were elemental and merely regional.
This blending of world cities into a fairly uniform global image is seen
by Mumford as an invisible world city.[2]

The more we take into account the global nature of urbanism and
industrialism, the less satisfying it becomes to study either in terms of
one country alone. Certainly, we can study cities structurally, their rate
and manner of growth and change, or their history in terms of countries
or wider regions. We can also study their economic bases and organizational life in national or regional terms. Such studies are highly necessary, but urban sociology is concerned with phenomena that extend
across national and regional boundaries. The great metropolis belongs
to the world, and needs to, if it is to effectively serve the country where
it is located. As observed by Kerr, who sees industrialism as an urbanizing force, the entire industrial urban complex assumes a one-world
aspect.

> To fulfill its logic, industrialism must sweep before it many of the be-
> havioral patterns of prior times, as it has certainly done with almost
> astonishing success. There are few things so changeable as "customs." In
> terms of the daily lives of men, however diverse they may be in parts of
> the world today, one can foresee with great clarity what they must be-
> come. The present can be penetrated best from the vantage point of the
> future because its motto of the future is *e pluribus unum,* and *unum* is
> fairly well known.[3]

DISTINGUISHING CITY, TOWN, VILLAGE

In most countries city, town, and village are defined in terms of
number of population, and this is done for public administration
reasons. These definitions may differ by country, by states, or by provinces
within countries, or they may differ from time to time. In some countries
any place above 1,000 or 2,000 inhabitants is called "urban." In the
United States it is any place of 2,500 or over, while it is any place of
5,000 inhabitants or more in India. For various administrative purposes
and for types of demographic comparison, identifying urban places in
terms of size is essential. Thus cities come to be grouped in classes by

---

[2] Lewis Mumford, *The City in History,* reviewed with two other urban books in an
article by Sylvia L. Thrupp, "The Creativity of Cities," *Comparative Studies in Society
and History,* Vol. 4, 1961–1962, pp. 53–64.

[3] Clark Kerr, "Changing Social Structures." See Wilbert E. Moore and Arnold S.
Feldman (Eds.), *Labor Commitment and Social Change in Developing Countries,* New
York, Social Science Research Council, 1961, p. 359.

size: 2,500 to 10,000; 10,000 to 25,000; and so on to those of a million or more.

For most sociological considerations it is usually sufficient to think of small cities in industrial countries as those from about 50,000 to 100,000; middle-size cities as those from 100,000 to 500,000. Often a city of 500,000 in a sparsely inhabited region would have the status of a metropolis. This would be less true of a middle-size city on the Atlantic seaboard of the United States, in Britain, or in Germany. Wherever located, cities of a million or more assume metropolitan character.

"Town" is a designation with many uses, although commonly it has reference to the comparatively small cities, 25,000 more or less. However, in the expression "town and country" the term "town" takes in all urban places. Any urban place may be the destination when a villager goes "to town." Moreover, an urbanite living in a residential area of a city, if he goes to the mid-city area, often called "downtown," may speak of "going to town." The meanings are various, but are usually evident in the context. As we use the term, no specific meaning is given to "town," and we follow the common usage.

"Village" also has many uses, although as we will use the term, it designates rural communities, more identified with agricultural than with industrial types of work. Sometimes a place is called a village and may be so by the legal definition of the state, although containing thousands of inhabitants. Often a housing development outside a city, or even within city limits, may be called a village. The idea of village is often associated by urbanites with a rural setting—trees, grass, and ample space— but rarely do these city-made villages capture the rural atmosphere. "Village" acquires still another meaning when used to identify areas found in some cities in which artists, poets, and various literary types locate.

Jane Jacobs, a widely quoted writer on urban matters offers these definitions of city, town, and village about which some may raise questions.

1. City—A settlement that consistently generates its economic growth from its own local economy.
2. Stagnant city—A settlement that formerly grew as a city, but has stopped doing so.
3. Metropolitan area—Economically, it means the same as "city." Politically, it means a city that has physically expanded beyond its former boundaries, in the process engulfing former towns and, in some instances, coalescing with other, formerly separate, cities.
4. Town—A settlement that does not generate its growth from its own local economy and has never done so. The occasional export a town may have generated for itself has produced no consistent self-generating growth thereafter.[4]

4 Jane Jacobs, *The Economy of Cities,* New York, Random House, 1969, p. 262.

THE RURAL-URBAN CONTINUUM

It is a truism that the cosmopolitan city is the most urban community in its region and the remote rural village would be among the least urban places within the region. If we assume certain traits to be more characteristic of urban places, while other traits are more characteristic of rural places, we may conclude that urban traits diminish with distance from the city and decreasing contacts with the city. Rural traits, on the other hand, diminish with nearness to the city. In these terms, many sociologists speak of a rural-urban continuum, the most rural places at one extreme and the most urban places at the other. Other places, according to their degree of urbanism and/or ruralism, would be distributed between the extremes of the continuum.

One difficulty with the continuum concept concerns the inability to measure degrees of urbanism found in different places. Duncan studied cities in the United States of 25,000 and under, taking account of such characteristics as occupation, level of education, married males and females, fertility ratio, median income, and others. As we would expect, he found minor differences between places in terms of their size.[5] Size alone is not a sufficient measure. The ways of life in places also needs to be considered. Moreover, a city of 5,000 or 10,000 half an hour from a metropolis might well be more urban than another city of the same size hours from the same metropolis.

Every sociologist knows that there are qualitative differences between the more urban places and the typical rural places. Some of these differences can be measured when comparing a particular small city with a large one. For example, there might be different work behaviors, different institutional behaviors, different small groups or "social set" behaviors. Social class structures are likely to be quite different. Also, different types of urbanism will be found in comparing cities such as Washington with nearby Baltimore, French-oriented Montreal with English-oriented Toronto, staid Liverpool with differently staid London.

Those who hold to the continuum concept could doubtless find other ways of testing the theory's validity. Dewey would compare places in terms of five "inevitable accompaniments of urbanization." Each of these, he avers, would be least evident in rural and most evident in urban places. These urban characteristics are pertinent here.

1. *Anonymity.* Urban people tend to be strangers to one another, contacts are transient and superficial. Not so with rural people.

5 Otis D. Duncan, "Community Size and Rural-Urban Continuum," reprinted in Jack P. Gibbs (Ed.), *Urban Research Methods*, New York, Van Nostrand, 1962, pp. 490–504.

2. *Division of labor.* Urban work is much more specialized than rural work and occupations are much more numerous.
3. *Heterogeneity of life.* Urban populations include a wide mixture of types, rural populations are more homogeneous.
4. *Impersonal relationships.* These are normal in cities, but in rural places closer acquaintance is expected.
5. *Symbols of status.* Urban status derives largely from outward visible evidences; manners, speech, dress, badges, place of residence, which is much less true of rural places.[6]

These characteristics of urban life, except for the division of labor, can not be easily measured statistically, but this is not a sufficient reason for discarding the concept. Despite the many difficulties, it has some value for discussion purposes. Dewey adds, "to argue, as has been done here, for reduced importance of the rural-urban continuum is not to seek its elimination from sociology."

QUALITIES AND DIMENSIONS OF URBANISM

Urbanism itself is mainly qualitative, much as many aspects of human life, especially those qualities of a person embraced in the term "personality." Realistically, we do not speak of the personality of a city, although that is often done, as when one city as an entity is compared with another. If one has an image of a particular city it is apt to be couched in personality terms. Verbs and adjectives may be used in describing a city such as one uses in describing persons. One may see the behavior of urban people as collectivities, and he may describe that behavior as he would the behavior of an individual, often in terms of praise or blame. Thus Kallen, after describing New York as a city that all other cities envy and imitate, against which no other city has been able "to set itself up as a rival," proceeds to call New York a most unthinking place. He complains that New Yorkers have next to no understanding of and little interest in the whys and the nature of their city. There is no conscious "idea of the city"; each inhabitant follows his own course of self-interest.[7]

Such complaints can be heard about any great city, indeed about any large urban place, often uttered by persons who would be unhappy living elsewhere. What may be praised by one may be condemned by another. Whether expressed by scholars or the less intellectual, they are judgments relating to quality.

[6] Richard Dewey, "The Rural-Urban Continuum; Real but Relatively Unimportant," *American Journal of Sociology,* Vol. 66, No. 1, July 1960, pp. 60–66.
[7] Horace M. Kallen, "City Planning and the Idea of the City," *Social Forces,* Vol. 23, No. 2, Spring 1956, p. 186.

Friedmann sees in urban life "a frame of mind, and a manner of thinking, speaking and behaving," in a habitat where any stranger is at home. These characteristics are most evident in large urban places.

> The spirit of the city arises from its social heterogeneity, a place where different languages are spoken, different customs practiced, different gods worshipped. Always it is a brilliantly exciting contrast to the monotony of the village in which life is bound to the cycle of the seasons. . . . The city has color and variety in its markets, bazaars, and workshops. It has the glittering bubble of entertainment; circuses, games, dancing girls, music, theaters, restaurants, where consciousness of self is brought to an acute sensibility. Ideas are formed, change in fads and fashions is the order of the day. News and discussion of news are essential to it. Here the present and the future interact. The true urbanite is always *en currant*. There is a place also for scholars who peer into the past and into cosmic space. Every major creative effort either originates or comes to full bloom in the city.[8]

Dimensions of urbanism, as used here, have reference to the relative presence of different aspects or characteristics. Dewey, in the citation above, gave five "accompaniments" of urbanism: anonymity, division of labor, heterogeneity of life, impersonal relationships, and symbols of status. While these are descriptive, other aspects should be considered. In the 11 "dimensions" which follow, the five characteristics mentioned by Dewey are included, some of them more than once. The dimensions appear in this order, although the order is not indicative of their relative importance.

1. *Division of labor and specialization*—resulting largely from economic competition and inventiveness in urban places.
2. *Man and his machines*—resulting from urban innovation and use of technology to increase production.
3. *Places and mobility*—relating mainly to changes in residence, occupations, jobs, and the social consequences.
4. *Man-made environment*—concerns the separation of urban man from the natural environment by his constructions.
5. *Implications of the clock*—relates to man's being separated from natural time and his use of mechanical time.
6. *The individual and familism*—concerns man's turning in cities from ascriptive familial control to individualism.
7. *Compulsions to form secondary relationships*—relates to the formation of voluntary bureaucratic groups for mass societal living.
8. *The proclivity for adaptation*—has reference to urban man's readiness to accept change, or expect it, and to initiate it.

[8] John Friedmann, "Cities in Social Transformation," *Comparative Studies in Society and History*, Vol. 4, 1961–1962, p. 88.

9. *Commitment to superlatives*—concerns the urban urge for beating records and for bigger, faster, and better material innovations.
10. *Money as the definer of values*—the transition from familial quasi-subsistence to the money economy.
11. *Writing, records, and bureaucracy*—the increasing use of all three are related to the growth of industrial urbanism.

1. *Division of Labor and Specialization*

In any society a division of labor may be found, but in the least developed societies it involves a division of tasks between males and females plus a division between the more able-bodied and the less able-bodied. The special tasks in such a society might be healing the sick or working with metals, tasks performed by particular individuals. All other work could be performed by most of the people. The child in such a society grows up in the presence of his life's work and he learns about all he needs to know before reaching adolescence. In about the same way, although the economy is more advanced, the boy in a Newfoundland fishing village would come to know much of his life's work before becoming an adult. He would learn by contact the whole gamut of tasks related to fishing, even to building the boats needed.

In the medieval city the guildsmen had their crafts and each craft had its "mysteries" which were learned by the apprentice from the master craftsman. Here was the beginning of a division of labor based on learned skills. As a precise division evolved between specialties and more easily learned crafts, there began to evolve a functional hierarchy in which specialization caused "one or another of these functions to predominate." [9]

Occupations in the preindustrial city, as in the middle centuries, were family properties. The son inherited his father's occupation, and he learned from his father the skill and the approved ways of work. In the industrial work system which prevails in the modern community, occupations are determined by the needs of the production process and are little influenced by occupational tradition. Many earlier occupations no longer exist. Present occupations are numbered in the thousands, and most of these continue to change with changing technology. They tend to be classified in broad categories as unskilled, semi-skilled, skilled, white-collar, supervisory and technical, managerial, self-employed, and owner. Entrance to any occupation is based largely on the level of formal education achieved. All occupations in a work place come to be integrated in a work process until, as Drucker observes, it is the plant, not the worker, that is the producer of goods and services.[10]

[9] John H. Mundy and Peter Riesenberg, *The Medieval Town*, New York, Van Nostrand, 1958, p. 10.
[10] Peter F. Drucker, *The New Society*, New York, Harper & Row, 1950, pp. 22 and 26.

It may be said of all occupations in the modern society that none is secure in the face of technological and other change. However, the higher an occupation is in the occupational hierarchy, the greater its security. Increasingly, all occupations above the unskilled level call for higher levels of skill and education. Moreover, the more efficient industry becomes, the more it will call for specialized occupations and the less it will be able to utilize unskilled workers.[11]

2. *Urban Man and His Machines*

While machines contribute to man's convenience and enable his level of living to rise, they are condemned by many as destructive of cherished values, and they have been charged with being physically and mentally damaging to man as a worker. There is little agreement about these charges. What is pertinent in the present connection is that the machine, seen collectively, in the course of less than two centuries has been instrumental in changing radically both the organization of society and the cultures of advanced countries, and is doing so in the countries which are industrializing. It has modified social values and changed vocabularies. It has increased the tempo of work and living, and rendered man more mobile.

In this process of change attributed to the machine, because of increasing surpluses, cities have grown and changed. "The very emergence of cities," says Sjoberg, "is functionally related to society's ability to produce a sizable surplus; and its orientation, quite late in history, to the industrial base." [12] He recognizes that, while the machine is a dynamic agent in the modern world, it is also man's servant if he learns to use it to his advantage, but in the process man must change most of his ways of work and to a large extent his ways of living. The machine:

1. takes the heavy labor element out of work
2. increases the productivity of a day's work and makes the products of work more widely available
3. renders obsolete many of the less productive traditional tools and ways of work
4. breaks down localisms and speeds the mobility of labor, capital, and materials.

What is pertinent for our study is that the machine is a recent urban creation. Its uses and changes are primarily urban. Some may answer that the rural man uses machines in agriculture. With very few excep-

[11] On division of labor, see Max Weber, *Social and Economic Organization*, Talcott Parsons (Ed.), New York, Free Press, 1947; paperback ed., 1964 (translated by A. M. Henderson and Talcott Parsons), p. 218.

[12] Gideon Sjoberg, *The Preindustrial City, Past and Present*, New York, Free Press, 1960, p. 328.

tions, these are also of urban invention and make. The mechanisms of transportation and communication are equally urban in origin and make.

Much of the older folklore in work culture, including fairy tales, related to early types of work or to the early tradesmen. Most of it was, one would assume, of rural village origin. And there were work songs. Modern work, associated with machines, is impersonal and does not inspire fantasy. Arendt notes how the machine takes tools from workers and itself uses the tools.

> There was never any doubt about man's being adjusted or needing special adjustment to the tools he used; one might as well have adjusted them to his hands. The case of the machine is entirely different. Unlike the tools of workmanship, which at every moment of the work process remain the servants of the hand, the machines demand that the laborer serve them, that he adjust the natural rhythm of his body to their mechanical movement.[13]

We need to see machines joined together to make factories, which is preface to the linkages between factories and all sorts of other work places for which the city is the setting. The influence of this milieu, by what Kerr calls the logic of industrialism, extends outward and "may even insist eventually on a single world economy." [14]

Writing as an economic historian, Lampard views machines in their relation to industry, industry in its relation to the life of urban places; and he sees urban places as adapting to technology and mechanisms.

> The mechanical inventions of the last two hundred years, for example, are a class of innovations representing many syntheses of technical and intellectual elements made available in the cultural stream of western Europe. . . . In short, industrialization was a phase of cultural history in which certain communities, and not others, became marked by an increasing differentiation of economic functions, skills, instruments, institutions, and regions. It was the ongoing specialization among men and machines which gradually transformed the techno-organizational base of society and, with it, the spatial order of economic activities.[15]

3. Urban Places and Mobility

Before the emergence of cities, people moving about especially as individuals, would have been regarded as most unusual. Even in the early medieval centuries in Europe the normal course was for the

---

[13] Hannah Arendt, *The Human Condition,* Chicago, University of Chicago Press, 1958, p. 147.

[14] Kerr, op. cit., p. 349.

[15] Eric E. Lampard, "The History of Cities in the Economically Advanced Areas," *Economic Development and Cultural Change,* Vol. 3, 1954–1955, pp. 87–88.

individual to remain in the bosom of his family. Nor did families move. Nor did one move from one occupation to another. Industrialism and its work system assumes mobility and could not function well without it. As for cities, they have always assumed and depended on the mobility of people. The work systems found in cities, even under the fixed guild orders, never quite prevented moving about. Indeed, guilds accepted mobility and tried to exercise control over it, as when apprentices, on completing their training, were expected to do a "wander year," requiring them go to other towns and seek work in their craft, returning home with knowledge of their work elsewhere.

The more industrial and urban a country becomes, the more conducive it is to mobility, and the more its cities attract strangers. For example, Dore mentions that in 1950 more than four of each ten inhabitants of Tokyo were born outside that city.[16] As we shall see elsewhere in this book, one out of five Americans changes place of residence every year, and the number of people who move from job to job is probably even greater. In countries undergoing industrialization, where cities are only beginning to grow, people are moving about more than normally. Spitaels found in Leopoldville, Congo, in 1957, that of 80,000 employed men and 23,000 jobless men over half had come from tribal villages.[17]

The very existence of cities not only attracts rural people, but those who arrive in the city may be stimulated to move again and again—from job to job, from one occupation to another, from one place to another—and, as their level of work or income rises or falls, their status is correspondingly affected. These are not characteristics of life and work in rural places.

4. Man-Made Urban Environment

Anthony Trollope in 1861 visited Milwaukee. Although then it had a population of about 45,000, streets had been laid out and amenities installed for three times that number. Trollope noted that scores of places of only a few thousand inhabitants were aspiring to become 100,000-size cities, "the pioneers of civilization, as they called themselves." [18] Eagerly they were encasing themselves in an urban setting which they hoped to make increasingly urban. These city builders separated themselves from the earth by paving the streets. They piped

---

[16] It was 43 percent for males and 42 percent for females. R. P. Dore, *City Life in Japan*, London, Routledge and Kegan Paul, 1958, p. 18.

[17] Guy Spitaels, "Considérations sur le chômage Léopoldville," *Revue de l'Institut de Sociologie*, Bruxelles, 1960–1961, pp. 57–58.

[18] Anthony Trollope, *North America*, Philadelphia, 1862, pp. 133–136, quoted by Charles N. Glaab (Ed.), *The American City, A Documentary History*, Homewood, Ill., Dorsey Press, 1963, pp. 208–211.

water to their houses and disposed of their sewage with other pipes. They soon learned to illuminate the streets and work places with gas light, enabling work to go on by night as well as by day. This beginning of man creating a new environment really started with the emergence of cities, but it moved with increasing speed as technology advanced.

As we shall note in later chapters, poets and philosophers have been saying for decades that urban man divorces himself from nature. He invented the clock and is able to time himself without looking at the sun, moon, or stars. He becomes only remotely informed about the seasons and what they mean to rural man. He begins to behave, now almost entirely, in relation to his scientific knowledge of things and his skill in manipulating mechanisms. Thus the urbanite lives in an environment of his own making. If he spends a holiday in the country, he finds himself in strange surroundings.

The urban environment becomes increasingly mechanized; indeed even the modern urban house is a mechanism with machines for performing most housekeeping tasks. It is heated or cooled by mechanical devices. What is true of the house is no less true of the work places and of city traffic, which is regulated by automatic lighting systems. The very movement of population in the metropolis into, from, and about the city presents an orderly aspect that takes on the character of being automatically regulated. Yet, as Mumford remarks, however encased urban man may be, he knows the world.

> Though the city is the best organ of memory man has yet created, it is also, until it became so cluttered and disorganized, the best agent for discrimination and comparative evaluation, not merely because it spreads out so many goods for choosing, but because it likewise creates minds of large range, capable of coping with them. Yes, inclusiveness and large numbers are often necessary; but large numbers are not enough.[19]

Mumford's complaint is that, while the city is man's greatest invention, man has yet to learn how to control and guide it. Actually man has not yet learned to control and guide his rural existence either, except by tradition.

5. *Implications of the Clock*

Urban man must be more precisely time-conscious than his rural cousin. He cannot today use the sun as time keeper, for his time needs are more exact and his basic needs are less related than those of rural man to the seasons. His going and coming is regulated by the watch on

[19] Lewis Mumford, *The City in History, Its Origins, Its Transformations, and Its Prospects,* New York, Harcourt, Brace & World, 1961, p. 562.

his wrist. Clocks are on the wall in his home and work place or they face him as he walks the streets. Kenneth Fearing, in a crime story, calls the clock an "unswerving measuring machine." "It both creates and blots out, doing each with glacial impersonality. It measures people in the same way it measures money. . . . When it says a man is right he is right, and when it finds him wrong he is through, with no appeal. It is deaf as it is blind." [20]

As mechanical time, the clock is no more exacting than the sun, but by night or day it makes time visible. Factory whistles, church bells, or other sounds make time audible. Says de Grazia, the clock makes time a commodity.

> The clock's presence everywhere and its tie to the factory with its rela-
> tively unskilled labor, soon gave rise to the idea that one was selling his
> time, as well (or rather than) as skill. The lightening of toil and simplifica-
> tion brought about by machines gave a related impression; that one was
> selling time rather than labor.[21]

Rural man never needed the clock and would not have invented it, any more than he would have invented the reaper. Urban man, due to the demands of commerce and industry, could not have functioned effectively without some exact device for measuring time. Blum says we become conscious of time "when we cease to contemplate and begin to be active," and the more active one must be, the more he becomes time-conscious. With this, he sees a "fundamental change in our attitude toward work." [22] This could not be said of rural man as well; his work demands much activity at some times, less at other times, but he can work without the clock.

To speak of urban man as being under the "tyranny of the clock," as many do, is failing to understand that a similar "tyranny" exists for rural man who paces his daily rounds with the "times and seasons." Clearly, the more he has contact with the city, the more he too becomes clock-regulated.

6. *The Individual and Familism*

Rural life is understandably more tradition-oriented than urban life. The repetition of things in the cycle of the seasons helps make it so. The economic circumstances are such that the family becomes the logical

---

20 Kenneth Fearing, *The Big Clock,* London, Zephyr Books, 1948, p. 9.
21 Sebastian de Grazia, *Of Time, Work and Leisure,* New York, Twentieth Century Fund, 1962, p. 310.
22 Fred H. Blum, *Toward a Democratic Work Process,* New York, Harper & Row, 1961, Chapter 3.

producing and consuming unit. Until the factory-farm and the industrialized plantation appeared, the family was the most typical work unit, a kin group. In the typical fishing village, until now when the technology of fishing is changing, the usual fishing crew was the father and his grown sons or some other combination of kinsmen. The individual family members shared in the family economy. On the frontier the family group, in the extended family sense, was weaker than in the Old World, but even with lone nuclear families on homesteads work was a family matter and economic decisions were familial.

There was, to be sure, a type of individualism on the land frontier in both Canada and the United States. Commager speaks of a "required nonconformity" that paid dividends. The individual did not shrink from dissent.[23] But he was speaking of individualism as it related to politics, not the inhibitions of tradition respecting economic life.

Turner saw the frontier as the milieu of a new individualism and American democracy, standing for qualities which he feared would be destroyed by urban life. He seemed to regard industrial organization and such groupings as trade unions as inimical to individualism and democracy. What Turner lauded was a frontier brand of ruralism, which for the time being happened to be less tradition-bound in political and economic terms, but it was still rural and familial.[24]

The individualism that emerged in the industrial city had a dispersing effect on the family. It separated the work place from the home, and it employed workers as individuals. Members of families found employment in different work places, often in different occupations. Workers came to be recruited and their labor used as individuals, not as family members. Under industrialism, for the first time, the individual family member was free to make individual choices, whether competing in school, in the labor market, or in the marriage market. As a result in our time, as Boskoff notes, "there are incongruous notions about what individualism means, and elements of the traditional morality give place to a "transitional morality." [25]

In such a situation, characteristic of the more industrial urban countries, there is concern about the effects of individualism on traditional family functions and structure. Whatever the problems and however viewed, they relate primarily to changes in urban centers. Mumford, for example, sees danger in the freedoms of the city. To him "the wholeness of the individual depends upon his association within a whole community." Freedom is not achieved by escape from the "claims and

23 Henry S. Commager, *The American Mind*, New Haven, Yale University Press, 1950, p. 20.

24 Frederick J. Turner, *The Frontier in American History*, New York, Holt, Rinehart and Winston, 1920; 3rd ed., 1958, p. 303.

25 Alvin Boskoff, *The Sociology of Urban Regions*, New York, Appleton-Century-Crofts, 1962, p. 291.

duties of life in the community," and to him, extreme "social detachment is death." [26]

7. *Compulsions to Form Secondary Relationships*

The one aspect of urbanism which marks the great difference when compared with ruralism is the presence in modern cities of the secondary organization, which came increasingly into use as cities became more industrial. Large secondary groups, also called "corporate organizations," became more and more evident, and were more needed as cities grew larger and as their organization became more complex.

While urban life detaches the individual from traditional ties to the family organization, it also tends to render him helpless and to some extent insecure in the mass urban agglomerate. If one cannot stand alone against the seemingly formless mass, he may find it wise to join with others. Thus we find in the city organizations of every sort: economic, political, social, cultural, recreational, and others. As Mann observes, one becomes a member of a primary group (family, clique, club) by birth or informal contact, but he chooses to join a formal or secondary organization in which he pays dues, votes, and participates somewhat impersonally.[27]

Formal secondary organizations may be public, quasi-public, or private. Normally, however, the private and voluntary type is referred to as a formal secondary group. Greer and Orleans identify such organizations as "parapolitical," a term which may be misleading, since most of these organizations are often politically active, and properly should be.[28]

Although formal secondary groups are more identified with urbanism, in the industrial urban countries where rural people become quite urbanized, rural secondary groups are also established. These are, for example, various agricultural cooperatives and rural electric power associations. In addition, there are the various organized groups which serve religious, recreational, cultural, or patriotic interests. Normally, such widespread organizations found in small places will have their head offices in some great city. It is the city where the leaders of different organized groups come most readily into contact with each other.

8. *Urban Proclivity for Adaptation*

When he visited San Francisco in 1868, Samuel Bowles found a city in the throes of growing—a city dominated by the recklessness of pros-

26 Lewis Mumford, *The Condition of Man,* New York, Harcourt, Brace & World, 1944, p. 253.

27 Peter H. Mann, *An Approach to Urban Sociology,* London, Routledge and Kegan Paul, 1965, p. 111.

28 Scott Greer and Peter Orleans, "Mass Society and Parapolitical Structure," *American Sociological Review,* Vol. 27, No. 3, October 1962, pp. 634–646.

perity, and rampant individualism—in short, urbanism in the raw. He saw the finest human qualities mixed with the shoddy, the stabilizing elements of rural life conspicuously absent.

> [He noted] much dash, a certain chivalric honor combined with the care-lessness of word, of integrity, of consequence; a sort of gambling, speculat-ing, horse-jockeying morality, born of the uncertainties of mining—its sudden heights, its equally surprising depths, and the eager haste to get rich—that all require something of a re-casting of relationships, new standards, certainly new charities, in order to get the unaccustomed mind into a state of candor and justice. People who know they are smart in the East and come out to California, thinking to find an easy wool-gathering, are apt to go home shorn. Wall Street can teach Montgomery Street nothing.[29]

San Francisco, as Bowles saw the city in gold-rush days, manifested in the extreme certain characteristics which have always been common to cities, especially in a period of boom and expansion when venturing is least curbed and even a proposition reaching to the clouds may find takers. Bowles saw San Francisco at a time when the normal curbing influences found in older cities had had no time to develop. What he did see at its height was an attitude favorable to risk, a quality native to cities.

Cities are historically the home of innovation. It is no accident that practically all technical inventions and a good share of the social inven-tions are urban creations. This is to be expected, for all forms of com-petition flourish in cities. The very concentration of population in cities sharpens the struggle for survival and achievement.

Besides being the arena where men venture and take risks and where innovation is at home, cities have always attracted persons of imagina-tion and venturesomeness. This combination tends to stimulate in cities an outlook which is receptive to the new, ready to accept and adapt to change.

9. *Commitment to Superlatives*

The engineer who makes a machine that will outdo earlier ma-chines is well aware that engineers in a rival enterprise will endeavor to bring out a machine that will outmode his creation. The race goes on. Production records established today must be broken tomorrow. The superlative in bigger, faster, better is never final. The city rewards cre-ativity for the important reason that creativity is the imperative need,

[29] Samuel Bowles, *Our New West*, 1869, quoted by Charles N. Glaab (Ed.), *The American City, A Documentary History*, Homewood, Illinois, Dorsey Press, 1963, p. 201.

else urban people could not subsist. But they are not content with subsistence; their wants also increase.

The superlative elements in the urban ways of work and styles of life come also to be evidenced in higher levels of sophistication. One from a great metropolis is often quick to remark about the superiority of his city over another city half the size. The booster in a small city, believing firmly that bigger equates better, strives for the growth of his city. The struggle to be ahead, to exceed all others, even to exceed one's self—we may call it the "superlative urge"—is certainly characteristic of the modern urban mentality. Even the intellectuals, including artists, accept this way of thinking and flee from the little city to the metropolis. They contribute also to the mentality of the superlative urge, often bringing reality out of the dream.

This competitive quality of urbanism, as it relates to things, whether it reflects striving for gain or merely for recognition, finds expression in visible evidence of "newest," "latest," "most up-to-date," while at the same time it downgrades the old-fashioned.

The use of the rural house goes on and on, but the urban apartment building is outmoded in three decades. In the metropolis a substantial brick and stone office structure of 20 floors is replaced by a glass and stainless steel building of 30 floors. Tenants are not attracted to the old building but they are quite ready to pay higher rents in the new one. The impressive new building is assured to attract more business. Urban shop windows come to be used not merely to display a wide array of goods, but they must also display goods in an artistic manner with originality, for window-shopping in the city assumes the character of a leisure activity.

When H. G. Wells arrived in New York for an American visit in 1905, it was on the same day an earthquake virtually destroyed San Francisco. He asked himself what would happen if a quake shook New York.

> I believe that these people would more than half like the situation. It would give them scope, it would facilitate the conversion into white marble in process already, it would settle the difficulties of the elevated railroad and clear out the tangles of lower New York. There is no sense of accomplishment or finality in any of these things, the largest, the finest, the tallest are so obviously no more than symptoms and promises of Material Progress, of inhuman material progress that is in the nature of things that no one would regret their passing.[30]

In such fashion, Wells concluded, San Francisco would rebuild, brighter, taller, and more impressive than before. However, this commit-

---

[30] H. G. Wells, *The Future of America*, New York, Harper & Row, 1906, p. 42.

ment to the superlative finds expression in many other ways; ever faster passenger trains, ever larger and faster airplanes, still more luxurious automobiles, more efficient mechanized kitchens. The oil tanker of 50,000-ton capacity is replaced by one of 100,000-ton capacity, and now bigger ones are promised. Every such technological change forces others to be made, but the point of pertinence here is that this "superlative-ness" centers in cities.

10. *Money as the Definer of Values*

Isolated rural peoples and tribal peoples sustain themselves on what is called a "subsistence economy," producing most of the consumer goods they need, although one village may barter with another. Trade does not involve money. They are able to put values on goods; ten head of cattle may equal one wife or one cow may be equal to three sheep.[31]

Doubtless, the earliest cities were mere barter markets. Money was not needed until strangers from more remote places arrived to buy and sell, by which time the market had come under control of some authority, such as a king who had coins minted, his image stamped thereon to insure their value.

For the most part, the early American frontiersmen managed with a quasi-subsistence economy. They were not commercial farmers but hunters and trappers. Settlers who later went to the frontier to be home-steaders saw themselves as commercial farmers or ranchers. In some cases they needed money. It is said, for example, that Sutter, on whose land grant in California gold was discovered, used a coinage of tin. An out-standing example of frontier coinage was the gold money minted by the Mormons in Utah. Without money, they could not have traded with the wagon trains passing through.[32]

Most rural people around the world are either on a subsistence or a quasi-subsistence economy, as is the case with most Newfoundland out-port fishermen. Whether trading work or selling fish, they reckon values in money terms but handle little cash. Rural people may be in the money economy but not participating wholly in it. As neighbors they lend and borrow or exchange work; the system assumes friendly relations and the giving and receiving of help.

When the stranger enters the market and when the number of strangers multiply, the use of money becomes imperative. To enter the money economy from a subsistence economy is to move into a wider

[31] For a discussion of barter trade in Africa, see Harold K. Schneider, "Economics in East African Aboriginal Societies," in Melvin J. Herskovits and Mitchell Harwitz (Eds.), *Economic Transition in Africa,* London, Routledge and Kegan Paul, 1964, pp. 53–76.

[32] Nels Anderson, *Desert Saints,* Chicago, University of Chicago Press, 1966, pp. 86–87.

market in the face of which the local subsistence economies are rudi-
mentary. Control of money, however, centers in cities and the value of
things money will buy is established by the urban markets. Largely because wealth accumulates in cities, levels of income there, and price
levels, tend to be higher than in rural places. Thus the rural people are
ever poor by comparison. Not only do wages in rural areas remain lower
than in urban industrial areas, but prices for urban goods and services
in rural areas tend to be higher.

11. *Writing, Records, and Bureaucracy*

The earliest record of writing, done about 3000 B.C., as mentioned
by Childe, was for the purpose of keeping accurate accounts in the
temple at Eroch in the Middle East. The priests who managed the
economy in this early city, made loans, for example, of seed to farmers
and they were paid back in kind, but with interest. Instead of entrusting
the facts to memory, a precise record was made, using symbols.[33] Apparently writing was used for such practical purposes long before it was
used for putting down ideas, and it began in towns, as it also developed
there.

Writing involves the making of records for future use, accounts of
agreements for future reference, commercial correspondence, testaments,
or creative productions. All of these are witnesses to be conserved. The
preserving of records was and is the beginning of bureaucracy. All three,
writing, records, and bureaucracy, are aspects of urbanism.[34]

Besides making and keeping records for ready reference, bureaucracy
is a system of order in the management of affairs. The order in some of
its manifestations is called management, and management is especially
concerned with the planning and control of man's work. Another function of records and bureaucracy concerns predictions regarding the operations of an organization, what is likely or what is possible respecting
tomorrow's activity.

There are many who see bureaucracy as not needed in many phases
of community or organization life. They are often unwilling to recognize
its importance for order in governments and corporations, or to concede
their own dependence on bureaucracies.[35]

There are those who rail against public bureaucracy but are often
unaware of similar faults in private bureaucracies, the bureaucracies of
giant commercial firms or industrial corporations. All such bureaucracies
have evolved apace with the growing complexity of industrialism and

---

[33] V. Gordon Childe, *Man Makes Himself*, London, Watts, 1936, p. 152.

[34] Sjoberg, op. cit., p. 244.

[35] For a criticism of public bureaucracy, see E. Strauss, *The Ruling Servants,
Bureaucracy in Russia, France, and Britain*, London, Allen and Unwin, 1961.

with the growth and complexity of cities. As urbanism and industrialism spread, the controls of bureaucracy spread to rural areas.[36]

URBANISM AS THE COSMOPOLITAN LIFE

As we have seen, urban life is anonymous, impersonal, highly competitive, extremely mobile, creative, ever changing and yet unpredictable. Many other characteristics could be added. Cosmopolitanism, for example, is very much a quality of urban life. In some respects, cosmopolitanism is the sum of the many qualities which identify the urbanized man who is at home in the great city, the rural man being seen as "out there."

Cosmopolitanism is something quite other than the concept "urbanized social organization," used by some rural sociologists when they observe how rural people take on urban ways.[37] The cosmopolitan is at the point in the urban milieu where urban ways take form and change. It is in part expressed by Mundy and Riesenberg who speak of "another side to urbanism than simply the history of the town itself. This side is the relationship of the town to the countryside."[38] They see the town as a center with specialized techniques and as being in a dominant position with respect to the countryside.

RURAL-URBAN INTERACTION

The cosmopolitanism of the city is no mere veneer, but is functional in various ways in the rural-urban relationship. Redfield and Singer, while recognizing that urbanism creates and initiates, insist that the relationship is not a one-way street. Over time and in diverse ways urban life must adapt to the rural hinterland.

> . . . we find that the processes of cultural interaction and "flow" are far too complex to be handled by simple mechanical laws concerning the direction, rate, and "flow" of cultural diffusion between "city" and "country." The cities themselves are creatures as well as creators of this process, and it takes a broad cross-cultural perspective to begin to see what its nature is.[39]

[36] For a theory of bureaucracy, see Lewis A. Coser and Bernard Rosenberg (Eds.), *Sociological Theory*, New York, Macmillan, 1964, pp. 463–518.

[37] Urbanized social organization is a central theme for Lee Taylor and Arthur R. Jones, Jr., *Rural Life and Urbanized Society*, New York, Oxford University Press, 1964.

[38] Mundy and Riesenberg, op. cit., p. 15.

[39] Robert Redfield and Milton B. Singer, "The Cultural Role of Cities," *Economic Development and Cultural Change*, Vol. 3, 1954–1955, p. 70.

Such influence as the countryside may have on the city is not necessarily a conscious and guided one. The two great segments of society act and react, each in its own way, to the same wider environment, and in so doing each may follow its own self-interest. While the city appears to be going its way alone, it must adapt to the same limitations that affect rural life, such as the climate, the variety and limits of natural resources, and its accessibility to markets. Nor is the city fully able, despite its sophistication, superior know-how, and initiating genius, to steer a purposeful, rational course, although it does keep on going, and although administered by law and management codes. Friedmann, however, sees the city as an essentially rational phenomenon, as indeed it often is in day-to-day matters.

> Money and accountancy govern its trade, and most things become essentially reduced to their value in cash—whether it be labor, a work of art, or a parcel of land. Universities pursue science, mathematics and philosophy (all three distinctive urban forms of mental activity) to the limits of reason and into the realms of ultimate doubt.[40]

All of urban life is not rational. Friedmann reminds us that there is the modern rational sector which dominates, but coexisting with it is the "folk sector." American cities have not only grown fast, they have become in material values ultraurban. But most of the builders of these cities and the architects of their industrial order were, as many still are, of rural origin, and much in the way of rural values and attitudes still finds expression in the nonwork institutional life of these cities. In this sense, we need to recognize that the line between urbanism and ruralism is not merely one between rural and urban places, geographically dispersed; the line extends into the city itself. It is much more evident in Canadian than American cities. Social and cultural life in Canadian cities is still under the surveillance of the so-called Lord's Day laws, like Blue Laws in the United States.

However, when rural and urban are compared in terms of the material traits of culture, the extent to which machines are used by rural and urban people, the access to radio and television, the transportation used, consumer preferences, and the amenities in the home, then the line between urban and rural weaves and often vanishes.

Writing about agriculture and rural life in Canada, Whyte concludes, "The complexity of rural and urban conceptual types makes accurate operationalization of these concepts extremely difficult." He finds that most criteria one might use to distinguish urban from rural, whether social, psychological, or cultural, fail to separate these opposing ways of life. The distinction is in large part an occupational one; the rural man

[40] Friedmann, op. cit., p. 89.

takes food or fibre from the soil, fish from the sea, or products from the forest. Urban man converts raw products into finished goods, or he sells services. While the two come more and more to have the same wants, the rural man usually must work harder for less ample returns. Thus, as Whyte observes, the two ways of life tend to converge.

> The urbanization of a traditionally rural society will be manifest in a convergence of rural with urban social characteristics. The convergence will be directly related to the rate of diffusion of scientific knowledge and advancement of technical knowhow in agricultural and other primary industries. It must be cautioned, however, that no single cause can be imputed. Other factors, both accountable and unaccountable are simultaneously operating to maintain or reduce rural and urban differences.[41]

Here we are reminded that pressure for change comes from the urban side of the society, while the rural comes increasingly to be shaped to the urban image. Thus there is no line denoting the outer reach of the study area of the urban sociologist. Nor does this intrude on the field of the rural sociologist, whose discipline becomes the more meaningful as he is fortified with knowledge about the urban community, its work and its life.

[41] Donald R. Whyte, "Rural Canada in Transition," in Marc A. Tremblay and Walton J. Anderson (Eds.), *Rural Canada in Transition,* Ottawa, Agricultural Economics Research Council, 1966, pp. 7, 8.

Urban communities and their functions | 2

ON THE DEFINITION OF COMMUNITY

In the previous chapter "community" was used without being first defined, but this was not an oversight. Like many terms that have wide usage, community also has many applications. Precisely because it is so much used it would be difficult to coin some more exact term to replace it. The new term might not be accepted or, if accepted, it too would very soon acquire a variety of meanings.

Hillery collected 94 definitions of community, but no universal, all-purpose definition resulted.[1] A similar effort was made by the German sociologist König, as he followed the concept, or its equivalent, in various languages. He encountered numerous obstacles, for applications of the term vary with languages. For example, the German *Gemeinde* is normally identified with an area, a *Gemeinde* being the equivalent of a county. It could hardly be used to identify, for example, the American community in London or the Hungarian community in New York, or the Swedish community in Paris.[2]

One major difficulty encountered in defining social science terms is the notion still held by some that a concept should be so defined that the definition will serve all purposes; in other words it should have a universal application. If one designed such a definition, he might be called on to defend it, a view which in the past led to considerable useless debate.

It is coming to be seen as unrealistic to make all-purpose definitions if in practice they do not serve specific uses. What community means to a sociologist doing an ecological study may not serve the needs of a geographer or economist doing their kind of research. The sociologist

[1] George A. Hillery, "Definitions of Community, Areas of Agreement," *Rural Sociology*, Vol. 20, No. 1, June 1955, pp. 111–125.
[2] Renée König, *Die Gemeinde*, Hamburg, Rowahlt, 1958, p. 24.

may be obliged to define community in one way to study juvenile delinquency and in a somewhat different way to study a race problem or even further to study the relationship between the flow of traffic and the distribution of housing by social class.

One characteristic in the definition of community (for whatever purpose) is commonality. While a community may have within it a great diversity of interests, there also are interests which are common to large sections if not to all of the inhabitants. All, for example, would expect reliable police protection, an adequate water supply system, and an efficient traffic control. Not all, on the other hand, would be interested in playgrounds or band concerts in the parks. Where the common interests make for community satisfaction, various specialized interests of particular sections of the population may very well make for friction.

A second characteristic of a community concerns the assurance of continuity, a balance of males and females and of age groups. This is also called "biological continuity." It does not exist in a "colony" of old people or the population of an institution. Of this continuity Arensberg and Kimball write:

> It is also an enduring temporal pattern of coexistence, an ordered time progress of individuals, from their births to their deaths, through roles and relationships of each kind known to their species or their culture. In short, it is the minimal common cast of characters supporting the drama of the biogram, in biology, in social science, its analogue of a way of life. This is its character as thing . . . an enduring natural unit of both process and organization in living phenomena . . . . a community is a natural sample, too, because it is a natural unit of the drama of successive repetitions of the life of an ongoing culture or society.[3]

In this sense, a community is a collectivity able to produce its own replacements and able to pass its culture to its own young.

To be sure, continuity may be characteristic of groups which are not biologically enduring. A corporation, which is a legal person, has its own means of insuring its existence, but this is not biological continuity.

No less important than commonality and continuity in defining community is the third element, territoriality. It occupies space, a particular identifiable bit of territory, whether formally shared by the members or not. One may wander far, but it is assumed that he is from some particular place. It is usual for one to have kin located in the place where he "belongs" but he may be a lone individual and still think of himself as belonging.

---

[3] Conrad M. Arensberg and Solon T. Kimball, *Culture and Community,* New York, Harcourt, Brace & World, 1965, p. 17.

THE CITY AS A COMMUNITY

Too often the idea of a community, if only by implication, suggests that the population therein is homogeneous, which may be so in a village, but the population of a city is anything but homogeneous. The great metropolis may have its racial minorities. Because of racial differences, a city may experience violence and riots. A minority group, due to poverty and bias, may find itself segregated or isolated in poor areas. Ethnic groups may voluntarily cluster in their enclaves, participating hardly at all in the wider community life. Commonality of interest hardly exists. Yet the city holds together, public services continue, the economic processes carry on, the daily movement of population, people going about their affairs, does not stop.

Life in the great city, however heterogeneous its population, does convey the aspect of continuity and, of course, the element of territoriality is present. Some would say that commonality finds expression in the subgroups and they can be identified as subcommunities, the well-being of each being dependent on various functional relations with the wider urban complex.

The urban community appears to be strikingly different from the small rural community with respect to awareness of its outer limits, and this applies especially to the tribal village. Those of the earlier community were conscious of the boundaries. The opposite tends to be true of the urban community. Except in legal terms, there is little interest in the boundaries. Economic, social, and cultural interests cross the line freely. Few in the great metropolis have any concern about the limits, but they know the center where all lines cross, where economic values are most concentrated, where tempo is greatest, and where competition is acute. The city-state had to guard its border, but when the nation-community emerged, guarding the border became its concern.[4]

Urban community organization is highly impersonal, quite the reverse of the rural community. Its larger groupings are secondary; most village groups are primary. Corporate enterprises and other large organizations in cities tend to supersede much activity in lesser communities.

It is in this impersonal and bureaucratic whole that urban community life functions. Looking at such a community with the eyes of an engineer, we can visualize it in terms of interrelated mechanistic networks—water supply systems; sewage and drainage systems; communications systems; the mechanical systems in houses, offices, and factories—and we can think of these as a behaving, integrated whole. Popenoe

4 Nels Anderson, "Diverse Perspective of Community," *International Review of Community Development,* No. 7, 1961, pp. 15–32.

remarks that community means many things to many men, and he offers
this definition, which has much in common with that by Wirth mentioned early in the first chapter.

> Let us define community as a sub-societal social unit which consists of
> persons who share a common geographic area interacting in terms of a
> common culture and which incorporates a range of social structures which
> function to meet a relatively broad range of needs of all persons who
> make up the social unit. Thus it is a kind of locality group (which is com-
> posed of all persons within a bounded territory) as opposed to a *func-
> tional* group (which is composed of persons bound together in order to
> perform a specific set of functions).[5]

To Popenoe, functional groups would include, for example, schools,
families, churches, banks, stores, governmental units, their operations
and interactions.

Gibbs would ask why we should expect a single definition to serve
all purposes.

> With increasing experience has come the recognition that no single
> definition of a city is suitable for all research purposes. Rather than con-
> tribute to the endless debate on the subject, as so many have done in the
> past, it is more realistic to grant that there are various ways of view-
> ing cities, all of which are relevant to urban research taken as a whole.[6]

SOME SALIENT ASPECTS OF THE URBAN COMMUNITY

While the notion of the urban community cannot be reduced to a
simple, well-defined statement, and one that is perhaps unnecessary,
there are several features of all urban communities which are highly
important and relevant to our study. Here we focus on the role of
strangers, communal networks, neighborhoods, social networks, social
order, and tolerance in attitudes.

1. *Strangers, Commerce, and Festivals*

We know that the city receives the stranger with comparative
unconcern, whereas his presence might be disturbing in the rural village. This is more true of modern than of ancient cities. But, since

---

5 David Popenoe, "On the Meaning of 'Urban' in Urban Studies," quoted by Paul
Meadows and Ephraim H. Mizruchi (Eds.), *Urbanism, Urbanization, and Change; Comparative Perspectives*, Reading, Massachusetts, Addison-Wesley, 1969, p. 70.

6 Jack P. Gibbs (Ed.), *Urban Research Methods*, New York, Van Nostrand, 1962,
p. 14.

even early cities were centers of commerce, ways were found to receive strangers, although they could not have been accepted as citizens. Fustel de Coulanges relates how difficult it was for the stranger to be granted citizenship in cities of ancient Greece; religious concepts stood in the way.

> Thus religion established between the citizen and the stranger a profound and ineffaceable distinction. This same religion, so long as it had its sway over the minds of men, forbade the right of citizenship to be granted to the stranger. . . . Sparta had accorded it to no one except a prophet; and even for this the formal command of the oracle was necessary. . . . Certainly there was no other public act when the legislator was surrounded with so many difficulties and precautions as that which conferred upon a stranger the title of citizen. . . . No one could become a citizen of Athens if he was a citizen of another city; for it was a religious impossibility to be at the same time a member of two cities, as it also was to be a member of two families. . . . Neither at Rome nor at Athens could a foreigner be a proprietor. He could not marry; or, if he married, his marriage was not recognized and his children were reputed illegitimate. . . . At first he could take no part in commerce. The Roman law forbade him to inherit from a citizen, and even forbade a citizen to inherit from him.[7]

We can be sure there were many strangers in those early Roman and Greek cities. While the citizens were relatively few, they were the owners of the property and the holders of power. They had practical reasons, perhaps business interests, for holding firm to the religious tenets that excluded those who owed their allegiance to other gods in other cities. With the changes that passing time brings, the circle of citizens in cities widened until today, when the stranger is readily accepted. To study the place of the stranger would be in large part a study of his contributions to urbanism.

A very different set of propositions would be needed to study the city as a mecca for recreation and where leisure activity becomes commerce. One would see the evolution of this urban function in the study of market days and fairs which have always had economic motivations but that were also occasions for ceremony, pomp, and merrymaking. Strauss calls attention to the role of ceremonials in European cities, the traditional ceremonials which are repeated each year, bringing crowds periodically to the city. They come to sell, to buy, but, no less, to have fun. Although the methods of commerce have changed in most cities of Europe, as Strauss observes, the ceremonials and festivals have become traditional and are annually repeated. They still serve leisure needs and

---

[7] N. D. Fustel de Coulanges, *The Ancient City,* Garden City, New York, Doubleday Anchor, 1955, pp. 195–196; 1st ed., 1864.

are still good for business.[8] They are associated with urban downtowns, where the stranger is most at home and where the city places its display structures to impress him.

2. *The Networks in Communities*

In a tribal community one belongs to a large family and he has many kinfolk. The nuclear family into which he is born is but a minor unit in that extended family, which, in turn, may be part of a linear kinship group, but a linear group also constitutes a network, perhaps one of several in the community. In terms of obligations, affinitive or economic, each individual has his indentity and status in both family and community. But the filial ties in his network are the stronger, so strong in fact that the family makes most of the major decisions that affect his life, even to choosing his marriage mate.

In the urban community the networks are no less present, but mainly it is the individual who makes use of them. The networks in the modern rural community are generally more familial than in the city, but the individual is far less bound to his family than in a tribal village. He has much more freedom, for example, in making decisions about his education, his occupation, and in choosing a marriage partner, and he has more freedom for making friendships in the community out-side the family.

Urban networks, those which are characteristic of the urban com-munity, tend to be of a secondary nature. While the ancient city de-fended itself against the outside by walling itself in, the modern city assumes an opposite stance; it builds roads to multiply contact with the outside. As it is able to establish contacts with other places, large or small, so its own work places are able to prosper. With the coming of modern industry a city was confronted with the need to extend its hinterland of outside contact. The size of a city came to be determined by its ability to obtain resources with which to work and a wide enough market hinterland. In such terms, each urban community could be seen as being identified with a network of exchange between itself and out-side places. Within each such modern city there evolved a second net-work of exchange interdependence; a network in the sense that work places serve one another as well as the widely dispersed market.

Gottmann's revealing study of the Atlantic seaboard, mainly from Boston to Washington, makes clear that between the dozens of cities and the hundreds of towns and villages in this region a multiplicity of net-works can be seen. Moreover, between these hundreds of communities can be discerned something like a division of labor. Every community is

[8] Anselm Strauss, "Spatial Representation and the Orbits of City Life," *Sociological Quarterly*, Vol. 1, No. 3, July 1960, pp. 167–180.

depended on in some ways by others, as it also depends on others. New York, in the dominant position for the region, is most involved in these interdependencies.[9]

Within such a complex matrix of impersonal networks for buying and selling are found the cultural and social networks, and every community, large and small, is involved in them to some degree. This does not prevent each community from having its own identity. But it may be questioned whether, even for the small community, one knows "where the line between inside and outside, and between insider and outsider, falls." [10] Only rarely is the line likely to be of much concern, since focus is more on the community center.

Briggs, for instance, observes that the interlocking of communities and the blotting out of old identities has been under way in Britain for decades. Once each main city had its own identity and each was surrounded by its own agricultural green. Then cities began crossing borders in search of wider markets. "Local newspapers began to increase greatly in scope and scale. The same branded goods began to be offered in shops in all parts of the country." [11] With the growth of boundary-crossing networks, urban communities come to be known by their central areas.

3. *The Ideal of the Neighborhood*

The idea of neighborhood applies to a limited area of residence occupied by a small number of families acquainted with one another. It is assumed, furthermore, that a neighborhood is an area of relative stability in terms of the number of people moving in or moving out. Those who idealize the concept of neighborhood residence, many sociologists included, are prone to think of the neighborhood in highly desirable terms, as a place of interfamily harmony. Firth found such fairly permanent neighborhoods on the island of Tikopia, but they turned out to be anything but harmonious. If a person from one small village visited the next small village he would take with him some gift and he would have news to relate about his own village neighborhood. Not only would any piece of news be material for negative gossip after his departure, there would be critical remarks about the quantity or quality of the gift he brought compared with the gift he took away.[12]

The neighborhood may be seen as a very small community, although even a small community may, due to the distribution of the in-

[9] Jean Gottmann, *Megalopolis, The Urbanized Northeastern Seaboard of the United States,* New York, Twentieth Century Fund, 1961.

[10] Conrad Arensberg, "The Community as Object and Sample," *American Anthropologist,* Vol. 63, No. 2, April 1961, p. 250.

[11] Asa Briggs, *Victorian Cities,* London, Odham Press, 1963, p. 45.

[12] Raymond Firth, *We, The Tikopia,* Boston, Beacon Press, 1965; 1st ed., 1936.

habitants, frequently consist of two or more recognized neighborhoods, one less opulent than the other. The neighborhood in a caste village is likely to be a precisely marked area occupied by a particular caste. Those of the higher castes would be at the city's center, those of the low castes at the edge. In his study of dialects in an Indian village, Gumperz found that the separations had remained fixed for so many decades that the different untouchable castes had dialect differences. Two such castes, their neighborhoods side by side, managed to have no social contact. Yet all castes in the village were economically integrated for production and consumption.[13]

West wrote about "Plainville," a small Midwestern rural town, and he gave considerable attention to neighborhoods. He found that families did not consider all other families living near them to be neighbors, only those with whom they "neighbored." He noted that the "party" telephone line had become a means of neighboring between housewives. With the same line connecting several households, four or five could carry on conversation.[14] Gallaher found that after 15 years neighborhood relationships in this essentially rural place had changed greatly. Proximity of residence had ceased to be an important factor. It depended more than before on contact by automobile. Rich farmers, however dispersed, neighbored with other rich farmers. The practice of neighbors helping neighbors with their work had more or less gone out of fashion.

> In the first instance, a man formerly identified his close neighbors as those with whom he maintained various reciprocal cooperative relationships such as borrowing (including labor) and visiting. Today, however, borrowing is giving way to technological self-sufficiency, and visiting patterns extend far beyond the community. The breakdown of this type of neighborhood which the farmer defines in terms of social interaction is attributed mainly to mechanization.[15]

The ideal neighborhood, if it ever existed, appears to be in the process of being overshadowed by the onrush of the urban style of life. Deveraux tells of 19 small places around Springdale in New York.

> Only five still have an operating church, only five still have a neighborhood store, only two have a local industry. Fully a third of the farms have been abandoned, and today only about half of the rural population is comprised of farmers and their families. While many of the people have left the community to seek their fortunes in the cities and while

[13] John J. Gumperz, "Dialect Differences and Social Stratification in a North Indian Village," *American Anthropologist*, Vol. 60, No. 4, August 1958, pp. 668–682.

[14] James West, *Plainville, U.S.A.*, New York, Columbia University Press, 1945.

[15] Art Gallaher, Jr., *Plainville, Fifteen Years Later*, New York, Columbia University Press, 1961, p. 140.

many of the retired farmers have moved to the village [Springdale] center, abandoned farms have been taken over by "shack people." . . . Small
wonder, under these circumstances, if the ties which operated to make the
rural neighborhood a cohesive unit have been so seriously weakened.[16]

In the cosmopolitan city, neighborhood has little meaning and most
efforts to build model housing projects to encourage neighborliness have
not succeeded. Kallen, who apparently feels that old-fashioned neighborhood relationships would be desirable, writes of this lack which appears
to be replaced by something like a city-wide consciousness.

In large tenements and apartment houses of the metropolitan city people
live next door to each other without ever meeting or speaking. The
"neighbor" is defined by other conditions of association than geographical
proximity. He is the person from your home town, your school or college
mate, your fellow worker in your trade or profession, your gymnasium or
card-table partner, your fellow bar-fly, and he may live at the other end
of the town from you. You may live at a maximum of social distance from
one fellow citizen with no geographical distance whatever; and you may
live at a maximum of geographical distance from another with the com-
pletest social intimacy.[17]

Under these conditions, neighborhood in the traditional rural sense
comes to be replaced in the city by social networks, of which more will
be said in the next section.

Early American cities, and Canadian cities too, as they emerged from
village status, tended to carry on affairs as if they had not entered a new
type of existence. Emerging cities continued to hold the "town meeting,"
usually manipulated, even in the village, by a few top families. From
Bridenbaugh we get this quote about the Lord's Day in Boston.

In February 1761 the Post Boy gave over its front page and part of the
second to printing the new Sabbath observation law passed by the General
Court, which prohibited work, sports, travel, entertainment in public
houses, unnecessary walking, loitering, or assembling in the streets on the
Lord's Day, and forbade shopkeepers to be open, hawkers to peddle, or
any public diversion after sunset on Saturday. Wardens enforced these
regulations with as much success in the Bay City as any urban center
would permit.[18]

Such moral controls characterized the colonial villages. In the cities
they gradually came to be modified. As cities became more liberal they

16 Edward C. Deveraux, Jr., "Springdale and Its People," *Journal of Social Issues*,
Vol. 16, No. 4, 1960, p. 13.
17 Horace M. Kallen, "City Planning and the Idea of the City, Considerations
Especially about New York," *Social Forces*, Vol. 23, No. 2, Spring, 1956, p. 188.
18 Carl Bridenbaugh, *Cities in Revolt, Urban Life in America, 1743–1776*, New
York, Knopf, 1955, p. 315.

became havens of escape for many who rebelled against the tight controls and scrutinies of village neighborhoods. However, the idea of restoring the old-fashioned neighborhood is still the bright hope of many. Indeed, the fiction of the model neighborhood way of life is still the bait offered by real estate dealers in promoting model suburban "villages," tempting families to escape the social chaos of the city.[19]

4. *Urban Community and Social Networks*

Kallen observed, as quoted above, that in the urban milieu, "The 'neighbor' is defined by other conditions of association than geographical proximity." The "other conditions of association" can be illustrated in the case of a highly urbanized man whose occupation for years has been that of a newspaper reporter in the city where he has lived four decades. His place of residence has always been near the city center in apartment buildings where one does not have neighbors on the basis of proximity. He would have no interest in being a good neighbor in the proximity sense, but he is known as a good neighbor among the many at all socioeconomic levels with whom he has acquaintance. His wife is a social worker or was until her recent retirement, although she is still active on various committees. Both participate in wider city activities.

Neither this man nor his wife could be described as socially isolated. Each has a circle of acquaintances and friends that both claim. These are acquaintances, close friends or not on the basis of choice, not on the basis of merely being neighbors in terms of physical proximity.

Bott, who made a study of families in London, would describe such acquaintance clusters as social networks.[20] Each individual in the urban situation tends to be the central point in a network which includes persons known in connection with one's work, including friends met on earlier jobs, former schoolmates, those from one's home town, acquaintances made in one's church or club. They are a selected cluster. Some may be close in one's network, others on the margin. One may, for reasons of his own, cut some from his network, while adding others. In like manner, he may be eliminated or "distanced" from the networks of others. In times of trouble these contacts may come to his aid, as he may go to them.[21]

In order to expand one's social networks the individual in the urban community may find it advisable to join various formal organizations,

[19] For a critical examination of the suburban movement, see Robert C. Wood, *Suburbia, Its People and their Politics,* Boston, Houghton Mifflin, 1959; also William H. Whyte, Jr., "The Consumer and the New Suburbia," in Lincoln H. Clark (Ed.), *Consumer Behavior,* New York, New York University Press, 1955.

[20] Elizabeth Bott, *Family and Social Network,* London, Tavistock Publications, 1958.

[21] For comments on networks, see George C. Homans, *Social Behavior,* New York, Harcourt, Brace & World, 1961, pp. 7–8.

those, for instance, which render him more secure in relation to his work, or those groups in which he can spend his leisure. If he is a war veteran he may join one of the veteran groups, or he may join a political party. Such are very necessary in the urban life. Among other functions, they serve, as Rose would say, to expand the alternatives available to the individual.

> The individual is only free as his society is structured to allow him to be. If the society has many groups with which the individual may affiliate, he has greater freedom of choice than in a society with relatively few groups.[22]

A social network is not, however, an organization. Rather it is a social grouping with the individual at the midpoint. To be sure, the social network is not entirely an urban type of group, but it is the kind of social constellation that finds its greatest utility in the city. Moreover, it is the type of constellation that any urbanite at any level can utilize. Such constellations, Southall suggests, are found among African tribesmen who migrate to towns. Many come to be detached from their tribal groupings but are not yet sufficiently adapted to form urban-type organizations.

> In some cases, informal networks of social relations form the interstitial links between families, kin groups, neighbourhoods, factories, and local authorities. They provide contexts for the induction of strangers into new communities. But this interstitial region may also be occupied by more clear-cut groups and associations, serving various functions and changing in this respect over time. They may provide kinship surrogates for persons accustomed in their rural homes to widely ramifying kinship systems which cannot be reproduced in towns and employment centres.[23]

5. *Order in the Urban Community*

A characteristic feature of any community is its way of ensuring continuity of its life and work. Much in life is taken for granted; a person will be on hand for work when expected, assuming that tomorrow life will continue about the same, and one's relationships with friends will not change suddenly. Life and work, also in the changing city, continue with considerable daily and weekly repetition, and one is able to enjoy a degree of security. This has doubtless always been true of community life, which is a cluster of ongoing behaviors, commitments, and

22 Arnold M. Rose, *Sociology*, New York, Knopf, 1965, p. 82.
23 Aidan Southall (Ed.), *Social Change in Modern Africa*, London, Oxford University Press, 1965, pp. 27–28.

expectations. However much things change, the continuing course of things in general is assumed.

If and when rules are made or ordinances enacted, very often they are intended to support and sustain ongoing patterns and processes, the more or less accustomed order of things. Here we are considering what appears to be an ever present feature of community life, urban or rural; there is an order, and the means are usually present to insure in the main the continuity of that order.

We can think of order as an essential product of the prevailing culture in the community, and we can think of the maintenance of order as an essential function of that culture. As the individual becomes identified with the culture of his community, learning what is expected of him, he helps to sustain it by his conformity. Order is thus the enforcement of rules established earlier and the expectations are no less defined by past experience. But the immediate situation, especially in the city, is a changing one. Urban people face the need to maintain the order while at the same time accepting modifications of it.[24]

To Wilensky, the urban community is mass society. "At the top, poorly organized elites, themselves mass oriented, become political and managerial manipulators responding to short-term pressures." [25] At other social levels people respond to the same short-term pressures, although they do not always respond in the manner as the elites. Leaders are not always strictly followed. In fact, leaders often take their cues as they observe the behavior of the followers. Moreover, in the urban community the leadership function tends to be performed in no small measure by institutionalized secondary organizations, most of them "legal persons." As Louis Wirth stated it:

> Since for most purposes it is impossible in the city to appeal individually to the large number of discrete and differentiated citizens, and since it is only through the organizations to which men belong that their interests and resources can be enlisted for a collective cause, it may be inferred that social control in the city should typically proceed through formally organized groups. It follows, too, that the masses of men in the city are subject to manipulation by symbols and stereotypes managed by individuals working from afar or operating invisibly through their control of instruments of communication.[26]

Actually, any society may be subject to control by ambitious persons or power groups, but in modern society mass communication affords

[24] Derived from Wood, op. cit., p. 92.

[25] Harold L. Wilensky, "Mass Society and Mass Culture, Interdependence and Independence," *American Sociological Review*, Vol. 29, No. 2, April 1964, p. 175.

[26] Louis Wirth, "Urbanism as a Way of Life," in Albert J. Reiss, Jr. (Ed.), *On Cities and Social Life*, Chicago, University of Chicago Press, 1964, p. 82; the article originally appeared in the *American Journal of Sociology*, July 1938.

the means for much wider contact. Also, respecting safeguards, the more kinds of large organizations there are, representing all sorts of interests, the more difficult it would be to capture complete control. The existence of a great variety and large number of such organizations attests to the complexity of the urban community, and this indicates an order under dispersed control.

Government becomes increasingly involved as the number and variety of private organizations in the urban community multiply. And yet, the government of a city, however many its responsibilities, tends to be most effective when it is able to perform by indirect means. This public performance role has been evolving through centuries of public service experience. Government and law function mainly to mediate, maintain, or enforce, or to provide services. The real order is the people going about their affairs and using their organizations in a customary manner. This order is found in the continuing social and economic behavior of the community. It carries on the customary ways even while accepting degrees of change.

Participating in this order is every kind of group, small and informal as well as large and formal. As Blumer observes, each group articulates in its own way and adapts, when necessary, to other groups. Most all share certain commonly sustained values and norms.

> An understanding of human groups which are organized in this manner requires little more than an identification of the controlling cultural definitions. Most large group activity and structure in human societies is an expression of such cultural definitions.[27]

Social organizations figure universally in the ordering of life in the community. In the most rural communities the primary group, mainly the family, is most utilized. In the highly urban community the large secondary organization (work and other economic, political, recreational, cultural, or social groups) tends to take precedence, although sustained by the various primary groups.

TOLERANCE IN THE URBAN COMMUNITY

Prejudice is descriptive of negative attitudes; one has a dislike for persons of a certain type. If one hates Negroes, or Italians, or communists, whether they be persons of good or bad character, he may be called prejudiced. Tolerance is expressive of an opposite attitude; one does not hate people because of race, national origin, or political views. Stauffer,

---

[27] Herbert Blumer, "Collective Behavior," in Joseph B. Gittler (Ed.), *Review of Sociology*, New York, Wiley, 1957, p. 130.

in his study of American attitudes toward socialists, anarchists, and communists, found that rural persons were the least tolerant and those in metropolitan places were the most tolerant. In the South the proportion of tolerant attitudes was Farm, 15 percent; Small town, 17 percent; Other cities, 19 percent; Metropolitan, 32 percent. For the East it was Farm, 26 percent; Small town, 40 percent; Other cities, 38 percent; Metropolitan, 50 percent.[28]

Between the extremes of general tolerance and blind prejudice there are, to be sure, degrees of tolerance and prejudice, and different types of both. However, the idea is widely accepted that more tolerance will be found in the city than in the rural village. But urban people may have their fixed and often irrational ideas about things. For example, Murphy reports that decades passed and many urbanites died before people were willing to recognize the elemental facts about pure water. Many who had agitated to have water piped into their cities opposed the idea of water filtration.[29]

When Anthony Trollope visited Canada in 1862, it offended him to observe the docility of French-Canadian peasants confronting their superiors. He mentioned how upper-class English expected such docility on the part of English peasants. Such self-humiliation, he remarked, is not characteristic of cities, for cities breed tolerance but not tolerance for servility. The gentleman must expect to be jostled in the urban throng.

> A crowd of greasy-coated town artisans with grimy hands and pale faces, is not in itself delectable; but each of that crowd has probably more of the goods of life than any rural labourer. He thinks more, reads more, feels more, sees more, hears more, and lives more. It is through great cities that the civilization of the world has progressed, and the charms of life been advanced. Man in his rudest state begins in the country, and in his most finished state may retire there. But the battle of the world has to be fought in the cities; and the country that shows the greatest city population is ever the one that is going most ahead in the world's history.[30]

This tolerance which makes the street as free to the grimy worker as to the gentleman does not mean the absence of prejudice. It does not mean that the white worker is willing to share his work place with a black worker or with a white worker who speaks a strange language. The white urban man may not object if he sees a black man and a white

28 Samuel A. Stauffer, *Communists, Conformity, and Civil Liberties*, Garden City, New York, Doubleday, 1955, p. 118.

29 Earl F. Murphy, *Water Purity*, Madison, University of Wisconsin Press, 1961, p. 24.

30 Anthony Trollope, *North America*, New York, Knopf, 1951, p. 50; 1st ed., 1862.

woman walking together in the street but, as ample examples have shown, he is likely to resist if a family of another race or nationality moves into his apartment house.

Sofer tells of Jinja, Uganda, a community of 10,000 to 15,000 inhabitants in 1954. The population was comprised of 2 percent Europeans, mostly British in administration and government; 45 percent Asians, mostly Indian shopkeepers and white-collar workers; and 53 percent Africans, sharply divided into tribal groups. Under the tight control of the governmental structures, an accepted relationship of coexistence was maintained as the racial mixture was learning to share the city.[31]

The city affords the opportunity for different types of people to share the streets and the markets, and to foregather, each with his own kind, to an extent that would not be permitted in the homogeneous rural village. Varying with different individuals, contact between the different types is possible and degrees of tolerance do develop. However, the stranger who fled the bias of his village does find some degree of freedom in the city, and sometimes more opportunity to meet others of his kind. The initial efforts in developing this aspect of urbanism may be confusing, as in Jinja.

> Jinja is not a European town, nor an Asian town, nor an African town. It is an urban area whose characteristics are largely a function of an inter-racial structure. The parts played by the different racial categories in producing the present situation are important for the immigrants mainly insofar as they facilitate or impose their participation and their formation into coherent groups in the existing and involved social structure.[32]

ESSENTIAL FUNCTIONS OF THE COMMUNITY

The substance of this chapter to this point has been an endeavor to define and describe the urban community and to present some of the salient characteristics of urbanism as a way of life. We turn now to a brief review of the functions of the urban community, first considering the functions of any community, urban or rural.

Any community is the unique locale where the essential culture traits are most at home, especially those having to do with distinctive norms and values. It is a place in which people share in their work

---

[31] Rhona Sofer, "Adjustment Problems of Africans in an Early Phase of Industrialism at Jinja, Uganda," *Social Implications of Industrialization and Urbanization in Africa South of the Sahara,* Paris, UNESCO, 1956, p. 616.

[32] Ibid., p. 616.

and, in some respects, share their problems. It is where they participate variously in the ongoing order. Children are born and trained and the old have some claim to security. Any community tends to be so constituted that it is able to cope with the problems of supply and safety.[33] Any community tends to assume collective responsibility for protection against such risks as robbery, theft, assault, and disaster. It must be able in the event of disaster to organize and regroup, so the usual course of life can get under way again.

In addition to the responsibilities assumed by any human community, a city may have certain wider functions. Kallen says that although "certain of the city's functions affect the welfare of the region and even, on occasion, the whole nation, its direct, immediate functions are services to its own citizens." [34] The reverse of this is equally true; while the immediate functions of cities are services to their own citizens, they also have functions for the service of their regions. Briefly, here are four of the more salient and unique urban functions.

1. *Leadership and Authority*

It has, probably, always been true that a king, or high religious authority governed or administered his domain from the vantage point of a city. In modern times, the corporation may have branch plants in many places, but its head offices will be in some great city. The trade union with locals throughout the nation is likely to have its head offices in the city where the seat of government is located. This holds no less for associations organized for political, cultural, social, or scientific purposes; their membership may be dispersed but their headquarters will be concentrated in great cities.[35]

Because of such a concentration of authorities and leadership roles in the great centers, persons of talent, including intellectuals, tend to be attracted from smaller places to cities. For similar reasons, wealthy families are most likely to have their places of residence in large cities where the most exclusive social circles are to be found, a phenomenon which is evident even in communist countries. Pirenne mentions how in medieval times the rural nobles, whose wealth was in landed estates and who owned rural castles, came to have town residences.[36]

---

[33] The matter of supply for London involves much of its activity; see William A. Robson (Ed.), *Great Cities of the World*, London, Allen and Unwin, 1957, pp. 55 ff.

[34] Kallen, op. cit., p. 186.

[35] On the ecology of voluntary associations and their headquarters in the United States, see Stanley Lieberson and Irving L. Allen, Jr., "Location of National Headquarters of Voluntary Associations," *Administrative Science Quarterly*, Vol. 8, December 1963, pp. 316–318.

[36] Henri Pirenne, *Medieval Cities*, Garden City, New York, Doubleday, 1956, p. 130; 1st ed., 1920.

2. Special Markets and Services

It is well known that a grocery store, a meat market, a garage, and other services at that level will be found in most villages and small towns. But a shoe store for women only, a haberdasher for men, a furrier, a large department store are found in cities. Very special stores for the elite trade, the medical specialist, the corporation lawyer, and the industrial engineering firm are more likely to be found in large cities. The more exclusive the market, the more likely it is to be in the great city.

3. Accumulations in the City

Cities, as already mentioned, are centers where talent and wealth accumulate. Because of the accumulation of wealth and talent, the symbols of art and knowledge accumulate in the museums and libraries found in large cities. Special skills of every sort and all the technical paraphernalia conducive to fostering skill will be there. All such capabilities and institutions serve wide regions. Regarding the function of cities, Ogburn writes:

> To the credit of the large city, then, are its economic advantages, which can be realized, thanks to the modern technology of production and transportation. Many observers have reported favorable reactions to the metropolis on other grounds as well. Here one finds the best in the artistic and intellectual life. Opera is heard and there are more and better concerts in very large cities than in smaller ones, many more exhibitions of painting and sculpture and more products for sale. . . .

> The largest city of a country generally contains more theaters than smaller cities. Publications emanate from great cities, where the editorial offices tend to be found . . . others like the metropolis for what it offers in recreations that may not be highly ranked as music, art and the theater.[37]

4. Diversion in the Large City

To "go to town" is an Americanism associated with leisure activity in an atmosphere of "joy unrestrained." The concept identifies the city as a place to which one goes for fun and diversion, escaping temporarily the strict controls of the rural community. The term also may be used by urban people. The idea of going to the town or city for diversion is very old and is historically related to commercial enterprise. For ex-

[37] William F. Ogburn, "Technology and Cities, the Dilemma of the Modern Metropolis," *Sociological Quarterly*, Vol. 1, No. 3, July 1960, p. 143.

ample, not only did "Simple Simon meet a pieman going to the fair," others met the pieman, and at the fair they were entertained by jugglers and singers. Fun-makers of every sort went from town to town where fairs were held. The fair, as we glean from Pirenne, gave to towns a periodic holiday spirit.

> They were centres of exchange and especially of wholesale exchange, and set out to attract the greatest number of people and of goods, independent of all local considerations. They may perhaps be compared with international exhibitions, for they exclude nothing and nobody; any individual, no matter what his country, every article which could be bought or sold, whatever its nature, was assured a welcome. Moreover, it was impossible to hold them more than once, or at least twice a year, so great was the necessary preparation involved. . . . But the important thing is that each fair was open to all trade, just as each seaport was open to all shipping.[38]

As does the city today, the fair that came to the medieval town served all levels from lowbrow to highbrow. It provided work for singers, dancers, jugglers, actors, musicians, fortunetellers, and fakirs. Such was the beginning of the entertainment industries. This role of the city as a provider of diversion is largely responsible for the negative image of town life held by many country people.

HOW URBANISM REACHES OUT

Today the rural man does not need to trudge his way to the fair to hear the jokes and watch the antics of entertainers. These and much more come to him by radio, television, or the movies. As a result, most traditional forms of rural amusement have gone out of style. As urban ways of leisure become rural ways, so the urban ways of work and commitment to the use of technology come to be taken over by rural people. Gallaher relates how some average farmers in Plainville became big farmers, using more and more machinery, but the poor farmers with too little land often lost out because their land lacks fertility or they lacked capital.

> The full adoption of technological changes for modern farms and homes, for example, poses several imperatives; more land, more live stock, increased mechanization, more capital, and greater management skill. Obviously, those who find it most difficult to achieve these imperatives are the approximate one and one half million farm families who live on substandard farms. Most Plainvillers are included in this number . . . for

[38] Henri Pirenne, *Economic and Social History of Medieval Europe*, New York, Harcourt, Brace & World, 1937, pp. 96–97.

them it is a question whether mechanical power can be efficiently adapted to their farms or whether income from their produce can even offset the expense of recommended soil-building chemicals, let alone permit them a standard of living which psychologically they already accept. And there still remains the most important question of all; can they ever compete with the more fortunate family farmers and the growing number of industrialized farmers short of outright full subsidy.[39]

Urban measures of efficiency and success are adopted by rural people, their adoption being compelled by the fact that both segments are on the same money economy and both compete in common markets. Rural children receive the same type of education as urban children and acquire similar aspirations. Rural areas in the countryside which, by their own standards, were quite self-sustaining in 1900 (before mass contact with the city by the mass media and the automobile) are now rated as poverty areas. Mitchell studied three such rural communities in northern England. Each in 1871 was a whole community with its own shops and its own craftsmen. All signs of self-containment have now vanished and, by comparison with urban communities, these places are economically depressed.[40]

By the outward extension of the urban-centered economy many rural areas find themselves in a weak position. Outlying communities that once had minor industries may suddenly find themselves with no industry at all because their little plants are no longer able to compete with the more efficient plants in cities. Most small industries that might operate in remote rural places can function more economically in urban places. Consider railroading, for example; many small places in Canada and the United States gained a livelihood by being railroad division points for servicing trains. With the coming of diesel engines, outmoding steam locomotives, longer trains can be pulled much greater distances. Many division points are not needed, another negative effect of the industrialism centering in cities.[41]

Since the beginning of cities the countryside has functioned in a service relation to them. Changes in the ways of life and work of rural people have been both stimulated and their course of change defined by urban influence. The difference is that in our time the contacts are much more numerous and they become increasingly varied. Rural people become urbanized in their ways of life, but it is not always possible for

   39 Gallaher, op. cit., p. 258.

   40 G. Duncan Mitchell, "Social Disintegration in a Rural Community," *Human Relations*, Vol. 3, No. 3, 1950, p. 303.

   41 For a moving account of how a long-standing railroad division point in Nevada was all but destroyed by dieselization, see W. F. Cottrell, "Death by Dieselization, a Case Study in the Reaction to Technological Change," *American Sociological Review*, Vol. 16, No. 3, June 1951, p. 360.

them to become equally industrialized in their ways of work. Those who cannot live by agriculture may find it better to migrate to cities. Farmers who have ample quantities of good land and can mechanize their work are most likely to prosper. The net result is that the country which is most urban and industrial will have a small proportion of its population in agriculture. Thus in the United States there are seven to eight industrial workers for each agricultural worker, while in such a country as India, with relatively little industry, there are seven to eight agricultural workers for each industrial worker.

Evolution of the urban community | 3

PERTINENCE OF THE CITY IN HISTORY

To better understand any community today, especially a complex city, it is helpful to know something about its yesterdays. But the past of cities is a long story reaching back 4,000 to 5,000 years, all of which may be of great human interest as knowledge, although not pertinent to the situation of a modern city. Most important for us are the recent centuries.

Yet, during these long-ago centuries various important developments began in cities and helped to fashion their ways of living, one outstanding example being the invention of writing. The institution of kingship, out of which civil government ultimately emerged, must have taken form very early because the city as market had to have its order. The king was the symbol of legitimate authority and writing enabled him to operate more effectively.

Self-government in cities, whereby major decision-making was shared by the different elite groups, apparently began with the Romans, but its more precise elements emerged in the Middle Centuries, when the guilds found a place in the council chambers. That must have been a slow development, but the details are not especially pertinent for our study. We know that ancient cities and some important medieval cities were states, a few even to the last century. Subsequently they became subdivisions of the modern type of state or province, but that evolution is only indirectly relevant.[1]

One generalization that can be made about the evolution of cities concerns their growth out of the rural life of their regions. In the course of decades in some countries, centuries in older countries, the biography

1 John Sirjamaki, *The Sociology of Cities,* New York, Random House, 1964, Chaps. 1 and 13.

44

of a city was linked with the history of its region. Despite many similarities, comparing cities around the world, each is unique. The life story of each is revealed in the material and nonmaterial traits of its culture. The city's link with its history is not always visible, but it may be compelling. Comparing Bombay with Madras, Chouhan sees deep-rooted differences. The latter, being less in the mainstream of commerce, has been less invaded by outsiders. Whereas in 1951 in Bombay 70 percent of the inhabitants were born elsewhere, 39 percent of the inhabitants of Madras were of nonnative birth. Also in 1951 there were in Bombay 168 males to each 100 females, while the ratio in Madras was 109 to 100.

Bombay, as pictured by Chouhan, has become so deluged by strangers in recent years that their presence has rendered invisible much of the city's old character. The opposite is true for Madras. Yet the regional character of Bombay has not been extinguished. Rules regarding marital relations continue and so do various functions of community life. He mentions, for example, that "Fortune tellers are [still] linked with the richest of the brokers." [2]

Modern cities are least tied to the past in matters of structure and technology. The means of transportation most used are technically new. Electricity is almost everywhere used for heat, light, and power. New also are the uses of concrete, metals, and glass in construction; and new are the means of communication. All of these are typically urban, and each of them has had a profound impact on community structure.

CHANGE PROCESSES AND TRADITION

To say that urbanism is often anti-tradition does not mean that urban thinking is generally anti-tradition. Vestigial traditional elements, for example, as they relate to manners and speech, may be strictly cherished. Berlin's dialect or that of certain American southern cities are examples. Wylie holds that among Frenchmen one finds notions about peasants which are rooted in traditional ideas about the soil and agriculture. He notes that certain French urban traits are reflective of such attitudes.

> One must also be aware of the French attachment to the soil. Probably most city people everywhere have a sentimental feeling for rural life, all the stronger if they have had little farm experience. At any rate, this feeling is particularly strong in France. However much the bourgeois may

2 Brij Raj Chouhan, "Cities and Tradition," in T. K. N. Unnithan, Indra Deva, and Yogendra Singh (Eds.), *Towards a Sociology of Culture for India*, New Delhi, Prentice-Hall, 1965, pp. 395–401.

condemn the boorish peasant and use the word "paysan" as an insult to
fling at awkward drivers in a Parisian traffic jam, still they feel a need to
attach themselves as closely as they can to rural life. They hang on to
the old family farm and manage to spend a few days a year there re-
newing the virtuous contact with the soil. There is an old tradition of
blasé city people from Marie-Antoinette to Jean Gabin, playing at being
farmers. Otherwise they are "déracinés"; they have lost their roots. The
"peasantism" to which Wright refers is based on this belief that the
strength and virtue of France depend on the strength and virtue of independent little farmers.[3]

There may be, as Wylie suggests, a lingering rural bias in the otherwise quite traditionless city. Most of the new cities of North America
borrowed English municipal traditions, which mixed with rural traditions of their own. Thus, nostalgic attitudes which reflect a rural image
of country life and growing things are still very much present in American cities, and they constitute one of the core motivations for the flight
from the crowded city to the suburbs.

Many aspects of the urban community, however, depart widely from
time-honored traditions. Childe visualizes the blacksmith who learned
to get metal out of ore, and who learned to make tools and things out
of the metal, as the first craftsman in history. Unless it was the potter
who made things of clay, the blacksmith was the first industrialist.[4] In
the New World he was first among inventors, making guns, clocks,
wagons, machines, and so on. In those countries where craftsmen still
use hand tools to make things, the tradition of the blacksmith carries
on. Industry came on the scene to make the tool a part of the machine
which man manipulated, a tradition-breaking arrangement. Then came
the corporation, a social invention for managing a total work situation.
Mundy and Riesenberg mention early corporations in France in which
during a crisis situation various associations were formed.

> From being narrow bodies of mill operators and owners, they became
> broad associations of shareholders in a common enterprise. The share-
> holders entrusted the operation of the mills to well-paid specialists, workers
> and officers. Later a real managerial group appeared, specializing in legal
> and financial affairs. Management developed the conception of the *honor*
> to describe the society as a whole. Similar to the modern corporation, the
> honor was a fictional legal person, theoretically perpetual. Its investors
> were liable only to the amount invested.[5]

[3] Laurence Wylie, review of *Rural Revolution in France, the Peasantry of the
Twentieth Century,* by Gordon Wright, *American Journal of Sociology,* Vol. 71, No. 6,
May 1966, p. 736.

[4] V. Gordon Childe, *Man Makes Himself,* London, Watts, 1956, p. 118; 1st ed.,
1936.

[5] John H. Mundy and Peter Riesenberg, *The Medieval Town,* New York, Van
Nostrand, 1958, p. 75.

This forerunner of the industrial corporation experimented with the complexities of making a formal organization for managing work operations in their more complex arrangements. We may assume that before the 1700s there had been various experiments with corporate management before expert knowledge accumulated to enable efficient use of such instruments. This special kind of learning was another breaker of tradition.

Another aspect of this evolution concerned learning to live in cities which were becoming bigger and more challenging than any man had known. In this mass society with its evolving mass industry the idea of trade unionism began to take form. But a century of trial and error had to pass before organized labor, despite the resistance of tradition, appeared. While one section of society was making strides in managing corporate industry another section of society, the workers, wrestled, for their own defense, with the intricacies of evolving trade unionism.

CONCERNING THE IDEA OF PROGRESS

Some who speak of evolution use the term interchangeably with progress. Ginsberg reminds us that there is a great difference. "Neither development nor evolution is the same as progress. Progress is development or evolution in a direction which satisfies rational criteria of value." [6] Man sets the standards of value, and much that is called progress in the industrial society has reference to material change in a desired direction. The businessman calls it progress if his city is growing, especially if his own business increases. The term has other uses, as we shall see.

In medieval times one did not speak of progress, in the sense that man can improve his condition by rational methods; that would have been regarded as radicalism. The idea began with certain philosophers in the seventeenth century, among them Pascal, a French mathematician (1623–1662). Pascal's thought is summarized here by Sampson:

> Man alone, of all forms of life, was endowed with sufficient powers both of memory and communication, to enable him to inherit a living body of knowledge from his predecessors, by beginning at the point where they left off, to proceed in each generation to add to the store that had been amassed through the ages. The notion received its most vivid illustration at the hands of Pascal. . . . And since knowledge was power—power above all over physical nature, as it seemed to those who lived to see the birth of a modern physical science—man was a creature able to exert increasing control over and independent of his environment.[7]

[6] Morris Ginsberg, *Essays in Sociology and Social Philosophy,* London, Heinemann, 1961, Vol. III, p. 30.

[7] R. V. Sampson, *Progress in the Age of Reason,* London, Heinemann, 1956, p. 39.

The arguments of that time involved a clash between those who held science as authority and the source of knowledge and those who regarded the ancients as authority and the source of knowledge. De Condorcet, writing a century later, is credited with being the most active of the proponents of the idea of progress. He visualized the possibility of man's infinite advance through purposeful and rational effort.

> The human species can be improved, firstly, by new discoveries in the arts and sciences and, consequently, in the means of well-being and common prosperity; secondly, by progress in the principles of conduct and moral practice, and thirdly, by the improvement of human faculty. This may be the result of improvements in the instruments which increase the intensity of change, the direction of the use of our faculties or perhaps also of a change in the innate organization itself.[8]

Much that is called progress, as well as change not called progress, would be included in any look at the evolution of the urban community. Also some developments called progress at one time may be differently viewed at a later time. Ekirch notes that during the American frontier period progress had ceased to be a mere philosophical idea, and came to be central to the American conception of *mission*.

> The faith of the early Republic in the general progress of democracy through the peaceful workings of the American example became transferred into a dogma of expansion—political and material. Against the opposition to expansion offered by the Indians and by the Mexicans, the concept of progress was used to prove that backward peoples must yield to the force of civilization or be crushed in its advance. To the expansionist's slogan of manifest destiny the idea of progress imparted a kind of historic background and a vision of a better future for all—conquerors and conquered alike.[9]

This notion that "might makes right" was not uniquely American; it found expression in the colonial policy of various European countries. Even the exercise of such a policy, whether called progress or not, would figure in any look at the evolution of a city or a country. As for cities, however we look at their evolution, we can see that progress is evident in the sanitation of cities, in their relative freedom from plagues, in the buildings erected for whatever use. Most work has been relieved of the drudgery element and the productivity of work increases. Levels of liv-

---

8 J. N. C. de Condorcet (*Esquisse d'un tableau historique des progrès de l'esprit humain*), English translation, *Historical Essay on the Progress of Human Reason*, London, 1795. Still a standard work on the subject, J. B. Bury, *The Idea of Progress*, New York, Macmillan, 1932.

9 Arthur A. Ekirch, Jr., *The Idea of Progress in America, 1815–1860*, New York, Peter Smith, 1951, pp. 37, 70.

ing rise, workers have more leisure, and education becomes more universal. Ayres states, "What the evidence shows is that humbug, crudity, and squalor have been decreasing for the population as a whole throughout modern times, as they have been decreasing through the history of the race." [10]

ON THE ANCIENT CITY

The little we know about ancient cities serves to pique the imagination. Records written long ago are seldom as revealing as we would wish. Exaggerated description was often accepted with relish. This is seen in a document of about the sixth century A.D. describing the Indian city of Sagala, included by Mukerjee in his study of Indian art and culture.

Sagala is seen as located in the country of the Konakas, "well-watered and hilly, abounding in parks, gardens, groves and lakes." The writer does not mention fields. The city is walled, protected by moats, and its gates are strong. It is called a peaceful city because all its "enemies and adversaries have been put down." It is a well laid out city, for its architects are wise, and its marts are filled with costly merchandise.

Within Sagala's walls, the ancient writer avers, are "hundreds of thousands of magnificent mansions, which rise aloft like the mountain peaks of the Himalayas." He tells how the streets are crowded with carriers, camels, and pedestrians and how strangers of many kind may be seen, including students, teachers, merchants, and holy men of many sects. Sagala was a free city.

> Shops are there for the sale of Barbaras muslin, of Kotunbara stuffs, and of other cloths of various kinds; and sweet odours are exhaled from the bazaars, where all sorts of flowers and perfumes are tastefully set out. Jewels are there in plenty, and guilds of traders in all sorts of finery, display their goods in bazaars which face all quarters of the sky.[11]

Without doubt, the streets of Sagala were crowded, more so than in our auto age, but then the crowds were taken for granted. And Sagala was cosmopolitan; men of all religions were there. It was enough of a regional city that leaders of the different religions resided there. Note that only the luxury markets were mentioned and the "hundreds of thousands of magnificent mansions." That would mean millions of

10 C. E. Ayres, *The Theory of Economic Progress*, Chapel Hill, University of North Carolina Press, 1944, p. 244.
11 Radhakamal Mukerjee, *The Culture and Art of India*, London, Allen and Unwin, 1959, p. 133.

inhabitants. Nothing is said of what so many did for a livelihood. Even modern students of ancient cities are vague about the work side, as often they are unrealistic in their estimates of the number of inhabitants in ancient cities, freely speaking of a million or a half-million, giving no thought to the matter of ancient cities providing themselves with food, fuel, feed, and water. Sjoberg mentions the problem of transportation in both ancient and medieval towns, and suggests that 10,000 inhabitants would be considerable for many of them.[12]

The cities of Greece and Rome, as considered by Fustel de Coulanges, were markets for their regions and in each region there were many villages. The leading cities were governed and in fact owned by clusters of families. "Several families formed the phratry, several phratries the tribe, several tribes the city. . . . The city was a confederation. Hence it was obliged, at least for several centuries, to respect the religious and civil independence of the tribes, phratries and families." [13] Strangers were welcome as traders or they were used as slaves, but they could not become citizens. The citizens were representatives of family lines. Each city had its gods and each family its household gods. One could be a citizen only of the city where his god or gods resided.

> Each city had its corps of priests, who depended upon no foreign authority. Between the priests of two cities there was no bond, no communication, no exchange of instruction or of rites. If one passed from one city to another, he found other gods, other dogmas, other ceremonies. The ancients had books of liturgies, but those of one city did not resemble those of another. Every city had its collection of prayers and practices, which were kept very secret; it would have thought itself in danger of compromising its religion and its destiny by opening this collection to strangers.[14]

In time the family-centered system encountered difficulty. Each family had attached to it an array of servants who had lower rank, although some had high responsibility and were able in managing affairs. Some in time became citizens. These came to be known as the clients. Lower down were the plebeians.

> At Rome the difference between the two classes was startling. The city of the patricians and their clients was the one that Romulus founded, according to the rites, on the Palatine. The dwellings of the plebs were in the asylum, a species of enclosure situated on the slope of the Capi-

[12] Gideon Sjoberg, *The Preindustrial City, Past and Present*, New York, Free Press, 1960, p. 323.

[13] N. D. Fustel de Coulanges, *The Ancient City*, Garden City, New York, Donbleday Anchor, 1955, p. 127; 1st ed., 1864.

[14] Ibid., p. 151.

toline Hill, where Romulus admitted people without hearth or home, whom he could not admit to the city. Later when the new plebeians came to Rome, as they were strangers to the religion of the city, they were established on the Aventine—that is to say, without the pomoerium, or religious city. . . . The plebs were a despised and abject class, beyond the pale of religion, law, society and the family. The patrician could compare such an existence only with that of the brutes. . . . The touch of the plebeian was impure.[15]

With the passing of time the clients pressured their way into the full rights of citizenship, becoming patricians. Following that, the plebs in the sixth century B.C., many having risen in status to skilled occupations and even to wealth in some cases, staged a type of revolution. To their advantage was the gradual decline of familism and the rise of the idea of the city being a republic governed more by civil than by tribal law. Methods of war were changing, the foot soldier was coming to be more important, and an army had come to be a host of men. Plebeians were needed and some plebs rose to high military rank. Thus the evolution of Roman cities was one of stages.

1. The initial step was made by the citizen aristocracy as they coerced the king and gradually took over his power.
2. The early servant class (clients, gentes) moved out of servant status to become shopkeepers, managers, and lesser officials or upper military officers, and were able in time to demand and gain a place in the circle of authority.
3. The plebeians, from a despised position, century by century gained more secure position, following the upward course taken by the clients and taking over former client roles, until they too gained citizen status.[16]

In such a manner, the social organization of Roman cities evolved.

EVOLVING SKILLS IN CITY MANAGEMENT

It may be presumed that, speaking generally, medieval cities were larger than ancient cities, and without doubt their organization for management was more complex. Increasing size alone results in complexity of administration for most organizations. But management skills change as men learn from past experience and as their relationships become more widespread. We know that advances were made in commerce between ancient and medieval times. The medieval city needed clock time and made use of it. Work organization became more complex and so too

15 Ibid., p. 231.
16 Ibid., pp. 237–245, 269–273.

the role of merchants. Cities were gradually changing from an economy of tribute to one of commerce. Increasing size and complexity were major evolutionary factors in this change.[17]

Ancient cities were, in many cases, able to organize for mass undertakings, such as building their walls, organizing disciplined armies, and maintaining government over tributary areas. Rome even constructed a system of roads and promoted economic development in conquered areas. What came down to us out of the experience of ancient cities, in particular from Greece and Rome? In regard to Greece, Wallbank and Taylor conclude, "It could almost be said that the Greeks taught us to live properly without learning the secret themselves. . . . And the Greeks gave us a most valuable political idea; the nobility of public service and the necessity of citizenship participation." [18] The lessons the Greeks taught the Romans, who in turn took the beginning steps in the development of law and public administration, were developed later by other cities of the West.

It would not be incorrect to say that in Rome at the height of Roman power, the emergence of public bureaucracy began. Perhaps the forms and methods were elemental, but the situation called for the making and keeping of records. This function was later taken over and further developed by the Church of Rome, through that period called the "Dark Ages."

While not fostering private industry, the goverment of Rome carried on a gigantic public enterprise in which the army constituted the work force. The returns, notes Heaton, came in three forms: 1) safety from the tribes that once harassed Rome, 2) rewards in the form of booty and tribute, and 3) business opportunities for Roman enterprisers who took contracts for building ships and for collecting and distributing tribute.

> Finally, the collection of these claims on the income of property of the vanquished called for a little army of administrators of high and low degree, for ships in which the tribute in kind could be carried to Rome, and for capitalists who were willing to finance the collection of the levies, the registration of wasted lands, the development of new ones.[19]

What is too often overlooked by historians is that during some four centuries of contact, Rome brought to the "barbarians" much knowledge

---

[17] On the pertinence of size and complexity, see Theodore Caplow, *Principles of Organization*, New York, Harcourt, Brace & World, 1964, pp. 25–28.

[18] T. W. Wallbank and A. M. Taylor, *Civilization, Past and Present*, Chicago, Scott, Foresman, 1950, Vol. I, p. 11.

[19] Herbert Heaton, *Economic History of Europe*, New York, Harper & Row, 1948, pp. 42–43.

about doing things. Rome's influence was definitely felt later when cities in the once-conquered areas began attaining size and self-government. While the Romans built roads, some still existing, and used the roads to carry away tribute, they left behind the concept of government by civil law, a valuable heritage.

MEDIEVAL REVIVAL OF CITIES

Cities under the control of Rome did not develop as centers of industry and commerce. Such development, which might have led to ideas about independence, were not encouraged by Rome. Cities occupied by the Roman legions were merely points from which control was administered or they were service stations for the collection of tribute. Not until 306 A.D. when the Empire was divided, Constantine ruling from the Adriatic eastward, did change begin. In the eastern region, its capital Constantinople, commerce was a province of the merchants operating under military protection.

After the fall of Rome commerce in the old Roman Empire came to a standstill and four centuries passed before trade began to revive. They were the "dark" centuries mainly for city development. Pirates dominated the Mediterranean shoreline and Norse raiders prevented trade from developing on the Atlantic side of Europe. Without trade, the towns stagnated. Rural areas, however, because of a favorable climate and fertile soil, could be self-efficient. Heaton notes, "The Roman Empire in the west ended with a class of great land owners exercising far-reaching power over *coloni* and slaves, with stagnant or decaying towns." [20]

Lacking trade with the outside, towns in western Europe lapsed into a state of isolation. There was little need of city-to-city commerce. The one wide-reaching organization, extending to all parts of the old Empire, was the Church. In most towns the bishop governed in secular as well as in sacred affairs. There was the secular nobility, to be sure, but their source of income was agricultural. While some ruled in towns, those who resided in castles on their estates were better situated. None during those dark centuries had much access to capital. Business and industry became so minor an influence, it was not difficult for them to hold traders in low esteem.

The whole Empire, abandoned after the Roman legions dissolved, was left to the ravages of the "barbarians." Many places were destroyed utterly and most of the surviving inhabitants were enslaved. The only

[20] Ibid., p. 58.

stabilizing force was the Roman Church, but its influence took hold only gradually, requiring two or more centuries.[21]

The rule of the Church came to be the only authority that kings, princes, and grand dukes would respect. In general, they accepted the Church ban on usury. Money gained through business, they learned to frown upon. As late as the fifteenth century it was resented if one gentleman of the nobility called another a merchant or a trader, but either would feel virtuous if he could win equal sums by gambling with cards. Not until the merchants began to enter the titled ranks did this attitude change.

However, as Mundy and Riesenberg indicate, the Church did encourage various economic ventures, such as developing certain land areas. Thus, while Europe was in poverty in terms of cash, it was not food-supply poverty. Even in the cities with minimal cash commerce the craftsmen still had work. They went on making cloth, shoes, harnesses, things of wood and metal, and the building crafts continued to function. The Church saw to that. This leadership was provided by the monastic orders which began about the tenth century.

> Primarily agrarian, these orders were able to mobilize ample resources for great purposes. Throughout the eleventh and twelfth centuries the monks invested in land mortgages. Capital was dear in those days, but land was plentiful and barely settled. But the primary activity of the clergy was not, nor could it be, lending money. The monks usually worked in partnership with the secular or ecclesiastical lords to develop lands and capitalize exploitations. These partnerships had implications that transcend economics.[22]

During those centuries of lean urban activity the customers of the weaver, tailor, shoemaker, and blacksmith lived not more than a day's walk from the town. The guilds were secure as they never had been under Roman rule. As Pirenne tells us, the areas of towns and their boundaries had not changed since they had been laid out by the Romans. Church authority followed the same area divisions. "In fact, from the beginning of the sixth century the word *civitas* took the special mean-

---

21 Only after this manuscript was completed did this writer come upon a book on medieval Europe by a French writer, Boissonnade. It takes account of Roman influence over four centuries in bringing industrial skills to the out-regions and Roman revolutionary influence in developing a new agriculture in these regions. A chapter is given to the ruthless destruction that followed the fall of Rome, Boissonnade gives full credit to the Roman Church for bringing order and stability, and he relates the later influence of the Church as it opposed economic development, the expansion of trade, and the growth of a more representative government in the cities. See P. Boissonnade, *Life and Work in Medieval Europe,* Trans. by Eileen Power, New York, Harper & Row, 1964, pp. 4, 26–30, 34–36, 46–48, and 150–158.

22 Mundy and Riesenberg, op. cit., p. 26.

ing of 'episcopal city,' to safeguard the existence of Roman cities." [23]

Pirenne points to the plight of Charlemagne's empire of the ninth century. Without a navy, there was no defense against the Saracen pirates on the Mediterranean or the Danish and Norwegian raiders of settlements along the shores and rivers of western and northern Europe. Nor did Charlemagne have the power to establish an army or to levy taxes against the many feudal princes that occupied his domain. The weakness of the Empire meant more power for the Church, and the towns were quite free. The economic base of "the state, as of society, was from this time on the landed proprietor. Just as the Carolingian Empire was an inland state without foreign markets, so it was essentially an agricultural state." [24]

Moreover, this inland empire took pride in being identified with the land. Commerce, mainly carried on by strangers, was held in low esteem. In the main, secular nobles lived in their castles surrounded by their peasants, whereas the bishops were at home in the towns. The two types of authority had little reason for clash. The bishops were in the stronger position because they held the weapon of excommunication, which even the highest of nobles could not ignore.

Constantinople in the meanwhile had become the leader in commerce, and because of her power, the ports of the Mediterranean opened to trade in the eleventh century. The second major development took place in the north, where the Scandinavians were finding it more lucrative to engage in trade than in coastal raids. Pirenne notes how trade contributed to change.

> It was only in the twelfth century that, gradually but definitely, western Europe was transformed. The economic development freed her from the traditional immobility to which a social organization, depending solely on the relations of man to the soil, had condemned her. Commerce and industry did not merely find a place alongside of agriculture; they reacted upon it. Its products no longer served solely for the consumption of the landed proprietors and the tillers of the soil; they were brought into general circulation, as objects of barter or as raw material.[25]

No less important was the effect commerce had on altering the outlook of cities. Tight restrictions and the limited activity sphere imposed by the Church were no longer accepted. It was not revolutionary change but a matter of particulars. Without being eliminated from the control circle in the medieval town, ecclesiastical influence was modified. Pirenne adds that the country "oriented itself afresh to the city."

[23] Henri Pirenne, *Medieval Cities*, Garden City, New York, Doubleday, 1956, p. 8; 1st ed., 1925.
[24] Ibid., p. 28.
[25] Ibid., p. 72.

THE MERCHANTS AND URBAN CHANGE

Cities are typically work places, and the "dark" centuries were dark mainly because cities were deprived of work, isolated from the outside. The arrival of the merchants, once the trade routes opened, brought pronounced change in about the twelfth century. Towns of the north were getting Bordeaux wine, fruits from Spain, and spices from the Orient. Western metalware and lumber were arriving in the eastern Mediterranean area. Mundy and Riesenberg relate how commerce expanded.

> . . . its significance is clearly illustrated by an entry in the book of a Stockholm merchant. In 1328, the good Esterling sold to a Swedish noble family:

1½ pounds of saffron derived from Spain or Italy	5 pounds of pepper from the Malabar coast
12 pounds of kummel and	3 pounds of anis from southern Germany
90 of almonds from the Mediterranean	
4¾ pounds of Indian ginger	3 pounds galangal from Asia
½ pound paradise from Africa	150 pounds of rice and
1 pound Singhalese cinnamon	4 pounds of sugar from Spain
	3 barrels wine, one Rhine and two French [26]

From these figures we can imagine the great number of merchants participating in serving one wealthy family. To be sure, much of the trade was in luxury goods, as is to be expected with such limited transport facilities.

For that period in Sweden, the merchant was regarded with wonder, as well as with suspicion. Hansson states, "He was rather a foreigner who spent much of his time traveling. He kept his family and stores behind water and palisades [protective post fences] in the rare merchant colonies of the time; the 'cities' of Birka near Stockholm, Kauping near Oslo, Hedeby near Lubeck." [27]

Being a stranger ever under suspicion, the pioneering merchant had to be resourceful. Always traveling with his wares at his own risk, he had to be a man of courage. Perhaps part of his security, such as he had,

---

[26] Mundy and Riesenberg, op. cit., p. 33.
[27] Borje Hansson, "Urban Activity, Urban People, and Urban Environment in Scandinavian History," in Nels Anderson (Ed.), *Urbanism and Urbanization*, Leiden, Brill, 1964, p. 145.

lay in the fact that he was a man of mystery, and robbing him might be bad luck. To many, he was a comic character. Apparently some feared his coming, believing he brought bad luck. "This vagabond of trade," quoting Pirenne, "by the very strangeness of his manner of life must have, from the very first, astonished the agricultural society." [28]

The merchant brought news from other places and he learned to make the most of the relating of news. In time he acquainted people who never traveled with some knowledge of and appreciation for moving about. The merchant, with little honor, and the knight, who was highly honored, symbolized mobility. Moreover, the merchant, not identified with local tradition, was outside all local value systems. His value system was strictly rational and linked with the rules of making money. He had no need to be concerned about status in local terms. His kind of realism in time came to be copied by others. Especially since he had money, he came to be looked to by others for help, an advantage he made the most of.

> The nobility never had anything but disdain for these upstarts who came from no one knew where, and whose insolent good fortune they could not bear. They were infuriated to see them better supplied with money than themselves; they were humiliated by being obliged to have recourse, in time of trouble, to the purse of these newly rich. Save in Italy where aristocratic families did not hesitate to augment their fortunes by having an interest in commercial operations in the capacity of money lender. The prejudice that it was degrading to engage in business remained deep-rooted in the heart of the feudal caste up to the time of the French revolution.[29]

It was that firm unwillingness of the titled nobility to engage in business or to initiate some industrial venture that left the field wide open for the merchants. Nor did they get the blessing of the clergy. With their proclivity for gaining wealth through merchandising, they were disturbing the old balance of life in towns, a stability which the clergy would preserve. Moreover, their trade was bringing money into the towns, and money going into different pockets was a breeder of new attitudes, another worry for the clergy. Still, for two centuries or more, the merchant was forced to reside outside the walls of the city. But he could not be kept out indefinitely. When merchants did enter the city and were able to form their guilds, these guilds became the dominating influence in town life. The merchant became a gentleman and in time he too was admitted to nobility status.

[28] Pirenne, op. cit., p. 86.
[29] Pirenne, op. cit., p. 86.

URBAN WORK IN EVOLUTION

Until machines entered the workshops late in the history of cities, work carried on in urban places was done with hand tools, and its ways were traditional. The son who took over the occupation of his father took over the secrets of his craft much as his father and grandfather had done. The respected craftsman was the old man. Industrialism reversed this. However, change in urban work ways from century to century was minor, and often even minor change was resisted. Those of a particular craft formed a guild. The guild was a cluster of families, each guild having a monopoly in its town. It resisted innovation as it resisted competition.

As an idea carrier in urban history the medieval merchant brought major change to the traditional work system. Doubtless he had always been the conveyor of change, but from the twelfth century on the merchant operated in an economy that was leaving the dead level. It expanded continually. To expand his business it was necessary to speed up the productivity of urban craftsmen.

The merchant brought raw materials from other places, or he brought different raw materials which called for work adaptation. He stimulated master workmen, each using his group of journeymen and apprentices, to produce greater quantities so they could earn more. Or the merchant established workshops in which numbers of trained workers were supervised by a master guildsman as foreman. He stimulated inter-city competition between guilds. He encouraged new and faster methods of work. In his efforts to get more goods at the lowest price, the merchant eventually turned out to be a disturber of the guild system.

By the sixteenth century the ancient guild pattern of the cities was being disrupted. There was conflict between guilds and, as Unwin found in his extended study of that system, most of the guilds were beginning to fall apart in the seventeenth century.[30]

Entering at the small end of the horn, the merchant's role continued to expand from being despised to being respected. His concern was that of getting money through trade, moving goods about. To get more goods to serve widening markets, he took the initiative in promoting a more productive organization for work. In time some merchants themselves operated workshops. This awakening stimulated technological inventiveness. In various ways the reviving cities became the centers of change, places where money was moving more freely. Not only were the guilds weakened, their rural counterpart, the feudal system, was

[30] George Unwin, *Industrial Organization in the Sixteenth and Seventeenth Centuries*, London, Cass, 1957. The first edition of the revealing study appeared in 1904.

weakened. The power of the bishop and the prince, says Pirenne, also declined. A new order was appearing. "There happened in the Middle Ages what has been happening so often since then. Those who were the benefactors of the established order were bent upon defending it, because it guaranteed their interests, as it seemed to them indispensable to the preservation of society." [31]

The upper-level opposition to change, even when titled families tried to benefit from it, gave rise to a lasting bias against the innovators, many of whom were outsiders and often were identified as Jews. The common expression in identifying them was "Jews and other merchants." [32]

CITIES AND TECHNOLOGICAL CHANGE

Whether in ancient, medieval, or modern times, if there is technical invention that leads to social change its point of beginning tends most likely to be in urban centers. In addition, those innovations called social inventions usually begin in cities (armies, civil law, bureaucracy). Inventions and other creations were comparatively fewer in ancient than in medieval times. The rate at which they appeared increased each century since the 1100s, until today invention is an ongoing function of industry.[33]

Each advance in technology served to increase the complexity of cities and augment their stationary properties. Sjoberg relates how cities evolved toward greater complexity with each step in technology.

> Although at any given level of technology the politically dominant social orders are those most likely to be highly urbanized, we must recognize that the extent of urban development has been dramatically accelerated by the shift from the preindustrial to the industrial level of technology. The Industrial Revolution, by vastly increasing the surplus of food and raw materials, has permitted the formation of full-fledged urban societies. A reasonable guess is that cities of preindustrial societies embraced 5 to 10 percent of the total societal population. Compare this with the situation today in highly industrial urbanized systems, where well over half the population is urban and where cities over a million have become almost commonplace.[34]

[31] Pirenne, op. cit., p. 121.
[32] Mundy and Riesenberg, op. cit., p. 46.
[33] See Lewis Mumford, *Technics and Civilization*, New York, Harcourt, Brace & World, 1934. In an appendix is a chronology of inventions from the tenth century on.
[34] Gideon Sjoberg, "The Rise and Fall of Cities, a Theoretical Perspective," *International Journal of Comparative Sociology*, Vol. 4, No. 2, September 1964, p. 13.

The modern city stands firm and grows as it finds more work to do. With improved technology and materials to work on, its growth may be rapid. Otherwise, it may stand still or even decline. The more favorably situated cities may continue to grow. However, all must adopt certain technological facilities to insure their health and welfare; sanitation, water supply, food inspection, and distribution, even systems of transportation and communication must be provided. Urban amenities, too, have been evolving over the centuries. In medieval times most houses lacked windows and few had chimneys for indoor cooking.

It would not be incorrect to say that since medieval times cities have acquired a new role. The transition to a new kind of urbanism is apparent in various perspectives of which five are noted.

1. Even before technology outmoded city walls, which were symbolic of isolation, cities were building roads to increase access to wider markets. Emphasis in the modern city is on contact.
2. Cities have always attracted population, but until recent times their growth was slow. Walled cities even discouraged ingress. Modern industrial cities regard population growth as one evidence of increasing prosperity.
3. Accumulations in cities are not new. Modern cities compete to exceed, not only in accumulating wealth, but in attracting or establishing museums, universities, and technical schools. They view with satisfaction their ability to attract artists, writers, and other intellectuals.
4. The modern city is not content in merely being an influence center in its region. It becomes an active center radiating its influence to outside areas, as it markets its wares and services and as it seeks to change outside ways of living.
5. To an extent never before possible, cities within themselves become increasingly self-stimulating. Competing industries stimulate technological invention. More than ever, as social change follows technological change, social inventions are needed, and social organization changes.

To a limited extent, the beginnings of most of these characteristics may be seen in the cities of any age. But, as Childe reports, change can be clearly seen when the cities of 3000 B.C. (in terms of archeological evidence) are compared with the cities of still earlier times.

And so by 3000 B.C. the archeologist's picture of Egypt, Mesopotamia, and the Indus Valley no longer focus attention on communities of simple farmers, but on States embracing various professions and classes. The foreground is occupied by priests, princes, scribes and officials, and an army of specialized craftsmen, professional soldiers and miscellaneous labourers, all withdrawn from the primary task of food production. The most striking objects now unearthed are no longer the tools of agriculture and the chase, and other products of domestic industry, but temple furniture, weapons, wheel-made pots, jewellery, and other manufactures turned out on a large scale by skilled artisans. As monuments, we have instead of farmhouses, monumental tombs, temples, palaces and workshops.[35]

Sjoberg writes about the now extinct Mesoamerican cities that were presumably at their height about 500 B.C. or later. Teotihuacan in Mexico may have contained 100,000 people scattered over 16 square miles. These cities were apparently not industrial, but ceremonial and administrative. Sjoberg assumes they had achieved writing, else they could not have attained certain evident achievements in mathematics and astronomy, nor have invented the concept of zero. There must have been a central urban area where the elites foregathered. But "in Mesoamerica, cities were created without animal husbandry [and] the wheel," and it appears that commerce was minimal. "One reason for this is maize, a superior grain crop that produced a food surplus." [36]

Mesoamerican cities were not trade marts and their technology was that of nonindustrial work related mainly to stone structures. Using crude tools, they achieved wonders with stone. In those early cities described by Childe and Sjoberg, if invention was encouraged, it apparently concerned luxury goods for the few or war weapons for the many. Invention touched general work only marginally. If we come closer in time, we find that the tools of the mason, the carpenter, the smith, the shoemaker, or the tailor have changed very little since medieval times. But many tools were radically changed by industry beginning around 1800. It was mainly in Europe after the sixteenth century where technology and science made greatest strides and commerce flourished, thus clearing the way for the oncoming industrialism, which was to make modern urbanism possible. Again from Sjoberg:

> Now the factory system with its mass production of goods and mechanization of activity, began to take hold. With it emerged a new kind of occupational structure; a structure that depends on highly specialized knowledge and that functions effectively only when the activities of the component occupations are synchronized. . . . Today as industrialism moves inexorably across the globe, it continues to create social problems. Many surviving traditional cities evince in various ways the conflict between their preindustrial past and their industrial future. Nonetheless, the trend is clear; barring nuclear war, the industrial city will become the dominant urban form throughout the world, replacing forever the preindustrial city that was man's first urban creation.[37]

[35] V. Gordon Childe, *Man Makes Himself*, London, Watts, 1956, p. 105.
[36] Gideon Sjoberg, "The Origin and Evolution of Cities," *Scientific American*, Vol. 213, No. 5, September 1965, p. 58.
[37] Ibid., p. 62.

THE DYNAMICS OF URBANISM SINCE 1800

Briefly, we need to consider that flowering period in the evolution of cities which began a decade or two before 1800 and is still continuing, although it may be entering another dispensation. Cities around 1800 were beginning to grow faster than the general population, drawing increasing numbers of people from rural areas. The chaotic growth of cities by 1850 had begun to attract the concern of scholars, more so of reformers, because the staid way of life of old cities was being threatened. Davis mentions how in all industrial countries the rate of growth between 1850 and 1900 exceeded the growth rate between 1800 and 1850. It has continued to climb until now he ventures we are on the way to seeing half the world's population living in cities of 100,000 or more by 1990.[38]

Twin factors, acting upon each other, have been involved in this phenomenal growth; the emerging industrialism providing ever more jobs and attracting more people to cities, while increasing population, in turn, stimulated increasing industrialization. Other factors, to be sure, also figured. The combination of a growing population and expanding industry quickened the tempo of life in cities, which was disturbing to existing patterns, both ecological and social.

That period, at least to 1850, we know as the Industrial Revolution. As we have seen already, it was preceded by at least three centuries of Commercial Revolution in Europe. By comparison, the Commercial Revolution was slow-moving. The Industrial Revolution was a drastic change-inducer. Polanyi here speaks of its effects on English towns:

> Before the process had advanced very far, the laboring people had been crowded together in new places of desolation, the so-called industrial towns of England; the country folk had been dehumanized into slum dwellers; the family was on the road to perdition; and large parts of the country were rapidly disappearing under the slag and scrap heaps vomited forth from the "satanic mills." Writers of all views and parties, conservatives and liberals, capitalists and socialists invariably referred to social conditions under the Industrial Revolution as a veritable abyss of human degradation.[39]

Urban society before 1800 had not been standing still; actually the rate of change had been accelerating since the twelfth century. Certain

---

[38] Kingsley Davis, "The Urbanization of the Human Population," *Scientific American*, Vol. 213, No. 3, September 1965, p. 41.

[39] Karl Polanyi, *The Great Transformation*, Boston, Beacon Press, 1967, p. 39.

technological and other advances had been made without which the Industrial Revolution could not have gotten under way. Men had already come to believe that the Golden Age was ahead and not in some remote past, and achieving it lay in their own hands. The new venture forward was of another kind, away from much that tradition implies and there could be no turning back. The past had little to offer for the solution of the problems that lie ahead. To Polanyi this crossing of a bridge was The Great Transformation, entering a new kind of economy with new technologies and a different value system.

> The transformation to this system from the earlier economy is so complete that it resembles more the metamorphosis of the caterpillar than any alteration that can be expressed in terms of continuous growth and development. Contrast, for example, the merchant-producer's selling activities and his buying; his sales concern only artifacts whether he succeeds or not in finding purchasers, the fabric in society need not be affected. But what he *buys* is raw materials and labor—nature and man. Machine production in a commercial society involves, in effect, no less a transformation than that of the natural and human substance of society into commodities. The conclusion, though weird, is inevitable; nothing less will serve the purpose; obviously, the dislocation caused by such devices must disjoint man's relationships and threaten his natural habitat with annihilation.[40]

Actually before the advent of the Industrial Revolution man was turning to the re-creation of his man-made environent. Now, as he became better equipped, he turned with equal ardor to new ways of exploiting his natural environment, often destructively. He was moved by curiosity and a passion for gain to explore and bring under his dominion every corner of the earth where new natural resources could be had.

Eagerness for material progress became Western man's most insistent purpose as gain became his most valued goal. Impatient with distances, he made better roads and invented more and more efficient modes of transportation. The railroad outmoded the canal barge and river boat. The automobile came to compete with the railroad, and now all forms of surface transportation are challenged by ever more efficient airplanes.

Motivated by the same impatience, but using other technologies, man has been able to overcome the communication obstacles inherent in distance. This trend began with the telegraph, was bettered by the telephone, and now has been supplemented by radio. The human voice, starting from any part of the earth, can reach a particular ear in any other part. Now with the same speed voices and pictures together can be communicated.

40 Ibid., p. 42.

While the great step forward brought new problems and new dangers, it enables many more people to live where fewer lived before. It brought greater health security than man had ever known and increased the life span by two times that of ancient man. Due to the insistence of industry to be more efficiently served, the demand for knowledge and skill has resulted in higher levels of education, the level of industry has risen, and this continues. This speeded-up evolution from the outset has been urban-centered.

Another aspect of this collective learning, often easily overlooked, concerns the skills that must be acquired by great agglomerates of people, which enable them to live in concentrated areas with a minimum of friction and social disorder. The agglomerate had to learn to put itself to work, clothe itself, house itself, and feed itself, which could not be done without mass organizations of different kinds. The arts of urban government had to be developed in different ways to serve new needs. Powers that the Lord of the Manor once held as a personal right no longer served to govern his community as it grew by the decade more heterogeneous in its life and more diversified in its work. The growth of urban government must be regarded as one of the achievements of The Great Transformation.

AS CITIES CONFRONT THE PRESENT

In his history of change in American cities between 1915 and 1966, McKelvey presents the views of various urban leaders. One can draw from these a conclusion which is far from optimistic. "Model" urban government is far from being achieved. The most challenging problems of an earlier decade are still present; the race issue, housing, flight to the suburbs, fair labor practices, and so on. While some of these problems may have abated, others have become more acute.[41] As we look through McKelvey's carefully documented report, we are forced to conclude that the same pessimistic viewpoints were held in 1930 and in 1920.

Cities in our industrial age are not likely to be pleasing to those who hold firm notions about what the model city should be. They are the places of the most competitive productive processes, the central points where rival interests clash, where the forces for change find their most dramatic expression. As Wade points out, many American cities began as one-man ventures or as investment schemes of groups of men, much as some American colonies began as investments. As cities grew they came to serve other uses, and they changed in design and structure

[41] Blake McKelvey, *The Emergence of Metropolitan America, 1915–1966,* New Brunswick, Rutgers University Press, 1968, pp. 184–198.

to meet new demands. They continue to change as they were doing between 1790 and 1830, the decades studied by Wade.[42]

American cities, built by practical men for practical purpose, were ever an offense to men with strong moral concerns, and there was a tendency among many men of moral concern to see virtue only in rural life. From Thomas Jefferson to James W. Emerson, to the historian Frederick J. Turner, cities were regarded as dangerous to democratic life.

When Josiah Strong, a widely read clergyman, in the 1880s, wrote of the growing industrial city as a threat, he was not a lone voice in the wilderness. He visualized what has now arrived, the time when the city would impress its image on the countryside. He recognized that in the early period of western settlement the country determined the character of the town. He was, of course, thinking of the small market town, not the industrial city fast filling with immigrants of other languages, religions, and ethnic stock.

> We must note also the order of the settlement. . . . In the Middle States the farms were the first taken, then the town sprang up to supply its wants, and at length the railroad connected it with the world; but in the West the order is reversed—first the railroad, then the towns, then the farms. Settlement is consequently much more rapid, and the city stamps the country, instead of the country stamping the city. It is the city and towns which will frame state constitutions, make laws, create the public opinion, establish social usages, and fix standards of morals in the West.[43]

Cities have not only gained the power, as Strong feared, they have gained the population too until more than three-fourths of the labor force are engaged in urban occupations. Were this not the case, a country like the United States with a rapidly expanding population would be hard pressed.

In other parts of the world too the city is coming to the rescue, as it is able to industrialize and draw surplus population from crowded rural areas. Bose writes of Calcutta, an Indian city that is making itself over as it becomes increasingly the haven for immigrants. To the outsider it may seem a chaotic place, but Bose sees an emerging order in the distance, although it may not be structurally visible for decades.

> Calcutta is not only a great seaport and today an increasingly diversified manufacturing center; it is also the cultural capital of the Bengali-speaking people of eastern India. Its cosmopolitan population embraces skilled

[42] Richard C. Wade, *The Urban Frontier, The Rise of Western Cities, 1790–1830*, Cambridge, Harvard University Press, 1959, p. 30.

[43] Josiah Strong, *Our Country, Its Possible Future and Its Present Crisis*, New York, Baker and Taylor, 1885, p. 206.

Sikh workers from Punjab, businessmen from Rajastan and Gujarat on the western side of India, highly educated civil service professionals from Kerala and Madras in the south and Hindi-speaking bearers and laborers from neighboring states; the population also includes native Bengali Moslems as well as the dominant Bengali Hindu population (whose numbers have been swelled since 1947 by the influx of 700,000 refugees from East Pakistan).

Calcutta is thus the scene of a major confrontation between the enduring institutions of old India—her caste communities and diversity of ethnic heritages—and the pressures and values arising from the process of urbanization that presages India's industrial revolution. What happens in Calcutta will strongly determine the character and tempo of that revolution throughout the entire country. The same can be said in all likelihood, about the roles that are played by the metropolises of other developing countries.[44]

This is not the same Calcutta one might have known several decades ago. The population is more heterogeneous, the life of the people is less dominated by caste restrictions, and the industrial ways of work, which make the greatest difference, are becoming firmly established. The past may hold compelling, although weakening, sway over family and nonwork life, but industrial work is of the present. As a consequence, caste rules have diminishing force in the urban work place; the untouchable has freedom that would not be tolerated in the village.

As the cities of the world face the present, we can think of them as having a mission; they are the final haven of millions in every world region who are surplus in rural places. Cities will continue to be criticized by some as the unfeeling destroyers of men, by others as corrupt and immoral, and by still others as the ugly habitats in which human beings are isolated from the beauties of nature. The charges, of course, are not new, they were even more loudly voiced during the nineteenth century. They will continue to be heard again and again, and they should be as urban man tries to make the city a better place to live.

City planner Lynch is optimistic about urban man's ability to make the urban community a good place both to live and work. "We need not look forward with gloom to the future of the city," or visualize the future in terms of some imaginary golden past. He speaks not, of course, about how cities are managed or the relationships between heterogeneous populations, but of the physical aspects of the urban community.

We cling to the notion of a world with an urban inside and a rural outside, divided between the exciting but dirty and disagreeable city and the

44 Nirmal Kumar Bose, "Calcutta, a Premature Metropolis," *Scientific American,* Vol. 213, No. 3, September 1965, p. 90.

placid countryside where people live in dull good health. The contrast is ceasing to have any validity. There have been artificial environments in the past that were cherished by their inhabitants with passionate attachment; most farm landscapes were of this kind. The sense of being at home does not depend on tidiness or tininess but on the active relation between men and their landscape, a pervasive meaningfulness in what they see. The meaningfulness is as possible in the city as in any other place, and probably more so. For perhaps the first time in history we have the means of producing an enjoyable environment for everyone.[45]

The future of cities as good places to live is indeed important, but this concern moves to the background as cities face their present gigantic task of finding work for the millions coming to them. These cannot be turned back. It is the urban mission to do what rural places cannot, and this may be their greatest challenge for some decades to come.

[45] Kevin Lynch, "The City as Environment," *Scientific American*, Vol. 213, No. 3, September 1965, p. 219.

Rural ways of life and the confrontation with urbanism | 4

SOME QUALITIES OF RURALISM

In North America the truly rural community, whose people typify ruralism, can be found in the more isolated areas. Or one can go back a century, for example, to the novels of Hamlin Garland, who describes farm life in the Middle West. One gets glimpses of the old rural scenes from the writing of Mark Twain's boyhood. One could go back two more generations to rural life in colonial times, for example, to the "Letters from an American Farmer," by de Crévecoeur, who sometime before 1779 wrote about the ways of life in a village. He describes the resourcefulness of the farmer in providing for himself and his family from his animals and acres. Independent in politics, interdependent with neighbors in his work, gregarious in his simple pastimes, the colonial farmer had little need of the town or very much liking for it. And he held himself in high respect.

> The rich and the poor are not so far removed from each other. . . . We are a people of cultivators scattered over an immense territory, communicating with others by means of good roads, . . . united by the silken bands of mild government, all respecting the laws without dreading their power. . . . We are all animated by an industry which is unfettered and unrestrained, because each person works for himself. . . . A pleasing uniformity of decent competence appears throughout our habitations. . . . There, on a Sunday, he sees a congregation of respectable farmers and their wives, all clad in neat homespun, well mounted, or riding in their own humble wagons.[1]

But these rural people, while reflecting folk culture, were not at the level of the peasant society in Europe. European peasants were then in

[1] J. Hector St. John de Crévecoeur, *Letters from an American Farmer* (1782), Toronto, Canada, Signet, 1963, p. 61.

a very different category from the original rurals in Redfield's model of elemental folk culture. The farmer is kinship oriented and homogeneous, but not extremely so. He is traditional, but mainly in matters of morals and religion. The farmer today, like the colonial farmer, does not accept uncritically the experience of the past generations as did the folk society. Moreover, as Redfield recognized, people of the later forms of rural society are more prone than those of the folk society to make rational approaches to the problems of the day.[2]

Redfield's concept of folk society would necessarily include people in communities who had not yet been sufficiently touched by modernizing influences to disturb their time-honored values and norms or to cause them to question their traditional ways and beliefs. We can think of the pure folk society as rural but, by comparison, the modern farmer, while he may retain certain folk society traits, is stages above in advancement, and this would hold even for farmers of the least developed of American rural communities.

The ruralism in the industrial country may change, but it is not thrown out of equilibrium in the way tribal ruralism is when outside ways and things are imported and even the approach of the money economy is disturbing. Forde calls attention to the effects on the subsistence village economy of African tribes when money and things bought with money enter the scene.

> Where cash payments are important, they provide the link between the rural household or village and the outside world from which comes the demand for payment of tax and the supply of manufactured goods, mostly of Western manufacture, that are fairly valued for their quality or the prestige they confer. These goods are associated in the minds of the people as a whole with the urban centres from which, whether imported or locally made, they came. It is their evergrowing place in the lives of the rural population that endows the earning power of money with such importance.[3]

While Forde does not use Redfield's term "folk society," he does see the African villager as rural in the most elemental sense. But the term "rural" applies to other types of communities as well, for example, that of the fishing folk in the Newfoundland outports who in many cases have hardly enough productive land for gardens or to pasture a cow and who for decades could not be reached by roads. These people had little need for wheeled vehicles and little need for money, although for more

[2] Robert Redfield, "The Folk Society," *American Journal of Sociology*, Vol. 52, No. 5, January 1947, pp. 293–308.

[3] Daryll Forde, "Social Aspects of Urbanization and Industrialization in Africa, a General View," *Social Implications of Industrialization and Urbanization in Africa South of the Sahara*, Paris, UNESCO, 1956, Introduction.

than a century they were on the money economy. In local relations they exchanged labor. The local merchant acted as agent for a bigger merchant, usually in England, who came periodically to buy fish and bring supplies. The local merchant kept the accounts, which ran from year to year with no final settlement; hence the fisherman needed no cash. Occasionally in the nonfishing season he went to the mainland and worked for cash in the woods or as a seal hunter. He was as rural as fishermen in New Brunswick, who also had small farms and when not fishing or farming, earned some cash in the lumber woods.

The modern farmer in the United States is no longer the stereotype one meets through the movies, radio, or television. His way of life, say Horton and Hunt, is no longer one of isolation, homogeneity, land tilling, and bare subsistence, but rather one of "commercialization and rationalization." [4]

THE VILLAGE HABITAT OF RURAL LIFE

Despite the trend toward urbanization in all world regions, well over half of the world's population still lives in villages, most of them engaged in the production of food and fibers. The majority of these villages are small and in most of them agriculture is still primitive by Western standards. They are elemental communities and, in general, their level of living is rarely above one of subsistence.

Perhaps the number of rural villages in the world exceeds three million. In 1961 in India alone there were 562,681 rural places of less than 5,000 inhabitants. Of India's 439 million people in 1961, fully 360 million, about 82 percent, were rural; not all, to be sure, were engaged in agriculture.

If we assume over half of India's rural population to be engaged in agriculture, that would exceed the population of Canada and the United States. Despite this, partly because of inefficient farm methods, there are occasional food shortages in India. For the United States in 1960 the farm population was 15,669,000 and it dropped to 12,954,000 by 1964. Productivity per worker is as much as 20 times greater than for most farm workers in developing countries where life centers in traditional rural villages. The early type of farm village has vanished from the American scene.

Through the centuries the thinkers who have expressed their views in writing have been respectful of the rural community, usually describing it as clean and wholesome when compared with cities. One of the obstacles to developing an objective rural sociology in Europe has

4 Paul B. Horton and Chester L. Hunt, *Sociology,* New York, McGraw-Hill, 1964, pp. 455–457.

been the romantic image these writers have presented of the countryside. Such romantic thought also has been articulated by urbanized scholars on the American scene. For example:

> Whether the ruralite is farmer or hunter or fisherman, he is in constant touch with nature. He sees nature not as the artist who observes her moods in the detachment of aesthetic appreciation nor as the scientist who seeks to know her secrets for their own sake, but as the practical worker who must wrest a living from the soil. He sees nature as friend and as enemy, as the ripener of crops and the sender of weeds, as the bringer of drought and moisture, of storm and sunshine. He must win her rewards through struggle and endure her caprices with resignation. . . . His varying tasks are set for him not by the commands of a master but by the exigencies of nature.[5]

It is true that the rural man is largely on his own, getting on as he is able with his natural environment. What he does as a farmer, and what he thinks, are determined largely by what his fellow farmers do and think. And the less advanced the agriculture, the more this is descriptive of the rural village. The homogeneity of the rural community is more than the kinship groups found there, into which the individual, especially in the less advantaged communities, is integrated. His daily routine and even most of his decisions are at one with the homogeneity of village thinking. But, little by little, as Boateng found among rural villages in Ghana, outside influence seeps in and village life tends to "acquire urban features." [6]

As outside influences begin to pervade, other changes are stimulated. Saal found that this was even the case for the relatively progressive farmers in the rural villages of Holland in an area specializing in the production of butter and cheese. Making these products had long been a monopoly of the women, but the farmers concluded that their cheese and butter would have a more uniform quality if produced in a factory. The factory was a success, but it left the housewives and daughters without a traditional occupation through which a young woman was once able to capture a desirable husband.[7]

The Dutch rural village is as modern as any but, as can be seen in the outdoor agricultural museum at Arnheim, this village has passed through a long evolution. In the earliest of reproduced farm houses, typical of the fourteenth century, the animals and the family shared

---

[5] Robert M. MacIver and Charles H. Page, *Society, An Introductory Analysis,* New York, Holt, Rinehart and Winston, 1949, p. 317.

[6] E. A. Boateng, *A Geography of Ghana,* Cambridge, Cambridge University Press, 1959, p. 17.

[7] C. D. Saal, "Causes of the Delay in Western European Family Research and Some Notes on the Investigation of the Dutch Rural Family," in Nels Anderson (Ed.), *Recherches sur la famille,* Tubingen, Mohr-Siebeck, 1956, p. 239.

the same room. The family reserved to itself the side of the room around a fireplace. The primitive tools and utensils were there. It is possible in the succession of exhibits to see the step-by-step development of the house and to reconstruct the evolution of the village from a semi-primitive stage to the present. Many rural villages in the world today would have to pass through several stages of evolution before reaching the level of the first, or earliest, of Dutch villages in the exhibit.

CHANGE AS SEEN IN VILLAGES

Of all human communities, the rural village is the least likely to initiate internal change, although this may happen in a time of crisis. In general, the longer the history of a rural village and the more its traditions reach into the past, the less ready it is either to initiate or to accept change. Ishwaran says of Shivapur, about which he wrote a revealing report:

> So far, in Shivapur there have been only one inter-religious, five inter-caste, and just one inter-sub-caste marriage in the last century or so. There are further changes in other areas of life. The rules for dining and drinking have been considerably relaxed. So also have the rules of purity and pollution. The former relaxation may be attributed to the modern modes of transport, the number of tea shops and the new egalitarian laws.[8]

Here change is induced by outside contact and is being encouraged by government, for which reason the Indian villager tends to be on the defensive against his well-meaning national authorities. Describing life in an isolated village of southern Italy, a village with a thousand years of history, Banfield found a deep-rooted fear and mistrust of government. These villagers, for generations in poverty, can only be changed through the patient and understanding forces on the outside. "Clearly a change in ethos cannot be brought about by the deliberate choice of the people of Montegrano. It is precisely their inability to act concertedly in the public interest which is the problem." [9]

Not all resistance to change in the rural village is attributable to the social inertia of the people. Their institutions, in which traditions are often fixed and rigid, may be responsible for the systematic exclusion of influences which might bring about change. It is well known that church control in French Canada, using the French language as a facility,

[8] K. Ishwaran, *Tradition and Economy in Village India*, London, Routledge and Kegan Paul, 1966, p. 25.

[9] Edward C. Banfield, *The Moral Basis of a Backward Society*, New York, Free Press, 1966, p. 156, paperback ed.).

for decades maintained the social isolation of most rural villages in Quebec.[10]

Siegfried, a French sociologist, saw virtue in the isolation policy of the church in Quebec, a way of preserving the "peasant" way of life. He noted that while American farmers suffered in the depression, peasants in Quebec villages were little affected; their poverty did not deepen. He remarked that the United States might have fared better in the depression had more of the farmers been peasants.[11]

In Canada's westward movement, French Canadians established a cluster of villages in the Red River Valley, a few miles north of the United States border. Here again the same policy of self-isolation was maintained. The English language was excluded, but the effort proved unsuccessful. Piddington, who made a study of these villages, found that "the church with its many associated institutions, educational and otherwise; the French language; political and moral attitudes toward *les Anglais,* exacerbated from time to time by the repercussions of minority status; the French-Canadian conception of kinship, with all that these imply," continued the struggle against change. "To sum up, French-Canadian culture continues to survive, though in a variety of new forms, which are themselves constantly changing." [12]

The case of French Canada illustrates the difficulties and costs of self-isolation in a changing world. With the lowest level of education in Canada, migrants leaving these villages were doubly handicapped in the labor market; their lack of English and lack of schooling consigned them to the lowest wages at the common labor level. The policy in French Canada has now been reversed. The economic costs of self-isolation were too great.

Normally the rural village in an urban industrial country, such as Canada or the United States, although it may be more conservative than the city, does not lag far behind in accepting change. It accepts, in the words of Taylor and Jones, the urbanized social organization.

> It applies to social structures which originated in cities but which have now been accepted by people outside cities as well. In the process of being accepted in open country areas the social organization characteristic of cities has often been modified, but qualities reflecting urban origin still dominate. Urbanized social organization is a system of human life tending toward universal social institutions for all members of the society.[13]

10 Horace Miner, *St. Denis, A French Canadian Parish,* Chicago, University of Chicago Press, 1939.

11 André Siegfried, *Canada, An International Power,* 2nd ed., London, Jonathan Cape, 1958, p. 114.

12 Ralph Piddington, "A Study of French-Canadian Kinship," *International Journal of Comparative Sociology,* Vol. 4, No. 1, March 1963, p. 21.

13 Lee Taylor and Arthur R. Jones, Jr., *Rural Life and Urbanized Society,* New York, Oxford University Press, 1964, p. 23.

The rural village in the less developed country also may be yielding to demands for change, although in a compromising manner. Ishwaran mentions how untouchables in Shivapur cannot be legally excluded from the tea shops, but inside they find they must drink from chipped and broken cups set in a special place for them; only the untouchables must wash their cups after use. Ishwaran mentions further pressures for change in the rural village.

> The role of the newspapers and the operation of government sponsored community development projects have also contributed considerably to the relaxation of the ancient rules. One often feels, as in the case of the tea shop example above, that the changes are more verbal than real, and that people speak in one language and act in quite another. Once again, we are driven to our central theme, the village today is the scene of change as well as continuity.[14]

ANTI-URBANISM IN THE RURAL VILLAGE

We would expect that even the most modern of rural villages would hold attitudes of bias against the city, much as many suburbs do, but here attention is on that type of bias which reflects rural cultural naiveté. For example, Schachter, found a strong anti-Rome bias among villagers in southern Italy. To them Rome was "the center of a foreign and hostile world." Rome was imposing education on these villagers for which they saw no need. They acecpted local public officials, but suspected those from the national government. Nationhood had little importance.[15]

Majumdar sees two sets of values in India, those associated with the town and the anti-urban values of the rural village. The rural attitude is expressed by the term *sahariya*.

> That is how abnormal behaviour, luxurious living, immoral conduct, atheism, and selfishness are dubbed, as *sahariya* . . . [town ways] and thus different from the patterns of their rural life. When a father refuses to send his son to a school in the city, he says, "I don't want him to become sahariya," which connotes a constellation of values different from the ones with which he is familiar and to which he has been tuned for generations.[16]

Bias against the town does not stop at this point. It is believed that most urban politicians are corrupt, that one who goes to the city must

14 Ishwaran, op. cit., p. 26.
15 Gustav Schachter, "Rural Life in Southern Italy," *American Journal of Economics and Sociology,* Vol. 24, No. 4, October 1965, pp. 422–423.
16 D. N. Majumdar, *Caste and Communication in an Indian Village,* Bombay, Asia Publishing House, 1958, p. 329.

expect to be cheated, and that laws made in the city always operate against the rural man.[17]

The bias of the rural man is likely to be as deeply sensed as it is irrationally expressed. The urbanite's bias against rural people is often expressed in sophisticated humor, unless the city man is personally inconvenienced. Not infrequently the urban intellectual motivated by some political ideology may charge rural people with stupidity, as being committed to localism, and stubbornly resistant to new ideas. Coulton quotes Gautier de Coincy, a priest in the thirteenth century, who described the miserable poverty of German peasants and saw them as lacking in the ordinary virtues of Christian men. So low were they in these qualities that he considered a peasant unworthy of better.

> True, on the one hand he works from morning to night; but, on the other hand he forgets God and constantly works on Sundays and holy days, "he has no more fear of God than a sheep, nor would he give a button for the holy laws of the Holy Church; he steals from his neighbor when he can; he steals from the parson. . . . Worst of all, many serfs hate the clergy even as Esau hated Jacob" . . . little do they love them and little less do they believe them.[18]

To those who had power over him, the peasant was a man to be held down and he could be punished with impunity. The law and the codes of conduct for the landowning nobility, who held the peasants as so much property, did not apply to these subjected strata. The lord of the estate took the best of the produce and the peasant subsisted as he could on what remained. The priest just quoted mentions how the diet of the peasants was mainly brown bread and porridge. Often the peasants shared their mud cottages with their animals. They wore homemade garments and handmade boots of untanned leather. The idealized chivalry of the feudal centuries was reserved for the nobility, but for the peasant, says Coulton, there was always brute force, and he was expected to produce.

> That is the one constant factor in medieval civil wars; both parties fought over the peasant's fields, forced the peasant into their ranks, and blackmailed the peasant when they had gotten the upper hand. For five centuries of European history the anarchical conditions of society discouraged savings, and pressed harder upon the laborious middle class (artisans) who were then the better-to-do peasants. . . . The villager's ignorance and simplicity put him at a fatal disadvantage.[19]

[17] Ibid., p. 299.
[18] G. C. Coulton, *Medieval Village, Manor and Monastery*, New York, Harper & Row, 1960, p. 21; 1st ed., 1925.
[19] Ibid., pp. 105–106.

The descendants of those peasants in England, Germany, Holland, and the Scandinavian countries today are both economically sophisticated and politically literate, and the most self-sufficient agriculturalists in Europe. Even though they have put aside most of their old peasant ways, they tend as a class still to be anti-urban, as much as farmers in the United States.

RURAL INDIFFERENCE TO URBANISM

The anti-urban bias of rural people is most likely to be evidenced at times of rural-urban contact, as in situations involving buying and selling, or in politics. Normally, for instance, it could not be said of the fisherman in a remote outport of Newfoundland that he gives much thought to invidious comparison. His work is absorbing and challenging, and he is the master of it. He finds fullness in his family-oriented community. His life may be repetitive with the round of the seasons, but it is not dull. Whether he is illiterate or not, he is an equal in a milieu where he can function fully and compete effectively. There is sufficient internal rivalry in his isolated community to make life worth-while. Anti-urban attitudes find expression at the point when mechanisms outmode the old methods of fishing and the long-accepted poverty of the fisherman leaves him helpless to acquire a bigger boat, propelled by a motor, and the more costly fishing gear. He is disemployed by technological advance.[20]

Gillin described the two kinds of native folk found in Central America, two opposite personality types, the phlegmatic Indian and the more energetic Ladino. The Indian takes life as it comes. "The Ladino . . . assumes that the universe, including its supernatural department, can be manipulated by man, that control and power can be established not only over things and other animals, but also over men." To the Indian the group is more important, but the Ladino is innately an individualist.

> The universe of the Indian does not extend backward to a remembered past. Even the Indians who live on the sites of the great ruins of antiquity

---

[20] A number of studies are in process in Newfoundland at this time. Of the reports published, two are pertinent, Tom Philbrook, *Fisherman, Logger, Merchant, Miner* (1966), and Melvin M. Firestone, *Brothers and Rivals, Patrilocality in Savage Cove* (1967), both published by the Institute of Social and Economic Research, Memorial University of Newfoundland, St. John's. One report in process is by Noel Iverson, and deals with government efforts to move fishermen from the remote outports to larger ports where they cease to be independent fishermen and work for fishing companies. These people, while idealizing the former way of life, are very articulate in condemning the new.

do not connect these with their own ancestors. Nor do they project changes for the future. According to the Indian scheme of things, life goes on in a timeless present, it has been this way as long as anyone knows. . . .

The typical Ladino, on the other hand, lives in a universe considerably more expanded both in space and time. His notions about the great world beyond the limits of his own community may be uninformed and naive from the point of view of modern science, but he does not believe that the world ends at the limits of his township. . . . The Ladino's strivings or drives are seldom entirely restricted to his local community, but are also oriented toward goals whose locus is in the larger outside world.[21]

We might expect to find the two types in any rural community, early or modern. A good share of the inhabitants of the mountain areas of Kentucky and Tennessee, a depressed region known as Appalachia, are identified as "hillbillies," lethargic folk content to let things drift. Ford mentions that most are committed to traditionalism and fatalism. "Both fatalism and other-worldliness share the premise that life is governed by external forces, over which humans have little or no control." While this outlook may mark the majority, many in the region do not share it, and gradually their efforts modify the outlook.[22]

A study by Leonard and Loomis of El Cerrito, a Spanish-American village in New Mexico, pictures a community which does not envy the Americano and his world of faster tempo and more things. El Cerrito people may have a low opinion of a nearby Spanish-American village but are negligibly interested in the works and ways of Americano communities.

The El Cerrito community began in 1822 as a huge Spanish land grant, much of which has been lost because of the inability to pay taxes. Most of the land is dry and hilly. The El Cerrito families, despite having 85,000 acres of land, have not developed herds. They have been content with being small farmers, each family with a few acres of irrigated land and a field for "dry farming." Their ways of work are steady, but not hurried. They do not imitate the Americano.

These natives can see neither sin nor moral corruption in idleness and leisure time. They see neither virtue nor common sense in keeping busy for the sake of occupying the hands and the mind. Work is simply a means to an end—a means of accomplishing that which is valued or desired, and as such these people realize its importance. Children are taught at an

21 John Gillin, "Ethos and Cultural Aspects of Personality," in Sol Tax (Ed.), *Heritage and Conquest,* New York, Free Press, 1952, pp. 196–198.
22 Thomas R. Ford (Ed.), *The Southern Appalachian Region,* Lexington, University of Kentucky Press, 1962, p. 16.

early age the necessity of labor and are given ample opportunity to put it into practice. But this necessity of work lies in what it will bring in a material way—money, land, independence. Furthermore, the accumulation of material goods adds little to popular esteem for the individual. The prestige of the man depends in no small measure on his contributions to the fiestas or his activities in the political life and activities of the group.[23]

RURAL-URBAN COUNTER-INFLUENCE

Town and country comprise a division of labor which has long existed and is likely to continue. While the nature of this relationship can be expected to change, it would be unrealistic to expect the elimination of rural-urban biases, although the bases for these may change. One basic difference between the rural and the urban community concerns ownership, use, and attitudes toward land. Through the generations, land ownership, even a small bit of land, has been a prized rural value. For the urbanite land is merely another commodity. Trollope was surprised to find that the economic attitude toward land among rural settlers in the Middle West in 1861 did not reflect the peasant attitude in Europe. In the United States, land was plentiful; the farmer could sell and find cheaper land farther west. Trollope found the farmers were more self-possessed, less servile, and quite resourceful compared with European peasants.[24]

It turned out that the typical American frontier farmer, for all his upstanding qualities and his knowledge about affairs in his country, developed firm ideas about what was good for town and country. He acquired a strong moral philosophy which was in some respects anti-urban. He came to regard bankers and large corporations with suspicion. He worried about the mass immigration of non-English-speaking people to the cities, certain they would lower the standards of what to him was Americanism. While he may have joined farmer organizations later, he feared the trade unions taking form among industrial workers. Such political power as he had was used to impose moral restraints on cities, the so-called Blue Laws. Broom and Selznick speak of the rural support for prohibition.

> Public opinion has a social base. Prohibitionist sentiment was not a matter of random individual opinion but was concentrated in native, rural, Protestant areas. It never gained significant following in large

[23] Olen Leonard and C. P. Loomis, "El Cerrito, New Mexico," in C. P. Loomis (Ed.), *Studies in Rural Social Organization in the United States, Latin America, and Germany,* East Lansing, Michigan, Michigan State University Press, 1945, p. 283.

[24] Anthony Trollope, *North America,* Donald Smalley and Bradford A. Booth (Eds.), New York, Knopf, 1951, p. 136; 1st ed., 1862.

cities, nor among immigrants and non-Protestants. The effectiveness of public opinion in determining governmental policy depends in large measure upon the social and political resources of its social base. The passage of prohibition legislation reflected the political and social importation of rural population in American life, especially in the state legislatures. Its repeal can be attributed in part to the growing dominance both of the political power of the city dweller and of the values and attitudes of urban life.[25]

In the United States and Canada, rural people have been politically literate from the outset. Rural Americans have used political power mainly in support of moral causes and to impose heavier tax burdens on urban people than on themselves. They have justified the latter with the argument that in economic matters the city always takes advantage of them. They have also tried to use their political power to impose moral controls on urban people, believing that the many immigrants settling in cities were a dangerous element to be on guard against.

This rural moral influence on legislation was even stronger in Canada. In Toronto, for example, streetcars were not permitted to run on Sunday until 1897, although "gentle people" were free to drive in their own carriages. An English observer, after a dull Sabbath in Toronto, wrote, "Religious rule has made Sunday a terror to the poor, unless one happens to enjoy going to church, walking about the quiet streets, reading or sleeping. . . . Most of the people disappear for the day, as if in a shell." [26]

Rural political power over Canadian urban life is gradually losing ground, although in some of the more rural provinces church organizations still have a firm control over education, each denomination contending with others for schools of their own faith, all supported by public funds. As far as quality of education is concerned, the results are far from satisfactory, for which reason church control of education in Canada is weakening.

The ways of rural life in Canada and the United States, although changing under the pressures of urban influence, tend to carry forward much that comes out of the past. The American rural community, for example, has a varied ancestry, especially English, German, and Scandinavian. This may be evident in the two sections which follow, the first dealing with the English village, and the second with a typical Danish village.

[25] Leonard Broom and Philip Selznick, *Sociology*, New York, Harper & Row, 1963, p. 294. The citation relates to the National Prohibition Law passed in 1920 and repealed in 1933.

[26] Quoted by J. R. Burnett, "Urban Community and Changing Moral Standards," in S. D. Clark (Ed.), *Urbanism and the Changing Canadian Society*, Toronto, University of Toronto Press, 1961, pp. 70–99.

THE ENGLISH RURAL VILLAGE

The small community in the United States, with some minor exceptions, evolved in the image of the English village. This is much more true in Canada, except in French Canada. Where the Americans, in some respects, might have departed from English tradition, the Canadians in "English Canada" would consciously transplant the village ways of the mother country. The traditional English notion that the village belongs to its inhabitants is quite general both in English Canada and the United States. The villagers claim maximum responsibility for their own affairs, which turns out not always to be an advantage in these days of enlarging organizations.

In both the United States and Canada certain basic elements of the rural village are similar; the codes of village government, the names of village officials (constable, justice of the peace), and concepts about the rights and duties of citizens are typical. And, while it may not be spoken or even recognized, much of English religious imagery was also transplanted. At the same time the rural villages absorbed traits of other peoples, evidencing a high degree of cultural diffusion in these new countries.

It needs to be emphasized that the transplanting of English culture was equally as strong in the cities of the Atlantic seaboard of the United States as in Canadian cities. Both copied the London style of life and for more than a century adopted English types of organizations: the urban social club, early "humane societies," the English type of theater, and later such London-originated organizations as the Salvation Army, Young Men's Christian Association, Boy Scouts, social settlements, charity organization societies, and others. During colonial times carriage styles, furniture styles, and society manners were to a large extent duplicated.

Doubtless, even in the colonial rural village, there were features which were not of English origin. Apparently the town meeting, for example, was a New England invention, although it failed to survive. The English institution, the poorhouse, was transplanted, but its character changed materially. Also the concept of the "lord of the manor" was absent.

The lord of the manor of the English village, usually the only one in the village with the status of "gentleman," emerged out of feudal times. Then he was owner of the land and virtually owner of the people on his estate who served him, but he was also responsible for their protection and welfare under the theory of *noblesse oblige*.

The established church, as Bonham-Carter notes, began acquiring a moral responsibility for the village and, for example, became responsible for education. The pastor, who went about declaring, forbidding, chastising, advising, and just generally intruding, could not be ignored even by the constable.[27]

The English village was a compact local society, more so than the early American village. Rarely were acquaintances made in neighboring villages. However, although the contact area of the peasant was quite restricted, his life was not dull. Trevelyan writes:

> Only a small proportion of the villagers of either sex ever visited town. Most people remained all their lives under the influence of Pan and his magic . . . for the common people, untouched by the skepticism of the town, the fairies still danced in the woods, though when the wayfarer came around the bush they had already vanished. Books in the village were few. . . . No city-made newspapers or magazines stamped a uniform mentality on the nation. In this isolation from the world at large, each shire had its own traditions, interests and character. . . . For gossip and sensation they were satisfied with the daily drama of their own village, with its poaching, affrays and smuggling adventures, its feuds and loves, its ghosts and suicides, its quarrels of miller and innkeeper, of parson and squire.[28]

Better roads and the automobile, easier access to the city and its labor market, and other changes have deprived the English village of the isolation which protected its uniqueness. The typical village, says Saville, no longer supports "a thatcher, a carpenter, two tailors, a boot and shoe maker, a blacksmith, a wheelwright, two masons, two dairymen, and a marine store-keeper." For recreation, the village takes up the city forms, with the result that its old way of life has about vanished.[29]

VEJEN, A DANISH RURAL VILLAGE

In the story of Vejen, a typical Danish village, can be seen how changes within the village were stimulated by changes outside until finally the original character of Vejen had about disappeared and Vejen became a modern small rural town, fully urbanized.

Quite unlike other parts of western Europe, the Scandinavian rural village in feudal times was not without a folk organization. Town life was all but absent. Hansson mentions how even the king had to travel about to collect his tribute which was consumed as he moved from place

---

[27] Victor Bonham-Carter, *The English Village*, London, Penguin, 1952, p. 150. Good, brief description of the early village.

[28] G. M. Trevelyan, *English Social History*, London, Reprint Company, 1948, p. 321.

[29] John Saville, *Rural Depopulation in England and Wales, 1851–1951*, London, Routledge and Kegan Paul, 1957, p. 23.

to place. The entire economy was initially based on agriculture. Each
hamlet had its council of old men and the wider organization was one
of clans. Clans had their meetings which were:

> . . . taken up by religious and cult ceremonies, judicial proceedings,
> trade and convivial activities. The viking age society was one of clans
> rather than individuals, and the law told at the thing [meeting] by the
> "lagman" took care of the interest of the clans. He who was not defended
> by his relatives was an outlaw. And even folks from other counties were
> outlawed to a certain extent.[30]

Early Vejen was apparently not greatly different. The peasants
worked land owned by the earl, whose job it was to administer things.
Or as duty called, he went forth to war with horse and armor. Peasants
who occupied land were farmers; those without land were thralls, or
laborers. The clergyman, who occupied a middle position between
peasant and earl, was rarely trusted by the peasants because he was
socially closer to the earl. He kept the record of taxes, military service,
and so on.[31]

For the peasants, the control unit in the hamlet was the *oldermand,*
an ongoing council of top farmers, whose meeting place was usually
around a wide flat stone in a grove. They levied fines if a cow broke
into a field or if some young person behaved improperly. Year by year
they saw to it that boundary stones between fields were in place, and
they supported church rules, although "belief and superstition were often
strongly mixed." [32]

In 1784 Vejen contained 114 inhabitants, and it was still tied to the
early ways of farming. Plows and harrows were of wood, wheels were still
without metal tires, and horses were unshod. Roads were primitive and
impassable in wet weather. Chairs were beginning to appear and the
record reports one clock in Vejen. A few families owned hymn books,
but none could read; the book was a prestige item. Vejen in 1801 had
296 inhabitants. By this time the peasants owned their land. They now
had iron, so the village had a blacksmith; they also had a weaver, a clog
(wooden shoe) maker, a wheelwright, a thatcher, one store, and an inn.[33]

By 1834 the population had reached 475, including 60 landowners.
Compared with earlier centuries, these farmers were prosperous, and
equipment had improved. There were 15 craftsmen of different kinds.

[30] Borje Hansson, "Urban Activity, Urban People and Urban Environment in
Scandinavian History," in Nels Anderson (Ed.), *Urbanism and Urbanization,* Leiden,
Brill, 1964, p. 144.
[31] F. Skrubbeltrang, *Agricultural Development and Rural Reform in Denmark,*
Rome, Food and Agricultural Organization, 1953, p. 9.
[32] Ibid., p. 12.
[33] Ibid., pp. 33–36 and 95.

Small industries included a tannery, a cloth weavery, and a brickmaking plant. The first school also had been established.

The census for 1860 shows considerable gain in Vejen; 751 inhabitants and 89 farms, although the size of the average farm was smaller. Livestock included 750 cattle, 718 sheep, 166 horses, and 149 pigs. Nonlandowners were no longer a submerged group; many were craftsmen. The traditional village council had been replaced in 1841 by a local civil government, a change brought about by the nonfarming majority. Now public officials had to keep records and be responsible for welfare, education, roads, collecting taxes, and regulating the sale of liquor. Different organizations were taking form; rifle clubs, singing and music groups, and social clubs emerged. A folk high school had started and villagers were interested in national politics.[34]

Each census report since 1860 marks some change in this community which began as the most elemental of rural villages. Population grew to 865 in 1870 and to 1,431 in 1890, reaching 2,110 in 1901, when only 833 inhabitants of Vejen were in agriculture, while 663 were in handicrafts and industry, and the rest were in other occupations including public service.

In 1906 there were 272 urban properties in Vejen and 158 rural properties of which only 50 were real farms. The spurt toward urban character came with the arrival of the railroad in 1874. In 1898, at the initiation of the nonfarming elements, a citizens' association was formed to promote development. By this time the farmers were joining various national farm organizations, mostly of a cooperative nature.[35]

By 1945 Vejen had about lost its rural character, only a fourth of its 3,664 inhabitants being identified with agriculture. The town had achieved the usual urban amenities: a water supply, sewers, electric power, paved streets, and the essential public buildings.

RURALISM CONFRONTING SOCIAL CHANGE

Much that has been written about the rural community in recent times, about ruralism as a way of life or agriculture as a way of work, concerns in large part the rural struggle against social and technological change. Rural familism has been especially challenged by demands for change. Regarding the already mentioned Appalachian region, Ford remarks that the rural family there "has retained its traditional functions to a far greater degree than in the industrialized parts of the nation. At the same time, the factors that have led to the preservation of familism have also served to retard the development of the more highly specialized

[34] Ibid., pp. 149, 154 and 160.
[35] Ibid., pp. 225–241.

institutional forms of industrial society." [36] This is the core challenge to both ruralism and the rural familism. Each becomes identified with a wider order of things from which there is no escape, and each must adapt to the wider order.

Seldom in human history did the family have greater opportunity for expression than on the frontier in North America, and here we take a passage from a book by an English traveler who visited the interior of the United States about 1817. It astonished him that ordinary people from the Old World were becoming self-sufficient individuals on the frontier. Although he had a low opinion of the Irish, he was impressed during his visit with an Irish homesteader in Ohio.

> The wife was at a neighbor's on a "wool-picking frolic," which is a merry-making of gossips at each other's houses, to pick the year's wool and prepare it for the carding. The son and daughter were married and well settled, each having eight children. He came to this place fourteen years ago, before an axe had been lifted, except to make a blaze road, a track across the wilderness, marked by the trees, which passed over the spot where the town now stands. A free and independent American, and a warm politician, he now discusses the interests of the State as one concerned with its prosperity; and so he is, for he owns 118 acres of excellent land, and has twenty descendants. He has also the right to scrutinize the acts of government, for he has a share in its appointment, and pays eight dollars a year in taxes—five to the General Treasury and three to his own county; in all four pence per acre. He still inhabits a cabin, but it is not an Irish cabin.[37]

On this frontier where land was plentiful, the extended family had little opportunity to develop. Each new family had an opportunity to stake out its own homestead and could be its own master on its own land.

Maine, well over a century ago, advanced the notion that the village originally was a rural community occupied by a collective family, and all authority rested with the family. Persons not born to the family might become members by adoption. In the course of time the nature of society became too complex for such familial control. As civil law began to emerge some authority previously held by the family was lost to the wider organization, the beginning of civil government.

> Nor is it difficult to see what is the tie between man and man which replaces by degrees those forms of reciprocity in rights and duties which have their origin in the family. It is contract. Starting at one terminus of history, from a condition of society in which all the relations of persons are summed up in the relations of the family, we seem to have steadily

---

36 Ford, op. cit., p. 149.
37 Morris Birkbeck, *Notes on a Journey to America*, London, 1818, p. 31.

moved toward a phase of the social order in which all the relations arise from the free agreement of individuals.[38]

Maine recognized that, with the evolution of the more complex society, the local family-centered society would have to give ground. The evidence was before him that this had been the trend. The trend has moved far since his day. As the urban community has advanced, the rural community has adapted. The demand for change continues to reach out from the more heterogeneous urban community. As Foster sees this trend:

> Cities are focal points of change. Most social and economic change begins among the upper classes and then spreads downward to the traditionally inarticulate lower classes and outward to the countryside. The cultural innovations of urban areas have prestige attached to them.[39]

Everywhere the rural village becomes less rural, agriculture becomes more mechanized, farming comes to be more rational in operation and more guided by scientific knowledge—all despite continuous resistance.

LIKELY PROSPECTS FOR RURAL LIFE

In connection with the President's National Advisory Commission on Rural Poverty, Glenn V. Fuguitt studied a sample of 570 rural villages in the United States. The sample was 1 out of 20 of all villages having in 1960 more than 500 but less than 2,500 inhabitants. These were villages located 50 miles or more from a metropolitan city. They contained a total of 386,601 inhabitants in 1960. It was found that of the 570 villages 269 were declining (having lost population since 1950). The Census data showed that for villages of 500 to 2,500 inhabitants, there were:

In 1950 11,162 with a population of 8,246,276
In 1960 11,295 with a population of 7,616,584
Average inhabitants per village in 1950 747
Average inhabitants per village in 1960 674 [40]

Income levels are lower in the declining than in the growing villages and the housing conditions are worse. Of the population in the declining

---

[38] Henry Sumner Maine, *Ancient Law*, Boston, Beacon Press, 1963, p. 163; 1st ed., 1861.

[39] George M. Foster, *Traditional Cultures, and the Impact of Technological Change*, New York, Harper & Row, 1962, p. 29.

[40] Glenn V. Fuguitt, *Rural Poverty in the United States*, Washington, D. C., Government Printing Office, 1968, p. 53.

villages, for each 100 inhabitants, 27 were under 15 years of age, 55 were 15–64, and 18 were 65 or over. For the growing villages of this sample the figures were respectively 31, 56, 13, and for United States cities, 31, 59, and 10. Fuguitt cites Nesmith who wrote that while these poor villagers would find life hard if they moved to cities, it will be as hard if they do not move.[41]

Urban ways have brought to rural people a new style of life which cannot be sustained by the old frugal rural economy. To prosper in agriculture, the farmer needs good land and many acres. He needs machines and scientific knowledge. Those who lack these essentials are poor and their villages are declining. We can expect the trend to continue unless planning, development, and rational control are provided by the government.

Control, urban-initiated, goes even farther. Cities and their industries impose themselves upon the rural environment. Their waste is dumped into the streams and fresh-water lakes. The need for the elimination and prevention of pollution results in controls established by government. While these controls benefit both urban and rural people, their very existence illustrates the extent to which the rural environment can no longer be considered separately.[42]

A more vital control over rural work and life will doubtless result from the increasing concentration of population in cities. More than likely, as population pressure increases, national governments will face the need of assuming food-supply responsibility, encouraging farmers to produce more of the kinds of food needed. Already this guidance has begun in some countries, where farmers are being subsidized to produce needed crops. If population pressure continues to increase, the government may need to establish firm controls over the production of food, as well as over the limited water supply. This is not an altogether new phenomenon. Urban controls over farmers did exist, to be sure, in medieval times.

> When Bologna granted to the peasants in her republic citizenship and liberty from their lords in 1257, the end of an age was signaled. The peasants were free. Once seignoral jurisdiction was destroyed, however, the villagers were open to town exploitation. In fact, the food-hungry towns of northern Italy often granted an ineffectual citizenship or freedom to peasants in exchange for producing strictly regulated crops to be

[41] Dwight A. Nesmith, "The Small Rural Town," in Alfred Stefferud (Ed.), *A Place to Live; The Yearbook of Agriculture, 1963,* Washington, D. C., U.S. Department of Agriculture, 1963, p. 179.

[42] On the matter of pollution, see Abel Wolman, "The Metabolism of Cities," *Scientific American,* Vol. 213, No. 3, September 1965, pp. 178–193.

sold at fixed prices. The village had lost an old master to become the slave of the town.[43]

Yet if in the future controls are placed over agriculture they are not likely to be of an exploitive nature. Other than this, we are not in a position to precisely estimate what these controls may be like. What is fairly certain is that the supply of food-producing land in the world cannot increase in acreage or in productivity to keep pace with the rise in population. This may call for controls to secure the most efficient use of available land. Dependence on the soil may be too crucial to leave the choice of crops and land use to the individual farmers. Whoever lives by farming may be required to learn the most efficient methods; his will most certainly be a skilled occupation.

[43] John H. Mundy and Peter Riesenberg, *The Medieval Town*, New York, Van Nostrand, 1958, p. 69.

Ecology and the human community | 5

SETTLEMENTS AND ENVIRONMENTS

In this chapter we will consider the way communities arrange themselves on the sites which they occupy, how men use the space which comprises their habitats. This is human ecology, the study of man in relation to the phenomena of space and distance. This approach is especially essential in the study of urban sociology. Thomlinson says pertinently:

> Human spatial distribution in and around cities as an influent and mediator of social relationships is probably the only major urban phenomenon that remains sufficiently separable to provide a legitimate intellectual rationale for the continuance of urban sociology as a distinct field. The only unique integrant of urban sociology is urban ecology.[1]

While recognizing the utility of human ecology in the study of cities, the phenomena of human ecology are evident in all communities, large or small, primitive or modern. Competition for space tends to be greater in cities, and in growing cities the uses of space change more rapidly, and urban man tends to be more efficient in changing the natural environment for his needs.

Gourou, a Belgian ecologist, stresses the thought that relations between *man* and the environment are less revealing than "relations between *men* and environment." One must consider people behaving and take note of how they manage in association to "modify the environment."

> Men, groups of men, are tied together by techniques of production and of organization in space, and their view of the environment is conditioned by their regional organized system of techniques, in other words, their

[1] Ralph Thomlinson, *Urban Structure*, New York, Random House, 1969, Preface.

civilization. Their view of the environment is in large part a subjective one. Thus, each civilization has its own particular view of ecology.[2]

The concluding thought might also be stated in reverse, "The view of ecology might be different for each particular civilization." When men settle, as frontiersmen in a new region, they meet at the outset the essential facts of geography: terrain, altitude, soil, plant and animal life. Ecologically, the different species of plant life share a habitat which is also occupied by a network of animal life. We can think here of the plant ecology and the animal ecology and their interrelations, or how they are affected when man enters the scene with an ecology of his own which throws the natural ecological order out of balance. If man brings in domestic animals, he more than likely eliminates the wild ones. He may deplete the soil by overcropping or cause erosion by clearing away the forest. If man turns to mining in this new habitat, he may lay much of the land to waste. To use Gourou's term, man may "violently" disturb the environment.

Under such circumstances, man's relation to his environment may be of interest to both geographers and ecologists as well as to the sociologist. Man makes his environment over if he expands a community until a village becomes a great city. By perfecting systems of transportation, he minimizes that geographic factor called distance. He may dredge a river and convert it into a harbor for large ships. He may minimize a mountain as a barrier by tunneling through it, as he overcomes a river barrier by building a bridge. And he may multiply the utility of a unity of space by erecting on it a building of 30 or more floors.

The geographic facts are doubtless much more an influence for primitive people and least so for urban and industrial people. Indeed, urban man with his structures has been able to surround himself with an environment of his own making. By his system of work and living, he is able to establish a community of several million within a geographical area on which fewer than 3,000 Indians lived before his arrival.

SOCIAL PREOCCUPATION OF GEOGRAPHY

A considerable number of geographers have been convinced that culture is in large part the product of the natural environment. In these terms, they have tried to explain not only the work ways of people, their family systems and their technology, but even their skin color.[3] Friedrich

[2] Pierre Gourou, stated in group discussion, see William L. Thomas (Ed.), *Man's Role in Changing the Face of the Earth,* Chicago, University of Chicago Press, 1956, p. 945.

[3] A work on environmentalism and environment is Franklin Thomas, *The Environmental Basis of Society,* New York, Appleton-Century-Crofts, 1925.

Ratzel was among the early and ardent environmentalists, and his influence was considerable. One of his disciples, Ellen Churchill Semple, wrote a book on geographic environment which had considerable influence for a time on American social scientists.[4] She was outdistanced later by Ellsworth Huntington who studied the effects of climate on certain mass migrations of history, and whose books still have popularity in paperback editions.

Huntington was not content with mere geographical determinism to explain migration and settlement; he added moral observations. He argued that migrants who ventured forth were of better quality than the stay-at-homes. The strong move greater distances, the weak fall by the way. He offered an explanation for two northern islands, Newfoundland and Iceland, both rugged of terrain, where the people live mainly by fishing. While Iceland has long had a government, a distinguished university, and many notable men, Newfoundland remained backward. Huntington holds that Newfoundland was settled by people of lower quality and less initiative than the Danes who settled Iceland. He failed to recognize that Britain for some three centuries discouraged settlements on Newfoundland. The management of its affairs was left almost wholly to the fishing merchants. Most of the people settled on land were not permitted to own it, and many still do not own the land they occupy. The situation changed in 1949 when Newfoundland became a province of the Dominion of Canada.[5]

Environmentalism, unfortunately, was not adequate to explain social and cultural phenomena which lay outside the field of geography. Certain earlier geographers were tempted to overextend the notion of environmental determinism, which is far less true of most geographers today.[6]

Most modern geographers recognize that man also lives in a social environment largely of his own making and he is armed with technology by which he is able to alter in certain ways the influences of the natural environment. The modern geographer proposes the concept of "possibilism" which recognizes that the geographic influences affect man, but within limits, and also that man can modify the natural environment, again within limits. The possibilists recognize that different peoples, exposed to the same environment, may respond differently. It is also evident that as a civilization advances people are less dominated by their immediate environment, and much less restricted than was primitive man to his immediate environment.

[4] Ellen Churchill Semple, *Influence of Geographic Environment*, New York, Holt, Rinehart and Winston, 1911.

[5] Ellsworth Huntington, *Mainsprings of Civilization*, New York, Wiley, 1952, Chap. 7, paperback ed.

[6] For example, see Alfred H. Meyer and John H. Strietelmeyer, *Geography in World Society, A Conceptual Approach*, Philadelphia, Lippincott, 1963.

This doctrine was the fusion of three sets of ideas; 1) the idea of man as a geographical agent, emphasizing, that is, the role of man in changing the physical environment; 2) the significance of historic factors, in the development of culture; and 3) a concept of resources based on the idea of plant and animal associations, derived from the growing science of plant ecology.[7]

GEOGRAPHY AND HUMAN ECOLOGY

When man settles in a geographical location he begins to have various relations with it. He makes use of the available resources or he may try to improve upon these resources, as when he makes the soil more productive for grain crops than when it was used merely for pasture. Different parts of his new habitat, he finds, are better used for one purpose than another. Different members in the settlement may engage in their special kinds of work, each finding the location most suitable for his purposes. Thus a pattern of uses develop in this habitat which different people share. The phenomena cease to be merely geographic and begin to be ecological. "It may be said," and we quote Theodorson, "that human ecology emphasizes the relationships between man and an environmental setting, while human geography emphasizes the physical environment itself and man's reciprocal relationship with that environment." [8]

More than does the geographer, the ecologist must take account of competition within and among species, whether the community be at the plant level, the animal level, or the human level. At each level, as numbers increase, the struggle for sustenance intensifies. But at the human level many of the adaptations are conscious; they tend also to be cultural adaptations. The geographer, says Hawley, observes the distribution of community phenomena in their visible aspects. "Human ecology, which is also interested in the relations of man to his physical environment, fastens its attention upon the human interdependencies that develop in action and reaction of the population and its habitat." [9] Ecology takes account of behavior and reasons for it.

Man makes things and they have meaning for him. They are called by names and become symbols used in communication. Ideas about things and their use can be communicated, whether these be roads, canals, bridges, buildings, fields and crops, fish plants, mines, or salt

[7] Clarence J. Glacken, "Changing Ideas of the Habitable World," in William L. Thomas, Jr. (Ed.), *Man's Role in Changing the Face of the Earth*, Chicago, University of Chicago Press, 1956, p. 85.

[8] George A. Theodorson, "Human Ecology and Human Geography," in Joseph S. Roucek (Ed.), *Contemporary Sociology*, New York, Philosophical Library, 1958, p. 339.

[9] Amos H. Hawley, *Human Ecology*, New York, Ronald Press, 1950, p. 72.

beds. The list is endless, but each item tells something, and clusters of items tell a great deal about the culture of a human community. All may be observed as facts for geography or for ecology, but the interest of the ecologist intensifies at the point where the interest of the geographer leaves off. Each of the many things made by man has some pertinence to his diverse use of space in his habitat.

Moreover, the ecologist may have greater interest than the geographer in changes that take place in the human community, especially in the detailed aspects of change, technological, economic, or social. Evans, for example, has studied the evolution of the rural village in western Europe. He finds that much of the peasant village culture of late medieval times has been lost. The ecology of these villages has changed radically. He urges an effort be made to gather information about their houses, dress, tools, dances, and songs before it is too late. Thus the ecologist may be able to make allowances "for the inheritance of traditions from the earlier phases of adjustment." [10]

Human ecology in the United States began as a sociological pursuit with the study of cities, although it is recognized that ecological phenomena relate to all human communities, in addition to the relations between communities. It is also recognized that there are ecological differences between rural and urban communities. One difference concerns the basis for the value put on land. Rural land is primarily valued for its fertility and also for its distance from the markets. The value of urban land, on the other hand, is based on *site,* where it is located with reference to the urban center. The quality of the land itself is largely irrelevant; urban land is so much space. Land use in the city is related to work, but not the rural kind of work. Even the urban man's thinking about land is divorced from rural land values, a fact that is reflected in the ecology of cities. Kolb suggests:

> In the city stress is more purely on extension and topography as conditions or means of functional activities, since the activities of the city essentially involve problems of space occupancy and spatial movement.[11]

"Extension" to Kolb apparently means distance or area on the level, while "topography" would relate to the up-and-down dimension, hills, for example, which ecologically would be barriers to effective land use. Topography would also relate to streams or water bodies which ecologically may be an advantage to a community, although in other respects

---

10 E. Estwyn Evans, "The Ecology of Peasant Life in Western Europe," in William L. Thomas, Jr. (Ed.), *Man's Role in Changing the Face of the Earth,* Chicago, University of Chicago Press, 1956, p. 234.

11 William L. Kolb, "The Social Functions and Structure of Cities," *Economic Development and Cultural Change,* Vol. 3, 1954–1955, p. 38.

they may be barriers to ready circulation. These are geographic facts, but their implications may be greater for ecology.

ECOLOGY AND SOCIAL DETERMINANTS

Changes in the ecology of the human community can be understood, to some extent, in terms of technological and economic considerations, or some techno-economic combination. Some ecologists would rule out certain emotional or sentimental behavior, which is not easily measured. The "human" in human ecology makes the difference. People do not always behave rationally. A suburb may oppose the nearby location of an industrial plant. As viewed by some it might bring in "lower-class" people, even foreigners or Negroes. Similarly a middle-class residential area may oppose widening a street to make an arterial highway; it might destroy the quiet of the neighborhood.

The techno-economic view of ecology may recognize that some social factors figure in ecological change; but despite the recognition of sentiment as a variable, they assume that all ecological change can be seen as economic. And, as put by Sirjamaki, most if not all such change is a product of human competition.

> *First,* is the fundamental interdependence of men; they must live in communities because they share the same human condition.
>
> *Second,* locality has an economic function; men locate their social, cultural and economic activities at certain places in their communities, which aid in realizing their objectives.
>
> The *third* is competition for limited space; human beings congest their communities by overcrowding the interior areas with people and buildings, thus constricting the spaces necessary for human movement. This congestion intensifies the competition for favorable location of activities and leads to inflation of land prices and rents, high costs of transportation, and additional time in communication and travel.[12]

This economic view assumes that, in general, both social and business uses of space respond alike to economic forces. It appears to be true that land used for business or industry derives its value primarily from economic competition; yet social pressure may result in excluding industry from certain streets or areas. Certain areas may be set aside for industry; yet social pressures may cause certain "noxious" industries (a slaughterhouse or soap factory) from locating there.

---

[12] John Sirjamaki, *The Sociology of Cities,* New York, Random House, 1964, p. 195.

With respect to land used for residential purposes, we find various contradictions to the economic-selection concept. Slums may be found on high-priced land near the urban center and may be so occupied for a number of years waiting for the land to be put to more profitable use. The value of middle-class residences may drop suddenly if one or two middle-class Negro families move onto the street. In an old city the demands of economy may call for the widening of certain streets. But these streets and some of the buildings on them, for historical reasons, may have a sentimental value to the citizens. Resistance is shown and the change is not made.

It needs to be mentioned that Durkheim gave some thought to the spatial distribution of people in communities. Halbwachs, a student of Durkheim, carried the thought further, thinking of men and their things as being distributed in space and of degrees of social distance between them. "This aspect of collective life is the subject matter of social morphology; i.e., the study of groups insofar as they are in the corporal world . . . insofar as they define themselves as things in space and as organic realities." [13] This thinking was tested by Paul Chombart de Lauwe in his study of areas and zones of occupancy in Paris, mentioned later in this chapter.

Whether this area of sociological research is called human ecology or social morphology, Firey has taken the position that one needs to give more attention to the influence of human sentiment in the uses of space in communities. He found in his study of Boston that a proposed ecological change may be sound from the point of economic values, but people may oppose it for sentimental reasons which relate to tradition. Or they may for social reasons make certain demands respecting zoning laws. While certain of these sentimental views may change with time, they may also stand for a long time as a block to total ecological planning.[14]

CONCENTRATION AND MOVEMENT

Whatever the size of a community, its essential institutions and functions will be clustered at the most central point, which is most accessible to the largest number of people. At the center are the main stores, banks, office buildings, and the key professions. If a city of 10,000 grows to 100,000, the same concentrations in the mid-area will be seen,

[13] Maurice Halbwachs, *Population and Society, Introduction to Social Morphology,* translated by Otis D. Duncan and Harold W. Pfautz, New York, Free Press, 1960, pp. 45 and 183.

[14] Walter Firey, *Land Use in Central Boston,* Cambridge, Harvard University Press, 1947, p. 3.

although there will be greater evidence of specialization. The establishments selling goods or services will be on the main streets or adjacent side streets, distributed according to their ability to meet location costs.

Areas of residence will also be differently distributed, depending in large part on how other space is used (industry, business, transportation, recreation, other types of residence). From the center to the periphery, they may show various degrees of concentration, but with the greatest concentrations near the center. In particular the lower class will be located in certain, often compact, slum areas, and the upper class may be concentrated (at least those who prefer inner-city residence) in "high-rise" luxury apartments on certain streets accessible to the center. In large cities, people living in their own houses increase proportionately with remoteness from the urban center. Rich estates are likely to be in the suburbs. Urban residential occupancy thus shows an ecological pattern reflecting both income and social class.[15]

The pattern also frequently reflects the division of labor. But, however many the parts in the community's pattern of space, the primary orientation of each part is to the community center. Moreover, each part or area tends to have some special function, and we can speak of a division of labor between the parts. Different types of business, of industry, of residence, with space used for such special purposes as public administration, culture, education, or recreation, become interdependent parts. Depending on the interdependence between the parts, the whole "sinks or swims together."

> Individuals, firms, industries, whole areas rely on the general prosperity for their particular welfare and are more closely tied to some "common bond of stable interest." Direct interdependence . . . is ecological; it arises from the necessity of overcoming structural and environmental frictions which may impede the smooth, efficient operation of differentiated parts. As a rule, the more specialized a function the greater its dependence on other functions to keep it regularly and fully employed. Operational interdependence of this type requires more comprehensive cooperation and coordination of functions and areas, giving rise to more complex "round-about" patterns of production.[16]

"Direct interdependence" to Lampard relates primarily to the sphere of work, big industries, in big cities. This interdependence, in less intense form, is found in smaller industrial centers as well. This press for concentration implies the moving about of large numbers of people. It means goods being moved, and it suggests varying degrees of access,

[15] Alvin Boskoff, *The Sociology of Urban Regions,* New York, Appleton-Century-Crofts, 1962, p. 97.

[16] Eric E. Lampard, "The History of Cities in the Economically Advanced Areas," *Economic Development and Cultural Change,* Vol. 3, 1954–1955, p. 90.

which becomes more difficult as concentrations increase. The very pressure to get more use of streets and sidewalks, stimulates the tempo of all movement. As Schnore observes, the ebb and flow of movement through the streets in towns assumes a type of self-directed regularity. Of the metropolis he says:

> The entire metropolitan complex manifests patterned movements in space. After all, one of the key features distinguishing the modern metropolis from large cities of the past is the ease and rapidity of exchange and movement, whether of persons, commodities or information. Moreover, smaller cities, which also enjoy the advanced transportation and communication facilities of the metropolis, share this complete ease of movement. The unique features distinguishing internal movement in the metropolitan community appear merely to reflect the enhanced complexity associated with a far-flung system of interdependent nucleii.[17]

TIME, DISTANCE, AND THE ROAD

In these terms we can think of the ecology of the urban community as a type of spatial order which reflects and influences the social and economic order. The different users of space tend to locate in areas of greatest advantage for their purposes, in areas of least inconvenience respecting transit and other movement. For residential location, for instance, people tend to settle in streets to and from which their transport needs will be best served, although their choices will also be determined somewhat by social preference.

However, despite all efforts made by municipal authorities to widen streets, congestion continues. If accessibility is made easier, congestion soon overtakes it. Although streets in big cities are many times more efficient than before the automobile arrived, the demands on these same streets have increased even more.[18]

In a very early study, which appeared in 1841, Kohl, a German economist, attempted to explain why communities are of different sizes and why they are distributed over the landscape according to their size. But he also wrestled with the matter of relationships between communities. Distributed around the large city, like satellites, were smaller

---

[17] Leo F. Schnore, "Urban Form, The Case of the Metropolitan Community," in Werner E. Hirsch (Ed.), *Urban Life and Form,* New York, Holt, Rinehart and Winston, 1963, p. 187.

[18] Gideon Sjoberg, "Comparative Urban Sociology," in Robert K. Merton, Leonard Broom, and Leonard S. Cottrell, Jr. (Eds.), *Sociology Today, Problems and Prospects,* New York, Basic Books, 1959, p. 347.

towns and villages. These clusters appeared to him as intercommunity networks.[19]

What Kohl observed is now commonly recognized as an ecological fact. The ecological pattern seen in an urban community does not stop at the political boundary of the city; the suburbs beyond the line are economically, socially, and culturally outlying areas of the city. The road that links the village to the small city also links the small city to the greater one. In the city it is the street and outside it is the road that provides access. Brunhes wrote:

> The larger the city the closer the network of roads around it and, conversely, the more the concentration of roads at a given point is favored by physical conditions the greater are the city's chances and opportunities of growing large. . . . The town creates the road and is dependent on it, but the road in its turn creates the town, or re-creates it, by displacing it or changing its form.[20]

It is assumed that where roads exist they are used to carry raw products to the city and finished goods away. From the materials carried to the town or from it we can know the work done there. The resources coming from the hinterland tell us also of work done. Cooley's theory of transportation, written about 1894, observed that wealth and population gather at breaks in transportation. Goods may arrive on an ocean vessel and be transferred to other carriers—one kind of break in transportation. Goods may arrive in bulk and be distributed in small lots, or packaged and distributed—another kind of break in transportation. Goods may change form, as when cotton is manufactured into cloth—still another break in transportation. The different kinds of work, fostered by the means of transportation and the movement of goods, make the town possible, and the town may become a city.[21]

It is related that in the colonial days a farmer living seven miles from a city needed a full day to deliver a load of stove wood to a house in the city. The cost of delivery was greater than the cost of cutting the wood. De Crévecoeur, a New York farmer, in a letter written about 1760 told of the hardships of farmers trying to take produce to the market. His farm was apparently less than 10 miles from a town, but farmers living 15 or more miles away would begin the journey at midnight, to

[19] J. G. Kohl, *Der Verkehr und die Ansiedlung der Menschen in ihrer Abhangigkeit von der Gestaltung der Erdoberflache,* 2nd ed., Leipzig, 1850.

[20] Jean Brunhes, *Human Geographie,* abridged and edited by Mme. M. Jean Brunhes Delamarre and Pierre Belfontaines, translated by Ernst F. Rowe, New York, Rand-McNally, 1952, p. 76.

[21] Charles H. Cooley, "A Theory of Transportation," in Robert C. Angell (Ed.), *Sociological Theory and Social Research,* New York, Holt, Rinehart and Winston, 1930.

be back home by the next midnight, an ordeal in winter. Farmers along the way would leave their doors open and have a fire in the hearth.

> The traveler, when cold has a right to stop and warm himself at the first house he sees. He freely goes to the fire, which is kept a-burning all night. There he forgets the keenness of the cold; he smokes his pipe; drinks of the cider which is often left by the hearth; and departs in peace. We always sleep in these rooms; at least I do, and have often seen mine full when I was in bed. On waking I have sometimes spoken to them; at other times it was a silent meeting. . . . Far from being uneasy at seeing my house thus filled while my wife and I are abed, I think it, on the contrary, a great compliment.[22]

De Crévecoeur mentions how farmers far from a market, although tilling fertile land, would be in deep poverty. Bowman, nearly a century later, writing as a geographer, mentioned the farmer's problem of access to market. A farmer growing vegetables or small fruits was inconvenienced if his farm was more than 10 miles from market, while a field-crop farmer could not afford to be much more than 20 miles from market. A sheep rancher or cattle rancher could be more distant. Hard-surface, all-weather roads, along with motorized transport, have removed most of these limitations. All ecological zones involving cost of movement in time and money have been extended.[23]

With moden road transport and refrigeration, eggs, dairy products, and vegetables can be hauled hundreds of miles. By the same token the farmer can go 20 or more miles to a town on shopping trips or for reasons of recreation, and he may even pace his work to city time. A negative result has been the decline of many small "road-crossing" hamlets where there once were the store, post office, school, and church. Today only a filling station may be needed. Urban intimacy with the hinterland, while eliminating many villages, tends to swell towns and cities, an ecological redistribution of people and trade.

For the city and its immediate environs, cost of transport, especially for business and industry, may be as influential as tax rates in deciding the location of a firm. It concerns the money and time cost from one point to another in the city. It also includes the cost of space for vehicles, and these costs force many firms to move from central to outer areas. Winnick makes the point in an if-it-were-otherwise observation.

> Clearly, were there no costs of transfer, there would be so little need for physical proximity and therefore much less economic justification for the

[22] Hector St. John de Crévecoeur, *Letters from an American Farmer* (1782), Toronto, Signet, 1963, p. 318.
[23] Isaiah Bowman, *Geography in Relation to the Social Sciences*, New York, Scribner, 1934.

city. Were it possible to traverse distance without time or cost of inconvenience, there would not only be a tremendous gain in economic welfare, but also a radical transformation in the geographical map of population and production. Urban concentration would tend to disappear.[24]

In the United States and Canada, as presumably elsewhere, the choice of space users is one between high transport costs and high rents. For certain firms proximity to the urban center is vital to their survival. The demand for space is so great that more and more tall buildings go up, which increases the load on the streets. However, erecting taller and taller buildings to relieve pressure, like building wider and wider streets to serve traffic, is not a solution. But many cities act as though it is. Now European cities, long aloof to the idea, are building skyscrapers because of pressure at the urban center. Not only in London but in small cities in England as well, one finds taller buildings being erected.[25] In the war-damaged but now rebuilt German cities skyscrapers rising as much as 15 floors are not uncommon; even taller ones are being erected in the cities of north Italy.

LAND USE AND AREA SPECIALIZATION

As already noted, in the larger communities in which there is great diversity in types of work, special activities tend to cluster. Lampard emphasizes the need for such clustering on the basis of the interdependence of functions. Because of efficiency, related establishments must not be widely dispersed.[26]

Lampard views the areal pattern of the urban community from the perspective of an economist, his attention being on work activity and the distribution of work places. With some modification, we can detect a comparable ecological distribution of public functions and establishments, of cultural functions and establishments and, of course, of residential areas. People tend to cluster for social as well as for economic reasons; on the basis of race, ethnic identity, social class, and so on.

Calcutta reminds us of the many social types there may be in a city of nearly five million. They may cluster according to region (even place) of origin, or be drawn together in terms of language, caste, religion, level of income, or home-industry occupation. Each group in its particular area retains something of its own subculture, yet all these clusters mix

24 Louis Winnick, "The Economic Functions of the City, Yesterday and Tomorrow," in Thomas P. Pearson (Ed.), *Proceedings of the Academy of Political Science*, Vol. 27, No. 1, 1960, p. 15.

25 Peter H. Mann, *An Approach to Urban Sociology*, London, Routledge and Kegan Paul, 1965, p. 79.

26 Lampard, op. cit., p. 92.

in the economic life of the city. Ecologically segregated, they tend no less to become increasingly economically integrated.

> Today Bengalis make up half of the population of Calcutta. For them, more than for any other ethnic group, the city is "home"; the average Bengali family of 5.4 members exceeds in size the average family of the city. The Bengalis used to maintain the old "native" quarter of the city, north of the Maidan as a distinctive Bengali quarter. There are now distinguishable concentrations of Bengali-speaking Hindus in every ward of the city . . . (distinguished by caste, origin, occupation). . . .

> The Kansari, or brassworker caste shows a comparable continuity of identity and residence in one ward in the northeastern part of the city and one ward in the south. . . . For centuries the brass water jars, cooking pots and eating bowls that are the work of such artisans have constituted the principal imperishable possessions of the Hindu household. . . .

> The descendants of the Brahmin and Kayastha zamindars (land owners in villages) have tended to follow the Western pattern of drift into the learned professions, letters and science, and into the civil service and accountancy. These families continue to be identified with the old native quarter of Calcutta, where they are numerous and influential. . . .

> The eastern and northeastern fringes of Calcutta, where the land is low and even now subject to flooding, were initially inhabited by Bengali fisherfolk and gardeners. . . . They usually belong to the Scheduled Castes . . . (untouchables). . . . Many of these low-caste people have lost their hereditary occupational identity and have joined the ranks of either skilled or unskilled labor. . . .

> The largest numbers [of the many male in-migrants] come from Uttar Predesh and Bihar. Both Moslems and Hindus, they speak Hindi, the stationary "national" language of India. These men live singly or in "messing groups" of five or so in the tenements and slums of the northern, eastern and southern reaches of the city.[27]

The distribution of people by type in Calcutta is not unlike the distribution one finds in cities of Canada and the United States, although in Calcutta the concentrations are greater. And in Calcutta, as in other large cities, habitation areas change shape as people move in or out. As in other great cities, the poor in Calcutta may be found in a great variety of small areas, some near the center of the city. As Smith reports, in Latin American cities and particularly Brazilian cities, the slums are found at the fringes. But in these cities, unlike Calcutta, the fringe areas

[27] Nirmal Kumar Bose, "Calcutta, a Premature Metropolis," *Scientific American*, Vol. 213, No. 3, September 1965, pp. 96–99.

are often within walking distance. Smith mentions that the rich live centrally, conveniently near the downtown area, where urban amenities are available.[28]

The pattern described by Smith is similar to the distribution existing before 1890 in most cities in the United States. In New York, for example, before 1840 large "shanty-town" slums existed at the outer areas of the city, but by 1890 there were slum areas near the urban center. The same was true for many other cities. The rich lived in or very near the central area but later when outlying areas acquired the essential amenities such as piped water, sewer lines, electric power, and paved streets, the upper-class families began locating in suburban places. Their in-town residences were taken over by business or the houses were made over for rooming houses or other residential use. The rich man's private house near the urban center vanished, often to be replaced by tall luxury apartment buildings where reside many of the well-to-do who have no wish to live in the suburbs.

Urban areas of residence, like those of work, or areas for leisure, take form as people are attracted together according to their interests. However, convenience may be another determining factor. But, what is convenient in Brazil may not be in France. What is spatially convenient in London was not found by Marris to be so in Lagos, Nigeria, but a definite ecological pattern still exists in each of these two cities.

> In a society where people can barely live within their income any disturbance creates difficulties. For the people of central Lagos, these difficulties are especially serious, because they depend so much on trade, which is notoriously hard to transplant. There is a danger that their family life will be impoverished as much as their livelihood, and in turn create new hardships as they are forced to abandon obligations to their kin. Good housing is needed, but the people become socially and otherwise detached if they move from the centre.[29]

These remarks by Marris concern an effort in Lagos to establish a housing development at the edge of the city. Families were moved from a slum near the center about to be cleared for city "renewal." Most of these families gained part of their livelihood by trade, which could not be done if they lived a bus ride from the center. Moreover, families in the housing project were cut off from their kin near the town center. The cost of bus fare limited the visiting that could be done. The inconveniences aside, what is happening as Lagos grows is that its central area widens. A housing site may have to yield to a business block, a cluster

---

[28] T. Lynn Smith, *Brazil, People and Institutions*, Baton Rouge, Louisiana State University Press, 1963, p. 73.

[29] Peter Marris, *Family and Social Change in an African City*, London, Routledge and Kegan Paul, 1961, p. 115.

of poor houses may be razed to make space for a new factory. The rich may move out voluntarily, while the poor may be pushed back. In much the same way, a business establishment at the town center, not able to meet rent costs, is replaced by one that can.

URBAN GROWTH AND COMPETITION FOR SPACE

In social terms, competition for residential space is concerned only partly with economic considerations; prestige values may be a factor, although these are most important for middle and upper classes. The norms for this kind of competition differ from the norms involving competition for business space. In either type of competition there is, to Kolb, a moral order, not found among animals. Man must learn to keep the rules and engage in competition too.

> But man competes in economic affairs as a seeker of culturally defined ends, and such ends if not normatively limited are infinite. Further, men are conscious of their economic activities so that if their ends are not normatively limited they know that each is in competition with everyone else; and conscious competition unless normatively achieved inevitably results in war of all against all. Thus moral order is necessary in human society, not to mitigate competition but to prevent or lessen open conflict.[30]

For most forms of competition, man needs a spot where he can be found as he also needs space upon which to stand. If he is a professional song writer he may need a small office at the city's entertainment center. In that same area will be found the promoters of "shows," but they need much more space. A whole building may be occupied by persons and firms active in show business. In and near this specialized area will be related establishments: hotels, special eating places, and the little shops of the sellers of theater tickets. But in any particular city the entertainment area of today may not be precisely where it was 50 years earlier. Its central point may have moved by one or two city blocks in one direction or another. In New York the entertainment center has moved step by step, in the course of a century, some 20 blocks in the uptown direction. Other areas, dressmaking, the fur center, the wholesalers, and other occupiers, competing for space, helped force the uptown retreat of the entertainment-hotel center.

This kind of space competition is most characteristic of fast-growing cities, particularly big Canadian and American cities where such change is less resisted by tradition than in Old World cities. London is one example where the uses of space change but the pace is slower. Robson

30 Kolb, op. cit., p. 35.

mentions how certain areas have been identified with special functions for many decades. In a way, each has become institutionalized. He mentions Fleet Street, the center for newspaper and press offices; Shoreditch, the furniture market; Barmondsey, the center for canned foods, biscuits, jams; Deptford, the area for ship repairs and supplies; The Temple, Gray's Inn, and Lincoln's Inn, the legal center; Barclay Street, the medical center; and Hatten Garden, the center for dealers in precious stones.[31]

Mayer, a geographer, speaks of these integrated and specialized areas as nucleations. The rivalry for space within areas or between areas, he sees as rivalry for proximity, each competitor faced with the need of being near the urban center. For some purposes, depending on cost, transportation can be substituted for proximity and transfer costs for rent. The choice will differ for each type of establishment. The same choice must be made whether the establishment is at the center or in some other area.

A firm or business which places a high value on accessibility or, as Mayer would say, proximity to its main clients or customers, may find that land values or rents at what to it would be the most desirable location are in excess of what it can pay. The firm or business must choose to locate where rents are lower. It gains on rent but loses a little on proximity, in that its location is not in the "life center." The demands for proximity would vary with different business firms.[32]

In the growing city competition for elbow room is continuous and all-embracing, affecting even the shoemaker with his shop in a basement and the slum family living in a back street. Mayer concludes that this competition which touches all areas is a "sorting-out" process, the cumulation of many individual decisions, as prices are made in the market. Mann would say that this process is inherent in the urban ethos. People compete for space as for goods, social values embodying a materialistic ethos being assumed. "Trade, commerce, and industry are economic activities of the city and in their ethos must dominate all things. It would then follow that what is good for trade, commerce, and industry is good for other aspects of living. If industry needs innovation then innovation as a value is a good thing."[33]

The ecological pattern results as many people, perhaps millions, make individual decisions respecting location in space, and we know that many economic decisions may be sentimentally motivated. Even

[31] William A. Robson (Ed.), *Great Cities of the World*, London, Allen and Unwin, 1957, p. 263. See the chapter on London.
[32] Harold M. Mayer, "Chicago, Transportation and Metropolitan Planning," *Papers and Proceedings of the Regional Planning Association*, Philadelphia, University of Pennsylvania Press, 1961, Vol. 7, p. 244.
[33] Mann, op. cit., p. 108.

when space planning, zoning for example, is imposed to guide or limit uses of space, the efforts are rarely completely effective. The ecological pattern tends to take shape without much guidance, or despite it. Also, without or despite guidance, the pattern is ever changing, often in unpredicted ways. The economic and technological factors that stimulate change are sometimes also unpredictable.

The evolution of the ecological pattern, as a product of competition for land in the community, is, much like evolution in nature, a consequence in large part of trial and error. We may say it is wasteful, but so far planners have not found a substitute.

ECOLOGICAL SUCCESSION AND EQUILIBRIUM

Britannia Mews, a story by Margery Sharp, concerns an alley between two fashionable streets in London and the succession of human types inhabiting it from about 1860 to 1920. In the alley, behind each property, was a substantial masonry stable (mews), each with space for carriage and horses on the ground floor and for servants' quarters above.

When the story begins the street was one of impressive private homes of rich families. In the 1870s or later the rich families began moving away to live in country homes from which they could commute to the city. The line of stables in the Mews came to be inhabited by poor families. In time, the Mews began to attract artists. The concentration of artists began to attract "arty" people, not all of them poor. In the final phase of the story, the old buildings were replaced by apartments. In less than a century the Mews move through a cycle, from a respected use back again to respectability, illustrating an urban process of structural change known ecologically as succession.

One type of succession relates to a series of occupants inhabiting a structure and making the same use of it—one family and then another occupying an apartment; a series of shopkeepers, of any kind, maintaining the same shop. With aging, the structure becomes outmoded and may not be kept in good repair. Rents may go down and successive occupants may be of lower socioeconomic class. A cluster of such structures may finally become a slum. Such is the history of many urban slum areas.

A second type of succession relates to the replacement of structures. An office building may become out-of-date and cease to be profitable. It is then replaced by a bigger office building with modern facilities. The slum may be removed and middle-class apartments erected, but these too are likely to deteriorate in the course of three or four decades.

A third type of succession involves a change of use. An abandoned church may be torn down and a modern apartment, a store, or a hotel may be erected on the land. In growing cities many sites used by business establishments were once occupied by the homes of leading citizens. In the growth of a city certain types of structures may no longer be needed. For example, Mayer mentioned that in Chicago warehouses are less needed than formerly, and factories are moving from large cities.[34]

As it relates to the man-made environment of the community, succession involves structural replacement. The entire physical part of the community (buildings, roads, bridges, water supply and sewer networks) is subject to decline, decay, wear, and may have to be replaced because of technological change. This applies to public as well as to private properties. Seen in these terms it is understandable why about a third of the structural work in the city has to do with replacement. Plumbing and water piping put in a building 30 years earlier may not only be outmoded but constant repair may be needed. The same holds for the old elevators and the heating system. An old building may still be strong in its primary structure, but to modernize it may be as costly as building anew. All such successions call for change in the distribution of facilities and of people, each an outstanding case of ecological dynamics.[35]

In the course of urban change and growth some streets on which little development has been experienced suddenly come alive with reconstruction. Urban growth is moving in that direction. Another area may be afflicted with decline. The near west side in Chicago was a depressed area for a generation, although located near the downtown. But it was and is isolated by the river. When expansion crossed the river the whole area was in a state of boom. In this case a whole area experiences structural succession.

Many German cities, destroyed by wartime bombing, had what many thought to be the first opportunity to build anew, to eliminate many short and winding streets. Opposition to radical change was considerable. People wanted to move back to the streets where they once lived. They would have new houses, to be sure, but they wanted stores and other services to be where they stood before. They opposed any new alignment of the streets. Planners found themselves balked to a great extent in their wish to change the use of various units of land.[36]

Apparently there is in the older cities of Europe a much greater demand for continuity of the elements in their physical environment than is found, for example, in American cities. The main hotel in Darmstadt after the war was built on the same site where a hotel of the same name stood since about 1300. It had been built anew several times, an

34 Mayer, op. cit., p. 244.
35 Boskoff, op. cit., p. 117.
36 See two articles on this issue, Fred C. Ikle, "The Effect of War Destruction on the Ecology of Cities," *Social Forces*, Vol. 29, May 1951, pp. 283–291; and Leo Grebler, "Continuity in the Rebuilding of Bombed Cities in Western Europe," *American Journal of Sociology*, Vol. 61, No. 5, March 1956, pp. 463–469.

example of structural succession, although the use of the structure did not change.

PATTERNS AND LAYOUT OF URBAN GROWTH

If we think of an ecological arrangement of the physical aspects of the community, including the man-made elements, as constituting a kind of order, then it is useful to discover the nature of that order. It is generally accepted that the focus of most of the competitive activity revolves about the urban center, the most used meeting point for the whole community. Does the arrangement of the center in one urban community bear any resemblance to the arrangement in other communities?

We know that the price of land and the level of rent are highest at the urban center and they diminish with distance from the center, but they diminish also with accessibility to the center. Each user of space tends to have his own condition which helps him determine the most optimum point to locate. Whereas it may be imperative for some occupiers to be at the center, it may be better for others to find more remote locations. This holds for various groups of occupiers: industrial, commercial, and residential.

A stable city that has experienced little growth over decades will tend to have a fairly crystallized ecological order. So a worker in a shop or a housewife, a native of the place, will know where everything is, and may be able to explain why the different areas of residence and business are here or there and not somewhere else. The whole array of things takes the form of a map in his head, although he may not think in terms of "pattern."

It is different with a growing community; the different areas jostle one another. Fast-growing areas tend to push outward, each in the direction most favorable to itself. The whole community expands. Different observers have identified three types of outward growth:

1. The city grows outward in all directions, unless growth is blocked in some directions by barriers such as hills or bodies of water.
2. Growth extends ribbon-like along the main routes of access, the space between the ribbons eventually filling. Some call this a starlike type of growth.
3. Growth extends outward along routes, but along the routes will be communities already established, some as old as the city itself. Each of these points begins to expand until the space in the direction of the city is filled. In time these once independent places become areas within the city, each such area still keeping its name and having its center.

Any description of the manner of city expansion may be valid, and it would be folly to hold that any one is universal. Some maintain that all changes in the process of growth, whatever the city, will be reflected in changing land values. Competition for space will be present in all areas of the community. People will settle where land is cheapest and where access is most promising.[37]

Ernest Burgess, first to attempt making maps showing the distribution of the many types of areas in the city, found a tendency in Chicago for types of areas to be distributed in something like concentric circles in terms of their distance from the urban center.[38] He recognized that the circles are only approximate, since types of barriers interfere. His distribution map for Chicago was not intended to have universal application. It was offered as a method. Burgess recognized that whatever the pattern of areas found in a city, growth will be affected by the natural lay of the land. A city crowded against the sea by mountains, as Rio de Janeiro, must either fill in water space to make land or growth must follow the canyons. Stockholm is a city built on islands and peninsulas but, despite water barriers, as Sidenbladh shows, it manages to orient itself to a central area, and its outward growth on the mainland approximates a circle.[39]

Very comparable to the Chicago areal study by Burgess is a mapping of areas in Paris by Chombart de Lauwe. Following the morphology concept of Halbwachs, he identified the various areas and groups of areas, the small areas being identified as *quartiers* and the groups of areas being classified as *secteurs*. Generally, he found that *secteurs* were bound by various barriers to free movement: wide avenues, railroad lines, water bodies, parks, hills. However, the *secteurs*, according to the types of use, arranged themselves in zones of varying width from the urban center outward. He identified seven of these *secteur* zones.

1. *Noyau de Paris;* the mid-town; hotels, special shops, certain institutions, monuments, some residence
2. *Tourists and strangers;* very cosmopolitan, rich and poor, refugees, students, artists, radical groups, railroad stations, overlapping in part the Noyau de Paris
3. *Residence and small enterprise;* small and medium commercial and industrial establishments; some areas of rich residence, also residence of other types
4. *Residence and large enterprise;* large industries surrounded by working-class housing, small semi-rural areas
5. *Residence and small suburbs; secteur* lines become very irregular, average distance ten kilometers from urban center

[37] William Alonzo, "A Theory of the Urban Land Market," *Papers and Proceedings of the Regional Planning Association*, Philadelphia, University of Pennsylvania Press, 1960, Vol. 6, p. 149.

[38] Burgess, op. cit., p. 55.

[39] Goran Sidenbladh, "Stockholm, A Planned City," *Scientific American*, Vol. 213, No. 3, September 1965, pp. 106–121.

6. *Lotissements* (building developments); self-sufficient suburbs begin, *secteur* line reaches out in fingerlike fashion along the main lines of transportation
7. *Zone of commuters;* larger suburbs, at various points the urban uses of land merge into the rural uses.[40]

Unfortunately, the ecological approach to the study of the community has been subjected to a considerable amount of dispute, much of it unworthy, and this has continued for three decades. Mann, a British sociologist, suggests that instead of arguing about the Burgess theory (or by extension, any of the competing theories), some research should be undertaken to test its validity.[41]

Patently, each city grows outward as the lay of the land and other circumstances permit, and the argument for the "star" theory, the "sector" theory, or the "concentric circle" theory may be suggestive but not very applicable to many situations. It may be more important to be aware of the changes in the spatial order of things within the urban community while growth is under way, or as growth ceases.[42]

In their introductory chapter to their study of the present and future of the American metropolis, Otis D. Duncan and associates mention that the ecological approach was used, but they add that no single approach is sufficient for the study of great cities and their regions. "The ecologist's orientation gives him an advantage in 'seeing things whole', it also requires that he be willing to exploit the methods and discoveries of related disciplines—demography, economics, geography, and sociology—putting them not always to their original uses but rather to those suggested by his own conceptual framework." [43]

THE UTILITY OF ECOLOGICAL METHOD

The ordinary urbanite may know his city well, although he will know best the downtown and his own area, but he will not be without knowledge about other areas. He may give information about areas he has not visited. He can tell where different industrial areas are and he knows

[40] Paul Chombart de Lauwe (Ed.), *Paris et l'agglomeration parisienne*, Paris, Presses Universitaires de France, 1952, Vol. I, p. 55.

[41] Mann, op. cit., p. 95.

[42] Among the more pertinent initial studies of urban growth patterns are Richard M. Hurd, *Principles of Urban Land Values*, New York, Record and Guide, 1923, pp. 30 ff.; Ernest W. Burgess, "The Growth of the City," in Robert E. Park (Ed.), *The City*, Chicago, University of Chicago Press, 1925; R. D. McKenzie, *The Metropolitan Community*, New York, McGraw-Hill, 1933, Part II; Homer Hoyt, *The Structure and Growth of Residential Neighborhoods in American Cities*, Washington, D. C., Federal Housing Administration, 1939.

[43] Otis D. Duncan, W. Richard Scott, Stanley Lieberson, Beverly Duncan, and Hal H. Winsborough, *Metropolis and Region*, Baltimore, Johns Hopkins Press, 1960, p. 3.

about areas of residence. The ecologist differs from the ordinary urbanite because he puts his information on maps, quite understandable to ordinary urban people. Maps may show how different categories of people are distributed by income, occupation, race, ethnic origin, and other factors. Information on the distribution of births, deaths, marital status, state of health, or crime can all be shown spatially.[44]

Ecological maps enable comparisons to be made measuring change, or spatial distributions can be made of comparable types of data. Strauss mentions, "When properly mapped, any given area will be symbolized by several populations, from just a few to dozens." But the types of information about an area, he adds, enable us to see problems as they relate to location.[45] If we are interested in the distribution of auto accidents, homicides, juvenile delinquency, the distribution can be compared with type of housing, level of income, level of education, and so on for different areas.

Actually, although ecological maps comprise only a part of ecology, they are increasingly used by city engineers, real estate dealers, planners, business executives, police inspectors, health officials, and the welfare agencies. They can be used to compare areas for a given time or to compare change over time in particular areas. These uses, says Wirth, enable us to "anchor the generalizations concerning society . . . more firmly in time and space, and physical reality." [46]

[44] See Thomlinson, op. cit., Chap. 2, for a discussion of the nature of ecological data and how it is collected and used.

[45] Anselm L. Strauss, *Images of the Modern City*, New York, Free Press, 1961, p. 59.

[46] Louis Wirth, *On Cities and Social Life*, Albert J. Reiss, Jr. (Ed.), Chicago, University of Chicago Press, 1964, p. 188.

Industrial urbanism and population | 6

CITIES AND POPULATION INCREASE

In 1850 only London and Paris had populations in the area of a million inhabitants, Paris with about a million and London with over two million. In 1968 not less than 50 cities in the world have more than a million inhabitants and half of these have more than two million. Actually, it is not certain how many cities with population of over a million there are. What is more important is the fact that the rate of urban growth is faster than the general population growth.

The world population is now about three and one-half billion and most estimates of future growth put the total at six to seven billion or more by the year 2000. The average annual rate of increase in 1850 was about 0.51 percent, but in 1960 it was 1.7 percent. This means that according to the 1850 rate of growth it would require about 135 years to double the 1,171 million inhabitants, the number then estimated, whereas the population will double in only 41 years according to the 1960 rate of increase. The rate of increase in some countries is well over 2 percent a year, but, for the most part, these are poor countries with low levels of education and technology and a low living standard. Davis and others, observing this trend, speak of a "population crisis." [1]

Concern about population growth has been expressed by thinkers at different times, but the recognition that the world is at the point of being crowded is fairly recent. Comparatively, there was considerable increase in population growth during medieval times after the twelfth century. As Pirenne tells it, this increase had the effect of stimulating economic and technological change. Commerce increased and cities grew. Under such conditions population increase was a boon.[2] Present and

[1] Kingsley Davis, "The World's Population Crisis," in Robert K. Merton and Robert A. Nisbet (Eds.), *Contemporary Social Problems*, New York, Harcourt, Brace & World, 1961, pp. 291–323.

[2] Henri Pirenne, *The Medieval City*, Garden City, New York, Doubleday Anchor, 1956, pp. 73–76.

prospective population increase, as we shall see, is much less than a boon.

Our attention must turn to population increase as it affects the cities of the world, and we emphasize "cities of the world," because the urban population problem cannot be comprehended in terms of any one region or country. Much as population growth in rural areas will be felt in urban places, so pressures in one world region make their impress on other regions. In every region it is the cities that are most beset by population growth at this time, and it is a problem that cities will not be able to put aside. They are the final refuge of human surplus. Davis estimates that half of the population of the world by 1990 will be found in cities of 100,000 and over.[3]

HOW CITIES GROW

Rome, once a city of power, was fairly static for many centuries. It had a population of 180,000 in 1800 and only 226,000 in 1870. Within its walls there were 14 districts, the same number as in the days of Constantine. It began to grow, however, after 1870; its population reached 580,000 in 1914 and 1,735,000 in 1953.[4] New York had a population of 79,000 in 1800, which grew to 7,892,000 by 1950. London in 1800 had 960,000 inhabitants, thus being the only English city at that time with more than 100,000.

Actually, big-city building did not begin in most societies until after 1850 and the growth has accelerated with each decade. The rate of urban growth has moved abreast with the growth and worldwide spread of modern industry. Indeed industrialism and urbanism must go hand in hand. If we accept the estimate that in 1990 half the world's population will be living in cities of 100,000 inhabitants and over, we can safely assume that another fourth of the population will be in cities with only slightly under 100,000. In the United States as of 1960, for instance, there were 117 cities of 100,000 inhabitants and over and 137 with between 50,000 and 100,000. There were in addition about 800 with between 10,000 and 50,000 inhabitants.

Much more is involved than mere columns of figures. It is alarming to many that at this time hundreds of millions are moving into cities, and this may go on for some decades. What is staggering about the flood toward the cities is that the masses of newcomers need to be urbanized in their way of life, and they need to learn the skills demanded in the industrial labor market. Even more staggering is the problem of finding enough industrial work to keep them effectively employed.

[3] Kingsley Davis, "The Urbanization of the Human Population," *Scientific American,* Vol. 213, No. 3, September 1965, p. 41.

[4] Guiseppe Chiarelli, "Rome," in William A. Robson (Ed.), *Great Cities of the World,* London, Allen and Unwin, 1957, p. 522.

LAND AREA AND RESOURCES

When the clergyman-scholar, Thomas Robert Malthus, in 1789 issued his essay on population he was not the first to write about the problem. What he did was to put down in understandable terms the elemental facts about natural increase, the same facts that apply to animals as well as to men. Their numbers, according to Malthus, increase faster than the food supply. Had he written about the natural increase rate of rats or flies there would have been no dispute, but he applied the same logic to human increase. The curbs to man's increase are disease, natural disasters, war, and the controls he imposes on himself.[5]

The "Malthusian theory" is still objected to by many who would accept it for animals but not for humans. They hold that human increase is a sphere apart, some holding that this matter is in the hands of God. A certain few say, in essence, "Let the increase continue, let competition be sharp and free; then the fittest will survive." Optimists are ready to believe that, whatever the increase, science and technology will find ways to provide the food.

Urbanized industrial countries, best able now to sustain themselves because they have ready access to the goods of the world, evidence little awareness of food shortages which exist elsewhere. If news comes of starvation in some developing countries, groups may organize to collect private donations, but these good-will efforts, commendably motivated, hardly touch the problem. For many people, these private efforts may even divert attention from the real challenge of the man-food problems in the world.

It is often heard that the surface of the earth is vast and that the possibilities of getting food from land and sea are infinite. Actually, only a small part the earth's surface is suitable for producing food, or even suitable for human habitation. For example, there are:

33,450,000,000   acres of land on the earth, which includes ice caps, mountains and deserts;

15,600,000,000   estimated acres of potential crop land, but this is generally recognized as unrealistic;

4,000,000,000   acres of tillable land on the earth, according to the most careful estimates and of this about

3,200,000,000   acres are already under cultivation, approximately one acre for each inhabitant in 1966.[6]

[5] Thomas Robert Malthus, *An Essay on the Principle of Population*, 7th ed., London, Reeves and Turner, 1872.

[6] *World Population and Resources*, Political and Economic Planning, London, Allen and Unwin, 1962, p. 31.

Here we must add an observation too often overlooked: cities and other communities, including industrial establishments, are least likely to be found on ice caps, mountains or deserts. These and other man-made users of space are most likely located on the low, fertile plains. These non-food uses of land utilize land at a rate far faster than the rate at which new lands can be brought into food-producing use.

Optimism about the sea as a source of food supply is often widely expressed; it is said to be "the great pasture where fish feed." We do not know the limits of the sea, but we do know that much of the sea can be likened to a desert under water. Likewise, we do not yet know the extent to which tropical marshes can be converted into food-producing land. We only know that the effort would be costly. In the meanwhile population increases faster with each decade.

While cities grow at a faster rate, the fact faces us that there are food shortages in certain areas even at the present time. Platt reminds us not only of shortages but of serious food deficiencies.

> Two-thirds of the world's present population is subsisting on a diet which is inadequate in both quality and quantity for full health and happiness, as well as for that minimal increase in productive effort which is indispensable for raising the level above subsistence. In helping agricultural people of this kind it is necessary, so to speak, to prime the pump. At the subsistence level a man may "tick over" like the engine of a stationary car, but unlike the automobile, he consumes and weakens his own tissues in the process.
>
> In order to raise the level of man's productive effort and to secure an effective return in terms of vigour, it is essential to supply additional food —that is, brought in—of good quality and substantial quantity. This is the first step in raising the level of efficiency; and if this could be achieved by an act of God overnight, the total increase of availability would have to be of the order of 25 percent.[7]

Food-producing land is unevenly distributed in and between nations and regions. This, in turn, helps account for the uneven distribution of the population and of cities and towns by size. Industry, too, since its location depends on accessibility to raw materials, is dispersed unevenly. In general, areas of good land become areas of dense population, which helps make them more attractive for industry—secondary industry especially.

GROWTH OF AMERICAN CITIES

In 1790 only about 3 percent of the population in the United States was urban but the proportion was up to 70 percent in 1960. Of the 179

[7] Ibid., p. 23, footnote quoting B. S. Platt, authority on food supply.

million population in 1960 only about 16 million were in agriculture
and the number in agriculture has since dropped to about 12 million.
A good share of the population not included as urban in Bureau of the
Census reports are living in areas identified as rural, but are not engaged in agriculture.

While urban growth in the United States has been phenomenal, it
has been uneven for the different regions. Larger cities along the Atlantic seaboard stabilized or lost population, the principal gains being
in cities from 15,000 to 50,000. In other parts of the nation almost all
cities of all sizes have gained, when comparing the 1960 with the 1950
census.[8]

It is to be expected that cities in different regions at different times
will have different rates of growth. They grow or decline as they have
more or less resources available, more or less work to do. In Table
6–1 are shown certain facts about the United States population from

Table 6–1   Population Change in the United States, 1800, 1850, 1900, 1950

	1800	1850	1900	1950
Total population (millions)	5.3	23.3	76.1	151.7
Urban population	6.1%	15.3%	39.7%	59.0%*
Percentage of occupied persons engaged in agriculture	71.8%	63.6%	36.8%	11.8
Number of urban places	33	236	1,737	4,023*
Births per 1,000 population	55.2	44.3	32.3	24.1
Children under the age of 5 per 1,000 white women, 20 to 44 years of age	1,342	892	666	587
Median age (years)	16.0	18.9	22.9	30.2
Foreign-born population	—	9.7%	13.6%	6.7%
Negro population	18.8%	15.7%	11.6%	10.0%

* By 1960 definition, the urban population in 1950 would be 64 percent and number of urban places in 1950 would be 4,741.

Source: William Peterson, *Population*, New York, Macmillan, 1961, p. 20.

1800 to 1950. Each line tells of a particular type of change, and these
are only a few of many change trends. Taken together they combine to
show a country in process of becoming urban and industrial.

More than in most countries, Americans tend to rate cities as better
or not so good in terms of their rate of growth. If two cities are compared
the bigger one will be regarded as better. Businessmen in smaller cities
are prone to include suburbs within their economic sphere. Indeed, the
census defines metropolitan areas as each containing a central city (or

[8] Based on U.S. Census reports, Series PC (1)-A and 1950 Census, Series P-A,
Statistical Bulletin, 43, May 1962, pp. 3–5.

twin cities) surrounded by urban communities. Here the concept is defined by Peterson:

> An Urbanized Area is made up of at least one city (or a pair of contiguous cities) of 50,000 or more, plus the surrounding densely settled, closely spaced, urban fringe. A Standard Metropolitan Statistical Area (or SMSA), as it is now termed, is defined as one or more contiguous nonagricultural counties containing at least one city of 50,000 or more (or, again, a pair of contiguous twin cities of at least this joint size), and having a generally metropolitan character based on the counties' social and economic integration with the central city.[9]

When a small city becomes an SMSA it joins the 225 metropolitan areas (as of 1960) in the United States. Among these can be found, for example, Albany, Georgia (75,680), Great Falls, Montana (73,418), Laredo, Texas (64,791), and Meriden, Connecticut (51,850). On top of the list is New York with over ten million inhabitants.

There may be great rivalry between central cities and their fringe areas, which, as shown in Table 6–2, grow faster than do the central

Table 6–2   Population Change for Standard Metropolitan
Statistical Areas in the United States, 1960 Over 1950

Component parts of SMSA's	1960	1950	Percent increase
The 225 SMSA's	116,584,421	92,138,060	26
Central cities	58,782,271	52,875,360	12
Areas outside cities	57,802,150	39,262,700	47

Source: Bureau of the Census, in *World Almanac*, 1966, p. 380. For the report based on early returns, see Henry S. Shrylock, Jr., "Some Results of the 1960 Census of the United States," *Rural Sociology*, Vol. 27, No. 4, December 1962, pp. 360–372.

cities. More important than the naked figures showing growth is information about the kinds of growth taking place. For example, there is the trend toward decentralization which helps to explain why in ten years central cities grew by 11 percent while their fringe areas grew by 49 percent.

URBAN GROWTH IN WIDER PERSPECTIVE

When a city becomes a metropolis and its real active sphere extends far beyond its political borders, population enumerations may be misleading. Many who figure importantly in its life and work may live

[9] William Peterson, *Population*, New York, Macmillan, 1961, p. 186.

twenty or more miles away. Mercantile establishments may have their warehouses in a far suburb and certain industrial enterprises may have their main workshops five to ten miles beyond the city limits. Great numbers of people, even in the urban fringe beyond the near suburbs, identify with the metropolis. Thus Davis observes that it is difficult to identify a particular urban population:

> As a society becomes advanced enough to be highly urbanized it can also afford considerable suburbanization and fringe development. In a sense the slowing down of urbanization is thus more apparent than real; an increasing proportion of urbanites simply live in the country and are classified as rural. Many countries now try to compensate for this ambiguity by enlarging the boundaries of urban places; they did so in numerous censuses taken around 1960. Whether in these cases the old classification of urban or the new one is erroneous depends on how one looks at it; at a very advanced stage the entire concept of urbanization becomes ambiguous.[10]

Table 6–3 shows that there are, as defined by the different world areas, 1,374 cities of 100,000 or more inhabitants. These 1,374 cities comprise every variety of urbanism. By the standards of Northwest and

Table 6–3   Population in World Areas, Number of Cities
of 100,000 and Over, and Percent of Population
in Cities of 100,000 and Over

World area	Total population (1,000's)	Number of cities with over 100,000 inhabitants	Percent of urban population	Percent of population in cities of over 100,000 inhabitants
Oceania	14,698	12	70	50
North Africa	53,736	15	34	22
Sub-Sahara	209,270	44	12	5
Northern America	197,596	169	69	50
Middle America	66,897	37	43	33
South America	144,728	88	47	27
Asia	1,593,876	481	19	14
Northwest and Central Europe	272,772	214	67	33
Eastern and Southern Europe	154,756	94	42	21
U.S.S.R.	221,465	220	45	26
World total	2,929,274	1,374	—	—

Source: Kingsley Davis, "The Urbanization of the Human Population," *Scientific American,* Vol. 213, No. 3, September 1965, p. 45.

[10] Davis, "The Urbanization of the Human Population," op. cit., p. 44.

Central Europe, many of the 481 cities in Asia would not qualify as industrial and urban. Many include hundreds, perhaps thousands, of small subsistence farmers or fishermen whose work is in the sphere of primary industry. We have no measure of the number of urban places of less than 100,000 inhabitants, but many of these are moving into the 10,000-plus class. How fast this growth takes place is seen in the figures for Mexico.

National population: 19.6 million in 1940, 33.8 million in 1960; increase from 1940 to 1960: 73 percent.

Population of Mexico City: 1.4 million in 1940, 2.2 million in 1950, and about 4 million in 1960; increase 1940 to 1960: 285 percent.

Cities of 10,000 and over held 22 percent of the total population in 1940 and 30 percent in 1950.

Cities of 10,000 and over increased from 97 in 1940 to 159 in 1950.[11]

Country-to-country comparison of places by size frequently offers difficulties. Comparison is easier for cities of 100,000 inhabitants and over than for cities of 50,000 and over and may become more confusing for cities of smaller size. Table 6–4 shows number of places by size for

Table 6–4   Number of Communities by Size: United States, 1960; India, 1961

Size of place (according to number of inhabitants)	United States	India
50,000 and over	333	246
10,000 to 50,000	1,566	1,338
5,000 to 10,000	1,394	3,421
2,500 to 5,000	2,152	—
2,000 to 5,000	—	26,565
1,000 to 2,500	4,151	—
1,000 to 2,000	—	65,277
Under 1,000	9,598	—
500 to 1,000	—	109,086
Under 500	—	351,650
Total population	179,323,175	439,072,582

Source: *Statistical Abstract of the United States,* Washington, D.C., Government Printing Office, 1962, p. 21; *India, a Reference Annual, 1964,* New Delhi, Government Publications Division, 1964, p. 22.

the United States and India. In the United States any place with under 2,500 inhabitants is called rural, but in India any place with under 5,000

11 Oscar Lewis, "Mexico Since Cardenas," in Richard N. Adams (Ed.), *Social Change in Latin America Today,* New York, Harper & Row, 1960, p. 287.

inhabitants is considered rural. An unknown number of hamlets of 500 inhabitants and under in the United States went out of existence with the coming of the automobile. In India, most small places are agricultural, within walking distance of the fields.

MOBILITY AND THE URBAN LIFE

As we have seen, the urban community induces population mobility, and without such mobility industrialism would languish. The Bureau of the Census reported that in 1949 nearly 25 million persons (not including persons under one year of age), or about 17 percent of the population, had moved from one residence to another within the state or between states. A large proportion of these moves were related to job changes.[12]

To Peterson, such a volume of place-to-place mobility is uniquely American. It is more evident in some states than in others, but in each region the volume changes from time to time and the streams of migration change in direction. Actually the census figure is an understatement, because many younger persons, as is customary, move two or more times during a given year.[13]

We also lack information about the reasons which impel Americans to move. Only the results are seen when the census is taken every ten years and it is learned that some places grew rapidly and some slowly, and others lost population. Where the greatest gains are reported it can be seen that industry has also made gains.

Whyte, in his study of the management profession, remarks that much of this moving about in the United States is reflected in social mobility. As migrants are able to rise occupationally they also rise socially. He seemed not surprised to find that in 1950 only 6.3 percent of Americans were still living in the places where they were born, and he stressed the thought that persons most likely to migrate are those who have had more education than others.[14] This would apply especially to those leaving smaller places.

Compared with the United States there is much less residential and job-to-job mobility in Western Europe. There it is more usual for workers to cling to jobs because their security increases with tenure. Workers are less likely than in the United States to risk migration in the hope of bettering themselves. Following World War II, however, coun-

---

12 U.S. Bureau of the Census, *U.S. Census of Population, 1950,* Vol. 4, Special Reports, Part 4, Chap. B, "Population Mobility," Table 1.

13 Peterson, op. cit., p. 176.

14 William H. Whyte, Jr., *The Organization Man,* New York, Simon and Schuster, 1956, pp. 269–271.

tries of Western Europe received a great influx of escapees and expellees from the Iron Curtain countries. Almost all of these went to the cities. There is much more of such venturing in developing countries now, especially for those countries which are being industrialized.[15]

Moving about and resettlement have special pertinence for urban communities. Those arriving in the cities tend to be of diverse cultural and ethnic origins. The great cities receive the greatest variety of immigrants, often coming from far places. Because of them the cities have been called "melting pots," which is important from the standpoint of population study. Here, for example, is a description of the many kinds of immigrant communities in Cleveland in 1940:

> In the anonymous masses that make up the living city, Cleveland is almost a Midwest anomaly. The white stock of native parentage comprises only a quarter of the population; eight percent are Negroes and the remaining 67 percent are either foreign-born or the offspring of foreign or mixed parentage. Once almost entirely Nordic and Celtic in makeup, Cleveland was transformed by the expanding steel industry into one of the most racially diversified communities in the United States. Forty-eight nationalities have representatives here; more than forty languages are spoken in the city. First in number are the Czechoslovaks, followed by the Poles, Italians, Germans, Yugoslavs, Irish and Hungarians. Where they concentrate in nationality groups, their native languages are spoken almost as commonly as English.[16]

During the generation since that description was written the process of integrating the ethnic mixture has gone far. The great change has been for Negroes: from the 8 percent indicated, they constituted 28.6 percent of the population for Cleveland in 1960.

CITIES AND THE SEX RATIO

It was once considered improper in Western countries for a lone woman to migrate from a village to a city in search of employment. This is still true in some developing countries. With increasing urbanization, however, this attitude in Western countries has mellowed. For example, in rural places in England and Wales in 1951 there were 983 females for each 1,000 males, while the urban ratio was 1,107 to 1,000. This imbalance was highest for the work-age group from 15 to 45 years.[17]

15 G. Beijer (Ed.), *Rural Migrants in Urban Setting*, The Hague, prepared by the Netherlands Ministry of Social Work and the European Society for Rural Sociology, Nihoff, 1963.

16 *The Ohio Guide*, New York, Oxford University Press, 1940, p. 217.

17 Peter H. Mann, *An Approach to Urban Sociology*, London, Routledge and Kegan Paul, 1965, p. 30.

Before the turn of the century if a girl from a rural place in the United States went to the city the prospects for employment above the unskilled level were meager. Today the rural girl has much more opportunity to acquire a high school education before migrating, and she has greater prospects to find skilled employment in the city. This explains, in part, why the ratio of females to males in cities tends to rise. Table 6–5 shows these ratios for selected countries. As may be seen,

Table 6–5   Urban-Rural Sex Ratios for Selected Countries

Country	Year	Area	Male	Female
United States	1950	Urban	94	100
		Rural	106	100
England and Wales	1951	Urban	91	100
		Rural	102	100
Canada	1951	Urban	96	100
		Rural	114	100
Israel	1951	Urban	102	100
		Rural	112	100
Ceylon	1946	Urban	139	100
		Rural	109	100

Source: *United Nations Statistical Yearbook,* New York, 1952, p. 15.

Canada is one extreme with 96 males to 100 females in cities and 114 males to 100 females in rural areas. At the other extreme is Ceylon, a relatively nonindustrial country, with 139 males to 100 females in cities and 109 males to 100 females in rural areas.

As of 1950 Rio de Janeiro had 2.4 million inhabitants of whom 40 percent were born elsewhere. Of the in-migrants the ratio was 88 males to 100 females. In this case there has been an influx of females from nearby areas.[18] Dore reports, on the other hand, that females outnumber males in both rural and urban areas of Japan by about 2 percent, and the migration of males and females to cities shows the same balance.[19] Generally the industrial city provides more kinds of employment to which women can turn than is possible in the village. Also there are more opportunities in the city for women to find jobs above the level of common labor.

In the United States, where agriculture has become increasingly mechanized, farming is almost wholly a man's work. There is little for the farmer's daughter to do except to stay at home and hope for marriage. She does, however, get an education, usually more than that of the average farmer's son. If she wants a career, she must migrate, which she

[18] T. Lynn Smith, *Brazil, People and Institutions,* Baton Rouge, Louisiana State University Press, 1963, pp. 146–147.
[19] R. P. Dore, *City Life In Japan,* London, Routledge and Kegan Paul, 1958, p. 20.

can do since her education is not significantly different from that of an urban girl. The following comparison of the urban and rural sex ratios for 1920 and 1950, prepared by Bogue, illustrates this situation in the United States:

Rural
   1920   109.1 males to 100 females
   1950   110.1   "   " 100   "
Urban
   1920   100.4   "   " 100   "
   1950   94.6   "   " 100   "

It was during these three decades when mechanization of agriculture made great strides and the war years offered increasing employment for women in the cities.[20]

The age and sex structures in different cities show marked contrasts. Two such examples are Geneva, Switzerland, a city of international organizations (156,900 in 1950), and Colombo, Ceylon (426,127 in 1953), a city in the process of becoming industrialized. Geneva affords a favorable labor market for women, particularly those with office skills or ad-

		Sex ratio
Geneva, Switzerland		
Proportion of males for the city	45%	90–100
Proportion of males for the nation	48%	96–100
Colombo, Ceylon		
Proportion of males for the city	61%	122–100
Proportion of males for the nation	53%	106–100

ministrative skills. Such a labor market for women does not exist in Colombo, at least not yet. Most of the work for women is unskilled.[21]

Poorly balanced sex ratios in urban areas may give rise to breaks with the traditional norms and affect family life. An excess of males may put the females in a favorable bargaining position in the marriage market and, as Southall noted in Kampala, may weaken the family-marriage traditions. The old model is losing support before a new one has taken form.

> The Uganda women undoubtedly have a very great influence in the type of marriage and family life which is prevalent in the urban areas. Many of them prefer to have a series of lovers and retain their freedom than to

[20] Donald J. Bogue, *The Population of the United States,* New York, Free Press, 1959, p. 159.
[21] Harley L. Browning, "Methods of Describing the Age-Sex Structure of Cities," in Jack P. Gibbs (Ed.), *Urban Research Methods,* New York, Van Nostrand, 1962, p. 138.

tie themselves to a lasting union. This meets the needs of the men temporarily in town, including, of course, those who are stably married but have left their wives behind. This group of women has a very low fertility, and, when children are born, they are often sent off after weaning to the relatives of either the mother or the father.[22]

Such examples of family breakdown, as industrial urbanization prevails in developing countries, do not necessarily indicate that the tribal family system is disorganized. More than likely, the stability of the tribal order may serve a useful function in preventing too rapid a malfunctioning of the family in the new cities.

BIRTH RATES

The rate of population increase (births per thousand over deaths) for 1954–1958 was 0.8 percent for Europe, while for Asia, excluding Japan, it was 2.3 percent; for Japan it was 1.1 percent; for Latin America it was 2.5 percent and for North America it was 1.7 percent. These figures, assembled by Jones, and quoted by Dentler, show disturbing rates of increase for some countries: Dominican Republic (1953–1958), 3.5 percent; Mexico (1960), 3.4 percent; Brazil (1961), 3.1 percent; Egypt (1957–1960), 3.5 percent; Algeria (1954–1960), 3.3 percent. The 1961 rate of increase for the world was 2.0, but was an estimated 0.5 percent between 1650 and 1950.[23]

It is well known that in the industrial urban countries birth rates in cities are lower than in rural communities. Especially in cities, birth rates are lower for high-income than for low-income families, and usually lower for women of higher education, most of whom are urban. As seen in Table 6–6, the number of children that have been born to white women in the United States has been decreasing since 1800. Note also that for the 1940–1950 decade there was a rise in the number of children but, uniquely, a greater rise in the urban sector (22 percent, rural, and 54 percent, urban), which somehow may be explained by the postwar "baby boom," but it may also be due to many young couples settling in cities after the war. In general, the number of children between 1800 and 1940 declined faster in the rural sector. The gap between the rural

22 A. W. Southall, "Determinants of the Social Structure of African Population with Reference to Kampala, Uganda," *Social Implications of Industrialization and Urbanization in Africa South of the Sahara*, Paris, UNESCO, 1956, p. 560.

23 Joseph M. Jones, "Does Overpopulation Mean Poverty?" quoted in Robert A. Dentler (Ed.), *Major American Social Problems*, Chicago, Rand McNally, 1967, pp. 483–492.

Table 6–6   Children Under the Age of 5 per 1,000 Women Between 20 and 44 Years of Age, White Population by Residence in the United States, 1800–1950

Year	Total	Rural	Urban
1800	1,231	1,319	845
1820	1,236	1,276	831
1840	1,070	1,134	701
1910	609	782	469
1930	485	658	388
1940	400	551	311
1950	551	673	479

Source: William Peterson, *Population*, New York, Macmillan, 1961, p. 217.

and urban birth rates in 1800 was 66 percent compared with 56 percent in 1940.[24]

In Canada, too, there has been a birth-rate decline from 45 per 1,000 population for 1851–1861 to 26 for 1961.[25] The concern of Canada's "English" element has been the high French-Canadian birth rate, which is a threat to their population majority. The English sector has been able to hold the lead, however (see Table 6–7), because of the influx of

Table 6–7   Ethnic Composition of Canadian Population, and the Number in Thousands and Percent, 1901, 1931 and 1961

Ethnic origin	1901 Number	Percentage	1931 Number	Percentage	1961 Number	Percentage
British	3,063	57.0	5,381	51.9	7,997	43.8
French	1,649	30.7	2,928	28.2	5,540	30.4
Other	659	12.3	2,068	19.9	4,486	25.8
Total	5,371	100.0	10,377	100.0	18,023	100.0

Source: Warren E. Kalbach, "Population Growth and Ethnic Balance," in Richard Laskin (Ed.), *Social Problems, A Canadian Profile*, Toronto, McGraw-Hill, 1964, p. 238.

non-French immigrants and the inability of the French sector to attract French-speaking immigrants. While the French part of the population increased between 1931 and 1961 (28.2 percent to 30.4 percent) and the British sector declined, the "other" group increased enough to hold the French-Canadian minority to less than a third of the total population for Canada.

Birth rates vary from country to country from year to year as do

[24] Wilson H. Grabill, Clyde V. Kiser, and Pascal K. Whelpton, *The Fertility of American Women*, New York, Wiley, 1958, for analysis.
[25] *Canadian Yearbook, 1963–1964*, pp. 227, 237 and 247.

death rates. At any time in any country, urban birth and death rates
will be very different from rural rates. Figures such as those shown in
Table 6–8 are assembled periodically by the United Nations. The selected

Table 6–8 Rural and Urban Birth and Death Rates for Selected Countries

Countries	Year	Births		Deaths	
		Urban	*Rural*	*Urban*	*Rural*
El Salvador	1966	48.5	43.5	12.1	8.7
Morocco	1962	47.2	45.6	14.8	20.3
Israel	1966	23.1	36.4	6.5	5.5
United States	1960	21.2	29.7	*	*
Japan	1965	19.6	16.3	6.3	8.9
United Kingdom	1965	18.1	17.9	11.7	10.8
Netherlands	1966	17.3	21.3	8.4	4.1
Canada	1966	16.9	26.2	6.9	9.1
Poland	1966	14.4	19.1	6.9	7.7
Hungary	1966	12.1	14.8	9.7	10.2

Source: *United Nations Demographic Yearbook,* New York, 1967, pp. 242–244 and
358–360.

* In this U.N. table no figures on urban and rural deaths for the United States
were given. Elsewhere in the same source the general death rate in the U.S. for 1966
is reported to be 9.5.

countries present some unique contrasts; in the two high birth-rate countries, El Salvador and Morocco, as in the two industrial countries, the
United Kingdom and Japan, the urban birth rate is higher than the
rural. The urban death rate is higher than the rural in six of the countries, notably in El Salvador.

Birth rates may differ in relation to the educational level of mothers,
or family income. This was found in an extensive health survey in the
United States in 1936 in which about 700,000 families, 623,000 of them
urban, were interviewed. Of 336,226 married women (16 to 44 years of
age) Karpinos and Kiser ascertained the number of children per 1,000
white wives, both on the basis of income and level of education. Their
data show that higher-income families have relatively fewer children,

Children per 1,000 wives with family income of:
  $3,000 or more   84.6
  Less than $3,000   132.9
Children per 1,000 wives with education level of:
  Some college or college degree   96.9
  High school   102.5
  Seventh or eighth grade   117.5
  Less than seventh grade   130.7

and the lower the level of education of women the greater the number of children they have.[26]

Later Kiser joined Whelpton in a study of 6,531 native white couples at completed fertility (wife's age, 40–44) in a Midwest city. Of these wives 18.8 percent were childless and 46.8 percent had had one or two children. Childlessness was greater for Protestant than for Catholic couples and lowest for Protestant-Catholic couples; it increased with lateness of marriage and decreased with higher educational level.[27]

Some reasons why birth rates are lower in urban than in rural communities are that children are more an asset in rural areas, more a burden in urban places, and the different ideals and aspirations of urban people and rural people influence their rate of fertility.[28]

DEATH RATES AND LIFE EXPECTANCY

A person's life expectancy depends on a variety of conditions: foods available, access to medical care, climate, and, among other conditions, style of life and kind of work. Although the average length of life for males in the United States rose from 46.3 years in 1900 to 66.9 years in 1964, and for females from 48.3 to 73.7 years, we know that for any year there are males and females, both rural and urban, who reached the age of 80 or 90 years.

When we speak of life expectancy we identify it with the total population of a region or nation. If the birth rate declines and the death rate does not rise there will be more elderly persons in the population and the median age of the population will rise. Horton and Hunt say:

> Life expectancy at birth has doubled in the last century and a half; life expectancy at age 60 has increased only a couple of years. In other words, infants today are far more likely to reach the age of sixty than infants a century ago, but people who have reached sixty today have only two more years of life remaining than those who reached sixty a century ago. Stated still differently, more people live to be old today, but old people today do not live much longer than old people used to live.[29]

26 Bernard D. Karpinos and Clyde V. Kiser, "The Differential Fertility and Potential Rate of Growth of Various Income and Education Classes of Urban Population in the United States," *Milbank Memorial Fund Quarterly*, Vol. 17, October 1939, pp. 367–392.

27 Clyde V. Kiser and Pascal K. Whelpton, "Social and Psychological Factors Affecting Families," *Milbank Memorial Fund Quarterly*, Vol. 22, January 1944.

28 Peterson, op. cit., p. 240.

29 Paul B. Horton and Chester L. Hunt, *Sociology*, New York, McGraw-Hill, 1968, p. 403.

The rise or fall of birth rates has more influence than do the death rates in determining the median age of a population. Birth rates often fluctuate rapidly. Between 1960 and 1966 Chile's birth rate rose from 25.4 to 30.6; New Zealand's dropped from 27.1 to 22.5; Poland's from 20.7 to 16.7; Canada's from 26.3 to 19.3; and that of the United States from 23.4 to 18.4. These changes may be due to World War II.[30]

India's death rate in 1961 was 11.4 compared with 9.0 in the United States, and her infant death rate (deaths per 1,000 live births) was 83 in 1961, compared with 28.8 in the United States. Actually, for India as for many developing countries, all births and deaths are not registered. The estimated Indian birth rate for 1951–1960 (annual average) is 41.7 and the estimated death rate for 1951–1960 is put at 22.8. Expectation of life for 1889–1900 was 23.6 years for males and 24.0 for females. For 1951–1960 it was 41.9 years for males and 40.6 years for females.[31] It is over 60 years in most Western countries.

For countries where birth rates are high and death rates are going down, population growth is high to the point of concern. Such a problem is evident in Africa:

> There is . . . a danger that a successful health policy may lead to such a growth of population that it may offset . . . the result of better farming and a more economic use of cattle. If that happens, African living standards will be depressed below their present level. They can also be raised permanently if the rate of increase in population can be kept below that of economic production. This means control which in Britain has been applied by delayed marriage and birth control after marriage.[32]

People with life spans under 40 years, as in India, tend to encourage early marriages. Child marriages are banned now in India, but they continue to be formed in isolated places. And in such places the birth rate is still high despite the family planning clinics.

In the industrial cities of the West, especially among the poor, throughout most of the past century birth rates were high, but the infant death rate was also high. In some slum areas half or more of the babies died. Cities then were hazardous for children. Ferguson mentions how the poor often regarded a high infant death rate as providential; the poor man with fewer to feed had so much to be thankful for.[33]

---

30 *United Nations Demographic Yearbook,* New York, 1967, pp. 231–241 and 352–357.

31 *India, a Reference Manual, 1964,* New Delhi, Government Publications Division, 1964, pp. 14–15.

32 T. R. Batten, *Problems of African Development,* London, Oxford University Press, 1960, Vol. II, p. 22.

33 Thomas Ferguson, *The Dawn of Scottish Social Welfare,* London, Thomas, 1948, p. 172. He notes that a typical children's disease was called "a poor man's friend."

Children's diseases have been all but eliminated from the more developed industrial cities and they begin to disappear from developing cities. This means that, even if birth rates go down a little, infantile deaths will go down even more and so population increases.

Data in Table 6–9, from a report by Benoit on a study of the Congo mining city of Elisabethville (122,000 inhabitants in 1957) indicate death

Table 6–9   Age Groups, Deaths and Death Rates by
Age Groups for Elisabethville, Congo, 1957

Age groups	Deaths	Death rates	Total population	
			Age groups	Percent
4 and under	639	21.9	Under 15	46.3
5 to 19	93	3.4	15 to 19	6.3
15 to 19	13	1.7	20 to 24	7.9
20 to 24	25	2.6	25 to 39	24.9
25 to 44	118	3.4	40 to 49	5.8
45 to 59	75	14.0	50 and over	8.8
60 and over	30	64.7	Total	100.0
Age not known:				
Children	24	5.3		
Adults	123	34.6		
	1,140	12.1		

Source: J. Benoit, *La population africaine à Elisabethville à la fin de 1957*, Elisabethville, Katanga, Fondation de l'Université de Liège pour les Recherches Scientifiques en Afrique Central, 1963.

rates for that city by age groups. The study was done before the revolution came to the Congo. The small number of persons of 40 years and over is striking. Most of the men in the labor force came from backland villages where persons over 40 are thought to be too near the end of their life span to migrate. Note that those who reached 60 years of age or more had a death rate of nearly 65 per 1,000, about three times higher than for children of four years and under. Moreover, for about one of every eight of the dead the age was not known. From this table it can be seen that the population in one of the world's largest mining areas, in which corporations tried to control mobility, is far from balanced. It is an area of younger families and an area from which non-family men are likely to return to their tribal villages when they approach 40 years of age.[34]

[34] J. Benoit, *La population africaine à Elisabethville à la fin de 1957*, Elisabethville, Katanga, Fondation de l'Université de Liège pour les Recherches Scientifiques en Afrique Central, 1963, pp. 68–70.

POPULATION AND THE HUMAN CONDITION

In 1960 about 70 percent of the population of the United States lived in cities, compared with about 40 percent in 1900. Looking at neighboring Canada, we see that of about 5 million people in 1901 about one third of the inhabitants were in cities of 1,000 or more, many small places claiming the title of "city." But in 1964, all of 70 percent of Canada's 20 million people were urban. While population in the United States grew from 76 million in 1900 to 180 million in 1960, Canadians increased by four times, and much of that growth was in cities. Together, these two North American countries, in six decades grew from 80 million to about 200 million. They were favored with land and other natural resources. Unlike the many tightly packed countries, they have not been until now much aware of the "man-land ratio."

The world population in 1900 was estimated at 1,608 million and in 1960 at 2,995 million. The rate of increase for the world as a whole is speeding up. In 1964, by United Nations estimates, the world's population was 3,220 million. More than likely, as modern medicine reduces death rates around the world and extends the span of life, old age may become as much a problem as the birth rate. If, for example, China's expectation of life of 30 years rises to 68 years, which is the expectation of life in Britain, the effects on population increase would be enormous. The world's population would be getting older and greater demands would be made on the evironment for food and other supplies, for this older population, amid other changes, will demand a higher level of living.[35]

By extending life, science adds consumer years to the pressure on the world's food supply. As Ogburn and Nimkoff point out, the number of people in the world getting 2,200 calories per day or less, compared with 3,200 calories in North America, increases. They add:

> Technical writers on the subject of food and population generally agree that the knowledge exists to produce and distribute adequate food for a 50 percent increase in population. The difficulty is rather the practical one of changing the habits and agricultural practices of such a vast population in remote areas in thirty years' time. . . . Science can blueprint vast increases in food supply by fertilizing the ocean and harvesting the food therefrom, by growing food in sand and water, and by utilizing chlorophyll as a factory for producing starches, fats and proteins; but to move from blueprints . . . is an undertaking now immeasurable in time, costs, and effort.[36]

[35] See Arnold M. Rose, "Population," *Sociology,* New York, Knopf, 1965, pp. 481–516.

[36] William F. Ogburn and Meyer F. Nimkoff, *Sociology,* Boston, Houghton Mifflin, 1964, 399–400.

While the world waits for costly, and slow-moving technology to solve the problem, the population in many countries increases faster than food, and food costs take 60 percent or more of the worker's budget. In the meanwhile, more people flock from hungering rural areas to the cities. Here the likelihood of getting food is greater, but food costs are higher.

Escape to the cities is no solution for the food problem, despite the beliefs of many. What it does, in theory, is to relieve pressure on the land, providing better conditions for more efficient agriculture. But the countries most in need of efficient agriculture are the most resistant to it. And even if they were receptive, the means are lacking to implement it. The people, as Chandrasekhar, the Indian demographer, insists, may be helplessly submerged. They must reach a certain economic level before they can make use of better agricultural methods. The cities receive the rural people in great number, but the economy is too weak to establish the needed industry. "Excessive population growth nullifies most programmes for improvement in education, public health, sanitation and rural recovery." [37]

Countries like Canada and the United States are less aware of population pressure, partly because they are favored with much food-producing land. Agriculture has become highly mechanized; more than a half-billion horses would be needed to perform the work now done by machines that originally replaced horses. In addition, the removal of the horses made many millions of acres available for food production. This means that North Americans have gained temporary respite from the pains of population pressure. During the interval they have become a highly urbanized and self-maintaining population. This region of the world has been able to achieve a high standard of living and to advance technologically. Food scarcity is not yet in sight.

Wolfbein calls our attention to some of the benefits coming to Americans in the course of becoming urbanized and industrialized. Among these are a longer life expectancy and the prospect of a longer work cycle. These figures suggest that the future will bring more leisure and time for personal development. The years outside the labor market include the years of childhood, schooling, and old age, more than a fourth of a man's life in the year 1900. Wolfbein estimates that it will be more

	1900	1950	2000
Average life expectancy at time of birth	48.2	65.5	75.2
Average work cycle expectancy	32.1	41.9	45.1
Average years outside labor market	16.1	23.6	29.1
Average years in retirement	2.8	5.7	8.7

[37] S. Chandrasekhar, *Population and Planned Parenthood in India*, London, Allen and Unwin, 1961, p. 19.

than a third of a man's life in the year 2000 when more time will be given to education. While urban industrial man shortens his work week, it is likely that his work cycle, the number of years he will be available for work, will increase.[38]

POPULATION SELECTION AND CONTROL

Concern about the population problem has led from time to time, at least in Western society, to movements or programs to do something about it. Myrdal, for example, relates the effects in Sweden when Karl Wicksell, a university student, went about advocating birth control, his solution for poverty. Except to shock people, his effort made little impression. Three decades later the birth rate in Sweden began dropping.[39]

Possibly the efforts of Wicksell and his associates had been stimulated by the birth-control movement then active in England under the leadership of Annie Besant and Charles Bradlough. In England, too, there was no immediate response, or very little. Population decline began only fifty years later.[40]

The equivalent of birth control today is "family planning," and India is perhaps the first major country to establish clinics for family planning. This program began in 1952 and in 1963 there were 2,720 clinics in rural places and 984 in urban places. In addition there were 7,233 contraceptive distribution centers in rural and urban public medical clinics.[41] There has not been time enough to permit an opinion about the effectiveness of the Indian experiment. Apparently there is more disposition to cooperate with the plan in urban than in rural communities. In Ishwaran's view, time is needed:

> In our opinion, the man in rural India is willing to understand the problem. He realizes the burden of a big family and its social and economic implications. Fortunately, no religious ideology of the Catholic type has hardened his attitude in respect to family planning. But he needs to be understood, guided and directed, and a change in his mentality can only be brought about by an appreciation of the cultural complex in which he is brought up.[42]

[38] Seymour L. Wolfbein, "The Changing Length of Working Life," in Eric Larrabee and Rolf Meyersohn (Eds.), *Mass Leisure*, New York, Free Press, 1958, p. 157.

[39] Alva Myrdal, *Nation and Family*, London, Routledge and Kegan Paul, 1945, p. 20.

[40] *Report of the Royal Commission of Population*, London, Stationery House, 1949, p. 36.

[41] *India, a Reference Manual*, op. cit., p. 102.

[42] K. Ishwaran, Editorial, "Planning and Population Control," *International Journal of Comparative Sociology*, Vol. 1, No. 1, March 1960, pp. 125–128.

Taeuber found an opposite public attitude toward the family planning program in Japan, called the 1949 Eugenic Protection Act, which reverses the wartime ban on abortion, sterilization, and contraception. "They are now legalized under carefully regulated conditions for a variety of hereditary and presumed hereditary deficiencies and malfunctionings and to protect the health of mothers against the hazards of excessive childbearing." [43]

She reports that the people at all economic levels, rural and urban, make use of the service.

The program in Japan is presumed to be one of selection as well as family planning. There are many who doubt the ability of a government to assume effective responsibility for selection and planning.

No headway has been made in Western countries to establish family planning programs, although more liberal legislation regarding abortions and about providing birth-control information is likely in the United States.

In a country with a high level of education and in which birth-control methods come to be common knowledge, it may be assumed that people acquire their own standards regarding family planning. Moreover, in a highly urbanized country, many of the influences which, in a rural situation, encourage large families are absent. Urbanism, as it becomes established, becomes itself a force for both family limitation and selection, in unpredictable ways and within limits, of course.

In this chapter we have not considered the different eugenic schemes advocated by various organizations for upgrading the population. By persuasion or by law the eugenists would encourage certain types to marry and have children, while the types deemed to be less desirable would be prevented from reproducing their kind.[44] The advocates of such selective breeding programs may, as they have in the United States, endeavor to influence national policy for the selection of immigrants. It was argued from about 1900 on that most of the serious problems of American cities were caused by immigrants from certain countries who were prone to crime, shiftlessness, and even creating the slums. On the other hand, immigrants from other countries were believed to have quite the opposite innate traits.[45]

This viewpoint was accepted by the Congress and it found expression in the 1924 Immigration Act, which limited immigrants from European

43 Irene B. Taeuber, "The Population of Japan," in Ronald Freedman (Ed.), *Population, The Vital Problem,* Garden City, New York, Doubleday Anchor, 1964, p. 222.

44 For a pro and con discussion of selective birth control and human evolution, see *Daedalus,* Vol. 91, No. 1, Summer 1961, which contains articles growing out of a conference on the issue.

45 See Peterson, op. cit., p. 45.

countries to 2 percent of the number from each such country in the United States as reported by the 1890 census (which was before the great flood of the "less desirable" immigrants began arriving). Now after four decades it is being recognized that the "quality" theory of the 1924 law was not supported by the facts. High quality, however quality is defined, tends to be distributed at random among all ethnic groups.

Urbanism and mobility phenomena | 7

Few words in the vocabulary of sociology are more variously used than "mobility." To the demographer it means change in the composition of the population. Some sociologists use it almost wholly to identify upward or downward movement in the social-class hierarchy, that is, social mobility. Once it was used more than now to describe the moving about of people in a city or metropolitan area, the kind of moving about which the term, "migration," does not seem to describe well.

Much of moving about within one's area or region of acquaintance seems to fit our term, "residential mobility," and much of that is incidental to "job mobility," moving from one place of work to another. If rural people move to cities and change from agricultural to industrial work, such moving could be called migration, also "urbanization." The usual meaning of migration suggests a rather long distance, going from one region to another or from one country to another. Our use of mobility for moving about and change of residence, whether short moves or long ones, is a convenience. If we speak of migration it will relate to particular long-distance moves, such as from country to country.

We begin with recognizing mobility as it figured in American land settlement, industrial development, and town building. We feel it pertinent to consider the influence of "the road" as an inducer of mobility, not in North America only, but generally, and we call attention to the pertinence of mobility to the development of the frontier.

MOBILITY AND INDUSTRIAL URBANISM

The settlement of North America, Canada and the United States, was a phenomenal experience in human history. People of different ethnic origins occupied a new land of rich resources. Within three generations they had become a unified people of mixed origins. The continent had become the world's largest commercial agricultural region. This could not have happened had there not been an equally phenomenal development of roads, railroads, and transport facilities. Nor could these have been had there not been the building of thousands of towns, some hundreds of which became cities.

The world has never known such a far-reaching building of towns and cities. Every little town, while serving as a center for trade, was intent on promoting industry. Many cities within a generation grew to be centers of industry. All of this development, first on the land frontier and then on the urban industrial frontier was marked by a never-ending mobility. Some towns rose and then vanished, and many industries rose and then fell, to be superseded by others. Capital moved from places of less promise to places that held out the promise of bonanza. The moving about of people, things, and finances reflected the spirit of an era that stimulated in people attitudes of "mobility-mindedness," an attitude which still persists.

We have read how these masses flocking to America were escaping poverty and political oppression in Europe. Allegedly, they came to find freedom. Handlin, however, insists that they came no less for economic reasons. Europe, too, was changing. Millions of peasants were being pushed off the land. They crowded into the cities of the Old World in search of industrial employment of which there was too little.[1]

In the past century, whether in America or Europe, cities would not have grown as rapidly as they did had they not received streams of job-hunting people from rural places. Today as industry expands around the world that old experience is being repeated. Cities attract people from rural areas in numbers so great that industry is hard put to create the needed number of jobs. The jobless mill about, going here and there. On the other hand, industry in the cities could not develop if these in-migrants did not appear. Such phenomena, including the milling about and moving of people, have been experienced in the United States.

We must add that among Americans, who take such mobility for granted, there is a tendency to rationalize about it, even to think of moving about in romantic terms. The stay-at-home may be reminded that it would be good for him to "take to the road." People persuade themselves that there is something commendable about changing jobs or moving about from place to place.

---

[1] Oscar Handlin, *The Uprooted, The Epic Story of the Great Migrations That Made the American People,* Boston, Little, Brown, 1951.

MOBILITY AND THE "INNATE" URGES

The first cities, we may assume, were markets where people initially met periodically to exchange goods. Craftsmen in the villages who made things of cloth, wood, clay, or metal brought their wares to exchange. Some located at the market place or nearby, becoming among the first urban residents. One of the first establishments was perhaps the inn where traders could find shelter. Merchants who brought goods from place to place were among the first migrants. When cities came under the control of rulers and the rulers founded armies, the soldier became a type of mobile person. During medieval times when knights were the soldiers, they wandered here or there serving one lord or another.

Hansson mentions how it became necessary for knights to have names and when they came to strange places the family crest stitched on a knight's cloak identified him as of the House of X or the House of Y or some other. Mobility brought Europe the need for family names, first for the nobility, and later for the poor villagers who might journey a few miles away for employment or for the young craftsmen who served their "wander year" away from home, getting experience in their craft as journeymen.[2]

Fiction writers have encased the rovings of the knight in an overly romantic setting, whereas often he was only a migratory worker on horseback, serving one lord or another. And while about it, he may have been on the lookout for a profitable marriage. Later, as Europe became more urban and commercial, other types of transients appeared on the scene, some of them migratory workers and others were wandering vagrants.[3]

From the romantic view of mobility, going to far places and seeing the new and strange, the idea of *wanderlust* came into the English language. The American frontier, for example, brought into existence a whole population of migratory workers called hobos. The stay-at-homes became the market for stories about such go-about workers: miners, woodsmen, cowboys, construction workers, harvest hands. The hobo was one who did any and all kinds of work, who came and went with careless abandon, who was never tied down.[4]

[2] Börge Hansson, "Urban Activity, Urban People and Urban Environment in Scandinavian History," *International Journal of Comparative Sociology*, Vol. 4, No. 2, September 1963, pp. 343–358.

[3] C. J. Ribron-Turner, *A History of Vagrants and Vagrancy and Beggars and Begging*, London, Chapman and Hall, 1887. This has been called a classical work.

[4] For bibliography on this theme, see Samuel E. Wallace, *Skid Row, A Way of Life*, Totowa, N.J., Badminton Press, 1965. Also see Nels Anderson, *The Hobo*, Chicago, University of Chicago Press, paperback, 1965 (1st ed., 1923).

THE ROMANTIC INFLUENCE OF THE ROAD

Most fairy tales are produced by people in isolation whose way of life changes little. The fairytale heroes often come from far places, or, like Sinband, they go to far places. Often, mentioned or implied, a road or route figures in these stories. In reality, the road exists, although it may be only a path, only if there is the mode of travel by which it is traversed; it is equally a road if one follows a route by water. One goes to places or people come from places. Goods are carried on the backs of men or of beasts, or are carried in conveyances. Even if one never travels the road he knows that "it leads from my door to everywhere." It symbolizes mobility and keeps alive the awareness of far places.

The tales about roads and travel that have been evolved by people in the Orient have given rise to many romantic myths. For example, one such indicates: "The introduction of silk into Persia was due, according to tradition, to a Chinese princess who was married into Persia and took some eggs of the silkworm and seeds of the mulberry tree hidden in her headdress, as she did not want to be deprived of silk." The secret of silk had been so guarded in China that few people in other lands, even if they knew of silk, were informed about its source.[5]

Among the various songs identified as part of the "hobo culture," many of them doggerel, we get such as this:

> So beat it, Bo, while you're young and strong;
> See all you can, for it won't last long;
> You can tarry for only a little spell,
> On the long, gray road to Fare-Ye-Well,
> That leads to Heaven, or maybe Hell,
> And nothing to do but go.[6]

We need to mention especially Whitman's long and oft-quoted ode to the road, to him a complex and intriguing institution. He mused, "I believe you are not all that is here, I believe that much unseen is also here." He saw the road as passing through time and space, into and out of cities, over waters and into mountains. But he warned that only the strong should enter upon it, this tester of flesh and spirit. Whitman's road never comes to an end and those who tread it never come to rest.[7] He might have agreed with Huntington who years later pictured the road

---

[5] J. W. Gregory, *The Story of the Road*, London, Black, 1928, p. 39.
[6] Credited to H. H. Knibbs, Anderson, op. cit., p. 198.
[7] Walt Whitman, *Leaves of Grass*, New York, Random House, 1944, pp. 165–178.

as a selecting or screening agent, whereby the weak fall by the way but the strong move on to success.[8]

ROADS IN HISTORY

Roman roads, regarded as a structural achievement, went into disuse after the fall of Roman power. One reason for their neglect was that they were built for military use; commercial needs would call for other routes. As a matter of fact, all roads fell into disuse from about the fifth to the twelfth centuries because pirates along the Atlantic and the Mediterranean cut off all trade to Western Europe. The way in which the cities dwindled, as observed by Pirenne, indicates how essential roads are for the survival of urban places.[9]

ROADS AND THE FRONTIER

One of the first issues debated in the American Congress concerned the demand of some that federal funds should be used to build a road from the Atlantic Seaboard to the Ohio Valley. Prior to 1810, westward settlement had been slow because of the difficult route through the mountains. Money was finally paid to the states, but the states, as then assumed, did not have the authority to build roads, so the money was given to the counties, each county building as it saw fit. Eventually the Cumberland Pike was finished. Until the railroad came after 1830 and the earlier opening of the Erie Canal, the Cumberland Pike was the main traveled route westward, reaching inland about 900 miles. Before the railroad, it was believed that the main access to the sea for the Middle West was by boat over the Ohio and Mississippi Rivers, and on that route would be the big cities. The seaport for the region would be New Orleans, not New York.

New York was saved by the Erie Canal. The work began in 1817 and was completed by 1825 for a water route to the central region. Boats could ascend the Hudson, cross by canal to Lake Erie, and so reach Cleveland. Once the canal was in operation, instead of $400 and forty days of wagon travel to take a ton of freight from New York to Cleveland, the trip was made in twenty days and the cost was reduced by 80 percent. According to the boast of some local editor, "They built the longest

8 Ellsworth Huntington, *World Power and Evolution*, New Haven, Yale University Press, 1919.

9 Henri Pirenne, *Medieval Cities*, Garden City, New York, Doubleday Anchor, 1956, pp. 30–58 (1st ed., 1925).

canal in the world in the shortest time with the least experience, for the least money and at the greatest public benefit." [10] Four decades later railroads outmoded the canal.

The Westward American movement was a running battle between cities. While New York struggled to outflank New Orleans, Boston was struggling to hold its own against New York. Pittsburgh faced the competition of other cities on the Ohio River. Later, the river cities, especially St. Louis, competed with Chicago, which had the greater advantage because of the railroads.

There was much resistance to the railroad in Europe and America. In England it was mainly from the canal companies. George Stephenson, who in 1815 demonstrated the feasibility of rail travel, found many anti-railroad canal friends in Parliament. Various German towns did not want the railroad at all, fearing it would bring factories and these would bring hordes of lower-class workers. Nor was there much interest at first in railroads in the United States, except as they might be used for portage service between canals. This attitude quickly passed. Rail miles reached 2,810 by 1849 and were up to 31,246 by 1860, more railroad than in all the European countries combined.

In the history of Pittsburgh and other river cities, it is evident how the Midwest economy was oriented to river transport. The growth impetus spread westward from Pittsburg, the first American iron city.[11] This was the outfitting point for expeditions going west by river or road. Wade describes the great stimulus to boat building and experimentation with powered vessels. One such steamboat, the *Enterprise,* on her own power reached Pittsburgh from New Orleans in 1815. But the coming of the railroad dampened this enthusiasm for river transportation.[12]

THE FRONTIER AND TURNER'S THESIS

The nineteenth century was perhaps the first time in history when people had before them a frontier with abundant land and opportunity whose only limits were in the imaginations and resourcefulness of men. If one made a fortune and lost it, he could begin again. There were those who visualized a new society emerging, each individual free to go his limit and all engaged in setting up a liberty-defending democracy. The prospect was inspiring to journalists of the day, and they made the fron-

[10] Quoted in E. C. Kirkland, *A History of American Economic Life,* New York, Appleton-Century-Crofts, 1951, p. 231.

[11] Richard C. Wade, *The Urban Frontier, The Rise of Western Cities, 1780–1830,* Cambridge, Harvard University Press, 1959.

[12] Ibid., p. 71.

tiersman who settled in the wilderness a hero without equal. Historians were no less impressed.[13]

Notable among the historians of the frontier was Frederick Jackson Turner to whom the pioneer was the great individualist and creator of the American ideal of democracy. For every virtue he saw in the land frontier, he saw some opposite quality in the emerging industrial city, which he failed to recognize as a frontier of another order. The society of the land frontier:

> was not a disciplined army, where all must keep step and where collective interests destroyed individual will and work. Rather it was a mobile mass of freely circulating atoms, each making its own place and finding play for its own powers and for its own original initiative. We cannot lay too much stress upon this point, for it is at the very heart of the whole American movement.[14]

It is not pertinent here to examine the Turner thesis in detail. Our main point is that the rapidly growing industrial city was also a frontier for technological inventiveness and the industrial production which speeded and facilitated land settlement. In the 1880's, the network of railroads, a product of industry, enabled thousands to reach the land frontier where hundreds struggled to get in the 1830's. Industry was making strong wagons to match the hard roads, and farm implements where only hand tools were available a half-century earlier. Roads and railroads provided access to markets that did not exist a few decades earlier.

Turner's thesis exalting the man who went forth with gun, axe, and hoe blinded him to the expanding urbanism of his day. The booming industrialism did not catch his attention, except negatively, as it provided work for hordes of immigrants. Neither did he recognize that the culture which was to be called American was also evolving in the cities, as was an equally important brand of individualism. And the urban-fashioned culture was also moving west and seeping through the land frontier. Turner did not see how his views "contradicted the notion that the West merely lagged behind the East and would gradually catch up as it passed through the appropriated stages of progress." [15]

It is understood that the land frontier stimulated the mobility of people, and improvements in the road (water, rail, highway) made move-

13 For example, see Robert E. Riegel, *America Moves West*, New York, Holt, Rinehart and Winston, 1956.

14 Frederick Jackson Turner, *The Frontier in American History*, New York, Holt, Rinehart and Winston, 1958, p. 306 (1st ed., 1920).

15 Anselm L. Strauss, *Images of the Emerging City*, New York, Free Press, 1965, p. 165.

ment easier. Among those who settled, many moved again, some several times. The urban community was promoting by its growth other types of movement. Urban mobility is largely stimulated by industrial growth and changes—changes in the occupations men live by. In general, increasing mobility is an accompaniment of expansion and expansion has characterized the frontier, urban and rural.

THE FRONTIER IN CANADA

The movement to the frontier in the United States, as industry developed, as the rate of iron and steel production enabled railroads to be built, came to be something like a "crash" movement, feverish and rapid. Two interdependent frontiers moved westward at the same time, land settlement and town-building. Land settlement, agriculture, stock raising, forestry, and mining needed the towns, and the towns, impatient to become cities, aspired to be industrial. The slave-holding, Southern plantation frontier moved slowly and stopped in eastern Texas. Railroad building and industrial towns were in the northern frontier which, as it extended westward, and expanded over the Southwest. Canada, represents a third frontier, which lagged for several reasons, each of which helps us understand better the expansion of the United States.

Most of Canada was held by a private corporation, the Hudson's Bay Company, until 1867, when the provinces formed a loose Dominion government. Prior to that each province functioned as a separate British colony, competing with the other provinces. The American government was a going establishment nearly seven decades before Canada gained limited autonomy. The Canadian government had very little land to give out for development purposes, while the U.S. government had much. The Americans developed iron and steel in great quantities, enabling industry to grow. Canada then lacked iron and coal. Industry did not begin to develop until after 1870, and that to a limited degree around the Great Lakes.

Railroad building to link the wide regions of Canada moved slowly because of the poverty of the provinces, but slow development was partly due to the inter-province rivalry. Moreover, the meager prospects for industrial development did not attract capital for railroad construction. Where construction was undertaken, rivalry between the provinces resulted in tracks of different gauge being laid, which, of course, hampered the moving of carloads from province to province; and there was an unwillingness in some areas to have connections with American railroads.[16] This policy was reversed after confederation, when industry began to

[16] Oscar D. Skelton, *The Railroad Builders,* Toronto, Brown, 1916, pp. 84–87.

develop. A Canadian railroad to the Pacific was not finished until 1885, whereas the American transcontinental contact was complete in 1869.

Unable to make a policy decision about Canada's status, and unwilling to take any sort of initiative, the Britain government sent Lord Durham in 1839 to conduct a survey and make some recommendations. All the provinces condemned his report, each for a different set of reasons. He warned his government about the ease with which Canadians and Americans crossed back and forth over the border. He called attention to the lack of Canadian identity and mentioned the failure of British efforts to encourage immigrants to settle in Canada. Among those who did immigrate, a good share of them crossed the border, since Canada had little to offer.[17]

Canada is now 70 percent urban and highly industrial but this development did not begin to take root until after World War I. Today Canadians are as mobile as their neighbors in the United States. One explanation suggested for the early industrial and urban advances in the United States as compared with retardation in Canada is that "the English colonies in America . . . were founded by groups of rebels, freethinkers and fugitives who sought to free themselves from the political, religious and economic pressures of England," while the Canadians, including the French-Canadians, were not rebellious,[18] at least in such terms.

MOBILITY, CHANGE, INNOVATION

Based upon much research into why people move about, we may safely conclude that some mobility is stimulated by romantic interests, without which the tourist industry would languish. The kind of movement which concerns us relates mainly to the mobility of families or individuals for practical reasons. There have been mass migrations in early historical times, due to climatic change in a region or persecution by enemies, but there was almost no mobility of families or individuals. This type of mobility began late in medieval times, but is more a characteristic of our industrial, city-building era. Normally, romantic mobility does not lead to resettlement; one ventures forth, looks, listens, compares, but returns home with souvenirs and a repertoire of stories.

Most of the mobility that leads to resettlement, the kind that brings new communities into existence, is related more to basic life interests:

17 C. P. Lucas (Ed.), *Lord Durham's Report on the Affairs of British North America*, Oxford, Clarendon Press, 1912, Vol. II, p. 272.

18 Jean C. Falardeau, "The Role and Importance of the Church in French Canada," in Marcel Rioux and Yves Martin (Eds.), *French-Canadian Society*, Toronto, McClelland and Stewart, 1964, p. 343.

finding employment, entering some new occupation, locating a more desirable place to live. Also, those who move, since there are drives as well as attractions, may feel compelled to escape low wages and unemployment, unsatisfactory housing, an unfavorable environment for children, unproductive soil. The different types of "pull" and "push" may vary with the situation of the individual or family.

Often mobility is induced, as in the 1870's and 1880's when agents from American industry went to Europe to recruit workers. Once the American railroads were in operation, they launched advertising programs. To them it mattered not whether migrants to the West settled on the land or in cities; the more people they could coax into the wide open areas, the better the future would be for the railway transportation business. The modern version of that sort of induced mobility, much of it since 1920, is the real estate promotion of suburban development, an especially lucrative business after the arrival of the automobile.

Much of mobility is stimulated by change. The availability of new tracts of fertile land at low cost may diminish one's interest in clinging to the old family farm. Technological change may stimulate mobility. Whereas the hazards and hardships of wagon traveling discouraged many from moving in the direction of the American frontier, the prospect of traveling on the railroad rendered mobility attractive. If one did not like Nebraska or California, he could return to Virginia or Ohio. Even greater place-to-place movement came with the perfection of the automobile and the building of hard-surface, all-weather roads.

The automobile, the tractor, and various types of labor-saving agricultural equipment wrought tremendous change in American and Canadian rural life and work. The possibility of increasing productivity with decreasing labor inputs released a large proportion of rural labor at a time when industrial employment in cities was increasing. The result was increasing country-to-city mobility. The migrant moved from his place of origin in reaction to rural change and at his point of destination in some industrial center he came into contact with urban change.

In North America, with its ample natural resources, men confronted opportunities for engaging in rewarding kinds of work. The creators of the "Kentucky rifle" produced the kind of gun the frontiersman needed. The demand exceeded their capacity to produce. The situation called for inventions to speed the work. Clockmakers found more demand than they could meet, so their little shops became factories. With an expanding economy, the industrial urban milieu generally becomes one of innovation and invention.[19]

19 On industrial inventiveness in the United States, see John W. Oliver, *History of American Technology*, New York, Ronald Press, 1956; and Mitchell Wilson, *American Science and Invention*, New York, Simon and Schuster, 1954.

For the American cities the market was the enlarging land frontier whose growth and change stimulated industry to produce more things and more newly invented things. So the city gave the farmer the iron plow. Cyrus McCormack, a migrant from the farm to the city, invented the reaper. Urban industry produced the windmill which enabled farmers to survive more easily on semiarid land. Barbed wire was an urban industrial creation which resulted in some open warfare between newly settled farmers and the cattlemen. The farmers were trying to protect their crops against the range cattle and the cattlemen wanted to prevent the farmers from moving in.

Commager, including town and country in his concept of the frontier, saw pioneering life as a great open field in which each individual was stimulated by new situations to engage in experimentation. Each new wave of settlers and each new wave of immigrants had to do its own experimenting. Every new community was at once a gamble and an opportunity. He speaks of the American as a gambler, especially as he established towns and enterprises. If one approach failed, he turned readily to another. He dared to do old things in new ways or to undertake what had never been done before. He had little patience with precedent or tradition unless they served some practical purpose. If something needed was lacking, he would improvise.[20]

Mobility was not only reflective of the pioneer's detachment from traditional controls and his flair for experimentation, but moving about may have stimulated favorable attitudes toward mobility. Although de Tocqueville thought the frontiersmen were crude in many respects, he admired their resourcefulness. The new world was so different from Europe where "no one seeks any longer to resist the inevitable law of his destiny," where the peasant could never think of being other than a peasant. This outlook, accepting change and mobility as part of one's way of life, was equally present in the emerging towns de Tocqueville visited around 1833.[21]

Foreigners visiting the United States between 1830 and 1860, while they made fun of American manners, were impressed with technical achievements as seen in the development of towns. They mentioned the Conestoga wagon or a ride on the Erie Canal and told of steam heating systems in hotels and of bath tubs in hotels. Dickens was especially impressed with the canal and railway system for taking passengers over the mountains between Philadelphia and Pittsburgh.[22]

20 Harry S. Commager, *The American Mind*, New Haven, Yale University Press, 1950, p. 12.

21 Alexis de Tocqueville, *Democracy in America*, Vol. I, New York, Knopf, 1946, p. 33 (1st ed., Paris, 1835–1840).

22 *Pennsylvania, A Guide to the Keystone State*, New York, Oxford University Press, 4th ed., 1950, pp. 90 and 391.

MOBILITY AND THE NEW NATIONS

A vast amount of literature is appearing which deals with the development of the "underdeveloped" countries, a term which is anathema to the young nations that have emerged from colonialism, most of them since World War II. What most of these countries have in common is their poverty, limited or undeveloped natural resources, and limited capacity for coping with their own problems. They share a common aspiration to become urbanized and industrialized in the shortest time possible. Shils speaks of their determination to become modern, democratic, technically progressive, economically self-sufficient; to establish bright, efficient cities, and to achieve commanding industrial status.[23]

These new countries are a new kind of frontier and are being plunged suddenly, as it were, from adolescence into adulthood, confronted with the common problem of functioning in the world of industrial urbanism, although bewildered by its cultural demands. They are in the dangerous situation of shaking loose from the things of the past before getting attached to the new. The technological, social, and economic evolution, which took three centuries in Western countries, these people are being asked to pass through in one or two decades.

All of these new nations have had a century or more of contact with one or another European culture, often planted in their midst by force. But only in a marginal sense did they share the life of the European culture with which they had contact, whether English, French, Dutch, Spanish, Portuguese, or German. They figured in the world economy only as sources of needed raw materials. Now they aspire to become self-sufficient peoples, too often with only vague notions of what that implies. For them, there is no century of time for trial-and-error experimentation. None of the more advanced countries had faced such a challenge.

Cities are springing up in the developing countries before any but the upper elites have learned the ways of urban life. Outside interests are being invited to establish industries in new nations before the constituted authorities have acquired the elemental knowledge for operating the type of public bureaucracy necessary to sustain industry. Decades were needed in the more advanced countries to learn these lessons.

All of these new countries are baffled by the increasing mobility of the people. Hance points out that in some countries of Africa a great deal of emphasis is placed on industry while little attention is given to agriculture. Or if attention is given, it is not to crops to feed the people

[23] Edward Shils, "Political Development in New States," *Comparative Studies in Society and History,* Vol. 2, 1959–1960, pp. 265–292 and 379–411.

but to commercial crops, for example, producing oils for export. Urban development is given priority over building needed roads. In many villages women and old men are left to carry the agricultural work while the able-bodied men languish in towns where unemployment exceeds industry's ability to provide jobs.[24]

Hance adds that resources exist in the African countries, but outside help is needed to develop these. For example, of electric power potential "the Belgian Congo alone has 21.5% of the world's total." There are few power installations and the work of providing them is beyond the governments' powers to finance and to manage.[25]

In these countries mobility is seen in all its forms and perhaps with all the usual consequences. Almost all of the migration is from village to city and very little of it is from city to city. The young are more numerous among those who migrate, and males predominate, much as during frontier times in the United States when young males predominated among those who went westward.

In most developing countries the industries most likely to receive capital support from abroad are not the kind that thrive in the cities. They are likely to be vast mining projects located in hilly areas remote from the concentrations of native populations, such as the copper mines in the Katanga and the tin mines in Malaya; or plantations remote from towns, large enough so that the workers live in company villages; or projects for taking special woods from the forests. These primary industries do not help a developing country acquire a skilled labor force such as is needed for secondary industries, most at home in cities. Such industries are developing in Latin American countries, but not fast enough to provide work for the supply of in-migrants.

A study in 1957 of Elisabethville in the Katanga mining region revealed that practically all of the sample of 4,121 men interviewed came from native villages, mostly outside the district, and 45 percent of these men had been in the area for less than six years. Of the population of the area, 40,000 in Elisabethville and about 100,000 in mining villages, apparently more than half were in-migrants. In 1940 the sex ratio had been 135 males to 100 females, but by 1956 it was down to 129 males to 100 females. All the communities then were under the control of the mining companies whose policy was to exclude migrants not of use to the area labor market.[26]

24 William A. Hance, *African Economic Development,* London, Oxford University Press, 1958, pp. 5 and 106.

25 Ibid., p. 12.

26 J. Benoit, *La population africaine à Elisabethville à la fin de 1957,* Elisabethville, fondation de l'Université Lièges Pour les Recherches Scientifiques en Afrique Central, 1963, pp. 7–9.

ON THE "LAWS" OF MIGRATION

If the "laws" of migration or the laws that control urban growth could be discovered, then presumably it would be possible to predict future migration and to understand the reasons for it. These laws could perhaps bring it under control, and control might give the means for selection. Governments, in establishing immigration policy, have indicated a wish for such knowledge.

The obstacles to discovering the laws of migration are the many variables which either facilitate migration (available transportation), impel it (food shortages or unemployment), or encourage it (widening labor markets). These or other variables are always subject to change.

An early effort to discover the laws of migration was made by Ravenstein in the 1880's.[27] In general, he found that most migrants heading for the city, usually go first to a smaller place and may move another time or two before reaching the large center. As each move is made gaps are provided for other migrants. Each flow of migrants tends to be countered by a movement in the opposite direction. Smith and McMahon, on the basis of their studies, found in the United States much what Ravenstein had found in England.

1. Younger age groups predominate among rural to urban migrants.
2. In cities of arrival the median age of migrants is lower than the median age of the resident population.
3. Younger migrants arriving in cities, in general, come from more distant places of origin than do older migrants.
4. In normal times females migrate to the city in a greater proportion than males.
5. Normally females migrate at an earlier age than males.
6. Of older age groups, more males than females migrate to the city.
7. Farmers who migrate from farms to the city usually have a higher level of education than farmers who do not migrate.[28]

These statements, quite generally known, are not presented by Smith and McMahon as laws. They merely tell us something about migration under conditions in the United States as of the present. A very different set of conditions prevailed in 1870, for example, when females were much less likely to migrate to the city.

Pons asked 3,534 natives in Stanleyville, Congo, about their arrival.

    [27] E. G. Ravenstein, "The Laws of Migration," *Journal of the Royal Statistical Society,* Vol. 68, 1885, pp. 167–235.
    [28] T. Lynn Smith and C. A. McMahon, *The Sociology of Urban Life,* New York, Dryden, 1951, p. 336.

As these figures show, the number of moves made by males and females from their tribal villages to Stanleyville are seen in percents. That 41.9 percent of the women were able to reach the city by one move was possible because many were wives whose husbands had found employment in the city. Also it is easier for men to move a distance, find temporary employment, and then move again.[29] The figures for the males appear to confirm Ravenstein's findings for England.

	Males	*Females*	*Total*
One move only	23.7%	41.9%	32.1%
Two moves	33.8	32.4	33.2
Three moves	21.2	13.9	17.8
Four moves	10.0	6.4	8.3
Five or more moves	11.3	5.4	8.6
Total	100.0%	100.0%	100.0%
Number	1,902	1,632	3,534

Germany, following the war, was burdened with refugees, and many people whose cities had been bombed were living in villages. Houses were crowded; often two families lived in apartments meant for one family. There was considerable tension and much moving, most of it to be near places of work. These figures from Nellner give some measure of the amount of movement in Germany in 1951. Many of those leaving cities went to suburban areas where houses could be erected cheaper and faster than in the cities.[30]

Movement into cities of 100,000 and over	414,560
Movement from cities of 100,000 and over	254,104
Movement into villages	1,514,335
Movement from villages	1,753,959

The postwar period lent impetus to suburban developments around German cities. The war scattered the urban population, and the slowness with which the cities were being rebuilt and the fact that priority was given to shops and other places of work resulted in outlying villages growing into suburbs.[31]

Although the study of migration continues, there is little interest in the laws of migration. The reasons for traveling are so much influenced

[29] V. G. Pons, N. Xydias, and P. Clement, "Social Effects of Urbanization in Stanleyville," *Social Implications of Industrialization and Urbanization in Africa South of the Sahara*, Paris, UNESCO, 1956, p. 257.

[30] Werner, Nellner, *Mitteilungen aus dem Institut für Raumforschung*, Bonn, Vol. 18, 1953, Table 4.

[31] An example is found in the study of a village near Cologne by Gerhard Wurzbacher and Renate Pflaum, *Das Dorf im Spannungsfeld industrieller Entwicklung*, Tübingen, Mohe-Siebeck, 1954.

by technical innovations in transport, by the changing modes of tourism, and the appeals of advertising, especially those of the airlines, that it is perhaps more useful to study "trends" than to search for laws.

"CIRCULATION," AN ASPECT OF MOBILITY

Without change of residence or moving to other work, the average American or Canadian travels about 2,000 miles a year, going places in his own automobile or by public transport. This is in addition to local work travel, shopping, visiting, and so on. Some may travel 10,000, 20,000, or more miles on vacation or business trips. This kind of moving about existed only to a minor degree in 1900. It is one kind of "circulation."

The American Automobile Association reported for 1965 that the private automobile "is used in 90 percent of all vacation and recreation trips." The mileage traveled by 75 million passenger cars was 700 billion miles. An additional 180 billion miles were traveled by 15 million trucks and buses. It was estimated that the interstate super highway system which "will comprise little more than 1 percent of the total U.S. road and street mileage . . . will carry 285 billion vehicle miles, or nearly 25 percent of the total 1,165 billion miles of travel estimated for 1975."

Before the automobile the young man who had never traveled may have been tempted by the sign in front of the recruiting station, "Join the Navy and See the World." Such an appeal would not be tempting now that youth know how to move about and they have seen distant places. The circulation horizon is extending and the strangeness of other places diminishes.

Circulation can also be seen in more limited terms. Let us take, for example, the development of Nordheim, Germany, which a few decades ago was rural and mainly agricultural. By 1960 Nordheim had become industrial, the main work center for the 16,462 employed workers in the Kreis. But nearly 5,000 of this work force lived outside Nordheim, mostly upon the farms. Formerly the rural people seldom went to Nordheim, but today, since so many of them have automobiles, Nordheim has become the center for their leisure-time activities. Most of the rural wives do their main shopping in Nordheim. The many localisms of the once rural Kreis have vanished and the whole area is now a single district for routine daily mobility, or circulation.[32]

A report for 1956 for the Detroit Study Area, a continuing research program of the University of Michigan, found that only six of each hundred adults of Detroit inhabit the houses where they were born. Most

---

[32] Edmund Mros, *Sozialer Dienst in Entwicklungsgebieten*, Bonn, Forschungsstelle der Forschungsgesellschaft für Agrarpolitik und Agrarsoziologie, 1962.

residents have lived in different sections of their city. These percentages show the types of residential movement from place to place in and about the city and its region, and from the outside. Moves from the metropoli-

Moves from outer region to central city (centripetal)	12%
Moves to outer region from central city (centrifugal)	46%
Moves between points within general areas (lateral)	34%
Moves from outside the metropolitan area	8%

tan area are not shown. These are moves made mainly during 1955, almost all being circulation within the region. The study also revealed that only one out of four Detroiters had lived in the same dwelling 10 years or longer.[33]

This kind of residential circulation is thought by some to be unique to American cities, when actually there is merely more of it than in cities elsewhere. House-to-house mobility is, to be sure, more difficult in European cities. A family in Cologne, Paris, or London may have to wait a year or longer before a desired dwelling can be found. As these figures

Number living in the suburb in 1931	26,685
Number not moving between 1931 and 1936	11,253
Proportion moving between 1931 and 1936	58%
Number moving out between 1931 and 1936	5,321
Number moving into suburb between 1931 and 1936	15,574
Number living in the suburb in 1936	31,054
Proportion changing addresses but remaining in the suburb between 1931 and 1936	18%

on moving in a Paris suburb show, there is considerable residential mobility even in a community where such moving is a major venture for a family.[34]

Another aspect of circulation concerns the daily mass movement of people in cities. Often half of the total population of an urban community have reason each work day to visit the urban center for work, leisure, or shopping; they walk in the streets, drive their cars, or ride the public conveyances. Owen finds that a tenth of every American dollar goes for this kind of circulation and he adds that two thirds of all motor transportation is found within an hour's radius of metropolitan centers.[35]

Daily mass circulation has probably always been an urban worry and it may be that, with the greater tempo of modern urban life, there will be increasing impatience with it. Moreover, in our time, different organized groups demand better access. Again, street congestion is a concern

[33] *A Social Profile of Detroit, 1956, Report of the Detroit Area Study,* Ann Arbor, University of Michigan Press, 1957.

[34] Paul Chombart de Lauwe (Ed.), *Paris et l'agglomeration parisienne,* Paris, Presses Universitaires de France, 1952, pp. 1–30.

[35] Wilfred Owen, "Automobile Transportation in the United States," *Annals of the American Academy of Political and Social Sciences,* Vol. 320, November 1958, pp. 2–3.

of most modern cities, not those of America alone. Green describes the serious problem in Manchester, England, for instance where 80 percent of the population leave home daily for short or long journeys, mainly to the urban center.[36]

This moving about, whether the seasonal change of residence or the daily circulation, can be seen as a type of group habit, especially in the large cities. In part it is prompted by various kinds of change. A person who gets a better job or is forced by a change in the labor market to accept a lower level job may need to move to another residence to be near his new place of work. A mobility mindedness develops. Wilson reasons that "physical mobility is only the external symbol of shifting, multiple group memberships and the associated ways of thinking and feeling." [37]

The going about of people in the course of living and earning their living is seen by Thomlinson as "routinization." They move about in orbits with some regularity. Under this term he also includes seasonal movements, like going on vacations or going away to school, though the persons involved retain their residence. The term could be extended to include what is here embraced by "circulation." [38]

SOCIAL IMPLICATIONS OF MOBILITY

It is related that in the community churchyard of a small town in Schleswig, that part of Denmark which is attached to the European mainland, there is a tombstone for some local worthy who died in the 1700's. Below the man's name and the vital dates is written, "He has been to Hamburgh." Less than 200 miles away, it was then a great venture to journey to that great seaport city. For most villagers of Schleswig there was, of course, no need to visit Hamburgh. During the next century, Hamburgh ceased to be so remote; young men from Schleswig were learning about job opportunities in that city.

As a country becomes more industrial and urban one consequence is greater mobility; today a person may travel around the world and still not find it sufficient for a line on his tombstone. Mobility, however, may lead to social distinction in other respects. Most migrants from the country to cities rise to higher income and occupational position. Some who had been laborers before, on reaching town, move into the skilled labor class. Some who become skilled workers may become foremen or super-

---

36 L. P. Green, *Provincial Metropolis, The Future of Local Government in Southeast Lancashire,* London, Allen and Unwin, 1958, p. 218.

37 Everett K. Wilson, "Some Notes on the Pains and Prospects of American Cities," *Confluence,* Vol. 7, No. 1, Spring 1958, p. 14.

38 Ralph Thomlinson, *Urban Structure,* New York, Random House, 1969, p. 110.

intendents. The white-collar worker may acquire more education and rise to a managerial position. To be sure, many who migrate do not rise above the unskilled level. However, Freedman has stated that the urban milieu stimulates a type of "mental mobility," a condition that in turn stimulates men to effort, which would hardly be likely in the village.[39]

Hauser puts the same thought in other terms, seeing large groups of arrivals in the city, from rural areas or foreign lands. The less trained take the lesser types of employment and live in the poorest areas. Some are able to rise occupationally which enables them to move to better housing, or the children of others rise to higher occupations than their fathers. As one wave of immigrants moves from the depressed areas and low-paying jobs, other immigrants take their place. In the growth of American cities there have been waves of in-migrants. He adds:

> Similarly, the shorter the period of settlement, the lower was the occupational level and income of the newcomers. The longer the period of settlement, the higher the educational level and income. Finally, with respect to social status, the common pattern was also visible. Each of the newcomer groups was in turn greeted with hostility, suspicion, distrust, prejudice and discriminatory practices. With the passage of time each of the newcomer groups climbed the social as well as the economic ladder to achieve access to the broader social and cultural life of the community and increased general acceptability.[40]

This, in broad terms is social mobility, moving up socially and culturally. It can be seen in mass terms or individual terms. A whole society may rise in its level of living, of education, of sophistication, or large sections of society, such as immigrant groups, may rise, and we may call this a climb from a low level to a high level of "general acceptability." In our competitive society social mobility is mainly associated with families or individual members of families. In Denmark Svalastoga found something like a balance in social mobility; the number of sons who rise higher than their fathers is generally matched by the number who do not rise as high as their fathers.[41]

This moving up or down in social status makes for the stratifications in society identified as social class, which in one form or other, is evident in all communities. Reissman mentions that "class has also been recognized as a divisive force in the city, for it created separate worlds in the

[39] Ronald Freedman, "Cityward Migration, Urban Ecology, and Social Theory," in Ernest W. Burgess and Donald J. Bogue (Eds.), *Contributions to Urban Sociology,* Chicago, University of Chicago Press, 1964, p. 198.

[40] Philip M. Hauser, "Urbanization, An Overview," in Philip M. Hauser and Leo F. Schnore (Eds.), *The Study of Urbanization,* New York, Wiley, 1966, p. 21.

[41] Kaare Svalastoga, *Prestige, Class and Mobility,* Copenhagen, Gyldendal, 1959, p. 10.

city and insulated them one from another." [42] But unlike earlier systems of social stratification, the lines between social classes in the industrial urban community are not tightly drawn. However, Gillin tells us that in the feudal rural society of some Latin American countries the class structure is still firm. The farm worker remains a farm worker, but if these rural people migrate to cities they find themselves in competitive relationships. Some are able to rise to higher incomes and occupations. This is becoming one of the expected rewards of mobility.[43]

Many of the rural migrants to Latin American cities may not achieve higher status through rising income; yet they still prefer the competitive milieu to the unchanging life of the countryside. In sophistication and otherwise, they feel superior to the peons they left behind, although, as Wagley notes:

> . . . they have not yet developed a new set of institutions to replace the old system. In the city there is seldom a storekeeper to extend credit. There are political leaders, to be sure, but the *Coronel*, the traditional political boss of the country people, is not present to tell them how to vote. They work for a company or corporation; thus they no longer have a *Patrao* in the traditional sense. They live the impersonal life of the city without the kinsmen and lifelong friends of the same neighborhood.[44]

Wagley would agree that, while some return to their villages, the majority do not. More than likely, they try to bring their kin to the city.

It is still firmly believed that in American society a person is able to rise in his lifetime from one occupational level to another, and then perhaps to rise to yet another occupational level. This would be less likely in a period of depression than of expansion, less likely in an old, stable community than in a rapidly growing community. Such mobility in one's lifetime would be somewhat unusual in the industrial countries of Europe where it is quite the accepted course for one to remain in a chosen occupation, although he may rise to more favored jobs within that occupation.

Van Heek studied the occupational structure of a textile town in Holland where textiles had been the dominant industry for more than three generations. Of 67 persons in management positions, he found that the fathers of 63 had been managers in the same town, often in the same enterprise, and 48 of these had grandfathers who had been managers in textile plants. The remaining four whose fathers had not been managers

[42] Leonard Reissman, "Class, City and Social Cohesion," *International Review of Community Development*, No. 7, 1961, p. 43.

[43] John P. Gillin, "Some Signposts of Policy," in Richard N. Adams (Ed.), *Social Change in Latin America Today*, New York, Harper & Row, 1960, pp. 23–28.

[44] Charles Wagley, "The Brazilian Revolution, Social Change Since 1930," ibid., pp. 210–212.

in textile plants were the sons of managers in other industries or of high public officials.[45]

Van Heek found a tendency in this town for sons of foremen to become foremen, although an occasional foreman was the son of a factory worker. If we had corresponding information for the same small city in the fifteenth century we would have found an occupational structure, with a guild for each type of work, in which the son not only followed in the occupation of his father, but performed the work in precisely the same way, and was respected because of it. In those days an occupation was inherited as a property right.

An expanding industrial society offers inducements to break with tradition, but, as Lipset and Bendix found, the more settled American industry becomes, the less possible it is for the individual to move up one, two, or three levels during his working life. In a period of economic expansion, upward occupational and social mobility may be expected to increase and new people will move into elite roles while others may fall back. "Just as there are changes in the demand for the various kinds of talent, there are constant shifts in the supply. No elite or ruling class controls the natural distribution of talent, intelligence or other abilities, though it may monopolize the opportunities for education and training." [46]

Denmark is a settled country of limited natural resources other than agricultural produce and does not hold out encouragement for rapid industrial development. Svalastoga finds that, by comparing generations, upward or downward social mobility tends to become balanced. Thus for each ten families, "four remain immobile from one generation to the next," two families move one step down and two move one step up. Of the remaining two, he notes, one moves quite far up and the other drops farther down. Whether upward or downward, individual status tends to be closely related to family status.[47]

Japan, a country that experienced industrial expansion over several decades, presents an opposite picture of generational mobility, as revealed in a study carried on by several Japanese universities in 1953. The trend is illustrated by two items from the findings:

> Sixteen percent of the interviewees were in white-collar occupations, compared with 8 percent of their fathers and less than 2 percent of their grandfathers.

[45] H. van Heek, "The Method of Extreme Types for the Study of Causes of Vertical Mobility," *Transactions of the Second World Congress of Sociology,* Vol. II, London, 1954, pp. 291 ff.

[46] Seymour M. Lipset and Reinhard Bendix, *Social Mobility in Industrial Society,* London, Heinemann, 1959, pp. 2–3.

[47] Kaare Svalastoga, "The Family in the Mobility Process," in Nels Anderson (Ed.), *Recherches sur la famille,* Güttingen, Vanderhoeck-Ruprecht, 1958, p. 295.

Two percent of the interviewees began their work life in agriculture compared with 28 percent of their fathers and 56 percent of their grandfathers.

As in the United States, the upward mobility of Japanese in their occupations was accompanied by rising levels of education.[48]

ASSIMILATION AND ACCOMMODATION

Persons or families moving from one place to another face the need
of adapting to the place of destination, which may be a considerable
problem in a neighborhood type of community but much less of a problem in an anonymous urban area. Newcomers from another country and
speaking another language must adapt to the total culture, including
the work ways of the country of destination, often the effort of a lifetime.
If the newcomers are of a different race, they may be able to adapt, but
may not be readily accepted. Whatever the characteristics of the newcomers, their likelihood of being accepted is much greater in an urban
than in a rural community.

The barriers newcomers face, both in their efforts to adapt and in
being accepted, tends to place them in an outsider category. They derive
a degree of psychological security by joining others of their own type and
origin. This is one of the understandable explanations of the various
enclaves found in large cities, the immigrant quarters or areas occupied
by racial groups. Regarding the immigrant areas, the parents may remain
there but their children, as they become adapted and accepted, tend to
move to other areas. They are assimilated by the majority, something
which is much more difficult for racially different people to achieve.

Geographical mobility of any kind is socially disturbing, to some
degree, to the established people in the places of destination. Even if the
newcomers are of the same kind, they must be adapted to; they may not
always be "like us." As Ogburn reasons, any number of people moving
into a community may disturb the economic balance. But the "home
people" may fear for their own way of life if the newcomers are of different ethnic origin, or race, or religion, or level of education.[49] When
the staid city of Bonn, long a quiet university town, became the seat of
the German government, many officials and public functionaries settled

---

[48] Japanese Sociological Society, "Social Stratification and Mobility in Six Large
Cities of Japan," *Transactions of the Second World Congress of Sociology*, Vol. II,
p. 414.

[49] William F. Ogburn, *On Culture and Social Change, Selected Papers*, Otis D.
Duncan (Ed.), Chicago, University of Chicago Press, 1964, p. 190.

there, outnumbering the original population. A sharp line developed between the old and the new citizens of Bonn. The old citizens became strangers in their native town. What was seen as progress to the newcomers, most of them sophisticated people from other German cities, was "destruction of the home town" to the old citizens. To the newcomers, who now are the majority, these "backward Rhinelanders" are not likely to be assimilated, but a relationship of accommodation exists.

Social mobility also may raise problems of adaptation and acceptance; in particular, this applies to upward mobility. The family or individual in the process of entering a higher social level may encounter types of discrimination which, in some respects, are not unlike the cool reception often accorded newcomers in the community. Such upwardly mobile aspirants may be assimilated in the community as a whole, but to enter a higher class may call for some cultural and other prerequisites which they may be acquiring but as yet do not have. Their children, however, may meet the requirements.

In the industrial urban community it is no longer seen as necessary for all types of people to be assimilated into the majority group. Catholics and Protestants come to accept one another as citizens, neighbors, fellow workers, and in other relations. This holds for persons of different ethnic origins. The relationship is one of *accommodation*. Each faction or segment has accepted the idea that conflict is of advantage to neither. Since neither group can eliminate or assimilate the other, they learn to accept a kind of continuing truce.

Wherever migration exists, the movement of people from country to city, from city to city, or from one country to another, it is to be expected that cities will be inhabited by people of different races, religions, and different ethnic origin. It is not likely that they can be melted into a homogeneous agglomerate. Instead, degrees of accommodation develop, an adaptation which is very old. Young and Mack add:

> The effects of accommodation may vary somewhat with circumstances. It may act to reduce the conflict between persons or groups as an initial step to synthesis of differences into a new pattern; in other words, it may lead to assimilation. It may serve to postpone outright conflict for a specific period of time, as in a treaty between nations or a labor-management agreement. It may permit groups marked by sharp socio-psychological distance to get along together.[50]

It should not be assumed that a community undisturbed by mobility, with a stable, homogeneous population, is a community without factions

---

[50] Kimball Young and Raymond W. Mack, *Systematic Sociology*, New York, American Book, 1964, p. 111.

and rivalries. The traditional caste community was little troubled with incoming strangers of other cultural or ethnic type. Moreover, social mobility was not possible, nor would it have been permitted. Yet such communities never came to the end of factional rivalry, although they were perfectly integrated socially, the integration being basically one of accommodation.

Urbanism and its incongruities | 8

URBAN CHANGE AND THE GUIDANCE ISSUE

In this chapter we shall consider criticisms aimed at cities in general, and large cities in particular. To begin with, we should indicate that there are two kinds of critics—the rural and the urban. It is to be expected that rural people through the ages would be critical of cities by which they are too often and too widely exploited. While country people in one village may hate those in the next, the two villages may be one in their distrust and dislike for the city fifty miles away. Yet sons and daughters of both villages may migrate to that city for employment with no intention of returning. We are more interested, however, in the criticism of people who know the city and are of it. These critics belong to the city and could not live elsewhere.

Few know the modern city better than Mumford, one of the most telling and persistent critics of it. To him, the very growth of the city is an aspect of its decline, and so it exposes our inability to understand urban reality.

> Those who work within the metropolitan myth, treating its cancerous tumors as normal manifestations of growth, will continue to apply poultices, salves, advertising incantations, public relations magic, and quick mechanical remedies until the patient dies before our failing eyes. . . . Slum clearance, model housing, civic architectural embellishment, suburban extension, "urban renewal"—has only continued in superficially new forms the same purposeless concentration and organic de-building that prompted the remedy.[1]

Mumford's viewpoint is akin to that of present-day critics who fault the American city fathers of 1850 for not displaying interest in establish-

[1] Lewis Mumford, *The City in History, Its Origins, Its Transformations, and Its Prospects,* New York, Harcourt, Brace & World, 1961, p. 560.

ing city parks and for accepting street patterns which proved to be a straightjacket once the automobile appeared on the scene. This view criticizes the shortsightedness of the grandfathers, even though they acted in good faith.

Various American philosophers have held similar anti-urban views. Emerson, for example, in 1840 wrote to a friend, "I always seem to suffer some loss of faith on entering cities. They are great conspiracies; the parties are all maskers, who have taken mutual oaths of silence not to betray each other's secret." Although Henry James admired London, Santayana called that great city a "Babel of false principles and blind cravings." Santayana loved humanity but he hated the big communities made by men. He saw the city as "levying a toll on everything transportable. However much they may collect and exhibit, they will never breed anything original." [2] Emerson, for example, knew that American cities were developing into industrial centers and he knew they were the necessary marts of commerce, yet they were repugnant to him. As for Santayana and his charge that cities will not "breed anything original," he certainly knew that breeding originality is one of the oldest functions of cities.

The novelist, Forster, in *Howard's End,* writes about London in 1910 and complains of London air being fouled by the odor of gasoline and how automobiles made it dangerous to cross streets. (Automobiles, at that time, were just coming on the scene.) He objected to the tearing up and rebuilding of streets. Man, he observed, was estranging himself from nature, so much so that in the great city it had become old-fashioned to speak of Pan. Indeed, London fascinated but he called it "intelligence without purpose and excitement without love." The touch of humanity is lacking and nature is excluded.[3]

In his *Confessions,* Rousseau relates his disappointment with Paris when in 1731 he saw it for the first time. It offended all his senses and had much to do with shaping his ideas about a more perfect existence, an escape to nature. But he was not able himself to escape Paris and its circle of intellectuals. His negative view of cities, in fact, echoes those set forth by many writers before him. Lowenstein found that many Roman writers had criticized cities, some of them viewing with disdain the showy display of Roman social life.[4]

Literary persons, with few exceptions, are constant critics of the city, and often are not too well informed about what offends them. The poet

[2] Morton White, "The Philosopher and the Metropolis in America," in Werner E. Hirsch (Ed.), *Urban Life and Form,* New York, Holt, Rinehart and Winston, 1963, pp. 86 and 91.

[3] Edward M. Forster, *Howard's End,* London, Arnold, 1910, p. 113.

[4] Susan Floess Lowenstein, "Urban Images by Roman Writers," *Comparative Studies in Society and History,* Vol. 8, No. 1, October 1965, pp. 110–123.

who did not know that the sewer ran under the pavement, who was furious when sewer gas began escaping, who was even more furious when the street near his apartment had to be torn up for repairs may be more typical than we know. Without mentioning critics, Knickerbocker wrote waggishly about the many kinds of complaints brought against cities, and observed that nevertheless the city manages to move on unguided. "The certain truth about American city life is that it has, at last, moved beyond comprehension, that it is changing. And nobody is in charge. At last, anything can happen." [5]

CRITICS AND THE URBAN FUNCTIONS

All communities have functions, but the cities have many; if they had none they would not exist. If they did not perform their functions they could not survive. If their performances did not stimulate hope, people would not flock to cities. But they are not utopias. When the utopian writer creates in his imagination an ideal city he excludes from it those human types he does not like. His utopia is regulated by a strict moral code, and everyone conforms to it. Sharp competition, so vital to cities, is excluded.

The real city is a place of competition and contest, and its aspirations are as heterogeneous as its inhabitants. People enter the real city mostly for practical reasons and the reasons are as varied as the city markets. The real city must be all things to all men. Each person utilizes those functions that mean the most to him.

The order of the real city is one of equilibrium in the face of diversity, which no utopia could tolerate. Knowledge and skills accumulate here, but there are many kinds of knowledge and skill. Here the debate over work, living, and art never ends. Each art form is at home here and each has its devotees. But, as Jacobs concludes, the city itself is not a work of art. It is the unfeeling milieu in which what is art and what is not art meet, argue, and compete. Art and life are not the same, and efforts to blend them lead to confusion.[6] The city is not the creation of any man or group. All who share its life are occupied with creating or recreating it, including those who resist this or that change. And never in this ongoing process are the hands of the dead absent. Thus change takes its course but never to the complete satisfaction of any individual or group.

Even the functions performed by the city, however old some may be, are never wholly satisfactory to all. These functions do not always serve

[5] Conrad Knickerbocker, "No Man's In Charge," *Life,* Vol. 59, No. 25, December 24, 1965, p. 37.

[6] Jane Jacobs, *The Death and Life of Great American Cities,* New York, Random House, Vintage, 1961, p. 272.

the city alone, for the city is a servant of its region, and the region makes claims upon it which may not always concern the residents. Nor do the functions preferred by the residents always meet with approval in the region. To perform its many kinds of roles, all necessary, the city is bound to offend. There have been American philosophers, Josiah Joyce, for example, who would have all urbanites flee to the provinces, "not in the sense of a cowardly and permanent retirement, but in the sense of a search for renewed strength, for the salvation of the individual from the overwhelming forces of consolidation." [7]

It has been difficult for urban thinkers to understand that it has become something like a "mission" for urbanism to supersede ruralism, and they themselves, if they settle in a rural area, help to speed the trend. They love nature, to which the rural person is often oblivious, but they want to enjoy the urban amenities in the country as well. John Dewey, a wise urban man, lamented the destruction of the old-fashioned type of rural community life, and he encouraged efforts, which proved futile, to reestablish the "neighborhood" in cities.[8]

The city, above all, is a place where people work, and most of its inhabitants are there because of their occupations. In the large cities there are thousands of places of work of every imaginable size and description. Yet a place of work which may be quite satisfactory for those using it can be objectionable to others. The very multiplicity of the places of work, with their noise and bad odors, the congestion they cause, and their unattractive appearance, renders the central city undesirable for residence. Hence, the modern flight to the suburbs, which Wood calls another type of anti-urbanism. This modern exodus to the suburbs to escape the incongruities of the cities comes itself to be one of the most challenging of metropolitan incongruities. The aim of the flight—to escape the economic responsibility one has to the city where one works, for the social community and democracy of the suburb—Wood concludes, is rarely realized. Suburbs rarely achieve either financial self-sufficiency and ideal democracy or the perfect old-fashioned social community.[9]

The critics of cities, philosophers, poets, or countrypeople, are still everlastingly dependent upon it. It is man's only social creation that faithfully reflects the diversities of human nature, the only human habitat where all types of humans can feel at home. We quote from an essay in *Time:*

> The ancient Athenians, true urbanites, delighted in the everyday drama of human encounter. For them the city was the supreme instrument of

[7] White, op. cit., p. 90.
[8] Ibid., p. 98.
[9] Robert C. Wood, *Suburbia, Its People and Their Politics,* Boston, Houghton Mifflin, 1959, p. 75.

civilization, the tool that gave men common traditions and goals, even as it encouraged their diversity and growth. "The men who dwell in the city are my teachers," said Socrates in Plato's *Phaedrus*, "and not the trees or the country." In turn, the city transformed them into something they had not been previously and could not have become without it—men who within a few generations produced more thought and works of beauty and value than the race had ever seen before.[10]

URBAN CHANGE AND THE IDEA OF WASTE

We never come to the end of hearing how wasteful urban man is, how everything built above the surface or constructed underground is due one day to be broken down or torn up because something more efficient (or more profitable) can be put in its place. This strikes many people as being wasteful. Such structural changes may have been forced by other changes, which also, in some other perspective, seemed wasteful, as when factories replace old machines with new ones.

Beauty is destroyed as grass and trees are replaced by a new street, or it is lost when a venerable historic building is replaced by one that will yield more income. Some may regret the replacement of the old kitchen stove by the electric range or the replacement of the family-size kitchen by the modern, tightly-packed mechanized one.

Winthrop makes the study of waste a scientific pursuit, and he names seven types of waste in modern life: 1) goods, 2) services, 3) time, 4) money, 5) labor, 6) technology, and 7) ideas.[11] He speaks also of the morality of waste. It may be argued that styles change and patterns of organization are deliberately promoted to outmode what was fashionable and displayed with pride yesterday. All of this, Winthrop would say, is accepted in the philosophy of waste of an affluent society.

> Mass democratic culture, under the influence of rapidly obsolescing techniques of production, encourages many forms of waste. . . . These are almost necessary prerequisites of Galbraith's affluent society. Quite different philosophies of waste would, of course, characterize economics of scarcity. Intentional communities and communitarian societies and groups arise essentially as protests against the characteristics of prevailing philosophies of waste found in the industrial, urban, bureaucratic and highly centralized societies.[12]

Building construction in the highly competitive modern city may result in more rapid replacement than in older, more tradition-conscious

[10] *Time*, November 14, 1969, p. 59.
[11] Henry Winthrop, "Waste as an Index of Social Pathology," *American Behavioral Scientist*, Vol. 10, No. 3, October 1961, p. 18.
[12] Ibid., p. 21.

cities. If a structure is not outdated by changes in style it may be out of demand because of new inventions, such as, new building materials and various new amenities. Building and rebuilding, repaving streets, putting in new sewers and water mains, laying lines of communication and transit underground, population being inconvenienced as sections of the city undergo reconstruction, all draw complaints about urban ugliness and waste. To Gottmann, this is calculated waste in which prospective gains are balanced against cumulative losses.

> A certain kind of planned waste is healthy for the economy of abundance in an industrialized society, and as long as it follows and supports the general tide of growth and progress it is a welcome factor of wealth. But if and when it interferes with the evolution of the rest of the way of life and appropriates for special use too large a share of the money, space, and time available to the population, then this waste must be eliminated. It is bound to be corrected in the field of activity it saturates, although similarly planned wastefulness may develop in other aspects of the nation's economy.[13]

WASTE IN COMMUNITY RESOURCES

It has been said of London that nothing gets done until it is too late, and whatever is done will be a compromise between barely enough and too little. Complaints alleging inaction may be heard from certain groups in any city. Perhaps the factories are dumping their liquid wastes and polluting the neighboring streams. The local government stands between two pressure groups: a civic-conscious, although not wealthy, minority demanding action and the wealthy industrial minority resisting any such initiative. The top taxpayers may be firmly united against any public activity that might increase the cost of local government. The reform groups continue making demands, and in the meantime vacant lots get piled with rubbish, recreation facilities are not provided, and the signs of neglect multiply. Ultimately the point of decision is reached and there is a burst of reform, but resistance remains strong.

An example of a city suddenly becoming aware of itself is seen in the awakening of Philadelphia, called "corrupt and contented" by Lincoln Steffens more than half a century ago and more recently called a "hotbed of inertia." As Tunley relates, this city began in 1682 as the "green countrie towne" of the Quakers and it was the center of American culture in 1775. In 1950:

> Except for a few islands here and there, the engulfing waves of blight had swamped large sections of the city. They were even lapping close to

[13] Jean Gottmann, *Megalopolis, The Urbanized Northeastern Seaboard of the United States,* New York, Twentieth Century Fund, 1961, p. 685.

the shores of America's most sacred shrine—Independence Hall. Industry was deserting the city, its rivers were clogged with silt and sewage, and its politics smelled higher than a twenty-year-old kipper. Most of the elite, as well as the middle class, had long since escaped to the suburbs. They had no truck with downtown Philadelphia except during working hours when they had to come to the center of the city to make a living.[14]

This was written five years after a liberal government came to power in Philadelphia. In the sixteen years since the revival began, much of the central area of the city has been rebuilt.

Most cities in the industrial countries are confronted with two problems each of which is menacing to public health: air pollution and water pollution, both in turn polluting the soil. The necessary controls cannot be realized; they demand immediate expenditures beyond the ability of industry and government to pay. The demand for action, unfortunately, has become a fad interest, the kind of interest that blows hot and cold. The real work of coping with pollution has only begun. National leadership and financing are needed and the pressure of law must be used against cities and industries. We all know that most streams and freshwater bodies, including the Great Lakes, as well as the shoreline of the Atlantic are polluted. The danger is that the urgent demand for action may abate in a year or so, even though the hazard increases. As an example of the extent of air pollution, in late November 1966 the population of much of the seacoast from New York to Boston was thrown into panic. A dome of fog and fumes hung over the area and the usual winds from the west that "whisk away the 17.6 million pounds of pollutants that New York alone spews into the air each day were nowhere to be found." [15] Many became sick and some might have died had the wind not come to the rescue.

In the great agglomerations where industry is concentrated and where increasing numbers are massing together, man is creating a hazardous environment. The complaint being voiced by increasing numbers is no mere emotional one. There is danger of damage to health and waste of life but, as Hall says of Paris, great cities are slow to take hold of big problems. Often many of the smaller problems also remain untouched. He mentions that in the suburbs of Paris, there is a lack of hospitals, libraries, culture centers, and theaters. One suburb has waited half a century for a public building in which the police and other services could be located, and he mentions overcrowding in areas of poor housing.[16] Most great cities move much faster in coping with their incongru-

---

[14] Roul Tunley, "Comeback of a Shabby City," *Saturday Evening Post,* December 5, 1959.
[15] *Time,* December 2, 1966, p. 29.
[16] Peter Hall, *The World Cities,* New York, McGraw-Hill, 1966, p. 80.

ities, but it would be unusual for any city to be ahead, or even abreast of, its more urgent problems.

URBAN APPEARANCES AND REALITY

Most of the objections to the city, or to a particular city, relate to some aspects which offend the senses. About this type of reaction, Jacobs remarks significantly, "The look of things and the way they work are inextricably bound together, and in no place more so than cities. . . . It is futile to plan a city's appearance, or speculate on how to endow it with a pleasing appearance of order without knowing what sort of innate functioning order it has." [17]

How a city works has to do with what it is used for, what people do there, how the city serves in meeting the needs of its many kinds of people. As there are many kinds of people, many different interests must be served, those that relate to work and production and those which concern leisure and consumption. Those who do clean work in neat establishments may object to the nearness of those who do dirty work in smelly or noisy places.

People who are offended by the city, with few exceptions, are those whose work is among the clean categories, and their work is rarely heavy or carried on in noisy places. Often for them the factories, foundries, freight yards, electric plants, or water works are unsightly and disorderly, although each may be a highly efficient and functionally necessary establishment.

The urbanized man is one who, while aware of the many incongruities of his city, recognizes that many must be accepted for utilitarian reasons. Perhaps in time they can be rendered less objectionable without diminishing their utility. He recognizes that the great evils which affect many must have first consideration. But the fully urbanized man is one of a minority. Often, as Dyckman has observed, even the most urbane citizens tend to see efforts at improvement in terms of old forms, in the image of the past.[18]

"Drabness" sums up much of the criticisms which relate to urban appearance. These are most likely to be heard in cities in the process of rapid change, where a whole block of shabby structures is replaced by bright, new, more efficient buildings, which makes other old blocks look shabbier. This was one of the consequences of rebuilding sections of downtown Philadelphia. In the course of a renewal project, nearby rows of old housing suddenly assumed the aspect of decrepit obsolescence.

---

[17] Jacobs, op. cit., p. 14.
[18] John Dyckman, "The Changing Uses of the City," *Daedalus*, Vol. 90, No. 1, Winter 1961, p. 116.

In the midst of such change people are stimulated to make comparisons. For cities gone stale by accepting things as they are, the stimulus of contrast is least present. Such is precisely the case in Britain, as Brogan points out; English towns possess a dead-level drabness, and it has become accepted. "There is a lot of unnecessary drabness that is the reflection of the taste, the energy, and the public spirit of the people." [19]

The acceptance of drabness may evolve gradually with time. For example, Halbwachs calls attention to many little islands of decay in Paris—here or there a cluster of old houses, decades out of date. Once each was a socially self-contained neighborhood. With change in the area, some families moved, but a hard core remained and their children or grandchildren were still holding on despite the decline of the old homes, hardly at all offended by the appearances so evident to others.[20] Prairie Avenue in Chicago was such a cluster in the 1890's but the forces of change were so compelling that its families abandoned the street, and the old homes were converted into rooming houses.

Briggs finds that many of the organizations which today are demanding city improvement did not exist a century ago. They are becoming increasingly the keepers of the community conscience. But he is talking about an exceptional elite in English cities who from about 1870 began to form organizations for "improvement." The leading spirits, many of them intellectuals, were concerned "not only with the contrasts between city and countryside but with contrasts within the city." [21]

THE COMPLEXITIES OF THE CHANGING SCENE

Opposed to the incongruities of urban places, often seen in terms of ugliness, is the concept of beauty and its entailing order. Every man is his own judge of beauty and his conception of it is rarely constant. Often what is accepted as beauty, at least by the elite, is confined to places reserved for it: parks, promenades, galleries, museums, etc., segregated as are the people or their places of work. Beauty as it is institutionally accepted is associated more with the leisure interests than the work interests of people.

Beauty as expressed by the pleasing aspects of a city seems not to have been a matter of great concern in earlier cities. Crowded streets, congested and dilapidated dwellings, dangerously unsanitary conditions were taken for granted. What we call sanitary conditions is something that belongs to recent decades. Again we take a bit from the already quoted

19 D. W. Brogan, *The English People,* New York, Knopf, 1949, p. 278.
20 Maurice Halbwachs, *La Mémoire collective,* Paris, Presses Universitaires de France, 1950, p. 139.
21 Asa Briggs, *Victorian Cities,* London, Odham's Press, 1963, p. 68.

essay in *Time,* the implication being that these conditions were common
to early cities:

> Babylon, for example, was the first great city of the ancient world; ac-
> cording to the Bible, it was "the mother of harlots and abominations of
> the earth." Ancient Athens, for all its architectural and intellectual glory,
> was scarcely more than an overgrown slum; the grandeur of Rome was
> overshadowed by its ramshackle ghettos, crime rate and traffic jams.
> Sanitation was so bad in the Paris of Louis XIV that two miles from the
> city's gates the traveler's nose would tell him that he was drawing near.[22]

And yet, as the essayist adds, "the truly great city is the stuff of leg-
ends and stories and a place with an ineradicable fascination." Something
of beauty, defined variously by different persons, is there and each person
finds his own kind. The poet may call the factory ugly; the industrialist
or engineer may think otherwise. To the sensitive aesthete, the freight
yards with their train-switching are a shambles, but it is a thing of beauty
to the railroader.

If we think of order as one aspect of beauty and consider the urban
community in relation to order, the questions that must be faced will
relate largely to aspects of efficiency: how well transportation is managed; how effectively food, water, fuel, power, and raw materials are supplied; how well education and training are related to employment; the
adequacy of housing and the related amenities; the adequacy of facilities
for leisure and culture. All of these are aspects of community living.
Order in the whole community, which is never perfectly achieved, will
be adversely affected if in these parts there is lack of order, or if there
is defective performance in some. Order in the community is the working
of a complex network of interdependent structures and functions. Green,
in his report on Manchester, found perfect order lacking. To him, the
city:

> . . . has become a vast, attenuated urban concentration, a sprawling giant
> which somehow must be housed, clothed, fed, transported, employed and
> looked after in sickness and health. Generally speaking, the technical
> means for satisfying its everyday needs are available, or the giant could
> not exist; but almost everywhere the management of these means are in
> the hands of lilliputian organizations set up to rule its predecessors. And
> the life of the giant city has a quickening pulse that demands a quicken-
> ing response to its needs.[23]

As size and complexity in organization increase, the more is the
order of the city likely to be in the hands of agencies of long standing,

---

[22] *Time,* November 14, 1969, p. 59.
[23] L. P. Green, *Provincial Metropolis, The Future of Local Government in Southeast Lancashire,* London, Allen and Unwin, 1959, p. 17.

operating under rules established for an earlier generation. Change can hardly be realized except in a piece-meal fashion; overall change initiated by such agencies, each in its own way, might be chaotic.

One of the problems of developing countries, the necessity to renew their older cities and to plan the newly emerging ones, may be more of a demand than they will be able to meet. In some of these cities the networks for service, management, and control, which in Western cities are taken for granted, are either unknown or are only now being experimented with. The bureaucratized world cities freed themselves after decades of many forms and procedures of the earlier ascriptive social order, which still prevail in less developed countries. Rodwin mentions that sometimes the problems of emerging cities, such as, control over land use, construction, water and food supply, and transportation, are challenges which exist, but are not recognized. They appear as incongruities only to the outsider.[24]

In a United Nations study of land-use policies in cities of developing countries, it was found that there is an all but discouraging unawareness of the knowledge a people must gain to effectively build, inhabit, and maintain a city.[25] Yet these people are striving to create cities as modern as are the Western cities; their attention, however, is more on the dream structure than on the underlying foundation of attitudes and habits. They are seeking shortcuts, as indeed they must. They cannot extend the period of trial and error over two or more centuries, as was done in the West.

URBAN SPACE AND CONGESTION

In the Middle Ages, when cities were compactly enclosed within walls, greater size was not regarded as a virtue. Migrants were not readily admitted, but the population, as the functions of the cities, did increase and new rings of walls had to be erected. In our day, perhaps because the tempo is faster, congestion is put high among the incongruities of the city. People outside the city have become more dependent than formerly on the urban center for goods, services, and decisions. The more the demands on the central city increase, as they continue to do, the more is congestion conducive to irritation. Despite the faults of the automobile as a space user, it enables the streets to be many times more efficient. Often the critic of the automobile may look with approval on the skyscraper which contributes even more to congestion.

Streets were crowded to suffocation in the days of horsedrawn vehi-

24 Lloyd Rodwin, "Metropolitan Policies for Developing Areas," *Daedalus,* Vol. 90, No. 1, Winter 1961, p. 132.
25 *Urban Land Policies,* New York, United Nations Secretariat, Document St/ SCA/9, 1953, pp. 173 and 210.

cles. Movement then was slower, the pavements worse, and the clumsy horse-drawn vehicles demanded more space than do automobiles. Nevins does not tell of the suffering of horses in the city or of the short life of an urban work horse, but he does call attention to the large number of horses needed in the days of the omnibus and horse-drawn streetcar. He also points out the great number of men needed to clean the streets after the horses.[26] Cresswell gives us this description of horse traffic in London in 1890:

> The whole of London's crowded wheeled traffic—which in parts of the city was at times dense beyond movement—was dependent on the horse; lorry, wagon, bus, hansom and "growler," and coaches and carriages and private vehicles of all kinds were appendages to horses. Meredith refers to the "anticipatory stench of its cab stands" on railway approach to London; but the characteristic aroma—for the nose recognized London with gay expectations—was of stables, which were commonly of three or four storeys with inclined ways zigzagging up the faces of them; (their) middens kept the castiron filigree chandeliers, that glorified the reception rooms of upper and middle class homes throughout London encrusted with dead flies and, in late summer, veiled by jiving clouds of them.[27]

It is interesting to note that for the same number of ton-miles 2,000 horses and 1,000 drivers were needed in a city in 1879, while fewer than 100 two-ton trucks and that number of drivers are needed today.

City planners and others with a professional interest in urban traffic problems belong to the age of the auto. It may also be, as some charge, that attention is given to traffic problems to the neglect of other problems. This attention creates favorable opinion about a "wide awake" municipality. Traffic counts provide impressive figures for planners. Coping with other problems, Jacobs implies, is more difficult. "It is questionable how much of the destruction wrought by automobiles on cities is really a response to transportation and traffic needs, and how much of it is owing to sheer disrespect for other city needs, uses and functions." [28]

Traffic congestion in cities, especially at certain points, as it again and again frustrates and is declaimed, is due to competition for space in the streets—people competing against vehicles and against the crowd. This, however, is merely symptomatic of the competition for work or residential space in the city. The competition for space, keener at hub points than elsewhere, and keenest at the urban center, is seldom noticed by the critics. According to Thompson's conclusions, merely to limit or

[26] Allan Nevins, *The Emergence of Modern America, 1865–1878*, New York, Macmillan, 1927, p. 81.

[27] H. B. Cresswell, *British Architectural Review*, December 1958, quoted in Jacobs, op. cit., p. 341.

[28] Jacobs, ibid., p. 339.

divert congestion would greatly disadvantage the users of land, while the widening of streets merely makes the congested points more accessible for more space users to crowd in.[29] Moreover, it gets us nowhere to blame congestion on a single cause, as does Fitch: "No other wheeled vehicle has approached the destructiveness of the automobile . . . For the automobile has not merely taken over the street; it has actually dissolved the living tissues of the city. Its appetite for space seems to be absolutely insatiable." [30]

THE GROWING CHALLENGE OF THE SLUM

A document issued by the United Nations defines the slum as a "building, group of buildings, or area characterized by overcrowding, deterioration, unsanitary conditions or absence of facilities or amenities which, because of these conditions or any of them endangers the health, safety and morals of its inhabitants or the community." [31] This would describe the conditions under which urban Europeans lived in the days of walled cities (crowded into narrow quarters, in dwellings with limited light and ventilation, their streets littered with filth) but the word, "slum," had not yet entered the vocabulary.

The slums that reform groups discovered a century ago in English factory towns were congested areas without amenities: inside rooms without ventilation, outside common toilets without a connection to the sewers, water available at a common tap in some back yard, with some families having to steal water. Apartments were crowded and so were the houses. Death rates were high. A century later Mann described a slum in Canada's brightest city, Toronto. He found area deterioration, a "confused" moral climate, and social disorganization.

> Adjacent to the main railroad tracks, heavily populated with truck depots, smoke-blackened industrial plants, and office buildings, and lying just west of the central business district, it is perhaps the least desirable residential section of Toronto. The air is heavily polluted, the side streets are littered or dirty, the roads are crammed all day with cars and lumbering trucks. Most buildings, including churches and recreational facilities, are ugly or depressing, and the majority of houses have deteriorated or are substandard.[32]

29 Wilbur R. Thompson, *A Preface to Urban Economics,* Baltimore, Johns Hopkins University Press, pp. 268, 308, and 366.
30 James M. Fitch, "In Defence of the City," in Thomas P. Peardon (Ed.), *Proceedings of the Academy of Political Science,* Vol. 27, No. 1, May 1960, p. 5.
31 *Urban Land Policies,* op. cit., p. 200.
32 W. E. Mann, "The Social System of a Slum; The Lower Ward, Toronto," in S. D. Clark (Ed.), *Urbanism and the Changing Canadian Society,* Toronto, University of Toronto Press, 1961, p. 42.

Such a slum may be found near the center of any modern city; in some cities it may be divided perhaps into two or three parts. The one described in Toronto tends to be removed as the central areas expand. However, there are different kinds of slums, and some would not be called slums by the poor who live there; for example, an area in Tokyo studied by Dore. Here not all families were poor and not all were in the lower occupations. Yet there were many shabby houses, streets were unpaved and muddy or dusty. Sidewalks were rows of paving stones and wooden gutters were rotten or missing.[33]

Manchester, England, famous in the history of the textile industry, came to be equally ill famed for its mass poverty and crowded, socially neglected slums.[34] The reformers of 1870 to 1890, shocked by such deprived areas, apparently loaded the term, "slum," with emotions similar to those attached to "ghetto" in the 1960's. The difference is that the ghetto in which Jews in medieval times were confined was clean and a social whole, in contrast to areas in the same cities where the non-Jewish poor lived. The ghetto included the rich, middle-class and poor Jews. It was internally well ordered.

Modern industrial cities contain various areas which are called slums; these are inhabited by ethnic-origin groups, racial groups, or by people of many types. When we take into account such characteristics as these, we find that slums, like other urban habitation areas, differ widely. Among these variable characteristics are:

1. *Appearance*—the condition of housing and other structures, adequacy, age, and state of repair.
2. *Location*—inside or outside of the city and the relationship to adjacent uses of space, transport, industry, etc.
3. *Economic status*—prevailing occupations and ways in which the inhabitants sustain themselves.
4. *Population density*—the extent to which inhabitants are crowded in dwellings and density in the area.
5. *Types of inhabitants*—if a slum is homogeneous, characteristically racial, ethnic, religious, or other; if heterogeneous, a certain mixture of personalities or social characteristics.
6. *Amenities*—water supply, sewage disposal, electric power, street paving, playgrounds, etc., and availability of these to the households.
7. *Health and sanitation*—the extent to which the area is able to keep itself sanitary and healthy.
8. *Deviant behavior*—the extent to which the area is, in fact, identified with crime or juvenile delinquency.

33 R. P. Dore, *City Life in Japan*, London, Routledge and Kegan Paul, 1958, p. 16.
34 Shena D. Simon, "Manchester," in William A. Robson (Ed.), *Great Cities of the World*, London, Allen and Unwin, 1957, p. 326. For a description of early slums in Birmingham, see Conrad Gill, *History of Birmingham*, Vol. I, London, Oxford University Press, 1952, p. 367.

9. *Style of life*—whether the area has unique sub-cultural characteristics, as, for example, a homogeneous ethnic area.

10. *Isolation*—the degree of isolation of the people from the wider community and isolation from one another within the area; also political isolation, which varies.

11. *Mobility*—the extent to which people move into the area, out of it or from house to house within it, and the extent to which social mobility is reflected in moving from the area.

It is not enough to identify a particular area as a slum; one needs to ask about the history of that particular area which, in most cases, has not always been a slum. The inhabitants may have assembled from former slums which have come to be used for other purposes. In the course of obsolescence and other change, this particular slum area may be put to other uses.

THE CASE AGAINST THE SLUM

When Zorbaugh studied a congested section of Chicago five decades ago he found many kinds of contrast. Within less than a mile of each other were the haunts of the homeless and the havens of the wealthy. From the apartments or houses of grand old families, one had but to cross two streets of the traffic that divides people to reach the gilded habitats of ill fame. Different, contrasting worlds existed then within waving distance, although a world apart socially.[35]

One thought standing out in Zorbaugh's study of the Gold Coast and the slum is that these extremely different areas of habitation are socially isolated from one another but they are not isolated from the economic processes of the city. Both are included in the ecological pattern of the city. Moreover, there are many shades between the extremes; all who are in the Gold Coast direction are not equally affluent, and far from all in the slum direction are at the bottom. Wherever people may be placed in this spectrum between affluence and poverty, all are participating variously in the total life of the community, and many are socially mobile.

Brace did not see the relationships between social levels when he described the shantytowns of New York, as he knew them in the 1860's. Dutch Hill, described by him, has been removed and the land area was occupied by tenements, later to be replaced by tall exclusive apartment buildings many of them now occupied by functionaries in the nearby United Nations complex. Nor did he see that the descendants of the

[35] Harvey W. Zorbaugh, *The Gold Coast and the Slum,* Chicago, University of Chicago Press, 1929, p. 128.

Dutch Hill shack dwellers, mostly German and other immigrants, would in three generations be among the middle and upper classes.[36]

During his active years, Brace was one of a dedicated generation of reformers, the first American generation to organize and evolve programs for ridding American cities of poverty and the slums. Although not social scientists, they were of the view that much more than religious approaches were needed to cope with the problems of the city. That generation, which was on the scene at the turn of the century, lent support to the efforts of the first American sociologists. Faults notwithstanding and despite scientific illiteracy, that generation of reformers encouraged a practical look at slums and poverty. A full generation went by before objective study of the slums and other urban problems began, such studies, for example, as that by Zorbaugh. In the meanwhile the slums in these same cities have reached unmanagable proportions and the poverty problem was never more baffling.

Protest against the slums and poverty continue, but the complaints come far less from the reform groups, more from groups at the poverty level, many of whom live in the present slums. The complaints of today resemble those of 1900 and before in one particular; the existence of the slum is blamed on the machinations of evil men or classes of men. However, the earlier protestors would have laws passed to condemn old houses and control rents, while the present demand is for national housing programs, or for liberal aid to private housing programs for the needy.

The challenge of the slums and of poverty has by now become a concern involving cities around the world, more especially in developing countries. Most new nations have pledged themselves to provide housing in their cities; this cannot, however, be more than a statement of policy for years to come, since money must first be used to develop industry. Cities in Latin America are surrounded by shanty settlements in ravines or on hills, as Rios reports for a Brazilian city.[37] In North Africa venerable old cities are crowded by people from the rural regions. Finding no place in the cities, they have created their own makeshift settlements outside. Many shacks are made of flattened oil cans and are appropriately called *bidonvilles*, French for oil-can towns. LeTourneau expressed the view:

> Sordid as they are, these miserable habitations are not worse than those
> which their occupants, once country people and now proletarians, left
> behind. Structurally, they are actually an improvement over the rural

36 C. Loring Brace, *Dangerous Classes of New York*, New York, Wynkoop and Hallenbeck, 1872, p. 151.

37 Jose Arthur Rios, "Rio de Janeiro," in William A. Robson (Ed.), *Great Cities of the World*, London, Allen and Unwin, 1957, p. 494.

dwellings in North Africa and are, moreover, marked less unhealthy, in spite of appearance than the overcrowded districts of the old medinas [in the cities].[38]

THE URBAN DECENTRALIZATION PROCESS

A slum, whether in the city or at the urban fringe, is a land area for which there is little demand by any occupant, residential or industrial. In the city it may be a residential area from which earlier occupants have moved. Its value for residential use, except for the poor, is low. The likelihood is it will be taken over for commercial or industrial use. The area is not inviting for the building of new residences. While the value of the land may be high and the prospects good, owners of the old houses elect to make no improvements. They collect what they can from low rents, while waiting for a profitable changeover to factories, offices, or some other use. This applies to most inner-city slums. Outer-city slums are likely to be on cheap, inaccessible land.

Thompson speaks of what is called the "awareness effect" of inner-city slums, "partly because the sight of slums offends the aesthetic sense of the upper classes as they commute through them between their suburban homes and their central city work places." Elsewhere he mentions how the same people are equally offended when they view areas abandoned by the poor, where the houses have fallen or have been removed, leaving wide empty spaces. The outward movement is called "sprawl," the decentralization of the city, which is displeasing to another set of critics: "They leave the city looking like an unmade bed, and rush out to mess up the countryside." Thompson mentions another group of critics, the "confirmed urbanites, impassioned and articulate, [who] may simply disapprove of suburbanites' taste patterns . . . and seek to apprise the city deserters of the error of their ways." Or they lament the taking over of miles of good farm land merely for residence.[39]

The automobile is blamed for decentralization. As more workers, formerly bound to the central city, gained higher incomes they were able to buy automobiles and so, with their own transportation, turned to the suburbs. An English professor, noting how the car has made living in the city difficult, tells how the private car affords escape also for Londoners. Thus Britain has all the problems which the auto brings, "though she is still a long way from achieving the levels of car ownership which obtain in many other countries.[40]

[38] Roger LeTourneau, "Social Change in the Muslim Cities of North Africa," *American Journal of Sociology,* Vol. 60, No. 3, March 1955, p. 530.

[39] Thompson, op. cit., pp. 126 and 321.

[40] Colin Buchanan, "Meeting the Challenge of the Car," *London Times,* September 19, 1966, p. 9.

In the rural economy out of which cities evolved, each community and each piece of private property had its borders within which it was presumed to have land enough for its needs. The interdependence of communities was not a concern. The interdependence of places today is many-sided and it enters all aspects of city-suburbs relations. Still in some industrial countries, the United States included, each community is politically independent of the rest, although in many ways dependent on the others. People and work plants that leave the city for the suburbs are politically free of the city but still dependent upon it. Many who condemn sprawl are unaware of this incongruity. Once most manufacturing jobs in the Boston area were in the city. Now seven out of ten are outside its borders. Relatively, Boston's tax income declines while demands for services increase. Other cities on the Atlantic Seaboard, New York especially, are caught in the same economic straitjacket.[41] A good share of the suburbanites are employed in the city, and every industry and commercial firm on the outside has reasons to use the streets of the city.

The results of this scattering without control are unsightly areas within cities and equally unsightly zones between suburbs, or between suburbs and cities. Mayer appears to be of the view that what seems to be a time of chaos, as the metropolitan region is viewed, is essentially a period during which a new spatial order is taking form around a dispersal of central points or nuclei. "If there is any form of structure at all, there must be nuclei, and presumably a hierarchy of nuclei, with the central business district of continuous importance as the main center of traffic generation." [42]

What actually is taking place in every metropolitan area is that the different types of occupants, industrial, commercial, and residential, tend to locate, each to its own advantage, forming an ecological distribution. But the ecological process moves slowly and never fully comes to rest. Often, even when a comparatively efficient order is reached it will not seem so to some.

When H. G. Wells saw Chicago in 1906, before the automobile had become a common sight and before decentralization began, he was offended by the grim factories and poor housing that bordered the railroad line for some thirty miles. Even then development extended far outward along the railroads.

> It was here I saw for the first time the enormous expanse and intricacy of railroads that net this great industrial desolation, and something of the going and coming of the myriads of polyglot workers. Chicago burns bi-

41 Gottmann, op. cit., pp. 438 and 496.
42 Harold M. Mayer, "Chicago, Transportation and Metropolitan Planning," *Proceedings of the Regional Planning Association*, Philadelphia, Wharton School, University of Pennsylvania, 1961, p. 246.

tuminous coal, it has the reek of outdoors London, and right and left of the line rise vast chimneys, huge blackened grain elevators, flame-crowned furnaces and gaunty and filthy factory buildings, monstrous mounds of refuse, desolate empty lots littered with rusty cans, old iron, and indescribable rubbish. Interspersed with these are groups of dirty, disreputable unsanitary-looking houses.[43]

In this bit of description, Wells made one concession—the sight of Chicago's grime reminded him of London. He failed to recognize that a great city is a giant work place and reflects the economic status of its region. Our interest in this observation by Wells concerns the outstretching arms of the industrial city along the railroad lines. It existed long before mass decentralization began, and has not changed greatly. Mass exodus is filling outside spaces between the railroad entrances, and the exodus involves many people and the many kinds of job-giving secondary industries. It is the running away from the center and filling the empty spaces outside which makes the city the abandoned back yard for residential purposes, while being the front yard for work and private money-making, making for ambiguity in the city-suburb relationship. One day, after much wasteful effort, the city and its suburbs are likely to be under unitary metropolitan control.

Apparently, until now, no city in North America, except Toronto, has established such a metropolitan control. That city and some dozen suburbs were required by order of the province of Ontario to form a metropolitan control. The suburbs retain local jurisdiction in minor matters, but all are under joint administration for traffic control, water supply, sewage, police jurisdiction, public institutions, and welfare and, more important, metropolitan finances. Other cities in Canada are being metropolitanized.

CONTINUITY OF URBAN INCONGRUITY

In this chapter we have been discussing objections to the city, some of them irrational criticisms, others quite informed. Criticism is an inevitable result of growth and change while, on the other hand, it may influence the direction and rate of growth and change. The absence of criticism in a city would imply that it was not concerned with either growth or change. But much of the criticism, especially as it relates to planning, is controversial. The planner who puts his ideas on a drawing board may favor straight lines and open areas, and wish to remove most traffic from central business areas, hoping thereby to diminish the crowds. For those of opposite view, Jacobs, for example, the central area is

43 H. G. Wells, *The Future of America*, New York, Harper, 1906, p. 59.

thought to be enjoyed by people only if the crowd is there. Nor would they wipe out all old buildings or eliminate the intimate little streets, or entirely ban the automobile. Jacobs sees the street as serving recreational as well as business needs. Her quarrel is with the planners who like their "vistas." [44]

While critics may disagree on questions of beauty and congeniality, they may be in full agreement about the pollution of air and water. But massive organization is needed to rid wide areas of such pollution, and public demand is just becoming loud enough. As we have noted, all cities are slow moving and old cities are hampered by cumbersome bureaucracies, so well rooted that they tend to be accepted. Chapman tells of the massive prefecture system by which all villages, towns, and cities in France are administered from a central organization in Paris, an establishment whose efficiency is measured by its ability to "hold the line" despite change.[45] It has been charged in fact that the prefecture system has changed very little since 1789.[46] While such deadening control comes to be accepted in countries where it has long existed, it would not be tolerated to such a degree in North American cities.

In North American cities, particularly in the United States, until recent decades, change and growth went forward with little public help and even less public control. It was assumed that the economic and social problems of the time were the normal consequences of population increase, industrial expansion, and finally the spreading out of cities. If there were slums and poverty, these have always been present in cities; they did not affect the great majority and most of those affected were able to rise to higher socio-economic levels, or their children would.

Today, after American cities have experienced a decade of deep depression, a major war and the ordeal of undeclared wars, as in Vietnam, and a never-imagined evolution in the technology of industry, the old viewpoints come under scrutiny and in many respects are found wanting. The industrial system, instead of being the cure-all in the labor market, is found to be a creator of unemployment. Nor is the slum a temporary condition for most of the poor who enter it; a good sized minority come to be identified as the permanent poor.

Instead of the government standing on the sidelines, it is being called on increasingly to give aid or assume regulatory functions. Large cities, unable to get needed administrative help from their states, must take their problems to the federal government, an unheard-of procedure before World War I. Nor has the federal government been able to avoid

---

[44] Jane Jacobs, "Downtown Is for People," in *Exploding Metropolis,* by the editors of *Fortune,* New York, Doubleday, 1958, p. 146.

[45] Brian Chapman, "Paris," in William A. Robson (Ed.), *Great Cities of the World,* London, Allen and Unwin, 1957, p. 431.

[46] Hall, op. cit., p. 81.

leadership in such major problems as meeting the needs of metropolitan government, and the elimination of air and water pollution.

The "sprawl disorder," irritating to so many in so many ways, and common to European and North American cities alike, is a cluster of problems and submits to no single solution. The shape and nature of great cities are changing. There is little to assure that planning efforts can bring the order which many hope for. What is certain is that with the increase of sprawl comes greater pressure for access to the urban center. It is known too that with population increase changes can be expected in the shape and the manner of the spread, as more people must find space for work and for living.

Finally, as in decades past, growing cities, whose way of life is ever competitive, may never come to rest. Resolving incongruities that offend merely clears the way for others as cities are confronted with more growth and more change.

The behavior of urban agglomerates | 9

COLLECTIVE COMMUNITY BEHAVIOR

When a once-small town whose population has increased asks a city charter from the state or national government, this is a collective action. Officials who represent the community, on receiving the charter, pledge the new city to accept and carry out certain municipal functions which affect the community's citizens, to provide certain services which individuals alone or groups of citizens cannot provide as well or as economically. There are many activities essential to community life in which groups or associations of citizens may engage. Groups of neighbors may join to pressure their municipal government, for example, to provide playgrounds for children. Industrialists, to carry on their activities with less frustration, may demand that certain streets be paved. Other groups of citizens may demand that neighborhood community centers be provided.

If a community has a long history, it also will have its collective events. There will be periodic ceremonies in which all classes of people participate. This too is a kind of activity for which the political authorities provide leadership, although the leaders of many groups may assume particular roles. Thus a community behaves as a center for work, but at times it turns to collective leisure and collective ceremonial behavior.

A community must continually behave collectively in matters of control; it must keep itself clean and orderly, and this calls for proper behavior by the citizens. Citizens learn to avoid creating fire and health hazards, lessons learned by children in the typical community. The authorities of a city have the responsibility to resolve conflicts, one of the oldest of community functions, and a universal one. Maintaining order is a continuing function of all organized groups, but riots and violent actions may call for the attention of the final community authority.

Thus various types of behavior assume a collective aspect and these

178

may be different for the different types of communities, from the village to the anonymous city. The larger a city becomes the more the population tends to be segmented into sub-populations. These may be identified by ethnic origin, race, social class, religion, or other, which to Hauser, marks the heterogeneity that emerges as cities increase in size. While each population type is adapted to the whole community, it tends to have its own values and behavior patterns. "The problem of intergroup relations is essentially an urban problem, or at least reaches its most critical manifestations in the urban area." [1] Seen in broad perspective, the different sub-populations, each with its sub-culture, is integrated into a single behaving agglomerate. The special behaviors of different groups tend to be expected behaviors, and predictable for each type of group.

Of course, such segmentations of people into socially contained continuing groups, each with a type of sub-culture, may also be found at times in non-urban communities. Berrman mentions five castes in a Himalayan village, the five parts in a division of labor which enables the community as a whole to function. Yet each caste remains somewhat isolated from the others.[2] Socially, the segmentation in the caste community tends to be fixed, the contacts needed for the integration of different types of work in the community carry on as the situation requires.

THE COMMUNITY AS A "PERSONALITY"

It is not uncommon in Europe to meet persons who have lived in the United States. They had worked and saved for years and then returned to their communities of origin, thinking to retire there. Meeting such a repatriate, one must expect to hear much about Cincinnati, Cleveland, New York, or some other city. Whatever the place, it stands in his memory much as a person, and he may use feminine pronouns, "she" or "her," in describing it. In this vein Henry James, long a resident in England, wrote about New York, describing that place as a fickle female, ever anxious to impress but with ever changing interests, gilding the temporary with gold. "I mean that she is serious, serious about any form whatever, or about anything but that perpetual, passionate pecuniary purpose which plays with all forms and devours them." [3] As seen by Wohl and Strauss, one can hardly regard a behaving community without in some measure visualizing it as a personal entity. One speaks of a town as "knowing" something or

1 Philip M. Hauser, "Urbanization, An Overview," in Philip M. Hauser and Leo F. Schnore (Eds.), *The Study of Urbanization*, New York, Wiley, 1966, p. 22.

2 Gerald D. Berrman, "Caste and Economy in the Himalayas," *Economic Development and Cultural Change*, Vol. 10, No. 4, July 1962, p. 387.

3 Henry James, *The American Scene*, 1907, quoted by Charles N. Glaab (Ed.), *The American City, A Documentary History*, Homewood, Illinois, Dorsey Press, 1963, p. 348.

"believing" something. It may be spoken of as "alive" or otherwise given personal qualities:

> . . . and the city may be endowed with a personality or—to use a commonplace—character of its own. Like a person, the city then acquires a biography and a reputation. Personified cities can be described with personal pronouns and, through the use of appropriate verbs, conceived of as having capacities for action and possession. And following this fashion of speaking, we may make the same allowances for, and judgments of cities that we are ordinarily inclined to make of people.[4]

Halbwachs wrote of communities behaving collectively in relation to their common memories, the latter a product of learning through shared experience. Drawing most of his illustrations from his own history-teeming Paris, he argued that without collective memory a city crowded with people would hardly be able to carry on so well. Particular memories shared by all are kept alive by the multitude of monuments, plaques on walls, place names, etc.[5]

THE CONSCIOUSNESS OF COMMUNITY

Collective memory implies collective consciousness, which means merely that many have the same ideas and feelings about certain things and tend to have uniform behavior with respect to them. The "we" of one village is a cluster of shared attitudes and memories when "those" of a neighboring village are being discussed. Describing the factions in an Indian village, Lewis mentions how the rival factions, each a kin group, enjoy relating their long list of grievances against other factions. But each faction is careful to avoid confrontation; one faction never knows when it may need the help of another. In this network of factions the rivalries, each an open secret in the village with no one ever forgetting them, do not, however, prevent the essential work of the village from getting done.[6] This kind of collective behavior, never absent in villages, serves both as a guide to social interaction and as a discipline for rule breaking.

The art of indirection, a collective behavior in small communities, is no less employed in sophisticated urban life and in high-level politics. As it serves to maintain attitudes of rivalry and to avoid open conflict, it

---

[4] R. Richard Wohl and Anselm L. Strauss, "Symbolic Representation and the Urban Milieu," *American Journal of Sociology*, Vol. 63, No. 5, March 1958, p. 528.

[5] Maurice Halbwachs, *La Mémoire collective*, Paris, Presses Universitaires de Paris, 1950.

[6] Oscar Lewis, "Aspects of Land Tenure and Economics in a North Indian Village," *Economic Development and Cultural Change*, Vol. 4, No. 3, April 1956, p. 291.

can be seen as a form of collective consciousness. One's awareness of his community and his identity with groups and fellows calls for acquiring the symbols of communication which are used by all. The Parisian behaves and thinks in ways which are unique to his community and which distinguish him, for example, from a native of the French-Canadian city, Montreal. Say Wohl and Strauss, one verbalizes the knowledge and values of his community.

> It seems safe to say that, without the resources of rhetoric the city dweller would have no verbal representation of his own or any other city. . . . To be comfortable in the city—in the widest sense of these words—requires the formation of one's relation to it, however unsystematically and crudely. Uncertainty about the character of the environment can only engender deep psychological stress.[7]

A consciousness of community is the awareness the inhabitants of a place have who belong there. Whether orally expressed or not, it is articulated in like behaviors, often like attitudes in like situations. In times of crisis it may be expressed in like collective response. To Briggs, this consciousness is the "sense of the city" which finds its outlet in the many kinds of organization developed by groups in the community. The interests and aspirations of some organizations may be in conflict with those of others. Nature lovers may be in conflict with the wild-game hunters, or the trade unions with the employers; each operates within the community and each appeals to the community for support. For Briggs, the urban man's "sense of the city" is a more cosmopolitan outlook than the rural man needs to have. The urban vantage point enables one to experience the wide and dynamic character of great aggregates of people. More than rural man, the city dweller senses the need to identify with various associated groups. A sense of the city finds expression automatically.[8]

DIVERSITY OF COMMUNITY BEHAVIOR

It would be surprising if community behavior did not vary with place, circumstances, and time. Any new condition to which the whole community must adjust is likely to bring change in collective behavior. Several illustrations of community adaptation follow. Each example presents a community behaving in relation to a particular situation. The case of Hebron shows a Mormon community confronted with the need of moving to a new location. The village in India is a tightly-knit, eco-

---

[7] Wohl and Strauss, op. cit., p. 532.
[8] Asa Briggs, *Victorian Cities,* London, Odham Press, 1963, p. 31.

logically-rooted community of factions unable to make a decision. The Newfoundland community turned from the hazards of fishing to a most dangerous type of mining but, despite dangers, the people continued to hold out. The accounts of Kingman and Chicago describe urban behavior in a period of boom.

1. *The Hebron-to-Enterprise Move*

When the Mormons began their systematic settlement of southern Utah in 1864 the object was to occupy all the land that was near any stream sufficient for irrigation. Taking possession of springs and streams in that dry region was no less important than occupying the land. Being sent to found a settlement was accepted as being called "on a mission." Families were selected and set to their locations by the Mormon authority (Church of Jesus Christ of Latter-Day Saints). Proud to be "called," they went to their locations, ten to fifty families, as many as were deemed necessary for safety and for the development task.

Hebron on Shoal Creek began with about a dozen families. After "starving it out" for several years, the Hebron families were comfortably established, living well as farmers and cattlemen. The land area was too small to provide farms for the next generation, the families of about 1890. Some of the men migrated to the mines, which caused concern because they were exposed to the company of the rough and ungodly. Some went to other Morman settlements to find land. The elderly parents were concerned both about the mining camp influence and the moving away.

Certain younger men, called "troublemakers," developed the idea that the Shoal Creek waters could be joined with another stream entering the canyon lower down. The two streams could be led to a wide flatland six miles below Hebron; this land was a "desert," but with the irrigating streams would become fertile and could provide farms for all. They also proposed building a dam to store these waters during the winter months. The scheme would make several times more land area available than at Hebron.

The older folks who were in authority answered that they had been called by the church to settle Hebron and to hold the place, and the call of the authorities was still binding. The younger men talked "progress;" they would have to abandon Hebron and live for a time in shacks in the desert, but in ten years they would be better off than in Hebron where all were sinking into poverty. The new community could not start without taking the irrigation water from Hebron.

The pro-movers appealed to the regional church leaders. The committee sent to "advise with the brethren" agreed that it would be wise to move. This did not satisfy the old folks and they appealed to the High Authority in Salt Lake. A member of the Inner Council came, blessed the people, released them from the 1864 call, and advised them to move. Families began moving about 1900.

Hebron had a population of less than 200 people. Enterprise, the new location, now has a population of about 2,000. While the anti-movers accepted the advice of the High Authority, the wounds opened by the move did not heal for years.[9]

2. Resettling an Indian Village

This case concerns Mallur, some 200 families or about 1,400 persons in the Mysore State of India.[10] Year after year since time out of memory the stream passing Mallur has risen to a flood and at times the village was inundated. After each such battle with high water there had been talk of relocating the village to higher ground nearby. But each year, the flood being over, the idea of moving was forgotten until the next monsoon. However, in 1948, Mallur experienced the worst flood anyone could recall. This time even the homes of the high castes were under water and there was the danger of an epidemic.

A public meeting was held and a large majority favored resettling. India now had its own government, which may have been a factor in the decision. An appeal was sent to the district administration asking that 64 acres of land be made available for the new village. In due course the land was made available to the village collectively. This was perhaps the first major decision made by the village in generations. The prospect and the experience must have been frightening to some who changed their minds about moving. Some may have been discouraged by the month after month debates in public meetings about the order of moving and the dozens of details.

It was decided that the layout of the new village, although being less crowded, would be exactly as that of the old, the same distribution of castes by streets and the same neighbors on each street. The lot of leading the meetings fell to the untiring local Congressman, most of his time being used to resolve disputes. Moving did not begin until 1950, two years after the flood. Of the 200 households, only 87 moved, including only one of the 16 untouchable households.

Those remaining in the old village not only found that they had the advantage of more room, but they began to feel that they were virtuous because they had not abandoned their ancestral home. However, the two villages, a short walk apart, were linked by various kinship ties. Most of

---

[9] Nels Anderson, *Desert Saints, The Mormon Frontier in Utah* (1942), Chicago, University of Chicago Press, 1966, pp. 383–386. Also, *Utah, A Guide to the State*, New York, Hastings House, 1945, p. 304.

[10] Summarized from an unpublished manuscript, K. Ishwaran, "Mallur, Internal Dynamics of Change in a Mysore Village," Toronto, York University.

the work ways and home routines carried over to the new village. But there were differences; something like a class consciousness was creeping in.

> The inhabitants of the new village have developed to a considerable extent the urban attitudes of independence and aloofness. We found evidence both of the existence of such attitudes and of dissatisfaction with such attitudes. One of our informants told us that the people in the new village did not care for each other as they used to in the old village. . . . In one case, an elderly lady in the new village had died at the time when her husband and son were away from home, and the ritual ceremony necessary for the occasion did not start for hours after the death because no neighbors turned up to help. The news of her death spread to the old village and it was from there that extended kinsmen came to help the bereaved family. . . .
>
> A more dramatic case contrasting the attitude of people in both villages was reported. A cattle shed in the new village had caught fire, and one could see from a distance the children fleeing from the scene. The flames were also visible from the old village. The people from the old village rushed to the spot, but none from the new village had bothered to come out. Before the people from the old village could reach the spot, the cattle had been burned to death.

Old villagers speak of those in the new village as "city" people, or as living for themselves. Despite the fact that the two villages are politically a single jurisdiction, there is rivalry between the new part on high land and the old part on low land. The new part has been more active in making and pressing proposals. It called for a new community building which has been completed and is located in the new village. But the temple remains in the old village, which stimulated the new village to have a temple of its own.

The rivalry, which in the old village was between family groups, is now caused by inter-village issues. The new village is seen as snobbish and dangerously modern, while those in the new village call the old villagers backward. Outwardly, the two parts get on well, but each within its area is on guard against the other.

3. *A Fatefully Benumbed Community*

A trend that seems fashionable in studies of depressed communities or areas, or of slum communities at the fringes of cities, is to speak of the people as lethargic, as inert, as lacking in (Durkheim's term) collective consciousness. Still others describe such people as alienated. The situation may be one of enduring stability at the poverty level, contrasted to continuing change in surrounding areas, the people accepting and even defending their insularity. Ford, describing the attitudes of isolated Appalachian people, speaks of their "retreat into fatalism and sectarian religion." They have adjusted psychologically to an environment that does not stimulate venturing.[11] This describes most fishing communities of Newfoundland, even St. Johns, the main city on that island, where the opening of a new store is seen as a mark of progress.

It is said that people adapt to conditions of continuing depression by adopting attitudes of fatalism and that these attitudes in turn cause them to fear the risks that change might bring. This may be illustrated in the case of St. Lawrence, a Newfoundland fishing village which in 1923 was destroyed completely by a tidal wave. The fishing people escaped the high water but, instead of leaving the place where they had lived for decades in poverty (by outside standards), they began rebuilding, most of them supported by meager relief funds for the next several years.

In 1932 an expert in such matters found the area to be rich in flourspar, a material used in making steel and aluminum. The mining company that was formed developed slowly, and a number of the fishermen turned from fishing to mining, earning 15 cents per hour. Not always able to raise funds, the company paid the workers with notes which circulated as cash until later redeemed. The company was forced to close in 1958. Since 1960 the Aluminum Company of Canada (Alcan) has been the sole operator in the area. The work force has increased to 240, and the old village has grown to about 2,000.

Flourspar mining is hazardous, particularly because of the radioactivity in the mines. Moreso earlier than at present, there was a lack of proper ventilation. Ian Adams, whose article is summarized here, reports that in the past two decades more than a hundred miners have died, most of them from cancer. At the time of the writing, he notes that seventeen others were grievously ill. The failure of the Newfoundland government to take action, except to appoint committees, is a long story, now on the way to becoming a scandal.

Wages are higher now, about $2.00 per hour, but the hazard has not been removed. Every adult in the community knows the risks of flourspar mining, and many of the miners appear to accept the prospect that they may be victims of cancer. The risk is greater by several times than that in fishing. But the depressed people in St. Lawrence do not move away, they do not seem capable of imagining themselves finding some other kind of work elsewhere in Canada.[12]

[11] Thomas R. Ford, "The Passing of Provincialism," in Thomas R. Ford (Ed.), *The Southern Appalachian Region,* Lexington, University of Kentucky Press, 1962, p. 30.
[12] Ian Adams, "The Forgotten Miners," *McLean's,* June 1967.

4. *Communities That Accept Change*

Redfield relates the case of a village in Central America which displayed a collective attitude quite opposite to that found in other villages of the region. For different reasons, which he considered, this village has acquired a respect for change and innovation which is unusual for that part of the world.[13] The new communities on the North American frontier were noted for this kind of an outlook. There are many stories of towns that were established before the arrival of the railroad. If bypassed by the railroad, they moved their structures to the railroad and began anew. Kingman, Kansas, was such an ambitious settlement, and it exemplifies a move for another reason.

Kingman began in 1872 on the north bank of the Ninnescha River. In 1878 another town calling itself Kingman began on the south bank. Each town had its stores, hotel, post office, and newspaper. Each worked furiously to outgrow the other. In 1880 the county had to select a town to be the county seat. Neither of the Kingmans alone had enough population to compete with other places in the county. Those on the north side offered free land for houses and business sites, and those on the south side floated their buildings across the stream. In this way, a united Kingman managed to become official headquarters for the county.[14]

Chicago stands out as a striking example of a city in which change and the pursuit of change assumed the character of a cult. From an isolated village in 1834, it grew to a city of about two million in 1900. Actually in 1850 it was a relatively unknown town. By 1860, the railroad having arrived, Chicago had 60 miles of streets paved with cedar blocks and boasted 60,000 buildings and a network of horsecars. It had become the main outfitting center for wagon trains moving west. It became and remained the principal labor market for that army of migratory workers needed in frontier development. With money in their pockets, they returned to Chicago to "blow it," for which reason that city came to be known among the genteel as a "Hellhole of Sin," or "Babylon of the West." [15] By 1870 Chicago had the most luxurious hotel in the West, the Palmer House, but it was still a city of wood with thousands of shack dwellings. A good share of these were swept away in 1871 by fire, but in two decades Chicago was built anew, bigger than ever, this time of stone and brick.

Charles Francis Adams of the Adams lineage in Boston visited the

13 Robert Redfield, *A Village That Chose Progress,* Chicago, University of Chicago Press, 1930.
14 *Kansas, Guide to the Sunflower State,* New York, Hastings House, 1937, p. 79.
15 Allan Nevins, *The Emergence of Modern America, 1865–1878,* New York, Macmillan, 1927, p. 79.

city in 1867. He was thrilled with the rush of life, the gigantic undertakings, the whole city alive, with no past to guide it and a wide-open future. All that he saw and heard was in contrast to his own placid Boston, the city that started the American Revolution and then lapsed into stolidity, preoccupied with honoring its own past. Boston had lost "much of her influence and all of her prestige." [16] Chicago started with an empty purse but in two decades had outstripped St. Louis, as New York had already outstripped Boston, favored by geographical situation.

But this upstart city, which dared to stage a world exposition in 1890, was no pet of the intellectuals and reformers. During the "World's Fair" Chicago authorities assured all visitors that the city was free and open. William T. Stead, an English editor, after his visit wrote his book, *If Christ Should Come to Chicago.* Several years later Rudyard Kipling arrived but to him Chicago was offensive, a barbarian inferno, with everyone working like mad trying to get rich, people running with telegrams, streets clogged with horse-drawn traffic, even the newsboys asking him, "How do you like our city?"

> A cab driver volunteered to show me the glory of the town for so much an hour, and with him I wandered far. He conceived that all this turmoil and squash was a thing to be reverently admired; that it was good to huddle men together in fifteen layers one atop of the other, and to dig holes in the ground for offices. He said that Chicago was a live town, and that all the creatures hurrying by me were engaged in business. That is to say they were trying to make some money. . . . He took me to canals, black as ink, and filled with untold abominations, and made me watch the stream of traffic across the bridges. He took me into a saloon, and while I drank, made me note that the floor was covered with coins sunk into cement. A Hottentot would not have been guilty of this sort of barbarism.[17]

This popular English writer was preparing a book to sell to Americans; most of them who lived far east of Chicago would be delighted with his account of that burgeoning city where few had time to read books. They would chuckle over his description of the Palmer House, that pile of marble with brass spitoons all about to serve tobacco-chewing guests sitting in plush chairs and talking big talk. Years later Carl Sandberg drew a different picture in his poem "Chicago." He saw that city as a brawny, daring youth who scorned effete cities. To Sandberg, Chicago was a "stacker of wheat," "builder of railroads," and "hog butcher to the world."

[16] Charles Francis Adams, Jr., "Boston," *North American Review*, January 1868, quoted in Glaab, op. cit., p. 191.
[17] Rudyard Kipling, *From Sea to Sea*, 1899, quoted in *ibid.*, p. 338.

THE PRIDE THAT COMMUNITIES SHOW

It would be unusual to find a town or city, even though its history has been brief and uneventful, which does not have a museum. If no more than in a corner of the town hall, there will be displayed the various proud possessions of the community, reminders of experiences lived through and crises overcome; or there will be some monument to the memory of the great names associated with the place. What is evident here has been called by various names: "city consciousness," "collective memory," or "community awareness." In a community living bonds of pride develop between the rich and the poor, the old families and the new, the native sons and the immigrants. They point with pride to what visitors must see, especially some new public building and, of course, a skyscraper, if there is one. Gottmann tells us that even Russian cities have their skyscrapers; and:

> It was the Russian authorities who directed the erection in the middle of Warsaw of the Palace of Culture which dominates the Polish Capital. In 1962 officials in charge of housing-program planning in Sweden told the writer how annoyed they were that small towns in Sweden, with 10,000 to 20,000 inhabitants only, each wanted a high tower. They were asking for a skyscraper, whether for apartments or any other use, but they needed it as a matter of self-respect.[18]

Some manifestations of community pride can be seen as behavior which is economically motivated, as when merchants in Jonesville do something to attract trade that might otherwise go to Smithville, a competing city twenty miles away. The institution of carnival, found in old cities around the world, in many instances, was initiated by medieval merchants to bring floods of customers to town. But in most of these same cities carnival has become an annual folk festival for parades, for dressing in costumes, and for two days or so of foolishness until all pockets are empty. These affairs are still good for business, but are not solely for that. Big festivals are a source of pride to a town, much as a native son or daughter who wins a gold medal at the Olympic games.

Wohl calls attention to a unique American expression of community pride, the tendency of an urban place to call itself a "city of homes and gardens;" or of cities to identify themselves with such rural virtues as neighborliness or "old-fashioned hospitality." He mentions that much of the glorification of rural life, as Thanksgiving festivals, picturing the

[18] Jean Gottmann, "The Skyscraper Amid the Sprawl," in Jean Gottmann and Herbert A. Harper (Eds.), *Metropolis On the Move,* New York, Wiley, 1967, p. 130.

harvest, farm scenes of the past, etc., is done by urban artists and writers for the entertainment of urbanites.[19]

Pride in one's town cuts across all human classifications, from the beggar to the club woman, from the janitor to the manager. These attitudes of pride can be shared by racial groups, ethnic groups, and all classes alike. Most big cities have their songs which are sung by all, whether *London Pride*, Berlin's *Unter den Linden*, or *Sidewalks of New York*. Brogan speaks of the aloof pride of the Londoner who:

> . . . may be mildly gratified on being complimented on the excellence of his subway system, but he would not be more than mildly irritated if he had to admit it was no better than New York's. He tolerates the chaos of the South London waterfront and the snail-like progress of the high-speed roads on the outskirts. He likes, but takes for granted, the comparative abundance of parks and squares, but in those parts of London which are least well off in this respect, local pride is just as deep and complacent.[20]

Urbanites are wont to speak with pride about the high points in their city's history; how the people rallied to combat a flood, how the city rebuilt after a great fire, how the railroad came and bypassed another town, and how that town "never grew after that." For ancient cities these events are elevated to the level of myth as, for example, the story of Romulus and Remus, the infants reared by a she-wolf, who became the founders of Rome. Stewart relates the story of how Herford, England, in 1189 bought its freedom from the king, and thereafter the first loyalty of the burgher was to his own little city. If he did voluntary work digging a ditch for his town it was as if he were working for himself. It was more important than giving free labor to the "Lord Bishop's dimence." [21] In this way, many events that affect communities as collective entries are honored annually, may inspire songs or pageants, or even cause the erection of monuments in their honor.

Long before tourism was born, if a city created a monument in honor of some local event or hero it was placed, as today, at some central point. Here it would be most accessible for the local people and most visible for visitors. It is in the midtown area where local ceremonials are staged, and here will be the most imposing public buildings. Whatever image the city has of itself will be articulated at its center. Perry tells of the hearty atmosphere exuded by the urban center of Fort Worth, Texas, cattle market and fun city for ranchers over a wide region, a town that declares

[19] R. Richard Wohl, "Urbanism, Urbanity, and the Historian," *University of Kansas City Review*, October 1955, quoted by Charles N. Glaag (Ed.), *The American City, A Documentary History*, Homewood, Illinois, Dorsey Press, 1963, p. 10.

[20] D. W. Brogan, *The English People*, New York, Knopf, 1949, p. 289.

[21] Cecil Stewart, *A Prospect for Cities*, London, Longmans, Green, 1952, p. 69.

itself in "big-hearted, loud-mouthed" terms. Fort Worth puts in full view whatever it wishes the out-of-town visitor to see.

> And the sturdy western folk with rawhide hands and high-heeled boots rub off in a town where they bank, buy and frolic. Fort Worth probably comes nearer expressing what the word "Texas" signifies to most outsiders than any city in the state. In its efforts to make a hit with the outside world, its problem is simple; it has simply to be itself, exuberant and whooping and friendly, since nearly everyone loves a western story.[22]

A world metropolis passes beyond the need of attracting visitors and striving to impress strangers, but it does not pass beyond living up to the proud image it holds of itself. Any stranger entering such a city will find spread before him whatever is on display for anyone to see. He will also see at its best whatever most interests him. In passing, he may look at the Eiffel Tower in Paris or the Nelson Monument in London, but if he is interested in fashions he can find the concentration of stores and indulge himself, or the night-club quarter where he can revel. In any case, whatever the stranger looks for in the great metropolis he will find at the urban center, and rarely does he see any other part of the city.[23]

Mumford sees a connection between "urbanism and monumentality," art once used to symbolize the greatness of the king. When the king moved from the urban scene, art was used to symbolize the city itself. Power has ever been resident in the city, at one time in the hands of the king, now in the hands of other authorities, secular and sacred. Whatever now is put on display there, in monuments, civic structures, private edifices, shops, tells what the place is like, how it makes its living; it tells of its evolution and may even reveal its hopes and aspirations. Proud behavior, moreover, is most artfully evident at the urban center, or most ingeniously concealed from all but the specialist or trained observer. Otherwise a city, Mumford suggests, would be to us "only a heap of baked mud and stones, formless, purposeless, meaningless; since without such cosmic representations, the common man could live an equally good or better life in a village." [24]

ON BELONGING TO THE URBAN COMMUNITY

Ferdinand Toennies was disturbed by the growth of great industrial cities in Germany. He saw a new way of life developing in the cities, and

---

[22] George Sessions Perry, *Cities in America,* New York, McGraw-Hill, 1947, p. 88.

[23] New York, in this connection, has become the great book and periodical publication center of the world, and a whole population revolves around it. It is the Mecca of artists, writers, and idea people. Says John A. Kouwenhoven: "New York is not an idea factory, nor an idea mine, nor an idea garden, but it is the world's point of highest velocity in idea exchanging." (*The Guide Book of New York,* New York, Dell, 1964, pp. 9–10.)

[24] Lewis Mumford, *The City in History, Its Origins, Its Transformations, and Its Prospects,* New York, Harcourt, Brace & World, 1961, p. 65.

he called it the *Gesellschaft* (society) type. City people, according to their special interests, joined organizations and informal groups. They lived as individuals in the crowd, each for himself, and family life was not dominant as in rural places, where he identified the way of life as *Gemeinschaft* (community). One belonged naturally to the rural community, identified with his kin, and his kin gave him standing in the community. A *Gemeinschaft* community offered the fullness of life, while one's life was fragmented in the urban *Gesellschaft* community.[25]

Although anti-urban in his thinking, Toennies was correct; one belongs in a different sense to the urban community. One does not, cannot, and need not identify himself with the whole community, yet he can live a full life in the city. Many since Toennies have made the same complaint about the city. Baker Brownell as late as 1950 complained that men remove themselves from nature "for a price." In the city they gyrate in a "fictitious solidarity of more or less massive groups." He would have all urbanites escape the city to live in small communities.[26]

Should modern society accept the notion that *Gesellschaft* is evil, the fact would still have to be faced that the world population is increasing, and there appears to be no place for the surplus except in the cities. It would be a considerable task to stop cities from growing. As they grow they must become more industrial. Despite the view of many that more and more people should be coaxed into *Gemeinschaft* type communities, it is not an idea that seems tempting. Increasingly people are escaping such communities.

The urbanite does not need to know his neighbors; if he has his circle of friends and acquaintances and if his work relations are satisfactory he can feel at home in the city. Nor does he need to know the mass of humans in the crowd. He can belong to the city and can identify himself psychologically and emotionally with it. If the team from his city wins at baseball or football, he shouts with the crowd, and vicariously he behaves as if part owner of "our team." He takes the side of his city in any contest the municipal authority has with state authority. He will be able to give an array of reasons why he would rather live in his city than in certain other cities that might be named. If his city has more advanced means of transportation or more modern office buildings than other cities, it gives him a feeling of satisfaction. In other words, merely residing in a place, in various ways, engenders loyalties. Depending on one's occupation, one may feel he belongs to the city. Thus the French professor, although his university may be 200 miles distant in a *province*, tries if he can to reside in Paris.

[25] Ferdinand Toennies, *Community and Society, Gemeinschaft and Gesellschaft,* (1887), translated by C. P. Loomis, East Lansing, Michigan, Michigan State University Press, 1956.

[26] Baker Brownell, *The Human Community*, New York, Harper & Row, 1950, pp. 6 and 20.

Perhaps because the city is man's own creation and because man is ever trying to improve upon it, he is attracted to cities and awed by them. Mumford mentions how the soldier and the engineer joined forces to make Rome the city that awed the world. He might also have mentioned the mechanic and the architect. "Rome attempted, not merely to cope with large quantities of people it had brought together, but to give its otherwise degraded mass culture an appropriate urgent guise reflecting imperial magnificence." [27]

In the rural community one shares the common life (whether willingly or not) as he participates in community-wide activity. One cannot do this in the city, but is more free to engage in activities of his own choosing. The urbanite fraternizes with those he chooses to know and the longer he remains in the urban community the more he becomes involved in his network of friends and acquaintances, kin not excluded. This idea was advanced two generations ago by George Simmel, except that he spoke of the circle of acquaintances.[28] Simmel recognized that the urban man may have one circle of friends in relation to work interests and other circles in relation to other interests, and the contacts in one circle may also be contacts in other circles. What is pertinent in the present connection is that one comes to feel that he belongs in a place where his friends and his family are. In such intimate terms he identifies himself with a place.

There are other aspects of the idea of belonging. Americans tend to think of the size of a city as important. A New Yorker is likely to feel himself disadvantaged if for occupational reasons he is asked to move to a smaller city such as Chicago or San Francisco. But this attitude, which emphasizes size of place, is reinforced by the conviction that a city smaller than one's own is likely to be a backward place. This viewpoint may be justified, if one is asked to move from a city with a population of a million or more to one with a hundred thousand where "small-town" traditions still hold firm. The big-city person has a type of sophistication, or, says Wilson, it might he called callousness. "Some call it evil." [29]

The attachment of the urban person to his city may be seen as a personality aspect evidenced by the development of attitudes which make him dependent on the urban milieu. He lives in the center of change and he acquires a degree of familiarity with the forces that make for change. Perhaps he identifies himself with certain of these forces, if only vicariously. In these terms he identifies himself with the scene itself, the urban

27 Mumford, op. cit., p. 214.

28 George Simmel (two essays), *Conflict,* translated by Kurt H. Wolff, and *Web of Group Affiliations,* translated by Reinhard Bendix, New York, Free Press, 1955, p. 163. Bendix mentions that he translated Simmel's "circle" as "group," which may not be what Simmel had in mind, that is, a scattered assortment of friends, not socially structured as we think of a group.

29 Everett K. Wilson, "Some Notes on the Pains and Prospects of American Cities," *Confluence,* Vol. 7, No. 1, Spring 1958, p. 4.

agglomerate that he knows. As mentioned before, he is proud of the super-latives boasted by his city. All this in one way or other contributes to a sense of belonging which he can claim, although may never articulate.

COLLECTIVE BEHAVIOR IN CRISES

Much as people or families do, communities have their critical ex-periences, and these are remembered. When the Russian army in 1947 blockaded West Berlin, there was terror in that city, but no panic. The water supply was short and most of the electric power from the Com-munist side of Berlin was cut off. The people readily accepted the emer-gency rationing of water, electric power, and food. American and British planes carried out the famous "Air lift," through which planes loaded with supplies arrived at a rate of every 150 seconds for week after week. Such a total blockade was never repeated, and the grateful people of West Berlin erected an imposing monument to the airmen.

Since the 1300's Torre Pellice, at the head of the Po River, in the mountainous western part of the Piedmont province of Italy, has been the home of an early Protestant group, the Waldenses. The movement started in France in the late 1100's and in time it joined with other small religious reform groups from Italy. For well over a century, even before the group had a name, a theology, or a common language these people survived in the rugged Cottian Alps which border France and Italy. Depending on whether they were hunted by the French or the Piedmont authorities, they crossed from one side of the mountain range to the other. In the long run they enjoyed longer periods of security on the Italian side. In 1386, after decades of quiet, their villages were raided in midwinter. Many were killed or perished in the cold and their property was stolen or destroyed. Over the next three centuries they experienced a number of such raids. In time they armed themselves and learned to defend them-selves in "the fastnesses of their mountains." Occasionally one of them would be caught to be burned at the stake for religious heresy. From the 1500's on the Waldenses were befriended by Protestants in Switzerland or by the non-Catholic governments. By the year 1600 they had become a French-speaking people with their own Bible in French.

During four centuries of unremitting religious antagonism and con-tinuous alert against raids, they came to make Torre Pellice, at the en-trance to the mountains, their control center. However, not until 1655 were they officially permitted to live there and not until 1848 were they permitted to have a church in Torre Pellice. Indeed for more than four centuries they were not permitted to have a cemetery for their dead. They buried their dead at night in unmarked graves. The Waldenses today are found in most of the Western countries, but wherever they are they regard Torre Pellice as their shrine city to which many come in their old age to retire. In this place they have their private monuments, museum, and library in which their story is kept alive.[30]

While they see themselves as Italians, the Waldenses are still a French-speaking people. For the lack of tillable land in their embattled region, they could not become farmers but engaged in various types of industry. Early in the last century they turned vigorously to education and were a generation ahead of their Catholic neighbors in building schools. They saw education as a resource. Even today in Torre Pellice the level of education of the Waldenses is four to five years ahead of their Catholic neighbors. Their young people enter the labor market, most of them, at the white-collar or professional level. The three terms most used, as Massucco-Costa found in her study of the Waldenses, by Catholics in describing Waldenses were "educated," "clean," and "hardworking," but on the matter of religion they used terms like "serious" or "intolerant."

Fritz, whose special interest has been the study of disasters, defines the term as "a basic disruption of the social context within which individuals and groups function, or a radical departure from the patterns of normal expectations." For the Waldenses through centuries crisis was a continuous experience, but there were the occasional assaults against them. Disaster in the sense of Fritz is the unexpected disruption which may be experienced by any people. It might be fire, flood, tornado, earthquake, or other. He notes that people may at first be thrown into panic and random fright behavior, only to recover and turn to remedial behavior, that is, helping others and in various ways coping with the situation, being ready to join organized efforts, accepting leadership, and working without stint or expectation of reward. While some may go about pillaging or robbing, the more common behavior is remedial; and this has been true throughout the history of the Waldenses' community.[31]

An outstanding example of behavior in the face of disaster is seen in the case of Galveston, Texas, which was destroyed by a tidal wave in 1900, with the loss of about 5,000 lives. This city which occupied a low-lying island was all but obliterated. Thanks to local leadership, Galveston was able to regroup and to brush aside the usual factionalism of the community. Even the old-fashioned alderman-type of government, when found to be unworkable, was abandoned and commissioners were named to assume responsibility for the different phases of the salvaging and rebuilding work. This form of municipal government, created to meet

30 Angiola Massucco-Costa, "Torre Pellice and Its People," in Nels Anderson (Ed.), *Studies in Multilingualism*, Leiden, Netherlands, E. J. Brill, 1969, Chap. 5.
31 Charles E. Fritz, "Disaster," in Robert E. Merton and Robert A. Nisbet (Eds.), *Contemporary Social Problems*, New York, Harcourt, Brace & World, 1961, pp. 651–696.

urgent needs in a crisis and intended for the emergency only, was continued in Galveston and has since been adopted by many other cities. The people of Galveston did not move to the mainland. Rather they raised the level of their island about eight feet and then surrounded the island with a sea wall well above high-water level.[32]

Almost every country has its examples of cities that were destroyed by natural or other disasters, and each case has its story of heroic collective action to rescue, salvage, and then rebuild.

Mass unemployment and depressions are also crisis situations but they rarely lead to heroic collective behavior, perhaps because only sections of the community are affected—the poor and those who are economically the least secure. The least affected and more affluent elements withdraw from most of their usual initiating activities. The unemployed may engage in protest marches and violent demonstrations. A depression divides the community into opposing factions, the "haves" against the "have-nots." If unemployment endures for years the community assumes a shabby appearance, the tempo of life slows down, while the attitudes at all levels, as Dean found in Minersville, evidence fatalism and cynicism.[33] Weiss and Riesman suggest that men caught by unemployment begin looking for work with a feeling of optimism, following all the obvious channels. Slowly, as one effort after another fails, they become pessimistic. The husband stops looking for work and sits dejected at home. Perhaps the wife tries to find employment, but often her efforts fail. The family then withdraws from most of its social contacts in the neighborhood.[34]

In Canada, as in the United States, since the 1950's many railroad division points have been discontinued because now diesel motors can pull longer trains greater distances than could the old steam locomotive. McAdam in the New Brunswick province of Canada (a few miles from the U.S. border) was such a railroad service point where more than a hundred jobs were eliminated by "dieselization." This was the major part of the labor force in this place. Some workers were pensioned ahead of retirement age. A few migrated and found employment elsewhere. But the majority, a stubborn and believing core, remains, some convinced that the ways of the railroad will change and that there will again be plenty of work in McAdam. With occasional odd jobs, this hard core, most of them home owners, have been able to hold fast now for two decades. Some are already too old to attempt migration. In the meanwhile they have not been adding to their pension credits. Their homes have lost value; even the best-maintained homes would have to beg for buyers. This hard-core

32 *Texas, A Guide to the Lone Star State*, New York, Hastings House, 1940, p. 227.
33 Lois R. Dean, *Five Towns*, New York, Random House, 1967, pp. 48–63.
34 Robert S. Weiss and David Riesman, "Social Problems and Disorganization in the World of Work," in Merton and Nisbet, op. cit., p. 508; see also Robert C. Angell, *The Family Encounters the Depression*, New York, Scribner, 1936.

group has just about lost interest in the future, except that they still believe that one day "the railroad will need McAdam again." [35]

An earlier study of the consequences of dieselization was made by Cottrell in Caliente, Nevada, which is located in a sun-parched canyon where no town is needed (which is somewhat true of McAdam) except to serve the railroad. The homes owned by the workers are a total loss. Most of the Caliente workers could, however, be absorbed by the railroad elsewhere, mainly in Las Vegas, Nevada.[36]

COLLECTIVE BEHAVIOR AND THE RIVAL TOWN

Gangrade reports an experience in a rural Indian village where he took the initiative in trying to persuade the community to build a school. He was aware that the community had the usual village factions and in this village it had long been recognized that a school was needed, indeed some years earlier land had been set aside for that purpose, but no one would initiate the action to get the work started. Gangrade managed to get the leaders of the lineal factions together and all agreed to join hands in getting the project under way, but none would volunteer to do the essential tasks, fearing to be accused of self-advancement by the others. After various stops and starts, the construction did get started. Gangrade had to leave for some days. He returned to find that work on the school had stopped, but no one would tell him the reason. After patient inquiry he learned that one of the committee in charge had been accused of buying materials at one cost and charging them at a higher cost. He persuaded the faction leaders to attend a meeting which became bitter and noisy. Accusations were met by counter accusations, grudges of long standing unrelated to the school issue came into dispute. Finally the religious leader stood up and said in essence that now that each had said his worst they had to think about what the neighboring village would say, how they would laugh if they learned what had been said. "They will say that we act like children," and he bound all to secrecy. Thereafter agreement was reached to start the job and finish the school. There were other quarrels and in the end outside authority took the lead in completing the school. But the village as an in-group was careful not to let the neighboring village know of their quarrels.[37]

35 A study of McAdam was made by Alick R. Andrews, *Social Crisis and Labour Mobility*, M.A. Thesis, Fredericton, University of New Brunswick, 1967.

36 W. F. Cottrell, "Death by Dieselization, A Case Study in the Reaction to Technological Change," *American Sociological Review*, Vol. 16, No. 3, June 1951, pp. 358–365.

37 K. D. Gangrade, "An Incomplete School, A Case Record of Rural Community Organization," *International Review of Community Development*, Nos. 13 14, 1965, pp. 95–118.

That the behavior in one community may often be determined by the presence of a nearby rival community is well known. A good example is found in a book on Nouville, France, by Berdot and Blanchard. Coutrain, the rival town, is younger than Nouville. Its site in a forest area was once used as a hunting lodge by the aristocracy. Both places are rural and both engage in the making of things of glass. The inhabitants of Nouville see themselves in many respects as superior to "those of Coutrain," which to them is a small isolated place. In Coutrain "those of Nouville" are regarded as snobbish and untrustworthy. If one from Nouville marries one from Coutrain, heads will shake and tongues will wag in both places.[38]

Such inter-community rivalry does not diminish as villages or cities grow in size, it merely finds other forms of expression. At this writing a sharp competition is under way between Saint John, New Brunswick, and Halifax, Nova Scotia, both equally good ocean ports, for the winter shipping between the sea and central Canada. In the summer the ocean-going vessels can reach Montreal, Toronto, and beyond by the St. Lawrence River and the Seaway. The rivalry is carried on by the public officials of the two port cities as they vie in making "deals" with shipping companies or gaining concessions from the federal government. But the people at all levels in the two port cities are keenly aware of the opinion each has of the other.

Briggs relates the long-standing rivalry between two English cities, Bradford and Leeds, and how it was displayed in 1858 when Leeds dedicated a new city hall. Previously Bradford had erected some public edifice which surpassed one in Leeds. The opening of the city hall of Leeds was a great event for that city. Queen Victoria accepted an invitation to be present, and police were borrowed from various cities, except Bradford, to control the crowds. The speech by Leeds' mayor addressed to the Queen was a shot at Bradford over her shoulder.

> We venture to hope that so excellent a judge of art as Your Majesty may find something to approve in the Hall in which we are now for the first time assembled, and may be well pleased to see the stirring and thriving seat of English industry embellished by such an edifice not inferior to those stately piles which still attest to the ancient opulence of the great commercial cities of Italy and Flanders.[39]

Between 1860 and 1900 there was sharp rivalry between St. Louis and the younger city, Chicago, for control of the Western markets. St. Louis waned, partly because of the growth of Kansas City, but mainly because of the rapid rise of Chicago as a railroad and industrial center.

---

[38] Lucian Berdot and René Blanchard, *Nouville, un village français,* Paris, Institut d'Ethnologie, 1953, pp. 260–262.

[39] Briggs, op. cit., p. 174.

Strauss cites documents which show that in 1848 Chicago was quite willing to recognize the ascendancy of St. Louis. But the tables turned five
years later when the citizens of Chicago began to see their city as the key
terminal for railroads from the East and the South, and the chief terminal
for lines to the West and Northwest. Favored by geographical situation,
Chicago's promoters could read their future in terms of thousands of new
settlements and millions of settlers.

> Men were, in addition, saying something new about the relation of cities
> to the entire western country. The St. Louis optimist believed that his
> city lay in a position to dominate the entire region of the West and
> Southwest; he thought this even if he was willing to believe that Chicago
> would dominate the region to the Northwest. In short, the cities were
> carving out commercial and social empires. It was partly a question which
> would be the richest empire, and partly who was to win that specific ter-
> rain from other cities.[40]

It often happens that the inhabitants of a town will hold a nearby
neighboring community in low esteem, and yet may have a more favorable opinion of another community which is more distant. Towns of
equal size may be located on opposite sides of a river. They agree in time
to share the cost of a bridge over the river. Once the bridge is in use, the
rivalry which previously had been somewhat friendly begins to intensify.
As both places grow, one will grow faster, and people from the other bank
will begin crossing the bridge to do their main shopping in the faster
growing place. A family doctor may locate in the lesser of the two places,
but a specialist would locate in the faster growing place. If a newspaper
starts it will be issued from the larger of the two places. Each community
will have its downtown area but the livelier downtown will be in the
faster growing community. If a factory comes to the area it will doubtless
elect to locate on the side of the river where the lesser community is because land can be purchased cheaper there, thus the lesser of the two
towns will become more associated with workingmen. Some better-to-do
families may decide to sell their homes and build better homes in the
more affluent town over the river, thus increasing its affluence.

This is the story of many closely situated places, although not always
separated by rivers, as in the case of St. Louis and East St. Louis, or Philadelphia and Camden. For the two there can be only one principal central
downtown area. The lesser city becomes economically identified with the
larger one but it cannot compete for prestige. Schmid tells of the rivalry
between St. Paul and Minneapolis, side by side from the start. In 1865
the population of St. Paul was 12,976 and that of Minneapolis was 4,607.

---

[40] Anselm L. Strauss, *Images of the American City*, New York, Free Press, 1961,
p. 156.

St. Paul, then the largest city in Minnesota, was selected to be the state capital. Minneapolis began to gain at a faster rate and by 1880 passed St. Paul for size (46,997 to 41,495). Rivalry was bitter. Each city had to have its own minor league baseball team.[41] In 1960 the population of Minneapolis was 482,872 while that of St. Paul, 313,411; but the rivalry goes on, although many have ceased to be aware of it. Many who live in St. Paul work in Minneapolis while many in Minneapolis have their jobs in St. Paul.

Such inter-community rivalry, like a family feud, may continue long after the original reasons for it have been forgotten. New reasons arise to sustain it. One example is mentioned by Simon in her history of Manchester, England. Manchester had been the official control center over a wide area in which were several villages including Manchester. The king himself was Lord of the Manor for this village. When industry came in the 1700's the first textile mills located in Manchester, across a small stream from Salford. Manchester continued to grow and was able, one after another, to annex the surrounding villages. But Salford, proud of its heritage, would not be annexed. Long ago the place lost its residential exclusiveness, and those who fought the good fight have long since been forgotten. Salford is now surrounded by Manchester, but the king is still Lord of the Manor there.[42]

One among several examples of American communities that would not be annexed by a growing city, is Evanston, Illinois, now completely surrounded by Chicago. It has long been the claim of the citizens of Evanston that they live in a town free of political corruption and free of foreign elements, although most people living in Evanston work in Chicago.

THE GREAT METROPOLIS IS DIFFERENT

Cities in the industrial countries are passing through an evolution, especially the metropolitan cities, which brings them into new ways of life. They are still all things to all men, but in a more dispersed and differentiated sense. If their functions change it is to become more varied and interlocked. Largely in relation to their functional changes they change in shape, to spread out more. Many observers have remarked that the name "city" no longer applies to places like Bombay and Calcutta, London and Paris, New York and Chicago. As for Holland, a half-dozen cities, a neighboring cluster, make up a single complex, much as a half-dozen cities in Germany's Ruhr district make up one cluster. Some have

41 Calvin F. Schmid, *The Saga of Two Cities,* Minneapolis, Minneapolis Council of Social Agencies, 1937, pp. 4–7.
42 Shena D. Simon, *A Century of City Government, Manchester, 1838–1938,* London, Allen and Unwin, 1938.

given the name "conurbation" to such clusters, while others prefer the term "megalopolis." With respect to the subject of this chapter, commu-- nities as entities capable of behaving collectively, megalopolis is anything but such a community. It has itself become a mass of somewhat inde- pendent, competing entities whose rivalries often stand in the way of effective metropolitan administration. Although admittedly, at a different level, these rivalries have much in common with that of the Indian village mentioned above where the factions could not come together to build a much-needed school. Mumford, who thinks of metropolitan order mainly in functional and appearance terms, holds that the more the experts try to bring about order the more confused things become. He sees a lack of vision, an inability to sense what a megalopolis is or what it might become. The remedies they apply are mere local applications that pro- long the ailments.[43]

In the United States and in Canada the conviction is growing that the megalopolis, the city and its satellites, can only confront its problem if and when whole urbanized regions are brought under the control of some new type of metropolitan authorities, as was done in Toronto, with the main city and a dozen of its satellites.

Anderson sees the megalopolis as a great body in the process of cre- ating itself, but which has not yet acquired a soul. It is "congeries of many overlapping and conflicting, often selfish and disputatious units." They cannot join one another in common efforts and if they are able to join in opposing the central city, without which they could not survive, then each does so for its own reasons.

> The entire metropolitan district, therefore, is politically amorphous, without structure or unity. It is not a corporate person. In the eye of the common law it does not exist; even in the field of politics, it speaks with many contradictory voices. It is a place of divided loyalties and conflicting allegiances. In short, it is a community that is not really a community.[44]

The issue is not merely one of rivalry, of inter-locality conflict, or of satellites trying to inconvenience central cities; it is rivalry outside the framework of a responsible control authority. To establish such authorities would not terminate inter-community rivalries. These are evidences of collective activity in communities. The function of the common authority would be to utilize rivalry, to integrate it and channel it into collective activities that serve the whole region. In this way, a megalopolis would be in a position to get things done despite rivalry between its localities and

43 Mumford, op. cit., p. 544.

44 William Anderson, "Political Influences of the Metropolis," in Robert M. Fisher (Ed.), *The Metropolis is Modern Life*, Garden City, New York, Doubleday, 1955, pp. 57–58.

its factions. Whether it will be able to achieve the various images that various idealists hold is another matter. The megalopolis is no longer a city in the old sense; the most it can be is an organization for managing its day-to-day affairs, planning as it can for the future. Its decisions and actions, as decisions and actions of cities have been, will more than likely be governed more by immediate practical considerations.

Social groups and classes in cities | 10

MAN AND HIS SOCIAL GROUPS

When we speak of a community we do so with an awareness that we are visualizing aggregates of people in a particular habit; they are a social organization. And we are also aware that any social organization that can be called a community is itself a cluster of organizations. It can be seen as an aggregate of families ranging from the affluent to the poor. Based on what we know, we would expect a community to be divided into areas or neighborhoods, which again range from the affluent to the poor. We would expect the people also to have their formal or informal groups held together by various common interests.

In any community, it is to be expected that the organized groups to which members of the affluent families belong, that is, professional people, leading business men, and top public officials, enjoy a higher degree of prestige than that accorded to organized groups whose members are skilled or white-collar workers. We tend to expect that those in the more affluent groups also have more influence in managing community affairs than members of less affluent groups.

In this comparison, two kinds of human groups are evident. The members of the more affluent groups and those of the groups of lesser affluence belong to different social classes. A social class is a category of people who belong at a social level because of particular generally accepted criteria: level of wealth, level of education, level of occupation, and (generally, but not always) family of origin. One belongs to a social class but not in the sense that he is the member of an organized group, although such categories are sufficiently real that, if one belongs to a particular social class he readily learns which groups are suitable for one of his social level. And the matter of joining groups becomes something of a "right" as far as some groups are concerned. To join lesser groups would hurt one's status. The groups one joins voluntarily become utilities in one way or other for him. Each group has a purpose and the members know the purpose, as they know one another. Membership is not amorphous, as in a social class.

One may use his position in a social class to advance himself in the competitive society in general terms. For advancing himself in particular terms, one joins special organizations, groups organized for particular purposes. Through such identities one orients himself and reorients himself to the changing scene. In the process one may rise to a position of leadership, and thus become one of the elite. This means in the words of Gould and Kolb, to attain eminence in some special field, to identify with the "governing minority and the circles from which" they are recruited.[1]

Those who do not belong to one of the upper classes may expend much effort through the groups they join to advance themselves. In European societies and in the more tradition-oriented societies those of the dominant classes have freer access to the elite jobs, management, for example, or public offices, than do aspirants from the lower classes. The more industrialized a society becomes and the more openly competitive, the more advancement is made in terms of personal achievement, and also the more the individual can use his membership in organized groups to promote himself.

SOCIAL STRATIFICATION SYSTEMS

It appears to be fairly universal, despite idealist views to the contrary, for people to impose systems of stratification upon themselves by which they rate themselves and others. Indeed, they may find it a satisfying preoccupation, especially that of rating others as inferior to themselves, or rating others comparatively as superior or inferior with respect to social, economic, cultural, or other qualities. As Wax puts it, in whatever society, whether at work or play, we "are forced to maintain subtle differences between ourselves and our inferiors and superiors."[2]

The social class system in Western Europe grew out of an earlier type of social stratification which divided all people into two categories, the nobility and the commoners. In time there developed a third category made up of the functionaries who in various offices performed the work of the king or of a lesser noble. The categories in this rural-urban feudal system have been called "estates," each estate being legally defined, po-

---

[1] Julius Gould and William L. Kolb (Eds.), *A Dictionary of the Social Sciences,* New York, Free Press, p. 234.
[2] Rosalie H. Wax, "Free Time in Other Cultures," in Wilma Donahue, et al., *Free Time,* Ann Arbor, University of Michigan Press, 1950, p. 15.

litically oriented, and representing a broad division of labor.[3] At the nobility level it extended from counts up to grand dukes. Rural people at the common level were lumped together largely as peasants. But in towns there were the different occupational groups, the guilds, which, with the coming of industrialism, became the important elements of a class system. The tripartite estate system prevailed, and as Svalastoga mentions for Denmark, was described in a document of the twelfth century, the *Rigsthula* of unknown authorship.

> Rigsthula describes the class of the thralls or slaves as having a darker and uglier appearance than the others, while the class of the earls or noblemen is described as lighter and more attractive than the rest. The thralls do the heavy manual work or work of a routine character, the farmers are the managers of the economy, while the earls are pictured as a well-to-do leisure class devoted to war and play, while at the same time retaining a monopoly on the art of writing. Swine and goats are the animals associated with the thralls, oxen those of the farmers, while the earls appear with hounds and horses.[4]

This rural system of stratification was destined to be replaced by a class system as the cities gradually grew and became industrial. The feudal agricultural ruling class was replaced in time by an industrial ruling class. It was this transition in Europe that provided Marx with the foundation for his ideas about social class evolution, in which he visualized an industrial proletariat coming finally into power.[5] What did happen and what is still spreading in the world is a social class system oriented to the industrial system of work.

Tribalism needs to be mentioned, not because it emerged from the family as the original type of stratification, but because it is still the most prevalent form in the developing countries. Tribalism is based on kinship, all members of the tribe claiming the same single ancestor, who may, in some instances, be thought to have been an animal. But all the fathers in the ancestral line, now existing in a supernatural realm, continue to be concerned about their living descendants. For the living descendants, the ancestral fathers are a powerful force, able to hinder or to help them. Stratification is based on age and sex, in most cases the male being dominant. The tribal member begins life at a level where he is thought to be negligible, but he gains status with age and experience, as he is able to serve the tribe, as he begets children, and as they beget

[3] T. B. Bottomore, *Sociology, A Guide to Problems and Literature*, London, Allen and Unwin, 1962, p. 92.

[4] Kaare Svalastoga, *Prestige, Class and Mobility*, Copenhagen, Gyldendal, 1959, p. 207.

[5] Isaiah Berlin, *Karl Marx, His Life and Environment*, New York, Oxford University Press, 1963, pp. 7–13 and 146–151.

children. Reaching old age, he is in the top category and sits in the council of old men where status is measured by the number and importance of his progeny.

These developing countries now aspire to become industrial. Already their cities, most of them established by the colonial powers, begin to grow and great numbers of tribal people are moving from their villages to these cities in search of employment. In a single leap, they are in the process of becoming acclimatized to urban ways of life. The transformation to city life in countries where tribalism exists is very different from the transformation in other developing countries, such as those, for example, in Latin America, or in culturally advanced countries, such as India.[6]

Caste is another system of social stratification, and, incidently, there are some 20 million tribesmen in India, many of them being slowly absorbed by the caste system, while castes take on some features of social class. The caste system, sustained by a systematic rationale, is not easily disturbed by the encroachments of industrialism and its class stucture. The system accepts change, although much of its effort is devoted to holding its structure firm.

Caste has been primarily associated with the peoples of India and Pakistan, but we can associate it also with rural life and agricultural work. We can think of it no less as a family system, a structure for religious order, and as a control over the division of labor. There are four basic castes in the *varna* system: Brahman, Kshatriya, Vaisya, and Sudra, which are known by different names in different regions, and there are various sub-castes. The untouchables have caste identities but are "outcastes" to the hierarchy. Here is Ishwaran's description of castes for a Mysore village.

> The caste is an institution whose membership is governed by the principles of a) birth, b) endogamy, c) occupation, d) purity and pollution, e) distance, f) interdining and drinking in that order. The specific contents of the classical model of the *varna* system is not of universal application, but its prinicples are. In Shivapur, its basic principles operate in all the crucial areas of the social system. Each caste and sub-caste group is, to some extent, an isolated island with its own patterns of behavior and values, although all of them are related to a larger social structure.

> But hierarchy is at the same time a subjective phenomenon involving the attitudes of the people themselves, and an objective phenomenon which an outsider can observe as revealed in the behaviour patterns of the

6 See, for example, Melvin J. Herskovits and Mitchell Harwitz (Eds.), *Economic Transition in Africa*, London, Routledge and Kegan Paul, 1964; and Richard N. Adams (Ed.), *Social Change in Latin America Today*, New York, Random House, Vintage, 1960.

people. Though in the classic caste model, the Brahman is supposed to be the highest caste, in our observation this is not true of Shivapur. Here it is the Lingayat who is in the highest group, both in terms of subjective popular attitudes and our objective appraisal of their behaviour.[7]

Caste serves to institute and maintain order in the community, each caste having its area of work, the lowest caste doing the most menial work for the least reward and the highest doing the most respected work. While inequality is institutionalized, there is a compensating equality; no matter how hard the times, all share (although unequally) in the food supply, and no caste may deprive another of its rightful work. All are governed by the same *Dharma* code of right living and dealing, governed by accepted rules and the collective expectations of the community, effective where one's conduct is ever visible to all.[8]

Caste members, including untouchables, who migrate to cities find themselves outside the sphere of rural work, employed in occupations that have no place in the caste system. Persons of different castes find themselves in the same occupations. But, unlike the tribal order, the caste system does not fall apart under the impact of urbanization. Its social and religious functions continue. A single caste may have among its urban members persons in different occupations, some with high incomes, others in need. The caste group may provide welfare for its own or engage in political activity. "By organizing in this way, caste has filled an important gap in the political life, and has provided an illiterate electorate with a direct link with the legislatures and political parties." [9] However, the caste ban on marriage with members of other castes is more difficult to enforce in the city than in the village. In this respect, the two systems are very little in conflict.[10]

Gould observes that, although members of a caste arriving in a city still retain caste status, caste intrudes very little into their occupational relationships. They actually become identified with a class system in economic matters while socially clinging to caste.

CHARACTERISTICS OF SOCIAL CLASSES

Bottomore identifies social classes as the "characteristic groups of the industrial societies which have developed since the 17th century." [11] It would be more precise to think of social class as an adaptation to the

[7] K. Ishwaran, *Tradition and Economy in Village India*, London, Routledge and Kegan Paul, 1966, pp. 16–17.

[8] M. N. Srinivas, et al, *Caste, A Trend Report and Bibliography*, Oxford, Blackwell, 1959, p. 135.

[9] Ibid., p. 145.

[10] Harold A. Gould, "Castes, Outcastes and the Sociology of Stratification," *International Journal of Comparative Sociology*, Vol. 1, No. 2, September 1960, p. 224.

[11] Bottomore, op. cit., p. 188.

work system introduced by industry, thus making the individual, and not the family, the work unit. It is achievement oriented and not ascription oriented, and in various ways counters earlier systems of work. Weber saw the industrial society as being doubly structured, being a social status system, on the one hand, and a social class system on the other. Social and cultural values predominate in the status structure, while economic values are uppermost for the social class system. He recognized that the structure called social class, the target of much emotional evaluation, rests upon a material base which really accounts for stratification distinctions.[12]

For government and industry, and all who are interested in the structure of the work system, it is convenient to classify income earners in terms of their occupations, from unskilled workers up to managers, owners, and officials. Cole sees this approach to social stratification as useful for comparing the labor forces of different countries and for measuring changes in the labor force. Levels in the occupational hierarchy tend to become social class levels.[13]

We can, and perhaps must, think of social class from two perspectives, each of which reflects a special phase of life and interest: 1) as stratification in relation to work, production, and income, mainly evidenced by one's occupation and the position of each occupation in the hierarchy of occupations; and 2) as social position, evidenced by consumption behavior, leisure activity, and other types of status identification, which may indirectly have a relationship to one's occupation.

The industrial work system quite impersonally makes its demands for labor, providing jobs at different levels from unskilled to highly technical, from those calling for little skill and education to those which require high levels of skill and education, often special training; and the pay ranges from low wages to high salaries. Such a stratification is found wherever complex industry has located. Moreover, the hierarchy of jobs is integrated into an effectively operating whole, and the management of such a work enterprise needs to be a bureaucratic one. Such an impersonal work system has its own order, which tends to identify people with occupation-income classes.[14]

In every work system people tend to be classified to some degree in relation to the value placed on the tasks they perform. The difference is that the industrial work system is more precise and is least influenced by traditional values. Also it changes with the same impersonality with which it operates. It is not fully free of manipulation and bias, but if

[12] Max Weber, *The Theory of Social and Economic Organization,* translated and edited by T. Parsons and A. M. Henderson, New York, Oxford University Press, 1947, pp. 424–429.

[13] G. D. H. Cole, *Studies in Class Structure,* London, Routledge and Kegan Paul, 1955, pp. 3–4.

[14] H. H. Gerth and C. Wright Mills, *From Max Weber, Essays in Sociology,* New York, Oxford University Press, 1946, pp. 196–198.

the system is misused the cost is likely to appear in diminishing productivity. However, our attention here is on the function of the system as it assigns persons to classes in relation to occupational and income level. Porter observes, that one method now used in determining class:

> . . . consists in devising a scale of occupations, through public opinion polling techniques. Because their occupations, or that of family heads, are the most generally known characteristic about people, and because occupation is closely related to income, it is thought that when people are arranged in a hierarchy of occupational prestige the subjective class structure has been revealed.[15]

The work-production-income aspects of class are identified by Porter, and by others, as the objective class structure, while the consumer-social aspects, which would include leisure, are identified as the subjective class structure. Porter, of course, recognizes that these two perspectives of social class complement each other.

ACCEPTANCE OF THE CLASS SYSTEM

Some sort of social stratification system is found in every society, primitive to modern. Rating others as higher or lower or rating oneself in relation to others appears to be universal. As an example, Hollingshead wrote that he found the people in Elmtown quite agreed that a social class system exists. They identified themselves with social classes and were able to name the classes. Moreover, they knew the characteristics of particular classes and were able, in their opinion, to identify others with specific classes. And Hollingshead noted that people in Elmtown believed that certain ways of living and behaving were associated with classes.[16]

Clement and Xydias found that 76 percent of the men and 70 percent of the women in a French city placed themselves in the "proletariat" (working class), while 22 percent of the men and 29 percent of the women thought they belonged to the middle class. Of the proletarian, 66 percent based their judgments on income alone. Of the middle class, 63 percent based their views on occupation and income. Of the few in the upper class, almost all identified social class for themselves in terms of education and family background.[17]

In his study of occupations in Britain, Martin asked respondents to rate themselves as belonging to the upper, middle, or lower (working)

[15] John Porter, *The Vertical Mosaic, An Analysis of Social Class and Power in Canada*, Toronto, University of Toronto Press, 1966, p. 12.

[16] August B. Hollingshead, *Elmtown's Youth*, New York, Wiley, 1969, p. 74.

[17] Pierre Clement and Nelly Xydias, *Vienne sur le Rhone*, Paris, H. Colin, 1955, Chap. 2.

classes. Of the top three occupational groups 70 percent put themselves in the middle class, as did 49 percent of all persons interviewed. Of the lower occupational groups, 65 percent placed themselves in the "poor" or "working" class. Martin found that upperclass persons tend to rate themselves toward the middle while those at the lower level tend to rate themselves toward the "golden mean." A fourth of the skilled workers put themselves in the middle class.[18]

In interviewing a thousand persons in a German city, Mayntz also found a tendency for the upper classes to put themselves in the middle class, but so did 18 percent of the unskilled workers. She found, moreover that: 4 percent said there were two classes, rich and poor; 46 percent said there were three classes, lower, middle, and upper; 16 percent named four classes but the names differed widely; and 34 percent spoke of five or more classes, though few could name them.[19]

Mayntz asked the respondents in the Germany city to arrange occupations in rank order. The median rating for each occupation is shown in the following list.

1. Factory owner	10. Bookkeeper
2. Bank director	11. Locomotion engineer
3. School official	12. Shop foreman in factory
4. Physician	13. Postal clerk
5. Pastor or priest	14. Salesman (in store)
6. City inspector	15. Textile worker
7. School teacher	16. Factory mechanic
8. Master baker	17. Railroad laborer
9. Storekeeper	18. Laborer, helper [20]

Top rating is given to the factory owner, which is to be expected; but some may wonder at third place for the school official and seventh for the grade-school teacher. These are respected personalities in the small German city. The bookkeeper, who often earns less, is placed above the locomotive engineer. The explanation is that such a white-collar worker has higher social status.

SOCIAL CLASSES AND THE COMMUNITY

As we suggested in the previous chapter, a community is an onward moving organization able to articulate itself. As an organization, it tends

18 F. M. Martin, "Some Subjective Aspects of Social Stratification," in D. V. Glass (Ed.), *Social Mobility in Great Britain,* London, Routledge and Kegan Paul, 1954, pp. 51–75.

19 Renate Mayntz, *Soziale Schichtung und sozialer Wandel in einer Industrie-gemeinde,* Stuttgart, Enke, 1958, pp. 86, 93 and 103.

20 Ibid., p. 119.

to be a socio-economic hierarchy of groupings, the leading personalities from the various groups, the elites, forming a loosely-knit core cluster which is not likely itself to be an organization. In a sense, the core cluster operates as keeper of the community conscience. Its members, each according to his own interest or the interests of his group, competes or cooperates. In a crisis, all may join hands; at other times their behavior is much like that of neighbors. The social consequences of the elite core cluster is great perhaps precisely because it is not organized, for it enables the diversity of community interests to be articulated. Marshall would doubtless say that whatever the social class structure of the community, it would be evident in the composition and behavior of this core cluster.[21]

In the continuing interaction of personalities as they participate in the core cluster of the community, different organized groups, as well as the various social classes, are involved. But, as Dahl found in his study of New Haven, with each passing decade change is evident in the mixture of personalities in the core cluster. Religious leaders who were the key figures in colonial times were not so conspicuously present a generation later. Representatives of early immigrant groups, or their children, were gradually moving from fringe roles or statuses toward central positions. More decades passed and the mixture of elites has again changed. A social class structure remains, but the personality mixture changes.[22]

It is sometimes argued that in small cities the core cluster of elites tends to become a closed control group, that it tends to dominate civic affairs, holds a monopoly over economic matters, and maintains an exclusive domination over social and cultural affairs in the community. Such were essentially the findings of Warner and his associates in their study of a small Midwest city. Foreigners, so they reported, found little opportunity to get ahead, and this was no less true for the offspring of poor families.[23] Warner and his students, in their study of "Yankee City," a small Massachusetts city, some years earlier, noted the membership in some 350 organized groups, formal as well as informal. Most of these memberships they identified with one social class or another. The membership of a few organizations (business, trade union, or political groups) included members from different social classes. Others, like the Red Cross, also cut across class lines, as well as racial and ethnic lines.[24]

In a rural New York town, Goodchilds and Harding identified 58

---

21 T. H. Marshall, *Citizenship and Social Class*, Cambridge, Cambridge University Press, 1950, p. 94.

22 Robert A. Dahl, *Who Governs?* New Haven, Yale University Press, 1962, p. 32.

23 W. Lloyd Warner, et al, *Democracy in Johnesvilles*, New York, Harper & Row, 1949, p. 130.

24 W. Lloyd Warner and Paul S. Lunt, *The Social Life of a Modern Community*, 2nd ed., New Haven, Yale University Press, 1950, pp. 307–308.

organized groups, most of them the groups found in many American and Canadian communities, that is, branch units of national organizations. In this small place the memberships came from different social levels, but the key personalities in each organized group were, in many cases, the same who held key positions in other organized groups. If not the elected officials, they were the informal leaders whose views prevailed.[25]

This tendency of the upper class and upper middle class to establish their exclusive groups is evident in cities as well as in smaller communities. In fact, the larger the community, the greater the possibility of forming a diversity of exclusive groups. Moreover, in the city the likelihood of group memberships to be identified with broad class divisions is greater.

ORGANIZED GROUPS IN COMMUNITIES

An organization (also called an association, a voluntary group, or some precise term, such as, corporation, club, fraternity, society, party, etc.) is an identifiable group. It has a name and membership, and its members are known to one another. It has a structure, with roles assigned to members, and a purpose for being. Organized groups, as already mentioned, are found in all communities, but in cities their number is great and their variety infinite. They are social tools, mechanisms, instrumentalities, used by their members for particular purposes. The larger ones in cities tend to be impersonal and to function in a secondary manner. They are a consequence of what Reissman calls the shift from an agricultural to an industrial society and constitute new bases for social divisions and a new "measure of a man's social worth." [26]

The industrial society evolves other dimensions and makes new demands, to which society responds by the formation of new groupings, oriented to new goals, and performing in new ways. Within a half century Finland changed from an aristocracy-peasant society dominated by landlords, clergy, and officials to one of trade unions, political parties, professionals, and other groupings not known before. With this change new bases for segmentation came. We quote Sariola:

> Since the value structures have become so institutionalized in the party system, it follows that to many Finns, the worth of individual assets and capacities has become secondary to collective ideals. This change from individualism to collectivism is gradual. Whereas the Bourgeois holds the belief that the upward and downward change of status depends upon the

25 Jacqueline D. Goodchilds and John Harding, "Formal Organizations and Informal Activities," *Journal of Social Issues,* Vol. 16, No. 4, 1960, p. 19.

26 Leonard Reissman, *Class in American Society,* New York, Free Press, 1959, p. 25.

performance of the individual, and the Social Democrats believe that he should be protected against the hazards of the wide discrepancies between status extremes in society by social planning consistent with individual freedom, the Communists deny the correspondence between achievement and reward and believe in a totalitarian arrangement of rewards.[27]

To the old rural aristocracy, the Finnish society that has been evolving since 1905 must appear chaotic and irresponsible. Actually, the industrial urban order has functioned with great efficiency. There is still a class system, and the groups found in and around Helsinki are quite like those found essential in other industrial cities.

Japan has also industrialized quickly and is now one of the most urban of countries. Dore finds, however, that the Japanese do not turn to voluntary groups with the zest seen in Finland and the same applies to the joining of trade unions. This reluctance:

> . . . may be partly explained in terms of the general characteristics of social relationships in Japanese society. The solidarity of primary groups implies feelings of separateness from people who do not belong to the group and a certain wary circumspection in one's dealing with them. A Japanese, who tends to make all his social relations as "personal" as possible, and hence also to confine his social relations to those which can be "personal," hesitates to enter into relations with strangers for specific recreational purposes.[28]

A good share of Japanese industry is of the small-shop type. In the small work places a type of familial relationship exists between workers and employers in which high value is placed on personal loyalties. It would be disloyal for a worker to join a trade union.

The family, as the basic and original primary group, is committed by all of its traditions to sustain the community. Even that primary group, the gang, generally viewed as deviating from community norms, is not without community loyalties. In the city the primary group is present in a great many forms. Various types of primary groups are found within the secondary groups. Indeed, these large formal groups could hardly function effectively without them. Likewise, the formal bureaucracy of a large public office or a private corporation could hardly function without the various primary group relationships within it.

[27] Sakari Sariola, "Defining Social Class in Two Finnish Communities," *Transactions of the Westermarck Society*, Abo, Abo Tidnings och Trycheri Aktiebolag, Vol. 11, 1953, p. 156.

[28] R. P. Dore, *City Life in Japan*, London, Routledge and Kegan Paul, 1958, p. 247.

THE UTILITY OF SECONDARY GROUPS

Formal groups hardly existed before the emergence of the industrial urban society, nor were they needed before the organization of society began to assume a more complex character. When the large city appeared, large organizations were needed to feed the people, transport goods, provide employment, and to manage community life. Large organizations, in other words, brought a semblance of order to the mass agglomerate. The common needs of the whole were supplemented by the many unique needs of special segments of the urban agglomerate. However, people still needed their more intimate primary groups [29] to get on better in the larger groups and in relation to the mass.

The secondary organization serves its members, who established it to perform collectively what they as individuals cannot do, or cannot do as effectively. Through representatives whom they select from among their number, it speaks for them, whether in relations with other large organizations or the public authority. The member is once removed from the relationship between his organization and others, hence it is seen as an indirect or secondary relationship.

An individual may belong to one such organization in his approach to the labor market (a trade union), to another in relation to his political interests (the political party), to still another in relation to his leisure interest (sport club, social club). An organized church serves his religious needs, and other needs may be served by other similarly organized large groups. Thus each large organization is a utility, used for a particular purpose.

The types and number of organizations in a city tend to be descriptive of its population, revealing much about the way of life of its people. Whether the secondary organization is incorporated as a legal person or not, if it is large enough to be formal and bureaucratic, its characteristics will include most of the following features:

1. *Identification.* The group will have a name, some type of emblem, perhaps ritual, a statement of purpose and, whether incorporated or not, it will have a constitution and by-laws.
2. *Sphere of activity.* The group is formed to achieve some particular purpose, to serve its members in some special area of interest and its method of operation will be oriented to this purpose, the area of interest to which it lays claim.

29 For an argument favoring a reappraisal of the primary group as it functions in mass society, see Elihu Katz and Paul F. Lazarsfeld, *Personal Influence,* New York, Free Press, 1955, pp. 41 and 44.

3. *Structure.* The organization of the group will be set forth in its constitution as to structure, while its method of operating will be spelled out in by-laws. There will be elected officers whose duties are prescribed and there will be committees for performing particular functions. Its internal structure becomes a hierarchy of roles which in various ways over time affords a status to each member.

4. *Records.* A formally organized group could hardly continue without making and keeping a record of its activities and finances, its members, and its contacts with other organizations. This becomes its history and, with pertinent documents, are preserved.

5. *Internal discipline.* For its own amicable functioning, the organization must have rules which are enforced without discrimination. These are self-imposed rules whose enforcement has been delegated to the elected officials.

6. *Rights and duties.* Within the rules and in relation to the goals of the organization, members enjoy specified rights and privileges. They share the duties and costs essential for the effective functioning of the organization, including the duty of loyalty and commitment to its purposes.[30]

Members do not need to know all other members in such a secondary organization, but they do need to know what the organization is doing, the problems on which it is working, and the progress being made. One function of the organization is to keep them informed. The members must acquire a broad and sophisticated overview of the community and the relation of their organization to it.

THE ELITES IN MODERN SOCIETY

To recognize the elites in a society, one would have to take account of the society, the time, and the circumstance. Someone has said that in a society of the blind a one-eyed man could be king. On the early American frontier illiteracy was general in many parts. Anyone who could read and write with moderate skill could not avoid being named town clerk. Svalastoga, a Danish sociologist, concludes that in the modern society there are at least eight major specific elites, and he adds a ninth, "general elite."

1. Charismatic elite: the popular heroes, the saints, the gods.
2. Power elite: those who excel in power or influence.
3. Wealth elite: the very rich, the millionaires.
4. Ascriptive elite: the "old" families, aristocracy of birth.
5. Artistic elite: the most recognized art producers.
6. Physical elite: the top people in sport and beauty contests.

[30] See Theodore Caplow, *Principles of Organization,* New York, Harcourt, Brace & World, 1964; also Robert Presthus, *Organizational Society,* New York, Random House, 1962.

7. Prestige elite: the holders of top prestige positions.
8. Scholastic elite: the holders of academic certificates or persons of similar standing.
9. General elite: the multidimensional top people, the "who is who" group.[31]

This area of interest can lead to many classifications of elites and to many views about their roles in public and private life. We would expect that the more developed and diversified a society and its economy become, the more opportunity there is for a large number of persons to become elites. In countries where labor is strongly organized, trade union officials may be among the elite.

As we have considered above, the elites in a city tend to be attracted to one another, forming a loose collective which we have called the core cluster. Mills noted how different elite types tend to meet in the entertainment spots of the city inhabited by "café society;" but there are other points of meeting, at clubs, gathering, etc.[32]

Getting things done in a community often means using influence to have public funds diverted to some purpose. If it is something for welfare, education, or culture, it is to be expected that the big taxpayers will put up resistance. The different organizations will line up for or against the proposal. In this regard, Presthus asked not only who the key individuals in two small cities were, but how each leader reacted to different issues over a period of several years. He used the now popular term "pluralism" to describe the sharing of community control by private and public bodies. He found that between key personalities in community elite groups there are give-and-take linkages. Each leading personality is in a network of relations with others. One any issue, his position depends of the stands taken or likely to be taken by other elites, influencing some, being influenced by others.[33] Theirs is the strategic art of getting things started or done. They are at the center of community life and are often better informed about pertinent issues and situations than are members of their own groups.[34]

Hunter and his associates, in their study of Salem, Massachusetts, asked their interviewees what characteristics one would expect to find in a community leader. The ten most frequently mentioned qualities were:

31 Kaare Svalastoga, "Elite and Social System," *Acta Sociologica*, Vol. 12, No. 1, 1969, p. 15. The aim of Svalastoga is to work out a formula to determine the number of each elite to expect per 10,000 population in different countries. He would recognize, of course, that some individuals would fit into more than one of the elite categories.

32 C. Wright Mills, *The Power Elite*, New York, Oxford University Press, 1956, p. 72.

33 Robert Presthus, *Men at the Top, A Study in Community Power*, New York, Oxford University Press, 1964, p. 19.

34 Ibid., p. 24.

1. Exercises power and influence, and this is known.
2. Has a moderate amount of wealth and property.
3. Enjoys good relations with major civic associations.
4. Residence is "satisfactory"; he is not a newcomer.
5. Is of "prime" age; he is not too young.
6. Is allied with major economic and political organizations.
7. Relations with the press are good.
8. Personal character and conduct meet community norms.
9. Hobby and leisure interests conform to social status.
10. Does not have any blemishes on record.[35]

There appears to be a tendency to go beyond reality in identifying the elites with initiative and energy, with having new ideas and the genious to have new things brought about. Salem is a town with a past, but it now has to settle for the status of a suburb. Its top families value the established and the stable life, and this appears to be reflected in the ten expectations listed by Hunter. An elite, determined to move things along, might not be welcome; they would migrate to livelier places where population and wealth accumulate. They are not wanted in a depressed city or region by those in power, and might be considered a nuisance. This seems to be confirmed by a study of Springdale, a rural town in New York. The people who run things in Springdale are members of the old families. The leaders of groups are past middle age, most of them having been in residence for more than twenty years. Although new-comers—teachers, lawyers, engineers, managers—had a much higher level of education and a more cosmopolitan outlook than the long-time residents, they were confined to minor roles in community affairs.[36]

Elites represent different interests in the community: economic (trade unions, manufacturers associations), political (the parties, patriotic groups), administrative, religious, and cultural. Each category has its own skills but all enjoy degrees of power as they are backed by numbers or wealth. Porter remarks:

> While elites exercise power by co-ordinating and directing relatively autonomous institutional orders, there must be some social mechanism by which the power activities of the various elites become meshed in the power system of the total society. It is this need for over-all co-ordination which limits the autonomy of the various elites. . . .

As organized groups encroach on one another or cooperate in various give-and-take arrangements, some are in positions of advantage today,

---

[35] Floyd Hunter, Ruth C. Schaffer, and Cecil G. Sheps, *Community Organization, Action and Inaction*, Chapel Hill, University of North Carolina Press, 1956, pp. 34 and 37.

[36] Edward C. Devereux, Jr., "Community Participation and Leadership," *Journal of Social Issues*, Vol. 16, No. 4, 1960, p. 38.

others in positions of advantage tomorrow. So the pluralistic community (or national) order remains in balance, even while change is taking place.

Porter sees specialization also as a force for bringing elites together, even in rival situations. Because of the interdependencies resulting from specialization there is the need for coordination.[37]

ELITES IN DEVELOPING REGIONS

Elites exist in every society, being a constituent part of each social order. In the less developed society their roles were and are more general. Nothing in the tribal village prevents the medicine man from also advising persons on family problems or making weather predictions. So also in the frontier community, the physician might also "doctor" animals and on Sunday act as preacher. The school teacher, because he could write and handle figures, might be asked to serve as county clerk. In the more complex communities the elites tend to be more precisely specialized. As rural areas become more urban and more exposed to industrialism, specialization at all occupational levels increases and the level of education at all these occupational levels tends to rise.

Community and other leaders in Canada's Atlantic provinces have nursed the hope that by increasing the level of education and training of the young, such inputs would initiate industrial development. Actually, a majority of those receiving the most education and training migrate elsewhere, mainly to the affluent industrial regions of Canada to enter the elite circles there. The depressed Atlantic provinces have their elites but, because of limited resources, they are too limited in number and type to absorb all potential recruits.

The situation is different in the new countries now eagerly trying to become industrial. Cities are growing and people are packing in, but industrial employment lags years behind. Much development is needed to attract industry but, with not enough industry stimulus to raise the skill level of the labor force, the preparation will lag. Nor will the industrial type of social class and big organization society develop. More than three centuries were needed to develop the industrial urbanism of the West. These new countries, most of them starting with greater handicaps, are trying to cover the same distance in a couple of decades. Their leaders, considering the technical difficulties only, tend to be optimistic. Often they make unrealistic promises which stir popular expectations. Heilbroner makes this observation:

> The immediate carriers of the torch for economic development, as contrasted with political independence, are apt to be not so much the poorest

37 Porter, op. cit., pp. 207–209.

classes as the leadership elite—a small but powerful group of political leaders, army officers, intellectuals. Here is where the drive for development is greatest, for these leaders understand, in a larger frame of reference than their illiterate or semiliterate countrymen, that only by a total economic severance . . . can the present lot of their countries be remedied.[38]

Those of the industrial urban countries could hardly find a more convincing reminder of the utility of the elites in their own society than to consider these new countries where core clusters of elite leadership are only now taking form. Too often these emerging elites are themselves ill-prepared to carry the burdens they are assuming. Those with technical know-how may lack economic and social know-how, or vice versa. Every new country faces a crying need for persons who can organize and direct. The many kinds of elites, so common in the industrial countries are often scarce in the new. Not only are they lacking, but few establishments exist for training them. To Shils, one of the most scarce of all elites in developing nations is the intellectual.

> Intellectuals are indispensible to any society, not just to industrial society, and the more complex the society the more indispensible they are. An effective collaboration between intellectuals and the authorities which govern society is a requirement for order and continuity in public life and for the integration of the wider reaches of the laity.[39]

Just as technically advanced industry cannot enter a developing country before the scene has been readied with the essential infrastructure, so the society of the developing country must achieve a minimum level of sophistication before the elites can be effectively utilized. But the paradox is that the elites are needed to start and guide this evolution.

CLASS, ORDER, AND PARTICIPATION

In our chapter dealing with ecology and the distribution of space occupancies in the community, we were confronted with firm evidence that the uses of land, clearly so for urban land, assume the form of a pattern. In terms of man's choices, residential areas reveal a pattern of distribution in terms of socio-economic class. Places of work tend to be distributed more on the basis of economic choice. The poor in the slums are not only segregated from the rich, the different groups or categories

---

[38] Robert L. Heilbroner, *The Great Ascent*, New York, Harper Torchbook, 1963, p. 69.

[39] Edward Shils, "The Intellectuals and the Powers, Some Perspectives for Comparative Analysis," *Comparative Studies in Society and History*, Vol. 1, 1958–1959, p. 21.

of the poor avoid other categories. This distribution tends to reflect social class distinctions, whether we identify classes as social status groups or as occupation-income groups.

Some such ecological distribution of people by residence, reflecting socio-economic stratification, has apparently been characteristic of cities through the centuries. In the early walled cities, people of different social categories (the class system had not yet arrived) often shared an area of only a few acres. Each individual or family within the wall, especially in the medieval city, could justify his presence there. From the gentleman of noble birth to the street sweeper, all had part in the community life. However low his status in the city's hierarchy, each member of that walled community belonged there by right; each performed a job which was essential to the community. Those belonging to the same occupation usually lived on the same street; thus a shoemaker and his family lived on a street with other shoemakers.

The earlier walled cities were like great households which had to have order to keep going. Mumford thinks that "the medieval mind took comfort in a universe of sharp definitions, solid walls, and limited views; even heaven and hell had their circular boundaries. Walls of custom bound the economic classes and kept them in their place." [40]

Even though the modern city is not pressed within walls, the house-keeping goes on; the social classes have their places, but the lines are less clearly defined. While the work system has become more extended, more complex, more technologically interdependent, and less dependent on the individual craftsman-producer, the social order has become more diffused and less tightly integrated. New instrumentalities from community participation have appeared on the scene, being needed to cope with mass industrial production and mass community living. The medieval craftsman had his guild to speak for him, but the guild could not survive in the industrial urban order. The individual now utilizes large formal secondary organizations, public as well as private.

THE DILEMMA OF COMMUNITY PARTICIPATION

In the United States, and to some extent in Europe, beginning about 1940, there was widespread interest in the study of community participation. It was concerned with, on the one hand, the extent to which people join voluntary organizations and become active members, and, on the other hand, their participation as citizens in public life. Generally, these studies revealed far fewer memberships and far less participation than

---

[40] Lewis Mumford, *The City in History, Its Origins, Its Transformations, and Its Prospects,* New York, Harcourt, Brace & World, 1961, p. 303.

the ideal model called for. One result has been considerable speculation about, and now considerable research into, the phenomena of alienation. Industrial employment is seen as alienating man from his work and urban living is viewed as alienating man from his fellows. But different categories appear to be less prone than others to participate in community life by joining organized groups. To take one example, Zimmer and Hawley found in their study of an industrial city that 45 percent of the urbanites compared with 25 percent of the suburbanites were members of secondary groups. They found that 70 percent of the owner-manager class, compared with 35 percent of the skilled workers were affiliated with organizations.[41] Other studies have shown that women are less ready to join organizations than are men, or that the joiners are mainly in the middle-age groups.

Summarizing the more important participation studies in the United States, Wright and Hyman report that joining is higher for urban and nonfarm people than for rurals, higher for Jews than Protestants, higher for Protestants than Catholics, and higher for the better educated.[42]

The elites are often those who make the greatest use of formal organizations, often belonging to a number of such and not infrequently providing the leadership for the organizations. Of those having memberships in such organizations, only a minority attend regular organizational functions. And of this minority, only a minority are noticeably active. Here is a state of affairs, viewed with alarm by some, which is perhaps not unique to any one modern industrial country or to our time. The majority seems content to leave the management of community affairs to the elites.

Buttressing this pattern, quite evident in the modern urban community, is the tendency of large sections of the middle and upper classes to leave the city for the suburbs, described by some as running away from community responsibility. They escape the city and its hostile competitions for a quiet haven outside. What they hope to find in the suburb is an elemental type of democracy nestled in idealized neighborhood life. Once in the suburbs, they find it easier to leave the complex problems to the experts. Says Wood, "If the expert is entrusted with the really tough problems, the suburbanite has the best of possible worlds; grassroots government run by automation. Under these circumstances democracy requires no democratic action of responsibility at all." [43] Perhaps this is true for the metropolis as a whole.

41 B. G. Zimmer and A. H. Hawley, "The Significance of Memberships in Associations," *American Journal of Sociology*, Vol. 65, No. 2, September 1959, pp. 196–201.

42 Charles R. Wright and Herbert H. Hyman, "Voluntary Association Memberships of American Adults, Evidence from National Sample Surveys," *American Sociological Review*, Vol. 23, No. 3, June 1958, pp. 284–294.

43 Robert C. Wood, *Surburbia, Its People and Their Politics*, Boston, Houghton Mifflin, 1959, p. 197.

Of course, participation in community life is not measured by organizational behavior alone; one also participates as a worker, a consumer, a church member, or as a neighbor, even as one who rears a law-abiding family. And each of these forms of participation contribute significantly to community order.

The family and industrial urbanism | 11

THE FAMILY CONFRONTS THE COMMUNITY

At the outset, as is generally recognized, the family was the community, the nuclear family of parents and children being the minimum unit. The individual hardly figured as a unit, viewed in the modern notion of an individual as having the right to make decisions on his own responsibility. Extended families were establishments of considerable size, including dozens of nuclear families. Its sphere of control included all the essential functions for insuring the well-being of the group.

We may assume that the increasing size of families led to food supply problems and control problems. Then the logical thing was for the heads of different families to join in forming some joint control. At that point the community began, and although founded to support the family, actually entered into competitive relations with the family. Such joint control arrangements, as creations of the family system are still found in tribal regions. Among the Ngombe in the Belgian Congo the chief and his aides are the heads of extended families. They are the community organization; the village, which performs certain functions, is no longer the sole province of the family.[1]

Communities that begin as auxiliaries to the family, doing what families cannot do, or cannot do as well, soon acquire other functions, even some previously performed by the family. In this process, the community as an organization for a wider group, however committed to the support of the family and its ideals, becomes a competitor of the family in the sharing of power. Thus any power exercised by the community is power that was previously exercised by the family, an observation made by Maine more than a century ago.[2]

[1] Alvin W. Wolfe, "The Dynamics of the Ngombe Segmentary System," in William R. Bascom and Melvin J. Herskovits (Eds.), *Continuity and Change in African Cultures*, Chicago, University of Chicago Press, 1959, pp. 173–176.
[2] Henry Sumner Maine, *Ancient Law*, (1861), Boston, Beacon Press, 1963, p. 164.

In this competition between family as organization and community as a coordinating organization, Maine recognized a change in the condition of the individual. Initially, he was totally identified with the family. Later he acquired a second identification, becoming a member of an organized community. It was the community organization that managed collective work activity and was responsible in times of war or other danger. In this second role the individual eventually acquired his status as a citizen.

Initially, as Maine saw the evolution of law, the individual belonged to his family, and his family to a greater kinship unit. The major decisions affecting his life were made by the elders in his family according to the codes of tradition. The relationship was one of *status*. With the increasing complexity of society it became increasingly expedient for individuals to act on their own. Law came to be written and impersonally administered. So agreements too came to be written. The emerging society, in its practices, came to be governed in many respects by *contracts* in which the individual, perhaps the family head, would be a party not as a representative of the family but as an individual among individuals.

The socio-economic implications of Maine's proposition have come to be wider than his mere application of it to civil law. It concerns the step-by-step deemphasis of the family, and we may safely assume it has survived a great number of serious deprivations in the process.

If we assume that the family has lost in many contests to retain functions and power, this does not warrant the conclusion that the family is disintegrating and losing all of its functions. Its most vital functions remain; there is its monopoly on reproduction, initial socialization of the young, and that of being the primary and most enduring affectional milieu. Goode puts this in other terms:

> In spite of the great number of divorces, and the large segment of our population that is hurt by marital disorganization, almost every adult does marry eventually. Almost every person who is widowed or divorced tries marriage once more, and even the children who had unhappy experiences in their own families grow up with enough faith to try marriage for themselves when they are grown.[4]

THE EFFECTS OF WORK CHANGE ON THE FAMILY

It is often brought to our attention how agriculture in North America was rendered more productive by the increasing application of sci-

---

3 Ibid., p. 163.

4 William J. Goode, "Family Disorganization," in Robert K. Merton and Robert A. Nisbet (Eds.), *Contemporary Social Problems*, New York, Harcourt, Brace & World, 1961, p. 458.

entific knowledge and the use of labor-saving machines. In most branches of agriculture per-man productivity has been so increased that the average output of two workers in 1970 equals that of six or more workers in 1870. The farmer with four sons can expect at least two to leave farming for industrial work. If the same farmer has three daughters he will have little in the way of farm labor for them to do, and one or two will migrate to the city.

Fortunately, the rate of industrial development in North American cities has been fast enough to absorb the labor surplus from agriculture. The general effects of such changes in the sphere of work on the farm family are well known. The idealized old-fashioned farmstead no longer exists, except to some extent among poor farmers on poor land. The urban family, in the meanwhile, has also been forced to adapt to changes in the industrial work system; for example, there has been an increasing proportion of women, especially married women, entering the labor market. The decreasing use of unskilled labor, occupational mobility, etc., bring changes to the work of all. Such changes often result in different family members having different occupations, different incomes, and different aspirations.

On the American scene, family stability was greatest among rural people in the days before farm machinery replaced hand tools. The Indian family, embraced within the caste system, and living in the agricultural village, approaches the ideal of a stable domestic unit. Singh sees this solidarity as being due in part to a tool-using economy. He adds the observation that where "practice," meaning the daily round of work and other activities, change little, the rules and beliefs by which individuals and families live tend to remain firm, since there is no demand for change.[5]

Indian beliefs and rules of life have been institutionalized in the caste system, in organized religion, and in the sacred literature. The family has ways of meeting crises. This institutionalization is rarely found in tribal societies. The habits of life in the tribal village make for a high degree of social continuity which is lost for tribesmen in towns. Izzett mentions problems the Yoruba tribesmen face in the city where the extended family weakens. A man's work is often irregular, still he is expected under the Western code to be responsible for his wife and children. According to tribal law, that is a worry for the wife's family. Indeed in the village his wife would have work and be self-supporting.

> This he frequently finds difficult to accept, and he does not regard his
> wife and children as having first claim on his wage or salary. He often
> feels his mother, his siblings or his cousins have prior claims. He expects

[5] Yogendra Singh, "Tradition and Modernity in India," in A. B. Shah and C. R. M. Rao (Eds.), *Tradition and Modernity in India*, Bombay, Manaktals, 1961, p. 54.

his wife, as under rural conditions, to contribute substantally to the family income, but the urban wife may have no qualification to obtain paid employment, and has insufficient capital to trade profitably.[6]

In this case the expectations of the tribal extended family run counter to Western expectations regarding the nuclear family being adopted in the West African city. Different notions and prospects relating to work and income are also involved.

Hansson describes the nuclear rural family in Sweden as of 1800 and earlier where, if the farm was large, the family might include other kin as well as employed persons. In that household the province of the wife as manager of her sphere of work was firmly recognized. She was:

> . . . mistress of the household . . . in the farm economy. She supervised and devoted herself to the manufacture of linen and woolen textiles. Hers were the duties of baking, brewing, and salting down. She ruled over the kitchen, larder and cellar. She worked in the cowhouse and took care of the small cattle and poultry. She commanded grownup daughters and maids.[7]

This description would apply in large measure to the housewife in colonial times or on the North American land frontier. If women's role or the roles of family members have changed as suggested here, we must look for some of the major reasons in work changes as they have intruded into the earlier ways of family living. Change, stated Ogburn, depends on regions, "their degree of industrialization, of their urbanization, and of their isolation." [8]

FAMILY AS SOCIAL INSTITUTION

We think of a social institution as an established and continuing system of roles associated with group form and behavior. To Truxal and Merrill the family is an involuntary social institution, which one becomes a part of by birth. Here they indicate what an institution does:

> The social institution uniquely combines the ideal and the practical aspects of human relationships. Institutions arise through the spiritual, as well as the biological and social, needs of human beings and are contin-

---

[6] Alison Izzett, "Family Life Among the Yoruba in Lagos, Nigeria," in Aidan Southall (Ed.), *Social Change in Modern Africa*, London, Oxford University Press, 1965, p. 311.

[7] Sorje Hansson, "Dimensions of Primary Group Structure in Sweden," in Nels Anderson (Ed.), *Recherches sur la Famille*, Tübingen, Mohr-Siebeck, 1956, p. 138.

[8] William F. Ogburn, "Why the Family is Changing," in ibid. p. 1.

ued by the same forces of reproduction, sex, affection, emotion, and the like. Institutions provide social patterns for channelizing many forms of behavior, which, if unregulated by some such sanctions, would mean chaos and the disintegration of organized society.[9]

No institution in any society is self-sufficient. Its structures, beliefs and behaviors intertwine with those of other institutions, the system of social stratification, religion, property, and others. For instance, the Indian family is integrated into the caste system, but the caste system is strongly oriented, on the one hand, to religion while, on the other hand, it is a system for managing the work of the community. As Ishwaran notes, all the rules of life are interrelated. The individual's mate in marriage is not only chosen by his family, but the family may try to select a mate from the same occupation and locality.[10]

The family as an institution is a model of different dimensions, the matter of staying together for reasons of livelihood being only one. Whether the family is nuclear or extended, status is important. The good family in a community need not be the most loved but it may be the most imitated if it is able to maintain itself well economically, if it is skillful in avoiding scandal, if it knows how and when to be helpful to neighbors, all of which evidences a firm inner solidarity. Criteria such as these appear to be pertinent to all cultural levels, perhaps moreso to the societies now emerging as new nations. But for most of these countries the institution of family is confronted with a painful and, to some extent, disintegrating transformation.

Every contact these emerging societies have with the culture the white man brings is often just another disturbing influence. The native who gets the white man's education is by so much detached from his origins, and if he qualifies to hold a job in the office of some white enterprise, he moves even farther from his own culture, becoming "detribalized." Thus he earns the dislike and suspicion of natives in his village of origin who have not had similar opportunities. He is called a "black European."

Wilson, writing about East Africa, in particular the Mombasa area, mentions how some natives come to accept the white man's church, which enables them to attend the mission school. The occasional energetic native may be sent away to get a white man's university education. He no longer accepts the basic beliefs of his family and village. For the native girl who goes through the mission school the risks are greater than for the young men. Her prospects for marriage are minor, and she may not

9 Andrew G. Truxal and Francis E. Merrill, *The Family in American Culture*, Englewood Cliffs, N.J., Prentice-Hall, 1947, p. 257.

10 K. Ishwaran, *Tradition and Economy in Village India*, London, Routledge and Kegan Paul, 1966, p. 108.

wish to marry a tribesman. Such situations multiply, and all are disturbing to the traditional family institution of a tribal way of life that is disintegrating.[11]

Fortunately, for such detribalized persons, the situation changes as their countries acquire nationhood status. They become citizens in their own right, as well as tribesmen, and so also acquire a status not possible under colonialism. This advantage for the detribalized may bring them more favorable attitudes in their villages. Notwithstanding this, the disintegration of the traditional family institution goes on, with no new model as yet to replace it.

THE FAMILY AND PERMEATING URBANIZATION AND INDUSTRIALIZATION

In the Latin American countries where initially settlement was mainly a matter of families getting extensive land grants, the upper-level feudal type of family was transplanted from Spain or Portugal. Here the establishment of an extended family was akin to a private village. The owner of the vast estate headed a family of various kin other than his wife and children, perhaps his concubines and adopted children. His manse was surrounded by families in his employ. The typical establishment had its chapel and priest, and sometimes a school or tutors for the children of the large household.[12] As Pierson portrays such households in Brazil, the inhabitants of those estates were living in a type of feudal society.[13]

It was not to the interest of the great landowners in the Latin American countries to encourage industry, but industry has increasingly pervaded the cities. Pierson observes that as urbanism waxes strong certain departures from the institutional family become evident. Beside the patriarchal there now are semipatriarchal and egalitarian families. "The peripheral elements have tended to separate from the familial system and attain autonomy in essentially monogamous relationships. . . . The nuclear family is increasing in importance; and concomitantly there has been a rise in individualistic behavior." [14]

The urban life, with its tendency to break up or diminish the influ-

[11] Gordon Wilson, "Mombasa, A Modern Colonial Municipality," in Aidan Southall (Ed.), *Social Change in Modern Africa,* London, Oxford University Press, 1965, pp. 110–111.

[12] William Henry Hudson, writing about his childhood, tells of living on such a vast estate, and in good middle-class terms he relates the daily life in that large household as ideal; *Far Away and Long Ago,* London, Dent, 1918.

[13] Donald Pierson, "The Family in Brazil," *Marriage and Family Living,* Vol. 16, November 1954, pp. 308–312.

[14] Ibid., p. 312.

ence of the extended family, may not operate with the same effect at all economic levels. Whether in the Brazilian cities or those in the United States, families at the working-class level are more likely to be fragmented than families of the upper class. The reasons are fairly self-evident. The transient nature of the occupations of common workers makes it difficult for large families to stay together. On the other hand, family cohesion is far less difficult for those having wealth and influence. Moreover, the upper classes hold the more secure and more rewarding occupations.

Modern work and living, as Halbwachs observed, encourage "uncomplicated families of which the hard core is the married couple." He recognized that with increasing frequency the married couple manages to remain childless.[15] Aubert sees the family in the urban milieu as more of a social utility than a social system, but his observations relate more to Norway than to the American scene. He regards the urban family as highly necessary to produce children and to socialize them, but its utility ends when the children depart to form domestic units of their own. Using the analogy of a ship's crew, Aubert states:

> The parents do not get new children when their offspring move away from home, as the skipper may get a new mate if he loses the old one. The eventual dissolution of the family is inherent in its biological and social function, and this perspective upon the future is built into its role structure. It is an obligation of the parents to prepare the children for independence, to teach them eventually "to stand on their own feet." It is impossible to grasp the structure of the family without a consideration of the time perspective. The role structure is continuously undergoing change.[16]

Aubert sees the nuclear urban family as having a limited existence, a cycle, which is not true of the traditional extended family. The latter is able to take birth and death, marriage and divorce in its stride. Like the crew of a ship, the extended family continues.

Changes in most highly industrialized countries are not greatly different from those found in the United States, although they may be more evident in the latter. Family changeover on the American scene is conspicuously visible. Dore describes the changeover of the Japanese family system from a highly agricultural to a highly industrial economy, much of it in two generations. In one specific area, he notes a radical change under way in the relationship between the mother-in-law and the daughter-in-law, in which traditionally the mother-in-law was dominant,

[15] Maurice Halbwachs, *The Psychology of Social Class*, London, Heinemann, 1958, p. 14.
[16] Vilhelm Aubert, *Elements of Sociology*, New York, Scribner, 1967, p. 83.

in a way often verging on tyranny. Under the traditional system the wife could not appeal to her husband who was duty-bound to take the side of his mother, for which the wife dared not to blame him. But in Tokyo:

> The young daughter-in-law, with her more recent schooling, is more up to date, more converted to the progressive attitude than her mother-in-law. The latter, in Tokyo commonly a country-born and country-educated woman who came to Tokyo soon after marriage, is often completely disoriented. The rapid changes in society in her lifetime, the backing given to new ideas by the school which, as an organ of the authorities, commands her respect; all these things have destroyed her confidence in the traditional ways before she has acquired knowledge of the new.[17]

Portugal could hardly be called an industrial country, or even a developing country, in the sense that it is striving to industrialize. There is a limited and not especially dynamic middle-class. However, in the peasant and working class, Willems found a strong tendency for nuclear families to detach themselves from their stem families. This trend, he concludes, is a practical adaptation to living conditions in a country of limited industrial employment. This may also explain why so many working-class Portuguese women are seen performing almost every type of common labor. In the course of becoming breadwinners, these women not only work with men, but they begin to evince attitudes of independence and self-confidence. The chronically low-wage urban labor market, apparently, may also affect family form and behavior. Willems found the working-class family in Portuguese cities to be "loosely structured and relatively unstable with a strong tendency toward anomie." [18]

However, it could not be said that the Portuguese upper classes and a good share of the middle class were without urban sophistication. Their type of society, conservative, aloof, and fearful of change, would not be at home in a modern industrial city; but, being wealthy, they are able to adapt without dissolution.

Changes with respect to marriage and the family are also evident in Britain, as the following figures show:

> *Marriage and divorce*—1,150 marriages to one divorce in 1871, compared with 10 marriages to one divorce in the 1950's.
> *Marriage rate*—for males, 59 per 1,000, for females, 52 in 1851–1860; for males, 68, and for females, 51 in 1951–1955.
> *Married women employed*—41 percent of the 6.9 million working women in 1950 were married, compared with 52 percent of the 7.6 million in 1959.

[17] R. P. Dore, *City Life in Japan,* London, Routledge and Kegan Paul, 1958, p. 129.
[18] Emilio Willems, "On Portuguese Family Structure," *International Journal of Comparative Sociology,* Vol. 3, No. 2, September 1962, pp. 64–69.

One measure of family change in the industrial urban society, as Dennis reports for Britain, is the extent to which women as wives have gained rights in court contests over husbands. For instance:

In 1870   Husband may not legally claim his wife's earnings.
   1882   Husband is not automatically owner of his wife's property.
   1886   Husband is no longer absolute guardian of the children.
   1925   Husband must consider wife's wishes regarding children.
   1935   Wife is entitled to full power of contract.
   1948   Procreation of children is no longer the chief aim of marriage; marriage is also for the companionship of the partners.

It is the view of Dennis that marriage in Britain declined with the rise of industrialism, as the family lost functions to industry and outside agencies. When the decline seemed beyond recovery, revival began. "Marriage was therefore rejuvenated and has been able to reach its present pre-eminence in Britain as the only producer of direct and immediate loyalty, commitment, and personal security." [19]

ON THE FUNCTIONS OF THE FAMILY

It may be said that the family survives because it is a type of group which is useful to man. We can think of it as a continuing system, or relationship. Ogburn in 1934 described the family as a function-performing social unit and he saw in the performance of these functions the social utility of the family. Each function served some particular human need. The essential functions, according to Ogburn, were:

1. Biological or reproductive
2. Protective—safeguarding family members
3. Economic—production and consumption
4. Religious
5. Recreational
6. Educational or training
7. Status conforming [20]

Various family sociologists have criticized these conclusions, but the objections appear not to recognize Ogburn's direct and uncomplicated

[19] Norman Dennis, "Secondary Group Relationships and the Pre-eminence of the Family," *International Journal of Comparative Sociology*, Vol. 3, No. 2, September 1962, pp. 80–90.
[20] William F. Ogburn and Clark Tibbitts, "The Family and Its Functions," *Recent Social Trends in the United States* (Report of the President's Research Committee on Social Trends, New York, McGraw-Hill, 1934, pp. 661–708.

explanation: that the family through history has been a work unit and that if it loses work functions its organization and behavior will be disturbed.[21] Today the family, once itself the entire community, has been caught up in a network of public or private agencies and enterprises for producing consumer goods and rendering services, and, while living its own life the family must adapt and coordinate with other types of organization. The latter have not only taken work from the family but they impose demands on the family as well.

Merrill, who recognizes that it is not necessary to focus on the precise list of functions given by Ogburn, suggests, however, that the family as a group must adapt as functions are lost, as new functions are added, or as the nature of functions change.

> The family performs a variety of activities in this fashion, including procreation, economic production, consumption, recreation, religious worship, education, and affectionate response. These activities are the functions of the family, the things it does or is supposed to do. The heart of any institution lies not so much in its structure as in the functions it performs and the values it enhances. When we say that the family is changing, we mean that it is ceasing to perform certain functions and is concentrating on others.[22]

In practically all societies the family retains a monopoly on the function of procreation. It is unable to meet modern demands for education from the elementary level on, but its work has not diminished at that lower level of education known as "socialization." Its function as a milieu of confidence and mutual moral support, called by some the affectional function, rises in importance. The modern family is expected to rear children for independent decision making, the very reverse of its traditional duty to sustain the age hierarchy, although that may still be found in upper-class families.

FAMILIES AND THEIR MEMBERS

Instead of being a relatively self-sustaining unit in a subsistence economy, the family in the industrial urban society has become a service unit in a wider social order. If children are produced at all, they are secularized for community participation as individuals. If the wife works,

[21] For such criticism, see Gerald R. Leslie, *The Family in Social Context*, New York, Oxford University Press, 1967, pp. 236–240; and Talcott Parsons, "The Social Structure of the Family," in Ruth N. Anshen (Ed.), *The Family, Its Function and Destiny*, New York, Harper & Row, 1959, pp. 241–274.

[22] Francis E. Merrill, *Society and Culture*, Englewood Cliffs, N. J., Prentice-Hall, 1965, p. 489.

she may have a different occupation from that of the husband. The children may turn to still other occupations, lower or even higher than those of the parents. Each member of the family thinks, at least in terms of work, in a different sphere of activity, one with its own imagery and work vocabulary.

This type of differentiation among family members is most likely to be found in middle-class or upper-class families. Individuals in working-class families, especially in European countries where it is still expected that children of working-class parents move into working-class occupations, are much less affected. Working-class parents are less sophisticated, alternatives in the labor market are fewer, and the cost of special education is excessive. The son of an unskilled worker living in a slum, the son of a Nova Scotia fisherman, or the son of a subsistence farmer in Appalachia may have aspirations but he is not likely to get a great deal of reinforcement from his family. Aubert, considering the limitations of the Norwegian fishing village, makes this observation:

> Today it is difficult for the grown-ups to know what they are going to prepare the young for, whether for roles available in the hamlet or for any one of the many that are waiting for them in the larger society outside. . . . In addition, it is unlikely that the young would decide in favor of a higher education; for example, they might find remunerative work outside the hamlet as fishermen, seamen, or in some other branch of unskilled labor. These choices have the additional advantages of flexibility, and at the same time they correspond better with the traditional ethos of the local community.[23]

Even when the family in modern society falls short of the sophisticated ideal, it is still pretty much a one-generation milieu within which much of the socialization of the young takes place. Thus the family as an effective service unit declines when the children disperse and it virtually ceases upon the death of the parents. Willmott and Young, in their studies of families in East London and in a London suburb, conclude that families stay together after the children marry thus challenging the one-generation-family theory. But the continuity of inter-generational ties in London is very far from reflecting the extended family model. Also, families in London are far less residentially mobile than in the United States.[24] Such extended bonds between parents and married children are indeed found in American cities but they are more characteristic of upper-class families.

Horton and Hunt are of the view that families of a lineage having

23 Aubert, op. cit., p. 215.

24 Peter Willmott and Michael Young, *Family and Class in a London Suburb*, London, Routledge and Kegan Paul, 1960; and Michael Young and Peter Willmott, *Family and Kinship in East London*, London, Routledge and Kegan Paul, 1957.

property interests in common will retain their bonds, even where friction exists. In the more common case, however, families may be held together by internal bonds even though the interests and personalities of members may be very different.

> It is united not by work and external pressures but by shared interests and affections. It shows a far greater variety, since no uniform set of marriage roles and duties are imposed upon all without regard for individual preferences and appetites. Such a family has a far greater potential for personality development and individual fulfillment than the traditional pattern. This potential, though not always realized, influences the form our family is taking.[25]

In the industrial urban society, the family stands between the strongly urged demands of the traditional model and the more rational, equally insistent demands to adapt. The demands to adapt are of two kinds: the family must adapt to the changing world outside itself, especially in the sphere of work, and it must achieve integration among its own members. Greer maintains that the family adapts to outside demands because adaptation is more rewarding than fighting back.[26] Adaptation of family members to one another as individuals appears to be the product of perceived demands within families, in part the product of searching for new ways of coping with family situations that no longer respond to the old ways. More will be said about this later.

THE CHANGING STRUCTURE OF THE FAMILY

Whether we look at the functions of an organization or its structure, we are confronting reasons for their existence. As the functions of the family identify it with what it does, so the structure identifies it with the form it must, or can, take for best performing the functions. After naming its key functions, Merrill remarks, "The contemporary family stands or falls on its success in performing these and related functions," and he adds that these functions find expression in the structure of the family.[27]

Whether the family type is one of monogamy, polygamy, polyandry, or other is not merely a matter of the whims of men. Often the economic situation, how the family earns its livelihood, is a determining factor.

25 Paul B. Horton and Chester L. Hunt, *Sociology,* New York, McGraw-Hill, 1964, p. 255.

26 Scott Greer, *The Emerging City, Myth and Reality,* New York, Free Press, 1962, p. 93.

27 Merrill, op. cit., p. 407; and he cites Robert F. Winch, *The Modern Family,* New York, Holt, Rinehart and Winston, 1963, Chap. 1.

However, as Goodfellow observed of the Bantu in Africa, a change in religion may affect family structure. He cited a village where although most families were of the extended polygamous type there were also nuclear families. "Wherever this is found it will be the clearest sign that the people are Christianized and have abandoned their old ways of life." Even so, he adds that changing economic conditions in Pondoland tend to reduce the number of persons in a household.[28]

The United States in 1800 was a country of large households; 579 persons per 100 households compared with 377 per 100 households in 1940. In 1800 there were 343 children per 100 households compared with 149 in 1940. These were predominantly nuclear families, but in 1800 there were in each 100 families 59 relatives, lodgers, or servants compared with 51 in 1940.[29] Today the American urban family only rarely has space for extra kin, and the likelihood of nuclear families or married couples living with their parents is comparatively rare.

The changing form of the family is also seen in Belgium where as industrialism increases family size declines. Delcourt notes that in 1846 the number of children per 100 married women was 182, but in 1947 it was down to 88. From Delcourt's data we can also see the rapidity of the change in household size. Comparing the figures for 1930 and 1947 households of one or two persons there is an increase from 37 percent to 47 percent of all households, while households of five or more members declined from 21 percent to 15 percent. Households of three or fewer persons increased from 62 percent of the total in 1930 to 71 percent in 1947.[30]

Persons per household	1930	1947
one	11%	16%
two	26%	31%
three	25%	24%
four	17%	14%
five	10%	7%
six or more	11%	8%

Table 9 shows the distribution in percentages of types of households in five rural prefectures and in six large cities of Japan. Here we see that one-generation and two-generation households comprise 86.1 percent of all households in the big cities compared with 48.1 percent of

28 D. M. Goodfellow, *Principles of Economic Sociology*, London, Routledge, 1938, p. 141.

29 William F. Ogburn and M. F. Nimkoff, *Technology and the Changing Family*, Boston, Houghton Mifflin, 1955, pp. 99 and 110.

30 Jacques Delcourt, *Famille et civilisation urbaine*, Bruxelles, la Pensée Catholique, 1960, p. 24.

Table 9   Composition of Households; Five Northern Rural Prefectures and Six Large Cities in Japan, (1920) *

Composition of households	Five rural perfectures	Six large cities
One generation	8.1%	27.4%
Two generations and one or no married couples	40.0	58.7
Two generations and two married couples	4.7	0.7
Three or more generations and one married couple	20.8	10.0
Three or more generations and two or more married couples	26.4	3.2
Total	100.0%	100.0%

Source: D. P. Dore, *City Life in Japan*, London, Routledge and Kegan Paul, 1958, p. 121.

* All the figures are based on a 1 percent sample of the 1920 population. This table in Dore's book also includes percentages for Shitayama-chu, a section of Tokyo studied by him. The figures are almost identical with those of the six large cities.

the households in the rural prefectures. On the other hand, the complex three-generation households comprise 26.4 percent in the rural areas but only 3.2 percent of the large city households. Apparently in Japan as in other industrial countries the industrial work system does affect large households.

THE URBAN MILIEU AND FAMILY SIZE

In the course of building larger cities and learning to live in them, we become committed to new ways of living. We learn to organize industry into larger units with the same eagerness that airplanes are made bigger to carry more people longer distances in less time. Workers, learning the arts of organization, concentrate on ever bigger trade unions. Anything measured by size, output, or speed is bound to be outdistanced; everything, that is, except that oldest of organizations, the family. Its ultimate test of utility calls for minimal size and termination when its basic job is done.

The evidence of this trend in family change is the extent to which the extended family has diminished in importance in communities that have become increasingly industrial. Whether the joint family of parents and married children found in Indian cities will survive further industrialization in that country remains to be seen. This does not mean that the basic utility of the family is diminishing; it implies rather that the family must become more knowledgeable in the accomplishment of its functions.

The model family as pictured in advertisements and otherwise is urban, or at least urban oriented. Its task, as idealized, is to rear the child for independent living. The school helps in this effort, but "where the family is concerned, the process seems rather to result in the freeing to a considerable extent of individual members to create new cultural and family patterns, independent of those of the family of orientation, and often radically different." Modern parents tend to regard the rearing of an independent child as a mark of success.[31]

In rural life through the generations the man with sons was deemed to be wealthy, and envied was the man with many. A wife who could not bear children could be replaced by another, and one who became polygamous was increasing his private labor force. For urban parents the opposite is true. Children are often an economic burden, a fact unheeded by rural-oriented religions. The very cost of rearing and educating children imposes a handicap on large families. It is no coincidence that out of such families come a good share of the untrained common workers.

The "dependency ratio" is the number of nonproductive persons (young, old, sick, etc.) per 100 productive persons. For Canada in 1961–1964 the overall dependency ratio was 87.8, but for rural areas it is 107.9, compared with 80.2 for urban areas. There are more children in rural areas and more workers without dependents in cities. This is evident in the following figures showing rural and urban family size for Quebec and Ontario:

	Rural	*Farm*	*Nonfarm*	*Urban*	*Total*
Quebec	5.1	5.7	4.7	4.0	4.2
Ontario	4.0	4.0	3.9	3.5	3.6

Each has a great city, but rural Quebec is mainly French, almost wholly Catholic, committed to elemental farming and large families.[32]

On the basis of their study of women in the labor market, Collver and Langlois find evidence that when women become wage earners their willingness to bear children diminishes somewhat. If employed women rise occupationally to more skilled types of work, the negative effect on fertility is greater. In most of the new developing countries the work provided by industry for women is mainly at the unskilled level with low per-worker productivity. To use a term from Collver and Langlois this is the "subsistence sector" of industry. Eventually in these regions the "modern sector" of industry may enable more women to enter more

[31] John R. Seeley, R. Alexander Sim, and Elizabeth W. Looslley, *Crestwood Heights,* New York, Basic Books, 1958.
[32] Donald R. Whyte, "Rural Canada in Transition," in Marc A. Tremblay and Walton J. Anderson (Eds.), *Rural Canada in Transition,* Ottawa, Agricultural Economics Research Council, 1966, pp. 18 and 52.

challenging occupations. They postulate, "The employment of women is particularly important in the underdeveloped areas today, not only because of its positive contribution to economic development, but also because of its negative effect on human fertility." [33]

ASPECTS OF FAMILY BREAKUP

Divorce is but one form of family breakup and the only kind on which reliable statistics can be had. Separations, which may be more numerous, can hardly be enumerated accurately. As for divorce, the United States is high among nations reporting. In the early 1960's there were 258 divorces per 1,000 marriages in the United States, compared with 238 in Egypt, 165 in Sweden, and 81 in England and Wales.

What is most pertinent is that divorce rates have been rising somewhat apace with the growth of urbanization in the Western countries. What would be of particular interest would be statistics over some time showing rural and urban divorce rates. In Western rural communities there is stern disapproval of family breakup, for which reason the figures on rural divorces, as Leslie concludes, are far from valid. Many rural applicants for divorce, if they do not get divorced in a city, migrate to a city later.[34]

Ishwaran compared divorce rates in Holland for places with under 5,000 and over 100,000 inhabitants (divorces per 10,000 married men). The rate for rural places in 1902–1906 was 2.3 but it was 22.2 for places of 100,000 or more inhabitants. For the 1951–1955 period the annual rate was up to 6.4 in rural places and 50.4 in cities. Even in this stolid country where religious influence is strong but where villages are highly urbanized, there is no way of knowing how much of rural divorce shows up in urban statistics.[35]

The bias against divorce in some circles is accompanied by a bias against remarriage; the divorced man or woman is seen as a poor choice. It turns out that, while divorce rates increase, the rate of remarriage also rises. Leslie, among others, concludes that in the United States "between 20 and 25 percent of all persons marrying recently have been entering marriage for the second or subsequent time." [36]

[33] Andrew Collver and Eleanor Langlois, "The Female Labor Force in Metropolitan Areas, An International Comparison," *Economic Development and Cultural Change,* Vol. 10, No. 4, July 1962, p. 367.

[34] Leslie, op. cit., p. 592.

[35] K. Ishwaran, *Family Life in the Netherlands,* The Hague, Van Keulen, 1959, pp. 57–58.

[36] Leslie, op. cit., p. 629. Among the more revealing studies cited are: Jessie Bernard, *Remarriage, A Study of Marriage,* New York, Dryden, 1956; and Paul C. Glick, "First Marriages and Remarriages," *American Sociological Review,* Vol. 14, December 1949, pp. 726–734.

We do not know, of course, the extent to which the permeating influences of urban values have figured in liberalizing attitudes toward the remarriage of divorced persons. However, as with the rising divorce rate, the remarriage rate tends to rise as the influence of urbanism spreads.

Goode shows that on the American scene the divorce rate per 1,000 marriages, as we would expect, varies widely with different sections of the population. For example, the rates are 257.7 for service workers, 180.3 for industrial laborers, but 67.7 for those with professional occupations.[37] Divorce rates by level of occupation and income should remind us that the sphere of work is not unrelated to family stability. The rates are highest among people who do the dirtiest, the lowest paid, the least respected, and least secure kinds of work in the community.

Marris also found in a West African city that divorce varied with occupational groups, that the rates tend to be higher for industrial workers than for the middle class.[38] It should be mentioned that great concern about divorce is largely found in Western society. In developing societies where the extended family is still strong, marriage breakup is no disturbing event, except in cities where Western law has been establishd.

THE CHANGING POSITION OF WOMEN

In the industrial countries it is fully accepted that upper-class women do not enter the labor market, although today they may circumspectly do so if they have acquired some professional competence. It was once a matter of pride for American farmers to keep their daughters out of the labor market. Prior to 1900 the industrial labor market had little to offer women except unskilled jobs. The typewriter opened the way for women to enter offices. World War I opened the way to certain better industrial jobs from which they had previously been barred, and World War II opened the gates still wider. The taboos still exist, but job opportunities multiply for women, and now it is quite accepted for women to take employment, marry, and continue working.

However, it is well known that women's wages, even for the same kind and quality of work, are lower than men's, and annual earnings are from a third to a half lower. The current Liberation Movement among women, centering in large American and Canadian cities, is demanding greater equality. However, it is confined to women in the more sophisticated occupations. It could in time spread downward to the lower occupations where most women work. Perhaps the majority of working

37 William J. Goode, *After Divorce*, New York, Free Press, 1956, p. 66.
38 Peter Marris, *Family and Social Change in an African City*, London, Routledge and Kegan Paul, 1961, pp. 51 and 114.

women accept existing conditions. Actually for many the job is secondary to marriage as a goal.[39] Most, if not all women who enter the modern labor market face the ambiguous position of their two roles. Many face the choice of a career of housekeeping and child-rearing. Some try to do both, and this Bierstedt calls the "woman problem."

> To reconcile two careers, one based on physiological fulfillment and the other on cultural creativity—this is the problem for which our society has so far found no satisfactory solution. Men and women alike, as we have seen, occupy many different statuses, but for women, the norms attached to these statuses pull them more frequently in two directions and leave them in conflict, caught between contradictory demands.[40]

In our educational system, girls and boys are taught the same basic subjects, as if both were being readied for the labor market. The assumption is that as each participates in the sphere of work the cost of education will be paid back. Both girls and boys envision participation in the labor market, but the industrial economy loses if women turn from employment to become wives and mothers. As Klein sees it there is a sacrifice on their part.

> Moreover, many young women—particularly those who have been trained for one of the highly skilled jobs or professions—feel personally involved in their work and committed to it. They are reluctant to give up their jobs at a point when they have just reached a reasonable level of proficiency.[41]

In a study by Morgan on the income and welfare of 773 working wives, only 34 of these were found to work because their husbands were moderately or seriously disabled. Of the working wives who were under 65 years of age, 146 had some college education, 290 had completed high school and 316 had less than 12 years of education; on the whole, a fairly high average level. When the husbands were asked their views about their wives working it was found that 342 were favorable, 266 were negative or ambivalent, and 143 were opposed.[42] Significantly, this last was a

[39] For figures regarding women in the labor market as reported in the 1950 Census, see Otos D. Duncan and Albert J. Reiss, Jr., *Social Characteristics of Urban and Rural Communities,* New York, Wiley, 1956, pp. 81 and 130; also Chester L. Hunt, "Female Occupational Roles and Urban Sex Ratios in the United States, Japan, and the Philippines," *Social Forces,* Vol. 43, March 1965, pp. 407–417.

[40] Robert Bierstedt, *The Social Order, An Introduction to Sociology,* New York, McGraw-Hill, 1963, p. 371.

[41] Viola Klein, "Married Women and Employment," *International Journal of Comparative Sociology,* Vol. 1, No. 2, September 1960, p. 256.

[42] James N. Morgan, et al., *Income and Welfare in the United States,* New York, McGraw-Hill, 1962, pp. 130–135.

special group of husbands, either out of the labor market or only marginally in it.

The views of husbands about wives working are difficult to assess. In general, it appears that husbands at the higher occupational levels are much less averse to their wives working than are husbands at the common labor level where traditional views about "the woman's place" are still strong.[43]

THE FAMILY LIFE CYCLE

Table 10 presents a picture which reflects stages in the family life

Table 10   Median Age of Husband and Wife at Selected Stages of the Family Life Cycle, in the United States for 1890, 1960, and a Projection for 1980

Stage	1890	1960	1980
Median age of wife at:			
First marriage	22.0	20.2	19.4–20.4
Birth of last child	31.9	25.8	27–28
Marriage of last child	55.3	47.1	48–49
Death of one spouse	53.3	63.6	65–66
Median age of husband at:			
First marriage	26.1	22.3	22–23
Birth of last child	36.0	27.9	29–30
Marriage of last child	59.4	49.2	51–52
Death of one spouse	57.4	65.7	68–69

Source: Paul C. Glick, David M. Heer, and John C. Beresford, "Social Change and Family Structure, Trends and Prospects," reprinted in Evelyn M. Duvall, *Family Development*, Philadelphia, J. B. Lippincott, 1962, p. 23.

cycle since 1890 in the United States. We include only the figures for 1890, 1960, and the projection for 1980. It should be noted that the period of the marriage partners' living together has lengthened by several years before separation by death. In 1890 it was likely in most cases that one spouse would die before the last child married. Many economic, social, cultural, and technological changes are reflected here. The 1960 family would be strange to the 1890 family and might even be called deviant in structure, functions, and ways of thinking. These are changes in the family, not family breakup. Nor can they be called pathological, except in terms of the cultural definitions of 1890. So runs the course of the nuclear family in the industrial society; it functions as a child-rearing

[43] The pros and cons of this question are presented in a book by F. Ivan Nye and Lois W. Hoffman (Eds.), *The Employed Mother in America*, Chicago, Rand McNally, 1963; see chapters by David M. Heer, Robert O. Blood, and Lois W. Hoffman.

unit. States Aubert, "The eventual dissolution of the family is inherent in its biological and social function, and this perspective upon the future is built into its very role structure."[44]

There is, to be sure, the cultural carry-over from one generation to the next. The spouses, as representatives of their own families of procreation, normally retain contact with their respective kin, while occupied with starting families of their own. Later they are themselves in a kind of "bridging" role between the family home and the new homes established by their own married children. But with the present generation the aging parents cannot presume to have "rights" in the homes of their children.

It is something new for parents to have up to fifteen or more years together after all the children have married. Perhaps the old father can work a few years before being retired, when he and the elderly mother become a problem to themselves. Seldom do the homes of their children have space for them, and just as often they will not intrude upon their children. They cannot very well, since they reared their children to be independent.

Leslie notes the widening gulf between married children and their retired parents. Citing various studies, he shows a steady decline in three-generation households, down to 2 or 3 percent in some cities.[45] Old age as a challenge increases with the lengthening of life. It means a population with more old people. In 1890 the median age of the American population was 24.6 years but in 1950 it was 31.6. In 1900 4.1 percent of the population was 65 years of age or over, as compared with 9.2 percent in 1960. The industrial urban society, putting great emphasis on work, is the only society to set people aside after they have passed beyond work. In primitive society the old are honored because of age. Willmott and Young tell us that 11 percent in a London poor area and six percent in the London suburb did not have children near to help them in case of illness.[46] Dore found that in Japan where the complex industrial urban life had begun less than a century ago rural expectations regarding the aged and their care are still firmly present among urban people. This is not surprising for such a homogeneous people; Japan has not been a melting pot for many kinds of immigrants of different backgrounds. Dore asked 70 parents of boys in Tokyo, which of their children would support them in their old age. Of these, 35 indicated the eldest son, 14 would depend on all their children, and 6 mentioned children and other kin. Even those who could rely only on kin support did not mention the social security system of Japan, although they were aware of it.[47]

44 Aubert, op. cit., p. 83.
45 Leslie, op. cit., p. 690.
46 Willmott and Young, *Family and Class in a London Suburb*, p. 74.
47 Dore, op. cit., pp. 131 and 149.

American attitudes regarding the care of the old are shown in Table 11. These data, based on Morgan's study of income and welfare, are from

Table 11   Attitude of American Family Heads on Care of Aged Parents

Attitude of head of family on government responsibility for the aged	Family heads	Percent of family heads
Relatives should have sole responsibility	773	28.9
Relatives should have primary responsibility, government helping if necessary	827	29.7
Relatives and government should share responsibility	247	9.0
Government should have primary responsibility, relatives helping if necessary	161	5.6
Government should have sole responsibility	648	21.8
Other answers, no opinion, or answer not ascertained	144	5.0
Total	2,800	100.0

Source: James N. Morgan, et al, *Income and Welfare in the United States*, New York, McGraw-Hill, 1962, p. 172.

a national sample. Note that more than a fifth of the households (21.8 percent) in this affluent country and in 1959, a year of full employment, opted for total government responsibility for aged parents.

SOME APPARENT FAMILY TRENDS

As Truxal and Merrill wrote in 1945, repeating a thought by Willystine Goodsell, written in 1934, "The traditional, patriarchal, authoritarian and indissoluble family is changing, giving place to a new equalitarian, and unstable family centered about affection and child-rearing."[48] If the family is evolving toward an egalitarian (or partnership) form we can be sure that this is an adaptation to the individuating forces in urban living and the industrial work system. The "unstable family" does not necessarily imply family disorganization; rather it should be seen as a flexible family, as flexible as modern life must be in a changing community.

Regarding the transition of the American family, Burgess has identified six principal areas of adaptation:

1. From a union held together by external pressure to one maintained by internal attraction.

[48] Truxal and Merrill, op. cit., p. 761.

2. From authoritarian and autocratic control (usually by the male) in husband-wife relations to a relationship which is mutual and permissive.
3. From traditional, static, and conventional designs to adaptive and creative ones.
4. From duty and respect in the family relationship to one of personal happiness and affection.
5. From subordination to family objectives in home life to the mutual self-expression of family members.
6. From the accommodation of different attitudes of husband and wife to a relationship of toleration and assimilation.[49]

Whatever the emerging family design, we can be sure it will not be the last, and we can be equally sure it will not be a family without problems. Most crucially, we may well expect that its daily concerns will center on orientation to the changing demands of industrial urbanism.

[49] Ernest W. Burgess, "Companionship Marriage in the United States," in Anderson, op. cit., p. 70.

Communities and their collective work | 12

THE POTENTIAL FOR COLLECTIVE ACTIVITY

Communities exist because they are needed to perform services, and these services are public work. A city engages in many kinds of work, some of which are not performed by smaller communities. The markets in a community must be regulated; without rules and order, conflict would increase. The thief must be curbed and robber bands put down. The community must be secure in its water and food supply. Roads and streets must be made passable. This is work that only the organized community can perform.

In the organized community there is also much work that private groups can perform, if they do no more than think up work, which can be performed by public means. Indeed, there is now emerging in the more advanced nations a Community Development (CD) movement whose purpose is to initiate private collective activity in communities. It is based on the belief that people have a potential for collective activity. Ross writes:

> This implies that groups of people, even those in situations which many people feel hopeless, can develop attitudes and skills which permit them to work effectively at the task of shaping their community more adequately to meet their needs. . . . Even in depressed neighborhoods, people have shown capacity to function as a unit . . . and where consideration has been given to development of skill in cooperative work, the achievements over a period of time have been considerable.[1]

This conception of community work is both worthy and possible, although it is also promotional. The Community Development expert

[1] Murray G. Ross, *Community Organization*, New York, Harper & Row, 1967, pp. 86–87.

aims at building community cooperation and neighborliness in areas where these qualities are not found, and not infrequently he is successful to a degree. He is concerned with how things should be. In this chapter, however, we shall limit our observations to things as they are.

The formally organized community, and our attention is primarily on the city, is a work-performing establishment, meeting the common needs of the people, whether in their work or leisure activities. The services performed by the city are not only for those within its boundaries; they serves others who are widely dispersed. If the city grows, that is evidence that more people are making use of it. And as it grows the demands for services increase in volume and variety. We may say that, beyond the obvious in such an observation, we must recognize that community living calls for group behavior respecting different public works, from those which are taken for granted (use of streets and roads) to those which call for particular organized behavior based on agreements.

Clearly, there are many differences in community behavior, both of public bodies and of private groups. If the community is in danger, there will be ready response (sometimes even heroic response) on the part of both public and private organizations. But if the crisis is one of unemployment, groups may disintegrate and the tempo of the community become sluggish. Community differences in behavior are seen in a study by Dean of five towns. She found that each had its own way of behaving. Let us look at three of these, the first prospering, the other two not.

1. *Factoryville*

Dean sees this place of about 80,000 as reflecting the industrial image of America which is revealed in the speeches of politicians or the utterances of leaders of industry and business. "This is a fully developed industrial community, and its felt problems are largely procedural. . . . The issues are not partisan or ideological, but practical and strategic." But Factoryville is grubby and slummy even while it bursts with growth. For those who fare well nothing else matters.

> There are several gloomy slum areas, within the city and on its edges. The streets are choked with cars and you can't find a place to park. Teenage boys in black leather jackets congregate on street corners and lounge about, trying to look tough. The people on the sidewalks look well fed but curiously shabby, as if they have taken on the grayish coloration of the shabby city they live in. And everywhere there is smoke and grime, those unlovely rewards of unceasing and expanding industrial activity.[2]

2 Lois R. Dean, *Five Towns, A Comparative Community Study*, New York, Random House, 1967, pp. 86–87.

2. *Minersville*

This is a coal mining town whose population, once 20,000, is down to about 7,000. While the tonnage output of the mines has not declined, 300 workers can now produce what 2,000 did ten years ago. The dominant industry is owned and controlled by forces far from the town, the mine owners and the United Mine Workers. Dean sees the place as insulated and the people as alienated. The mining companies have produced the isolation of the place, and a parochialism has taken possession.

> Insularity and alienation, compounded by more than a decade of economic decline, have blunted social awareness and induced languor in Minersville's local leaders. And the usual corrective—replacement of the old and disenchanted by the more daring and vigorous young—has not been available, because the young have departed in droves, and continue to do so. Thus the vicious circle is complete; from isolation to insulation and alienation, to languor, and around in perpetual feedback, with no indigenous leaders to break the chain.[3]

It might be asked what more imaginative indigenous leaders might do in such a situation, or how government might be used to revive a primary-industry community, whether it is mining, pulp and paper production, or fishing. Coal mining is in the process of being technically revolutionized.[4] It is to be expected that Minersville would have a down-at-the-heel appearance and would behave accordingly.

3. *River City*

This place had 20,000 inhabitants in 1920 but was down to 9,000 at the time of the study. Dieselation took away many railroad jobs and the woodworking plants passed into history with the disappearance of hardwood timber. There remain several agriculture servicing small industries and River City is again what it once was, an area market town. Dean notes that while the economy is down, morale is not, because River City in spirit and tradition is still "ante-bellum Southern and it seems to expect that 'The South' will rise again." This place, as we read the report, is inclined to live at peace with its old habitat, its history, and limited prospects. It may look run down, but does not feel so.

> Although River City is insulated, there is little of Minersville's languor; and in place of Minersville's passive alienation, there is in River City a

[3] Ibid., pp. 50–51.
[4] On this technological revolution, see Thomas Kennedy, *Automation Funds and Displaced Workers,* Cambridge, Harvard University Press, 1962.

passionate determination to succeed, the odds notwithstanding. Where Minersville is mired in its own lassitude, River City is a dedicated seeker after its own proud past. Except for a few gracious old residential neighborhoods, River City's physical appearance is decidedly tacky and unkempt. The downtown store fronts are old and dusty.[5]

Dean, having a more urbane sophisticated outlook, would see much in these small cities that the local people would not be aware of or concerned about. Of the other two towns in her group, Hometown is a slow-growing industrial community of about 50,000 and is stable in its morale. While it takes on urban character, its rural links remain strong. Newtown, the fifth in the group, is a planned residential suburb outside a metropolis, without industry, but also without history. Its inhabitants are mostly middle class. All sorts of organizations are present, but Newtown hardly qualifies as a whole community. Its working people have their jobs elsewhere.

THE NEEDS AND FUNCTIONS OF COMMUNITIES

Weber visualized communities, especially cities, as first emerging under the rule and protection of a lord or prince. The community, as he perceived the situation, was a domain to be exploited, and trade and the protection of trade were important aspects of the city. "However, the lord or prince might also hope to profit from the local settlement of tradesmen and mechanics capable of paying taxes and, as soon as the market settlement rose around the market, from land rents arising therefrom."[6]

Most others living in the emerging city were there for about the same practical reasons as the lord or prince. The craftsmen made things to sell, the farmers brought their produce, traders from elsewhere came to buy and sell, even the entertainers performed for a livelihood. As a market and a place of residence, the emerging city itself made demands on those living there. Or in other words, those living in the place had certain common needs which the community as an entity had to serve. If a storehouse was needed to protect goods against the weather, the lord or prince must have taken the initiative, as he also, being in the position of leader, must have taken the initiative in establishing standard weights and measures.

If walls had to be built to protect the city (and the wealth collected there) from armed bands, the safety of all would be involved, but getting it done depended on the initiative of the lord or prince, who had also to defend his citadel at the city center. As Mumford puts it: "Insofar as it

[5] Dean, op. cit., pp. 64–65.
[6] Max Weber, *The City,* translated and edited by Don Martindale and Gertrud Neuwirth, New York, Free Press, 1958, p. 67.

had a quasi-military use, the primitive citadel was rather a holding point, where the chieftain's booty, mainly grain and possibly women, would be safe against purely local degradations—safe that is to say, against the attack of resentful villagers." [7]

Despite the life and death power held by the lord or prince over his subjects within the city and the villagers without, he also had a responsibility for the well-being of the whole collectivity. Was his city supplied and secure in its water and food stores, in the supply of raw materials needed by the craftsmen who made things? How were strangers treated who came to buy and sell? Was the city within the walls filthy and stinking, or tolerably clean? As a collectivity, the city had the function of protection, of supply, of internal order. The ruler who made the rules had himself to abide by them even when ruling in his own self-interest. Writing about primitive Eastern cities, Coe notes, for instance that the well-being and survival of the cities gave a sense of security to the rice farmers whose work made the city secure.[8]

Community functions arise in the course of collective efforts to cope with continuing common needs. Supply is a never-ending need; so too are order and protection. It does not matter whether the city is ancient, medieval, or modern, whether governed by a king, by an aristocracy, or whether it is self-governing. These functions are necessary and must be collectively performed. They are performed to meet common needs, although they may differ in their mode of fulfillment from one community to another; and they are common to all settled collectives. However, when we look at modern communities we find that certain functions which may have been of little challenge, say to seventeenth-century cities, assume a serious aspect today. Traffic, transportation, the pollution of streams and the atmosphere, to name only a few, have become serious problems to which communities today must seek collective answers.

THE EVOLUTION OF COLLECTIVE PUBLIC WORK

As we have stated in different contexts, the city is a place where many kinds of work are performed. The city has other uses, to be sure, but work is basic to all of them. Tasks that are done by the community as a whole, normally for the benefit of the community as a whole, are public work; building the city wall, centuries later removing the wall and making a street where it stood, digging drains so water can wash the waste away, bringing pure water in through a network of pipes, maintaining a police

[7] Lewis Mumford, *The City in History, Its Origins, Its Transformations, and Its Prospects,* New York, Harcourt, Brace, & World, 1961, p. 36.

[8] Michael D. Coe, "Tropical Forest Civilizations," *Comparative Studies in Society and History,* Vol. 4, 1961–1962, pp. 71–72.

force, providing for different types of inspection, these are types of public work entrusted to the authorities who have been elected to govern. Each office, bureau, or department of that government has no other reason for being than to perform some special kind of work for the community, such as, constructing and maintaining facilities or providing services.

All of these functions, perhaps only in elemental form, were once performed under the authority residing in the citadel, but were later the responsibility of a more dispersed authority, the top families. In time the authority came to reside in the citizens and was by them delegated to chosen officials. Much of this evolution in the West has taken place since about 1800. As Simon describes in her history of government in Manchester, England, achievement of total citizen control did not come without a step-by-step contest between the smaller group holding power and the citizens demanding an equal share of it.[9]

The institution of municipal government in British cities in 1838 was beneficial mainly to property owners, which meant that only property owners were elected to office. Most of the working people were illiterate. Illiteracy at that time was not presumed to be a handicap for most of the available industrial labor. This attitude began changing slowly after 1870 when the government assumed responsibility for elementary education. Elementary education had been under way in the United States already for nearly half a century. Indeed, the American teacher was the secular missionary of the frontier where local government was needed and much used. In Canada, where no federal government existed until 1867, elementary education was left to the initiative of various churches. In the United States the public school system, supported by gifts of public land, provided the elementary education for a literate electorate, the better to make use of civil government at the local level.

However, in American cities popular government and responsible citizen control did not come easily. For urban government more sophistication is needed than for small town or village government. Moreover, in the cities men of competence, with an aptitude for management, turned to industry and commerce rather than to government. Those with an interest in politics found the way clear to make politics a business. Corruption in urban government became general, in the South as well as the North. This condition, with occasional scandals, came to be roundly but ineffectively condemned by reformers in the 1890's. What brought change was the work of the "muckrakers," certain journalists who in popular writings exposed the evil doers in public office who not infrequently were in collusion with businessmen and public contractors.

Part of the blame for public corruption rested on the informed citizen

[9] Shena D. Simon, *A Century of City Government, Manchester 1838–1938,* London, Allen and Unwin, 1938.

who took such conditions for granted. Civic groups that act as the community conscience had not yet come into existence, although they did begin taking form at about that time. It was the muckrakers who stirred people to found such voluntary civic groups. Among the journalist critics the name of Lincoln Steffens stands out.[10]

Beginning about 1910, American city government, of necessity, had to become more efficient and responsible. Business interests have not ceased in their efforts to use the municipality for private gain, but the watch-dog activities of organized citizen groups make for tighter control. With this change there has been a rise in the quality of the personnel in public service. Higher standards are set for the recruitment for public service, and upper-level public servants come to be professional in their standards and methods of work. In short, public administration has come increasingly under the surveillance of bureaucratic procedures.

Freedgood calls attention to important changes in the composition of the population in American industrial cities. Immigrants of many origins were conspicuously present in these cities in about 1900. Many were illiterate and few spoke English. The situation gave rise to a type of political machine which, while serving the immigrants, used them to keep itself in power. Urban politicians now have different constituencies—at least better educated ones—to deal with.

> The machine fed on the immigrants, but it also helped them—with jobs, with welfare services and personal favors, with Christmas baskets and dippers of coal—and the immigrants in turn were generous with their votes. . . . Reduced immigration gave the city time to absorb the earlier newcomers, reduce the language barriers, educate them and their children, and raise many of them into the middle class. This, along with federal social insurance, reduced the dependence of the big-city masses on the political machines.[11]

While this may be true of immigrants in the great industrial cities of the northern states, it does not explain irresponsible and often corrupt government in the cities of the southern states. In the southern cities the Negroes comprised the bulk of the lower working class, but the whites controlled the government.

In the course of their evolution, from the time when cities were ruled by kings to the present when the cities of the West are, in general, governed by representatives elected by the citizenry, the essential functions of collective urban living have continued to be performed. It is true that they were not always efficiently performed and the benefits have not always

10 See Lincoln Steffens, *Shame of the Cities*, New York, McGuire Phillips, 1904; and *Autobiography of Lincoln Steffens*, New York, Harcourt, Brace, 1931.

11 Seymour Freedgood, "The Strength in City Hall," in *The Exploding Metropolis*, by the editors of *Fortune*, Garden City, New York, Doubleday, 1958, p. 65.

been equitably shared. The evolution, though always involving much contest, has been in the direction of increasing efficiency in administration and in a more equitable distribution of public benefits. As Lord Bryce wrote in 1888, after considering the state of corruption in American cities at the time:

> It is probable that no other system of government would have been able to cope any more successfully, on the whole, with the actual conditions that American cities have been compelled to face. It may be claimed for American institutions even in cities, that they lend themselves with wonderfully little friction to growth and development and to the peaceful assimilation of new and strange peoples . . . progress has been made, and substantial progress, from decade to decade.[12]

This evolution still continues, largely in consequence of the rising level of education, to where there is a widening awareness of the functions and operations of government.

THE DILEMMA OF THE INDUSTRIAL CITY

The industrial city is the dominant form in North America and is normally the center of a metropolitan area. Lesser cities, towns, and villages within its area tend to identify with its economic, social, and cultural life. In the United States there are more than 200 such metropolitan areas, each with its central city or twin cities. It would be hard to find a small community that does not lie within the metropolitan sphere of a city. In medieval and ancient times when cities were states in their own right, each city laid a proprietary claim on a varying number of outlying communities and ruled them. Today the "rule" is absent but the hold of the city continues. The main difference is that the modern city is itself a subordinate unit of the province or state or, as in Britain, the national government. The charter from the state indicates the functions the city may perform and the conditions under which its government will operate, but the state retains control over taxation and unusual expenditures. This may not seriously inconvenience small cities but large cities are often hindered by such controls and may be victimized by political bias in state legislatures.[13]

Fortunately for the United States and the non-French part of Canada, the English concept of local government was followed, the assumption

12 James Bryce, *The American Commonwealth,* New York, Macmillan, 1895, Vol. 1, p. 666.

13 George S. Blair, *American Local Government,* New York, Harper & Row, 1964, pp. 70–76.

being that the maximum governing responsibility should rest with the local community. The American city, although fashioned after the English model, "sailed alone" in developing its structure. Its problem was to adapt to a new environment, absorb many kinds of people, and grow with the minimum of interference from higher public authority. As a collectivity, it began with the minimum of experience. It is beyond an informed guess to postulate what the evolution of these same cities might have been under such a prefecture system as that in France where 38,000 cities, towns, and villages are governed by the prefectural branch of the ministry of interior in Paris.[14]

After a century of experimenting, much blundering, not a little corruption, considerable well-meant but often short-sighted guidance from the states, and despite continuous political bias on the part of the rural populations, American cities have achieved a high level of municipal efficiency. In most cases the government of great cities (New York, Detroit, Chicago, Los Angeles) is more efficient than the state governments to which they are responsible. Crouch and McHenry cite, for example, the many charter changes made by Los Angeles, which indicate how one city has been continuously venturing and experimenting, making some mistakes, but not slipping into lethargy.[15] To be sure, as evolution in nature is a wasteful process, there has been waste in the evolution of effectively managing the industrial city in the West, as much as there has been incalculable waste in the evolution of industry itself.[16] But in the process, the efficiency of the city as a system for performing many kinds of work has increased.

PUBLIC SERVICES AND EXPECTATIONS

We can assume that in the history of communities people looked to the organized authority to perform tasks that they could not perform as individuals, as families, or in small work groups. If the water supply was insufficient, or being polluted, it was a concern of all. The authority for the community, if only a council of elders, would be expected to take action. A ditch might be dug to bring in a more adequate supply of water. Perhaps all able-bodied men would be called on to contribute

14 See Brian Chapman, *The Prefects and Provincial France,* London, Allen and Unwin, 1957, p. 173. He calls attention to the inability of the prefecture system to adapt to economic and technological change. It governs more on the basis of precedent than experiment. Local initiative is not encouraged.

15 Winston W. Crouch and Dean E. McHenry, "Los Angeles," in William A. Robson (Ed.), *Great Cities of the World,* London, Allen and Unwin, 1957, p. 303.

16 On the political problems engendered in the process, see William S. Sayre and Nelson W. Polsby, "American Political Science and the Study of Urbanization," in Philip M. Hauser and Leo F. Schnore (Eds.), *The Study of Urbanization,* New York, Wiley, 1965, p. 146.

labor. As for pollution, the council of elders might appoint someone to police the water supply to prevent pollution. In medieval walled cities safety from fire was important. For the safety of all, the city authorities established certain rules. Citizens, round the clock and through the week, had to take turns as watchers, doing public service as volunteers but with authority. In time this work became a full-time occupation of paid public servants. Rural villagers may be expected to keep the road passing their property in good repair. But streets in cities are better kept by the use of a public works crew, and the organized community is better able than individuals to build a bridge where it is necessary to keep traffic moving.

Beals mentions three levels or types of public labor in a Sierra Tarascan village, types that are still found in rural places and were prevalent in small towns during frontier times. The first is public work for which the organized community pays, mainly relating to the physical appearance and workability of the community, which would include building a masonry wall, paving the street at the town center, etc. The second is repetitive work that all citizens do under public supervision and for which they receive no pay, such as cleaning irrigation ditches. The third is the public work one does on his own property or on roads and streets along his property, like removing noxious weeds, keeping fences in repair, or removing garbage.[17] These are housekeeping tasks needed to make a community livable, few of which can be performed by citizens in cities.

Here we give Walker's list of services provided by the city of Chicago which, while not exhaustive, gives us some indication of the public services of modern cities.

Airports	Ambulance service	Advance sewer planning
Construction	Boiler inspection	Crime detection laboratory
Hospitals, clinics	Bridge operation	Electrical inspection
Housing	Dead animal removal	Local transportation
Libraries	Education	Motion picture censorship
Planning (space)	Fire department	Occupational training
Police, courts	Milk inspection	Plumbing inspection
Poor relief	Rat and pest control	Parks, playgrounds, beaches
Public docks	Slum clearance	Venereal disease control
Recreation	Smoke abatement	Ventilation inspection
Subways	Super highways	Waterworks system
Welfare of infants	Swimming pools	Welfare administration [18]

Some of these services came under the government jurisdiction during crisis situations and have continued, perhaps taking on additional related

[17] Ralph L. Beals, *Cheran, A Sierra Tarascan Village,* Washington, D.C., Institute of Social Anthropology, 1946, p. 109.
[18] Robert A. Walker, "Chicago," in William A. Robson (Ed.), *Great Cities of the World,* London, Allen and Unwin, 1957, pp. 203–205.

duties. Some services are extensive departments which also perform services not on the list. Each public service, whether in this list or included among the functions of listed offices or departments, constitutes acceptance by the municipality of a particular responsibility. Of course, all services found in one city may not be found in another. One city, for example, may operate a public slaughter house, another city may generate electricity, or another may operate public bus and subway lines. The wide differences in services merely point to the extent to which government is seen as an instrumentality for getting things done.

It is assumed by some that when a community becomes more affluent, a greater number of services will be performed in a more efficient manner. However, during the Depression when federal funds were made available for relief labor to be used on public projects, it was found that many normally affluent cities had neglected various essential services. Some lacked an adequate sewage system, while others needed to modernize their street paving. Many had never built community centers and even more lacked play fields, swimming pools, and other facilities for leisure. Butte, Montana, was especially deprived. Absentee owners had taken billions out of the copper mines, but the city had not developed much beyond the status of a mining shacktown. Some $50 million of federal funds were used to provide such essential services as sewers.[19] It is expected that large cities, more enmeshed in bureaucracy than small cities, will respond more slowly to demands for new services or demands to revitalize existing services. However, despite size, large American cities, less under the influence of traditional practices, are more responsive to changing needs than European cities where old things and ways are respected. Sinclair calls London, for instance, a city governed by men long dead, where "incompetence and maladministration" are tolerated, where nothing gets done until it is too late, and is only half done then.[20]

TECHNOLOGY AND PUBLIC SERVICE

From Bridenbaugh's study of American colonial cities we get the impression that Boston was governed much after the fashion of an English village. The elected officials were indeed city fathers who usually did the accepted and expected. They were advised by top citizens and then issued instructions. If citizens were unduly inconvenienced, they had the right of complaint and petition, something seldom necessary. For example, in 1713 the Boston Council issued an order instructing citizens to grade the

[19] *Copper Camp, Stories of the World's Greatest Mining Town, Butte, Montana,* New York, Hastings House, 1944, p. 11.

[20] Robert Sinclair, *The Big City, A Human Study of London,* London, Reynal and Hitchcock, 1938, p. 11.

streets, higher at the center so the water would run to the gutters; this was work that householders had to perform.[21] Elsewhere Bridenbaugh reports on early fire protection. The Council in each city organized the volunteer fire brigades, but every householder had to have a leather bucket ever ready. As cities grew, the brigades became so untrustworthy that insurance companies pressured city councils to establish fire departments with paid firemen. The early councils gave much attention to the digging of wells to provide water for households and for fighting fire. Later it was necessary to employ a supervisor of wells, to keep the wells in his district "Sweet, Useful and in Good Repair." [22]

As cities grew, the wells ceased to serve and more complex ways of obtaining water were adopted. The traditionless American cities, even in the heyday of their corruption, found a way. They suffered plagues, until they learned to provide sewers, and furthered technology in both their systems of water supply and sewerage. In other respects, cities were impelled to adapt both to new scientific knowledge and technological advance. For example, it was once believed by many that the function of a sewer was to drain off surface water, not to carry away household waste. Murphy mentions that Boston in 1833 was the first to use sewers to carry all sewage, and he adds that this was not done in Paris until 1880.[23]

Much of the demand for keeping up with technology in transportation was due to the initiative of private transit companies changing from omnibuses and horse-drawn streetcars to electric street cars, and from surface to subway lines. To these, the cities responded as they did to the railroads, and later to the motor vehicle. Efficient transportation began with piling more people and things in urban centers, causing higher structures to be erected. Still more efficient transportation began drawing people and industry away from the central areas, while at the same time increasing their importance, and the demand at the center caused buildings to go still higher. Lines of communication, along with more traffic, were forced underground. All sorts of inventions in construction and amenities appeared. Steel structures for buildings and new types of cement, glass, and other building materials came to increase the efficiency of the ever taller structures. American municipal government proved ever able to respond.

But change in other public services was slow. As late as 1853, when the development of Central Park in New York began, there were few parks in American cities, nor was there any demand for them. There were few playgrounds as late as 1900, but again, there was no demand. Garwood tells of Kansas City being embarrassed in the 1880's when a local

21 Carl Bridenbaugh, *Cities in the Wilderness, The First Century of Urban Life in America, 1625–1742,* New York, Knopf, 1955, pp. 61 and 159.

22 Ibid., p. 63.

23 Earl F. Murphy, *Water Supply,* Madison, University of Wisconsin Press, 1961.

citizen gave 1,300 acres far out of town to be a city park. It remained undeveloped for years. Today the city has spread around it and Swope Park has become a valued property.[24]

The idea of street lighting was accepted only slowly and cautiously. First there were individual oil lamps here and there. A leap forward came with the arrival of electricity. With each technical step ahead the lighting system became more complex. It was not until the 1900's that most of the advances in public lighting came. During most of the 1800's many cities were still ineffectively experimenting with whale oil lamps, much of the work being let to private contractors. But, as Gill reports for Birmingham, England, that city and others were accepting street lighting as a public service.[25]

Through the same kind of experience, cities found that private companies could not be relied on to provide a city with its water supply. Only sixteen American cities in 1850 had public water works, but by 1897 3,196 American cities had their public water systems.[26]

Moreover, as American cities grew, the problem of fire protection moved out of reach of the early volunteer pump and bucket brigades and, as noted above, these volunteer groups were often more interested in plunder than in extinguishing fires. Under pressure from businessmen, New York was the first city to establish a professional fire department. That was in 1865, and Philadelphia followed in 1870.[27]

PUBLIC SERVICE AND THE REFORMERS

If we look again at the list shown above of public services provided by the city of Chicago, we can well imagine the conditions under which each of these services came to be a public responsibility. For example, "dead animal removal" was much in demand in cities before the automobile appeared. A city of three million needed no less than a million horses and the work life of an urban horse was short. In the course of a year thousands died in the streets. The horse is gone, but the service continues on a reduced scale, most dead animals removed in cities now being dogs and cats. The demands for occupational training and vocational education comes often when unemployment is high, or it may come in a period of full employment on demand from employers. Such services as libraries, museums, parks, playgrounds, housing for the poor, etc., are usually initiated by the reform-minded part of the population.

[24] Darrell Garwood, *Crossroads of America, A History of Kansas City,* New York, Norton, 1946, p. 204.
[25] Conrad Gill, *History of Birmingham,* Vol. I, London, Oxford University Press, 1952, p. 367.
[26] Murphy, op. cit., pp. 27 and 31.
[27] Fred K. Vigman, *Crisis in the Cities,* Washington, D.C., Public Affairs Press, 1955, p. 7.

In American cities the period of reform came in about 1890. The call was for playgrounds, cleaning up the slums, establishing community centers, improving the schools, and for cultural facilities such as libraries, museums, and concert halls, acquainting the immigrants with the American way of life.[28] Seen in retrospect, we are tempted to regard the reformers as a very unrealistic lot. With no conspicuous exceptions, the social, moral, and cultural problems, in their minds, were attributed to greedy and evil men; the avaricious landlord, the ruthless employer who kept wages down, and the conniving, corrupt politician. Many reformers believed that, with the aid of charity and a change in the hearts of men, the major social problems would disappear. The failings and weaknesses of the poor could be greatly reduced by establishing community centers (settlement houses) where the people of the different classes might mingle. There were, to be sure, a great many reformers, and they tended to form groups; those advocating playgrounds, those wanting parks and promenades to add beauty to the city, those concerned primarily with slum housing, those who would develop the cultural side of city life, and still others who would make the city clean and healthy. But all to some degree have helped to add particular services to those performed by municipalities. Although successful in achieving their goals, some reformers managed to become nuisance characters. Briggs, for instance, writes of the efforts of such reformers to get pure water for London.

> The advocates were often amateurs, men like Chadwick himself, who "seized on an abuse with the tenacity of a bulldog" and believed that he was battling against Fate itself, or Charles Kingsley, who identified sanitary reform with the will of God. The moral strength of Victorianism often lay in its reliance on amateurs rather than on professionals to get things done. At the same time, delay in implementing legislation was made worse by the tardiness of Victorians to develop skills for managing growing cities—engineering skills for example, and medical skills. The noisy opposition to Chadwick made the most of his dogmatism, his eagerness to provide non-expert answers to highly complex technical problems.[29]

American cities, it should be stated, moved fast in stimulating the skills needed for doing things that served the needs of practical men,

[28] Such books as the following were bench marks of that period:
    1880 Charles L. Brace, *Dangerous Classes of New York*
    1885 Josiah Strong, *Our Country*
    1890 Jacob A. Riis, *How the Other Half Lives*
    1892 Jacob A. Riis, *The Children of the Poor*
    1893 Jane Adams, et al., *Philanthropy and Social Progress*
    1893 B. O. Flower, *Civilization's Inferno*
    1893 C. D. Randall (Ed.), *History of Child Saving in the United States*
    1894 William T. Stead, *If Christ Should Come to Chicago*
    1897 Charles R. Henderson, *Social Spirit in America*
    1897 George E. Waring, *Street-Cleaning*
[29] Asa Briggs, *Victorian Cities*, London, Odham Press, 1963, p. 21.

many of whom were the villains in reform literature. They were not out of harmony with the colonial and frontier image of the city as a place where men work and compete in their work. In the city, as they saw it, every man took his chances. One neither asked nor gave quarter. What the reformers began demanding, only after city building had spread across the continent, were public services that served other than the work interests of people. In the city, it was demanded, the common man should also be reasonably secure in his health and have places where his children could play. Public services should be there, no less, to serve the cultural and leisure interests of people. At the time all services of this sort were outside the ken of the practical-minded. This appears to be true as well of other countries. Amsterdam waited decades to get a new town hall and opera. "Practical" needs come first.[30]

ON LEARNING TO USE GOVERNMENT

As idealized, the good citizen under democratic government is one who is informed about his government, and in various ways participates in community decision making. He pays his taxes, he votes, he participates in political groups. The modern city is such a democracy; indeed, a modern city could hardly function were it not at least a limited democracy. Yet we know full well that the conscientious citizen does not have the time to inform himself regarding all he needs to know to participate intelligently in public affairs.

Greer reports on an effort in metropolitan St. Louis to establish a plan for governing the city and its suburbs. Only 21 percent of the voters in the city and 40 percent of those in the suburbs went to the polls. The proposal was defeated by a two-to-one majority. Full information about the plan had been disseminated by newspapers and broadcasts. Despite this effort, it was found later that only the occasional citizen had a clear idea about the plan or its purpose.

Mostly, so Greer noted, the voters acted on reasons which had little relation to the facts. He concludes that the machinery of government tends to attract the attention of amateurs and those with public good will, but who at the same time are not very realistic. There are the politicians in search of some niche from which to climb, and Greer mentions the old men, many of whom oppose any change. The informed citizens who are able to see things in clear perspective are often not heeded. Real advance in public polity comes slowly, and often by accident.

[The gains] must survive the attack of that which exists. Their sponsors grow tired, but new generations come on. These efforts to make the

30 J. P. Wildschut, "Amsterdam," in Robson, op. cit., p. 134.

Heavenly City may be compared to fish eggs, spawned by the million, lost and devoured by other organisms, but occasionally producing a new model, which could not have been predicted or designed, but may have virtues of its own.[31]

As might have been expected, suburbanites, fearful of big city domination, were more than two to one against the proposed plan. Many who voted took their cues from the declared positions of certain groups or personalities. It is also possible that the outspoken support given to the plan by certain reform groups stimulated opposition voters.

It may be that we need to reconsider the notion that the individual is the unit in the democratic management of urban affairs. If we assume that his motivations to participate are alert and active, the magnitude of the urban complex is beyond his comprehension. He knows it is there for his service, but it is rarely capable of serving individuals except when they come with complaints. If the individual is interested in depolluting the atmosphere he does better to join with groups engaged in fighting for public measures against pollution. Some have described the interest groups as playing a game that never ends, because the stakes and alignments are ever changing. Government is influenced in one direction or another, as the public interest asserts itself in the course of the contest. As groups, the contestants know how to use government.

[The contest] may have very high stakes, including ideological goals, public offices and jobs, economic gains and losses, and provision of desired services. There are a variety of participants seeking various of these stakes, including party leaders, public officials, organized municipal bureaucracies, non-governmental interest groups, officials of other governments, and ordinary voters. The contest is carried on by certain generally understood "rules of the game," some formal and some informal. . . . There are many varieties of strategies open to the various participants.[32]

In these terms, the "order" in government, like that in the market, can be ideally shown on an administrative chart, but its functioning is never that precise and patterned. An ever-changing system itself, it must be so to function in the midst of ever-changing groups of many kinds. Government, as it renders services, is not a mechanism narrowly divided. It is involved with every type of organization within its embrace, whether the organization be economic, social, cultural, or political.

---

[31] Scott Greer, *Metropolitics, A Study of Political Culture*, New York, Wiley, 1963, p. 200.

[32] William S. Sayre and Herbert Kaufman, "Governing New York," quoted in Sayre and Polsby, op. cit., p. 131.

THE INTERDEPENDENCE OF PUBLIC
AND PRIVATE WORK

Wellington, New Zealand, is located in a hilly area. The private dairy company, delivering milk from house to house, found it uneconomical to climb a hill to serve a scattering of families. The conservative city government behaved as a socialist government would be expected to; it assumed the task of delivering all milk in the city. What had been private work for private gain became a public service. The authorities could not stop with milk delivery alone but began altering the price structure of milk products. The municipality also went further than the dairymen had done in setting standards for insuring the purity of the milk.[33]

As the above situation illustrates there is always a division of labor between work that is private and work that usually is, often must be, or by popular choice becomes the work of the government. Some kinds of private work are dangerous and government may have to assume responsibility for safety. Some kinds call for highly skilled labor, and government is looked to for education and training service. Some kinds need ample supplies of water, or roads, or an abundance of electric power; if private industry cannot meet the need, government may have to accept the responsibility. Such public services, taken for granted in an urbanized country, may be lacking in developing countries. An advanced industrialism must wait until the needed "infrastructure" is provided by government. First, a physical, technical, and cultural environment congenial to advanced industrialism must be provided.[34]

Some kinds of work may be either public or private and, with time, may change from one to the other. Examples abound, such as the operating lines of transportation, printing plants, plants for generating electric power, quarries and stone-crushing plants, recreation facilities, airports. Whether such work is private or public would depend on the circumstances in each case. Medical care, with all its infrastructure (medical schools, drug distribution, hospitals, plants for making drugs or appliances) may be a public service and a public responsibility, as when government provides care for the elderly and poor.

The Tennessee Valley Authority (TVA) is a world-renowned example of a public work organization. Not only is it engaged in producing electric power but it manufacturers fertilizer, reforests eroded lands, and does other regional rehabilitation work. It is also a "yardstick" for determining the fair cost of generating and distributing electric power, this being the main reason for the continuous propaganda against TVA by private elec-

[33] Ralph Brookes, "Wellington," in Robson, op. cit., p. 620.
[34] See a series of papers in Melvin J. Herskovits and Mitchell Harwitz (Eds.), *Economic Transition in Africa,* London, Routledge and Kegan Paul, 1964.

tric facilities. While altogether public plants produce only about five percent of the power generated in the nation, all serve as yardsticks, and the argument for and against such public work, Blair notes, goes on, but there is no clear and final resolution.[35]

Whether a kind of work is public or private, its organization is likely to be substantially the same, and its methods and tempo fairly similar. In the interest of efficiency, a public or private work organization demands about the same bureaucratic setup. If we look at the regulation functions of government, for example the regulation of insurance companies, we are confronted with a relationship between two bureaucracies, one private and the other public; neither can be less efficient over time than the other.

WORK ORGANIZATION AND BUREAUCRACY

It is well known that all types of private work, faced with keen competition, come increasingly to be dominated by the canons of efficiency, and most areas of work tend to be organized into larger and larger operating units. It follows that the management of work enterprises necessarily comes to be more complex and their operation more bureaucratic as they become more specialized in their internal division of functions. There comes to be greater interdependence between work places. These trends are imperative both for the management and predictability of the performance of work organizations.

Development in the organization of government follows a similar pattern. Indeed, much of the development in the bureaucracy of public work, meshed with that of private work, is inescapable because of the interdependency between the two spheres of work. Often those who condemn bureaucracy in government fail to recognize similar bureaucracies in the great world-circling private corporations, and the many similarities between the two.

Sjoberg finds in his study of the preindustrial city that urban communities very early faced the need of keeping and filling records, of using financial records in planning and ordering public administration. While the efforts were of a fumbling nature, at least the need for some order in public departments was recognized. Like any other social invention, generations of experiment were needed before impersonal bureaucracy was achieved.[36]

When the structure of a bureaucracy assumes the character of a mechanism whose utility increases as it is impersonally used, it is a challenge to the ascriptive traditions of work.[37] Bureaucracy, in the legal and

[35] George S. Blair, *American Local Government*, New York, Harper & Row, 1964, pp. 491 and 496.

[36] Gideon Sjoberg, *The Preindustrial City, Past and Present*, New York, Free Press, 1960, p. 237.

[37] Ibid., pp. 238–239.

rational sense of Max Weber (and he had government bureaucracy in mind) was rarely achieved in the preindustrial city where jobs were sold and sometimes a man's job could be inherited by his son. Persons acquired jobs by right of political patronage, on the basis of class or family identity, conditions that still prevail in some Latin American countries where it is assumed that one elected to office has the right to give jobs to his kin and friends, a practice which in the view of Davis is a barrier to dependable government there.[38]

The strictly impersonal, achievement-oriented imperatives of bureaucracy were accepted comparatively readily by business and industry. But acceptance in government was difficult, especially in large cities, as Rios found in Brazilian cities.

> Patriarchism still exerts a tremendous influence in politics. The state has not overcome the institution of the family, which absorbs many of its functions and permeates public relations with its peculiar styles and ways of action. Power, therefore, is not only obtained through elections or impartial choice, but through the elaborate system of personal connections. Consequentially, Brazil presents problems which do not exist in European countries.[39]

The work system of private enterprise can function effectively if it is amenable to the demands of bureaucratic management, but its efficiency may be far less effective if it must operate in relation to a public bureaucracy whose practices are uneven and unpredictable and whose integrity is often open to question. Developing countries, eager to industrialize, are usually governed by men who understand that industrialism brings with it new work disciplines which apply to the public as well as the private sphere, but their situation is ambiguous. As Shils points out, they stand between the expectations of a tradition-devoted people and the demands of a new order to which they are committed but which the people cannot yet understand. The people have many things to learn, most of which are considered elemental in the more industrial countries.[40]

CITIZENSHIP AND POPULAR VIGILANCE

It can be argued that government, especially in cities, becomes ever more involved in the total life of the citizens. As government performs services that affect them sometimes directly, more often indirectly, the

38 Kingsley Davis, "Colonial Expansion and Urban Diffusion in the Americas," *International Journal of Comparative Sociology*, Vol. I, No. 1, March 1960, p. 49.

39 José Arthur Rios, "Rio de Janeiro," in Robson, op. cit., p. 506.

40 Edward Shils, "Political Development in the New States," *Comparative Studies in Society and History*, Vol. 2, 1959–1960, p. 273.

citizens increasingly look to it for help for training and rearing the young, for security for person and property, for health and sanitation service, for providing and aiding in the supply of water, food, and fuel, for services and facilities related to leisure time, and even for services and facilities related to art and culture.

It can also be argued that government, like industry, becomes ever bigger, increasingly complex, and its control centers become less approachable for the ordinary individual. Much is said about the individual, lost in the masses, becoming an atom with only the identity of a number, being jostled about by forces he cannot control and rarely understands. The individualism that marked the frontier or the medieval town is lost. By these massive forces, man is alienated from all the old interests that had meaning for him.

It is not certain how much of the idealized individualism men actually enjoyed in medieval times or on the frontier was lost when men exhausted the land frontier and then turned to building great cities and establishing massive industries. Whether we approve of the results or not, creativity is still more evident than ever, both in the building and rebuilding of cities and in the technological development of industry. Citizenship was more meaningful in 1900 than it was in 1850, and by 1968 it has acquired dimensions unimagined in 1900. It is argued that citizenship is ceasing to be a value and it is not practiced as formerly. Actually, people were saying the same thing in 1900.

In Marshall's view citizenship, in its long evolution, has proceeded through three stages of struggle for rights: civil rights, political rights, and social rights, in that order.[41] Each of these rights involves a particular type of relationship between the citizen and his government, and there are many ways in which the exercise of these rights may be evident. Voting, however important, is only one. One participates by paying taxes and obeying the law, by writing complaint letters to public officers, but probably most effectively, by being identified with formal organizations that represent his interests. In this vein, Greer has noted three types of participants in community life: "community actors," who get personally involved in public life and organized groups, "neighbors" who involve themselves in matters of personal interest, and the "isolates," who comprise the majority, the "disengaged from the organizational structure." Isolates may read the local newspaper, but "they are ignorant and incompetent with respect to the local community's affairs." [42]

We need not ask here whether the "isolates" are relatively more predominant today than in grandfather's day. Is the isolate, in political

41 T. H. Marshall, *Citizenship and Social Class*, Cambridge, Cambridge University Press, 1950, pp. 10–12.

42 Scott Greer, *The Emerging City, Myth and Reality*, New York, Free Press, 1962, p. 120.

terms, an isolate as church member, family member, or neighbor? One may not be concerned about voting, and yet he may be active in his trade union. If he is a "rod and gun" devotee, he may vigorously support activities to pressure government into doing something to depollute streams. There are many ways in which the citizen through organization may make his public interests known to government.

The facts of modern community life and how the citizen should share in it obviously do not always fit the conventional pattern which is held up as the model, and which is here summarized by Blair:

> Expressed in terms of desirable principles, the governmental machinery within the metropolitan area should be so organized that 1) political decisions are made through processes in which all citizens can share; 2) political decisions are made by an informed citizenry through discussion and vote; and 3) political decisions are made so that the process of public discussion is a continuous phenomenon.[43]

Were citizens to wait for public services on the basis of this informed, all-participating approach the results would be disappointing. Needed bond issues, however urgent, rarely get approved by citizen vote. City fathers and government officials are more likely to be guided by the moves and moods of pressure groups. If a big slice of public funds is allocated to some development to please industry, a smaller slice will be given to appease the "good citizen" groups. In the industrial urban community Galbraith observes that the struggle of interest groups and vested interests for public benefits results in the needs of industry having highest priority; the hospital or the playground must take lesser priority.[44] This does not always mean political corruption, nor does it mean that the individual has ceased to be of consequence. Nor does it mean that popular vigilance has abdicated. Vigilance finds other ways of expression through interest groups and vested interests, which in terms of their own self-interest resist the efforts of opposing interest groups and vested interests. In the course of the contest the programs for public service tend to expand and multiply. These programs, becoming professional, become themselves a new kind of pressure influence, demanding growth and diversity.

43 Blair, op. cit., p. 561.
44 John K. Galbraith, *The New Industrial State,* Boston, Houghton Mifflin, 1967, p. 345.

Work in the industrial urban life | 13

INDUSTRY AS CHANGER OF WORK

It is not enough to say that the culture of a people depends in large part on their major type of work. Many kinds of work, like the cultures in which they are found, are local in some measure. Rural cultures, which depend on the raising of cattle and the tilling of soil, may differ considerably in details, although they will have many traits in common. The cultures of fishing people, who gain their livelihood from the sea, will also have much in common, but from one region to another there will be significant differences. Also, of course, there are considerable differences between the cultures of these two groups.

Industrial work differs from these in that it tends toward uniformities throughout the world. More than the many kinds of preindustrial work, industrial work is increasingly associated with machines and technics. Wherever in the world a textile mill is placed into operation, it must be operated very much like any other textile mill anywhere. To a large degree, the same vocabulary will be used, even though vocabulary similarity is more evident in the world-circling communication industries and the mass media.

The similarities which mark industrial work tend to be an outgrowth of the nature of the work itself and the mechanisms used. A like industry making rubber products, automobiles, steel products, or electrical appliances has a fairly similar division of labor from country to country, and the organization of work for each type of industry is about the same. Moreover, there is similarity in the tempo of the work in each type of plant. These and other similarities are necessitated by the standards of efficiency which prevail in each type of industry. If such standards are taken lightly, unit costs of production rise and the enterprise may not be able to compete in world markets.

Because of certain unrelenting qualities inherent in it, industrial work has been described by many as both demeaning and destructive. Much of this work is seen as monotonous and routine, although that is much less true of the more modern industrial plants. The old complaint about long hours is no longer heard, but there are those who still see industry as subordinating men to machines. There were those also who believed that men of evil intent were using machines to subordinate men.

Few of these humanitarians were able to understand that industrial work is different, that it must, for example, be impersonal. The rules and practices of the small workshop cannot serve in the factory. Industrial work would fail if it were to be ascriptive and familial. Yet many students of industrial work continue to be offended by its cold impersonality and often they lend vocal support to various schemes for introducing "human relations into industry." However, to others including Friedmann, a French sociologist, such "fine sentiments, personal affirmations, however elegantly expressed, make no solid contribution." [1]

What too often the critics fail to recognize is that the population is increasing at a very great rate. More and more people must flee from rural areas to the cities to earn their livelihood in the industrial sector. Industries must increase in number and to serve humanity they need to be efficient. Doubtless, ways will be found to make industrial work more humane, and indeed that is what is happening. But the industrial system, to serve humanity better must grow bigger and more productive, must continue to be impersonal and bureaucratic.

In all countries where industrialism is now firmly established, the factory and its work system, inducing continuous change, has not only disturbed traditional ways of life and work, but continues to do so. The major fears and complaints of 1850 were replaced by new fears by 1900. These in turn have been pushed into the background by the present fear of automation, which now appears in its proper place in the evolution of the industrial work system, and will be considered later.

WORK ASSUMES NEW DIMENSIONS

When Joseph Conrad in his sea stories glorified work, seeing it as the symbol of "man's involvement in life," he was thinking of the work a sailor performs aboard a ship, each man having definite tasks which, when well done, identified him with the total crew. His work makes him one with his shipmates.[2] Work in an industrial order also identifies the worker

---

[1] Georges Friedmann, *Industrial Society, The Emergence of the Human Problems of Automation,* New York, Free Press, 1964, p. 19.

[2] G. Geddes, "The Importance of Work to Conrad," *Queens Quarterly,* Vol. 73, No. 4, Winter 1966, p. 560.

with his fellows, somewhat personally in the immediate work unit, but impersonally with the entire enterprise. To the contrary, the ship's crew is a single unit, much like a family. Only the captain remains in the sphere of secondary contact. To maintain control, he must remain detached.

Wells takes issue with those who write eulogistically that preindustrial people identified with their work. Through the ages, he reminds us, work has been used to punish man. He recognizes that there will always be those who love their work, but most men in the industrial society see work as the only way to secure a livelihood. He adds that only in the world of insects has nature produced a worker type, that is, the bee, a worker by instinct.[3]

It is a matter of concern among Westerners who write about the work system of industry that those who have jobs in the system regard their work merely as a means to an end. And many call it alienation. Unrealistically, according to many critics, those who perform tasks that are dirty, heavy, or repetitive are expected to have a devotion to their work, to get some inner satisfaction from it. More than a century ago Marx wrote that a worker who does not get satisfaction from his work is detached from it, he works with his hand while his thoughts turn elsewhere. "He is at home when he is not working, and when he is working he is not at home." [4]

The old expectations about identity with work have little meaning in the industrial work system. It is a market in which workers sell their time and skill, usually for an hourly rate of pay. They work for money to meet the cost of living, and for most workers, living is in another sphere. This, then, is one of the dimensions of industrial work, it is normally not "lived with;" one lives outside his work. Even if conscientious on the job, the job is marginal to living as it provides the means for living.

Lewis relates how the Mexican peasant is too proud to ask a big land owner for a job. He uses some indirect way to make his wish known. Also he will not work for a man for whom he has no respect, which is generally true in rural communities.[5] It would be unusual for an industrial worker in a city to have any personal concern about his employer or care to know personally the foreman placed over him. He will find ways to get on with his cohorts in the work place, but may have little interest in knowing them socially away from the work place. He avoids talking about his family and other private matters, and he does not pry into the

3 H. G. Wells, *Work, Wealth and the Happiness of Mankind,* London, Heinemann, 1933.

4 *Karl Marx, Selected Writings in Sociology and Social Philosophy,* edited and translated by T. B. Bottomore, New York, McGraw-Hill, 1956, p. 169.

5 Oscar Lewis, *Life in a Mexican Village, Tepotzlin Revisited,* Urbana, University of Illinois Press, 1951, 110–111.

private lives of his fellow workers. Such acquaintance may come only after working together for a long period of time.

In the industrial work place the individual is there on his own, apart from his family, which enhances somewhat the impersonality of the industrial job. Moreover, the relationship between worker and employer is contractual, as it needs to be in the more heterogeneous and anonymous urban milieu. A careful record is kept of the time worked and the rate of pay for each particular level of work. This, says Bottomore, is consistent with relationships "between economically independent individuals." [6] The contractual relation involves not only worker-employer relations but all seller-buyer relations. In the contractual sphere little is left to memory or to good faith, it must be written on paper. A trade union, for instance, always demands a written contract.

Another dimension of industrial work concerns the relative lack of limits that may be imposed on the units a machine can turn out in an hour, or the ability of computers to solve intricate problems, or the heights of buildings, or the impact of the mass media, or the per-man output on this job or that. Nor is there any limit in sight for the tempo of life in the industrial community. As contracts divorce man from the old status relationships, so mechanisms in their environment and their outputs outmode all earlier notions of a fair day's work. In Mumford's words, "Organic processes are purposeful, goal-seeking, and self-limiting; indeed, all organisms have built-in controls that serve to coordinate action and limit growth. The expanding economy, like the technological system on which it is largely based, has no such limitations." [7] In contrast to the industrial economy, the organic processes mentioned by Mumford are clearly operative in the case of rural work. The farmer's work for the year is measured out by the seasons and each kind must be done in a particular season. There are obvious limits with which he cannot argue when he sets out to make two blades of grass grow where one grew before.

WORK AND MAN'S IDENTITY

Martin Luther propounded the idea that any kind of work needed in the community was a worthy *Beruf* or calling, that all kinds of work were interdependent, and that the humblest calling was as important in the eyes of God as the highest. Through his work one attained salvation. [8]

6 T. B. Bottomore, "The Ideas of the Founding Fathers," *Archives europeènnes de sociologie*, T. 1, No. 1, 1960, p. 40.

7 Lewis Mumford, *The City in History, Its Origins, Its Transformations, and Its Prospects*, New York, Harcourt, Brace & World, 1961, p. 545.

8 For a presentation of Luther's views about work as a phase of religious living and the blessings that follow faithful performance, see Klara Vontobel, *Das Arbeitsethos des deutschen Protestantismus*, Bern, Franke, 1946.

This idea went far in Germany to raise humble occupations to a status of respect. Even occupations such as that of chimneysweep were followed with pride. Workers often identified themselves by their distinctive hats or other features of dress. In our day there are different ways by which occupation identifies a person. Those in one occupation will know quickly if another belongs from his vocabulary. However, as Hughes observes, there are many kinds of occupations and occupations change so rapidly, few people know the characteristics of people according to craft. We tend to group people in socio-economic categories by which they are indirectly identified with levels of work: laborers, skilled workers, white-collar workers, specialists, managers, etc. But it is done in terms of visible marks of status, how they present themselves as consumers. "This," says Hughes, "has been so longer than we sociologists, with our love of stereotypes of the past against which we highlight the present, allow." [9]

Edwards, introducing a volume of government statistics on occupations, wrote of the value of a person's work history. It tells much about the kind of person he is (or was). Knowing the occupations held, we can be fairly certain about his level of education, his level of living, even the sort of house in which he lives. "And when life's span is ended, quite likely there is no other single set of facts that tell so much the kind of a man he was and the part he played in life as a detailed and chronological statement of the occupation or occupations he pursued." [10]

In the community occupations come to be appraised as high or low in prestige. The caste system illustrates not only how occupations in the Indian community were rated, but also how the people who did them were rated. Those who did the dirtiest work, cleaned toilets, handled dead things, etc., were regarded as unclean and untouchable, and their children were required to do the same kind of work. At the upper extreme, the Brahmins had the most respected occupations, those of teacher, priest, and administrator. Caplow adds that heavy work is rated low, but light work is high in esteem. But in the industrial society other criteria are also important. Working for a big firm carries more respect than working for a struggling employer. One who starts work at nine o'clock in the morning is presumed to have higher status than one who starts his work day at eight o'clock. [11]

In the modern community people are still rated as high or low, depending on their occupations, but if the occupation of a man is not known precisely, some related method for rating him is used. Caplow says that we have many ways of defining status in terms of "economic function."

[9] Everett C. Hughes, *Men and Their Work,* New York, Free Press, 1958, p. 7.

[10] Alba Edwards, "Comparative Occupation Statistics in the United States," *Population,* Washington, D.C., Bureau of the Census, 1943, Preface.

[11] Theodore Caplow, *The Sociology of Work,* Minneapolis, University of Minnesota Press, 1954, p. 22.

The urban dweller tends to define his own relationship to his fellows in functional terms, since other means of identification with the community are attenuated. Then too, the separation of home from work place and the necessity for causal interaction with many unrelated people requires various shorthand methods for recognizing others, of which occupational designations are the most convenient after sex, age, and race.[12]

Those who are in occupations and who fraternize with others in the same occupation tend to acquire very precise criteria for rating one another. The good carpenter, crane operator, seaman, fisherman, pilot, aviator, etc. knows the more efficient and less efficient in his own craft, but, even while rating some higher and others lower, he shares with them all an identification with the craft, and a pride in his craft.

COMMUNITIES AND THEIR OCCUPATIONS

We know that the lives of people in a herding community, who do a minimum of farming, will be largely associated with animals: cattle, sheep, or goats. Their work vocabulary will enter their social conversation, and the things relating to their animals will enter the imagery of religion, and the religious ceremonies. This holds true even for remote fishing villages. We are not surprised to find it so, but we may be surprised to find the same tendency for work and the vocabulary of work to be present in an industrial community. Abegglen relates a visit to a silk-producing town of 30,000 in Japan, an hour from Tokyo. In this town there are more than 750 plants, ranging in size from 15 to 80 workers, with about 11,100 people employed altogether. Most of the plants are operated as if the owner, his relatives, and the hired workers were one large family. The men find work in other occupations, while the women make silk; and silk production gives the place its identity.[13] It helps to fashion the social life of the silk workers as well.

In the early decades of American industry there were many small places identified with one kind of industrial work, such as, Thomaston, Connecticut, where clocks were made, and Lancaster, Pennsylvania, where a cluster of German blacksmiths first began making the famous "Kentucky rifle." This latter industry started from the demand for a gun that would be able to shoot long distances accurately, would be light to carry, and inexpensive to own. Bridenbaugh wrote, "So vital was the town's gun-making industry that in 1776 it was summarily taken over by the Conti-

12 Ibid., p. 30.
13 James C. Abegglen, *The Japanese Factory,* New York, Free Press, 1960, pp. 70–72.

nental Congress. Today only two gunsmiths remain of this once flourishing business." [14]

With economic change the blacksmiths turned from making guns to other work, equally necessary and more lucrative, like making wagons, the kind of sturdy wagons needed for rough terrain. European wagons were too frail and the European cart could not be used. So came the Conestoga wagon, suited to haul heavy loads where roads hardly existed. The smith and the wheelwright had important frontier occupations.[15] Other wagon models later displaced the Conestoga model, when wagonmaking became a major industry in the Middle West, especially in Michigan and Indiana.

It was pertinent to both the community and the enterprise that the wagon industry developed a number of specialized occupations. It was no coincidence that automobile manufacture began in the region where wagon making had concentrated. The skills of the wagon makers were transformed to automobile manufacture, other skills being added. In time the skills for metal working replaced the wood-working skills. Since the automobile was more complex, auxiliary industries grew out of its manufacture, such as the making of rubber tires. Akron became the rubber city.[16]

Also there are one-industry towns, such as the steel-producing town, Gary, one-industry meat-packing towns, as Omaha, even cutlery towns, for example, Solingen, Germany, and perfume making towns as Grasse in France. In 1963 France produced 20,178 metric tons of perfumes, sold around the world. Much of the basic material was produced at Grasse. Toledo, the still-fortified hill city in Spain was once a famous sword-making town. They still make swords by the same old methods, not for the knights but to sell to tourists.

THE DYNAMISM OF INDUSTRIAL WORK

Modern work differs from preindustrial work in that it is highly impersonal, necessary largely because it is more starkly competitive, and competitiveness is seen as imperative to progress. Impersonally, worker competes with worker, employer with employer. The loser is expected to take his loss with the same level-headed equanimity that the

14 Carl Bridenbaugh, *The Colonial Craftsman,* New York, New York University Press, 1950, pp. 117–118.

15 Ibid., p. 119. Both the Conestoga wagon and the Kentucky rifle are reported in *Pennsylvania, A Guide to the Keystone State,* New York, Oxford University Press, 1950, p. 247.

16 *The Ohio Guide,* New York, Oxford University Press, 1940, p. 167.

winner takes his gain. However, we have reached the point in the most industrial countries when people are beginning to question the principle of competition. The competition that gives the industrial institution its dynamism is creating social costs that are staggering, for example, incurable unemployment, and poverty in the midst of plenty. Sultan writes, "It should not be surprising that an institution that promised, and attempted, so much should itself become a source of criticism; first to outsiders for what it promised to do, and second, to insiders for what it failed to do." [17]

Competitive work in the cities, with more and more people crowding in for their own survival, can hardly be other than dynamic. New kinds of work or better ways of doing old things must be found, each of which had little place in preindustrial work systems. Being ahead of others becomes a virtue. In this environment man is free, as Mumford observes, to drive himself; the inhibiting controls of tradition are absent.

> Man's capacity to impose work on himself not merely gave him greater security and freedom but made possible a more highly organized kind of society; not by accident perhaps was the original step from tribal societies to civilization accompanied for long by the enslavement of large groups, until all men were ready to submit to the slavery of work itself for the purpose of the wider and completer liberalism that results from the economic division of labor. But in origin work and play have the same common trunk and cannot be detached; every mastery over the economic condition of life lightens the burdens of servile work.[18]

It is this work system with all of its dynamic promise that the less developed countries are asking for, but for which they are so ill-prepared. Lambiri tells of the arrival of a textile mill in a rural community in Greece. This mill in 1950 opened with 62 workers and employed about 1,000 in 1957. It had been assumed that female as well as male labor would be used, but local tradition frowned on the idea of women taking industrial jobs. While the mill brought clock regulation to the community, which was inconveniencing, the employment of women was a moral issue.[19]

Indeed the dynamics of the industrial work system, once established in a nonindustrial environment, disturb all phases of established life, and adaptation may be a problem for decades. Presthus, who observed the adaptation process in Turkey, made these generalizations:

[17] Paul E. Sultan, *The Disenchanted Unionist,* New York, Harper & Row, 1963, p. 4.

[18] Lewis Mumford, *The Condition of Man,* New York, Harcourt, Brace, & World, 1944, pp. 4–5.

[19] Jane Lambiri, "The Impact of Industrial Employment on the Position of Women in a Greek Country Town," *British Journal of Sociology,* Vol. 14, 1963, pp. 240–247.

The patriarchal Turkish family system, which honors age and the authority of the father; the historic idealization of the military, with attending emphasis on obedience, rank and its prerogatives; the educational system which often makes the teacher's authority rather than the objective evidence the test of truth; a stratified class structure reinforced by widespread illiteracy and a consequent monopolization of political skills by a small elite—all provide a special framework for highly structured interpersonal relations.[20]

Presthus also notes that these different established control systems are interrelated, that disturbance to any one affects the others. Apparently Japan is an exception among newly industrialized countries. There the rural family system carries over from village to city and from agriculture to industry. Urbanization is much less than total rejection of ruralism. The family makes the transition without a total transformation. Abegglen notes that much of the feudal order is still present in worker-employer relations, and impersonalism, as found in Western industry, is found mainly in the larger Japanese industrial establishments, although the impersonal trend increases.[21]

One very crucial point, though, is that the very commitment of industrial work to competitive dynamism puts a premium on those aspects that take the heaviness out of labor, because it is uneconomical to use hand labor for drudgery work. Friedmann writes:

> One of the points on which many thinkers correctly agree is the service rendered by industrial mechanization in freeing man from difficult, disagreeable and brutalizing tasks. He is ceasing, and will cease more and more, to be used as a physical motor, as a brute force. The worker-slave of matter is increasingly rare. Even under the system of private profit it is usually in a businessman's interest to introduce mechanized processes of handling materials, transportation, etc.[22]

SOME VALUE ATTITUDES TOWARD WORK

A person from a Western country, reflecting the Western attitudes toward work, may be offended when observing the ways among people in less developed countries. Purcell, for instance, questions the charge of laziness, often applied to the Malayan who avoids taking a job toiling by the clock for a Chinese industrialist. The same Malayan may work dili-

20 Robert V. Presthus, "Weberian Versus Welfare Bureaucracy in Traditional Society," *Administrative Science Quarterly,* Vol. 6, No. 1, June 1961, p. 14.
21 Abegglen, op. cit., pp. 142–133.
22 Friedmann, op. cit., p. 392.

gently, when necessary, in his own rice field. But this is work in a milieu of personal relations, often seasonal, not work with a never-ending regularity.[23] Industrial work, being so foreign to such peoples, may be considered, in some cases perhaps, as degrading. Beaglehole found that the Polynesians are quite ready to do the white man's kind of work for pay, but they are often perfunctory about it, doing what has to be done, just enough and no more. "Anything is good enough that just works. . . . Indifference is the attitude to one who wants perfection." [24] However, others who know the Polynesians assert that they do their own traditional types of work well.

What may be called the Puritan attitude toward work in the West often was mixed with the assumption of religious obligations on the part of the employer. It was not uncommon in New York and other cities during the first third of the past century for employers of white-collar labor to start the work day with prayers. Such attitudes and practices are illustrated in this document of 1852 which sets forth the rules for office workers in a British textile mill.

1. Godliness, cleanliness and punctuality are the necessities of a good business.
2. This firm has reduced the hours of work, and the Clerical Staff will now only have to be present between the hours of 7 A.M. and 6 P.M. on weekdays.
3. Daily prayers will be held each morning in the Main Office. The Clerical Staff will be present.
4. Clothing must be of a sober nature. The Clerical Staff will not desport themselves in raiment of bright colours, nor will they wear hose unless in good repair.
5. Overshoes and top shoes may not be worn in the office, but neck scarves and headgear may be worn in inclement weather.
6. A stove is provided for the benefit of the Clerical Staff. Coal and wood must be kept in the locker. It is recommended that each member of the Clerical Staff bring 4 pounds of coal each day during cold weather.
7. No member of the Clerical Staff may leave the room without permission of Mr. Rogers. The calls of nature are permitted and the Clerical Staff may use the garden below the second gate. This area must be kept in good order.
8. No talking is allowed during business hours.
9. The craving for tobacco, wines or spirits is a human weakness, and as such is forbidden to all members of the Clerical Staff.
10. Now that the hours of business have been drastically reduced, the partaking of food is allowed between 11:30 A.M. and noon, but work will not, on any account, cease.
11. Members of the Clerical Staff will provide their own pens [doubtless quill pens]. A new sharpener is available on application to Mr. Rogers.

[23] Victor Purcell, *Malaysia*, London, Thames and Hudson, 1965, p. 42.
[24] Ernst Beaglehole, *Social Change in the South Pacific*, London, Allen and Unwin, 1957, p. 156.

12. Mr. Rogers will nominate a Senior Clerk to be responsible for the cleanliness of the Main Office and the Private Office, and all Boys and Juniors will report to him 40 minutes before Prayers, and will remain after closing hours for similar work. Brushes, Brooms, and Soap are provided by the Owners.[25]

Employers assumed control over the private lives of workers, as well; for example, they made sure that clerks attended church on Sunday. We learn from a well-documented study by Fitton and Wadsworth of the mills of the Strutts and the Arkwrights, then regarded as model employers. They show that both children and adults would be "fined" (some of their pay would be withheld) if the employers learned that they had misbehaved in public. Employers called it a public service to employ children; it saved them from wrongdoing.[26]

Behind the religious and social facade of making work a rewarding virtue, the employer virtuously made the work pay. American thinking then was very similar. Adams writes of that attitude in New England as it prevailed in the days of his own grandfather.

> If you did not work hard and were not shrewd, you did not achieve a rising scale of success, and, if you did not do that, you were inevitably, for some reason, not in God's favor. To rise meant to leave the wage class and become a property owner, and property for the most part meant land. So, to rise socially and to be a successful American, and in New England where the Puritan influence spread, to be one of the elect of God, you had to know the value of property. An odd complex thus developed, of local patriotism, good citizenship, duty to God, and the wisdom of the serpent, with the success and moral virtue measured by money.[27]

Although less encumbered with religious coloring, the American concept of work has not changed greatly. But we find similar ideas about work in countries not spurred on by the Puritan Ethic, for example, Japan and Israel. And Redfield found an eagerness for work in a Yucatan village: "The people are not concerned with salvation. The villager is closer to Benjamin Franklin than he is to Wesley. He is concerned with earthly affairs, he sees the gods as rewarding man for his prudence and piety with good fortune on the earth and in this life." [28]

25 Herbert J. Holland, St. Andrews, New Brunswick, submitted this document which appeared in *The Telegraph-Journal*, June 5, 1965, Saint John, New Brunswick, and gives permission for its use here. The document contained information on salaries. Senior Clerks, after fifteen years of service, received the equivalent of $3.15 weekly.

26 R. S. Fitton and A. P. Wadsworth, *The Strutts and the Arkwrights*, Manchester, Manchester University Press, 1958, pp. 182–184 and 224–260.

27 James T. Adams, *The Americans*, New York, Scribner, 1943, p. 71.

28 Robert Redfield, *A Village That Chose Progress*, Chicago, University of Chicago Press, 1950, p. 158.

PERSONAL RELATIONS AND IMPERSONAL WORK

In the rules for the office staff of the early English textile plant, as presented above, we note that Rule 8 banned talking on the job. We can be sure that those repressed clerical workers found ways to communicate, nevertheless. For half a century American prisons also imposed silence on prisoners, but despite the strict rules, as every prison official knew, a system of communication known as the "grape vine," was perfected.[29]

While the modern industrial work place tends to be impersonal, no effort is made to ban person-to-person communication. However, the nature of the work tends to limit socializing, and what communication is indulged in rarely leads to social interaction between workers after they leave their place of employment. Lipset calls attention, however, to one exceptional group of workers, the printers, who were among the earliest to form trade unions, even when barred from doing so by legal mandates. He states, "In addition to extensive social relations between printers away from the job, there is also more socializing among printers on the job than we find in most occupations." [30]

Work has always been important as a social activity and as a definer of social status. What needs to be recognized is that, however impersonal industrial work becomes, it still affords opportunity for various kinds of social interaction. Hall would say that workers turn easily to social interaction that is unrelated to the work itself, for which reason it may be the more tension-relieving. The system affords "extraordinary effective ways of getting work done, and of getting a multitude of workers to act in a coordinated fashion." [31]

Industrial work to be effective is marked by order and precision, and it makes demands upon those who perform it. The order necessary for operating the places of work in a community imposes demands for order and precision in other aspects of community life. The worker still carries his watch when on holiday, and work in the house tends to be coordinated with the schedules in the factories. However informal one's social activities are when not at work, he is still not isolated from the rhythms that radiate out of work places. The very fact that one works, even if the nature of his work is not known, enables him to socialize in off-the-job relations

29 For example, see E. H. Johnson, *Crime, Correction and Society*, Homewood, Illinois, Dorsey Press, 1965.

30 Seymour M. Lipset, Martin A. Trow, and James S. Coleman, *Union Democracy, The Internal Politics of the International Typographical Union*, New York, Free Press, 1956, pp. 70–71.

31 Oswald Hall, "Gender and the Division of Labour," *Implications of Traditional Divisions between Men's Work and Women's Work in Our Society*, Women's Bureau, Department of Labour of Canada, Ottawa, 1964, p. 28.

with a degree of security. The industrial worker in the urban society who feels secure in that he is employed, also enjoys another kind of security. His fellow workers comprise a group whose members have been selected by the employer. He is bound by the informal and formal rules of work to cooperate and coordinate his activities with them and he may actually enjoy the fellow-worker role. But he leaves behind that social sphere when his work day is over. From then on, his socializing is with persons of his own choosing, who may be fellow workers, but more often are not. Those with whom he socializes off the job are usually a mixture of people, some with occupations rated higher than his own, and others with occupations rated lower.

WORK AND PERSONALITY

While work and personality are intimately related, the specific relationship between the two varies with the level of work in the occupational hierarchy. At the lower level the job makes no demands on, and may supress the expression of, personality; and at the upper occupation level, where the job makes only stereotyped demands, personality becomes one of the values among the criteria for recruitment and promotion.

Ten Have, a Dutch psychologist, makes the following comment on the effect of work specialization on the personality:

> [Work] may be satisfying in some sphere or spheres of personal life, it may help to develop some potentialities, or it may render a gratification of some vital needs, nevertheless, it seems less than a vocation. If I am not mistaken, today it means much less. Therefore, if work is to have full meaning, a person needs more than a job; he needs a supply of significant experiences and activities, out of his hours of work.[32]

Blum appears of the view that a worker can be a well-balanced human if he has satisfactory nonwork interests. He found that workers in a meat packing plant are quite able to put their work out of mind at the stroke of the clock when they start home. Once at home they try "to get something done." They have a way of speaking of themselves as cogs in a machine, although the work is not physically tiring or dull. Blum seems to suggest that things would be better if industrial workers did have some emotional interest in their jobs and more contact between their work and other phases of life.[33] Durant, an English economist, who wrote

[32] T. T. Ten Have, "Automation, Work and Leisure," *Range,* No. 15, Hilversum, Holland, Philips Telecommunicatie Industrie, 1960, p. 9.

[33] Fred H. Blum, *Toward a Democratic Work Process,* New York, Harper & Row, 1953, pp. 99, 120, and 194.

of leisure as a problem, called its separation from work an "evil necessity." "Only when this division ceases, when leisure is complementary and not opposed to work, can its problems, as we know them, be solved." [34] This is asking that the clock be turned back. In preindustrial work systems the work place embodied the qualities of a social center; work and leisure were one. Such systems, however, could never meet the increasing demands made on industry by the growing population.

In the upper-level occupations it is expected that one give the whole of himself to his work, but first he must acquire the most valued traits in right measure and master the approved manner of role performance. Personality is valued, but the demand is for a specially tailored and tinted kind of personality. What does not blend must be put aside. Bensman and Rosenberg identify some of the requirements the "would-be success" in business must meet:

> The would-be success learns when to simulate enthusiasm, compassion, interest, modesty, confidence, and mastery; when to smile, with whom to laugh, and how intimate or friendly he can be with other people. He selects his home and his residence area with care; he buys his clothes and chooses style with an eye to their probable reception in his office. He reads or pretends to have read the right books, the right magazines, and the right newspapers. All this will be reflected in the "right line of conversation" which he adopts as his own, thereafter sustaining it with proper inflections. His tone is by turns disdainful, respectful, reverential, and choleric, but always well attuned to others. He joins the right party and espouses the political ideology of his fellows.[35]

These personality expectations are certainly precise but not more demanding than those one would have to meet for unity with the society of intellectuals in New York or those which one had to meet to be accepted by London's aristocracy in the seventeenth century. The main difference is that the front office personality is mandated less by work-place considerations than by drawing-room values, although the two overlap.

However, this work-place personality, Whyte's "organization man," for business reasons must also display social and community interests, and he is expected to lend at least a show of support for social welfare interests. He is expected to be anti-labor but he must also know when, how, and to whom he expresses his views. As he honors good work, he is also expected to support "good works," and Whyte suggests that this attitude comes to be genuine, that there is growing commitment to what he calls the "Social Ethic" (the Puritan Ethic minus religious over-

[34] H. W. Durant, *The Problem of Leisure,* London, Routledge, 1938, p. 31.

[35] Joseph Bensman and Bernard Rosenberg, "The Meaning of Work in Bureaucratic Society," in Maurice R. Stein, Arthur J. Vidich, and David M. White (Eds.), *Identity and Anxiety,* New York, Free Press, 1963, p. 183.

tones). "One's ambition is not a personal thing that craves achievement for achievement's sake, or an ego that demands self-expression. It is an ambition directed outward, to the satisfaction of making others happy." [36]

There is evidence, then, that the industrial work system manifests two stances regarding the utilization of worker personality. Among lower-level workers personality has little utility and industry allows little opportunity for expression. Among upper-level workers personality has a market utility, but in this area the market personality assumes the character of a stereotype which restricts individualism.

OCCUPATION AND SOCIAL CLASS STATUS

The industrial society, confronted with the complexities of the industrial work system, is itself forced to use stereotyping in order to conceptualize something like an understanding of a whole; otherwise, communication would not be possible. Let us look at stereotyping with respect to occupations. Not even the citizen whose information is above average can know all the occupations in the industrial urban community. He may have considerable knowledge about a few occupations, those closely related to his own, but his knowledge about others will be limited. Yet he tends to acquire notions about many occupations and is able to rate each higher or lower in what amounts to a hierarchy of ratings. Svalastoga tested 1,009 men and 212 women on 75 occupations in Denmark. He divided the ratings into nine classes ranging from upper-upper to lower-lower. As judged by the respondents, the ratings were on a 1 to 5 scale. We include here only the top, middle, and low ratings for each of the nine classes.

Upper-upper (1.00 to 1.16)

0. None among the occupations listed

Middle-upper (1.17 to 1.48)

1.	Ambassador	1.20
2.	Prime Minister	1.30
3.	Administrative head of ministry	1.45

Lower-upper (1.49 to 1.96)

5.	President of Supreme Court	1.53
6.	Chief physician, 7. Professor	1.59
9.	Manager of business or industry	1.95

Upper-middle (1.97 to 2.60)

10.	Ship owner	2.00
17.	Graduate engineer	2.22
25.	Department head in private firm	2.58

[36] William H. Whyte, Jr., *The Organization Man,* New York, Simon and Schuster, 1956, pp. 9, 14, and 115.

Middle-middle (2.61 to 3.40)

26. Professional assistant to Minister   2.64
33. Elementary school teacher   2.87
44. Count working as Office Clerk *   3.39

Lower-middle (3.41 to 4.04)

45. Actor   3.43
55. Grocer with two employees   3.80
60. Clerk in store or office   3.98

Upper-lower (4.05 to 4.52)

61. Shop assistant   4.17
64. Carpenter and joiner   4.36
69. Truck driver, taxi driver   4.51

Middle-lower (4.53 to 4.84)

70. Husbandman (farmer)   4.53
74. Unskilled worker   4.67
75. Shoeshiner   4.79

Lower-lower (4.85 to 5.00)
None among occupations listed

* Member of lower title noble family [37]

In Table 12 we see how Danes tend to rate people as upper, middle, or working class in terms of annual income. As in other countries, Svalastoga found that the prestige of an occupation rests only in part on what people know about the work involved. Danes, like Americans, come to rate occupations in consumer display terms.

Table 12   Danish Classification of Persons on Basis of Income

Annual income	Upper class	Middle class	Working class
4,000 Kroner	0.4%	7.9%	90.0%
8,000 "	1.4%	17.1%	80.4%
16,000 "	5.9%	67.7%	25.2%
32,000 "	43.6%	52.5%	3.0%
64,000 "	82.8%	15.0%	0.8%
128,000 "	93.5%	4.5%	1.0%

Source: Kaare Svalastoga, *Prestige, Class and Mobility*, Copenhagen, Gyldendal, 1959, p. 170.

In the United States Hatt and North made a similar test of 90 occupations. The prestige distribution, as we note here, is quite similar to that for Denmark for the 32 occupations which are comparable.

[37] Kaare Svalastoga, *Prestige, Class and Mobility*, Copenhagen, Gyldendal, 1959, pp. 74–78, and 154.

Danish occupations in rank order from a list of 75		Comparison with Danish of American occupations in rank order from a list of 90	
Ambassador	1	5	Diplomat in U.S. Foreign Service
Prime Minister	2	3	State governor
Head of a Ministry	4	4	Cabinet Minister, U.S. government
President of Supreme Court	5	1	U.S. Supreme Court Justice
Chief physician, hospital	6	2	Physician
Professor	7	7	Professor
Managing director of firm	9	19	Member, board of directors
Ship owner	10	26	Owner of factory, 100 employees
Attorney (district court)	16	18	Lawyer
Graduate engineer	17	23	Civil engineer
Clergyman, national church	24	15	Minister, 21 Priest
Professional assistant to Minister	26	13	Department head, State government
Elementary school teacher	33	35	Public school teacher
Accountant	37	28	Accountant in large business
Farmer (owner-operator)	46	38	Farmer (owner-operator)
Journalist (news reporter)	47	47	Reporter on daily paper
Policeman	52	54	Policeman
Grocer with two clerks	55	48	Manager, small store in city
Salesman, commercial	59	52	Traveling salesman
Clerk, store or office	60	65	Clerk in store
Shop assistant (mechanic)	61	59	Garage mechanic
Carpenter and joiner	64	57	Carpenter
Truck driver, taxi driver	69	70	Truck driver, 76 Taxi driver
Agricultural laborer	73	74	Farm laborer
Unskilled worker	74	79	Dock worker, 84 Janitor
Shoeshiner	75	88	Shoeshiner

In Denmark, as in the United States, the economy is highly industrial and about the same proportion of the population is urban. Both countries have high levels of education and standards of living. In the United States the types of industries are much more numerous and so are the types of occupations.[38]

OCCUPATIONS AND SOCIAL MOBILITY

We think of social mobility as change of social status, usually upward; one's income increases and he is able to enjoy a higher level of living and may be enabled to move in other social groups. This may mean that one has moved from a lesser to a higher occupation, in which case social mobility is partly or wholly the result of occupational mobility. Occupational mobility, however, may be encouraged or forced by technological changes in industry. Some types of work are eliminated and

[38] Paul H. Hatt and C. C. North, *Opinion News*, Vol. 9, September 1, 1947. Taken from pertinent table which was reproduced by Leonard Broom and Philip Selznick, *Sociology*, New York, Harper & Row, 1963, p. 200.

workers may turn to other, perhaps related, occupations, which may be rated higher or lower. Or occupations may be modified. Thus when cigars were made by hand, cigarmaking was a proud skill, but when cigarmaking machines arrived this became a semi-skilled occupation. On the other hand, to the benefit of workers, when machines were introduced into construction work, it became possible for common laborers, as machine operators, to be rated as skilled workers.

Much occupational mobility entails the movement of workers from one kind of work to another, but at the same occupational level. However, workers in the course of these moves often do change from one occupational level to another, perhaps earning more money. This may lead to upward mobility. One's status rises as he makes more money, even though he does not move to a better neighborhood. One may also remain in the same neighborhood even if his occupational status lowers.

Peasants of Europe during the nineteenth century migrated in large numbers to North America. Because of population increase or changes in agriculture, large numbers sought employment in cities. The American land frontier beckoned and new industrial cities offered a gambling chance to get ahead. Not only was all Europe stirred by stories of untapped wealth, but the whole Atlantic Seaboard teemed with excitement about opportunities in the New West from 1840 on.

> [For the generation coming to power in 1840, there] was the welling up of primitive pagan desires after long repressions—to grow rich, to grasp power, to be strong and masterful and lay the world at its feet. It was a violent reaction from the narrow poverty of frontier life and the narrow inhibitions of frontier religion [of earlier decades]. It had had enough of skimpy, meager ways, of grubbing along hoping for something to turn up. It was consumed with a great hunger for abundance, for the good things of life, for wealth.[39]

This is a description of the mood of America in the early decades before "social mobility" entered our vocabulary, although it had already taken root in our social heritage. What is now often identified as purely American has increasingly become characteristic of industrial society everywhere. People who have lived for generations with the accepted notion that one stays at his level in society are suddenly confronted with the idea of upward mobility. Indeed, it appears to have come to be a conviction that all men, if the way is open, will strive to climb and strive to attain abundance and power. But the conviction goes further, assuming that all have some measure of capacity for upward mobility. Barber puts it this way, "Through the mobility ethos a potential moti-

[39] Vernon L. Parrington, *Main Currents of American Thought,* Vol. III, New York, Harcourt, Brace, & World, 1930, p. 11.

vation of some or even many individuals becomes a compulsory life goal for all . . . [but although] practically everybody feels committed to upward mobility as a central life goal, a majority fails to achieve it." [40]

The idea of upward mobility, of achievement through competition is the central dynamic of the industrial work system. An increasing number of thinkers see this element in the cult of success as unrealistic. Not all are able to climb to the top, not all wish to, perhaps not all should, and it may be that this "middle-class" concept needs reexamination. A thought from Porter is to the point:

> I have tried to argue that the modern period of industrialization has created low levels of motivation, working-class culture, educationally deprived areas, and outmoded educational arrangements and curriculum content for societies based on the culture of science and technology. Cumulatively these dysfunctions constitute a major manpower problem for these societies taken separately, or as a set of societies drawing on common reserves of human resources.[41]

Some put the argument more bluntly: the cult of upward mobility for all, with its standard expectations and uniform measures, fails to take account of the natural differences between humans and overlooks or ignores the different levels of aspiration. These expectations are put impersonally to all alike, as if all humans were like clocks which can be universally synchronized with a single great time piece.

When industrialism brings its work system to a developing country its impersonal achievement values often fail to be understood. Instead, members of top families will hold top jobs, members of lesser families the middle jobs, and members of the lowest families will have the lowest jobs. Moving up may be as unthinkable as being moved down. Such was found by Harbison and Ibrahim in the industries of Egypt. The industries did not redefine the stratification system of the society but reflected it and its established social class values.[42]

Much that would be true of the work system in an industrial country is not possible in most countries being industrialized. Egypt's labor force is mainly agricultural. Other primary resources are lacking. The urban labor force is underemployed and much of the male labor force is engaged in nonproductive work. Of the whole urban labor force, 21 percent are in domestic employment and 75 percent of the domestic workers are

40 Bernard Barber, *Social Stratification*, New York, Harcourt, Brace, & World, 1957, p. 345.

41 John Porter, "The Future of Upward Mobility," *American Sociological Review*, Vol. 33, No. 1, February 1968, p. 19.

42 Frederick H. Harbison and I. A. Ibrahim, "Some Labor Problems of Industrialization in Egypt," *Annals of the American Academy of Political and Social Science*, Vol. 305, May 1956, pp. 114–124.

male. In this area of employment for which male workers can hardly be found in Britain, for example, Egyptian men have a monopoly. Job opportunities for women, even in offices, are limited. Offices too are overstaffed by Western standards. White-collar workers comprise 24 percent of Egypt's labor force, while the "proletariat in factories and workshops" comprise 18 percent of Egypt's employed workers. Most of these are in small shops. Pressure on the labor market is so great and the growth of mass industry so slow that the prospects for upward mobility are all but absent.[43]

THE MOBILITY TREND IN OCCUPATIONS

One long-standing complaint against the industrial work system concerns the relentlessness with which it outmodes occupations, changes occupations, or creates new ones. This is a normal consequence of industrial growth, and in a country of industrial expansion one measure of such mobility is seen when the occupations of sons are compared with those of fathers. Lipset and Bendix found that in the United States a third of the sons are in occupations higher than those of their fathers, the fathers considered being those in handwork occupations.[44] As shown in Table 13, from a study by Morgan, et al, we note that

Table 13   Occupational Level of Spending Unit Heads Compared With the Occupational Level of Their Fathers *

	Occupations of fathers			
Occupation of spending unit heads	White-collar workers	Skilled and semi-skilled workers	Unskilled workers	Farmers
White-collar workers	65%	35%	26%	27%
Skilled and semi-skilled workers	25	48	39	35
Unskilled workers	9	16	30	19
Farmers	1	1	5	19
	100%	100%	100%	100%
Number of cases	670	706	469	851

* Of 2,875 heads, incomplete information on 177.

Source: James N. Morgan (Ed.), *Income and Welfare in the United States*, New York, McGraw-Hill, 1962, p. 335.

43 For the figures on Egypt's labor force, see a report by L'Institut d'Etudes de Développement Economique et Social, "La Société urbaine egyptiènne," *Tiers Monde*, T. 2, No. 8, avril–juin 1961, p. 187.

44 Seymour M. Lipset and Reinhard Bendix, *Social Mobility in Industrial Society*, London, Heinemann, 1959, pp. 15, 19–21, and 58.

65 percent of the white-collar workers in the United States, based on their nation-wide sample, had fathers in the white-collar occupations. Of these sons who were family heads, 35 percent were in occupations lower than those of their fathers. Of family heads in skilled and semi-skilled occupations, 35 percent were in white-collar work, a level higher than their fathers. Of those spending unit heads whose fathers were un-skilled workers, 65 percent were in higher occupations. Of those whose fathers were farmers, 62 percent held jobs at the skilled or white-collar levels.

In Table 14, also from data assembled by Morgan, et al, we see that the level of education of spending unit heads tends to be higher than

Table 14   Spending Unit Heads Compared With Fathers for Level of Education

Educational mobility of heads, compared by education level with their fathers *	Percent of each mobility group whose occupations, compared with those of fathers, are clearly:		Number of spending unit heads
	Higher	Lower	
Heads have same level or education as fathers, or less	19	20	1,964
Heads have one level more education than fathers	33	17	721
Heads have two levels more education than fathers	36	12	322

* Levels: 0–8 grades, 9–11 grades, 12 grades, some college.
Source: James N. Morgan (Ed.), *Income and Welfare in the United States,* New York, McGraw-Hill, 1962, p. 343.

the level of education attained by their fathers. About 33 percent of these sons have one or more levels of education more than their fathers. They are in a better position than the fathers for upward occupational mobility.

As it is to be expected, occupational mobility is lower in Britain; hence there is a high migration of trained sons to Canada and the United States. Glass and Hall report that 69 percent of the sons in Britain are at the same occupational level as their fathers. Of the rest, 39 percent have occupations higher than their fathers and 61 percent have occupations that are lower.[45] British leaders complain about the "brain drain" to America where the demand for scientists, engineers, and other highly trained types exceeds the supply. This is due to the rapid technological

[45] D. V. Glass and J. R. Hall, "Social Mobility in Great Britain, A Study of Inter-generational Changes in Status," in D. V. Glass (Ed.), *Social Mobility in Great Britain,* London, Routledge and Kegan Paul, 1954, p. 184.

development of industry, and the likelihood of supply overtaking demand is not yet in sight.

What concerns many sociologists is that too few persons have an interest in social and occupational mobility. A large segment of the population is not thrilled with the aspiration model offered it, as some assume people were thrilled a century ago when the frontier was wide open. Such are seen as examples of alienation. In this regard, Porter states:

> In the light of evidence that levels of aspirations and attitudes to education vary so much by class one wonders how it could ever be claimed that, as part of the common value system, all Americans are achievement-oriented or share in a great quest for opportunity. Middle-class investigators seem genuinely puzzled about how the lower or working classes do or should react to the realities of their own class position. Evidence is presented that they are deviant, depressed or despaired and adopt a devil-may-care attitude. These would be logical reactions if working-class people had indeed internalized middle-class norms, and were not blessed by any kind of "false consciousness." [46]

MARGINAL GROUPS IN THE LABOR FORCE

A division of labor is an arrangement for including persons in certain work categories and excluding others. Once an occupation assumes organizational form, its members may set up standards for entrance and perhaps elect to bar certain types on the basis of race, religion, sex, or some other criterion. Our attention here turns to conditions which may be imposed by the work itself. For example, factory jobs may be such that they cannot be performed so well by women as by men; by old men as by young and able men; by youth who lack work experience; or by the crippled and mentally deficient.

We shall consider here the three categories of workers which, by the nature of industry itself, tend to be disadvantaged in the modern labor market. We shall not consider the various other types who are in the labor market marginally, and are identified by Miller as the "new" working class.[47] Our focus will be on youth, employable women, and elderly workers, because we can see in them the impersonality of industry in the labor market.

1. Youth Entering the Labor Force

Each preindustrial work system, such as, the crafts in medieval towns or the rural systems, supported built-in methods of inducting youth into

46 Porter, op. cit., p. 13.

47 S. M. Miller, "The New Working Class," in Arthur B. Shostak and William Gomberg (Eds.), *Blue-Collar World,* Englewood Cliffs, N.J., Prentice-Hall, 1964, pp. 2–8.

the life of work. The period of adolescence, compared with that in the industrial society, was short. The youth in the tribe was trained in the skills necessary for the work he was to do before reaching adolescence. In his early teens he was ready to work with men. The youth of today who would enter a profession must be educated and trained until his mid-twenties or longer, entering his occupation at an age when the primitive tribesman was in the final decades of his life span.

In the industrial society, much of the learning must be done, not in the work system, but before entering it. Even if one is relatively certain about the work he wants to do, there is considerable guesswork in his preparation for it, because even while he is training the nature of the occupation may be changing. This may be frustrating, says Dansereau, and somehow he thinks society is to blame.[48] Or perhaps the young person is given too little training and enters work life at a low level where there is the least security and where guidance is least likely to be provided.

The teenage son of a blue-collar (working-class) father, entering employment at the common labor level may have less trouble adapting because of his lower aspirations and expectations than would the teenage son of a white-collar father. But he is also less likely to enter his first job fortified with formal schooling and his chances for promotion might well be less than for the middle-class youth. What needs to be recognized is that it is not in the nature of industry to assume responsibility either for education or training. Industrial work has passed beyond the stage of using apprenticeship, the total method of training in the old guild system. Even though some occupations in the industrial order still make use of apprenticeship, especially in European countries, they now require a greater measure of formal education than was needed in preindustrial times. Industrial training is costly and complex. The unanswered question concerns how much of the training cost industry should assume when the young person enters the labor market after leaving school.

Hollingshead sees young people as entering the labor market somewhat at their own risk, and as being put to dirty work or "other monotonous, always menial, and often hard jobs . . . 8 to 12 hours a day." [49] There is nothing new about the young worker having to "eat his peck of dirt." Blucher, in a study of apprentices in Germany, found that they work up to 60 hours a week, which is illegal, but that nobody complains, not even the apprentice.[50] Had he asked members of the trade union, the stock answer would have been that this hardship, which apprentices learn to make light of, is good discipline.

[48] H. Kirk Dansereau, "Work and the Teenage Blue-Collarite," in Arthur B. Shostak and William Gomberg (Eds.), *Blue-Collar World,* Englewood Cliffs, N. J., Prentice-Hall, 1964, p. 183.

[49] A. B. Hollingshead, *Elmtown's Youth,* New York, Wiley, 1949, p. 377.

[50] Viggo Graf Blucher, *Freizeit in der industriellen Gesellschaft,* Stuttgart, Enke, 1956, p. 19.

The Glasgow public schools in January 1947 graduated 1,349 boys. Ferguson and Cunnison in 1950 undertook to interview these boys, few of whom had changed addresses. Only two of the total number had continued their schooling, although some others were attending evening classes. The following figures tell of trial and error in the labor market:

20 percent found jobs the first year
50 percent found jobs before the end of the second year
78 percent were employed by the end of the third year
10 percent were still holding their first job
. 39 percent had worked on two jobs
26 percent had worked on three jobs
21 percent had worked on four or more jobs [51]

2. *Women in the Labor Force*

While the responsibility may be imposed by society, it is not in the nature of industry to assume responsibility for training the young, although the young may be utilized by industries that need unskilled labor. Notably the textile industry in the past followed the policy of using the labor of both women and children, cheaper than the labor of men. In all preindustrial societies women had their spheres of work, and status in the division of labor. The earliest work afforded women by the industrial system, besides yielding low pay, was menial, routine, and quite without any prospect of advancement. It contributed negatively to their status.

In the leading industrial countries at the present time, women have access to many types of employment from which they were barred four or five decades ago. Their exclusion from certain occupations was not mainly because the industrial work system could not use their labor but was due to the fact that: 1) many occupations were presumed to be exclusively for men (such as, physician, barber, lawyer, secretary); and 2) certain popular notions prevailed about what was proper work for a woman. Today, the issue of the relation of women to work touches very little on the access to education for women or the social prohibitions.

The two most-often-voiced complaints women have regarding the modern work system are: 1) while they have access to many types of employment, they do not share with men the same prospect for upward mobility; and 2) rarely do women performing similar work receive the same remuneration as do men, an inequality that prevails even in unionized workshops.

On the other side, it is argued that, with few exceptions, women

[51] T. Ferguson and J. Cunnison, *The Young Wage Earner*, London, Oxford University Press, 1951, pp. 2, 11, and 88.

have mixed motivations when they enter the labor market. They are caught between two demands: the demand of society that they perform the social role of bearing and rearing children, a role for which industry can properly make no allowances, and the role of a career which, Myrdal and Klein maintain, is a direct challenge to the role of the wife-mother housekeeper.[52]

In most industrial countries about a third of the labor force is made up of women. In Canada women comprised about 30 percent of the labor force in 1963. They held 39 percent of the clerical positions in 1951 as compared with 43 percent in 1961. As in the United States, about 50 percent of the employed women are married. Again, as in the United States, the percentages of women in most types of employment are highest in cities, and they are higher for women with higher education.[53]

Girard gathered information in French cities on the amount of time employed married women give to the job and to housework, a measure of what they give in time to their two roles. These figures show that the larger the home load, the less time they have for the job. A mother with three or more children has a 12-hour day and 7-day week.[54]

		Job hours	*Total hours*
Married	no children	50.1	77.3
Mothers	one child	44.5	83.6
Mothers	two children	36.9	83.5
Mothers	three or more children	34.3	84.0

In 1959 women comprised 31 percent of the labor force in the United States. Of the more than 12 million employed women, 33 percent had children under six and 20 percent had children between six and seventeen.[55] Klein, who studied working wives in Britain, found that married women generally wanted to be identified with the employed. When Klein interviewed husbands she found that the greatest opposition to wives holding jobs were voiced by working-class husbands. But 56 percent of all husbands were favorable to wives working and husbands of higher level occupations and education were among the more favorable.[56]

[52] Alva Myrdal and Viola Klein, *Women's Two Roles, Home and Work,* London, Routledge and Kegan Paul, 1956, pp. 5–6.

[53] *Implications of Traditional Divisions Between Men's Work and Women's Work in Our Society,* Ottawa, Women's Bureau, Department of Labor in Canada, 1964, pp. 5–8.

[54] Alain Girard, "Le Budget-temps de la femme mariée dans les agglomerations urbaines," *Population* Vol. 13, No. 4, octobre–décembre 1958, p. 614.

[55] Jacob Schiffman, "Labor Force Activity of Married Women," *Monthly Labor Review,* Vol. 83, No. 8, August 1960, p. 829.

[56] Viola Klein, "Married Women in Employment," *International Journal of Comparative Sociology,* Vol. 1, No. 2, September 1960, pp. 259 and 261.

Hall and McFarlane, in their study of the transition of young persons from school to work, their attention primarily on high school students in Toronto, point out that the transition is much easier for girls. Most girls enter occupations at the white-collar level for which much of their training is received in school. Boys are advantaged if they have attended high school, but they must train for their line of work in the work place.[57]

In the article by Porter, already mentioned, in which he deals with the urgent demand in the United States and Canada for highly trained persons as physical scientists and engineers, he asks why the educators fail to encourage women to enter these fields.[58] Apparently here is a last remnant of the social bias for which the industrial work system cannot be blamed. Winthrop identifies this failure as a case of social waste. "The force of this point is increased if we recognize that household labor-saving devices make it unnecessary for women to allocate two hours to services in the home when one will suffice." [59]

3. *Old Age and the Exit from Work*

In the industrial society the life span increases, but the honor that traditionally came with age decreases. The level of industrial advance can so be measured. The industrial work system belongs to the young and able and makes no concessions to age, as preindustrial work systems did and still do. There is no little evidence that most workers face old age with dread, knowing that their status declines with their lessening worth in the work place. This attitude is betrayed in the well-meant efforts in North American society to encourage respect for the old who have entered their "golden years," and are called "senior citizens."

In tribal society, indeed in most nonindustrial countries, the elderly still command respect, mainly for the reason that they hold traditional authority, or they control family property. The same is true in our society for old persons whose families hold wealth and power.

Morgan reports the attitudes of 2,997 spending unit heads, a sample of the American population. He asked about their willingness to have their aging parents live in their homes. Of these:

    280 were favorable
    532 gave qualified answers
    288 gave "it-depends" answers

[57] Oswald Hall and Bruce McFarlane, *Transition From School to Work*, Ottawa, Department of Labour of Canada, Report No. 10, 1962, p. 66.

[58] Porter, op. cit., p. 19.

[59] Henry Winthrop, "Waste as an Index of Social Pathology," *American Behavioral Scientist*, Vol. 10, No. 2, October 1961, p. 20.

1,788 were definitely unfavorable
109 gave no answer

This does not mean an unwillingness of children to help their parents; rather they object to sharing their lives with the passing generation.[60]

The likelihood of the elderly being socially "put on the shelf," is much less for persons in the upper occupations. Often when the less-than-skilled worker must retire at 65, the highly skilled worker, or the technician, the manager or high public official may carry on until 70 or older. The same is true for persons in the self-employed occupations. People who have devoted their lives to work, whose status is largely a function of work, do not want to stop, even if economically secure. Riesman believes this "is not simply a legacy of the Puritan Ethic; it is rather a legacy of industrialism itself, of the structures it has created. Work may not be an active presence in the life of these workers, but its absence would be an active absence." [61]

IN THE EMBRACE OF TECHNOLOGY

It is to be expected that any change in man's way of work, since it will bring change in his socio-cultural way of life, will give rise to anxiety in the minds of some, if not many. We can believe that whoever made the first knife of metal was not loved by the makers and users of stone knives. Most early labor-saving mechanisms were greeted with alarm, if not violence. The latest "threat" is automation, which has stimulated much concern among thinkers. Arendt has written that it was no longer a question of "whether we are masters or the slaves of our machines, but whether machines will serve the world and its things." She foresaw, in 1957, the coming of mass unemployment.[62] Since then this fear has taken another turn. The first threat was seen as against the working class. Now comes the computer which appears as a threat to the white-collar class, including the scientists. Were that the case, and this the panic writers overlook, then these mechanisms would also starve because a disemployed labor force would not be able to buy. Walter Buckingham reasons, automation, including computers, is another step in the rationalization of work, and a new step in the mechanization of work. It is a giant step since it promises to be a mechanism for regulating other mechanisms.[63]

60 Morgan, op. cit., p. 159.
61 David Riesman, "Leisure and Work in Post-Industrial Society," in Eric Larrabee and Rolf Meyersohn (Eds.), *Mass Leisure,* New York, Free Press, 1958, p. 370.
62 Hannah Arendt, *The Human Condition,* Chicago, University of Chicago Press, 1958, pp. 4 and 151.
63 Walter Buckingham, *Automation, Its Impact on Business and People,* New York, Harper & Row, 1961, pp. 4–5.

Imaginative writers have fashioned such an image of automation and its possibilities that even some social scientists visualize direful consequences, as if at last a mechanism has come that will subordinate all men to machines.

For those who fear automation, it should be reassuring that the persons best informed do not show concern, as for example, Diebold who wrote one of the first books on the subject. His worry was rather that too much was being written about the elaborate controls and too little attention was being given to the knotty problems of automating work.[64] Some observers, like Simpson, recognize that technological advance increasingly frees workers "from drudgery, unpleasantness, tension, fatigue, tedium, muscular effort. . . ." But they are deprived of identity with their work. Whether one needs to be identified with his work, however, is questionable.[65]

What appears to be happening is that as automation is approached the demand for skilled workers increases and unemployment, except for the unskilled, is no serious challenge. What is serious in an affluent labor market is that most of the unskilled unemployed are rejected. Many can enter the labor market only if their skill level can be raised. There is yet another worry expressed by some that man may create machines so perfect that they will relieve him of both the need to work and to think, that man's robots will displace him. Ten Have answers "that man doesn't lose any of his powers—neither his bodily nor his mental powers—when he endows other things or creatures with them, or does *not* impoverish himself, but multiplies his original forces by providing other things with them." [66]

In the present trend toward automation, which is only beginning, and in the coming of the computer we have the extreme examples of what industrial work is coming to be. We still know little about what the effects will be on social life and culture. However, we do know that the emerging work system will be identified with urbanism, and it will give man much more leisure than he has ever known before.

[64] John Diebold, *Automation, The Advent of the Automatic Factory*, New York, Van Nostrant, 1952, p. 2.

[65] George Simpson, "Western Man Under Automation," *International Journal of Comparative Sociology*, Vol. 5, No. 2, September 1964, p. 200.

[66] Ten Have, op. cit., p. 5.

Industrial urbanism and leisure | 14

A GIFT FROM INDUSTRIAL WORK

In all industrial countries since the turn of the century the normal hours of work per day or week have diminished, giving employed people more leisure. Employers did not plan for it, nor did the labor unions demand it. No one had been aware that it was coming, educators had not prepared for a way of life of less work and more leisure. When thinkers who are concerned about trends did become aware of increasing leisure they saw it as a disturbing new element in community life. Persons who are involved with welfare and public morals saw the growing leisure as a moral threat. Actually, it has turned out to be a baffling challenge.

Kettle has remarked that in Canada, while the number of workers in the labor force has been increasing greatly, the total number of hours worked by all workers has increased little.

> In fact the Canadian labor force increased by 32 percent from 1946 to 1965, but the total number of hours they worked increased only 13 percent. . . . In the same period output increased by 141 percent. The main reason production rose so fast was the increase in productivity; output per man-hour increased by 114 percent. . . . People who worry about technological unemployment ask, in effect, How much longer can this go on? The answer is a long time yet.[1]

In the United States the average work week dropped from 53 hours in 1909 to 40 hours in 1964, and during that interval a considerable part of the American labor force gained 10 paid holidays and vacations with pay.

As is well known, American iron and steel plants, as late as 1907,

[1] John Kettle, "In Praise of Work," *Canada Month*, Vol. 8, No. 3, March 1968, p. 17.

worked an 84-hour week, seven 12-hour days. In the same plants the 40-hour week has now become standard, a gain of 44 hours for the worker. With more free time, these once submerged workers, their wages much higher, enjoy a level of living which was out of reach of the foreman in 1907. In 1907 the steel worker dared not lose a day lest he fall below the minimum needed.

Regarding the worker in a steel plant, Galbraith points out that he too has been brought within the benefits of industrial change. ". . . where his precurser in the steel towns worked to make a living, he works to satisfy his constantly expanded wants. The result is obvious. With more pleasant work and expanded wants, a man is somewhat more likely to choose more work than more leisure." [2] There is considerable evidence that, despite gaining the 40-hour week, many workers elect to work extra hours. In the event wages are high and working conditions favorable, the idea of working extra hours may be tempting to one who would use the money on the family vacation.

ON THE FEAR OF LEISURE

Heinila, a Finnish sociologist, wrote of the hard life of workers in Finnish preindustrial society. Hard labor put its stamp on life. If one had leisure, which often came by chance, he had to use it for resting so he would be ready again for work. Leisure was precious and one used it wisely.[3] It was used to serve work ends. It is, on the other hand, the present tendency for leisure to become an end served by work which causes concern. For example, Meerloo warns that too many people become leisure minded. "In a world of mere leisure and no work discipline, our unleashed instincts would gain again." He voices a view, still not uncommon, that the basic disciplines of life are those imposed by work. They keep the hands busy and the mind well occupied.[4]

This view is also voiced by Toynbee who sees that "the previous equilibrium between leisure and life" is disturbed. There comes a new orientation toward work which brings a "new attitude toward leisure. . . . Then leisure must have an absolute value in itself." [5]

Toynbee sees danger in the "cultural proletarianization of life" as leisure is bestowed on common people "without regard to the recipient's

[2] John K. Galbraith, *The New Industrial State*, Boston, Houghton Mifflin, 1967, p. 364.

[3] Kaveli Heinila, *Leisure and Sports*, Helsinki, Institute of Sociology, Publication No. 5, University of Helsinki, 1959, p. 205.

[4] Joost A. M. Meerloo, *The Rape of the Mind*, New York, World Publishing, 1956, p. 216.

[5] Arnold J. Toynbee, *A Study of History*, Vol. IX, London, Oxford University Press, 1955, p. 604.

capacity or incapacity for making use of it." He argue
needed "to learn how to make use of any new gift. The mis.
by a majority of its possessors was, notoriously, a new thi.
thinking of misuse in terms of upper-class values. Toynbee adi.
ever, that "in the days when leisure had been a monopoly of a n
a minority of that minority had always misused it." [6]

The views of Toynbee are quite akin to those of many intellectuals
who see the use of leisure in high-culture terms. Give much leisure to
the masses and they will turn to spectacles and circuses. This according
to the argument, has the effect of lowering the level of culture. Certain
reformers also argue that much leisure should not be given to the masses
"before they are ready for it;" but they do not offer suggestions about
how people can learn to use leisure before they have it. The intellectuals
would conserve what to them are the socially inherited refinements, while
the moral reformer would channel new leisure activity into the old
grooves of piety or middle-class morality, as traditional convention demands. It is to be expected, Galbraith observes, that handing more leisure
to the masses will be "regarded with misgiving" by the cultivated classes.
"Accordingly, a reduction in the standard work week must always be
considered dubious social policy, inducing moral or spiritual weakness." [7]

THE CULT ASPECT OF RECREATION

There is a vast and growing literature on recreation, most of it written by professional recreationists who provide the guidance in schools
or in public recreation areas, such as, playgrounds, playfields, swimming
pools, or community centers. In some communities they identify with
the school system but in larger cities they are in a department of recreation. Often they are the ardent promoters of all sorts of play activity
for all age groups.

Often the recreationist cooperates with the various private groups
who endeavor, as the Boy Scouts and other youth organizations, to provide wholesome activity for the young. Certain churches may engage in
the same work. Their conception of recreation would be quite in line
with the definition offered by Fitzgerald, "Leisure is time and recreation
is the expression of human interests in free time." Many leisure pursuits,
he holds, could not be called recreation. "Vice, gambling and juvenile
delinquency, in the main, take place during leisure when people are free
to do what they want to do. But they are not recreation. Neither are
leisure activities undertaken for ulterior motives, such as advance in the

---

[6] Ibid., p. 610.
[7] Galbraith, op. cit., p. 272.

economic scale, recreation." [8] If this conception of recreation is related to work at all, it is in the terms of using wholesome play to make one more fit for work.

Thus, Nash, a professor in the field of recreation, looked askance at mass leisure, spectacles where great crowds sit and yell while trained athletes, like gladiators, fight it out in the field. This to Nash was seen as a moral threat, a social ailment called "spectatoritis." He demanded that people of all ages be active, "get into the game." To him "rocking-chair sitting before radio or television is not enough. . . . Recreation means staying in the game. To rest is not to conquer, and to rest is not to enjoy full happiness." [9] Such is the cult of recreation.

While any study of leisure must take recreation into account, its implications are much wider. The implications of leisure relate in large part to work, to the uses of time, to the values involved in work and leisure, and they also concern leisure as a major provider of work.

AN EFFORT TO DEFINE LEISURE

The Greek word for leisure was *schole* but, we are told, the Greeks had no word for work except the negative *ascolia*, literally not-leisure. The Roman word for leisure was *otium* and they also had no word for work except the negative *negotium*. For the Greeks and Romans, the social distance between *schole* and *ascolia* as between *otium* and *negotium* was great and unbridgeable. To the citizen the pursuits of leisure were as duties. The citizen occupied himself with talking politics, sharing public control tasks, taking an interest in art and literature, and managing his estate.

The old distinctions between work and leisure and the names for each, de Grazia reminds us, have been lost, and we appear to be as unclear about leisure as the old Greeks and Romans were about work, for example:

> Leisure [seen in the old sense] is the state of being free from everyday necessity. A man in that state is at leisure and whatever he does is done leisurely. Play is what children do, frolic and sport. . . . Adults also play, though their games are less muscular and more intricate. . . . Men play games in recreation. . . . Recreation is activity that rests men from work, often by giving them a change. . . . When adults play, as they do, of course, with persons, things and symbols, they play for recreation. . . . Work can be taken in its modern sense as effort or exertion done typically

[8] Gerald B. Fitzgerald, *Community Organization for Recreation*, New York, Barnes, 1948, p. 31.

[9] Jay B. Nash, *Philosophy of Recreation and Leisure*, St. Louis, Mosby, 1953, pp. 174–175.

> to make a living or to keep house. . . . Leisure, it should be clear, remains unaffected by either work or recreation. It is outside their everyday world.[10]

These distinctions clearly leave out categories of activities which are neither work nor recreation. This definition of leisure, in the opening sentences at least, is essentially that long held by the Catholic Church; one contemplates the divine, an ideal to which few can aspire.

Still another definition comes from a group of West European scholars who in 1954 organized a seminar for the study of leisure. It was generally accepted that leisure was the time left to the individual after meeting his obligations to work, family, and community, time to be used by him for "relaxation, diversion and personal development." The definition recognized three kinds of time: 1) time used for work and work-related activity; 2) time used to meet obligations to family and community; and 3) time, called leisure, used by the individual for "relaxation, diversion and personal development."

Only the first of these uses of time relates to work, the other two are nonwork, but only the third was identified as leisure. It corresponds to "recreation" in the English-speaking world. But "recreation" was not admitted because it was thought to be too loaded with moral implications. No term could be found for the second type of time use, "meeting obligations to family and community." Some called this type of activity "nonwork," others saw it as "semileisure." [11]

The following definition is offered for leisure and its components. The term, "recreation," is too deeply rooted to be replaced, especially by "leisure," often used with a different meaning. The term, "chores," offered in the absence of a better word, has been used in this sense by others.

> *Leisure* refers to the total of the individual's time not used for work or work related activity. It is his nonwork time.
>
> *Recreation* is activity engaged in by the individual alone or in the company of others purely for enjoyment, diversion, or personal development. Recreation is one use of one's leisure time.
>
> *Chores* refer to activities and duties performed by the individual for or with others in his family, neighborhood, and community. Such activities are performed during one's leisure or nonwork time. They may involve work but it is not work related to one's occupation. These activities, while not recreation, may yield recreational satisfactions.

[10] Sebastian de Grazia, *Of Time, Work and Leisure,* New York, Twentieth Century Fund, 1962, pp. 246–247.

[11] Joffre Dumazedier, "Problèmes actuels de la sociologie du loisir," *Revue Internationale des Sciences Sociales,* Vol. 12, No. 4, 1960, p. 568. Also Nels Anderson, *Work and Leisure,* London, Routledge and Kegan Paul, 1961, Chap. 2, and *Dimensions of Work,* New York, David McKay, 1964, Chap. 8.

In his study of leisure activity among the Finns, Heinila uses the term "chores" to identify such activities as gardening, working at one's home, helping neighbors, doing church work, etc.[12] The separation of leisure into these two types of activity avoids the ambiguity of mixing such activities as painting furniture in one's home or mending the garden fence with dancing or ball playing and of identifying all as recreation.

LEISURE AS TIME USE

It is not unusual for work and leisure to compete for time in one's day. There is also competition during one's nonwork time, for example, between chores and recreation for diversion. In many ways the individual, even children, must make choices between what is expected of one and what one wishes to do. One must so route himself through duties and appointments, that he does not "lose time.[13] The Puritan Ethic is laden with precepts about the importance of "man's measure of time" and the proper uses of it. These are religious precepts, well recognized by Durkheim who points out that religions generally, in one way or other, stress the importance of the man-time relationship.[14]

The Puritan work philosophy placed high emphasis on man's limited measure of time and the importance of using it well. One was taught as a child how he would have to "work out his salvation," and there were many maxims to learn about time, such as "time is money," and "time idled makes the devil smile." While such expressions may not be heard in this generation, time dedication is still firm. Leisure was opportunity to invest time in self-improvement, and that conviction is still with us. The evidence of this time awareness in cities everywhere is the watch on the wrist. Ogden Nash quipped:

> Consider the man without a watch,
> He's like a soda without a Scotch.
> Of the male character I can give you the gist;
> It's a reach for the watch or a glance at the wrist.[15]

Contrary to Fitzgerald's notion that leisure activities are not recreation "if undertaken for ulterior motives," Stephen, a century ago, mentioned how London businessmen would attend parties, but in the processes of socializing they would improve the precious minutes by making

12 Heinila, op. cit., p. 206.

13 For further comment on this thought, see Nels Anderson, "Leisure and Adult Education," *International of Adult and Youth Education,* UNESCO, Vol. 15, 1965, pp. 187–192.

14 Emile Durkheim, *The Elementary Forms of the Religious Life* (1915), New York, Free Press, 1965, pp. 20–23.

15 Ogden Nash, *Collected Verses From 1926 On,* London, Deat, 1952, p. 198.

desired contacts. "The true final cause of evening parties, it may be argued, is not pleasure; they are frequented as the Stock exchange is frequented, with a view to ulterior profit." [16]

In any case, the medieval craftsman who worked all his waking hours had no need of the clock. The modern man, often in need of doing much on a tight schedule, must keep moving. He is buying time or selling it or asking for the time of someone. The worker gives his time at an hourly rate. As Soule remarks, one comes to think of sleep in terms of hours and he marks the hour he must return from some recreation.[17]

Mumford suggests that clocks were first used by churches in towns to call people to prayers. Different mechanical devices were used to announce the minute to ring the bells. The bells had other uses and came to be a means for marking the start or the end of the day in work places. This was the first step to putting hands and faces on clocks. The making of clocks with wheels progressed until a clock was small enough to be carried in the capitalist pocket. When the second hand was invented precise uses were waiting for it. The clock became "the outstanding fact and the typical symbol of the machine; even today no other machine is so ubiquitous." [18]

Unlike rural man whose daily round is guided by the position of the sun, and whose work schedule is paced by the seasons, urban industrial man can, in large measure, detach himself from natural time and feel secure with his more precise mechanical time piece. With this mechanism he can pace the activities of an entire factory and use it to integrate the work of many machines. It has become, says Mumford, "the new medium of existence." One no longer eats when feeling hungry "but when prompted by the clock." [19]

Preclock people are time-conscious in a different way, usually in ways consistent with their needs. Middleton tells how the Lugbara of Uganda manage their relations to time. They tend to reckon it "mainly by generations of men, the seasons, the stars, the moon and the sun," in other words, in terms of what is visible. "All these phenomena occur at regular intervals. Events that do not recur are not on a measured time scale." [20]

Like most other clockless people, the Lugbara's body is his timepiece regarding his day and night needs. The seasons and the rhythms in plant and animal life guide and time him in matters of work. He may

16 Leslie Stephen, "Vacations," *Cornhill Magazine*, Vol. 20. August 1869, pp. 205–214, quoted in Eric Larrabee and Rolf Meyersohn (Eds.), *Mass Leisure*, New York, Free Press, 1958, p. 282.

17 George Soule, *Time for Living*, New York, Viking, 1955, p. 93.

18 Lewis Mumford, *Technics and Civilization*, New York, Harcourt, Brace & World, 1934, p. 14.

19 Ibid., p. 17.

20 John Middleton, *The Lugbara of Uganda,* New York, Holt, Rinehart and Winston, 1963, p. 21.

not know what 9:00 A.M. is or 12 noon by the clock, but these hours figure approximately in his daily routine, and he may sense their arrival to the minute.

The influence of mechanical time, by which urban man is detached from the pacing influences in nature, is an influence that attaches him to the rhythms of man-made mechanisms. One's going and coming is paced by his daily round of appointments, all regulated by the clock. Some call it an enslavement to machines, and it may be for those who cannot adapt. Without it he would lose time. Without the clock, the world's work could not go on as well as it does. With it, a man in New York knows the precise minute to telephone a colleague in Singapore who needs certain instructions before boarding a plane for Australia. Thus the clock facilitates the saving as well as the use of time. It is merely a more precise method of using time in work or leisure.

De Grazia calls the clock a machine that has enabled man to gain leisure or free time, that tells how much leisure he can have away from work. Leisure, being time measured out by the clock, is not really free.

> If we but say "free clocked time," the illusion vanishes. Clocked time cannot be free. The phrase connotes, and justly so, that the "clockedness" has a purpose and a collectivity that is at odds with freeness and individuality. Clocked time requires activities and decisions that must always be referred back to (synchronized with) the machine and its ramifications in the industrial culture. Thus whatever free time we have is unfree from the start. That we oppose it to work really indicates that we really regard work as the dominant obligation.[21]

This is saying in effect that, however much one may enjoy the feast, he cannot put aside the fact that a feast must be worked for.

SEPARATION OF WORK FROM NONWORK

In the preindustrial systems the idea of leisure would have little meaning. Work and play intermingled except for festival occasions. Those who labored went about their work and nonwork intermittently. The interruptions were occasions for talk, some joking, even argument. The medieval craftsman worked from "sun to sun," but his work day was not all mere labor. When the factory came and workers were hired at an hourly rate the employer expected an hour of performance for each hour of pay. It was his loss if part of each hour was used for anything but work. Still more compelling, industrial work is group activity. What is done in one shop or by one work unit relates to what is done in other

21 De Grazia, op. cit., p. 325.

parts of the same enterprise. The work unit that trifles may delay the schedule of other work units. While work time in the industrial enterprise was on the way to becoming time for work only, work itself was becoming impersonal. It has been separated step by step from its earlier base and work ways. Three major stages are discernable:

1. The movement of industrial work from the home to the factory marked its separation from the domestic milieu in which it was familial or family-controlled activity.
2. The nature of work in the industrial enterprise is more duty intensive than work at home had been. All time-consuming activity not contributing to the work process must be excluded. This divorce has been identified as the separation of leisure activities and interests from work.
3. The equally necessary trend toward the impersonalization of industrial work has resulted in the separation of the personality of the worker from both the task and the product. This condition, as many believe, makes for the alienation of workers.

As a result of these three types of separation, some see the result as a separation of work from living; work ceases to be an end-interest and becomes more a means, serving interests outside the work place during one's leisure time. Weiss and Riesman put this thought in terms of leisure being identified with living, and one who goes *out* to work must cross the line that separates the two spheres.

> The notion of "job," of work as an activity separated from other activities of life, is a characteristic of the modern industrial society. And even here, it is not as all embracing as many of us would, on first thought, believe; the salesman's job, for example, continually intrudes into the time most people set aside for leisure activities.[22]

The separation is never total, keeping work and leisure in closed-off compartments, the work compartment cool and formal, that of leisure marked with warmth, relaxation, and humor. The influence from each penetrates the other. It would be unreal for one at leisure to put work fully out of mind or for one at work not to give a passing thought to leisure. Not even the worker for whom the job is a mere means to an end, a mere source of income, would find it satisfying to put the job totally out of mind when at leisure. For a grandfather work may have been an 84-hour week in a steel plant. For a grandson it is a 40-hour week in the same plant at more than three times the income. The clock tells him he has 44 hours of time for himself and more money to spend

[22] Robert S. Weiss and David Riesman, "Social Problems and Disorganization in the World of Work," in Robert K. Merton and Robert A. Nisbet (Eds.), *Contemporary Social Problems*, New York, Harcourt, Brace & World, 1961, pp. 459–515.

on leisure. For him to give prior attention to the 44 hours of his "own time," does not, or hardly could mean, putting the 40 hours of earning time out of mind.

Another example of changes under way in the uses of time by Americans, of separating work and leisure in our ways of thinking, is in the types of activities engaged in and the amount of time spent on each. As Table 15 indicates, there were in 1950 a total of 876 billion hours on

Table 15   National Time Budget and Time Division of Leisure, 1900, 1950, and 2000, in Billions of Hours Annually

Use of time	1900	1950	2000
Total population, millions	75.9	151.7	330.0
Total time for entire population	667	1,329	2,907
1. Sleep	265	514	1,131
2. Work	86	132	206
3. School	11	32	90
4. Housekeeping	61	68	93
Percent, work	(13)	(10)	(7)
Percent, school	(2)	(2)	(3)
Percent, housekeeping	(9)	(5)	(3)
5. Preschool population, nonsleeping hours	30	56	110
6. Personal care	37	74	164
Total, non-leisure related hours	490	876	1,794
7. Daily leisure hours	72	189	375
8. Weekend leisure hours	50	179	483
9. Vacation	17	35	182
10. Retired	6	24	56
11. Other, including unaccounted	32	26	16
Total, leisure related hours	177	453	1,113
Percent, nonleisure related hours	(74)	(66)	(62)
Percent, leisure related hours	(26)	(34)	(38)

Source: Mary A. Holman, "A National Time-Budget for the Year 2000," *Sociology and Social Research*, Vol. 46, No. 1, October 1961 as indicated in percents added here. Marion Clawson, "How Much Leisure, Now and in the Future," in Charles C. Charlesworth (Ed.), *Leisure in America, Blessing or Curse?* Philadelphia, American Academy of Political and Social Science, Monograph No. 4, 1964, p. 10.

the work side of the line (including as nonleisure sleep and personal care), and 453 billion hours on the leisure side of the line. The contrast with the division of time in 1900 is quite apparent.

Because of the increasing abundance of leisure time, its separation from work becomes more clearly remarked. Lee cautions, though, that while there is increasing recognition of a separation in the thinking and behavior of industrial people, it needs to be kept in mind that the two types of activity continually interpenetrate. The shift from work-oriented thinking to leisure-oriented thinking does not mean that the leisure-living interests have the field to themselves. They are bound to the work system, and in this relationship work is not downgraded. Leisure, as he sees, is more free of clock control than work can be, but control by clock still persists. "How inconceivable to imagine Western man in an environment not dominated by clock consciousness. We . . . live by what time the clock tells us it is." [23]

MORAL IMPLICATIONS OF LEISURE

It is to be expected that as industrial man acquires more leisure and more money to spend during leisure time, a situation develops which is inviting to commercial types of entertainment, and to industries making things for use in connection with leisure activity. Money making in the sphere of leisure activity has continually come into conflict with the normative order. Says Durant, those who offer entertainment for a price must be guided by profit considerations. "The machinery of amusement is run by businessmen actuated by business motives. Their concern is not primarily with the character of the entertainment they provide, for it is merely a means to the end of making profits. For them, good or bad means profitable or unprofitable." [24]

Many people who are interested in the problems of leisure would agree with Durant's view of commercial amusement. Thus, Nash said of commercial entertainment that it has a "predisposition toward sensationalism, money-mindedness, and crowd-mindedness. . . . Commercial amusement often seeks out, exploits, socializes, and makes dominant the low common denominator, and the masses, rendered passive, seem momentarily helpless." [25] As long as there are changes in business enterprise or in technology (automobile, airplane, radio, television, etc.), we can expect changes in leisure activity, and protest can be expected from those who feel that the moral order is threatened.

In any industrial urbanized nation where all behavior is in the process of change, there will be diverse viewpoints ranging from ultra conservative to ultra liberal about what is or is not moral. The great public is made up of many lesser publics. What the educators at the university level would offer in the way of radio and television programs would offend religious fundamentalists at one extreme and literary intellectuals at the other extreme. Douglass and Crawford quote a state-

[23] Robert Lee, *Religion and Leisure in America*, New York, Abingdon Press, 1964, pp. 23–29 and 209.

[24] W. H. Durant, *The Problem of Leisure*, London, Routledge and Kegan Paul, 1938, p. 22.

[25] Jay B. Nash, op. cit., pp. 60–61.

ment by Frank Stanton, President of the Columbia Broadcasting System which merits inclusion for its frankness.

> It has also been said . . . that the television is ruled by two tyrannies; the tyranny of the majority and the tyranny of the merchantilists; that, on the one hand, its sole purpose is to drug the great masses of citizens and, on the other hand, it is the tool of greedy men who will foist anything on the public if it will serve their purpose in selling things that nobody wants. . . . Both because of the technical limitations on the number of channels and because of the economic demands of the medium, it is impossible to have separate channels to serve every worthwhile minority.[26]

Among the many differences between leisure and work is the tendency for leisure activity to be much more determined by individual choice. We can predict to a large extent what a hundred workers in an enterprise will be doing during any coming week. Their work is interrelated, the job itself is largely "in command." It would be next to impossible to predict how the same hundred persons will spend their leisure during any coming week. This is undoubtedly one of the great values of leisure, however uncertain it causes some to be about the leisure of others, it is also the worry of private organizations that strive to influence the uses people make of their leisure. They want people to be occupied in ways they feel are the right ways. This is one reason why many organizations encourage people to find leisure-consuming hobbies. Lundberg, Komarovsky, and McInerny, whose revealing study of leisure has too long been unrecognized, said of the keep-busy cult:

> As a method of bridging the gap between birth and death, *keeping occupied* . . . undoubtedly keeps many out of mischief. The people most completely in its sway are not infrequently the pillars of society. Among other things, it prevents philosophic meditation and other morbid reflections which tend to afflict some preachers, professors, artists and others who won't work according to the formula. Nevertheless, the charmed circle is unpleasantly suggestive of a squirrel cage and its activities, suitable rather to the brain of a squirrel than to the brain of a man.[27]

It is often charged that the large organizations for guiding youth are dominated by the elderly of the upper and middle classes who really feel that yesterday's moral standards must be insisted upon, especially

---

[26] Paul F. Douglass and Robert W. Crawford, "Implementation of a Comprehensive Plan for the Wise Use of Leisure," in James C. Charlesworth (Ed.), *Leisure in America, Blessing or Curse?* Philadelphia, American Academy of Political and Social Science, Monograph No. 4, 1964, p. 51.

[27] George A. Lundberg, Mirra Komarovsky, and Mary A. McInerny, *Leisure, A Suburban Study*, New York, Columbia University Press, 1934, p. 16.

regarding sex. Foote answers that young people are also capable of making moral rules. He speaks of sex as a game played by all categories and those who engage in sex play also make the rules. Without rules, the game could not go on.[28]

Bertrand Russell pointed out the Western double standard of morality, which has been handicapping to girls in matters of work as well as leisure. The father, who expects his son to "sow some wild oats," may oppose his daughter going to a city to enter the labor market, a moral attitude that has had much to do with discouraging girls from entering certain occupations. That attitude was much more true three decades ago, the period Russell may have had in mind, than today, but the use of leisure time is still far from free of moral considerations.[29]

HOW PEOPLE USE LEISURE TIME

In a study of Ecuadorean Indians living in their traditional village culture, Salz attempted to determine what changes could be expected if they turned from agricultural to industrial work. In this connection, he gave some thought to leisure. He concluded that the idea of leisure does not exist among these people, and yet much of their activity is not directly related to work. In the Ecuadorean day, work and nonwork are mixed. One works for a spell, stops to talk, works again, sits and perhaps dozes, then engages in some foolishness, but the work gets done. There is no leisure separated from work in the Western sense.[30]

Western man's leisure is given to a great variety of activities; they are largely determined by the individual, although he may be influenced by his peer groups and by social class standards. Goodchilds and Harding in their study of a New York rural town, found 33 organized groups, each in some way concerned about leisure (recreation). Here is how the urbanized population in that rural place spend free time:

1. *Spectator.* The average person spends about 25 hours a week viewing television. Most attend movies; 63 percent watch parades and attend carnivals and 53 percent attend sport and school functions.
2. *Socializing.* About 80 percent spend time visiting friends or relatives in planned or informal activities.
3. *Card playing.* About 50 percent play cards for fun or money.

28 Nelson N. Foote, "Sex as Play," *Social Problems,* Vol. 1, No. 4, April, 1954, pp. 159–163.

29 Bertrand Russell, *In Praise of Idleness and Other Essays,* London, Allen and Unwin, 1948, p. 19.

30 Beate R. Salz, *The Human Element in Industrialization, A Hypothetical Case Study of Ecuadorean Indians,* special number of *Economic Development and Cultural Change,* Vol. 4, No. 1, Part 2, October 1955, p. 102.

4. *Active sports.* Some 60 percent, mostly males, engage in sports; 31 percent go hunting and 22 percent go fishing.
5. *Hobbies.* Over two thirds have hobbies; 42 percent make something, 21 percent garden, 15 percent engage in artistic or musical activities, 12 percent collect things.[31]

From this report it is evident that the 33 organizations comprise a type of leisure-time network through which social status comes to express itself. The investigators also report that "the individuals who engage in any particular activity tend to be more highly involved in the organizational life of the community than the non-doers." In another study, de Grazia obtained, in terms of numbers of times mentioned, a rank order of activities. Of 21 activities mentioned he found viewing television heading the list, followed by listening to the radio, listening to records, pleasure driving, going out to dinner. Significantly, the top three activities are enjoyed in the home.[32]

Concerning the interest in leisure among steel workers in Toulouse, France, Larrue asked workers if they engaged in this or that activity often, sometimes or never. To one who does not know the steel-mill proletariat in France, Table 16 may be informative. Listening to the radio is not included because of fairly total coverage. Nor is television mentioned because it was only beginning to reach steelworkers in 1957. Note that fishing ranks high compared with hunting; this is understandable since traditionally hunting was a gentleman's sport and even today not much hunting is done by workers because of the high cost involved.

Havighurst holds that one's way of using leisure is determined somewhat by his life outlook. He mentioned two viewpoints; one starts with heedless childhood, followed by heedful adulthood, and closes with a heedful contemplative old age.

> The other view sees creative productive work as the most valuable use of time at any age. The child is encouraged to learn it as early as possible. The adult is expected to continue it as long as possible. Inactivity is valueless, except as rest in preparation for a new period of activity. Contemplation is viewed with suspicion as being not far removed from mere vegetation. And, according to this view, a person might as well be dead as merely a vegetating man.[33]

[31] Jacqueline D. Goodchilds and John Harding, "Formal Organizations and Informal Activities," *Journal of Social Issues,* Vol. 16, No. 4, 1960, p. 26.

[32] Sebastian de Grazia, "Tomorrow's Good Life," *Teacher's College Record,* Vol. 61, No. 7, April 1960, p. 383.

[33] Robert J. Havighurst, "The Nature and Value of Meaningful Free Time Activity," in Robert W. Kleemeier (Ed.), *Aging and Leisure,* New York, Oxford University Press, 1961, p. 310.

Table 16   Leisure Activities of Male Metal Workers, Toulouse, 1957

Activity	Often	Sometimes	Total	Never
Trips to the country	62%	21%	83%	17%
* Work around home	27	52	79	21
Sport, as spectator	34	36	70	30
Movies	31	31	62	38
Fishing	28	31	59	41
Games (like bowles)	32	17	49	51
* Marketing	—	—	45	55
Sitting in cafes	15	17	32	68
* Gardening	11	16	27	73
Theater	7	17	24	76
Dancing	9	8	17	83
Sport, as participant	14	—	14	86
Art activity	—	—	13	87
Hunting	7	5	12	88

Reading:

Popular journals	29%	Serious journals	20%
Crime novels	22%	All other	14%

Source: Janine Larrue, "Loisirs ouvriers chez metallurgistes toulousaines," *Esprit*, 27 année, No. 274, juin 1959, p. 956.

* By our definition these activities would be chores, all others in the list would be recreation.

Havighurst questions the value of studies of leisure that merely produce lists of activity; it is also important, he mentions, to ask what the types of activity mean, that is, what satisfactions different activities yield. He suggests, in this connection, six characteristics and scales by which satisfactions may be measured.

1. *Financial cost of a leisure activity.* The scale ranges from $500 (joining a country club) to activities costing very little (card playing or fishing).
2. *Feeling of having much versus having little leisure.* The scale ranges from having too much to none at all.
3. *New experience versus repetition.* The scale ranges from ever looking for new experience and novelty to liking to do the same things over and over (gardening, playing cards).
4. *Vitality versus apathy.* The scale ranges from a vigorous interest to the apathetic in which one expects nothing from the leisure experience.
5. *Expansion versus constriction of interests and activities.* The scale ranges from expansion to a decreased or zero interest and activity.
6. *Things versus other values.* The scale ranges from "predominant interest in things" to "no interest in material objects or in working with materials." [34]

[34] Robert J. Havighurst, "Leisure Activities of the Middle-Aged," *American Journal of Sociology*, Vol. 63, No. 3, September 1957, p. 154.

It must be recognized that whoever seeks to measure the meanings of leisure activities is dealing with elusive material. Havighurst finds that different activities yield different satisfactions for different persons. Even the same activity may yield for any person different satisfactions under different circumstances.

LEISURE AND THE TIME BUDGET

If one is asked how he used his free time over the past week, he would find it difficult to answer, as he would also find it difficult to list all the money outlays during the week which could be called leisure costs. One has much less difficulty in telling his sources of income over a week or month, but what he did with his own time and the money spent on it is quickly forgotten. For this reason some students of leisure have concluded that the time budget is the only correct approach. The idea is that a person is asked to keep a daily record on which he reports how each hour, half hour, or quarter hour was occupied.

The difficulties with the time budget are obvious; few people will remember to fill in the blanks on the time budget sheet. Usually the record is kept for the seven-day week. The second obvious difficulty is that persons willing to keep a time budget for a week are likely to be those of the middle occupational groups or above, not of the working-class occupations. Table 17 is an example of a time budget which comes from a study done for an American broadcasting company and reproduced by de Grazia. Note that "leisure" is used in the table in the sense of "recreation," and the term "chores" is used to identify one of the nonrecreation items. Space does not permit the time uses for Saturday. For this national sample the males had on the average 3.6 hours of leisure and the females 4.5 hours on the week days. For the week males and females would have approximately 30 hours of recreation-leisure.

Clarke asked 574 men of different occupations how they would use two extra hours of each day, that is, additional leisure time. The responses reflect social-class or occupational-level attitudes.

Of those at the white-collar and professional level:
   28 percent would rest or sleep
   28 percent would read or study
   29 percent would give the two hours to extra work
    9 percent would do tasks around home

Of the unskilled to skilled handworkers:
   40 percent would rest or sleep
   13 percent would read or study

Table 17 Amount of Time Between 6 A.M. and 11 P.M. Devoted to Various Activities, Males and Females, 20–59 Years of Age, Spring 1954, in Hours

| | Average weekday | | Sunday | |
Activity	Males	Females	Males	Females
Total hours	17.0	17.0	17.0	17.0
Away from home	(9.7)	(4.1)	(5.5)	(3.9)
At work	7.2	2.0	1.2	0.3
Travel (work-connected, other)	1.4	0.6	1.3	1.0
Shopping	0.1	0.4	0.1	0.0
At restaurant, tavern, barber, etc.	0.3	0.1	0.1	0.1
At home of friend, or relative	0.4	0.6	1.4	1.4
Leisure (games, sport, church, etc.)	0.3	0.4	1.4	1.1
At home	(7.3)	(12.9)	(11.5)	(13.1)
Leisure other than reading	2.1	2.7	4.0	3.5
Reading	0.8	0.8	1.1	1.1
Miscellaneous work at home	0.6	1.2	0.8	0.7
Household chores and housekeeping	0.2	3.0	0.2	1.7
Eating or preparing food	1.2	2.5	1.3	2.5
Dressing, bathing, etc.	0.6	0.9	0.7	0.9
Sleeping, resting	1.8	1.8	3.4	2.7
Leisure activities	3.6	4.5	7.9	7.1

Source: Sebastian de Grazia, *Of Time, Work and Leisure,* New York, Twentieth Century Fund, 1962, p. 444.

> 9 percent would give the two hours to extra work
> 16 percent would do tasks around home

There were other answers but, significantly, there was almost no mention of giving the two extra hours to recreational activities.[35]

ASPIRATIONS AND USES OF LEISURE

Svalastoga interviewed students at the University of Copenhagen as to the uses they expected to make of their future leisure, after leaving the university and entering work activities. As seen in the distribution below, ten areas of activity were considered; family, career, education, etc. Within some of these areas two or more activities were listed, 25 in all, with one category for "other." Each student was given 1,000 time tokens, all to be distributed, according to choice, in different amounts to the different activities. The tokens stood for a measure of how much

35 Alfred C. Clarke, "The Use of Leisure and Its Relation to Levels of Occupational Prestige," *American Sociological Review,* Vol. 21, No. 3, June 1956, p. 306.

of one's future leisure would be given to each activity. The same schedule was used by the University of New Brunswick on a sample of 306 students (224 males, 82 females). The Danish sample included 203 males and 72 females. The figures here are percentages of the total number of tokens, 275,000 for students at the University of Copenhagen and about 306,000 for those at the University of New Brunswick. What stands out is that 39.6 percent of the Canadian tokens compared with 32.9 percent of the Danish were assigned to family interests. Tokens for recreation were 24.7 percent for New Brunswick students and 24.8 percent for Copenhagen students, for each group only about a fourth of all the tokens.

	University of New Brunswick	University of Copenhagen
Family		
1. Family life in general	12.3	13.3
2. Personal interaction between spouses	9.5	5.5
3. Rearing children	8.3	8.9
4. Providing children with education	5.7	3.3
5. Providing family with house and garden	3.8	1.9
Career		
6. Providing for one's career in general	9.2	6.1
7. Providing for a secure old age	2.5	1.2
Education		
8. Learning more after leaving university	4.9	7.5
Science		
9. Independent scientific activity	1.4	3.1
Mass communication		
10. Activity as lecturer, popularizer, etc.	1.3	1.3
Art		
11. Art, literary interests, active or passive	2.9	5.5
Religion		
12. Ecclesiastical, other religious activity	2.6	1.9
Politics		
13. Participation in political organizations	1.0	0.9
14. Reading, hearing political talks	1.3	1.7
15. Work for greater social equality	1.1	1.1
16. Work for greater individual freedom	0.8	2.5
17. Work for minimum welfare security for all	0.6	2.7
Personality development		
18. Development by reading and conversation	4.9	5.9
Recreation		
19. Travel	6.4	6.6
20. Hobbies	2.8	2.3
21. Interaction with friends	4.5	7.0
22. Restaurants, night clubs, etc.	2.2	0.7
23. Cards and other games	1.2	1.0
24. Sports, indoor exercises, dancing	5.1	3.3
25. Just reading, doing nothing	2.5	3.9
Other	1.2	0.9
	100.0	100.0

There are differences, to be sure, when the aspirations of males and females are compared or when the choices of liberals and conservatives are contrasted. For those figures space is not available here. What is especially striking is that the leisure aspirations of the two groups are so similar.[36]

URBANISM AND VACATION PHENOMENA

Clawson writes that the "total of paid vacations in the United States has risen from 17.5 million weeks in 1929 to 78 million weeks in 1959, or from .37 of a week per worker to slightly more than one week." Also there are six or seven general holidays, like Christmas, for which an increasing number of workers are paid.[37] In some European countries there are ten or more paid holidays, and paid vacations are also on the increase, due partly to the growing strength of trade unionism. Clawson might have added that a good part of the 17.5 million paid vacations in 1929 were enjoyed by upper-level white-collar workers, and that very few of these more privileged workers received vacations in 1900.

Vacations are not characteristic of preindustrial societies. As Vontobel reports in her study of work and leisure, preindustrial Germany, in adopting the Protestant Ethic, accepted some church holidays but not the idea of leisure.[38] In the industrial West the growth of the vacation idea is a breakaway from that Protestant heritage and the Puritan tradition. Historically, though, vacations were always the luxury of the nobility, eventually to become the luxury of the nontitled aristocracy as well, and in time to become a proprietary right of officials and top white-collar workers. As a social invention, vacations have always been identified with urban life, their uses and usages determined by the urban elites. As with the preindustrial aristocracy, vacations still mean escape from the city to the country for enjoyment purposes.

But the entire process of taking vacation and using it has evolved into somewhat of a cult. There are certain right times to go on vacation, right sorts of places to visit (one must always leave home for vacation), right things to do, and right rewards to realize. One who spends his vacation at home resting and perhaps doing things around the house can expect a frown from his boss, who believes that he paid for the

36 Kaare Svalastoga, "The Measurement of Desirability, The Time-Token Method," *Sociologiske Meddelelser*, Series 4, University of Copenhagen, 1957, pp. 83–98, for the Danish study. For the comparative study, see Nels Anderson, "Measurement of Values and Future Leisure," *Acta Sociologica*, Vol. 12, No. 4, Autumn 1969, pp. 177–185.

37 Marion Clawson, "How Much Leisure, Now and in the Future," in Charlesworth, op. cit., p. 6.

38 Klara Vontobel, *Das Arbeitsethos des deutschen Protestantismus*, Bern, Franke, 1946, pp. 66–69 and 84.

vacation and wants his man back refreshed and suntanned, ready to "tackle the job with new vigor."

De Grazia estimates that in 1960 1.5 million Americans were away on vacation each day of the year, and two of each three vacationing families were away from home about four days. "All told, these vacationers go by car for a distance of over a thousand miles round trip, have twenty days a year available to them, take two vacation trips, over 90 percent of them in the United States." [39]

In terms of money cost, vacations are the most expensive item in the national leisure budget. It has become as common to save for one's vacation as it once was to save for Christmas presents. Indeed, vacations have made tourism the most important single industry in some countries (Austria, Italy, Spain), and a money-loss problem for countries such as Germany and the United States from which many money-spending tourists come. Cullingworth estimates that Britain had about 30 million paid vacationers in 1962, an increase of 5 million over 1955. In 1961 nearly five million of these holidays were spent abroad, despite efforts of the government to discourage such journeys by limiting the money one might spend. [40] During 1967, and still, efforts are being made by the U.S. government to discourage vacationers from going abroad and taking dollars out of the country.

Vausson speaks of an aspect of the summer vacation craze in France which is seldom noticed by those who write on the subject from the urban viewpoint. He mentions how the farmers in France often feel harassed by the crowds that come from the cities on weekends or holidays; they go tramping through the countryside, walking through fields without concern, even disregarding the protests of farmers. Whether short vacations or long ones, Vausson notes that the proportion increases with the size of the city. In small towns few take vacations and in rural villages almost none. He estimates that in 1957 about 10 million urbanites made vacation journeys, and about half of these went to other countries, mainly Italy, Spain, and Switzerland. [41]

Miller and Robinson write about the increasing trend in the United States for vacationers to seek out rough, wild areas away from the cities: "parks, forests, wildlife areas, historic spots, resort sections, beaches and mountains," places where they can go boating, fishing, camping. The number runs into the tens of millions. [42]

In this regard we need to recognize that there are, in this age of

[39] De Grazia, *Of Time, Work and Leisure,* p. 117.

[40] J. B. Cullingworth, "Planning for Leisure," *Urban Studies,* Vol. 1, No. 1, May 1964, pp. 1–25.

[41] Claude Vausson, "Vacances à l'étranger," *Esprit,* 27 année, No. 274, juin 1959, pp. 1017–1029.

[42] Norman P. Miller and Duane M. Robinson, *The Leisure Age,* Belmont, California, Wadsworth, 1963, p. 207.

mass, affluent leisure, many areas of the earth's surface unsuited for agriculture and uninviting for industry, which now prove to be ideal "escape areas" for leisure activities. Mountain recesses that have known poverty for years, sandy beaches where formerly only a few fishermen eked out a living, forested lake regions only sparsely inhabited heretofore; all such areas are eagerly sought out by the tourism-vacation industries. Luxury hotels rise where only shacks were before. With the luxury hotel comes the gambling casino and the stylish night club. Here are towns of a new sort to which all social classes flock, and here are accommodations suited to any purse, and even elaborate camping grounds for families coming in their own automobiles or with trailers or tents.

LEISURE IN THE COST COLUMN

There is hardly any leisure activity that can be enjoyed without spending money, unless it be dozing in the shade, which is frowned upon. A careful effort to measure the cost of leisure in the United States was made by Saunders and Parker for 1953, 18 years ago. There seems not to have been another such total survey since. Their estimate of $30 billion, about a tenth of the 1953 consumer budget, would have to be doubled for 1970. However, their study does remind us of the difficulty of attempts to measure leisure spending because leisure permeates other costs; household, social duty, work-connected spending (e.g., use of the family auto).[43] And equally important, there is the difficulty of isolating spending for recreation and spending for other kinds of leisure activity. For the man who enjoys such activity, is spending money on the garden a recreational activity? Like leisure itself, leisure spending touches the whole of one's life and mixes in with all consumer spending. Nonetheless, some writers have, with not more than marginal success, made estimates. Miller and Robinson assembled leisure cost estimates from a variety of sources. Some of these convey the impression of magnitude:

> $39 billion for travel and tourism
> $40 billion for autos, of which perhaps a third could be charged to leisure use
> $10 billion for alcoholic beverages, a good part for leisure
> $ 2 billion for boats and boating
> $ 1 billion for private swimming pools
>
> there are 85,000 bowling alleys and 40 million bowlers
>> 55 million television sets in use and three times that number of radios [44]

[43] Dero A. Saunders and Sanford S. Parker, "$30 Billion for Fun," *Fortune*, Vol. 49, No. 2, August 8, 1954.
[44] Miller and Robinson, op. cit., pp. 202–214.

Like other forms of consumer spending, almost all aspects of leisure spending assume a commercial character, not merely the activities that are called "purchased" recreation. And this applies in varying degrees to the diverse guided types of activity carried on by private groups. Taken as a whole, leisure activities, those related to chores as well as to recreation, may be regarded as work-providing. The tourism-vacation area of leisure is served by practically every basic industry: steel, rubber, machinery, all means of transportation, electronics, as well as those providing food, drinks, and clothing. It is to be expected, however, that various kinds of leisure costs, alcoholic drinks for example, will be viewed with alarm by some groups, as much television viewing or gambling is a worry to other groups. And there are many who complain that there is too much spectator leisure participation and not enough of "playing the game."

Were leisure spending in any country to be reduced by as much as 10 percent, the hurt to the leisure industries would be felt by almost every other industry, as much as if every household returned to the kitchen, the living room, and the bedroom of 1890.

PUBLIC RESPONSIBILITIES FOR LEISURE

As we have considered elsewhere, there is hardly any aspect of man's work, especially in the urban community, that does not depend on government for providing facilities and service, if not some degree of control. Leisure industries, as work organizations, making things for recreation (sports equipment, boats, camping outfits, and toys) are enterprises for work in much the same sense as plants producing furniture, washing machines, or wearing apparel. They use the public amenities, the streets, and other facilities of the community.

Public participation is equally present in the performances of people during leisure, as one of the consuming aspects of community life. With respect to leisure activities government is looked to for guidance and sponsorship, on the one hand, and for regulation and protection, on the other. It acts in its capacity as corporate parent through the school and other agencies, teaching children how to play games, how to swim, etc. It provides specialists to organize group games and competitions. Many private organizations and groups are also involved in guiding people in their leisure, but it is only the public units concerned that provide the corporate parent service. It stands guard against the gamblers who would "fix" ball games and regulates in various ways the operations of commercial entertainments.

Prior to the Great Depression, American government at all levels evinced only a casual interest in matters of recreation, but, says Riesman, the importance of leisure had hardly been recognized. When millions were unemployed and some 3.5 million unemployed workers were provided with public jobs, then communities began using this labor to build swimming pools, develop play fields and playgrounds, sports arenas, facilities for winter games, community houses—facilities that had long been established, for example, in German cities. Through the depression, Americans discovered leisure as reality.[45]

Confronted with a depression, local, state, and federal government turned avidly to providing leisure facilities that "could not be afforded" during the affluent years. The Work Projects Administration (WPA), established to provide work for the jobless, had to find work of many kinds. Unemployed artists were assigned to paint pictures, make sculptures and other creative objects to be placed in schools and other public buildings, thus establishing a precedent in public service. The effort by WPA to foster theater productions in large cities turned out to be controversial, but music, folk dancing, and other social activities, and the recreation facilities, reports Wector, did much to make many communities leisure conscious.[46]

This same program built or improved 100,000 miles of farm-to-market and other country roads, thus eliminating many rural isolates, at the point when rural people were beginning to become automobile and tractor users. With the coming of motor vehicles, all roads, to an extent never before imagined, have come to be used for leisure purposes, especially on holidays and weekends. To meet the demands of tourism and other leisure needs, all the industrial countries are finding it necessary to extend good roads into the once inaccessible poverty areas where formerly such roads were not needed. They have now become popular leisure time retreats.

There are in the United States 178 national parks, ranging in size from a few to many thousand acres, altogether 25 million acres. In 1925 these public places for leisure received no more than 400,000 visitors in a year; they received 80 million visitors in 1960. While, on the one hand, good roads and the automobile eliminated thousands of hamlets in the United States, the same roads and automobiles made it possible for many millions of urban people to venture freely into the outdoors.[47]

Good roads provided by government, however helpful to city people wishing to enjoy rural outings, do not serve rural people in the same measure. Most public facilities for leisure use are found in the towns and

[45] David Riesman, *The Lonely Crowd,* 2nd ed., New York, Doubleday, 1956, p. 329.
[46] Dixon Wecter, *The Age of the Great Depression, 1929–1941,* New York, Macmillan, 1948, p. 224.
[47] See Jack Schaefer, "Your National Parks," *Holiday,* Vol. 26, No. 1, July 1959, pp. 46–54; and Marion Clawson, "Statistics on Outdoor Recreation," *Resources of the Future,* Washington, 1958 and op. cit.

cities, not in extremely rural areas. Country people must go to the near-est town for recreation, which is seldom convenient. In the meanwhile, new recreations in town have outmoded the old rural recreations. Saville points to Britain as a typical case. He states that as country people ac-cept "what may be called urban values," they devalue the old rural pas-times, and government in rural areas cannot afford to provide urbanlike recreational facilities.[48]

ON TRENDS AND PROSPECTS FOR LEISURE

Majumdar describes, in a study of an Indian rural community, how the country people spend their free time, without feelings of guilt, sitting together in groups, joking, telling stories, gossiping, perhaps doing some gambling. "Any villager who goes to Lucknow collects the latest news on the city and it is shared with the other villagers in these evening talks." But Majumdar recognizes that there are more and more visits to the city and slowly urban influence is making itself felt in rural ways of leisure.[49]

Not only does radiating urbanism tend to revolutionize rural ways of leisure, urban ways never cease changing. What with advertising new leisure activities and interests and with social class competition ever present, the dynamics of leisure in their particulars become most unpre-dictable. Veblen, who wrote not of leisure but of the antics of the "leisure class," saw leisure activities as a competitive pursuit.

> And as this leisure class sets the pace in all matters of decency, the result for the rest of society also is a gradual amelioration of the scheme of dress. As the community advances in wealth and culture, the ability to pay is put in evidence by means which require a progressively nicer dis-crimination in the beholder. The nicer discrimination between adver-tising media is in fact a very large element of the higher pecuniary culture.[50]

Veblen saw that leisure in other aspects than dress was equally a display contest common to all classes. Kerr calls attention to the prospect that more leisure in the future will be used in refresher education and personal development. The work week by 1984 may be lowered to 34 hours, but may not go much lower. As work hours diminish, it is likely

48 John Saville, *Rural Depopulation in England and Wales, 1851–1951,* London, Routledge and Kegan Paul, 1957, p. 36.

49 D. N. Majumdar, *Caste and Communication in an Indian Village,* Bombay, Indian Publishing House, 1958, p. 301.

50 Thorstein Veblen, *The Theory of the Leisure Class* (1st ed., 1899), New York, Modern Library, 1931, p. 187.

that work will itself become more highly valued, and for reasons of work more people will return periodically to universities for further study.[51]

There is also the prospect that the heedless pursuit of leisure activities which happens to be in style, and is now encouraged by advertisers, will diminish as levels of education rise and as drudgery and routine are removed from industrial work. For increasing numbers, a new work orientation could develop. Galbraith offers a view somewhat in line with this thought.

> There is no intrinsic reason why work must be more unpleasant than non-work. Presiding over the console that regulates the movement of billets through a steel mill may be as pleasant as sojourning with a connubial fishwife. To urge more leisure is a feckless exercise so long as the industrial system has the capacity to persuade the people that goods are more important. Men will value leisure over work only as they find the uses of leisure more interesting or rewarding than those of work, or as they win emancipation from the management [by advertisers] of their wants, or both. Leisure is not wanted *per se* but only as these prerequisites are provided.[52]

As work in the future becomes more scarce and valued, leisure will be weaker in competition with work for one's time. Mannheim sees the need for government sharing the responsibility for providing the facilities for leisure in the community, but he warns that there may be danger in passing to government the control over leisure practices, behaviors, and interests. Control by any authority is difficult because of the wide variety of views about the uses of leisure, from radical to conservative, and the many views about moral behavior.[53] Work, being more precisely utilitarian, can be controled, but leisure interests and activity lean in the direction of art, expressing more the spirit and the spontaneous urges of each individual. Creativity, whether of things or of ideas, may be stifled by the usually uniform control of any authority. This does not mean that our leisure is not under controls, social and otherwise, but in our society these are for the time being fairly tolerant controls.

[51] Clark Kerr, "The New Leisure, The New Wealth, and the New Community," in Stanley Scott (Ed.), *Metropolitan Area Problems,* Berkeley, University of California Press, 1960, pp. 35–42.

[52] Galbraith, op. cit., p. 365.

[53] Karl Mannheim, *Freedom, Power, and Democratic Planning,* New York, Oxford University Press, 1950, pp. 269–270.

Urban people and their livelihood | 15

CITIES, WORK, AND THE FOOD SUPPLY

The charge that cities are parasitic is not new. Urban people cannot produce their food supply, the fuels they need must be brought in, and so too the raw material with which they work. The work of processing materials and providing services is about the only way urbanites have for making a livelihood; they must make things to sell, or they sell services to their suppliers. How much a city may grow will depend on the size and productivity of its area of supply. They cannot grow, says Coe, unless there is access to the food, and he mentions that some cities in rich areas fail to grow because adequate roads are lacking.[1]

Great cities are sensitive as are most major industries. They can grow only where locations are favorable and they must have access to abundant supplies of food, fuel, fibers, metals, and other essential materials. What is abundant in one geographical region may be much less or much more than abundant in another region. Thus the size of a city and its level of affluence depends on the extent and richness of its supply area, usually referred to as its hinterland. Its area of supply also tends largely to be the market hinterland for its goods and services.

Thompson who conceptualizes cities in economic terms, in terms of exports and imports, sees their growth occurring in four stages:

1. *Stage of Export Specialization,* in which the local economy is the lengthened shadow of a single dominant industry or even a single firm (saw-mill town, mining town, center of fishing and fish processing).
2. *Stage of the Export Complex,* in which local production broadens to other

[1] Michael D. Coe, "Tropical Forest Civilizations," *Comparative Studies in Society and History,* Vol. 4, 1961–1962, p. 67.

products and/or deepens by extending forward or backward in the stages of production, by adding local suppliers and/or consumers of intermediate products.

3. *Stage of Economic Maturation,* in which the principal expansion of local activity is in the direction of replacing imports with new "own use" production; the local economy fills out in range and quality of both business and consumer services.

4. *Stage of Regional Metropolis,* reached when the local economy becomes a node connecting and controling neighboring cities, once rivals and now satellites, and the export of services becomes a major economic function.[2]

These stages, of course, are approximate. The first stage would describe most towns and small cities in depressed areas or regions. The industries are of the primary sort which make extensive use of low-cost unskilled labor. To enter the second stage calls for establishing secondary industries, producing finished products for the market, which enables the use of greater amounts of skilled labor, which serves to raise the economic level of the economy.[3] Of course, the growth of the economy may stop or stagnate between any of these stages; movement from one to another is not inevitable.

Our examination of the ways in which urban communities gain their livelihood needs to take into account the conditions under which a livelihood is gained, whether in small or large cities or in villages, in affluent or in depressed areas. In the Maritimes of Canada or the Appalachians of the United States gaining a livelihood is much more of a struggle than in British Columbia or California. The difference is reflected in the annual income of families, up to 30 percent lower in depressed than in affluent areas. Where affluence is present, the houses, stores, work places, public utilities, and artifacts generally present much to be seen and experienced which is absent in depressed habitat areas. The people have less to do with, less to feed upon in depressed than in affluent areas. They must work harder to receive less.

Even in the more affluent communities there are glaring inequalities in the distribution of both opportunities and income. In the great cities the contrasts are more visible; the slums and the best housing, the poor shopping area and the elite shopping area are rarely far apart. In both wide affluent regions as in wide depressed regions we find harsh inequalities between rural and urban people, the rural having the lower incomes and the lesser advantage in the distribution of economic and social benefits.

[2] Wilbur R. Thompson, *A Preface to Urban Economics,* Baltimore, Johns Hopkins Press, 1965, pp. 15–16.

[3] Ibid., pp. 16–17.

RURAL AND URBAN SOCIO-ECONOMIC CHANGE

Thompson's four stages of urban change and growth end with the emergence of the metropolis, which may well be the beginning of an even more complex stage of organization and development, through which cities themselves become embraced in an even larger techno-economic pattern of relationship and control. This may be what Handlin visualized when he states:

> The differences between city and country have been attenuated almost to the vanishing point. The movement of people, goods and messages has become so rapid and has extended over such a long period as to create a new situation. To put it bluntly, the urbanization of the whole society may be in process of destroying the distinctive role of the modern city.[4]

The challenging fact confronting us is that the economic worth of an individual or family becomes less than ever a private consideration. The worth of the individual or family must be seen in the collective terms of producing and consuming. A worker whose full capacities are not used in production is less of an asset. If he is able and willing to work but is not employed, or if his labor is inefficiently used, or if he must depend on welfare for part of his livelihood, then he is a burden to the whole economy. All this is obvious and is being said in many ways. Our point is that the same logic applies to communities.

Riley sees communities, economically, as intricate, continuing entities. He estimates that it would take a hundred years to liquidate a large insurance company because at least three generations are involved in its assets. The obligations of the company would concern people in a great number of cities, towns, and villages, and these people would be of different socio-economic classes. This relatedness of the economy may also be seen in the continuing community system. In terms of social dimensions, there is continuity in three wide areas: the demographic, the system of norms and values, and ideologies.

1. The community is a demographic phenomenon; people are born and people die, some move in and some move away, or they move about and cluster within the community. They enjoy or endure different standards of living, as they also display different levels of competence in the labor market. They may be racially or ethnically different, but they continue.

4 Oscar Handlin, "The Modern City as a Field for Historical Study," in Oscar Handlin and John Burchard (Eds.), *The Historian and the City*, Cambridge, The M.I.T. and Harvard University Presses, 1963, p. 24.

2. These people "live according to complex systems of rules and regulations—perhaps most of them written—which have to do with such basic activities as making a living, forming new families, socializing the young, coming to terms with the supernatural; and these arrangements are called social institutions."

3. People have their ideologies, that is, their ideas and beliefs about things; homogeneous groups have their idea patterns, expressed perhaps in their unique vocabularies. This continuing and changing aspect of community life can be identified as a system of values.[5]

Riley relates these continuing dimensions to the efforts of people to earn a livelihood, a dominating element in the mesh of community life to which every individual contributes and on which he depends. We can see the force of continuity in the following description of caste and family in an Indian community. New ideas and practices enter but the old are not pushed aside. Work ways and customs continue, changing only step by step. Such is the case with the changing role of the Washerman.

The Washerman caste renders several ritual services both for the upper and for the lower castes. The women of the caste perform the purificatory rituals to rid women of all castes from the Brahmin down to the Irivas (untouchables), of menstrual and birth pollution. Even the goddesses menstruate and have to be purified. The men perform certain rites in honour of minor deities of the lower castes and these are accompanied by songs.

As ritualists, they have to study various magical formulae and from this it is an easy transition for them to turn to the practice of magic, both white and black. Literacy becomes a need for them and it helps a smaller number of them to become physicians. The Mayur Washerman's medicine shop in the bazaar, however, is an innovation, a part of the process of urbanization. The Washerman-physician now becomes a trader, a new role for which his tradition provides no model.[6]

What is happening in this Indian community, as in communities around the world, is that economic and technological change afford new ways of earning a livelihood, and the benefits of such change may fall even to people of low degree, in this case the Washerman caste. As new ways of work emerge and old skills are slowly outmoded, Friedmann notes, more and more people must exert themselves in learning new skills, which normally opens the way for rising productivity levels and

[5] John W. Riley, Jr., "Basic Social Research in the Institution of Life Insurance," *American Behavioral Scientist*, Vol. 6, No. 9, May 1963, p. 7.

[6] A. Aiyappan, *Social Revolution in a Kerala Village*, New York, Asia Publishing House, 1965, pp. 85–86.

rising standards of living.[7] Moreover, as the level of skills in a community
rises with new types of production, the community itself may be in the
process of moving from a lesser to a higher economic level, as concep-
tualized in Thompson's four stages. Towns and small cities, much more
than large cities, and more than their individual inhabitants, are tied
to their natural resources and their immediate hinterlands. Those inhabitants who wish to remain or must remain become identified with the
economy of their community.

CITY SIZE AND LEVEL OF INCOME

After reviewing various studies, as well as available statistics on income by size of city, Thompson finds evidence of a step-by-step rise in
annual family income by size of city (2,500, 10,000, 50,000, 250,000,
500,000, above 500,000). For 1949 the range was from $2,400 to $3,000,
roughly a rise of $75 for each successive size. The figures are not without
inaccuracies because cities of any size group vary in their degree of being
industrial.[8]

Whereas the small city is likely to be dominated by a single industry,
the city of a half million or more will have a diversity of industries and
the large city will support a still more varied labor market. It is able to
use many skills for which there is no demand in the small place. In the
large cities are the most efficient facilities for skill training, and, while
attracting many who are unskilled, they attract the most talented and
ambitious. Here will be the head offices of giant corporations, the great
laboratories, and the habitations of the rich. In the large city are found
too the great social distances between rich and poor, "the basic degree
of interpersonal income inequality within the whole metropolitan area." [9]

In her report on a study of five towns, Dean concludes that the small
cities must be seen in more than economic terms. They tend to be "sub-
servient sub-systems performing adaptive and integrative functions for
the larger society . . . having adaptive and integrative functions of their
own." She calls the small town or city the "microcosm in terms of which
the national community is comprehended and evaluated." As a case of
subservience, she cites Minersville, a coal mining town which has long
been exploited by absentee owners, a town in Thompson's "stage of export specialization." Minersville has been in that condition to the point
where local initiative has about disappeared; the inhabitants regard

7 Georges Friedmann, *Industrial Society, The Emergence of the Human Problems of Automation*, New York, Free Press, 1964, pp. 184 ff.
8 Thompson, op. cit., pp. 88–89.
9 Ibid., pp. 106–107.

themselves as being exploited, with no means of their own to mend matters.[10]

The nearer a small city is to the status of Minersville, the less urban will be its way of life and the less diversified its labor force. Such a town, with a primary industry that produces something of value for export, holds no inducement for secondary industry and therefore does not prosper. Often it lacks paved streets and other amenities, and both the family income and the level of education are low. Most of the youth who finish high school feel impelled to migrate.

In a study of rural and urban characteristics, Duncan and Reiss show the average earnings of males and females for 1949 in cities of three size categories. Note that for the small cities the annual earnings

	Males	Females
Cities of 3,000,000 or more	$3,078	$1,603
Cities of 10,000 to 250,000	2,692	1,121
Cities of 2,500 to 10,000	2,354	839

of female workers was 36 percent of the male earnings and it was 42 percent for cities of 10,000 to 250,000, while for cities of 3,000,000 or more female earnings were 53 percent of male earnings.[11]

Of course other factors than size of city influence inequality of income. Wage and salary levels in Canada tend to be lower for all categories of labor than in the United States. This is despite the fact that many industrial establishments in Canadian cities are extensions of similar industries in the United States. Certain trade unions in Canada are affiliates of American trade unions. However, as seen in Table 18, the

Table 18   Selected Measures of Income per Capita for Canada
and the United States, in 1964

	Canada	United States	Canada as percentage of United States
		Income per capita *	
Gross national product	$2,444	$3,272	74.7
Net national income	1,825	2,677	68.2
Personal disposable income	1,643	2,248	73.1

* Each country in terms of own dollars.
Source: *Towards a Sustained and Balanced Economic Growth,* Ottawa, Economic Council of Canada, 1965, p. 53.

[10] Lois R. Dean, *Five Towns, A Comparative Community Study,* New York, Random House, 1967, p. 6.
[11] Otis D. Duncan and Albert J. Reiss, Jr., *Social Characteristics of Rural and Urban Communities,* New York, Wiley, 1956, p. 96.

net income of the Canadian is 73.1 percent of that of an American. Of the gross national product, the average income per employed person was $7,500 (Canadian dollars) in Canada and $9,400 for workers in the United States.[12]

INCOME DISTRIBUTION AND INEQUALITY

We can understand that towns or cities in deprived areas, compared with urban places in fertile environments, will grow slowly and experience weak economic development. The distribution of urban places, from weak to strong, tends to reflect the unequal geographical distribution of natural resources. Aside from such inequalities about which man can do little are the inequalities inherent in the labor market of every community, where different rates of pay are offered for different levels of work. Moreover, the competitive labor market is more favorable to the skilled than the unskilled, more favorable to the young than the old, is less generous to females than males, and often (for reasons of bias) racial, ethnic, religious, and other minorities are socially disadvantaged in the labor market.

The labor market, even in the best of possible worlds, tends to sort people out, with the result that incomes are unequal. The percentage of families and income-receiving individuals in the United States for 1960, and their distribution according to income level, is seen in Table

Table 19   Families and Individuals, by Income Levels, Before Taxes, for the United States, in 1960

| | Percentage distribution | |
Income in dollars	Families	Individuals
Under 1,000	5.0	33.6
1,000–1,999	8.0	20.4
2,000–2,999	8.7	12.8
3,000–3,999	9.8	10.2
4,000–4,999	10.5	9.3
5,000–5,999	12.9	6.0
6,000–9,999	30.8	6.5
10,000 and over	14.3	1.2
Total	100.0	100.0
Number in millions	45.4	10.9

Source: *Poverty and Deprivation in the United States*, Washington, D.C., Conference on Economic Progress, 1962, p. 95.

[12] *Towards a Sustained and Balanced Economic Growth*, Ottawa, Economic Council of Canada, 1965, p. 53.

19. Many of the individual income receivers were elderly persons. For 1960 in the United States $4,000 was the dividing line for families; those receiving less were deemed to be in deprivation, which would total 31.5 percent of the 45.4 million families in the United States. For individuals, those with less than $2,000 income were in the deprived category, 54.0 percent of the 10.9 million.[13]

When we look at incomes for Canada the same unequal distribution appears (Table 20). Here we note that 46 percent of the income recipi-

Table 20 Distribution of Nonfarm Incomes by Income Class, for Canada, in 1961

	Income recipients	
Income in dollars	Number in thousands	Percent
Under 1,999	976	20.3
2,000–3,999	1,237	25.8
4,000–5,999	1,302	27.2
6,000–7,999	711	14.8
8,000–9,000	313	6.5
10,000–14,999	188	3.9
15,000 and over	73	1.5
Totals	4,800	100.0

Source: *Distribution of Nonfarm Income by Size, 1961,* Ottawa, Dominion Bureau of Statistics, 1964, Tables 1 and 2.

ents received less than $4,000 in 1961, whereas about 80 percent were receiving less than $4,000 in 1955 (evidence of wage and salary rise); 5.4 percent in 1961 had incomes of $10,000 and over compared with 1.6 percent for 1955. The total income was $14 billion in 1955 compared with $23 billion in 1961. In 1955 there were 875,000 in the agricultural labor force and of these only 215,000 earned sufficient money to make income tax returns. Of the farm owners in this group, as Porter remarks, only 35,000 made enough to be taxed. Canada's rural prosperity is enjoyed by a limited number of farmers, the rest are poor.[14]

Inequalities between farm and nonfarm (including urban) families in the United States for 1950 and 1960 are presented in Table 21. Two trends are shown respecting farm operating families; first, their average income declined from 65 percent of the average urban income in 1950 to 56 percent of average urban income in 1960. This helps to explain the

[13] *Poverty and Deprivation in the United States,* Washington, D.C., Conference on Economic Progress, 1962, p. 95.

[14] John Porter, *The Vertical Mosaic, An Analysis of Social Class and Power in Canada,* Toronto, University of Toronto Press, 1966, p. 109.

Table 21   Families and Individuals in the United States by Income
and Number for 1950 * and 1960

Characteristic	1950	1960
Income, all families and individuals	$ 4,444	$ 6,845
Nonfarm (and urban) families	5,232	8,049
Farm-operating families	3,382	4,518
Individuals	2,147	3,232
Families and individuals, in thousands		
All families and individuals	48,890	56,060
Nonfarm (and urban) families	34,140	40,830
Farm-operating families	5,650	4,540
Individuals	9,100	19,690

* Excluding Alaska and Hawaii.
Source: Helen M. Lamale, "Workers' Health and Family Living Standards,"
Monthly Labor Review, Vol. 86, No. 6, June 1963, p. 677.

decline in farm operating families from 5.65 million in 1950 to 4.54 million in 1960, a drop of 20 percent.[15]

The problems associated with the inequalities of income come glaringly into focus in a country as the population increasingly becomes industrial and urban. The American rural family of 1800 was in large measure living on a subsistence economy, in deep poverty by present standards, but it was not seen as something to worry about. The economic prospects of the family bettered as the number of children increased. Even in that day the large family was not greatly disadvantaged in the growing towns. Today the working-class family in the city is likely to be among the disadvantaged. This is evident from Table 22 showing the

Table 22   Children in Poor and Nonpoor American Families,
in 1965

Characteristic	Poor families	Nonpoor families
Families with children		
1 to 2 children	43%	64%
3 to 4 children	34%	29%
5 or more children	23%	7%
Number of families, in thousands	4,319	28,550
Number of children, in thousands	13,937	55,692
Mean number of children per family	3.23	2.30

Source: Harold L. Sheppard, *Effects of Family Planning on Poverty in the United States,* Kalamazoo, Michigan, Upjohn Institute for Unemployment Research, 1967, p. 2.

number of children in poor and nonpoor American families. The poor families have the responsibility for nearly one child more, on the

[15] Helen H. Lamale, "Workers' Health and Family Living Standards," *Monthly Labor Review,* Vol. 86, No. 6, June 1963, p. 677.

average, than the nonpoor families. The table also shows that families with more than four children are more likely to be among the poor. Yet at the same time 43 percent of these families had only one or two children, and 7 percent of the nonpoor families had five children or more.

The number of dependent children clearly also has a bearing on economic inequality. Whyte conceived a "dependency ratio" for different provinces of Canada (number of persons under 20 and over 70 years of age per 100 persons between 20 and 69 years of age), and here is

	Rural	*Urban*	*Total*
All Canada	107.9	80.2	87.8
Quebec	125.9	82.5	92.0
British Columbia	95.9	78.0	82.5

shown the average for Canada, for Quebec, the poor province, and for British Columbia, the affluent province. For British Columbia the urban sector shows a dependency ratio of 78 per 100 employment age (20 to 69) persons, about 18 fewer than for the rural sector. For urban Quebec the ratio is more than 43 lower than for the rural sector.[16]

ON DISPARITIES BETWEEN COUNTRIES

In the world of our time with its globalizing industrial urbanism, no country can enjoy economic growth in isolation, nor can it keep pace with social and cultural change. While, on the one hand, the advanced countries differ widely in their ways of life and standards of living, taken together, a great gap separates them from the so-called underdeveloped countries. The more advanced depend on the less advanced, as they are also depended on by the less developed, the burden of whose attempts at development they cannot avoid sharing. They must share with the less developed both their wealth and their know-how. However, Gunnar Myrdal has complained:

> There is still a tendency to discuss the world economic problem from the narrow point of view of the small minority of mankind in the nationally highly integrated and prosperous countries, and to do so in terms all too exclusively of their trade and payments problems. By far the most glaring evidence, however, of the failure of international integration, according

[16] Donald R. Whyte, "Rural Canada in Transition," in Marc A. Tremblay and Walton J. Anderson (Eds.), *Rural Canada in Transition,* Ottawa, Agricultural Economics Research Council, 1966, p. 18.

to our definition of this ideal, is the relatively great poverty of so many countries, with such large populations. As a matter of fact, the world trend seems to be towards even greater inequality.[17]

Inequality, as between established nations and emerging ones, concerns the socio-cultural as well as the economic dimension. The economic dimension is most widely used because it is the most easily quantified. Apertet compares countries on the basis of fuels used for energy, all types reduced to tons equivalent of coal (TEC's), the number of TEC's used per capita. For example, the consumption for each of the following countries is: United States, 7.6; Canada, 5.2; Great Britain, 4.7; Belgium, 3.8; Germany, 3.2; France, 2.4; Japan, 0.9; Mexico, 0.7; Greece, 0.4; Brazil, 0.4; and India, 0.2.[18]

Table 23 presents a comparison for ten countries on per capita income and per capita consumption of energy (gas, oil, electric power,

Table 23   Population, Annual per Capita Income, Daily Calories per Capita Food Consumption, and Annual per Capita Energy Consumption, for Selected Countries and the World

| | | | Per capita consumption of | |
Countries	Millions population	Per capita income *	Food calories	Energy TEC's †
United States	180.7	2,289	3,100	8.79
Canada	17.8	1,543	3,100	7.90
United Kingdom	52.5	1,084	3,200	5.12
Belgium	9.2	987	2,900	4.27
West Germany	53.4	967	2,900	4.02
Netherlands	11.5	803	3,000	3.04
Italy	49.4	509	2,700	1.57
Japan	93.2	341	2,200	1.42
India	432.6	62	1,800	0.15
Nigeria	35.1	84	—	0.05
World	2,995.0	—	—	1.53

* U.S. $ equivalent.
† Tons equivalent of coal.
Source: *Science and Technology for Development*, New York, United Nations, 1963, Vol. I, p. 38.

coal in TEC's). In general, where per capita income is high, the consumption of calories and energy, "calories for machines," tend also to

[17] Gunnar Myrdal, "The Conditions of Economic Integration," in David E. Novak and Robert Lekachman (Eds.), *Development and Society*, New York, St. Martin's Press, 1964, p. 318.
[18] J. Apertet, "De nouvelles sources d'énergie pour les pays insuffisament développés," *Tiers Monde*, T. 2, No. 5, janvier–mars 1961, p. 3.

be. These may not be adequate measures but, whatever their merit, they show the more industrial urban countries in a position of advantage.

Country-to-country comparisons of incomes and expenditures may be deceiving. Looking at Table 24, we can see that it would be impossible

Table 24   Income and Expenditures of Workers in Japan, Germany, and Venezuela

A. *Japan, in 1964,* averages (360 Yen = $1)

Income per family (month)	62,142
Expenditure per family (month)	52,433
Worker income, plants under 100 workers	26,182
Worker income, plants over 500 workers	31,827

B. *Germany, in 1965,* averages (4 D-Marks = $1)

Income per male worker (month)	454
Income per female worker (month)	309
Income of 4-person family (middle level)	1,107
Income of 4-person family (higher level)	2,106
Expenditure, 4-person family a month (middle)	981
Expenditure, 4-person family a month (higher)	1,919

C. *Venezuela, in 1961,* (rural and urban) average monthly (4.5 Bolivares = $1)

Income, all workers	950
Income, urban workers	1,231
Income, rural workers	453
Expenditures, urban	1,119
Expenditures, rural	400

Source: *Labor Development Abroad,* Washington, D.C., Department of Labor; for Japan, January 1966, pp. 13–26; for Germany, November 1966, pp. 18–29; for Venezuela, September 1966, pp. 13–22.

for four skilled industrial workers, a Japanese, a German, a Venezuelan, and an American, to agree about the benefits they derive from their incomes; the variables involved are too numerous. The dollar income of the American (valued in D-Marks) would be four times that of the German worker, but his standard of living would not be four times higher or more comfortable. Nor can we say that the Venezuelan urban worker whose monthly income is nearly three times that of a like Venezuelan worker in a rural village is three times better off than the rural worker. Several marked differences are evident when we compare things in the worker's home, the worker's level of education, the possibility of woman rising above the unskilled level, etc. Of workers in the labor force in Germany, 36 percent are women. Their proportion is 33 percent in Japan and 23 percent in Venezuela. German women are found in most occupational groups.

It is safe to say that the industrial work system in any country has its own development history, which is part of a wider development history. Not all the incongruities found in one country would be equally present elsewhere. But it would be unrealistic to expect anywhere the absence of inequality, even though it differs from country to country.

AFFLUENCE, POVERTY, AND THE POVERTY CULTURE

Many people in the industrial countries have held to the view that if there is full employment and rising wages, poverty is no great challenge, except for the unemployable. It was believed that affluence at the top would "trickle down" and all social and economic levels would benefit proportionately. This, as we increasingly see, is not true. Industrial advances that enable some in the labor force to benefit may exclude others from the labor force. This encourages the argument that the excluded ones are more or less permanently excluded, that they tend to form a poverty class with a culture of their own; they are therefore in the larger community but not of it, an excluded and self-insulated category of people.

Glazer notes a second paradox of industrialization; the proportion of people in poverty has not changed greatly over the past three decades but writings about poverty and studies of poverty have multiplied several times since about 1964. It might be added that almost nothing was written on the subject, certainly not by most social scientists, during the Great Depression when unemployment for a decade hovered around 10 million in the United States. Glazer also reminds us that the amount of dependency in Britain, in terms of percentages, is not less than in the United States, but there is less anxiety about poverty there.

> I would say that one of the reasons for the difference of response in the problem of poverty in England . . . is that a floor of service has been built, a standard floor for the entire nation, beneath which theoretically no one can fall. This floor is by definition designed to provide adequacy. . . . The mechanisms by which it is provided consist of a variety of elements, such as old age pensions, unemployment insurance, family allowances, national health insurance and the like, and it turns out . . . that despite the artful construction, people do slip below the floor.[19]

In practical terms, we can identify poverty, although inadequately, only as expressive of income. By adding the essential costs for food, shelter, transportation, and other needs, an estimate of the amount of

[19] Nathan Glazer, "A Sociologist's View of Poverty," in Margaret S. Gordon (Ed.), *Poverty in America,* San Francisco, Chandler, 1965, p. 15 (Conference on Poverty, University of California, Berkeley).

income needed by one person, two persons, three persons, and so on can be calculated. It depends on how much is included, whether the budget can be called generous or niggardly. By using a tight-minimum budget we might estimate that 10 percent of American families and individuals are living below the poverty line (incomes less than needed for the budget). For instance, according to a budget prepared by the Department of Health, Education and Welfare, a total of 34.5 million persons in 1963 were in poverty, that is, about 18 percent of the population. That budget allowed $3,130 for a family of four with a male head. The income needed for a farm family of four with a male head was put at $1,925.[20]

Miller summarizes some of the major points of poverty statistics for 1963, based on families with incomes of less than $3,000.

1. Seven million families and five million unrelated individuals were in poverty. Their aggregate income was $11.5 billion below their estimated minimum requirements.
2. There were two million families with female heads. Their aggregate income deficiency was about $5 billion. These comprised a fourth of all poor families.
3. Two million families (a fourth of the total) were headed by persons who had full-time employment, but earnings were not adequate.
4. One and one half million families were headed by persons who had full-time jobs, but employment through the year was irregular.
5. There were two million nonwhite families (a fourth of the total, few of whom have full-time employment). Forty percent of these families had female heads.
6. One and one half million families and individuals were aged persons.[21]

It is hardly necessary to elaborate upon the thought that poverty is a relative concept and, like social class, is measured in terms of income and expenditures. And, again like social class, those in poverty do not do the rating; poverty is seen solely in relation to the incomes and expenditures of others. To Lundberg it reveals the gap between socio-psychologically defined wants and one's ability to meet these wants.[22] Galbraith adds that people are in poverty when (for time and place) they do not have what is regarded as the minimum in their community. "There is no firm definition of this phenomenon, and again, save as a tactic for countering the intellectual obstructionist, no precise definition is needed."[23]

[20] Herman P. Miller, "Changes in Number and Composition of the Poor," in ibid., p. 84. Miller cites figures from Mollie Orshansky, "Counting the Poor, Another Look at the Poverty Profile," *Social Security Bulletin,* Vol. 28, January 1965.

[21] Miller, ibid., p. 86.

[22] George A. Lundberg, Mirra Komarovsky, and Mary McInerny, *Leisure, A Suburban Study,* New York, Columbia University Press, 1934, p. 12.

[23] John K. Galbraith, *The Affluent Society,* Boston, Houghton Mifflin, 1958, p. 323.

LIFE SPAN AND THE EARNING CYCLE

Moore suggests that workers in developing countries upon entering industry are rarely aware of their most elementary problems. The industrial worker is expected in the industrial urban society to accept certain responsibilities for himself, which are quite different from those of the tribesman in his village. He must learn how to ask for a job, how to get on with fellow workers, how to handle his money, and how to plan for his future, all commonplace and taken for granted in the industrial society.[24]

In an industrial society man is brought up to think of time and money in terms of how they concern him for the present and for the future. He plans for his children far into the future, not as the farmer who thinks in terms of this season and the next. He must visualize trends, changes, and prospects involving an array of elements: occupation, social position, old-age security, etc. These crucial elements of orientation must be confronted anew by each generation but in the dynamic industrial situation the orientation efforts of the young may clash with the accepted standards of the old. Gallaher mentioned how the older generation in Plainville was concerned by the disregard evinced by the young for their own future. When the young were asked about their plans for old age, they would answer, "The government will take care of you when you are old." [25]

The tribesman does not show concern about his life cycle either, but he does not need to; the rules for progress from infancy to old age are built into the tribal culture and are sustained by customary law. In recent decades it appears that such a set of rules may be taking form in the secondary industrial urban culture. Increasingly public and private institutions are taking the responsibility for the individual's life-cycle problems, with the support of civil law. The rules set down the minimum of schooling one must have before entering the labor market, the minimum training needed for various occupations, the minimum age when one may enter paid employment, and the age at which one must retire. Other rules are effective within the work system itself relating, for example, to safety and the measure of a fair day's work.[26]

A tribesman, in his unchanging milieu, is confronted with a life

24 Wilbert E. Moore, *Industrialization and Labor,* Ithaca, Cornell University Press, 1951, pp. 113–119.
25 Art Gallaher, Jr., *Plainville, Fifteen Years Later,* New York, Columbia University Press, 1961, pp. 33–35.
26 On the life cycles, see Nels Anderson, *Work and Leisure,* London, Routledge and Kegan Paul, 1961, Chaps. 6–8.

course that calls for little decision making; his father can teach him all that he needs to know. In an industrial society, despite the evolving system of rules, the individual worker can and must make many decisions. There are many occupations and occupations are ever changing. Much that one learns is soon outmoded, and one must continually keep up with what is new. Wilensky suggests that mobility in occupations, which may include "12 different jobs in a 46-year work life," contributes greatly to a lack of interpersonal obligations to kin and increases the need for individual decision making.[27]

Even with the securities of collective insurance, the industrial worker is never free of social obligations and he must make decisions about his future and take the consequences. If he is concerned about others, he more than likely will give prior thought to his spouse and children. He comes to recognize that in his own old age he has only a moral claim on his children for help, unless he lives in a small community where community social pressures are sharply felt by his own descendents.

It was Rowntree, in his study of income and living among the poor of York, England, who conceived the idea of the "poverty cycle" which weaves up and down across the "poverty line." According to him, there are four stages in the cycle:

1. At marriage the husband's earnings are usually adequate, a little more than adequate if his wife works.
2. As children arrive and the husband's income does not rise, the family deprives itself more with each additional child, sinking below the poverty line, and may receive assistance.
3. As the children find employment, income rises and the family again crosses above the poverty line.
4. The children marry and establish families of their own. The elderly parents get on well until the husband's income, because of old age, declines. They are not able to save and so fall again below the poverty line.[28]

Riesman and Roseborough call attention to another aspect of the life cycle of families. It relates to housing and material goods. The newlyweds may start housekeeping in a small apartment with the minimum of household things. They may be content for a time to live in low-cost quarters on a poor street. Both may be working and saving. They may decide to move to a better apartment on a better street when the first baby arrives. They may get rid of some pieces of furniture and buy better furniture. The family may have to move again to get more space if

27 Harold L. Wilensky, "Life Cycle, Work Situation and Participation in Formal Associations," in Robert W. Kleemeier (Ed.), *Aging and Leisure*, New York, Oxford University Press, 1961, p. 225.

28 B. Seebohm Rowntree, *Poverty, A Study of Town Life*, 2nd ed., New York, Longmans, Green, 1922.

the number of children increases to three or four. In the course of years, if family income increases and the social wants of the growing family increase, there may be social reasons for moving to an even better apartment.

Riesman and Roseborough observe that, since most families are subject to pressures for style change, possessions from time to time become outmoded and are moved to back rooms or discarded. The process of replacing is continuous, but so is the process of accumulation. The peak is reached at the point when the first child marries, perhaps taking some possessions from the parental home to start a household of his own. This is the "domestic package," all the possessions the parents have accumulated and have on their hands after the children leave. If they have more things and more space than they need, there begins the process of "dismantling," a concern even of working-class parents when finally left alone. It may call for moving to a smaller apartment and then a still smaller one. The evolution and devolution of the domestic package thus takes on the character of a "consumer cycle." [29]

THE ECONOMIC WORTH OF A MAN

Man is an acquisitive animal. He tends to accumulate many things of worth: land, houses, stores, work places, vehicles, household goods, ornaments, and things to wear, or money in the bank and paper assets. Some accumulate skills and knowledge, or even a recognized right to a job. In depicting the caste hierarchy of an Indian village, Dube tells how each caste, even the untouchables, have community rights. One caste may not take the work of another. Upper caste households have their continuing obligations to lower caste members in work-exchange arrangements. "According to the size of the land holding of the cultivator, one or more Madiga (untouchable caste) families attach themselves to him." These rights of economic worth, to be sure, would have no recognition in the next village.[30]

The Council of Economic Advisors estimated that if an American in 1963 would live on supplementary income (earnings from types of property), he and his wife would need property to the amount of $19,000. The income from this "worth" would hardly support even a frugal couple. Actually, the average net worth of all American families in 1962 was not $19,000, but about $4,700. For low-income families the average net worth

[29] David Riesman and Howard Roseborough, "Careers and Consumer Behavior," in Lincoln H. Clark (Ed.), *Consumer Behavior,* Vol. II, New York, New York University Press, 1955, pp. 6–9 and 17.

[30] S. C. Dube, *Indian Village,* London, Routledge and Kegan Paul, 1961, p. 69.

[31] "Poverty in America," *Monthly Labor Review,* Vol. 87, No. 3, March 1964, p. 286, being a summary of pertinent sections of the Report of the Council of Economic Advisors, January 1964.

was about $1,000, and in most cases this was an equity in a house.[31] Actually, as is well known, it is no easy matter to estimate the economic worth of families in a nation. Morgan, et al., on the basis of a nationwide survey, found that the median economic worth, or economic assets, was

12 percent had no assets at all
10 percent had less than $1,000
14 percent had assets from $1,000 to $4,999
22 percent had assets from $5,000 to $9,999
26 percent had assets from $10,000 to $24,999
14 percent claimed assets over $25,000

not $4,700 but about $8,000. The figures in this distribution show that not over 40 percent of all American families had assets sufficient for their security, while 22 percent reported less than $1,000 or none at all.[32]

Table 25 presents a picture of the financial complexities of Japanese workers who must live carefully to meet costs. The figures shown reveal

Table 25　Expended Incomes of Workers' Families by Source, in Cities of Japan, Averages for March 1951 *

Actual income and balance with other receipts	Office workers		Other workers	
	Yen	*Percent*	*Yen*	*Percent*
Number of workers in sample	1,307		325	
Actual income				
Earnings of household head	13,739	82.7	10,656	80.0
Earnings of others of household	1,301	7.8	1,954	14.8
Work done at home for pay	271	1.6	180	1.4
Rent, interest, etc.	154	1.6	42	0.3
Social security benefits	64	0.4	79	0.6
Gifts of money received	144	0.8	134	1.0
Other types of income	530	3.2	254	1.9
Balance of other receipts				
Withdrawal of savings or sale of assets, less savings	529	3.2	−50	−0.3
Borrowing, less repayment	63	0.4	121	0.9
Money from loan payments, less loans	65	0.4	53	0.4
Other receipts, plus balance at March 1, less balance at March 31	−245	−1.5	−235	−1.8

* Receipts balanced against spending.
　Source: *Consumer Price Survey,* Tokyo, Statistical Bureau, Office of Prime Minister, March 1951, p. 23.

32 James N. Morgan, et al., *Income and Welfare in the United States,* New York, McGraw-Hill, 1962, p. 443.

what Japanese office workers and other workers earned and spent during March 1951. Note how much higher the monthly earnings of Japanese workers were in 1964 as indicated in Table 24 above. It appears that for the Japanese worker living is a matter of getting money from many sources. For one thing, it is not unusual for workers to borrow from fellow workers.[33]

SPENDING AND CONSUMER BEHAVIOR

Not all of our spending is merely to secure food, clothing to keep warm, and a house sufficient to afford protection against the elements. We think of an individual as being in poverty if most of his income must go for these bare necessities. Meeting these needs for the affluent takes a minor part of their financial outlay. Any spending has socio-economic implications because of the interdependence of production and consumption. In describing this relationship, Galbraith speaks of the "dependence effect," more consumption stimulates more production activity, and also the other way around.

> Increases in consumption, the counterpart of increases in production, act as suggestion or emulation to increase wants. Or producers may proceed actively to create wants through advertising and salesmanship. Wants thus come to depend on output. In technical terms, it can no longer be assumed that welfare is greater at an all-round higher level of production than at a lower level. It may be the same. The higher level of production has, merely, a higher level of want creation, necessitating a higher level of want satisfaction.[34]

Leisure spending, as it mixes with social spending, is often an effort to satisfy such induced wants. The lady's hat, new last year, would seem "outlandish" if worn this year. Such sophisticated, socially prompted consumption increases as the economy of a society improves, although it increases unequally in a direct relation to the levels of income.

Because of these changes in consumer behavior, it is necessary in the industrial society to continually study what people need to buy in order to live at some recognized level. Government departments must periodically obtain information on prices charged for hundreds of items deemed to be necessary for an "economy" budget, a "level of comfort" budget, even a "subsistence" budget. Such studies began with the Department of Labor in 1946, and have continued, pricing goods and services of all kinds in about 40 American cities. This information is used continuously in

33 R. P. Dore, *City Life in Japan,* London, Routledge and Kegan Paul, 1958, p. 56.
34 Galbraith, op. cit., p. 158.

wage bargaining between management and labor.[35] Behind such public budget making is the widely accepted assumption that those who work must have money to supply other than creature wants, such as, higher levels of education and the satisfaction of cultural needs. The standard budget, adjusted for any size or type of family, as much as a wage and salary scale, enables families and individuals to identify themselves securely with their community. It becomes the common yardstick both for trade unions and management groups.[36]

Budgets, like wage scales or occupation categories, also enable reliable comparisons of standards of living as, for example, between different years or for comparisons between countries. This is illustrated in Table 26 which shows income, consumer expenditures, and other outlays for

Table 26   Income and Outlay for the Private Sector, Great Britain and the United States, in 1960

	Great Britain (million pounds)	United States (billion dollars)
Income from all sources	22,900	453.9
Consumer expenditures	16,608	328.7
Food	29%	21%
Drink	6%	3%
Tobacco	6%	3%
Clothing	10%	10%
Housing	9%	13%
Household goods	5%	4%
Vehicles	4%	5%
Public transport	4%	1%
All other	27%	40%
Transfers abroad	0	0.3
Taxes on income	3,624	91.2
Savings	2,668	33.7
Savings as percent of income	12%	8%
Total outgoings	22,900	452.9

Source: Richard and Giovanna Stone, *National Income and Expenditure,* London, Bowles, 1962, pp. 56–57.

Britain and the United States. One significant item in consumer outlays is food, 29 percent for Britain and 21 percent in the United States. Of the savings, 74 percent in the United States is saved by individuals, while in Britain 58 percent is saved by companies.[37]

Estimates about the earnings of whole nations are bound to vary greatly, which is seen when we compare some of the budget items from

[35] See Helen H. Lamale and Margaret S. Stotz, "The Interim City Workers' Family Budget," *Monthly Labor Review,* Vol. 83, No. 8, August 1960, p. 785.

[36] Ibid., p. 789.

[37] Richard and Giovanna Stone, *National Income and Expenditure,* London, Bowles, 1962, pp. 56–57.

the above table by the Stones for about 1960 with those of Newman for 1959. Regardless of the specific percentages, these figures show that an American spends less of his income for food and more for housing than does an Englishman.[38] However, as seen in this summary from Lamale,

| | Great Britain | | United States | |
	Housing	Food	Housing	Food
Stone's estimate	9%	29%	13%	21%
Newman's estimate	14%	31%	17%	23%

although the American worker earns more, he also spends more liberally, perhaps as a result of the influence of advertising. The average American in 1960 had a total income of $6,173, but at the end of the year he had a deficit of $261. This does not mean that he was slipping in the direction

Expenditures for current consumption	$5,630
Gifts and contributions	313
Personal insurance outlays	336
Net change in assets, liabilities	155
Total expenditures	$6,434
Money income after taxes	$6,090
Other money receipts	83
Total income	$6,173
Account balancing difference	$—261

of poverty; on the contrary, he was probably spending freely because of his confidence in future income.[39]

ON THE AMBIGUITY OF SAVING

The old notion that any man, whatever his income, can do some saving, and that if he fails to save he is improvident, is still firmly advocated by some, despite its unreality. McCormack asks about the self-respecting poor, those known to her in Canadian cities, "whose children are neat and attend school regularly. But their incomes are precarious." They make every sacrifice to keep above the poverty line. Nonetheless, they fall below occasionally, because they cannot save for the spells of un-

[38] Dorothy K. Newman, "Housing in Britain and America," *Monthly Labor Review*, Vol. 82 (two parts), No. 5, May 1960, pp. 449–459, and No. 6, June 1960, pp. 561–568.

[39] Lamale, op. cit., p. 780.

employment or the costs of illness.[40] Despite Canada's rich natural resources in land, there are many poor areas where farming is an occupation with meager prospects. And the unskilled poor in the cities are not better off than in American cities. These people cannot save, although their condition is less hopeless, for example, than that of the unskilled poor in the cities of India where the per capita national income per day is about 20 cents.[41] Bhutani mentions that where a majority cannot save, however they may wish to, India's industry can develop only slowly. There are few accumulated savings on which to build. Americans are not tied to such a low subsistence level, but they are confronted with greater pressures to consume. As Morgan found in his study of income and welfare, about 50 percent of the American spending units have saved, but only an average of $500 during the five-year period ending with 1959. Only 13 percent had saved over $5,000 during that five-year period.[42]

For industrial urban people in Western countries the urge to save is far less pressing than when industrialism was getting started. Now it is industry, through the wiles of efficient advertising, that is building up a different attitude toward saving. Much of the saving done by ordinary people is for deferred spending: for Christmas presents, for a vacation, for the children's education, or for a down payment on an automobile. For the young, money is for spending and buying status. Whyte noted this in the behavior of boys in a Boston slum. If one of them won $60 in the "numbers" game, saving would have low priority. "The sixty dollars that comes from a ten-cent, three-number hit is used to pay off debts, to buy an outfit of clothes, to treat his friends, to give some to his parents, and to gamble again." [43]

Svalastoga in 1957 asked the Danes how they would use the money if they won 10,000 Kroner ($1,500) in a lottery. The same year Blume asked low-income Germans what they would do with DM 50,000 ($12,500) received unexpectedly. The following columns list the answers in percents. It needs to be kept in mind that German places had been bombed and many Germans were inadequately housed, which is evidenced in their spending choices.[44]

The industrialism we know could hardly have started, or its start would have been slow indeed, had not great numbers of people during

40 Thelma McCormack, "Poverty and Social Action," *Canadian Forum,* Vol. 46, No. 550, November 1966, p. 172.

41 D. H. Bhutani, "The Socio-Economic Background and Productivity," *Indian Journal of Social Research,* Issue No. 1, April 1964, p. 19.

42 Morgan, et al, op. cit., p. 430.

43 William F. Whyte, *Street Corner Society,* Chicago, University of Chicago Press, 1943, p. 141.

44 Kaare Svalastoga, *Prestige, Class and Mobility,* Copenhagen, Gyldendal, 1959, p. 169, for the Danish case; Otto Blume, *Ständiger Ausschuss für Selbsthilfe,* Cologne, for the German case.

	Danish answers	German answers
Buy furniture, clothing, etc.	53%	10%
Save some or pay off debts	31	25
Build or rebuild a house	15	54
Give some away, mostly to kin	11	14
Acquire a new business or a farm	10	0
Improve existing properties	9	21
Buy an automobile or a motorcycle	9	8
Travel, emigrate, take a vacation	8	8
Improve one's education	1	0
Buy stocks or bonds	0	19
Give to good causes	0	8
Other, including no answer	7	4
Total percents	154%	180%

the nineteenth century been committed to the idea of saving. The money put in banks was then put to work, for as Heilbroner states, "Saving is the cast by which a society releases some portion of its labor and material resources from the tasks of providing for the present so that both can be applied to building for the future. . . . [S]aving means the freeing of labor and resources from consumer-goods production so that they may be applied to capital-goods production." [45] There is no doubt that Americans are able to save, but most of the personal saving is done by persons in the upper-income brackets. Many who are sure of their jobs or other income do not try to save, and we can estimate at least a fifth who could not save if they wished. Galbraith remarks that those of low income and the "dissavers" are depended on by industry for spending. This is

> . . . the role of the individual in the industrial system and the accepted view of his function. The individual serves the industrial system not by supplying it with savings and the resulting capital; he serves it by consuming its products. On no other matter, religious, political or moral, is he so elaborately and skillfully and expensively instructed.[46]

TREND TO COLLECTIVE SAVING AND SPENDING

It was true that saving by individuals at the outset enabled the industrial system to get started and to grow, as do the young, by trying and failing at many tasks, but through it all gaining experience and stability. Now we recognize that the industrial system not only has the capacity and know-how to grow under its own direction, but it has the capacity to save

---

[45] Robert L. Heilbroner, *The Great Ascent,* New York, Harper Torchbook, 1963, p. 75.

[46] John K. Galbraith, *The New Industrial State,* Boston, Houghton Mifflin, 1967, pp. 37–38.

out of its gains for further development. This is a kind of corporate, collective, impersonal saving. The great mass of people in the industrial urban societies of our time are most useful to the industrial work system if they put their money into circulation. As they consume, they make work for the production processes. The growing emphasis on leisure activity stimulates consumption, especially "conspicuous consumption," in ways that give pleasure.

If a country is at war and the industrial processes are needed to produce war goods, then it becomes expedient to encourage people to consume less. Even industrial advertising may echo this advice. However, if an economic depression or recession comes then it becomes socially proper for people not to save, but to spend and consume, creating possibilities for work. There is no contradiction between these contrary types of advice. Each serves the industrial work system in its particular situation. While industry, at a high level of production, can manage its saving problem, it would be helpless if all spending units suddenly turned (which seems unlikely) to saving in the sense of the Puritan Ethic.[47]

But the corporate savings of the industrial system offer no return in security to workers and their families, other than wages or salaries. Should the worker become unemployable he would be left without resources. It has been the growing awareness of this security risk that has stimulated various forms of public intervention, for example, unemployment insurance, which is a reserve fund assembled under government management from a tax placed on workers and employers. This is a form of collective saving, resisted by industry, but indirectly depended on by it. The public old-age pension system is another form of compulsory saving, and health insurance yet another.

The industrial worker, earning a wage or salary in the impersonal labor market is no longer the member of a tiny kinship type of community, living mainly on an uncomplicated subsistence economy. He is a member of a great community whose economy is complex, often beyond his comprehension. It is controled by forces residing not in his city only, but those reaching afar. To survive in this milieu he must learn to exercise his rights as a citizen, a knowledge he acquires as he learns to make use of his secondary organizations. Marshall calls this a new type of citizenship, "a secondary system of industrial citizenship parallel with and supplementary to the system of political citizenship;" but this learning moves at a slow pace.[48]

The industrial worker, particularly in the skilled occupations and above, learns that his level of income and standard of living depend not wholly on his relationship with his employer. Both are involved in various

47 Ibid., pp. 220–223.

48 T. H. Marshall, *Citizenship and Social Class*, Cambridge, Cambridge University Press, 1950, p. 44.

wide reaching market relationships which neither can control. Government in various ways becomes a partner in this relationship. The complexity is beyond the understanding of most workers, but even they come to be aware of the role of government as the provider of some measure of security. To such, the work place comes to be, as Dubin observes, less an interest in itself than a means of livelihood. The individual's interests come to be identified with concerns quite unrelated to the work place. He somehow acquires a willingness to leave to the government the management of his own long-term security.[49]

CHALLENGES TO THE INDUSTRIAL WORK SYSTEM

The industrial work system, despite the efficiency it has attained in the more developed countries, is confronted by two challenges, neither of which can be ignored. The first concerns problems at home. While it affords high levels of income and standards of living for the majority who work, it also by its growing efficiency excludes large numbers from these benefits. It is this challenge which is bringing forth today such a flood of literature on the "culture of poverty," a protest wave which is not without foundation.

The second challenge concerns the many new developing countries with their low living standards and their limited prospects to improve their own condition. Yet they are in the world economy. Much as depressed regions in the United States or Canada or Brazil are a burden to the affluent regions in these countries, so the economies of affluent nations are tied to the plight of the relatively depressed less industrial countries. The industrial countries, still far from perfection, are at least two centuries in advance of the emerging nations. They have not achieved their degree of advance without high cost and much suffering. Their position of advantage was earned. The know-how they take, and must take, to the new countries is the result of generations of trial and error.

These new nations do not have two centuries in which to catch up. The common desire in most of these countries is to industrialize. Until they are able to, they will remain a burden to world urbanism as a way of life and world industrialism as a way of work. In some countries much has to be done before industry can get a foothold. Before the urban amenities, electric power, water supply, sewers, roads, schools, and training facilities can be had the tools and equipment must be brought in. Heilbroner adds that developing countries, until they can negotiate an in-

[49] Robert Dubin, "Industrial Workers' Worlds," *Social Problems,* Vol. 3, No. 3, January 1956, p. 135.

dustrial take-off, must raise capital, and their prospects for raising capital are limited.[50]

We cannot here do more than to mention these challenges, both of which remind us of the global interdependence of industrial work systems. This interdependence is not merely technical, or merely economic, it is no less social and cultural.

[50] Heilbroner, op. cit., p. 83.

Industrial urbanism and welfare | 16

DEPENDENCY AND THE WORK SYSTEM

We have seen how the industrial organization by which the modern society sustains itself is characterized by interdependence. Every society is interdependent, but this society manifests types of interdependence that circle the globe. There are different divisions of labor from those in the subsistence-economy village to the world-embracing communications system or the different transportation systems. As never before, communities are becoming more interdependent, as are world regions.

In the two previous chapters we took account of interdependence in work places and between work places, but we also saw interdependence in the division of industrial man's time between work and leisure. Leisure, for example, has made more distinct the dividing line between production and consumption, leisure has been separated from work. We recognized that leisure and leisure spending are made possible by work for income, but leisure activities become increasingly important as creators of work. Whole industries have emerged for no other purpose. While some artistic people would take issue, we venture that the demands for leisure-use goods and services have done more than the more utilitarian factors to bring art into the production of goods and services. Evidence for this will be found if one compares the advertisements in periodicals of today published for the social and cultural elites with those of 1900 to about 1910.

Doubtless, there have always been types of interdependence within the categories or classes of people in different societies. This is most precisely evident in a caste society, in which each caste is dependent on the others. Occupations, which mark the social distinctions in our class society, are arrayed in a hierarchy from the high to the low and they betoken degrees of interdependence socially and culturally much as in the places of work. Perhaps never before have the upper classes been more inconvenienced by the shortage of household servants; the industrial work system

344

encourages people to turn from domestic services to other work. The old interdependence between social classes is breaking down to be replaced by some other.

We have noted that any system of social stratification is one of in-equality, the social-class system being more strictly so; but in our society there is developing a political system of equality which can be and is being increasingly used as a countervailing force against the extremes of interclass inequality. The instrument for insuring equality, of course, is government, and its mediating influence is increasing.

The industrial work system, as we have seen, is both impersonal in its operations and neutral respecting the influences or issues that bedevil human society. The methods and goals of the industrial work system are largely the goals of the owners. The owners of an industrial enterprise may be thousands of individual stockholders, some of whom may be employed as workers in the enterprise. We see the enterprise as the im-personal provider of work at different skill levels. It is still the widely-accepted belief that persons at any skill level, willing and able to work, can find employment, if not in one enterprise, then in another. Recruit-ment in the industrial labor market is done largely on the basis of techno-logical determinants, but social determinants do intrude. If there is a choice, white people may be selected over the dark-skinned, the native-born over the foreign-born, the young over the old, or the more educated over the least educated.

It is becoming glaringly evident that the more efficient industry be-comes the more it excludes the least qualified, including those who are the least trained, as well as those excluded for reason of social choices. These then join the ranks of the "permanent poor." At the same time, as Thompson observes, skilled workers, reasonably secure in their employ-ment, have little concern about those who are kept out. They "regard themselves as the exploited and underprivileged and still look to the rich to carry the burden of unemployment and welfare." [1]

Here, as we consider it in this chapter, is another aspect of human interdependence. The poor are no longer merely the halt and the blind, the lame and the lazy; many are included who would have been normally employed a few decades ago. The work system, a system of inequality, ex-cludes them.

ON STAGES OF ECONOMIC CHANGE

Rostow visualizes six stages in economic growth, beginning with traditional society and ending with the "age of high mass consumption." The stages after the family-bound, fatalistic traditional level are:

[1] Wilbur R. Thompson, *A Preface to Urban Economics*, Baltimore, Johns Hopkins Press, 1965, p. 189.

Second, called "preconditions for take-off," when a society begins to improve its technology and produce some surplus for trade.

Third, the "take-off" stage when the economy begins to function on its own momentum, is able to sustain itself, operate rationally, accumulate capital, and improve its technology.

Fourth, called "the drive to maturity" when industry grows and spreads out, surplus accumulates and technology develops rapidly.

Fifth, called the "age of high mass consumption" when goods and services are available in abundance. All societies move through these stages but few have reached this point.

Sixth, the stage of "post-maturity" in which interest turns to matters of equality and welfare. This final stage is seen as an economic and technological plateau.

In addition to these economic changes, the society ceases to accept the further extension of modern technology as an over-riding objective. It is in this post-maturity stage, for example, that through the political process, Western societies have chosen to allocate increased resources to social welfare and security. The emergence of the welfare state is one manifestation of a society's moving beyond technical maturity; but it is also at this stage that resources tend increasingly to be directed to the production of consumers' durables and to the diffusion of services on a mass basis, if consumers' sovereignty reigns.[2]

By Rostow's estimate, countries like the United States, Germany, France, and Britain were emerging from stage four at the beginning of this century and are all now in, or entering, the fifth stage. He sees Russia as only now leaving stage four. Like other evolutionary models, for example, that of Herbert Spencer, followed by many sociologists in the last century, Rostow's idea of stages would be confronted with many contradictions if tested against a sample of some fifty nations, all trying to industrialize, although from different pre-take-off levels. This does not mean that the six-stage model does not have considerable utility for comparison; but it might be baffling to evolve valid measures for the rates at which all these countries are evolving. Will it be possible for some to reach only the fifth stage? or not even the fourth?

American thinking about welfare, before the shock of the Great Depression (1929-1941), was still in line with village thinking of a half-century earlier. These views have been changing as they must change with most Americans becoming urbanized. Owen has noted a like change in Britain, where more people are living their lives in congested cities.

It would be out of the question to translate to an urban environment the network of relationships, personal and institutional, that made rural

2 W. W. Rostow, *The Stages of Economic Growth,* Cambridge, Cambridge University Press, 1960, p. 11.

England an ordered society. Thus those who sought to improve the lot of their fellows faced a situation in which some of their traditional methods came to seem grossly inadequate, if not actually mischievous. Direct alms-giving and neighborhood charity, which in a village could be carried on without fear of being unduly imposed upon, now served to encourage the professional mendicant.[3]

THE CHARITY ORGANIZATION MOVEMENT

In England, more than in any other Western country, the trial-and-error growth of industry and the chaotic expansion of cities so disturbed the traditional urban order that men and women of conscience began to be alarmed. Almost everyone who worked was poor and most heads of families who worked were in a condition of deepest poverty. They lived a blind-alley existence which many came to recognize as their lot in life. By comparison, the poverty of industrial cities today would be considered affluence.

Woodroofe records that not only did the urban poor of England accept their lot, they were expected to do so by the upper classes, a surviving attitude from rural feudalism. Thus in 1807 when an education bill came before Parliament, a Mr. Giddy warned that it would teach the working classes to "despise their lot in life . . . render them fractious and refractory . . . [and] insolent to their superiors." [4] This view was voiced by many even fifty years later.

In preindustrial England it was assumed that every family and individual belonged to a community. If one wandered away and fell into need, he was expected to return to his home parish. If one became a vagabond, begging and perhaps stealing, he might be beaten or even hanged. When industry began settling in cities, this surplus rural labor supply was needed in urban places. But since the alleviation of their poverty was not seen as a community responsibility at the outset, such responsibility came to be accepted only gradually. By 1850 the accepted view was that aid for the poor was a responsibility of private charity.

Woodroofe's study mentions innumerable private charity groups in London, most of them small and each of them an independent effort. A study by Sampson Low of "The Charities of London, 1861" revealed that, while public aid to the poor in metropolitan London had been about 1.5 million pounds, the charity output of the many private groups had been about 2.5 million pounds, and a decade later it was estimated that

[3] David Owen, *English Philanthropy, 1660–1960,* Cambridge, Harvard University Press, 1964, p. 92.

[4] Kathleen Woodroofe, *From Charity to Social Work,* Toronto, University of Toronto Press, 1962, p. 15.

the competing private groups were giving out "seven million sterling a year." The more far-seeing reformers were becoming concerned, certain that charity itself was also a problem.

The movement toward organizing charity groups to bring all private givers into a collective got under way in different cities. The Society for Organizing Charitable Relief and Repressing Mendicity, established in London in 1870, may not have been the first, but for Americans it was the model. It stood for more and better charity, with high standards and firm discipline.

> Charity given indiscriminately and thoughtlessly demoralized; it encouraged habits of thriftlessness and dependence and these, the Society considered, were a root cause of poverty and pauperism. True Charity, administered according to certain principles, could encourage independence, strengthen character, and help to preserve the family as the fundamental unit of society. This was the ideal of Charity Organization to which the members of the Society pledged themselves in 1870.[5]

Well over a thousand charity groups were invited to join the Society, but only a small minority were willing to submit to such a central control. It became in time the Charity Organization Society (COS) and the self-appointed judge of private charity service, seen by many as a community conscience service. Owen concludes that the COS did raise standards of private welfare during the four decades of its sway.[6] In the United States the Charity Organization movement, before running its course, took the first major steps in raising welfare practices from the emotional level of "Lady Bountiful" to that of social work as a profession.[7]

CHARITY AND THE SELF-SUFFICIENT MAN

Over the past century there has been a steady evolution in thinking about poverty and the needs of the poor, about ways and means for meeting the problems of poverty. The direction of this change can be described as going from charity to welfare. Significantly, the term, "charity," is rarely found today in the more substantial books dealing with poverty and the problems of the poor. We speak rather of welfare, whose elements are little related to charity.

Charity assumed that an individual, however motivated, when ex-

---

5 Ibid., pp. 26–28.

6 Owen, op. cit., pp. 239 ff. He remarks that in Britain where the COS began as something like a revolutionary movement, it finally became a conservative force "frozen in what was virtually its original form and . . . [was] doggedly resistant to the changing social climate."

7 Woodroofe, op. cit., p. 54.

tending help to someone in need, was ideally "giving of himself with the gift." Whether the giver was religiously motivated or socially motivated, or rewarded by inner satisfaction, giving was idealized as a human relationship in which the recipient was also benefited morally. Presumably he was inspired to strive harder. But there was always the expectation that he should be grateful to the giver. Obviously, when the charity agency appeared, the direct contact between giver and recipient was lost, but the recipient was still expected to be grateful and to show his gratitude by taking any kind of work, living frugally, perhaps turning from unrighteous ways of living, and even humbling himself before a grasping employer.[8]

At the same time, in the urban world of work men were acquiring attitudes of self respect. Men who worked were beginning to recognize that in the industrial labor market they were victimized unless they could jointly demand a greater share of the product of industry and thereby achieve higher standards of living. However, this development was not a central concern for the forces of charity. The proponents of charity accepted the human condition, including the economic order, as good; they believed that any person who worked hard and was provident could achieve an adequate level of security. This concept was central to the American ideal of "rugged individualism." Mitchell suggests that the ideal of the self-sufficient individual put one on the high road to success, had become institutionalized in the educational system, as the ideal of charity had been institutionalized in religion. The concept of public welfare as a right, as it came to the fore in the Great Depression, contradicted the then prevalent approach to poverty.[9]

Charity thinking does not recognize aid as a right. Charity assumes that aid to the poor is mainly a local matter. The welfare concept sees need as related to the industrial work system, the control of which resides in the great cities, rarely in small communities where industrial plants may be located. Furthermore, the reach of welfare may be nationwide. The philosophy of welfare sees the problems of poverty and the poor in wider terms than are necessary for the traditional folk perspective of charity thinking. For example, employment might be the solution of poverty for some families, but it is not enough if unskilled workers earn less than needed for a minimum budget. Nor is employment the answer for some three of each ten poor families whose heads are not in the labor market, or for many detached individuals.[10] The welfare approach must take into account the complexities of urban living. The poor family in the urban milieu seldom has a network of kin upon which to lean, and

---

[8] Owen, op. cit., pp. 165–166.

[9] William Lloyd Mitchell, *Social Security in America,* Washington, D.C., Robert B. Lane, 1964, p. 6.

[10] Robert J. Lampman, "Income Distribution and Poverty," in Margaret S. Gordon (Ed.), *Poverty in America,* San Francisco, Chandler, 1965, pp. 102–114.

the old notion of getting one's neighbors to help him does not have much meaning in the urbanized society.

GENERAL WELFARE AND SOCIAL WELFARE

"Some members of the affluent society," says Seligman, "especially those who might have experienced rough times in their youth, or those whose parents were poor immigrants, are apt to be somewhat bemused by the recent concern over poverty." [11] These people relate how they climbed out of poverty and if the poor today cannot do the same, it must be due to their laziness. Many of these cited by Seligman were among the poor during the Great Depression, but they climbed up just the same. That same attitude was loudly voiced in the early 1930's. Chambers mentions how the argument was heard on all sides that the unemployed "can find work if they look for it." [12]

If one receives public benefits in the form of social welfare, it is to be expected that he be qualified, that is, able to meet the stipulated conditions. But public benefits in our complex economy are of many kinds. Public money is used for building roads to serve particular industries, building a park on public demand, purchasing agricultural surpluses, subsidizing shipping or airlines, giving allowances for dependent children, financing scientific research, etc., all of which are forms of public benefits. Altmeyer adds to this list the use of public money for "the post office, public works, public education, homestead grants and poor relief."

Some forms for the "general welfare" are regarded with respect, while those benefits allocated to "social welfare" generally are not.

> Protective tariffs, low postal rates to publishers of newspapers and magazines, and subsidies to railroads and shipping companies have also been justified on the grounds of promoting the general welfare. More recently, carrying out this responsibility has resulted in such governmental activities as insurance on bank deposits, guarantee on home mortgages, loans to banks and insurance companies to maintain their solvency, as well as subsidies to farmers and price supports for their crops.[13]

11 Ben B. Seligman (Ed.), "Introduction," *Poverty as a Public Issue,* New York, Free Press, 1965, p. 6.

12 Clarke A. Chambers, *Seedtime for Reform, American Social Service and Social Action, 1918–1933,* Minneapolis, University of Minnesota Press, 1963, pp. 143–145. He cites studies carried out during the Great Depression, which show that little work could be found: for example, Clinch Calkins, *Some Folks Won't Work,* Harcourt, Brace & World, 1930; Helen Hall, *Case Studies in Unemployment,* Philadelphia, University of Pennsylvania Press, 1931.

13 Arthur J. Altmeyer, "The People and Their Government," in Cora Kasius (Ed.), *New Directions in Social Work,* New York, Harper & Row, 1954, p. 55.

Public money given to social welfare is regarded by many economists as philanthropy because there is no visible *quid pro quo,* a viewpoint which is well stated by Dickinson in a book on the subject edited by him. By his definition of a "definite or immediate *quid pro quo*" we would have to regard the many millions of acres of public land given to the railroads prior to 1870, for which there was a payout without a payback, as philanthropy.

> At the present time I would say that what I mean by philanthropy is this; giving money away to persons and institutions outside the family without a definite or immediate *quid pro quo,* for purposes traditionally considered philanthropic. If we were in a position to measure philanthropy completely I would look for numbers which measure all types of transfer payments without a *quid pro quo,* excluding transfers between members of the family.[14]

Boulding has contended that a *quid pro quo* is present in many types of philanthropy; the middle aged pay for the care they received by rearing their own children, and the student pays back for help in his education as he makes use of skill and knowledge gained. This is a "disguised exchange, exchange, that is, over a period of years." [15]

It fails to make sense to regard social-security benefits as philanthropy, especially since the recipient has already invested his money into them. Hardee maintains that philanthropy cannot be judged, as some economists do, from a one-dimensional viewpoint. He argues that the private sector and the public sector of welfare become increasingly integrated and variously involved in the industrial system. All types of funded wealth become part of the total wealth upon which the industrial order leans.[16] Titmuss puts the thought in other terms, for he sees "needs" as social. The needs of the poor, the many kinds of needs of many categories of the poor, are not outside the market, for they also buy and consume.

> "Needs" may therefore be thought of as "social" and individual"; as interdependent, mutually related essentials for the continued existence of the parts and the whole. No complete division between the two is conceptually possible; the shading of one into the other changes with time over the life of all societies; it changes with time over the cycle of the needs

[14] Frank G. Dickinson (Ed.), *Philanthropy and Public Policy,* New York, National Bureau of Economic Research, 1962, p. 15.

[15] Kenneth E. Boulding, "Notes on a Theory of Philanthropy," in Frank G. Dickinson (Ed.), *Philanthropy and Public Policy,* New York, National Bureau of Economic Research, 1962, p. 60.

[16] Covington Hardee, "Philanthropy and the Business Corporation, Existing Guidelines—Future Policy," in Dickinson, ibid., p. 104.

of the individual and the family; and it depends on previous notions of what constitutes a "need." [17]

In the preindustrial rural society (and in the tribal society still), the idea was firmly recognized that the individual shared the life and work of the community, but if he was not able to work, whether in part or wholly, he still had a claim on his community for sustenance. These people also thought of *quid pro quo,* but they saw it in life-span terms, not in terms of the "definite and immediate." In the secondary industrial urban community, after having been pushed into the background, social welfare responsibility has begun to gain recognition, but in a new form.

ON FEAR ABOUT PUBLIC WELFARE

As sections of the American public, especially those who write about poverty and unemployment, see a danger in automation, another large section of the same public is concerned and fearful about public welfare. This latter fear found vigorous expression in the 1930's when the idea of social security was being adopted. That fear of public welfare programs has been associated until recently with the concept of the "welfare state," a concept which in 1968 is seldom seen, especially in the current literature on poverty. Attention turns now to the "War on Poverty," which, as most observers agree, comes with too little and is generally a little late.

Some of the criticism of the "War on Poverty" is ideological. It is seen by certain critics as a fear-motivated program committed to maintaining things as they are. It is recognized or feared that the poverty population may not continue to remain docile. Miller and Rein speak of the concern in the Office of Economic Opportunity to reach youth with more training and education. The attitude is:

> We want to do "something" about our youth. The "something" may mean that we are mainly interested in social control, rather than helping youngsters obtain decent jobs. The various programs in the War on Poverty can degenerate into devices to reduce our fears of delinquency and rioting, to police the poor, not to develop them. This danger persists because an underlying theme among many connected with the War on Poverty, especially at local levels, is that the purpose of the programs is to provide settings which administer control over youth and to "resocialize" them for "living in society." [18]

[17] Richard M. Titmuss, *Essays on the Welfare State,* London, Allen and Unwin, 1958, p. 39.
[18] S. M. Miller and Martin Rein, "The War on Poverty, Perspectives and Prospects," in Seligman, op. cit., p. 300.

It would be a mistake to assume that fear of the poor acting up is accompanied by any willingness to touch the work system which is on the way to creating even more unemployment. Whatever basic changes in the work system may be needed, these are also feared even among those who recognize that such changes may now be on the way. They are also aware that only the national government is in a position to bring about such changes.

Owen speaks of the fear among the private or voluntary agencies for welfare in Britain that their future would be made insecure by the coming of the welfare state, although they had helped to create it. Their fear was not unlike that of the affluent opponents of total public welfare. "Yet when the situation became more stable, the voluntary agencies found themselves as heavily occupied as ever, in some cases carrying on much as before, in others closely matched with the statutory services." Owen concludes that the welfare state is one of the cardinal facts of our time, and the situation is one that provides tasks for both public and private service agencies. He implies that the need for the private agency relates to various special services.[19]

The notion is entertained by many that if ordinary people are secure in their creature wants, that if they are certain of not being without shelter and food, they will be put at ease and cease to strive. The belief is conveyed in the folk expression, "If you give them their corn, and grind it too, then they will never go to work." That idea in more elegant terms has been used to argue against all proposals for social security. Insecurity for the poor is a middle-class value still. They not only fear public welfare for this reason, but they also see danger in raising public welfare benefits to the level of rights. As Bendix describes public welfare, it "underwrites a minimum standard of living for the weaker members of the political community, raises the recognized legal rights of the lower classes, and hence redefines the status citizenship in their favor." [20]

It is very possible that fear of public welfare explains in part the often ardent support given by so many of the upper and middle classes to fund-raising drives to support the private welfare agencies, especially those joined in the Community Chest of a city or town. According to their economic and social prestige, business leaders and industrialists are made chairmen of fund-raising committees. A community well "organized" for such a mass collection of funds is one in which every employer makes out his list of employees and each is told what would be a suitable contribution. Even public agencies fall in line with this pressure. The amounts collected in an industrial city are minimal compared with the need, but

19 Owen, op. cit., p. 526.
20 Reinhard Bendix, "The Lower Classes and the 'Democratic Revolution,'" *Industrial Relations*, Vol. 1, No. 1, October 1961, p. 96.

the annual mass effort serves to keep alive the illusion that the city "has a heart," and is caring for its needy. Seeley remarks:

> The religious mandate to "charity" becomes the civic duty . . . and the problem of the private conscience . . . becomes a matter of published performance and group "standards." The collection plate or the beggar's extended hand . . . is succeeded by a virtual private tax with social penalties not only for the miserly who do not give at all but for the non-conformists who wish to give otherwise or to some other cause.[21]

On the one hand, the private agencies, fearful of their own continuing existence in the face of growing public welfare, make use of the arts of advertising and pressure organizations. On the other hand, business and industrial leaders, fearing the growth of public welfare, conspicuously support the private welfare services. Notably their support was much less ardent before public social-security programs appeared on the scene.

IDEOLOGIES AND PUBLIC WELFARE

Opponents of public welfare proposals are prone to use social arguments in countering welfare schemes. Thus the Social Security Program, when debated in the 1930's, was called a threat to the "rugged individualism" so basic to the American frontier. This and other public programs were also called a disguised form of "creeping socialism." It turns out in fact, that the ideology of radical socialism did not figure in all countries now called welfare states.

In Japan, since the Second World War, there has been a strong trend toward the welfare state in public services, as Dore observes, but the motivations are quite unlike those in Western countries.

> The moral arguments most easily invoked in Japan belong to a general context of benevolent despotism, or more properly, perhaps, state paternalism. . . . Modern welfare-state philosophy in Japan, being thus the product of political battles fought not in Japan but elsewhere, is not surrounded by the same complex of moral conviction and political partnership as in the West. It is accepted as something like democracy, to the development of which Japan is committed in her general commitment to "progress." [22]

Dore's thought is that Japan is accepting the welfare state not because it has been demanded by the people—such demands have been mini-

21 John Seeley (Ed.), *The Community Chest, A Case Study in Philanthropy,* Toronto, University of Toronto Press, 1957, p. 296.
22 R. P. Dore, *City Life in Japan,* London, Routledge and Kegan Paul, 1958, p. 72.

mal—but that the step is taken as a practical measure, it being sensible, and good for the state. The transition from the earlier feudalism to capitalism has been smooth. Dore adds that the nineteenth-century Western doctrine of *laissez faire* "has never been held as a central dogma by any party or class." It was never advocated that "it is only by giving free rein to the acquisitive instinct of each that one can best insure the economic betterment of all." [23]

Bremme finds that public welfare in France is expressive of the revolutionary concepts, Liberty, Equality, and Fraternity, written into the French Constitution in 1791. Later, when organized groups in France became concerned about the weak, sick, and orphaned, they did not press demands on the government. Since the control of all local government is centralized in Paris and local public decision-making is minimal, there has been an unwillingness to entrust welfare to the centralized public bureaucracy. Rather organized groups retain control in private hands. Welfare in France does benefit from government surveillance but the programs are operated by private societies.[24]

On the other hand, in Britain where there is a strong tradition of local government and where familiarity with the working of government is widespread, demands for welfare programs were demands for government initiative. Bremme relates how the British "Welfare State" of 1948, based on the Beveridge Plan, evolved slowly, and was influenced by the following:

1. From the French Revolution came the idea of freedom, equality, and brotherhood.
2. The utilitarian philosophy of Jeremy Bentham and his school of thought contributed the principle of the greatest good to the greatest number.
3. Socialism, in particular the British non-revolutionary Fabian brand, promoted the idea of a national social service and a minimum-of-existence level.
4. Sidney and Beatrice Webb, authors of the Minority Report of the Royal Commission on Poor Laws and Relief of Distress (1909), and later J. M. Keynes promoted the schemes of labor market controls to achieve full employment.
5. From the German security system, initiated by Bismarck in 1884, came the idea of social insurance.[25]

These observations about the roots of the welfare state in Britain would apply for the most part to the development of public welfare in other Western countries as well; each has been influenced by developments in other countries. We find a similar evolution of public welfare in other English-speaking countries, especially so in Canada and some-

[23] Ibid., p. 71.
[24] Gabriele Bremme, *Freiheit und Sicherheit*, Stuttgart, Enke, 1961, pp. 124–128.
[25] Ibid., p. 42. For a discussion of the Beveridge Plan, see William H. Beveridge, *Social Insurance and Allied Services*, London, Stationery House, 1942.

what so in the United States. In certain Western industrialized, urbanized countries socialism was an influence, but it would be unrealistic to ignore various other influences, for example, industrial urbanism itself, which gave rise to socialism. For Bismarck, the establishment in the 1880's of accident, old-age, and sickness insurance was seen as a means of relieving the anxieties of industrial workers. But the action was also a tactic whereby Bismarck weakened the position of the opposition socialists. Briggs has observed for example, that critics who feared this type of public welfare said it would make the workers dependent and in the power of the state.[26] What Bismarck did was not original, since German workers had been experimenting for half a century with various kinds of group insurance. These groups continued to function although under the aegis of government protection and guidance. They were not superseded by any government system.

Socialism was more of a factor in establishing the welfare state in the Scandinavian countries, but much of the credit goes to the Scandinavian trade unions. These countries have been strongly socialist for half a century, but they have also been strongly religious and considerably under the influence of the Protestant Ethic. As they became more urban and industrial, they also moved in the direction of a state-guided control of alcoholic drinking.

In a study of two Finnish communities, a small agricultural town and an industrial city, Sariola points out the wide-ranging welfare services provided in each of these communities.

> Both communities engage in a wide range of social welfare activities and employ, besides administrative personnel, such functionaries as physicians, nurses, midwives, inspectors in various fields, home economists, home nurses and youth workers, architects, constructors, etc. Schools give free lunches, health inspection, dental care, vaccinations, etc.
>
> The extensive security measures include maternal, child unemployment, disability, old-age assistance, etc., that conform to the national security welfare policies. Strong and specialized cooperative agencies are found in both communities in such fields as merchandising, dairying, cattle breeding, milling, farm machinery, credit, transport, etc.[27]

As another example, Fleisher points to Sweden as a most advanced welfare state with a high standard of living, and no longer a country with a high emigration rate. Rather, with increasing industrialization, Sweden is re-

---

[26] Asa Briggs, "The Welfare State in Historical Perspective," *Archives européennes de sociologie*, T. 2, No. 1, 1961, p. 248.

[27] Sakari Sariola, "Defining Social Class in Two Finnish Communities," *Transactions of the Westermarck Society*, Tidnings och Trycheri Actiebolag Abo, Vol. 11, 1953, p. 157.

ceiving immigrants. Of the national income, 16 percent is allocated to public welfare services. A good share of this money goes to medicare services and children's allowances.[28]

Clearly, in the United States there has been a gradual drift in the direction of welfare-state commitment. If any ideology has been involved, it is the retreating ideology of *laissez faire* and a faith in the rugged self-sufficient individual. Each concession to collective welfare has been in the nature of a compromise resulting from a confrontation with a crisis. Myrdal, the Swedish economist, speaks of the waves of conversion experienced by Americans when they are in the midst of a crisis; they feel that they must do something, as in the War on Poverty.

> A dramatic change in American attitudes toward the social problem is under way. The nation is finally—and rather suddenly—becoming prepared to accept the welfare state. This implies an intellectual as well as a moral catharsis for the majority of Americans who are prosperous and secure. They cannot conceal from themselves any longer that there is in the United States a large "underclass" of poor and destitute people in the urban and rural slums who are largely cut off from the life and aspirations of the nation.[29]

SECURITY AND THE RISKS OF LIFE

The evolution of the city and of industry is a continuous and endless story in risk taking. Whoever invented a new tool, or machine, or a new method of performing a task risked failure, and perhaps did fail frequently before achieving his goal. No doubt, he risked the ridicule of others. The innovator confronts a challenging situation. Normally, however, he is not empty handed but is sustained by degrees of knowledge which raise risk above the level of mere chance.

In this connection, McClelland's discussion of certain psychological experiments carried out in four countries (the United States, Japan, Brazil, and India) are of interest. For the experiments, boys were asked to toss rings so that they would fall over pegs, the boys being permitted to stand at any distance from the pegs. It was found in all four experiments that the boys with the greatest skill would toss from a middle distance which involved moderate risk. "They did better only under conditions involving some degree of competition, some risk of doing worse than others or of not getting a sense of personal achievement." McClelland calls this "high *n* Achievement," and applies this principle to entrepreneurs and other venturing people.

[28] Wilfred Fleisher, *Sweden, The Welfare State*, New York, John Day, 1956, p. 228.
[29] Gunnar Myrdal, "Preface," in Ben B. Seligman (Ed.), *Poverty as a Public Issue*, New York, Free Press, 1965, p. v.

Therefore, if people with high *n* Achievement are to behave in an entre-
preneurial way, they must seek out and perform in situations in which
there is some moderate risk of failure—a risk which can, presumably, be
reduced by increased effort or skill. They should not work harder than
other people at routine tasks, or perform functions which they are certain
to do well simply by doing what everyone accepts as the correct traditional thing to do. On the other hand, they should avoid gambling situations, because, even if they win, they can receive no sense of personal
achievement.[30]

McClelland takes the position that achievement motivation can be instilled
in children. His notion that achievement motivation can be taught has
encouraged some to hope that such instruction might be useful to the
many unemployed workers in the United States, the central concern of
the War on Poverty.

Sheppard and Belitsky undertook a "job-hunt" study of 309 male and
146 female "blue-collar" workers who had been unemployed at some time
during the previous several months. They were asked about their job-hunt
experience: how soon they started the search, possible employers con-
tacted, fears and anxieties experienced, degree of confidence with which
they went about the search, and general knowledge they had about job
possibilities. The findings were about what anyone acquainted with job
hunting would expect: skilled workers found jobs easier than the unskilled or semiskilled, experienced skilled workers fared better than less
experienced skilled workers, younger workers fared better than workers
over 39 years of age, those with "high achievement motivation *and* values"
fared better than others. The observation is made though, that "if there
is going to be any payoff from increasing the jobseeking activities of
workers, there have to be jobs available to begin with." [31] Although the
study did not deal with those who remain jobless because of lack of skill
or some other reason, such research doubtless lends comfort to some who
believe that anyone can find work if he looks for it.

In 1963 there were an estimated 34 million Americans in poverty and
of these nearly 5 million were persons living alone. Of the other nearly
30 million half were children, and of the household heads about 9.5 million had been employed during 1963 only part time or not at all.[32] Most
of these would be described as having low achievement motivation, but
it is also becoming common knowledge that most of these people are in

---

[30] David C. McClelland, "The Achievement Motive in Economic Growth," in
David E. Novack and Robert Lekachman (Eds.), *Development and Society*, New York,
St. Martin's Press, 1964, p. 183.

[31] Harold L. Sheppard and A. Harvey Belitsky, *Promoting Jobfinding Success for
the Unemployed*, Kalamazoo, Michigan, Upjohn Institute for Employment Research,
1968, pp. 13–14 (pamphlet).

[32] Herman P. Miller, "Changes in the Number and Composition of the Poor," in
Gordon, op. cit., pp. 86–88.

a pasture without much grass. They too are confronted with the risks of life, but the odds are against them.

As the efficiency in the industrial work system increases, the more exacting the requirements become at the point of recruiting. Every employer wants the best applicants available, and those who cannot qualify are helpless. However the risks may be minimized. Gregg states, "Man's search for security reflects his desire to avoid the adverse consequences of risk. . . . In the more advanced countries, man has sought refuge by pooling his risks with others similarily inclined." [33] This means that workers are less at the mercy of life risks if they are insured, as against unemployment, sickness, and old age. They may also minimize risk by joining trade unions. But many who are among the least employable are not members of trade unions and seldom are unions concerned about them.

It is not the function of public welfare programs to relieve the citizen of all risk. It is assumed that he accepts the usual responsibilities of life as he competes with others and that he must sometimes make decisions which involve some degree of venturing. One function of welfare is to protect the citizen against the extreme negative consequences of risk. Another function is to take measures that will insure fair treatment in the labor market. A third expected function is for the government to initiate measures, through financial controls or public work programs, to insure full employment and to avoid extreme unemployment. In such a fashion, all public welfare is designed to soften the shocks of risk. These public measures are means by which the cost of risk is spread among large numbers of people. It is not something for nothing that government gives. But the government insures the integrity of such programs. It is, says Durand, a French authority on welfare, "welfare by cooperation between the state and the citizen." [34]

PUBLIC WELFARE, RURAL AND URBAN

A century ago in the United States it was well known that in a depression rural people were better able than industrial urban workers to weather an economic crisis. The opposite is true at the present time. As decade by decade agriculture has become mechanized, as the farmer becomes increasingly influenced by scientific methods, the family-farm ideal is pushed into the background. Agricultural industry is able to produce more and more with fewer workers. Farms increase in size and the farm

[33] David W. Gregg, "On the Expansion of Basic Research in Risk and Insurance," *American Behavioral Scientist,* Vol. 6, No. 9, May 1963, p. 11.

[34] Paul Durand, *La politique contemporaine de securité sociale,* Paris, Dallon, 1953, pp. 16–17.

population decreases. The small farmer with few acres and little capital, as Gallaher observed, finds himself in the poverty class.[35]

Whereas a century ago about half of the American families lived on farms, in 1963 farm families comprised but 3.1 million of 47.4 million families in the United States. But in 1963 when 16 percent of the urban families were in the poverty category (incomes under $3,000) 43 percent of all farm families were so classified.[36]

Weaver, in a paper about housing for the urban poor in 1965, remarked that of 9.3 million poor American families, over 5 million lived in the larger cities and have become "the city's most enduring trademark."

> Most important, though, the poor have been the main object of the democratic city's greatest purpose; to provide the fullest opportunities for the civilization of man. The American city has, on the whole, performed this civilizing function rather well. It has escalated millions of immigrants to relative affluence. . . . But, in recent years, we have come to see that this historic role of the city has deteriorated badly. Its humanizing function seems to have broken down. In some cities neighborhood blight and poverty have existed, hand-in-hand, for three generations or more, and for the people involved, escape from the slum and the clutch of impoverishment no longer seems likely.[37]

The transition from an agricultural society and economy, so striking in the United States, is equally evident in Canada's evolution. There, also, are wide stretches of good land where agriculture has been modernized and where farmers prosper. Also in Canada are areas where the land is not so productive or where it is not possible to join several little family farms into one great farm. There are wide regions, the Atlantic Provinces, or "Canada's Appalachia," for example, where quasi-subsistence farming still prevails. Many of these farmers are obliged to seek outside employment to make ends meet, and many families must depend in part on public assistance. There are many who think of these farmers as lacking ambition as well as imagination. It is true that their level of education is low and they do not have most of the skills demanded by the labor market. There is a high birth rate among them and many of their children will have to migrate to cities. Having low levels of education, they have low levels of aspiration. Says Abell, the farmer, especially the poor farmer, "does not ascribe to the expand-or-expire dogma." Were it otherwise, most farmers would have no choice but to leave agriculture. For those

[35] Art Gallaher, Jr., *Plainville Fifteen Years Later*, New York, Columbia University Press, 1961, p. 255.

[36] Mollie Orshansky, "Counting the Poor, Another Look at the Poverty Profile," *Social Security Bulletin*, Vol. 28, January 1965, Table 2.

[37] Robert C. Weaver, "Poverty in America, the Role of Urban Renewal," in Gordon, op. cit., p. 323.

who elect to remain, who accept a lower aspiration level than urbanites set for themselves, there are compensations. "Some who remain in agriculture have a frame of reference in which religious values, familism and other intangible 'social' values outweigh economic considerations," so Abell reasons. There is help for the needy farmer in Canada, as in the United States, but the farmer on poor land rarely qualifies for such aid. Abell points out for Canada:

> Some live on farms passed on to them from relatives, carry on little or no farming and wait for the "mail-box" money which is that regular cheque from the Government which goes to all Canadians who qualify on the basis of being parents, or of being 70 years of age or older or of being "unemployed" from seasonal part-time jobs or on any one of several other bases.[38]

It must not be overlooked that the stimulus and much of the guidance for this trend in farm modernization is urban, much as good roads in the industrial nation come from urban not rural demand. So it is with welfare programs; they evolve in response to urban demand, not to serve rural people. Actually rural people often oppose such proposals. However, when such welfare measures are established and if rural people benefit from them at all, it is rarely on a par with urbanites. Fernback writes:

> If the production of abundance automatically brought prosperity, those who produce our food and fibre surely would be most prosperous. . . . What is more, the desperate plight of those who work on farms for wages no longer can be ignored. By any yardstick, they are the most impoverished and exploited group in the labor force. They receive the lowest wage of all, an average of barely 90 cents an hour. Moreover, they are denied the benefit of virtually every federal and state social welfare and labor law enacted over a generation. They are excluded from the protection of the federal and most state wage and labor laws, and of most state workmen's compensation laws.[39]

Rural people in an urbanized world region are subject to controls and decisions which originate in urban centers. It is no accident that their incomes and welfare allowances are, compared with industrial workers, a third to a half lower. They receive only minor mention in the many

[38] Helen C. Abell, "The Social Consequences of the Modernization of Agriculture," in Marc-Adelard Tremblay and Walton J. Anderson (Eds.), *Rural Canada in Transition,* Ottawa, Agricultural Economics Research Council, 1966, p. 189. Family allowance checks for children under 16 are sent to all families, not the poor alone. In 1965 pension checks were paid to all Canadians of 70 and over. The entrance point has been lowered each year; in 1970 it has reached the limit of all Canadians of 65 and over.

[39] Frank L. Fernbach, "Policies Affecting Income Distribution," Gordon, op. cit., p. 125.

studies of poverty now appearing, although it is recognized that a considerable segment of the urban poor are of rural origin.[40]

ON THE "BURDEN" OF PUBLIC WELFARE

All public money when distributed, as mentioned above, takes the form of public benefits, and there are many categories of beneficiaries. The funds received by any group of beneficiaries will be protested by other groups. For example, funds allocated for aid to agriculture goes in large part to the more affluent farmers and to "agribusiness" projects; very little goes to the poor farmers. But affluent farmers, as Gallaher mentions, object vigorously if public relief benefits are paid to poor farmers.[41] Industry, while receiving lucrative contracts from the government, views with alarm all but minimal benefits distributed to the poor. Such self-interest behaviors are normal in any healthy democracy. Excessive demands, on the one side, and excessive resistance, on the other, tend to determine the middle course, which democratic governments usually take.

What each government does in the interest of public social welfare is determined by a mixture of factors, and this mixture like the economy of a country, is ever changing. This is despite the fact that whatever the public social welfare services performed by different levels of government, the course taken tomorrow may be largely influenced by the practices and policies of yesterday. Also, the kind of services provided may be determined by the socio-economic crises which may demand unusual action.

Moreover, public welfare services for the poor are of many kinds. The poor, like others, have various needs; they have different liabilities and handicaps and, as Table 27 shows, they fall into many categories. The persons listed in the categories of this table are counted, each of them, in but one category. One included as "aged" would not also be counted as "disabled." Morgan's study shows that of seven categories of poor families or spending units (755 of a national sample of 3,000), the seven groups differ widely in equities, savings surrendered, and the percentage receiving assistance. We need to keep in mind that no family or individual adjudged to be poor is so identified for one reason alone.[42]

Estimates of the cost of public social welfare are difficult to make because for some programs the cost is shared at three levels of government. The figures shown in Table 28 for 1935 and 1963 are for federal costs. The expenditures grouped here do not include those public ex-

---

40 Oscar Ornati, *Poverty Amid Affluence*, New York, Twentieth Century Fund, 1966, pp. 157 and 121.

41 Gallaher, op. cit., final chapter.

42 James N. Morgan, et al, *Income and Welfare in the United States*, New York, McGraw-Hill, 1962, pp. 203 and 216.

Table 27   Categories of Families in Poverty in the United States,
Property Equity, Savings Surrendered, Percent Receiving
Assistance, in 1959

Likely causes of poverty (main cause in each case)	Number of poor families	Equity in farm or home	Savings surren- dered	Number receiving assistance
Head of the family is:				
1. Aged	127	$ 3,300	$119	29
2. Disabled	65	3,600	182	40
3. Single and has children	86	1,000	24	38
4. Worker under 49 weeks in 1959	65	1,900	160	17
5. Self-employed business- man or farmer	91	12,000	125	6
6. Non-white	128	1,200	24	17
7. Other	183	4,300	185	17
All poor families	755	$ 3,000	$120	23

Source: James N. Morgan, et al., *Income and Welfare in the United States,* New
York, McGraw-Hill, 1962, pp. 203 and 216.

Table 28   Federal Welfare Costs in the United States,
in 1935 and 1963

Types of program	Millions	
	1935	1963
Total	$6,503	$65,904
Social insurance and related programs	384	25,735
Public aid (assistance)	2,998	5,516
Veterans' programs	450	5,385
Other welfare programs	139	1,483
Health and medical programs	544	5,657
Education (various aids to)	1,989	22,128
All welfare expenditures as percent of Gross National Product	9.5	11.6
Per capita welfare expenditures	$50.33	$345.67

Source: James N. Morgan, et al., *Income and Welfare in the United States,* New
Review, Vol. 86, No. 6, June 1963, p. 688.

penditures which have an indirect welfare character such as aids to agriculture or locating government facilities in depressed areas. It needs to
be kept in mind that 1935 dollars were worth less than half the 1963
dollars, but even with this allowance the table shows the direction which
public spending for welfare is taking.

When we speak of welfare today, attention is on public expenditures;
the comparatively small amounts collected and distributed by private
agencies attract little notice. Public welfare has become largely a matter

of federal spending, that is 65 to 70 percent national funds, 25 to 30 percent state or provincial funds, and 3 to 7 percent local or municipal funds. The responsibility for contact with the recipients or clients is necessarily local.

There is in every industrial country competition between the different service agencies or departments, each with its special program: old-age pensions, accident and disability payments, allowances for children, veterans' benefits, mothers' pensions, survivors benefits, unemployment insurance, and public assistance. According to changing needs and changing public policy, the percentage of total appropriations allocated to any one program may be increased or decreased compared with other programs.

It is well known, of course that there are powerful pressure groups supporting well-organized opposition to the "welfare-state trend" and they focus their opposition against one program or another. While public authorities cannot ignore such opposition, neither can they ignore the range of evident need. As Titmuss observes, through the silent pressure of need the state commitment to welfare becomes firmly established; the "welfare state" comes to be built into the economy.[43]

MEDICAL CARE, A NEW IMPERATIVE

Among other dramatic changes in the process of emerging, along with the evolution of industry and of the urban community over the past century, has been the growth of a medical service based on scientific discovery and various technological achievements. The evolution of medicine and medical care is well documented and well known. One seldom-mentioned aspect of this evolution though is worthy of notice as it concerns the use of this growing body of knowledge and skill by the lower socio-economic levels of society. In the days when barbers were the surgeons and many ailments were treated by taking "bad blood" from the patient, it was perhaps good that the poor did not turn to the physician in time of illness. The poor, as many of them still do, managed to get on without the physician. With the advance of medicine, the idea has spread that all people should take advantage of the knowledge and skill of medicine, the poor included.

In the meanwhile the art of medicine has become more and more of a profession, increasingly specialized. Those who enter this respected oc-

43 Richard M. Titmuss, *Commitment to Welfare.* (New York, Random House, Pantheon, 1968). The more rapid movement of Canada than other countries toward total welfare state status can be seen by examining the trend in hospital and welfare statistics as reported in the *Canada Yearbook* (Ottawa, Dominion Bureau of Statistics), sections on welfare and hospitals. Here can be seen how Canada, although less financially able, is adopting medicare more rapidly than the United States.

cupation, for whom learning was once an apprenticeship, must spend years in study and training. The medical profession and the great industries that serve it have become an integrated giant complex with many of the characteristics of a monopoly. In the course of this evolution, all levels of the industrial urban society have been converted to a faith in modern medicine as a means to lengthening and saving life. Once converted to this faith, the poor find that medical care has been priced far out of their reach. The awareness of the unavailability of adequate medical care for the working and lower classes has resulted in various organized attempts to make medical care a public service. The medical profession and the industries for making medicine and appliances, at great cost, have resisted this trend.

The ends to which this resistance may go is illustrated by the strike of physicians in Saskatchewan in 1962. Much as a trade union might, the physicians withheld their services from their patients and from most of the hospitals in that Canadian province.[44] In some towns the inhabitants divided, one group supporting the provincial medicare scheme and damning the doctors, the other group, mainly the middle and upper classes, supporting the doctors. A Toronto paper described what happened in a small town called Bigger, "Today Bigger is no longer a community in any except the geographical sense of the word. The citizenry has been split into two utterly incompatible elements by passionate but only dimly understood differences over the Saskatchewan Medical Care Act." [45]

This example of doctors going on strike illustrates how desperately serious medical practitioners are about the independent status of their profession. They warn that medicare will destroy the sacred "doctor-patient" relationship, although that idealized relationship, due to crowded schedules and specialization, rarely exists anymore, execpt for those with the money to claim more of the physician's time. The old professional pride is apparently genuine with physicians. It is understandable that the profession should put up vigorous, even vicious opposition. In many ways it is to be expected that, for them, the drive for medicare is seen as evil, even as stated by Annis, a leader in the American Medical Association.

> Here, as in many other countries, the proposals for government health care did not arise as a separate and distinct issue—based purely and simply on medical care problems. There is no medical crisis here, nor is the country confronted with any serious critical shortages which require radical changes in our system of health care.

[44] See articles by William Cameron, "Storm Over Saskatchewan," in the *Canadian Forum*, July 1962, and by Henry Copperstock, "Doctors on Strike," *Canadian Forum*, August 1962.
[45] Jeannine Locke, "Our Town Will Never Be the Same," Toronto, *The Daily Star*, August 4, 1962.

Like other plans in other nations, the proposal in this country arose as part of a trend based on the philosophy that individual freedom and initiative must be subordinated to government authority and regulation. This "big brother" concept, if allowed to spread unchecked, undermines self-reliance, and fosters the habit of turning to government for the solution of all problems.[46]

As large industries tend to outgrow the individual owner and corporate ownership takes over, so medicine tends to outgrow the family-doctor ideal. Roemer sees two trends for the future:

First, it seems quite clear that economic support for the health services will be increasingly collectivized. As we have seen, this may take many forms, but the principal ones are bound to be the insurance device and public taxation. There are endless varieties in these economic mechanisms, but the forces of our economy, at least in the health services, favor the path of taxation and its use at higher levels of government. . . .

The second general trend is clearly toward greater organization and systematization of technical services. Even if there were no movement toward collectivation of finances, this medico-social organization would continue, but the economic evolution accelerates it.[47]

Roemer concludes that the ordinary needs for economy and efficiency cannot be met by the present wasteful management of medical services with excessive duplication of equipment, costs which are added to medical fees. Roemer adds that people are quite aware that the medical profession is not serving as ideally as it is supposed to. Few, however, are aware that the medical profession is itself caught up in a growing structure which lacks organization, and that it does not have the organizing skills that are needed.[48]

WELFARE ASPECTS OF FULL EMPLOYMENT

Urbanized industrial societies are learning, however slowly and often grudgingly, that the open competitive labor market, providing jobs according to the willingness and abilities of job seekers, is efficient but wasteful. In such a labor market it is taken for granted that some will suffer due to their lack of skill, low aspirations, laziness, or stupidity. To

---

[46] Edward H. Annis, "Government Health Care, First the Aged, then Everyone," *Current History*, Vol. 45, No. 264, August 1963, p. 109. The issue contains other articles on the same subject.

[47] Milton I. Roemer, "The Future of Social Medicine in the United States," *Occasional Papers in Social and Economic Administration*, No. 4, London, Edutext Publications, 1967, Pamphlet 17.

[48] Ibid., p. 18.

defend the competitive labor market, it is necessary to assume that jobs are available in sufficient number at all skill levels, especially many jobs at the low-wage unskilled level, which is no longer true. The more efficient industry becomes the more selective becomes its recruitment policy, which means that a growing percentage of the least able in the labor market are excluded. Thus in 1967 when many were calling it a year of full employment, it was less than full employment for some four million Americans at the lower-skill levels. Their labor was not being used by the work system.

During the Great Depression in the United States, if one said that the government should assume some responsibility for creating work for the unemployed, he risked being called a Communist or a crank. After a long generation it is coming to be recognized that the industrial work system cannot be left to the vagaries of *laissez faire*. Too much is at stake in the mass society. If government must participate in the management of the money market, it can no longer stand aloof from giving guidance and protection to the labor market. Failing to utilize the labor force to the full imposes an unwarranted burden on the total economy. Not to find use for the unemployed, who must be supported anyhow, is a cost all others must share.

Minsky has called attention to the interdependence of public and private work, the line between the two becoming more indefinite. He proposed public work programs at minimum wages above the poverty line, but a phase of the program was designed to upgrade workers of low skill.

> Once such an artificially created tight labor market existed, the pattern of excess demands for labor resulting from generalized measures to expand aggregate demand would indicate the job training and work relocations that should be undertaken. The training and relocation programs are really valuable within the contexts of tight labor markets. Lifelong learning for all is a necessary policy objective in our complex and ever-changing economy and society. Programs making this possible and appealing to all should be instituted. But this is not solely or even primarily a concern of the war on poverty.[49]

This is no emergency public participation of government in the labor market, merely generating employment in depressions. The demand for such public responsibility is continuous. Many workers, securely employed today, may be less securely employed a decade hence. Minsky concludes:

> The way to end the biggest chunk of poverty is to generate jobs at adequate incomes for the people in poverty. Some improvements in transfer

[49] Hyman P. Minsky, "The Role of Employment Policy," in Gordon, op. cit., p. 199.

payments, such as children's allowances and medical care for all without means tests, would help, but the basic approach must be to provide jobs for all who are willing and able to work—taking their abilities as they are.[50]

Unemployment is a luxury the industrializing Communist countries will not permit. They have managed—in many respects, overmanaged— economies. They also have poverty. If one is able to work, there are ways to employ him, so potential labor is not lost. A well-regulated American economy, according to Riesman and Weiss, cannot afford unemployment either. If a country has a million unemployed a year, that means a million man-years of labor lost which, if not used in producing goods, might be used to provide public facilities and needed public services. In such terms, welfare is good business.[51]

THE PROFESSIONALIZATION OF PUBLIC WELFARE

Public welfare programs, whatever their nature, like other functions of government, must be operated according to accepted standards of administrative efficiency. Whether a particular program is concerned with the sick, the blind, needy families, the unemployed, or the retraining of the jobless, it is operated in non-sentimental terms, no less so than public programs for maintaining parks and playgrounds, regulating the traffic, or inspecting food and water supplies. Moreover, each kind of program constitutes a professional approach to a particular kind of public responsibility.

The social worker is such a professional. Once, says Woodroofe of the social worker, he worked for private groups, fighting "ignorance, idleness, disease, squalor and want . . . once regarded as a doer of good works . . . [he] has become an accepted part of the machinery of the State." [52] Previously, he worked as a well-meaning volunteer and no training was deemed necessary, a viewpoint still held in rural parts of the United States and Canada. However, the entry of government into social welfare, mainly since about 1920, has served to make a profession of social work. A college degree is now required plus a year or more of special training.

Titmuss sees the social worker as the key functionary in all public welfare programs, the point of contact between the people and the pro-

50 Ibid., p. 200.

51 Robert S. Weiss and David Riesman, "Social Problems and Disorganization in the World of Work," in Robert K. Merton and Robert A. Nisbet (Eds.), *Contemporary Social Problems*, New York, Harcourt, Brace & World, 1961, pp. 459–515.

52 Woodroofe, op. cit., p. 209.

gram. The job of the social worker in public service is not merely one of giving something away, as many still believe. This is a specialized work, becoming more complex, with an expanding division of labor. Hence it "becomes less intelligible to the lay councillor or public representative." [53]

As medicare and public health become a responsibility of government, a vast organization serving millions replaces (without displacing) the physician working alone. The physician becomes a functionary in a dominant public role surrounded by various paramedical professions: administrators, nurses, laboratory technicians, and others. Roemer notes that public medicine is now made up of five interrelated activity areas: 1) health insurance, 2) medical practice, 3) hospitals and other health facilities, 4) public health services, and 5) categories of health care programs.[54]

Social work, in like manner, comes to be integrated with related professions and cannot be ignored as in the private-charity days. On physical or mental health matters there is the contact between social work and the health-care complex. Contacts may be necessary with unemployment insurance or the employment service. Other contacts may be with the police. The different services, old-age insurance, aid to the blind, physical rehabilitation, vocational training, recreation centers, and the schools, may again and again be in contact with one another. The trained social worker is a specialist, having a dominant role in the welfare network, much as the physician figures in the network of the health system.

With growing complexity, not only of government as a whole but no less of its many departments, the ordinary citizen in need is helpless, not knowing where to go or whom to ask. Social workers, says Howard, "are experts in working with people. The principles of social work should be useful and applicable in efforts to achieve social action, as in any other human endeavor." [55] A major function of public welfare is to give expression to the human side of government, to work efficiently and yet display an understanding for the problems of people, which at the professional level can be done without sinking into maudlin sentimentality.

[53] Titmuss, op. cit., p. 27.
[54] Roemer, op. cit., p. 3.
[55] Donald S. Howard, "Social Work and Social Reform," in Cora Kasius (Ed.), *New Directives in Social Work*, New York, Harper & Row, 1954, p. 173.

Social control in urban society | 17

THE CONTROL CHALLENGE OF MASS SOCIETY

As the world's population becomes increasingly urbanized and as more and more people concentrate in cities with populations of over a million, it should not surprise us if mass-behavior problems emerge. Indeed, mass-behavior problems come to our attention in the news daily. In ideological conflict, crowds organized into mobs become political weapons. Those in political power in a government may use mass demonstrations as evidence of popular approval of their policies and practices. The political opposition may use mass demonstrations as evidence of popular unrest.

Great numbers of people in the ranks of the poor are usually unorganized. If and when leaders, able to articulate their grievances, call them together, they may become emotionally aroused and turn to rioting. Students in large universities, under similar circumstances, may emerge in mass protest, which can also lead to rioting and the destruction of property.

Such mass behaviors are pertinent to our consideration of social control. They are also pertinent because they concern social control and order in large cities, an order which is increasingly challenged by these demonstrations, although some demonstrations, while not challenging government, may be efforts to pressure government to take action against others. For example, trade unions in some countries may march enmasse to the public authorities demanding that certain controls be imposed on employers, or they may demand that price controls be imposed. Or mass demonstrations may have the purpose of bringing grievances to public attention, to get public support for demands being made on government. Negro mass demonstrations have had the aim of impressing upon government the need of fair employment and housing legislation.

With rare exceptions, such challenging mass demonstrations take place in large cities and generally in the crowded urban centers where the greatest number of activities involving the greatest number of people take place. This means that, besides being most accessible for gathering, a mass demonstration at midtown can result in the maximum amount of inconvenience. One measure of order in a large city, the kind of order that makes the midtown most accessible to the greatest number, is the extent to which public authority can prevent the various disorders which hinder ready access. Mass demonstrations are disruptions of order, as often they are intended to be, and demonstrations which become riots are more so.[1]

Mass activity leading to mob violence and rioting, as behaviors in urban communities, are maladies of the secondary society. Living unnumbered generations in small communities, men acquired ways of maintaining order. In most relationships, they have learned to maintain order in cities, except as great numbers gather under leadership and the crowd becomes a mob. This kind of mass behavior leading to violence beyond rational control is seen by many as a challenge to secure urban living. This is not to say that there is no reason for angry mass demonstrations. Minorities held for decades in positions of low status, feeling themselves fenced in, may find in mass demonstration the only means to getting their needs considered. In such a manner workers finally gained the right to form trade unions, and in like manner the Negro is demanding a measure of equality.

However spectacular mass demonstrations may be, and there have been mass uprisings in cities over the centuries, they comprise a small part of the many kinds of behavior in cities which occur under fairly effective control. Even while a mob of a few thousands is on the rampage in a particular area, a million or more in other areas of a city are going about their affairs. These continuous aspects of control are our concern in this chapter.

THE IMPLICATIONS OF SOCIAL ORDER

A child is born into a situation in which people own certain things and these things have their places, a situation in which grown-ups have established order. Here each person understands what others are about, and what one does is understandable to others. Each adult knows today what he will be doing and where he will be tomorrow, and with about the same certainty he knows where others will be and what they will be

1 On this subject, see Ralph H. Turner and Lewis M. Killian, *Collective Behavior,* Englewood Cliffs, N.J., Prentice-Hall, 1957, Chaps. 3–13.

doing. He is aware of his status with respect to others, and knows the
rules for buying or selling and for interacting with others. This is the
social order into which one is born. To Horton and Hunt, it is in addition a network of rights and duties.

> Unless we can depend upon police officers to protect us, workers to go
> to work on schedule and motorists to stay on the right side of the road
> most of the time, there can be no social order. The orderliness of a society
> rests upon a network of roles according to which each person accepts cer-
> tain duties toward others and claims certain rights from others.

Social control, on the other hand, concerns the methods by which
one born into a social order, be it a tribal village or a city, is socialized.
He is taught what to believe and how to properly behave. It takes in all
"the means and processes whereby a group or a society secures its members' conformity to its expectations." [2]

The most elemental method of social control involves interaction
between two persons (a dyad); Ego (the individual) and Alter (the other
person) may each try to influence the other. Each is in a position to
cooperate or not, and either may be in a position to impose negative
sanctions (punishment) or to bestow positive sanctions (rewards) on the
others. Each presumably is motivated by self-interest, and each may adapt
to the influence of the other. Both Ego and Alter however, are also behaving in relation to the social order. To Catlin this constitutes a "balance" where people, objects, and their movements follow a particular
course and most of the constructs one sees and touches have reason for
being there. For those who move among them, the arrangement of the
constructs have meaning. To one oriented there, the slum and its people
and their distribution constitutes order no less than in the case of the
"gold coast" milieu. This constitutes what Catlin calls the *modus vivendi:*

> . . . by which man is able to accommodate his physical, psychological, and
> economic needs in a fashion consistent with some measure of accommo-
> dation with his neighbors. This balance has been effected in a fashion
> consistent with the fundamental laws which are the formulations of the
> constants of human nature and which govern human conduct. It is a bal-
> ance supported by the presence of all those persons who are interested in
> its maintenance against any intruding and adverse individual or group.[3]

The order to which people adapt includes more than people in their
continuing relations. It includes the physical milieu in which they be-

---

[2] Paul B. Horton and Chester L. Hunt, *Sociology,* New York, McGraw-Hill, 1968,
p. 127.

[3] George E. C. Catlin, "Introduction" to Emile Durkheim, *The Rules of Sociological Method,* 8th ed., New York, Free Press, 1958, p. xxxv.

have, constructs in their places and the usual uses to which each is put, the things used, and the supplies of goods consumed. While this order changes, and changes more rapidly in the urban community, it continually retains sufficient equilibrium that the changing life within it is not disorganized.

Man in this situation, while adapting, may himself also be an agent of change; man must learn to accept change and still retain a degree of equilibrium. Aubert writes:

> It becomes advantageous to deviate from traditional norms, such as those which define proper and prudent behavior of rural folk, and instead take up a new way of life like that found in the cities where employment opportunities are better. What originally emerged as the consequence of an opportunistic strategic choice may soon become ensconced in norms and role patterns which define the new behavior as proper and moral, as well as lucrative. However, norms may create a resistance to change, and sometimes this resistance can only be broken if normative patterns are first loosened up.[4]

The social order into which man is born and to which he must adapt is normative in that it demands conformity in behavior and belief. But it is also innovative and changing, especially so in the urban community, and whoever is socialized or adapted to the social order must continually resocialize himself. This process of identification with the social order is one, as seen by some, notably Parsons, in which the individual "internalizes" the norms, behaves in harmony with them, and affirms this behavior to a degree which makes his behavior and his utterances predictable.[5] However, the internalization of a norm appears to be a matter of degree, and conforming behavior respecting a norm may be ambivalent, especially in the rapidly changing environment.

CHANGING BEHAVIOR IN THE URBAN MILIEU

Wrong sees sociology in its emergent stages as a protest against partial views of man and his behavior: economic man as gain seeker, political man as power seeker, self-perserving man as security seeker, religious man as God seeker, and libidinal man as pleasure seeker. Such images, says Wrong, have their value if "not taken for the whole truth."

> In recent years sociologists have been less interested than they once were in culture and national character as backgrounds to conduct, partly be-

4 Vilhelm Aubert, *Elements of Sociology*, New York, Scribner, 1967, p. 142.
5 Talcott Parsons, *The Structure of Social Action*, New York, McGraw-Hill, 1937, pp. 378–390.

cause stress on the concept of "role" as the crucial link between the individual and the social structure has directed their attention to the immediate situation in which social interaction takes place. Man is increasingly seen as a "role-playing" creature, responding eagerly or anxiously to the expectations of other role-players in the multiple group settings in which he finds himself.[6]

In responding to meet "the expectations of other role-players," one may in some situations disregard his internalized norms, but he may also have mixed motivations. What one is expected to do and what he must do may both be in conflict with what he wishes to do in a particular situation. What he actually does may be quite something else. "The view that man is invariably pushed by internalized norms or pulled by the lure of self-validation by others ignores—to speak archaically for a moment—both the highest and the lowest, both beast and angel in his nature." [7]

In this analysis of human behavior in which man may be "social but not entirely socialized," Wrong views the human in a complex environment, impinged upon by a great mixture of influences, some of which may contradict one another. The conflict may be likened to that of a merchant seaman who is often a behavior problem on shore leave, but on the ship at sea his behavior is predictably ideal. Ship regulations define every detail of his work and there is unvarying regularity in his timetable.

Were cities ordered culturally as ships are, they would not be the havens of strangers or the abiding places of heterogeneous populations. People of different cultural backgrounds and different languages brush elbows on the street. Some speak of this as a tolerant milieu, and it is that if we think of tolerance as expressive of indifference. This is one reason why intellectuals and other less-conforming types escape the village for the city. Some of these, White observes, find the city "not civilized enough." Some adapt to the city readily, while still others find it much "too wild, too vulgar, too ostentatious, too uncontrolled." [8]

We need to consider the kinds of social control found in the urban community, primary controls or those which are realized in personal interaction, and those of a more formal type which are compelled by the forces of the urban order of things. We look first at primary group controls.

---

6 Dennis Wrong, "The Oversocialized Conception of Man," *American Sociological Review*, Vol. 26, No. 2, April 1961, p. 190.

7 Ibid., p. 191.

8 Morton White, "Two Stages in the Critique of the American City," in Oscar Handlin and John Burchard (Eds.), *The Historian and the City*, Cambridge, MIT and Harvard University Press, 1963, p. 88.

THE CONTROL FUNCTION OF PRIMARY GROUPS

A child is born into the family, the most universal of primary groups, and the most depended on for the guidance control of the young. Normally he remains a member of this group through life. In earlier stages of human history one dared not leave his family, since without family one was a nonentity and the hand of every man was against him. But even in those times, as today, one could choose to belong to peer groups. Whatever the groups, they would be small and the relations in them would be primary. Such is also the case with social control; it is informal and often spontaneous.

> The members of the group react to the actions of each other. When a member irritates or annoys the others, they may show their disapproval through ridicule, laughter, criticism, or even ostracism. When a member's behavior is acceptable, a secure and comfortable "belonging" is his usual reward . . . [one who has been disciplined] must earn his way back into group acceptance through penitence and renewed conformity.[9]

The small informal group, how it serves the individual, how as a minute collectivity it fits into the larger community, and how it may be used for social control ends, is an important research interest among sociologists. It is in small groups that much of city life, whether at work or leisure, is experienced. This, for example, is told by Whyte in his study of a street gang in Boston.[10] It would be unusual for one who has adapted to urban life to be without various primary group relationships. As Warner found in Jonesville, a small Midwest city, the small groups dominate community life, both at the adult and youth levels.[11] It is this domination that makes small town life stifling for some people. In the large city one can escape most negative social controls of the class-defining primary group. Urban groups are varied and operate in various spheres. Gould observed a greater freedom of small group formation in the cities of India compared with the caste-bound villages. "Each of the two forms of social stratification is associated with a particular kind of civilization." The rural ascriptive type is associated with the agricultural and the urban achievement type is associated with the industrial civilization.[12] And each type influences the formation of many primary group ties.

[9] Horton and Hunt, op. cit., p. 130.

[10] William Foote Whyte, *Street-Corner Society*, Chicago, University of Chicago Press, 1943.

[11] W. Lloyd Warner (Ed.), *Democracy in Jonesville*, New York, Harper & Row, 1949.

[12] Harold A. Gould, "Castes, Outcastes, and the Sociology of Stratification," *International Journal of Comparative Sociology*, Vol. 1, No. 2, September 1960, p. 221.

Bureaucracies, as we have noted elsewhere, are administrative organizations for getting work done, for making and keeping records. They insure efficiency and predictability, but they are impersonal in their operation and neutral to all social values or emotional interests. However, it is well known that even the most efficient bureaucracy could hardly function were it not permeated by a great variety of informal relationships and fellowship interaction between peer groups. By the so-called "grapevine" and other communication devices between the levels of an organization, most decisions are made informally before being put on paper. The informal personal bureaucracy operates with little restriction in the shadow of the formal impersonal bureaucracy. Caplow writes of the peer group, a primary group of equals, as it functions in large organizations, and as the spirit or soul of secondary organizations.

> Peer groups are necessarily factional. The larger organization often attempts to suppress them or denies their existence. Although the peer group is as old as human society, it was not much analyzed until about thirty years ago, when studies of factories revealed the existence of peer groups that regulated the daily output of workers. They were at first regarded as perverse and pathological; however, as further studies demonstrated their functions, it was gradually perceived that peer groups do not represent a breakdown in the larger organization, but are essential components of it.[13]

Taylor calls attention to the many ways in which informal groups operate among workers in an industrial enterprise. For instance, they may set the standards for what they think is a fair day's work. In a conflict situation, they may stand together against the foreman, although some may know that the foreman is in the right. They may shun the person who pushes too hard to "get ahead." Despite its faults, the informal organization is often useful for the efficiency of the formal one. It allows for a reasonable degree of socializing in the place of work, and helps relieve the dullness of some work routines. "Often it is a facilitating mechanism and intended to support the official bureaucracy." [14]

SOCIAL CONTROL AND SOCIAL ORDER CHANGE

Among other functions of social control in modern society is that of adapting to changes in the environment. Invention after invention re-

13 Theodore Caplow, *Principles of Organization,* New York, Harcourt, Brace & World, 1964, p. 19.
14 Lee Taylor, *Occupational Sociology,* New York, Oxford University Press, 1968, p. 91. In this connection Taylor cites Peter M. Blau, *Bureaucracy in Modern Society,* New York, Random House, 1956.

sults in changing the industrial work system. People are deprived of their old occupations and must learn new ones. The small labor-intensive workshop is priced out of existence and workers must turn to the capital-intensive industrial plant. The concentration of low-paid workers in factories brings about congested areas of low-quality houses, and a slum is created. On the other hand, rising wage rates for skilled workers enables a large section of the labor force to move up socially. These are types of social order change.

As used here (at least until a better name is found for it), the social order is that vast organization of organizations by which the industrial urban society supplies its creature needs, stratifies itself into numerous, ever-changing echelons for producing goods and services, educates itself in the "right" ways to consume goods and services and to use leisure. It is, on the one hand, the complex of things and, on the other hand, it is the complex of behaviors and beliefs which enables the society to use and enjoy the whole of it. Once it was called "the system" by rebel intellectuals, but to present-day disciples of discontent, whose art it is to use it and damn it at the same time, order is identified as "the Establishment." Galbraith remarks:

> Not inappropriately, the rejection extends not only to the economic, social and political views of the Establishment but to its clothing, conventional housing and even to the soap, depilatory apparatus and other goods, the production of which is the sanctioned measure of success. All these are eschewed by the dissidents in a highly visible manner.[15]

The social order, be it static or changing, is ever an educative system. In the static society its educational function is mainly confined to the rising generation. Elsewhere in a changing milieu each change is a demand for new learning, and all age groups become involved. In the sphere of production something new must be learned with each technological innovation and each rearrangement of the work process. In this learning some move rapidly ahead while others lag behind. In the sphere of consumption, learning and adaptation is no less competitive and takes the form of display.

Learning in the changing order is a matter of gaining knowledge, becoming skilled in the ways of getting on, acquiring know-how, and taking on the cultural concomitants of new roles. One does not become a skilled worker merely by learning to use the tools, or rise to a higher social level by putting on better clothes and driving a better automobile; nor can one become even a "hippie" without learning the vocabulary and the right way to use it. In any large community, as Shils points out,

15 John K. Galbraith, *The New Industrial State,* Boston, Houghton Mifflin, 1967, p. 324.

there are levels of capability and there are many "whose 'antennae' are short, whose intelligence and imagination is either limited or has not yet been aroused," and there are whole sections of the people who lag behind.

> For such persons, who are many in the world, the need for affection, for self-maintenance, can be gratified largely in personal primary groups, . . . or in working collectivities. Much of the order they need, as well as the affection and rewards they desire . . . is found in such circles of small radius. Their minds must be prodded by education and exhortation to seek the wider reaches of the cosmos and society, and in most instances these do not have much impact.[16]

Profound changes in the social order, which call for changes in ways of work and living, and changes in social expectations, may occur in any society, advanced as well as backward. But the advanced society is more inured to change, is more "case-hardened." It is not only more experienced in adapting to the new but may take pride in keeping abreast. In the new nations the opposite is true. Even minor changes may weaken the whole fabric of a traditional culture. Blumer sees three stages in this painful process.

1. *Undermining of the established social order.* The ways in which industrialization is thought to undermine a preestablished social order are legion. . . .
2. *Setting new relations for people.* A second major kind of social change conventionally attributed to industrialization is that of bringing people together in unfamiliar forms of association, thus requiring them to forge new relations. . . .
3. *Consolidation of an industrial order.* Scholars of industrialization usually endow it with intrinsic tendencies which are declared to move persistently to mold a given type of social order. . . . In the long run these imperious tendencies are held to triumph; thus there emerges a social order with a distinctive character.[17]

The imported political ways a new order brings to a traditional society are not less complex than are the industrial ways. Cowan found that the chief-headed tribal council of West Africa clashed with the Western notions of impersonal, bureaucratic government. "The complex system of social interaction with the tribal unit was regulated and adjusted by behavioral prescriptions which were frequently derived from magico-religious sources." Formal government violates all traditions of

---

[16] Edward Shils, "Charisma, Order nad Status," *American Sociological Review,* Vol. 30, No. 2, April 1965, p. 203.

[17] Herbert Blumer, "Industrialization and Race Relations," in Guy Hunter (Ed.), *Industrialization and Race Relations,* London, Oxford University Press, 1965, pp. 225–230.

personal loyalty and extends its benefits to strangers as to natives.[18]

Developing countries differ widely in their ability to adapt to the oncoming industrial order. Willner reports the versatility of the Javanese, many of them migrating to cities and "rising in the world." In the following item she writes mainly of Javanese in the upper occupations.

> Members of these groups voice alternately and even simultaneously the desirability of "modernization" and "return to our traditional values" while increasingly adopting consumption, recreation and association patterns barely distinguishable from those of the European community with which they increasingly fraternize. They inhabit new houses in new suburbs, drive large cars and purchase, however prohibitive the price and regardless of quality, imported in preference to domestic articles. Mixed sports, receptions, and even cocktail parties are replacing the traditional family or clan gathering with its segregation of sexes.[19]

This industrial social order, as it influences behavior and compels behavioral change, is quite amoral. He who acts in the right manner and the wrongdoer alike come under its influence, and either may prosper.

CHANGE AND SOCIAL PERSISTENCE

When we look at the "social" in social change we become aware of its many-sided character. To illustrate, take the case of two Congo tribesmen, uncle and nephew, who left their village and found work in an urban factory. In terms of ascriptive tribal culture, the uncle, being older and of the next higher generation, was in a dominant position vis-a-vis the nephew. In time the nephew, being more imaginative and alert, became a subforeman, which meant that he had to give orders to the uncle, an impersonal relationship by the rules of the work place. The nephew felt compelled to favor the uncle, with the result that both were discharged. Had he not favored the uncle he would have received severe criticism on returning to the village.

Conflicts of this nature appear in many guises in the course of social change. The old ways, rooted in habits of behavior and thought, do not always readily yield. Confronted with change, some institutions face greater adaptation demands than others, or some institutions are able to adapt more readily than others. According to Ogburn these different rates of change are due to a cultural lag between fast-moving and slow-moving change, a notion that has considerable validity, even though not

[18] L. Gray Cowan, *Local Government in West Africa*, New York, Columbia University Press, 1959, p. 2.

[19] Ann Ruth Willner, "Change in the Javanese Town-Village Life," *Economic Development and Cultural Change*, Vol. 6, No. 3, April 1958, p. 229.

universally applicable.[20] Dore describes how in Japan, for instance, the persistence of family-linked statuses and behaviors of earlier origin have carried over to nonfamily organizations in the urban community. Duty and obedience in such organizations are equated with filial piety: as the worker bowing to the boss in the same way as to his father, or the student bowing to the teacher, or workers to the trade union leaders. This is true to different degrees in most old countries, including European countries. Dore sees such behaviors as having early origins. In some countries still, obeisance is a behavior which is practiced with some degree of pride; it serves to remind one of his social position vis-a-vis others.[21]

Obeisance, which became a fine art in some cultures, would hardly originate in an industrial urban culture, but it may persist in a culture that becomes industrial and urban, although, while persisting, it may lose some of its original force for social control. We may identify it with earlier persistent qualities of social stratification systems. Warner speaks of the persistence of a social-class consciousness in the top ranks of a society. "The American social class system persists partly because, through the activities of its members, it is capable of attaching new members to its group and forming them into a variety of personalities which fit the system." [22] The preferred new members are those born to the class.

The persistence of behavior and attitude patterns is no better illustrated than in the case of many Southerners who have learned in their up-bringing that the Negro must be "kept in his place." In his study of a Southern town, Hill reports the practice of the whites to call Negroes, even elderly ones, by their first names. No Negro in that town at the time of this study would dare to hale a white man into court, whatever the grievance. He would have to persaude another white man to sponsor his complaint. But while the higher classes cling to their forms and approved codes, they cannot in the modern society, as customary at one time, forbid imitation.[23]

It would be difficult to draw a line between what may be called commendable tradition and negative, change-inhibiting tradition, which may persist in families, places of work, and institutions. In some of its aspects tradition is venerable, and certain old practices ought to continue, although agreement on what is venerable and what should continue would be difficult. For example, should the medieval authoritarian role of the husband and father continue? And what of the insistence of some trade unions that apprenticeship, inherited from the ancient guilds,

20 William F. Ogburn, *Social Change*, New York, Viking, 1922.

21 R. P. Dore, *City Life in Japan*, London, Routledge and Kegan Paul, 1958, p. 94.

22 W. Lloyd Warner, *American Life, Dream and Reality*, Chicago, University of Chicago Press, 1962, p. 225.

23 Reuben Hill (Ed.), *Eddyville's Families*, Chapel Hill, Institute for Research in Social Sciences, University of North Carolina, 1953, p. 111 (mimeographed).

continue, although in some cases it is a wasteful method of learning an occupation? On the other hand, what of pageant-like ceremonials, such as university graduations, and all of the "impractical" aspects of weddings? Or of family reunions? Or national holidays? Here is an item from Horton and Hunt:

> Of all sources of truth, tradition is one of the most reassuring. Here is the accumulated wisdom of the ages, and he who disregards it may expect denunciation as a scoundrel or a fool. If a pattern has worked in the past why not keep on using it?

> Tradition, however, preserves both the accumulated wisdom and the accumulated bunkum of the ages. Tradition is society's attic, crammed with all sorts of useful tools and useless relics.[24]

Our past is not only institutionalized in "the Establishment," our churches and schools, but in the structures we make and our use of them, in our manners, and even in what we may think are our own codes of right and wrong. The changes we make or try to make in our social patterns are compromises between the old and the new. Even the radical intellectual respects the old in his vocabulary and in his uses of speech.

RELIGION AS A CONTROL AGENT

It is well known that churches and other organizations in the sphere of religion act as conservers of tradition. They impose and defend their codes of conduct which come out of the past, absolutes that cannot be compromised. They are enforced formally by the organization and informally by the members. Most of the great religions are rural in origin or at least they acquired their codes and structure before the great industrial city appeared, and by implication their norms and values retain an invisible rural orientation.

Wilson sees churches as upholding the "universality of religious prescriptions" exerting pressure on men to square their professions with their practice. In short, "The church becomes an instrument of justice, sometimes interpreting and applying God's law before the courts apply man's law to redefine and rectify human relationships." [25] This does not mean that the church in the complex community is fully effective amid the less traditional secular influences.

Religious systems, for example, endeavor to minimize the strivings

[24] Horton and Hunt, op. cit., pp. 5–6.
[25] Everett K. Wilson, *Sociology, Rules, Roles, and Relationships*, Homewood, Illinois, Dorsey Press, 1966, p. 463.

of class against class in competition for earthbound values. Fromm regards the social class system, which permeates even the church, as an institutionalized order in its own right. "The more mixed and institutionalized the class structure is, the more will different sets of norms be
explicitly related to different classes, as for instance, norms for free men
or for serfs in a feudal culture, or for whites and Negroes." [26]

A religious organization, at any rate, a Christian organization, aims
to be a guide in man's conduct, although in the urbanized society it can
hardly go beyond exhorting people to behave properly. In a rural society,
however, a church may also carry on active guidance functions and may
even impose correctional treatment for deviants. A church may, as many
churches did in American frontier times, operate much as a private government. The Mormon church did that in the extreme during its period
of settlement in Utah. There were church courts at different levels, but
initially they handled civil as well as ecclesiastical matters.[27] When Utah
gained statehood and control over its courts the church courts discontinued handling civil cases but they continued to handle cases of moral
conduct for a decade or two. Church authorities still use membership
loyalty as a leverage to guide the Saints (more properly, the Church of
Jesus Christ of Latterday Saints) in political elections. But top leaders
are mainly of the wealthy and conservative class, while the majority of
the membership supports the more liberal candidates.

While the businessmen leaders of the Mormon church strongly support modernism, individualism, higher levels of education, and democracy, church control flows from the top down. Church decisions handed
down are voted on but only to be "affirmed." The Mormon is free to be
an individual, with only moral restraints in the secular sphere, but as
a church member his individualism is severely limited. He acquires the
ability of keeping the two notions of democracy in separate spheres, as
O'Dea points out. He can be himself in relation to political democracy,
and also one "of the tithing" in church democracy. "In terms of church
government, there has resulted a democracy of participation within the
context of hierarchical organization and authoritarian operation." [28] One
can be a member in good standing and a free citizen and never face that
contradiction between democracy and authoritarian control. More than
likely, other religious organizations, in their efforts to adapt to changes
in modern life, find other ways of wielding their influence. But it increasingly appears that, on the whole, the strength of their influence for
control purposes is declining.

26 Erich Fromm, *Man for Himself*, New York, Rinehart, 1947, p. 241.
27 Nels Anderson, *Desert Saints, The Mormon Frontier*, 2nd ed., Chicago, University of Chicago Press, 1966, Chap. 13.
28 Thomas F. O'Dea, *The Mormons*, Chicago, University of Chicago Press, 1957,
p. 243.

SOCIAL EXPECTATIONS AND CONFORMITY TYPES

One of the functions of systems of social stratification is to divide people into categories which generally reflect the division of labor in a society. Keller speaks of a class system as having a social core, those at the top who make the decisions, who define the values, and determine the norms. "Classes grow out of the social division of labor; the social core grows out of the various subdivisions of the expanded and stratified community." As people are designated high or low, clean or dirty, skilled or unskilled according to their level in the work hierarchy, they are also rated as low, middle, or high in matters of taste, aspiration, and adaptability.[29]

Presthus, writing about large organizations, mainly those producing goods and services, suggests three types of people, the "upward-mobile," the "ambivalents," and the "indifferents," each a different type of personality and each evincing different behaviors.

> The upward-mobiles are those who react positively to the bureaucratic situation and succeed in it. The indifferents are the uncommitted majority who see their jobs as mere instruments to obtain off-work satisfactions. The ambivalents are a small perpetually disturbed minority who can neither renounce their claims for status and power nor play the disciplined role that would enable them to cash in on such claims.[30]

Most typologies of people having two extreme types usually need to have in between a third type of person who cannot be identified with either extreme, or who may waver, now toward one extreme, now the other. But the hard-to-achieve extreme will be much smaller than the group at the other extreme. In Presthus' three-part classification, they are the "indifferents," those with least concern about upward mobility. Some observers would call many among the indifferents "alienated."

Viewing the behavior types in the modern society from the outlook of social psychology, Thomas postulated three types. He identified the "philistine" at the conservative extreme and the "bohemian" at the other extreme. The philistine is usually more economically secure and better established socially. He stands for the arts and beauty, and for cultural change so long as it does not operate to his disadvantage. He is usually a conformist and he expects conformity. His thinking usually reflects what Galbraith calls the "conventional wisdom." To the bohemian con-

[29] Suzanne Keller, *Beyond the Ruling Class,* New York, Random House, 1968, pp. 44–47.

[30] Robert Presthus, *Organizational Society,* New York, Random House, Vintage, 1962, p. 15.

formity is something less than a virtue.[31] To him, the philistine is a "stuffed shirt."

The bohemian does not bow to the conventional wisdom. Thomas sees him as venturing, often irrationally but with zest, in one direction or another; he is ever ready to change to another course.

> The choice of a scheme by a bohemian depends on his momentary standpoint, and this may be determined either by some outburst of a primary temperamental attitude or by some isolated character attitude which makes him subject to some indiscriminately accepted influence. In either case, inconsistency is the essential feature of his activity. But, on the other hand, he shows a degree of adaptability to new conditions quite in contrast with the philistine, though his adaptability is only provisional and does not lead to a new systematic life organization.[32]

In a situation deemed to involve no social risk the philistine may deport himself as a bohemian, or a bohemian at times may exhibit the attitude of a philistine. Perhaps the youthful bohemian may become a middle-aged philistine. And the philistine, if rich, may become a collector of art objects and so vicariously touch bohemian life. Between these two types, so conspicuous in cities, Thomas postulated a third type, "the creative man" without whom a city of bohemians would be a chaotic place, and a city of philistines as deadening as Utopia.

To speak of social control in the urban community it must be kept in mind that there are many behavior codes, that norms differ from one category of people to another. There is a multitude of different expectations to which each individual is subjected. Categories of people differ in their understanding of the norms, or of certain norms, and their respect for them. This is to be expected in the urban society whose people have come together out of a great diversity of backgrounds. As a result it is also to be expected that social control will be more variegated and tenuous.

CONTROL POSITION OF THE MARGINAL MAN

In the heterogeneous urban society the trend of change is more likely to be in the direction of greater heterogeneity than toward greater homogeneity. A family gains wealth and finds its way into a higher social class; marriages across class lines occur; the son of a laborer becomes a lawyer

    31 Edward H. Volkart (Ed.), *Social Behavior and Personality, Contributions of William I. Thomas to Theory and Social Science,* New York, Social Science Research Council, 1951, p. 159.
    32 Ibid., pp. 160–161.

or an architect; a Jew marries a Christian or a Negro marries a white person; these are cultural mixtures which place each person involved in a new relationship with his own cultural background and in a strange relationship with a second cultural category in the community. He becomes a marginal person with respect to both groups, and may be stimulated to carve a niche for himself. He may also discover and ally himself with others in the same half-and-half situation.

One may also move into a marginal role merely by changing his occupation, as when an Indian from the untouchable sweeper caste becomes a schoolteacher in the village where he was born; legally he holds his position but socially he belongs wholly not even to his own caste. But precisely for this reason, if he is a person of capability, he may be sought after to help get things done. Wilson tells of the position of the "detribalized" African native who has gained some education and is able to hold a clerical job. He cannot be fully accepted by the whites from the colonial power, nor can he return to the culture of his tribe, but he is in a favored position if his country rises from colonial status to nationhood.[33]

Cowan writes about certain natives in West Africa who have had the opportunity to become more Europeanized than others and have learned some of the ways of Western civil government introduced by the outsiders. They acquire the vocabulary and tricks of political behavior and are able to push themselves into political roles and come to be accepted as leaders talking the language of impersonal democratic national government, even while being identified with the traditional authority of local chiefdoms.

> The charismatic leader has been able through the force of the personal charisma which surrounds him to reconcile some of the opposition between these two forces in African society. He has provided the necessary bridge between the purely traditional and the purely secular forces of government. . . . The function of the charismatic leader has been to provide a popular substitute for the traditional loyalties which are no longer applicable to the new representative institutions demanded by the Western democratic state.[34]

During the period from 1879 to 1910, large American industrial cities (Boston, Chicago, Cleveland, New York, and others) contained a great variety of immigrant groups, all unschooled in the ways of democratic government. Out of these marginal minority groups indigenous leaders came to the fore. They had a genius for serving people in trouble

[33] G. Wilson, "An Essay on the Economics of Detribalization in Northern Rhodesia," *Social Implications of Industrialization and Urbanization in Africa South of the Sahara*, Paris, UNESCO, 1956, p. 153.

[34] Cowan, op. cit., p. 239.

because they had skill in using the machinery of government. To the poor and uninformed they were useful functionaries, to the middle and upper classes they were a lot of "ward heelers" who traded service for votes. They did serve an important leadership function only to largely disappear once the level of political literacy of immigrants and their children was equal to others in the city, and political leaders of stature rose out of these immigrant enclaves.[35]

During the Great Depression the unemployed in Canadian cities were advised to go to the land where at least they could meet their needs for food. Many families who did so suffered privation, being as much in need as the poor in cities. Out of their midst came self-appointed, dedicated religious leaders, and various evangelical cults took form. Similar cult groups organized in the cities. Together they assumed the character of a socio-religious movement. They joined hands in a type of morale-sustaining, self-help endeavor. They saw themselves as disregarded by the affluent and unwelcome in the respectable churches. Mann described these cult groups as emphasizing "heavenly rewards, religious status, and comradely fellowship," which supplied a partial answer to social inferiority and economic vulnerability.[36]

While these minor sects preached the same fundamentalist gospel, they were unable to integrate as a political force. There were many leaders and small "inner circles." Each local leader "commonly enjoyed a position of almost unlimited importance." But it was a "counsellor-patient relationship . . . between leader and follower." The cult groups with strong leaders tried vigorously to expand in competition with other cult groups.[37]

Conspicuous among the marginal personalities in urbanized society are the intellectual elites, or intelligentsia. It is not always clear how they or the cult leaders figure in the control of society, although they cannot be called unimportant in a social control system. Keller sees their role as diverse: "to criticize, debate, challenge, and teach, to question established opinions, to explore new ideas, and to widen the experience and limited knowledge of men." [38] They have served kings and presidents and have supported rebels, speaking out or writing whether asked to or not.

Such elites are prone to cluster in certain great cities, among the artists and other bohemian types. Their way of life in Greenwich Village, once New York's "Latin Quarter," was studied by Ware, and she describes the "village" in its heyday before World War I.

[35] See Harold D. Lasswell, *Who Gets What, When, How,* New York, McGraw-Hill, 1936.
[36] W. E. Mann, "Sect, Cult and Church in Alberta," quoted in Bernard R. Blishen et al., *Canadian Society, Sociological Perspectives,* Toronto, Macmillan, 1961, p. 364.
[37] Ibid., p. 361.
[38] Keller, op. cit., p. 290.

The first group of villagers had been made up of individuals of exceptional independence, who had faced social problems with earnestness and had sought positive solutions. When the community had come to contain a large proportion of persons of ordinary caliber whose positions reflected the social situations from which they had come more than the personal quality of the individuals, the negative desire to escape took the place of any positive quest, and social earnestness gave way to a drifting attitude.[39]

For any Latin Quarter, as in Greenwich Village in the period mentioned by Ware, there is a full assortment of intelligentsia, those who make their mark as well as many who do not.

LAW AS THE ULTIMATE CONTROL AGENT

Schur calls the law a control mechanism that permeates and stands behind the various others, although there is no precise rule about when it should be used and to what extent. It is "at once an embodiment of high ideals and a means by which men can deal with the quite mundane and often messy conflicts and problems that arise in everyday living." [40] Bottomore, after describing social control as society's way of managing its members, adds that control is either by social pressure or by force, the two methods being variously interrelated.

> The ultimate sanction of law is physical coercion and physical force may enter more or less prominently into all the types of social control; public opinion may become mob violence, religious sentiment may turn to religious persecution and the burning of heretics. On the other hand, physical coercion itself is usually most effective where it can be justified by widely accepted values; and even in the most extreme case of rule by force, the ruling group itself must be bound together by other means.[41]

In the industrial urban society, large organizations created by the state, although private in purpose, are authorized to exercise certain controls over their members. A large organization, incorporated or not, if in a position of strength, may not only control its members, it may endeavor to impose restrictive controls over nonmembers, as when a medical association or a trade union effectively bar even well qualified persons from work. Etzioni, for example, noting the legitimate and non-

[39] Caroline Ware, *Greenwich Village*, quoted in Paul K. Hatt and Albert J. Reiss, Jr. (Eds.), *Reader in Urban Sociology*, New York, Free Press, 1951, p. 394.

[40] Edwin M. Schur, *Law and Society*, New York, Random House, 1968, pp. 72 and 202.

[41] T. B. Bottomore, *Sociology, A Guide to Problems and Literature*, London, Allen and Unwin, 1962, p. 211.

legitimate power exercised by private groups, points out that it is the function of the law to intercede to hold such groups in line.[42]

Aubert observes that the institutions of the law, like those of social class, interpenetrate other institutions. Whether the law is invoked or not it stands there, an effective power sustaining the accepted norms.

> Law is engaged in a battle against deviations from the rules of the other social institutions; it also offers a technique for solving conflicts which the separate institutions are unable to settle by their own means. Law thus puts force behind the norms of other institutions. However, while the norms of social stratification accept . . . the fact that actors in the various sectors of society are ranked above and below each other, law purports to treat everyone equally, even when it is not engaged in an attempt to remedy existing social inequalities.[43]

Civil law, as we recognize it, is largely the outgrowth of custom, and without it nonascriptive civil government could hardly exist. To MacIver law is much older than government. "Every society at every stage of civilization rests on a firmament of law that is vastly greater and much more intricate than any ever devised by government, one that is too great and too intricate to be completely overthrown even by the most revolutionary of governments." [44] Homans also mentions that as societies change, their ways of using the law also change but, whatever the changes, there remains the division of labor between formal law and the informal rule of custom.

> As societies grow in size, activities like religion, war and law enforcement are delegated, first to individual specialists, and then to specialized organizations, but the original basis of control always persists. Many small societies show an admirable obedience to law without having anything like law officers. Even in our own society external control is concerned with relatively few, though perhaps important, crimes, and in dealing with them can be effective only when supported by controls other than the formal law.[45]

For many people, the policeman, the most trusted and the most belabored of all public servants, symbolizes the law. To the criminal he is Public Enemy No. 1, and we see the policeman portrayed as a blockhead again and again in the movies and television, especially in detective

---

[42] Amitai Etzioni, *A Comprehensive Analysis of Complex Organizations,* New York, Free Press, 1961, p. 14.

[43] Aubert, op. cit., p. 226.

[44] Robert M. MacIver, *The Web of Government,* New York, Macmillan, 1947, p. 65.

[45] George C. Homans, *The Human Group,* London, Routledge and Kegan Paul, 1951, p. 284.

stories. Often he is used by parents to frighten their children. On his beat, says Greer, "he stands for the norms and must provide the surveillance and enforce the sanctions that maintain the rights and duties of the passerby." [46]

It is also well known that if the policeman were not on his beat, even for half a day because of a strike, the city would be in a panic as in Montreal in 1969. Such an action is more feared than a strike of medical practitioners. Thus, Johnson would say, if the policeman only walks his beat he is a force for control; he makes arrests only when he must and he knows that many who should be arrested know how to avoid him.[47]

PRIVATE ORGANIZATIONS AS GOVERNMENT

We have seen the formal, secondary group as an instrument for getting things done in the agglomerated society. The private industrial organization produces goods and services. As organizations relate to social control, the economic organization for work, for its influence on the labor market, is not without some control influence. But more important for the present subject is the organization whose central purpose is social, moral, cultural, artistic, patriotic, nature loving, and so on. Such are often called voluntary associations and often some aspect of control is crucial for them. Even an organization such as a trade union, although mainly economic in its purposes, will lend strong support to problems involving housing, recreation, health, and education, which would not attract business or industrial organizations.

In Jonesville, a town of less than 10,000, Warner found 133 organized private groups, and these reflected the social class structure as well as the organized effective control of the community. Not all adults in Jonesville were members of such voluntary associations, but some top influential people were members of several groups.[48] Forming and joining such groups is a characteristic of urban life. Apparently the more heterogeneous a community becomes, the more people feel the need of these special-interest organizations through which they can articulate their demands and protests. The more an urban man becomes integrated into the life of the community the more use he finds for various organizational memberships.[49]

[46] Scott Greer, *The Emerging City, Myth and Reality,* New York, Free Press, 1962, p. 60.

[47] Elmer H. Johnson, *Crime, Correction and Society,* Homewood, Illinois, Dorsey Press, 1964, p. 239.

[48] Warner, op. cit., pp. 116–120.

[49] Robert A. Nisbet, *Community and Power,* New York, Oxford University Press, 1962, p. 71. The earlier edition was titled *The Quest for Community.*

Keller suggests that, with the growth of population and with the growing diversity in the division of labor, the need for organization becomes imperative. With this growth and diversity the various elites appear, either to be active in forming groups or to voice the aspirations of such special-interest associations. She mentions such elites as moral or religious leaders, educators, and opinion leaders.[50]

While many organizations may not have been started by elites, they may become the milieu from which elites emerge, perhaps to form other associations. Each member of an association knows of others, and a new group may grow to have hundreds of members and become itself a formal organization, but its purposes will doubtless relate to some type of community control for which it will make demands and exert pressure on the public authority. Such organized groups, depending on their numbers or prestige, tend to become partners with government in managing the affairs of the community. We call *pluralism* the arrangement by which formal groups as private government sit at the table with the elected leaders of government who represent the entire community. Through such associations the individual is fortified vis-a-vis the central authority, and these "cellular organisms" each exert some kind or degree of pressure.[51]

One method of testing how groups, more particularly group leaders, function in the control of the organizational community is that offered by Hunter in his study of the power structure in a Southern city. His purpose was to identify the key personalities, those most likely to get things done, or most able to oppose and block the proposals of others.[52] Following Hunter's method, Miller studied a Western city, and still later a city in England. The columns presented here show the types of personalities by occupation who, in community opinion, were the local key personalities. Note that no trade unionist is named in the American cities and that seven of those in the English city were not in finance, industry, or big business. A look at the voluntary associations in each of these cities would doubtless show that these key leaders and their close allies would have memberships in the more influential associations.[53]

50 Keller, op. cit., pp. 215 and 227.

51 Milton R. Konvitz (Ed.), *Law and Social Action, Selected Essays of Alexander H. Pekelis,* Ithaca, Cornell University Press, 1950, p. 68.

52 Floyd Hunter, *Community Power Structure,* Chapel Hill, University of North Carolina Press, 1954.

53 Delbert C. Miller, "Industry and Community Power Structure, A Comparative Study of an American and an English City," *American Sociological Review,* Vol. 23, No. 1, January 1958, p. 12. For a later and similar study, see Delbert C. Miller, "Town and Gown, The Power Structure in a University Town," *American Journal of Sociology,* Vol. 68, No. 4, January 1963, p. 443.

Pacific City	English City	Southern City
1. Manufacturing executive	1. Labor Party leader	1. Utilities executive
2. Wholesale owner and investor	2. University president	2. Transport executive
3. Mercantile executive	3. Manufacturing executive	3. Lawyer
4. Real estate owner executive	4. Bishop, Church of England	4. Mayor
5. Business executive (woman)	5. Manufacturing executive	5. Manufacturing executive
6. College president	6. Citizen, party leader	6. Utilities president
7. Investment executive	7. Manufacturing executive	7. Manufacturer, owner
8. Investment executive	8. Manufacturer, owner	8. Mercantile executive
9. Bank executive investor	9. Trade union leader	9. Investment executive
10. Episcopalian bishop	10. Civic leader (woman)	10. Lawyer
11. Mayor, lawyer	11. Lawyer	11. Mercantile executive
12. Lawyer	12. Society leader	12. Merchant, owner

In a similar vein Presthus compared leadership in two small cities, one fairly prosperous and the other less so. By asking people in all walks of life to name the leaders of influence a list of names was obtained for each city. Then a list of problems having to do with health, education, street improvements, and such, which had been faced in each city during the previous five years, was obtained. The problem was to "read the record" on each key personality, what he did or did not do with respect to each of these problems. It turned out that these key persons did not operate solo but more often through the different organized groups in the city. Individual (elites) do stand out as control forces, Presthus concludes, but pluralism is not to be underestimated.[54] In theory at least, all private groups have access to the circle in which formal decision-making for managing the community is done.

THE MASS MEDIA AND SOCIAL CONTROL

The American city in 1850 impressed foreign visitors with being a quiet place; the only sounds that reached any distance were the ringing of church bells. The newspaper existed but only a minority read it. Today a message can reach millions through the printed page, the radio, the movies, and television, joining the village and the city into a single

[54] Robert Presthus, *Men at the Top, A Study in Community Power,* New York, Oxford University Press, 1964, p. 9.

audience. These mass media, say the Gouldners, "no longer depend on literacy." All can listen, but it is almost always to voices from the city, which express "the urban, the sophisticated points of view." [55] Abu-Lughod relates how in an Egyptian village rural people who cannot read gather in various stores to listen to the radios while the storekeepers and officials get their news from the daily press. The radio may not widen the horizon of the villagers greatly, since much of the news has little meaning for them, but it takes them at least one step out of their original isolation.[56]

In speaking from the city, the mass media present the same programs to ruralities and urbanites from the low classes to the top. We need not evaluate here the content of the mass media message, but we must recognize the media as having great potential for influencing behavior and values. Vidich and Bensman, speaking of a New York rural town, remark that:

> Few individuals read only the local weekly paper; the majority subscribe to dailies published in surrounding cities. . . . The mass culture and mass advertising of television and radio reach Springdale in all their variety. Television, particularly, is significant in its impact because, for the first time, the higher art forms such as ballet, opera, and plays are visible to a broad rural audience. . . . The intrusion of the mass media is so overwhelming that little scope is left for the expression of local cultural and artistic forms.[57]

Whatever control influence may be attributed to the mass media, all types of people in both rural and urban spheres are similarly exposed. It doubtless makes for much uniformity. There are contradictory opinions about the quality of the outpourings. Wilensky is of the view that one's level of education makes a difference in what he hears, views, or reads, but not much difference, "the good, the mediocre, and the trashy are becoming confused; high brows and low brows divert themselves alike." He concludes that to be integrated, one must learn to live with propaganda, with "advertising, speedy obsolescence in consumption." [58] One might ask, as many do, that if control is to be established over the mass media, by whose standards would such control be governed?

55 Alvin K. Gouldner and Helen P. Gouldner, *Modern Sociology*, New York, Harcourt, Brace & World, 1963, p. 613.
56 Ibrahim Abu-Lughod, "The Mass Media and Egyptian Village Life," *Social Forces*, Vol. 42, No. 1, October 1963, p. 101.
57 Arthur J. Vidich and Joseph Bensman, *Small Town in Mass Society*, Princeton, Princeton University Press, 1958, pp. 85, 104, and 314.
58 Harold L. Wilensky, "Mass Society and Mass Culture, Interdependence or Independence," *American Sociological Review*, Vol. 29, No. 2, April 1964, pp. 181 and 193.

THE CONTROL ASPECT OF WRITTEN RECORDS

Population increase in cities, increasing diversity of interests and occupations, and the individuating effect of moving in crowds results in a high degree of anonymous behavior. This is deplored by many who see anonymity as inducement to wrongdoing. On the other side, anonymity is seen as privacy or a kind of tolerance in human relations. Parsons suggests that anonymity is somewhat indifferent to diversity, is flexible, and permits change. It is "the necessary price of dynamic openness to progressive change." [59]

In order to function with the order needed, this kind of society, in most of its contacts, formal and transient, has been evolving that type of formal control which we call bureaucracy. Whatever else it may be, bureaucracy is a system for making and preserving records, pertinent information retained for future reference. Without this function a bureaucracy would be next to useless. The records in the files of public and private offices have now become a control device with scores of uses. They tell what was said by whom and when, they name the witnesses, they show precisely what was paid and what is due, they contain one's school record and his work record, they give information about every formal contact one has had with a public office or private agency, and they preserve even those telltale records called fingerprints so feared by every major offender.

To the criminal, even the "one-timer" with a minor conviction, a "record" is a fearful thing, especially when he must find a job. But people with "nothing to hide" may be equally conscious of information about them to be found in many files. The sophisticated citizen who is much in the public eye learns the importance of putting desired information "on the record," and he learns how to keep unfavorable information "off the record." Private agencies, as well as governments, have come to recognize the importance of "privileged" personal records and they are kept in confidence. However, the secrecy of records is never complete, certain private records can be viewed by order of a court. While most public records are confidential, they still may be used impersonally for statistical purposes. The main point is that people may often be seriously concerned about the uses made of information about them which has been recorded in public or private files. In their concern, a degree of social control results.

[59] Talcott Parsons, *The Social System*, New York, Free Press, 1951, p. 309.

SOCIAL CONTROL, AN URBAN QUESTION

Much that is written about social problems and deviance from the norms is associated with urban life. The primary controls identified with small groups are common to rural and urban societies. But the secondary controls mentioned in this chapter, those which inhere in large formal organizations and in the civil law, are of urban origin, although they now extend to rural society as well. When we considered the problems of control and change, it had to do with various aspects of the change-over from rural to urban ways. The dynamic urban life demands adaption on the part of seasoned urbanites as well as newcomers to the city. People adapt to change at different rates. Those slowest to adapt, or unwilling to adapt at all may point the accusing finger at those who adapt too readily. But there are behaviors which are deviant by any standards, robbery, for example.

There have always been those who see the city itself as a problem, and it is that in so far as it not only exists but often thrives without much guidance from man. Men, coming under its influence, tend to behave at times in unpredictable ways. Human behavior in the early rural community was often quite predictable although rural life was never without its deviants. Brownell, who would have us all return to something like the old rural community life sees urban man in a whirlpool that can only pull him under.

> For direct cooperation in the community, the elite accept the vast but often fictitious solidarity of more or less massive groups. In these great groups a man is related for the most part to people he does not and cannot know well. They are abstract and usually fragmented persons as far as they enter his experience. The solidarity of such a group is specialized. It is abstract. It can be expressed only by indirection and far-fetched symbols. Cant, falsehoods, or just talk may then replace the native solidarities of action.[60]

But cities, says Jacobs, have always symbolized freedom from the less free life of the rural and primitive places.

> In real life, barbarians (and peasants) are the least free of men—bound by tradition, ridden by caste, fettered by superstitions, riddled by suspicion and foreboding of whatever is strange. "City life makes free," was the medieval saying, when city air literally did make free the runaway serf. City air still makes free the runaways from company towns, from

---

[60] Baker Brownell, *The Human Community*, New York, Harper & Row, 1950, p. 20.

plantations, from factory farms, from subsistence farms, from migrant picker routes, from mining towns, from one-class suburbs.[61]

Arriving in the city, these newcomers, like those who manage to escape a slum existence, must learn the changing ways of the city. As often as not, they do not do well at it. The control system is there, but it does not stand like the Rock of Ages; changes in the norms are under way through the workings of one hand while the other hand is occupied with enforcement. Some writers, Becker especially so, see something like hypocrisy in society's behavior toward deviants.[62] In the case of such students of deviancy so much criticism is made of the derelictions of society that, doubtlessly unintended, the impression is conveyed that the delinquent is really the victim. He is seen as deviant largely because society defines what deviancy is.[63]

[61] Jane Jacobs, *The Death and Life of Great American Cities,* New York, Random House, 1961, p. 144.

[62] Howard S. Becker, *The Outsiders,* New York, Free Press, 1963.

[63] For an examination of this issue and some of the personalities involved, see Alvin W. Gouldner, "The Sociologist as Partisan, Sociology and the Welfare State," *The American Sociologist,* Vol. 3, No. 2, May 1968, pp. 103–116.

The urban habitat and urban planning | 18

ENVIRONMENTAL AND WELFARE PLANNING

In 1900 it would have been unusual to hear a businessman or even a high public official talk about urban planning. It was of interest only to a few intellectuals and high society people. The dominant theme then was "the City Beautiful" which concerned mainly the showplace aspect of limited spots at the urban center occupied by impressive buildings, imposing monuments, artistic fountains, perhaps a promenade and a park. The rest of the city was given little attention except by volunteer welfare workers who spoke of slums and poverty.

Today planning is a respectable term at all levels and in all circles; business and industry, social welfare and recreation, education and health, as well as being a professional pursuit of engineers, architects, and social scientists. An expression like this from a mortgage and housing corporation official in Toronto would have been strange reading in 1900.

> The end product of all our civic endeavors—the city itself—is not merely a matter of governments and their planners, although they have a prime role in the development. It is equally a matter for industry, and all the voluntary associations that make up our democratic way. The city, like the garden, has to be redreamed periodically, reviewed, recast, renewed, revived. What we now have in buildings, streets, shops, institutions, is quite recent in the history of mankind; they do not represent the alpha and omega, the beginning and the end, of city growth.[1]

That idea is gaining wide acceptance. Whatever planning may mean, it is never finished; the best for one generation is already "dated" for

[1] Remarks by Stewart Bates, President, Central Mortgage and Housing Corporation, to the University of Toronto Round Table on "Man and Industry," November 3, 1958, p. 7.

the next. Another view is that planning is rarely local and cannot isolate itself. Thus Soule sees planning in national terms, the slum is part of a city and the city is central to a region but the regional belongs more to the nation than to any state.[2] A region may include parts of several states. It is rarely that states can cooperate on planning either to utilize or conserve natural resources, or control industry to insure continuous employment. Such planning needs to be a joint effort of the public and private sectors, but the leadership and control must be public. A book edited by Warner focuses on the large city with the networks of cities in mind. The nation to this group of writers is a nation of cities. Much about urban planning that was orthodox two decades ago is absent in this volume. Instead, the primary attention is on planning for work and welfare.

> At present, American society influences the way people live in three strong ways; by the kinds of jobs cities offer, by the kinds of physical settings cities possess, and by the public services cities furnish. National and metropolitan employment are not generally dealt with as ingredients of urban planning, yet they are the first subjects that must be mastered if physical planning and public services are to be complementary. The world of urban work not only determines the personal income of city dwellers, it also is a major determinant of urban styles of life.[3]

Those who take this wider look at urban and metropolitan planning are strongly of the opinion that planning in the wider sense (counting people in) cannot be realized if left to local and state governments. The task is far too complex and must be assumed by the national government. The problems, says Dyckman, have changed radically and are now changing moreso.

> We have moved from an era of great rural-urban differences to one in which the greatest social and economic differences may be found within the city itself. The cities in turn have tended to grow together in large supercity systems. These in turn are linked in a national jet airport network, in which the small city airports feed the regional jet ports. The latter are linked in a world system. Corporate mergers and reorganization have produced new international grants, usually headquartered in New York.[4]

The very title of this book, "The Industrial Urban Community," commits us to a wider look at planning than the mere physical and

2 George Soule, *Planning U.S.A.*, New York, Viking, 1967, p. 16.

3 Sam Bass Warner, Jr. (Ed.), *Planning for a Nation of Cities*, Cambridge, The M.I.T. Press, 1966, p. iv.

4 John W. Dyckman, "The Public and Private Rationale for a National Urban Policy," in ibid., p. 24.

spatial, important as these be. The habitat is a proper interest for those specialists concerned with things and structures and their arrangement. But people are there too, in all sorts of group arrangements, engaged in all sorts of activities, which give meaning to the physical layout.

IMPLICATIONS OF BEAUTY AND ORDER

A prime demand of community habitants is the practical one that the arrangements of things serve their convenience. If there is a market place, it should be most accessible to the greatest number. This also may be true of the church and the school, but these would not push the market place aside. Meeting these demands of convenience gives to the community an aspect of order. People also have some degree of expectation regarding the attractiveness of things in their community, an expectation to which the term, "beauty," may be assigned, meaning that which pleases, or at least does not offend.

Beauty, which is art and order to Hayakawa, is a quality of its own. "Indeed, sometimes the internal order and neat relationships of the parts to each other in a novel may be so impressive that we enjoy it in spite of a lack of sympathy with the kinds of incidents or the people portrayed." [5] Beauty, besides being visually pleasing, reflects the order that satisfies because it serves with minimum inconvenience, but this second quality is not always the primary test of beauty for many planners.

Iverson describes the initial plan for New Ulm, Minnesota, which was the idea of one of the German farmers, one of the idealistic group who settled there in the early 1850's. The area comprised 9,000 acres (land bought at $1.25 per acre, worth more than $500 per acre now). Christian Prignitz, who died before the planning profession was born, would have a town with work for all, with big elm trees (New Elm named for Ulm (elm), Germany). It was a community that would accept the change that growth would bring, a good place to see and to live in. This idea of beauty, Iverson reports, is still present in New Ulm.[6] The idea of beauty in the New Ulm plan related not to the scene alone, but it served the work needs of the farmers, due in time to be prosperous. This is, says Mumford, what most people expect, even though they do not talk much about it. "But for even the humblest person, a day spent without the sight or sound of beauty, the contemplation of mystery, or

[5] S. I. Hayakawa, *Language in Thought and Action*, New York, Harcourt, Brace & World, 1949, p. 152.

[6] Noel Iverson, *Germania, USA*, Minneapolis, University of Minnesota Press, 1966, p. 62.

the search for truth and perfection is a poverty-stricken day; and a succession of such days is fatal to human life." [7]

Not only do planners, architects, engineers, and others differ among themselves regarding a plan as it relates to the urban community, people who are not experts will have different views. The art-conscious tourist, looking at the downtown of a city, will have opinions very different from those of a real estate man, or a taxi driver born in the slum of that city. No matter how a city is built or may be rebuilt there would be disagreement. Thus Greer and Miner suggest that what planners strive for is "intrinsically right," but they fail to serve the diversity of views because there are so many ideas about beauty and order. [8]

PLANNING SCHEMES AND THE METROPOLIS

There is probably no world city that can be called the result of a plan, and there is probably not one that is today being guided in its growth and changes, in complete terms, by a plan. However, plans do exist for most world cities, plans in the sense of there being long-term objectives. Since even the wisest planner is not able to foresee all contingencies that lurk in the future, ten, five, or even two years ahead, the enforcement of plans turns out to be one compromise after another. Washington, D.C., began as a planned city, but the plan envisioned a much smaller city, not the metropolis which today is much hampered because of the plan.

The best known of cities founded by kings is Versailles, initiated by Louis XIV in 1661. It survives as a showpiece symbolic of a period in art and architecture and, like many royal plans, a monument to an individual. Greer has a good word for some of those cities "planned by mandate;" they allowed space for work, play, and living. [9] He would probably say that of Mannheim, Germany, started in 1720, 136 squares enclosed by a wall. Today, however, the old Mannheim is surrounded by the new and much of its old pattern is blotted out.

Certain American cities began as planned communities. For example, William Penn gave Philadelphia its austere gridiron pattern in 1682, and James Oglethorpe in 1733 designed a unique plan for Savannah. What was thought to be a sophisticated plan for Washington, but now called a "mess," was laid out in 1791. Buffalo in 1804 and Detroit in

[7] Lewis Mumford, *The Condition of Man,* New York, Harcourt, Brace & World, 1944, p. 420.

[8] Scott Greer and David Miner, "The Political Side of Urban Development and Redevelopment," *Annals of the American Academy of Political and Social Science,* Vol. 352, March 1964, pp. 63–73.

[9] Guy Greer, *Your City Tomorrow,* New York, Macmillan, 1947, p. 1.

1807 began as planned cities, but went on growing in a *laissez faire* fashion. The "heaven-revealed" plan for Salt Lake City and other Mormon towns, with uncomfortably wide streets, dates from 1847. It was designed mainly for an agricultural people.

The typical American town plan of straight streets and rectangular plots of land is a heritage of public land ownership. Land was given or sold by the government on the basis of the "section," a square mile which, however subdivided, comprised rectangular units and no curves; even those imposed by nature were ignored by the engineer. Bowles mentions how San Francisco, with its many hills did not fit the gridiron pattern but, just the same, streets went straight up steep hills and straight down.[10] The unimaginative grid town pattern lives on to the everlasting distress of architect and planners who would have street patterns fit the contours of the land.

Except in Latin America where the plaza-centered town of Spain was copied in some cases, cities in the New World were little influenced by those of the mother countries. In the United States planning was limited mainly to expediency decisions, meeting problems as they came. However, around 1900 two opposite types of planning movements got under way, the City Beautiful and the Garden City. The City Beautiful concept began in Chicago with the 1893 World Fair. Of this Jacobs writes:

> The aim of the City Beautiful was the City Monumental. Great schemes were drawn up for systems of baroque boulevards which mainly came to nothing. What did come out of the movement was the Center Monumental, modeled on the fair. City after city built its civic center or its cultural center. . . . However they were arranged, the important point was that the monuments had been sorted out from the rest of the city, and assembled into the grandest effect thought possible, the whole being treated as a complete unit in a separate and well-defined way. People were proud of them, but the centers were not a success. For one thing, invariably the ordinary city around them ran down instead of being uplifted.[11]

The Garden City idea is traced to England and to a man named Ebenezer Howard, who would have the working class leave the city to establish more spacious communities outside. In his plan these would not be commuters' suburbs but whole communities with factories to provide employment. Various such projects were initiated in England

---

[10] Samuel Bowles, *Our New West,* Hartford, 1869, quoted by Charles N. Glaab (Ed.), *The American City, A Documentary History,* Homewood, Illinois, Dorsey Press, 1963, p. 200.

[11] Jane Jacobs, *The Death and Life of Great American Cities,* New York, Random House, 1961, p. 24.

and the United States, only to be swallowed later by the expanding city. The idea may have stimulated interest in suburbs. The suburban movement speeded without guidance, once low-cost rapid transit from the city center out was available. Whereas the City Beautiful idea was concerned only with the heart of the city, ignoring the rest of the body, the Garden City aim was to escape the city and was not concerned with the whole of which it was a part. It aimed to bring urban life and work to the country in what Howard called a "perfect combination." Tunnard suggests that the country according to this notion of planning would be the "unhappy partner in this forced marriage." [12] Like the City Beautiful with fluent champions still, the Garden City idea lives on and is ever popular among those who think of city planning in terms of escape; Howard's book [13] still has ardent readers.

THE URBAN COMMUNITY AND ITS REGION

As we have noted, planning for the urban community is no longer limited to structures and spatial arrangements with an eye to beauty and order, even though there are increasing numbers of experts who concentrate on special fields: transportation, parks and open spaces, or the "heart" of the city. The wider vision considers not only the habitat but planning for full employment, health and recreation, and livable houses. We noted, too, that planning to make the urban community a good place in which to live is no mere local matter, for communities are linked together in interdependent networks. Each town and city has its own hinterland which is an aspect of itself. Paris, as the tourist sees it, is only part of a metropolitan expanse of 5,000 square miles and an agglomerate of 8.5 million people. Redick sees the borders of Rangoon, Burma, as indefinite. The region of that city assumes a different shape for each service performed; the dispenser of the service is in the city, the recipients widely dispersed.[14]

We think of the central city and the metropolitan region as serving each other in a symbiotic relationship. To speak of a region assumes a city central to it. However, this does not apply to one of the most ambitious regional development schemes, the Tennessee Valley Authority,

12 Christopher Tunnard, *The City of Man*, New York, Scribner, 1953, p. 236. A summary of these movements is found in Thomas Adams, *Outline of Town and City Planning*, New York, Russell Sage Foundation, 1936.

13 Ebenezer Howard, *Garden Cities of Tomorrow*, 3rd ed., E. J. Osburn (Ed.), London, Faber and Faber, 1945.

14 Richard W. Redick, "A Demographic and Ecological Study of Rangoon, Burma, 1953," in Ernest W. Burgess and Donald J. Bogue (Eds.), *Contributions to Urban Sociology*, Chicago, University of Chicago Press, 1964, p . 40.

which embraces a river valley and spreads into seven southern states. No metropolis commands this region, although in time one of the larger cities may become one. This great project for reclaiming depressed areas was established by the federal government as a public corporation in 1933. Its purpose was to reclaim wasted and eroded farm lands, reforest the denuded hills, and produce electric power in abundance.[15] Soule pronounces the TVA a world famous example of reclaiming a region laid waste by man and of capturing unused resources. Its power plants in 1965 produced nearly 15 million kilowatt-hours of electric power, and have brought to the valley industries that could not have been tempted before.[16]

The TVA illustrates what the wholeness of a natural region means and the importance of conserving the resources contained therein. The region of a metropolis need not be a natural geographical area; nor does its position need to be in a river basin where commerce meets the ships from the sea, as Montreal, for example, or Portland, or Calcutta. The region of a city, as that of New York, may reach over valleys by land transport. London, for instance, is no longer a city at a key point in a river valley. Its region is only partly the land area of its back yard, its front yard is global, which is true of other world cities. For such a great city to carry on its far-flung functions, considerable elbow room is needed. Its growth and changes may assume diverse, seemingly illogical aspects, as Robson notes looking at Greater London and its 143 authorities, mostly local and many created to meet some long-ago need. But there is often no authority for coping with today's urgent urban problems. For example, he says there is no attempt to control the location of in-dustries or building developments. We could say the same for 1970. There are limited controls but total control is not likely. The many planning authorities in the London metropolitan region make for con-fusion when confronted with wider planning needs, which Robson de-claims. This, too, is a continuing perplexity in a metropolitan region where the best plans of today will be outmoded a few years hence. Selfish interests may resist a good plan, but all who resist may not do so for selfish reasons.[17]

Metropolitan planning in Britain is only now accepting a wider perspective, but this is equally true of the United States, where as yet no single planning authority for metropolitan regions exists. This need can be met only on the initiative of the federal government.

[15] Philip Selznick, *TVA and the Grass Roots*, Berkeley, University of California Press, 1949.

[16] Soule, op. cit., p. 129.

[17] William A. Robson (Ed.), "London," in *Great Cities of the World*, London, Allen and Unwin, 1957, p. 292.

REGIONAL CHALLENGES TO PLANNING

As industrial countries become more populous, as their cities grow and more space is taken for residence and work, the more precarious becomes the man-land relationship. It is expected that, with population growth, the food supply problem of the world will tighten, but the water and clean air supply for urban agglomerates is already tightening. Europe's rivers, especially the Rhine, have become so polluted that fish life has about vanished. Along the Atlantic Seaboard in the United States, cities compete for water, but the water sources are being polluted and, at great cost, water must be purified. As cities and industries grow, more pollution is thrown in the environment. The turning point from indifference to public interest came in 1964 when the Governor of New York announced that New York was launching an anti-pollution program. The press took up the cry and the anti-pollution fad was launched.[18]

Various other writers have been calling our attention to the growing hazard of water pollution, mainly since about 1960, pointing to the vanishing fish life in North American streams and freshwater bodies. Most streams and rivers in the populous parts of the United States have become a hazard for bathing and less attractive for camping or water sports. Among these writers, Mitchell Gordon has noted a most severe crisis respecting the supply of fresh air and clean water.[19]

Gottmann reminds us that along the Atlantic Seaboard, on a twentieth of the land area of the United States live a fifth of the population, the pearl of the urbanized areas in the world. Men have created here the most productive of urbanized industrial regions. Now the health and general welfare of the millions living here is facing a critical challenge. "The people are now wealthier, better educated and better endowed with technological means than ever. They ought to be able to find ways of avoiding decline of the area." [20]

For a metropolis to keep itself clean and healthy means to establish strict control over the water for leagues around. If the air is polluted to the extent that nylons are disintegrated by the fumes from factories, or if lungs are infected by pollutants in the air, that calls for control over all establishments and machines that exhaust fumes. More control is

---

[18] The Governor's message is well reported in *The New York Herald-Tribune,* December 29, 1964, p. 18. More pertinent to the present is George R. Stewart, *Not So Rich as You Think,* Boston, Houghton Mifflin, 1968.

[19] Mitchell Gordon, *Sick Cities,* New York, Macmillan, 1963, pp. 84–95.

[20] Jean Gottmann, *Megalopolis, The Urbanized Northeastern Seaboard of the United States,* New York, Twentieth Century Fund, 1961, p. 12.

needed than can be legally imposed, for example, in Britain, Canada, or the United States. In central Canada is a smelter whose fumes have destroyed vegetation for miles around, impoverished farmers, killed live stock, and endangered the health of people. It has not been resolved whether control is a responsibility of the province or the Canadian government. Alderson mentions how wide-reaching problems cannot be met because each small area insists on planning control for its own district. And these groups are in most cases too small for effective and expert operation.

> Because of their smallness they cannot afford the necessary specialists. Because of their smallness, there are too many of them either for effective cooperation or effective coordination by the central Government. Lastly, because of their smallness, it is common for people to live under the jurisdiction of one planning authority but to work under the jurisdiction of another.[21]

If Britain is plagued by too much decentralization of planning authority, France exemplifies the other extreme. National Planning there is balked by an ingrown, traditional proclivity for centralized decision making, but economic planning for the diversities of a nation calls for degrees of local and regional decision making. The plans for the economic guidance of France have provided for regional offices, and plans have been worked out for regions. But decision making does not get transferred from the head offices at Paris to the regions, nor is the region always consulted when Paris makes decisions. Bauchet notes that "More often than not, the regional development associations are simply a screen for the big organizations in Paris. Local authorities have less and less control over the decisions of the private financiers." [22] While every city is problem laden at any time, those with acute problems at this time are the most developed of cities. They are faced with the urgent need to deal with water and air pollution. These cities, much as other cities around the world must also provide housing for the poor. If not aware of it now, most cities will be asked to provide out-of-city recreation areas. More and more as the world's population concentrates in urban centers, as they are now doing, cities will be increasingly plagued by the problem of water shortage. Those responsible for planning will find their efforts increasingly resisted by vested interests who argue, as does Hayek, that public planning is an invasion of individual freedom.[23]

[21] Stanley Alderson, *Britain in the Sixties, Housing,* London, Pelican, 1962, p. 154.
[22] Pierre Bauchet, *Economic Planning, The French Experience,* translated by Dauphne Woodward, London, Heinemann, 1964, p. 57.
[23] Friedrich A. Hayek, *Individualism and Economic Order,* London, Routledge and Kegan Paul, 1947, p. 27.

THE SOCIAL IMPERATIVES OF PLANNING

Such urgent problems as air and water pollution, housing for the masses, and recreational space for an urbanized population, are the concerns of settled communities. They are in part the consequences of communities not having "lived right," of neglect, and heedless self-interest. A commission of wise men laying out a new city could avoid most of these ills and fashion a city in which people would be able to live the good life. Such a city has been laid out in the Orinoco Valley of Venezuela, three hundred miles from Caracas. It is known as Ciudad Guayana. The city is near a falls in the river where power can be developed, and the region is rich in minerals, metals, and petroleum. There is no problem of space planning because the government owns the land and the organization in control is a public corporation on the order of the Tennessee Valley Authority. Rodwin, whom we quote, and other professional planners are guiding the development. This is an informal group operating with a free hand. They are trying to build a city that will be a pleasant home and will afford the good life, but they are not yet sure what the drawbacks of a drawing-board city will be. Ciudad Guayana grows and is prosperous, but who can predict its future? "All in all it is a unique situation; a new city planted by a tour de force in an isolated frontier region." Rodwin tells of some of the problems encountered in the development of the city:

> The persistent shortages of staff . . . made it clear that one of the hardest tasks is to determine not only what must be done but also what problems the policy-maker must live with, given the constraints and opportunities. For the same reason it has proved even more difficult to innovate than appeared possible at first. Experiments must be few and critical and adequate means must be devised for getting feedback from them.[24]

In the planning of this city consideration was given not only to space uses and arrangements, but to employment, living conditions, and public amenities. What makes this an unusual planned industrial city is that the social imperatives are not being overlooked. But social planning cannot foresee future needs and tastes. This phase must be a step-by-step matter; yet the answers must be sought in advance.

Such an outlook had no place in the City Beautiful approach to laying out the downtowns in American cities when, as Pomeroy remarks, the engineers were more in control than now.

[24] Lloyd Rodwin, "Ciudad Guayana, A New City," *Scientific American*, Vol. 213, No. 3, September 1965, pp. 130 and 131.

If the "City-Beautiful" people had *not* been effective by reason of being somewhat visionary, the engineers probably did more damage to cities by reason of the fact that they *were effective*. They were interested in widening streets and building things and somehow tended to overlook what might be called the soul of the city, to which the city-beautiful people had to some degree been sensitive.[25]

Of the time Pomeroy has in mind, around 1900, the ordinary engineers and architects sold their services to the landowner who erected buildings on their properties, and the buildings wanted were the kind that would be the most profitable to the owners, whether used as residences or work places. These owners were not concerned with beauty as expressed in design or arrangement. If an owner's land could not be used for industry, there was the possibility of erecting low-cost tenements, which were in demand, especially if located near factories. This was the history of many of the smaller slums in American cities, the so-called "interstitial" areas. Tenements occupied high-value land until the opportune time when they would be replaced by more profitable buildings.

An area which may be identified as a slum by official standards is presumably eligible to be replaced by some urban renewal project. Gans describes "federal and local housing standards which are applied to slum areas" as reflecting the "value patterns of upper middle-class professionals." He adds that life in the slums is evaluated by professionals by the same middle-class values.[26] Earlier planners, their attention on City Beautiful appearance, ignored the slum, whereas city planners a generation later saw it as a public virtue to remove slums, leaving the dispossessed families to find new quarters. Today, in theory at least, it is seen as a responsibility of a renewal project to help the dislocated to find other housing and, as far as possible, better housing. There is emerging an official attitude towards slums and their dwellers, even though reflecting middle-class values, which assumes it a public responsibility to improve things, and this is new.[27]

A unique feature of British town and country planning since about 1950 has been the tendency to make sociological studies of cities and their regions as supplementary to the more technical studies relating to streets and structures. One such that should be noticed was done by Glass and associates of Middlesbrough. In this study the town was seen in relation to its suburbs, taking account of social, cultural, and educational needs.[28]

[25] Hugh R. Pomeroy, "The Planning Process and Public Participation," in Gerald Breese and Dorothy E. Whiteman (Eds.), *An Approach to Urban Planning*, Princeton, Princeton University Press, 1953, p. 36.

[26] Herbert J. Gans, *The Urban Villagers*, New York, Free Press, 1962, p. 309.

[27] Ibid., pp. 321–328.

[28] Ruth Glass (Ed.), *The Social Background of a Plan*, London, Routledge and Kegan Paul, 1948, p. 12.

Middlesbrough managed for centuries without the benefit of planning, but now it was becoming urban in a new way. People were moving about more and a degree of decentralization was taking place. Questions were being asked about where people should live and where industries should be put, about conserving the old and still be in step with the new. The change taking place needed to be brought under a degree of guidance, but what guidance? Instead of the topsy-turvy aspect, Glass saw the need of pulling "the parts together." [29]

Injecting the social imperatives into planning is illustrated by the trend under way in Toronto. This is the only metropolis in North America which has been relieved of the city-suburbs struggle. The eleven or twelve suburban towns have been joined with Toronto under a single metropolitan authority, and this authority has responsibility for sewerage and water supply, transportation, housing and building control, recreational areas, welfare, health, education, and other general urban functions. Yet in Toronto, as in other cities, there are happy promotors who believe a bigger city is a better one, and they talk of a metropolitan area of seven million by 1981. A Toronto paper warns that much is to be done to make the city a better place to live, and calls attention to some urgent but neglected social challenges.

> If that happens, Toronto could become another megapolitan chaos, an asphalt jungle, a prison for its people. But if we can plan to seize this great potential and channel it intelligently we have the chance to produce a really fine city, one that will work well and be a source of pride and pleasure to its citizens. It is a tremendous challenge, a great responsibility and a wonderful opportunity.[30]

THE SUBURBS AND THE CENTRAL CITY

Large industrial cities are decentralizing ever faster as low-cost rapid transportation becomes available. Central cities are losing population and industries to the suburban communities by which they are surrounded; especially in the United States this is becoming a serious problem. A considerable share of the working population in upper occupations have their jobs in the central city and their residences outside. Industries that move attract to suburban areas a good share of the skilled and semiskilled workers. Central cities are losing the community leadership elites and are also losing income. Central areas, as a result, are becoming excessively populated with the very poor.

In Table 30 we see how the ten largest cities fared in relation to their metropolitan areas. There were 225 Standard Metropolitan Statis-

29 Ibid., p. 15.
30 Toronto, *Globe and Mail*, September 26, 1966, p. 8.

Table 30   Population in the Largest Metropolitan Areas in the
United States, and Percentage of Area Population in
Central Cities, in 1960 and 1950

| | Population in the metropolitan area | | Central city as percent of the metropolitan area | |
Cities by size rank	1960	1950	1960	1950
1. New York	10,694,633	9,555,943	72.9	82.6
2. Chicago	6,220,913	5,117,868	57.7	69.9
3. Los Angeles—Long Beach	6,038,771	4,151,687	46.7	53.5
4. Philadelphia	4,342,897	3,671,048	46.6	56.4
5. Detroit	3,762,360	3,016,197	44.4	61.3
6. San Francisco—Oakland	2,648,762	2,135,762	41.8	53.8
7. Boston	2,595,481	2,410,572	26.8	33.3
8. Pittsburgh	2,405,435	2,213,236	25.5	30.5
9. St. Louis	2,104,669	1,755,334	35.6	48.8
10. Washington, D.C.	2,001,897	1,464,089	38.6	54.9
Total	42,815,818	35,552,008	51.1	61.7
For the 225 metropolitan areas	116,584,421	92,138,060	50.4	57.4

Source: *The World Almanac,* 1966, 380–382.

tical Areas in the United States in 1960. For almost all of these cities
metropolitan growth has been mainly outside the central city; the central cities lost population or gained at a slower rate. The extreme case
among the ten cities shown here is Boston, 801,444 in 1950 declining to
697,197 in 1960. For St. Louis the population declined from 856,796 to
750,026. Many use the emotionally loaded word "sprawl" to describe
this trend, but the trend is quite normal. The difficulty is that the central city is politically isolated from wide areas which are economically,
socially, and culturally parts of itself.

Canada and the United States have inherited the English tradition
of strong local government which, however precious in preindustrial
times, no longer serves. Canada is breaking the tradition by forming wide
metropolitan public authorities. A similar trend appears to be likely in
the United States. Britain is also beginning to break with the tradition.
For the 10 million people in the 2,525 square miles of Greater London
there is now a single police control and a regional transportation authority. However, for most of the everyday relations between a city and its
region, the British metropolis is no more free of problems than the American. After his study of city-suburb relations for Manchester, Green
wrote:

> There is no authority charged with the fundamental responsibility of
> *regional* planning and control over development. . . . Its planning ob-
> jective is the balanced local community of housing, commerce, industry

and recreation; an objective completely outmoded by the transformations of the region's social and economic structure. . . . The local communities are necessarily unbalanced, specialized and dependent; and their function and character can be understood only in the context of the region.[31]

It may be said that with the exodus, especially of the elites, to the suburbs, as many are insisting, the large city has assumed a community consciousness of a secondary, conventional sort. Now it is recognized that the suburban growth is also affecting town life outside. Smith claims the once self-sufficient town is losing out.

The point here that needs emphasizing is the fact that the towns have been drawn into the national community and made a part of it. In the process they have lost many of their traditional characteristics. In some towns, as Granville Hicks observed [*Small Town*, 1946], "the old controls have disintegrated, and no new controls, whether operating from within the individual or imposed from the outside, have been developed." [32]

Actually, the many parts of the metropolitan area are linked in matters of economic exchange, of cultural values, and in their leisures, but this is not the old personal linkages of a century ago. The 1956 survey report of the Detroit Area study found that whereas formerly it was usual for newcomers to settle first in the central city and then move outward, today they are just as likely to settle first in a suburb. Moreover most house-to-house moves are outward, from the central city to a near suburb, from a near suburb to a far one.[33]

While all the parts of the complex metropolis are interlinked in their exchange patterns, each also has a type of subordinated identity. People try to escape to middle-class or elite suburbs to gain space and the illusion of a rural atmosphere. But these escapees who live on and by the central city are too urbanized to accept rurality in fullness. Furthermore, if they wished to find the idealized rural small town they would be hard put, for every remote village strives to be identified with urban ways.[34] Even if the urban escapee finds the suitable suburb, he will not enjoy it for long. The suburb of the upper elite tends slowly to be invaded by the lesser elite, becomes crowded, and the upper elite must escape once more. As a concomitant trend, urban expansion leads

[31] L. P. Green, *Provincial Metropolis, The Future of Local Government in Southeast Lancashire,* London, Allen and Unwin, 1959, p. 201.

[32] Page Smith, *As a City Upon a Hill,* New York, Knopf, 1966, p. 301.

[33] *A Social Profile of Detroit, 1956,* Report of the Detroit Area Study, Ann Arbor, University of Michigan Press, 1957, p. 17.

[34] Smith, op. cit., concluding chapter stresses this thought.

to other than residential encroachments on suburban space as, for example, by industry and commerce.[35]

Suburbs tend increasingly to be specialized occupational areas outside the city. Residential suburbs tend to be occupied by socio-economic levels of population: upper class, middle class, working class, with here and there a suburban slum. Other suburbs are the so-called industrial parks, and various areas are set aside for recreation. They represent so many more or less independent units, seldom cooperating with one another, even on common matters, but they usually agree in opposing the central city in rivalries that are never resolved.

Dye is one who believes that by discussion competing suburbs can come to agreement, that even suburbs and the central city can resolve their problems by discussion. "Bargaining is made possible by the fact that conflict, while a basic form of interaction among metropolitan communities, is not necessarily of a non-zero type." He sees harm in imposing decisions on rival communities; they are often not comprehensive solutions, and may even ignore the virtues of political diversity.[36] There is almost no evidence that major decisions have been reached by such bargaining, or evidence that suburbs have successfully bargained with central cities. On the other hand, there are many cases of the most patient efforts failing. The metropolitan consolidations in Canada were imposed by provincial authority.

TRANSPORTATION AND METROPOLITAN PLANNING

Medieval cities were less concerned about making roads than building walls. Modern cities cannot tolerate walls but lay great stress on roads. Farmers were never great road builders. Before the arrival of the automobile agricultural groups usually opposed bond issues for road building. Before the railroads came, in the United States as in Western Europe, great emphasis was placed on building canals, but it was an urban demand. The first roads built in England and the United States were the semiprivate toll roads, which were promoted by business and industry in the cities. The rural attitude in the industrial countries is presently highly favorable to good roads, especially among farmers who own tractors and automobiles.

The five types of transportation (cheapest to costliest per ton-mile) are water routes, pipelines (mainly for oil or water), railroad, highway, and air routes. The efficiency of each of these carriers, with time, has

---

[35] Harold M. Mayer, "A Survey of Urban Geography," in Philip M. Hauser and Leo F. Schnore (Eds.), *The Study of Urbanization,* New York, Wiley, 1966, p. 99.

[36] Thomas R. Dye, "Metropolitan Integration by Bargaining Among Sub-Areas," *American Behavioral Scientist,* Vol. 5, No. 9, May 1962, p. 11.

increased in meeting the transportation needs of industries and cities. Industry is indeed the creator of the pipelines, railroads, and airplanes.

It is in order here to mention pipelines as they are used to transport fresh water to cities, a form of transportation that is rarely noticed. For big cities this carrier may deliver more tonnage than the others combined, often over hundreds of miles. The average daily per capita consumption in the United States is about 130 gallons. How much is used depends less on domestic demand than on the amount and types of industry in a city. Domestic uses, however, have tended to increase, more than doubling since 1900.[37] From information assembled by Gordon, 25,000 gallons of water are needed to make a ton of paper, 65,000 gallons for a ton of steel, and 200,000 gallons for producing a ton of rayon fiber.[38] This gigantic job of underground transport, exceeding all urban surface transport, may be used in some form, as some experts predict, as a flow-carrier for goods entering or being shipped from the metropolis.

Insofar as conveyance need causes a problem of transporting live bodies and goods, it is less one of movement between widely separated points and more one within central cities or their metropolitan areas. The problem is seen in degrees of traffic congestion at in-city points during peak-load hours. It is largely a consequence of the industrial work system which requires that all places of work, being interconnected, begin and stop at strokes of the clock. Dyckman sees the problem getting more acute as a population becomes affluent.

> Improvements in living standards have contributed almost as much to the growth of cities as contemporary urban traffic conditions. Expectations of greater comfort and convenience, as well as the ability to sustain higher costs have affected the choice of both residence and mode of travel. The transportation plight of cities—at least in the prosperous, developed countries of the world—is a condition people have themselves brought about by taking advantage of individual opportunities.[39]

Continuous pressure to improve transportation and the increasing prospect of more people acquiring motor conveyances had enabled cities to spread far in a short time. For central cities the consequences have been evidenced by decreasing residential population, increased shopping in out-lying areas, and loss of income for downtown business. Planners, says Dyckman, are divided. Some would halt the spread and encourage more concentration in the central city, claiming that the spread aggravates the transportation problem. Other planners defend decentralization.

---

37 Earl F. Murphy, *Water Purity*, Madison, University of Wisconsin Press, 1961, pp. 6–7.

38 Gordon, op. cit., pp. 84–114.

39 John W. Dyckman, "Transportation in Cities," *Scientific American*, Vol. 213, No. 3, September 1965, p. 163.

They argue that a degree of congestion will give rise to more efficient forms of transportation, and perhaps would reserve the urban center more for people and less for motor vehicles. They would find ways to move more people into and out of the central city with less friction and less loss of time. This would call for much "controlled timing and phasing of movement and many other adaptations more drastic than those proposed in present transportation plans." [40]

In the transportation difficulties of the changing city are reflected various other problems which arise as increasing numbers gather in urban areas. The challenges of transportation cut across every other aspect of planning for the good life in the urbanized society, whether planning for work or leisure. Changes are ahead of which we have only an inkling at present. Dyckman suggests that controls over transportation may be matched by controls over the uses of land in cities and between cities. [41]

Transportation in all its forms removes far places from their self-sufficient isolation, and provides access to the village, to the town, and on to a city. The more roads and the farther they reach, bringing and taking away more goods and people, the more important becomes the terminal city. Its importance can be measured by the demands it makes for transportation, as the utility of a city is measured by the efficiency of its transportation. These facilities for transportation are, along with the water supply, the highest public cost in a city. Thompson suggests that urbanites pay an invisible or seldom noted "price" for this, and that the cost has been increasing. [42]

THE PLANNING POTENTIAL OF URBAN PLACES

Kevin Lynch sees four deficiencies as standing between the modern metropolis and its achieving an environment conducive to the good life, and he looks upon that environment which extends far into the rural outland as if it were a birthright of the city. The four faults are:

1. ". . . the burden of perceptual stress," referring to noise, heat, polluted air.
2. ". . . lack of visible identity. A good environment is richly diverse" but the urbanite is rarely aware of this. He needs freer access to all the parts, and prideful acquaintance with them.
3. "A third source of distress in our cities is their illegibility." The urban environment needs to be made more inviting as well as more accessible. The

40 Ibid., p. 165.
41 Ibid., p. 174.
42 Wilbur R. Thompson, "Toward a Framework for Urban Public Management," in Sam Bass Warner, Jr. (Ed.), *Planning for a Nation of Cities*, Cambridge, The M.I.T. Press, 1966, p. 231.

present chaos induces alienation, but this can be removed by development efforts.

4. There is the rigidity of the city, "its lack of openness." The citizen needs more contact with his city and to share the task of changing it. Individual action makes for growth.[43]

Much that Lynch would do to make a city more vital and more inviting has to do with the arrangement of urban functions, the placing of structures, but he speaks too of new kinds and routes of transport, making the "system of movement" easier. "Many new highways and transit lines will be built by public agencies in our metropolitan areas in the next 20 years. The alignment and details of these routes could easily be planned to make traveling a delight as well as a necessity." And he adds that we can now begin "to convert the real existing metropolis into an environment in which men will take pride and pleasure . . . a work of art, fitted to human purpose." [44]

As with many who focus on regional planning, Lynch speaks of the "human purpose" of urban people. If a natural scene is to be preempted it is to be made pleasing to the urban eye. Gutkind, writing about regional planning in Britain, insists that "agriculture must have the same rights as industry," but he is thinking of rights as defined by urbanites when he adds that "agriculture must be integrated into the complete structure of our urbanized social and economic life." The "must" is seen in urban terms.[45]

Rural people did not invent most of the machines which enable the farmer to produce more with less labor, nor did they discover the scientific principles by which their animals are made more productive and through which an acre can be induced to yield more. The road system which farmers use did not come by rural demand or rural technology. The general rural attitude has ever been negative to much that is called progress in cities, although rural people usually come to accept progress. Nor is the rural man a planner in the wider sense, his perspective usually being local. Mitrany calls attention to the Communist impatience with the backward-looking peasant or farmer. Communist efforts to place agriculture on a par with industry as a work system has often taken the form of force-supported programs, large collective farms, and these plans have rarely been effective.[46] The same goals are being reached in such countries as Australia, Canada, New Zealand, and the United States, but

[43] Kevin Lynch, "The City as Environment," *Scientific American*, Vol. 213, No. 3, September 1965, p. 209.

[44] Ibid., pp. 214 and 219.

[45] E. A. Gutkind (Ed.), *Creative Demobilization*, New York, Oxford University Press, 1944, pp. 1–120.

[46] David Mitrany, *Marx Against the Peasant*, London, Weidenfeld and Nicolson, 1952, p. 223.

mainly by farmers on good land. Whether by force or persuasion, where farmers are still peasants the changeover will take time. Friedmann, however, relates the many difficulties encountered in Italy in moving peasants to new land where they have better houses and equipment. They cling to their old ways and a generation may be needed to achieve the goals which have little meaning and little importance to tradition-oriented rural people. Many of them may be suspicious of the program because it comes from the city.[47]

In the United States and Canada the urbanization of the rural population moves rapidly of its own accord. Farmers on good land, owning large farms are faring well both economically and technologically, while farmers on poor land and inefficient small farms are a deprived people. The small farmers, the majority in some regions where planning is most needed, are rarely interested in such schemes. Taylor and Jones identify the effective farmer with "agribusiness." They profit most from public rural-aid programs.[48]

It must be added that rural-urban planning as seen from the urban side is not always realistic. Most planners of today have almost no first-hand knowledge of rural work and life. What Brogan says of the knowledge of the average Briton about rural work and life and the farmer's world would apply to 100 million Americans.

> As a consequence, there is no country in the world in which feeling for the soil as a factor of production is so rare as in England, or where knowledge of farming as a way of making a living is as much a specialized knowledge, in which the most romantic or unrealistic views of country life can be advanced with less fear of brutal contradiction from people who know what agriculture, as an economic and social system involves.[49]

THE COSMOPOLITAN HEART OF THE CITY

If the much-traveled person talks about the cities known to him, the known portions of Paris, Barcelona, Bombay, or even New York would not exceed more than a few square miles, the midtown or downtown of each city. This section tends to be much alike everywhere, having, with minor variations, similar functions and amenities. The differences in world cities and the unique characteristics of each increase with distance

[47] F. G. Friedmann, "The Impact of Technologically Advanced Civilizations on Underdeveloped Areas," *Confluence*, Vol. 4, No. 4, 1955, pp. 397 and 401–404.
[48] Lee Taylor and Arthur R. Jones, Jr., *Rural Life and Urbanized Society*, New York, Oxford University Press, 1964, p. 209.
[49] D. W. Brogan, *The English People*, New York, Knopf, 1949, p. 275.

from the center. Even in one's own city it tends to be usual to make comparisons with other cities in terms of certain features identified with the heart area; the opera, the entertainment street, the city's "Chinatown," its key hotels, night clubs, the leading newspaper, imposing public buildings, and so on.

If we consider all the books about city planning and the impressive articles which appear in popular or even professional journals, most are found to deal mainly with the heart area. The City Beautiful urge lives on but in a more sophisticated form. The midtown area never ceases to fascinate because this is the one spot in which all who enter the city have a proprietary interest. In no other part of the city is the street so much a property of strangers and homeguards alike, nor, as Wilcox noted half a century ago, is the street more an institution than in the urban center. Here private interests from all distances and directions meet in work or play. Martindale adds that "the value of the street as a symbol does not stop here and one could as well use it as a point of departure to all urban life." [50] The street leads to the road and the road to the country. Wherever the urbanite may live in the metropolis, if only in a slum several blocks away, "going to town" means visiting the core area, and the visit may be satisfying if he does nothing more than walk with the crowd. In this regard, Jane Jacobs sees the street as a special kind of neighborhood, enjoyed by everyone at his own level.[51]

Planners would take the crowd off the downtown street. When they draw plans for the ideal downtown they picture people on the street, one or two here and there. In the Orient, streets are chronically crowded in the midtown area and this is accepted. Everything crowds into the streets of Indian cities (cows, cars, handcarts, rickshaws, carriages, oxcarts, etc.) and all moving things take their pace as they can. Sacred cows hold up traffic, and they are tolerated. Peddlers are free to spread their wares on the sidewalk. Western cities do not permit such indiscriminate use of streets, but for them congestion assumes other frustrating forms.[52] The congested center to Sert is a "value of confusion" and "bedlam." He would clear away all the noise and jostling and bring in "plants, water, sun and shade, and all the natural elements friendly to man." Naturally he would exclude motor cars and fumes.[53]

[50] His introduction to Max Weber, *The City*, translated and edited by Don Martindale and Gertrud Neuwirth, New York, Free Press, 1958, p. 62. Cited is Delow F. Wilcox, *The American City, A Problem in Democracy*, New York, Macmillan, 1904.

[51] Jacobs, op. cit., Chap. 7.

[52] On traffic in Indian cities, see J. D. N. Versluys (Ed.), "Introduction," to *The Implications of Industrialization and Urbanization*, Calcutta, Delhi, Unesco Research Centre, 1956.

[53] J. L. Sert, "Centres of Community Life," in J. Tyrwhitt, J. L. Sert, and E. N. Rogers (Eds.), *The Heart of the City*, London, Lund Humphries, 1952, pp. 3–16.

WORK ROLES OF THE URBAN CORE

The June 1968 issue of *Esquire* contains a picture-sketch article about six cities in need of rehabilitation, most of the attention being on the downtown areas. The problem is seen to be one of making the downtowns more attractive and so better for business. New Orleans is concerned about her $200 million tourist trade; Chicago's downtown is hurt economically by the continuing exodus of the middle-class whites; Omaha has a plan to create a whole new midtown around two great skyscrapers, each a hundred floors tall; and we are shown the plan for Washington to renew its central area.

Such urban redevelopment plans characterize much of the urban planning interest in American cities. While they represent a striving for convenience and make various concessions to art, their main purpose is to make the central area a more satisfactory work place. Most of these plans aim to achieve their ends by erecting taller buildings.

Hoover and Vernon, in their study of Central New York, indicate the importance of sensitive enterprises, some with nationwide or worldwide business, having their headquarters in this area. Here are concentrated the top influentials in finance, utilities, special services, communications, and mass media. Management must be near experts and advisors.

> This factor alone would not draw the business elite physically toward their outside advisors were it not that face-to-face interchange is the only adequate means of communication for much of the executive's work. Here we have once again the situation encountered in the analysis of communication-oriented manufacturing and of the financial community; delicate negotiations and subtle, complex ideas not easily entrusted to the telephone or the letter. In this respect, the Manhattan central business district has a clear advantage over any other location in the Region, since its working population is so densely packed in a tiny land area.[54]

The horde flocking to the midtown for the work day returns for the evening to spend leisure time. This makes work for others whose task it is to transform the area into a fun spot under the lights. Mack and McElrath speak of the many special functions of the midtown. "Wide-reaching activities are originated in, funneled through or transformed by the urban posts of command and coordination. This centralizing function is evidenced by the presence in all modern cities of a substantial tertiary

[54] Edgar M. Hoover and Raymond Vernon, *Anatomy of a Metropolis*, New York, Doubleday Anchor, 1962, p. 97.

labor force." [55] And this is the highest paid of any labor force.

Functions performed in the midtown district cannot be performed, or certainly not as well, elsewhere. For instance, Jersey City is only about a mile from the Wall Street area on the other side of the Hudson River. Nevertheless, Farmer points out, a square yard of land in the financial district of New York has a higher value than an acre in parts of Jersey City. Once a delightful residential town, Jersey City is now an area of slums and warehouses. The crucial work of New York's center cannot risk moving even that short a distance, which could be traveled in ten minutes by ferry. It could be converted into an ideal middle-class housing district, but it remains a slum and factory district.[56] Here it is pertinent to note that, even if tunnels and bridges are built, rivers remain barriers to easy movement in most cities.

HOUSING IN THE INDUSTRIAL URBAN COMMUNITY

It was possible in the medieval town for a family to own its house and for ownership to remain in the family two or more generations. In most cases then the house was also a work place, and the work of the family did not change, or rarely changed, from one generation to the next. Under industrialism the work of a man may change once, twice or more in the course of his active life, and he may be identified with a whole series of work places. For work reasons, he may have to change his place of residence again and again. Now he may be able to move to a better residence, later he is forced into a worse one. The married couple needs more room as the family grows and less space when the children depart. The home of the average modern family is one of the impermanent facts of life.

Moreover, it has become uneconomical for the average modern family to own its home, unless the home be in a remote suburb, part of the cost of which is continuous commuting to one's job. Owning a home in the city may be practicable for those in the high income brackets. Even for them home ownership may become a burden. They find it easier to live in a rented apartment. In the modern community, building and owning residential buildings and managing residences owned by others has become both a profession and a complex industry. The dwelling has become a consumer good, a commodity in a competitive market. Housing comes to

55 Raymond W. Mack and Dennis C. McElrath, "Urban Social Differentiation and Allocation of Resources," *Annals of the American Academy of Political and Social Science,* Vol. 352, March 1964, p. 27.

56 John J. Farmer, "The Rise and Fall of Jersey City," *The Reporter,* August 13, 1964, p. 47.

be identified with socio-economic class levels. Family status is proclaimed not only by the type of family automobile, it is also evidenced by the residence in which the family lives and the quality of the street.

Another aspect of the dwelling in the modern community, reflecting the fact that the house is a competitive commodity, relates to modernity. The new apartments of 1970 are equipped with amenities and gadgets not known in 1940 or even in 1950. Like the automobile, the urban house is continuously going out of date. The dwelling that attracted top priority tenants in 1940, a decade later would not attract such tenants. Such a residential building, at its peak in 1940, might be occupied by a much lower socio-economic class in 1970. A street of such buildings, after three decades of aging, may experience decline to the point of neglect, and become a street of slumlike residence. This has been called the "filtering-down" process by which the poorest families are ever occupying the oldest houses. The point is finally reached when the old buildings cease to be profitable investments, although they occupy high-value land. In many American cities the point of economic loss is reached when such a street is likely to be redeveloped as an urban renewal project. So, as Gans described, the West End slum in Boston was renewed. According to the renewal plan, the old neighborhood was broken as families were moved to other parts of the city. The new dwellings would attract families able to pay much higher rents, the face of the city would be brightened, and more taxes would come into the public coffers.[57]

It tends to be assumed by planners that when houses get old they will be occupied by tenants of lower and lower income level. Vernon states:

> The housing which will become obsolescent and ripe for downgrading over the next twenty years will be drawn largely from stock built between 1910 and 1930, during a period when the Region's population increased by about 4,000,000. Much of this housing will be turned over for low-income use; and much of it is located in the outlying parts of the Core counties and in the Inner Ring. The obsolescence rate of the block of housing built before 1930 promises to be especially high because most of it was built without regard for the existence of the automobile.[58]

Vernon's observations relate to New York, but the downgrading process of which he speaks is true of most American cities. If there are plans for redevelopment or slum removal they will involve houses which will less easily be downgraded. Planning for good housing for all has never been achieved in any country, Communist or capitalist. Moreover, demand is unpredictable. The housing needs of a family may change several times

57 Gans, op. cit., Chap. 13.
58 Raymond Vernon, *Metropolis 1985*, Garden City, New York, Doubleday Anchor, 1963, p. 198.

between marriage and the retirement of the spouses, and it changes as the fortunes of the family rise or fall. Add to this the residential mobility of families from outdated houses into those with the latest in fixtures and amenities. Because of this unpredictability, Dentler maintains, "City slums cannot be eliminated solely by enforcing housing codes or by prosecuting landlords. They cannot be eliminated solely by building public housing alternatives." [59]

Breese writes about housing needs in the developing countries where cities are growing and industrialization is increasing. No new government is able to undertake the housing task. Limited funds there must go to meet other needs.[60] Poor-man houses that are acceptable in most European cities, for example, despite their lack of amenities, would be called slums in American or Canadian cities. Working-class housing, say in San Francisco or Toronto, may be better appointed than working-class housing in Liverpool or Marseilles, but they would still be poor compared with lesser middle-class dwellings. The easy answer is that where the market does not provide better housing, there government should do the job. Seligman reminds us, though, that this may be too much even for an affluent government.[61]

POLITICS AND THE PLANNING CHALLENGE

The realistic social scientist or planner may often be irritated by the too-often unrealistic social reformer, but he may have even less confidence in the "practical" politician who is usually governed by considerations of expediency and whose perspective is generally more immediate than long-term. Marris, describing a slum removal project in Lagos, Nigeria, which had not been a conspicuous success, noted that business leaders and politicians were quite happy about the project. Their attention was more on the "removal" than on the people displaced.

> The overriding aim was to rebuild the most conspicuous neighbourhood in Lagos to the standard Nigerians had set for themselves, as a matter of pride, and a symbol of the progress they were determined to achieve. And by this token of their intentions rather than their present wealth, they hoped the foreign visitor would judge them.[62]

[59] Robert A. Dentler, *American Community Problems*, New York, McGraw-Hill, 1968, p. 72.

[60] Gerald Breese, *Urbanization in Newly Developing Countries*, Englewood Cliffs, N.J., Prentice-Hall, 1966, p. 126.

[61] Daniel Seligman, "The Enduring Slums," *Fortune*, December 1957, reprinted in Edward C. McDonagh and Jon E. Simpson (Eds.), *Social Problems, Persistent Challenges*, New York, Holt, Rinehart & Winston, 1965, pp. 9–14.

[62] Peter Marris, *Family and Social Change in an African City*, London, Routledge and Kegan Paul, 1961, p. 119.

Public officials are of two kinds: the elected ones who make initial decisions and the public functionaries who make administrative decisions. Either type of decision may have political implications, but the functionary is more identified with the bureaucracy of government. He is frequently accused of being dominated by the elected officials, but he is more often blamed for tardiness in getting things done, or for increasing the complexity of the machinery of government. Wildschut notes that in Amsterdam, a city with a traditionally clean government, even with an efficient master plan the city fathers cannot always carry out the most desired projects. Ideal projects get postponed again and again while others start quickly. Everybody wants the new city hall and the public opera, but the electric power plant or some improvement on the water front to help business gets higher priority.[63]

The fact remains that if there is to be planning for cities and their regions, it must become a public responsibility. Oules, a French economist, would keep the political "mystique" out of all social and economic planning. "If we wish to 'demystify' economic problems and make the economy truly democratic, all economic questions must be taken out of politics." Most important is economic planning for which great effort must be made to learn the effective techniques and to apply them.[64]

The problem of polluted streams and lakes left to private planning would likely fail, and the same holds for the housing problem. Public control is the least evil of the alternatives. Control can still be influenced by organized groups, and even groups that condemn politics are themselves often equally political. Were they not so their community influence would be minimal.

ORDER, BEAUTY AND THE GOOD LIFE

More need not be said about urban complexity and the continuity of change, especially unpredictable change, in the urban scene. The scene at any time, despite earlier efforts to establish order, becomes one of inconveniences. Saarinen, for example, blamed the grandfathers for the faults he saw in American cities of 1940.[65] How were the grandfathers to foresee the automobile, the use of steel and concrete in construction, the diverse uses of electric power and other innovations? Unpredictable changes, even looking a decade ahead are more hazardous for planning than in 1900. It would be most surprising if the grandchildren of this

63 J. P. Wildschut, "Amsterdam," in Robson, op. cit., pp. 18–19.

64 Firmin Oules, *Economic Planning and Democracy*, translated by R. H. Barry, Baltimore, Penguin, 1966, p. 347.

65 Eliel Saarinen, *The City, Its Growth, Its Decay, Its Future*, New York, Reinhold, 1945, p. 250.

generation will not have much to blame on their grandfathers.

However, this generation of planners, more than those of 1900, have begun to recognize that planning must be more than a "grand design." It must be more concerned with the whole community than with the core, and one must think more in terms of the various needs of people. But even today there are critics who charge planners with more interest in plans than people. Jacobs says that there is more interest in the uses of space for business than in the informal human uses during nonwork hours. She sees many plans as "an exercise in cures irrelevant to the disease." [66]

With more of the world's population entering urbanized existence, with more of the world's labor force entering industrial employment, and with the prospect of rising standards of living and of increasing mobility, planning for the good life is bound to increase in complexity and decrease in predictability. The increasing demand of people for access to nature will doubtless continue to be destructive of natural things until, as McHarg complains, beauty will be found only in the cemetery. "The modern metropolis covers thousands of square miles, much of the land is sterilized and water proofed, the original animals have long gone, as have primeval plants, rivers are foul, the atmosphere is polluted, climate and microclimate have retrogressed to increasing violence." [67] Others voice the call. Many, among them Brownell, complain that urban people lose interest in nature.

> They learn to remove themselves from the close, compelling influence of natural things. They abstract their thoughts and interests and even their activities from the green context and spiritual milieu of life in Nature, and reside in massive agglomerations or in other ways remote from rural interests. But they have not taken with them into these agglomerations the stable, human community or the naturally integrated life. They have renounced nature for a price.[68]

Many would describe this viewpoint as being an idealistic notion of a rural stability that never existed or, at least, no longer exists. This does not gainsay that something like a return to nature is desirable for more urban people. It is a goal not easy to attain. But those who plan for the good life must also strive for higher living standards, full employment, and for all a greater access to leisure, learning, and the essential securities of life.

[66] Jacobs, op. cit., p. 154.
[67] Ian L. McHarg, "The Place of Nature in the City of Man," *Annals of the American Academy of Political and Social Science*, Vol. 353, March 1964, p. 3.
[68] Baker Brownell, *The Human Community*, New York, Harper & Row, 1950, p. 6.

Name Index

Abegglen, James C., 270, 273
Abell, Helen C., 360
Abu-Lughod, Ibrahim, 392
Adams, Charles F., 186
Adams, Ian, 185
Adams, James T., 275
Adams, Richard N., 205
Addams, Jane, 257, 390
Aiyappan, A., 321
Alderson, Stanley, 26, 404
Allen, Irving L., Jr., 39
Alonzo, William, 107
Altmeyer, Arthur J., 350
Anderon, Nels, 19, 26, 135, 183, 297, 298, 332, 382
Anderson, William, 200
Andrews, Alick R., 196
Angell, Robert C., 195
Annis, Edward H., 365, 366
Apertet, J., 328
Arendt, Hannah, 11, 291
Arensberg, Conrad M., 25, 30
Arkwright, Richard, 275
Aubert, Vilhelm, 228, 232, 241, 373, 388
Ayres, C. E., 49

Banfield, Edward C., 72
Barber, Bernard, 282, 283
Bates, Stewart, 396
Batten, T. R., 126
Bauchet, Pierre, 404
Beaglehole, Ernst, 274
Beals, Ralph L., 253
Becker, Howard S., 395
Beijer, G., 119
Belitsky, A. Harvey, 358
Bendix, Reinhard, 153, 284, 353
Benoit, J., 127, 145
Bensman, Joseph, 287, 392
Bentham, Jeremy, 355
Berdot, Lucian, 197
Beresford, John C., 240
Berlin, Isaiah, 204

Bernard, Jessie, 237
Berrman, Gerald, D., 179
Besant, Annie, 130
Bhutani, D. H., 339
Bierstedt, Robert, 239
Birkbeck, Morris, 84
Bismarck, Otto von, 356
Blair, George S., 251, 261, 264
Blanchard, René, 197
Blood, Robert O., 240
Blucher, Viggo, Graf, 287
Blum, Fred H., 14, 277
Blume, Otto, 339
Blumer, Herbert, 36, 378
Boateng, E. A., 71
Bogue, Donald J., 121
Boissonnade, P., 54
Bonham-Carter, Victor, 80, 81
Bose, Nirmal Kumar, 65, 100
Boskoff, Alvin, 15, 95, 105
Bott, Elizabeth, 33
Bottomore, T. B., 204, 206, 268, 387
Boulding, Kenneth E., 351
Bowles, Samuel, 16, 17, 400
Bowman, Isaiah, 98
Brace, C. Loring, 171, 257
Bradlaugh, Charles, 130
Breese, Gerald, 419
Bremme, Gabriele, 355
Bridenbaugh, Carl, 32, 254, 270
Briggs, Asa, 30, 165, 181, 197, 257, 356
Brogan, D. W., 165, 189, 414
Brookes, Ralph, 260
Broom, Leonard, 78
Brownell, Baker, 191, 384, 421
Browning, Harley L., 121
Brunhes, Jean, 97
Bryce, James, 251
Buchanan, Colin, 173
Buckingham, Walter, 291
Burgess, Ernest W., 107, 242
Burnett, J. R., 79
Bury, J. B., 48

Cameron, William, 365
Caplow, Theodore, 52, 214, 269, 376
Catlin, George E. C., 372
Chambers, Clarke A., 350
Chandrasekhar, S., 129
Chapman, Brian, 176, 252
Chauhan, Brij Raj, 45
Chiarelli, Guiseppe, 111
Childe, V. Gordon, 20, 46, 60
Chombart de Lauwe, Paul, 94, 107, 149
Clarke, Alfred C., 308
Clawson, Marion, 302, 311, 315
Clement, Pierre, 147, 208
Coe, Michael D., 248, 318
Cole, G. D. H., 207
Coleman, James S., 276
Collver, Andrew, 236, 237
Commager, Henry S., 15, 143
Conrad, Joseph, 266
Cooley, Charles H., 97
Copperstock, Henry, 365
Coser, Lewis A., 21
Cottrell, W. F., 42, 196
Coulton, G. C., 75
Cowan, L. Gray, 378, 385
Crawford, Robert W., 303
Cresswell, H. B., 168
Crouch, Winston W., 252
Cullingworth, J. B., 312
Cunnison, J., 288

Dahl, Robert A., 210
Dansereau, H. Kirk, 287
Davis, Kingsley, 110, 116, 262
Dean, Lois R., 245, 247, 322
de Coincy, Gautier, 75
de Condorcet, J. N. C., 48
de Crévecoeur, J. Hector St. John, 68, 97, 98
de Grazia, Sebastian, 296, 300, 306, 309
Delcourt, Jacques, 234
Dennis, Norman, 230
Dentler, Robert A., 122, 419
de Tocqueville, Alexis, 143
Deveraux, Edward C., Jr., 31, 32, 216
Dewey, Richard, 6, 7, 8
Dickens, Charles, 143
Dickinson, Frank G., 351
Diebold, John, 292
Dore, R. P., 120, 170, 212, 228, 235, 241, 336, 354, 380
Duncan, Otis D., 6, 108, 239, 323
Durand, Paul, 359
Durant, H. W., 277, 278, 303
Durham (Lord), 141
Durkheim, Emile, 94, 184, 298
Dyckman, John W., 164, 397, 411
Dye, Thomas R., 410

Edwards, Alba, 269
Edwards, John N., xii
Ekirch, Arthur A., 48
Emerson, Ralph W., 65, 158
Etzioni, Amitai, 387
Evans, E. Estwyn, 92

Falardeau, Jean C., 141
Farmer, John J., 217
Fearing, Kenneth, 14
Ferguson, Thomas, 126, 288
Fernback, Frank L., 361
Firestone, Melvin M., 76
Firey, Walter, 94
Firth, Raymond, 30
Fitch, James M., 169
Fitton, R. S., 275
Fitzgerald, Gerald B., 295, 298
Fleisher, Wilfred, 356
Flower, B. O., 257, 390
Foote, Nelson N., 305
Ford, Thomas R., 77, 83, 185
Forde, Daryll, 69
Forster, Edward M., 158
Foster, George M., 85
Franklin, Benjamin, 275
Freedgood, Seymour, 250
Freedman, Ronald, 151
Friedmann, F. G., 414
Friedmann, Georges, 266, 273, 231
Friedmann, John, 8, 22
Fustel de Coulanges, N. D., 28, 50

Galbraith, John J., 161, 294, 317, 331, 336, 340, 377, 383
Gallaher, Art, Jr., 31, 41, 42, 332, 360, 362
Gangrade, K. D., 196
Gans, Herbert J., 406, 418
Garland, Hamlin, 68
Garwood, Darrell, 255, 256
Geddes, G., 266
Gerth, Hans H., 207
Gibbs, Jack P., 27
Gill, Conrad, 170, 256
Gillin, John P., 76, 77, 152
Ginsberg, Morris, 47
Girard, Alain, 289
Glacken, Clarence J., 91
Glass, D. V., 285
Glass, Ruth, 406, 407
Glazer, Nathan, 330
Glick, Paul C., 237, 240
Goodchilds, Jacqueline D., 210, 211, 306
Goode, William J., 223, 238
Goodfellow, D. M., 234
Goodsell, Willystine, 242
Gordon, Mitchell, 403, 411
Gottmann, Jean, 29, 162, 174, 188
Gould, Harold A., 206, 375
Gould, Julius, 203
Gouldner, Alvin W., 392, 395
Gouldner, Helen P., 392
Gourou, Pierre, 88, 89
Grabill, Wilson H., 123
Grebler, Leo, 105
Green, L. P., 150, 166, 408, 409
Greer, Guy, 399
Greer, Scott, 16, 233, 258, 259, 263, 389, 399
Gregg, David W., 359
Gregory, J. W., 136
Gumperz, John J., 31

Gutkind, E. A., 413

Halbwachs, Maurice, 94, 107, 165, 180, 228
Hall, J. R., 285
Hall, Oswald, 276, 290
Hall, Peter, 163, 176
Hance, William A., 144, 145
Handlin, Oscar, 134, 320
Hansson, Borje, 56, 81, 82, 135, 225, 283
Hardee, Covington, 351
Harding, John, 210, 211, 306
Harwitz, Mitchell, 205, 260
Hauser, Philip M., 151, 179
Havinghurst, Robert J., 306, 308
Hawley, Amos H., 91, 220
Hayakawa, S. I., 398
Hayek, Frederick A., 404
Heaton, Herbert, 52, 53
Heer, David M., 240
Heilbroner, Robert L., 217, 218, 340, 343
Heinila, Kaveli, 294, 298
Herskovits, Melvin J., 205, 260
Hicks, Granville, 409
Hill, Reuben, 380
Hillery, George A., 24
Hoffman, Lois W., 240
Holland, Herbert J., 275
Hollingshead, August B., 208, 287
Holman, Mary A., 302
Homans, George C., 33, 388
Hoover, Edgar M., 416
Horton, Paul B., 70, 125, 232, 233, 372, 375
Howard, Donald S., 369
Howard, Ebenezer, 400, 401
Hoyt, Homer, 108
Hudson, William H., 227
Hughes, Everett C., 269
Hunt, Chester L., 70, 125, 232, 233, 239, 372, 375, 381
Hunter, Floyd, 215, 216, 390
Huntington, Ellsworth, 90, 136, 137
Hurd, Richard M., 108
Hyman, Herbert H., 220

Ibrahim, I. A., 283
Ikle, Fred C., 105
Ishwaran, K., 74, 130, 183, 205, 206, 226, 237
Iverson, Noel, 398
Izzett, Alison, 225

Jacobs, Jane, 5, 159, 164, 168, 175, 176, 394, 400, 415, 421
James, Henry, 158, 179
Jefferson, Thomas, 65
Johnson, Elmer H., 276, 389
Jones, Arthur R., Jr., 21, 73, 414
Jones, Joseph M., 122
Joyce, Josiah, 160

Kalbach, Warren E., 123
Kallen, Horace M., 7, 32, 33, 39
Karpinos, Bernard D., 124, 125
Katz, Elihu, 213

Kaufman, Herbert, 259
Keller, Suzanne, 383, 386, 390
Kennedy, Thomas, 246
Kerr, Clark, 4, 11, 316, 317
Kettle, John, 293
Keynes, J. M., 355
Killian, Lewis M., 371
Kimball, Solon T., 25
Kipling, Rudyard, 187
Kirkland, E. C,. 138
Kiser, Clyde V., 124, 125
Klein, Viola, 239, 289
Knibbs, H. H., 136
Knickerbocker, Conrad, 159
Kohl, 96, 97
Kolb, William L., 92, 192, 203
Komarovsky, Mirra, 304, 331
König, Renée, 24
Konvitz, Milton R., 390
Kouwenhoven, John A., 190

Lamale, Helen H., 326, 337, 338
Lambiri, Jane, 272
Lampard, Eric E., 11, 95, 99
Lampman, Robert J., 349
Langlois, Eleanor, 236, 237
Larrue, Janine, 306, 307
Lasswell, Harold D., 386
Lazarsfeld, Paul F., 213
Lee, Robert, 302, 303
Leonard, Olen, 77
Leslie, Gerald R., 231, 237, 241
LeTourneau, Roger, 172, 173
Lewis, Oscar, 117, 180, 267
Lieberson, Stanley, 39, 108
Lipset, Seymour M., 153, 276, 284
Locke, Jeannine, 365
Loomis, C. P., 77, 78
Loosley, Elizabeth W., 236
Low, Sampson, 347
Lowenstein, Susan F., 158
Lucas, C. P., 141
Lundberg, George A., 304, 331
Lunt, Paul S., 210
Luther, Martin, 268
Lynch, Kevin, 66, 412, 413

McClelland, David C., 257
McCormack, Cyrus, 143
McCormack, Thelma, 338, 339
McElrath, Dennis C., 416, 417
McFarlane, Bruce, 290
McHarg, Ian L., 421
McHenry, Dean E., 252
McInerny, Mary A., 304, 331
MacIver, Robert M., 71, 388
Mack, Raymond W., 155, 416, 417
McKelvey, Blake, 64
McKenzie, R. D., 108
McMahan, C. A., 146

Maine, Henry S., 84, 85, 222, 223
Majumdar, D. N., 74, 75, 316
Malthus, Thomas R., 112
Mann, Peter H., 16, 99, 103, 108, 119

Mann, W. E., 169, 386
Mannheim, Karl, 317
Marris, Peter, 101, 238, 419
Marshall, T. H., 210, 263, 341
Martin, F. M., 209
Martindale, Don, 415
Marx, Karl, 204, 267,
Massucco-Costa, Angiola, 194
Mayer, Harold M., 103, 105, 174, 410
Mayntz, Renata, 209
Meerloo, Joost A. M., 294
Merriam, Ida C., 363
Merrill, Francis E., 231, 233, 242
Meyer, Alfred H., 90
Middleton, John, 299
Miller, Delbert C., 390
Miller, Herman P., 331, 358
Miller, Norman P., 312, 313
Miller, S. M., 286, 352
Mills, C. Wright, 207, 215
Miner, David, 399
Miner, Horace, 73
Minsky, Hyman P., 367, 368
Mitchell, G. Duncan, 42
Mitchell William L., 349
Mitrany, David, 413
Moore, Wilbert E., 332
Morgan, James N., 239, 242, 284, 290, 291,
    335, 339, 362, 363
Mros, Edmund, 148
Mukherjee, Radhakamal, 49
Mumford, Lewis, 13, 15, 59, 157, 190, 192,
    200, 219, 247, 248, 268, 272, 299, 398,
    399
Mundy, John M., 9, 21, 46, 54, 56, 59, 87
Murphy, Earl F., 37, 255, 411
Myrdal, Alva, 130, 289
Myrdal, Gunnar, 327, 328, 357

Nash, Jay B., 296, 303
Nash, Ogden, 298
Nellner, Werner, 147
Nesmith, Dwight A., 86
Nevins, Allen, 168, 186
Newman, Dorothy K., 338
Nimkoff, Meyer F., 128, 234
Nisbet, Robert A., 389
North, C. C., 280, 281
Nye, F. Ivan, 240

O'Dea, Thomas F., 382
Ogburn, William F., 40, 128, 154, 225,
    230, 231, 234, 379
Oglethorpe, James, 399
Oliver, John W., 142
Orleans, Peter, 16
Ornati, Oscar, 362
Orshansky, Mollie, 360
Oules, Firmin, 420
Owen, David, 346, 349, 353
Owen, Wilfred, 149

Page, Charles H., 71
Parker, Sanford S., 313
Parrington, Vernon L., 282

Parsons, Talcott, 231, 373, 393
Pascal, Blaise, 47
Penn, William, 399
Perry, George S., 189, 190
Peterson, William, 118, 123, 125, 131
Pflaum, Renate, 147
Philbrook, Tom, 76
Piddington, Ralph, 73
Pierson, Donald, 227
Pirenne, Henri, 39, 41, 54, 55, 57, 59, 110,
    137
Platt, B. S., 113
Plato, 161
Polanyi, Karl, 62, 63
Polsby, Nelson W., 252
Pomeroy, Hugh R., 405, 406
Pons, V. G., 146, 147
Popenoe, David, 27
Porter, John 208, 217, 283, 286, 290, 325
Presthus, Robert, 214, 215, 272, 273, 383,
    391
Prignitz, Christian, 398
Purcell, Victor, 273, 274

Randall, C. D., 257
Ratzel, Friedrick, 90
Ravenstein, E. G., 146, 147
Redfield, Robert, 21, 69, 186, 275
Redick, Richard W., 401
Rein, Martin, 352
Reiss, Albert J., Jr., 239, 323
Reissman, Leonard, 151, 152, 211
Ribton-Turner, C. J., 135
Riegel, Robert E., 139
Riesenberg, Peter, 9, 21, 46, 54, 56, 59, 87
Riesman, David, 195, 301, 314, 315, 333,
    334, 368
Riis, Jacob A., 257
Riley, John W., 320, 321
Rios, Jose Arthur, 172, 262
Robinson, Duane M., 312, 313
Robson, William A., 39, 102, 402
Rodwin, Lloyd, 167, 405
Roemer, Milton I., 366, 369
Rose, Arnold M., 34, 128
Rosenberg, Bernard, 21, 278
Rosenborough, Howard, 333, 334
Ross, Murray G., 244
Rostow, W. W., 345, 346
Rousseau, J. J., 158
Rowntree, B. Seebohm, 333
Russell, Bertrand, 305

Saal, C. D., 71
Saarinen, Eliel, 420
Salz, Beate R., 305
Sampson, R. V., 47
Sandberg, Carl, 187
Santayana, George, 158
Sariola, Sakari, 211, 212, 350
Saunders, Dero A., 313
Saville, John, 81, 316
Sayre, William S., 252, 259
Schachter, Gustav, 74
Schaefer, Jack, 315, 316

Schaffer, Ruth C., 216
Schiffman, Jacob, 289
Schmid, Calvin F., 198, 199
Schneider, Harold K., 19
Schnore, Leo F., 96
Schur, Edwin M., 387
Scott, W. Richard, 105
Seeley, John R., 236, 354
Seidenbladh, Goran, 107
Seligman, Ben B., 350
Seligman, Daniel, 419
Selznick, Philip, 78, 79, 402
Semple, Ellen Churchill, 90
Sert, J. L., 415
Sharp, Margery, 104
Sheppard, Harold L., 326, 358
Sheps, Cecil G., 216
Shils, Edward, 218, 262, 377, 378
Shrylock, Henry S., 115
Siegfried, André, 73
Sim, R. Alexander, 236
Simmel, Georg, 192
Simon, Shena D., 170, 199, 249
Simpson, George, 292
Sinclair, Robert, 254
Singer, Milton B., 21
Singh, Yogendra, 224
Sirjamaki, John, 44, 93
Sjoberg, Gideon, 10, 20, 50, 59, 61, 96, 261
Skelton, Oscar D., 140
Skrubbeltrang, F., 82, 83
Smith, Page, 409
Smith, T. Lynn, 100, 101, 120, 146
Socrates, 161
Sofer, Rhona, 38
Soule, George, 299, 397, 402
Southall, Aidan, 34, 121, 122
Spencer, Herbert, 346
Srinivas, M. N., 206
Stanton, Frank, 304
Stauffer, Samuel A., 36, 37
Stead, William T., 187, 257
Steffens, Lincoln, 162, 250
Stephen, Leslie, 298, 299
Stephenson, George, 138
Stewart, Cecil, 189
Strauss, Anselm L., 28, 29, 109, 139, 179, 181, 198
Strauss, E., 20
Stone, Giovanna, 337
Stone, Richard, 337
Stotz, Margaret S., 337
Streitelmeyer, John H., 90
Strong, Josiah, 65, 257
Strutts, Jedediah, 275
Sultan, Paul E., 272
Sutter, John, 19
Svalastoga, Kaare, 279, 280, 309, 311, 339

Taeuber, Irene B., 131
Taylor, A. M., 52
Taylor, Lee, 21, 73, 376, 414
Ten Have, T. T., 277, 292
Theodorson, George A., 91
Thomas, Franklin, 89

Thomas, William I., 383, 384
Thomlinson, Ralph, 88, 109, 150
Thompson, Wilbur R., 168, 173, 218, 220, 322, 345, 412
Tibbitts, Clark, 230
Titmuss, Richard M., 351, 364, 368, 369
Toennies, Ferdinand, 190, 191
Toynbee, Arnold J., 294, 295
Trevelyan, G. M., 81
Trollope, Anthony, 12, 37, 78
Trow, Martin A., 276
Truxal, Andrew G., 225, 226, 242
Tunley, Roul, 162
Tunnard, Christopher, 401
Turner, Frederick, J., 15, 65, 139
Turner, Ralph H., 371
Twain, Mark, 68

Unwin, George, 58

Van Heek, H., 152, 153
Vausson, Claude, 312
Veblen, Thorstein, 316
Vernon, Raymond, 416, 418
Versluys, J. D. N., 415
Vidich, Arthur J., 392
Vigman, Fred K., 256
Volkart, Edward H., 384
Vontobel, 268, 311

Wade, Richard C., 64, 65, 138
Wadsworth, A. P., 275
Wagley, Charles, 152
Walker, Robert A., 253
Wallace, Samuel E., 135
Wallbank, T. W., 52
Ware, Caroline, 386
Waring, George E., 257
Warner, Sam B., Jr., 397
Warner, W. Lloyd, 210, 375, 380, 389
Wax, Rosalie H., 203
Weaver, Robert C., 360
Webb, Beatrice, 355
Webb, Sidney, 355
Weber, Max, 10, 207, 247, 262
Wecter, Dixon, 315
Weiss, Robert S., 195, 301, 368
Wells, H. G., 18, 174, 175, 267
Wesley, John, 275
West, James, 31
Whelpton, Pascal K., 123, 125
White, Morton, 158, 160, 374
Whitman, Walt, 136
Whyte, Donald R., 22, 23, 236, 327
Whyte, William F., 339, 375
Whyte, William H., Jr., 33, 118, 278, 279
Wicksell, Karl, 130
Wilcox, Delos F., 415
Wildschut, J. P., 258, 420
Wilensky, Harold L., 35, 333, 392
Willems, Emilio, 229
Willmott, Peter, 232, 241
Willner, Ann Ruth, 379
Wilson, Everett K., 150, 192, 381

Wilson, Gordon, 226, 227, 385
Wilson, Mitchell, 142
Winch, Robert F., 233
Winnick, Louis, 98
Winsborough, Hal H., 108
Winthrop, Henry, 161, 290,
Wirth, Louis, 2, 27, 35, 109
Wohl, Richard R., 179, 181, 188, 189
Wood, Robert C., 33, 35, 160, 220
Woodroofe, Kathleen, 347, 348, 368
Wright, Charles R., 220

Wrong, Dennis, 373, 374
Wurzbacher, Gerhard, 147
Wylie, Laurance, 45, 46

Xydias, Nelly, 147, 208

Young, Kimball, 155
Young, Michael, 232, 241

Zimmer, B. G., 220
Zorbaugh, Harvey W., 171

Subject Index

Acceptance of class system, 208–9
Accommodation, aspects, 154
Adaptability, urban, 16
Affluence and poverty culture, 330–2
"Agribusiness" as rural planning, 414
Agriculture and technology, 142
Alienation in community, 220
Ambiguity of saving, 338–40
American cities, growth of, 115
Ancient cities, knowledge of, 79
  types of, 60
Antiurbanism, rural, 74–5
  suburban, 160
Areas of residence, 95
Arnheim Rural Museum, 71
Aspects of family breakup, 237–8
Aspirations for future leisure, 309
Assimilation, and accommodation, 154
  and strangers, 156
Attitude patterns, persistence, 380
Attitudes of tolerance, 36–7
Authority, urban, 39
Automation and mechanization, 291
Automobile and decentralization, 173

Beauty and cities, 165–6
  conceptions of, 165
  destruction of, 161
  and the good life, 421
  and order, implications, 398
Behavioral types in society, 383
Belonging to the community, 191
Bias against medieval merchants, 58–9
Birth control movement, 130
Birth and death rates, 124
Birth rates, 122–4
  American, 122
  Canadian, 123
  and education of mothers, 124

Birth rates (cont.)
  and income, 124
  industrial urban, 122
  religion of parents, 125
  rural families, 123
Bohemians and philistines, 384
Boundaries, community, 26
Britanny Mews, London novel, 104
Bureaucracy, and peer groups 376
  evolution of, 261
  public and private, 261
  and public service, 61
  and records, 20, 393
Burden of agricultural efficiency, 361
Burden of public welfare, 362–4

Calcutta, area pattern of, 99
Canadian frontier, 140
Canals and railroads, 137
Carnival and its festivals, 188
Carolingian Empire, weakness of, 55
Caste, and continuity, 179
  and neighborhood, 31
  as social stratification, 205–6
  and untouchables, 206
  in the urban setting, 206
  and work system, 269
Central city and its suburbs, 407
  work roles in, 416
Ceremonials, in cities, 25
Challenge, of emerging nations, 342
  of industrial work system, 343
  of poverty and unemployment, 342
Change, in occupations, 9
  in social order, 378
  and social persistence, 379–81
Change processes, urban, 45
Changing position of women, 238
Charismatic leadership, 385

Charity, and Great Depression, 349
  and its organization, 347–8
  and self-sufficient man, 349
  transition to welfare, 349
Chicago, dynamics and growth, 186
Children, death rates of, 127
  and the family, 236
Chivalry and the peasants, 75
"Chores," non-recreation leisure, 297
Chronic American nobility, 116
Church, and commerce, 55
  and medieval economy, 33–4
  as private government, 382
  in rural villages, 72
"Circulation," and nobility, 148
Cities, accumulations in, 40
  ancient, medieval, 49
  confront the present, 64–5
  decentralization of, 115
  as diversion centers, 41
  functions of, 38–9
  innovation in, 16-7
  mission of, 66
  in new nations, 144–5
  pluralism in, 215
  and pollution, 403
  and population increase, 110–11
  refuge for population, 111
  and regional government, 251
  and river transportation, 138
  and sex ratio, 122
  stages of growth, 318
  and superlative urge, 17
  and technology, 59
  work competition in, 272
Citizens and government, 258–9
Citizenship, aspects of, 263
  evolution of, 50–1
  industrial, political, 341
City, as a community, 26
  critics of, 157–66
  in history, 44–5
  management, rise of, 51–2
  mission of, 66
  neighborhood in, 32
  official definition of, 4–5
  size and levels of income, 322
  and tolerance, 37
  as a work place, 160
City Beautiful, limited perspective, 406
  movement for, 400
City-building, era of, 141
City center, its problems, 414
City consciousness and pride, 188
Ciudad Guayana, a pleasant city, 405
Civil law, beginning of, 85
Civil service, changes in, 250
Civilization and waste, 161

Class conflict and religion, 381
Class status and occupation, 279
Class system, acceptance of, 208
Classes and interdependence, 345
Clocks, functions of, 13–4
  regulation of work, 277
  "tyranny" of, 14
  use of and leisure, 299
Coexistence, as tolerance, 38
Collective behavior, in crises, 193
  community action, 244
  functional, 196–9
  learning, 64
  memory, 180
  saving and spending, 340–2
Colonial cities, services in, 254
Colonial farmers, 68
Commerce, and the church, 54
  medieval, 53
Commercial Revolution, 62
Communities, confront change, 181–7
  difference in behavior, 245–7
  ecology of, 92
  land use in, 113
  needs and functions, 247
  occupations in, 270
Community, collective activity in, 244
  collective memory in, 180
  commonality in, 25
  and continuity, 25
  definitions of, 24–7
  and depression, 195
  disaster behavior in, 194
  functions of, 38
  as a "Gemeinde," 24
  order in, 34–5
  as a "personality," 179–80
  and social classes, 210
  and society, 2
  types of behavior, 178–80
Companionship model of family, 243
Competition, family and community, 223
  for urban space, 103, 168
  in work places, 271, 367
Compulsions of organizations, 16
Concentration and movement, 94
Concentric circles and urban layout, 107
Consciousness of community, 181
Consumer spending, Britain, U.S., 337
Consumption ad industrial output, 341
  and social values, 337
Continuity, of change itself, 175
  in communities, 25–34
  of space patterns, 95
Continuum, rural-urban, 6
Contract, evolution of, 223
  and industrial work, 268
Corporate saving and workers, 341

Cosmopolitanism, modern 21
Council of old men, 82
Crises and collective behavior, 193–6
  and community pride, 189
Culture of the folk, 69
Custom and law, 388

Danish rural village, 81
Death rates, of children, 126–7
  by country, 124
  fluctuations in 126
  and life expectancy, 126
Decentralization of cities, 407
  also called "sprawl," 177
  consequences of, 411
  urban and suburban, 173
Deficiencies of urban environment, 412
Delay in facing urban problems, 163
Democracy and the frontier, 15, 138
Dependency ratio, 236, 327
  and the work system, 344
Depressed areas, elites in, 185, 195
Depression and community, 196
Detribalization, defined, 226
Developing countries, bureaucracy in, 262
  economic levels of, 328–9
  elites in, 217–8
  industrial challenges, 342
  industry in, 144
  problems of, 167
Deviants, views about, 395
Dilemma of social participation, 219–21
Disasters defined, 194
  and communities, 195
Disparities between countries, 195
Diversion centers, urban, 40
Diversity of community behavior, 181–7
Division of labor and specialization, 9
Divorce, and occupational groups, 238
  rates, trends, 237
"Domestic package" and family, 334
Dual nature of classes, 207
Dynamics of urbanism, 65
Dynamism of industrial work, 271–3

Ecological aspect of social class, 219
  balance, 89
  method and uses, 108
  order and growth, 106
  patterns and change, 104
  succession, 104
  theory and community, 107
Ecology, and civilization, 89
  plant and animal, 89
  social determinants, 93
  and social morphology, 94
  and sociology, 92
  and "sorting out," 103

Ecology (*cont.*)
  of time and distance, 96
  of urban congestion, 99
Economic growth, stages of, 346
Economic worth, and the family, 334–6
  and the individual, 334
  and the rights involved, 334
Economy of urban growth, 318
Ecuadorean Indians and leisure, 305
Education, and government, 249
  and social order, 377
Elites, in the community, 210
  in depressed regions, 210
  in developing countries, 218
  in modern society, 214–7
  types of, 214
Employers, moral attitudes of, 274
Employment determinants of, 345
Energy consumption by countries, 327
Engineers, and city planning, 405
English rural village, 80
Entertainment, and sport, 3
Entertainment centers, urban, 40
Environment, artificial, 67
  man-made, 12, 89
  and settlement, 88
Environmental planning, national, 405
Environmentalism, geographic, 90
Equilibrium and succession, 104
"Establishment," and the order, 377
Estates, feudal stratification, 203
Ethic, puritan or social, 278
Ethnic areas, Calcutta, 65
Eugenics movement, 131
Evolution of contract, 233
Evolution and progress, 47–8

Fads, nature and utility, 3
Familism, rural, 84
Family, aspects of breakup, 237
  changing structure of, 233–5
  and children, 236
  and civil law, 85
  and community, 222
  companionship model, 244
  diversity among members, 232
  and "domestic package," 334
  and economic worth, 333
  functions of, 230
  and income levels, 325
  and the individual, 14, 223
  institution of, 225
  Japanese, 228, 234
  life cycle of, 240
  and its members, 232
  nuclear, urban, 228
  poor and nonpoor, 326
  religious influence on, 234

Family *(cont.)*
  size and economic worth, 326
  social networks of, 33–4
  and urbanization, 227–30
  and work change, 224
Family planning, India, 130
  Japan, 130
Farm population, changes, 70
Farming as a skill, 87
Fathers and sons, occupations of, 284
Fear, of the city, 65
  of technology, 292
Female migration, Africa, 121
  attitudes toward, 120
  family status, 122
  rural-urban migrants, 120
Fertile land, distribution of, 113
Feudal social system, 204
Fishermen and merchants, 70
Folklore and roads, 136
Folk society and culture, 69
Food, deficiencies of, 113
  and housing costs, 338
  needs in world, 128–9
  supply, and government, 87
  supply, new sources of, 113
  supply, and work, 318
Formal organizations, characteristics, 213
  and law, 387
Formal secondary groups, 16
Freedom and urban life, 394
French-Canadian population, 123
  village, 73
Fringe areas and suburbs, 116
Frontier and farming, 78
  Canadian, 140
  family on the, 84
  and individualism, 15, 139
  and settlement, 143
  theories of the, 139
  and tradition, 142
Frontiersmen, traits of, 143
Full employment and welfare, 367
Functions, of cities, 159
  communities, 38
  the family, 230

Garden City movement, 400
Gemeinschaft as rural life, 191
General and social welfare, 350
Generational mobility, 153, 284
Geography, and environmentalism, 89
  and human ecology, 91
Gesellschaft, as urban life, 190–1
Getting things done, 215
Ghetto in medieval Europe, 170
Government, and bureaucracy, 262
  of critics, 408

Government *(cont.)*
  and food supply, 87
  functions of, 249
  and service for leisure, 314
Great Transformation, 64
Gridiron pattern in cities, 400
Growth and decline of areas, 105
Guilds, medieval decline, 54, 58

Health, and safety services, 256
Heroism in crises, 193
Heterogeneity of urban society, 384
Hill-billies, an area type, 77
Hobos and the frontier, 136
Home ownership, burden of 417
Horses in cities, 168
Housing, industrial urban, 417
  and slums, 418
Human ecology defined, 92
Husbands and working wives, 239

Iceland, Newfoundland compared, 90
Idea of the city, 7
Idea of progress, 47–8
Ideal of the neighborhood, 31
Immigrant areas in cities, 119, 250
Immigrants, assimilation of, 154
  and social mobility, 282
Immigration, induced, 142
Impersonal industrial work, 276
Implications of beauty and order, 398
Income, and birth rates, 124
  and city size, 322–4
  inequalities of, 324–6
  as measure of poverty, 330
  rural levels of, 85
Indians and Ladinos, 76
Indian village, change in, 72, 74
  resettled, 183
Incongruities, urban, 156–76
Individual, and family, 14, 213, 223
  social networks of 33
Individualism and frontier, 138
Industrial city, dilemma of, 251
Industrial efficiency, risks, 359
Industrial order, new countries, 379
Industrial Revolution, 62
Industrial work, and class, 207
  competitive, 272
  dynamism of, 271
  and the family, 267
  and rural culture, 265
Industrial worker and security, 332
Industrialism, global, 4
  and urbanism, 62, 111
Industrialization, permeating, 139, 227
Industry, as changer of work, 265
  distribution of, 113

Industry (*cont.*)
  and social order, 378
  and urbanization, 227
Inequality of incomes, 324–6
Innovation and mobility, 141
Institutional family, 242
Intellectuals as elites, 218
  as elite leaders, 386
Interaction, rural-urban, 22
Interdependence, and class system, 345
  of communities, 174
  of work system, 95, 344
Internalized norms and control, 374
Inventions and cities, 59, 142
"Isolates" and "community actors," 263

Job-hunt, methods, 358
Jobs, growing demand for, 111
  opportunities for women, 238

"Keep-busy cult," 304
Key leaders in cities, 391
Kipling, views on Chicago, 187

Labor force, marginal groups in, 286–9
Labor market for women, 129, 288
Ladinos and Indians, 76
Land, attitudes toward, 78
  areas and resources, 112
Land use, economy of, 93
  and leisure, 312–3, 315
  pattern in Calcutta, 100
  pattern in Paris, 107
  values, ecological, 92
Law, and customs, 388
  and other institutions, 388
  ultimate control agent, 387–9
"Laws" of migration to cities, 146
Leaders, characteristics of, 216
Leadership and authority, 39
  in communities, 390
  political, 176–8
Learning process in society, 377
Leisure, and class competition, 316
  commercialization of, 306
  and consumer spending, 314
  definitions of, 296–7
  and double standard, 305
  and education, 316
  and fear of, 294
  and government, 314, 317
  increase of, 293
  interdependence with work, 344
  and land use, 312
  and metal workers, 307
  moral implications of, 303–5
  separation from work, 301
  and social status, 306

Leisure (*cont.*)
  trends and prospects, 316
  uses of, social, 305
Leisure time and occupation, 308
  how used, 307–8
Life cycle of the family, 240
Life expectancy, at birth, 125
  changes in, 125
  and death rates, 126
  year 2000, estimates, 129
Life span and earning cycle, 332–4
Life outlook and leisure, 306
Lord of the Manor, 81
Loyalties of urbanities, 191

Machines and urban man, 10–11
Malthus, theory of population, 112
Man and his environment, 88
Man-made environment, 12
  and succession, 105
Man's identity and work, 269–70
Marginal man, position of, 385
  social status of, 384–7
Marginal groups in labor force, 386–91
  elderly persons, 290
  women, 288
  younger persons, 286
Market rivalry of towns, 198
Markets and services, urban, 40
Marriage and divorce, Britain, 229
Married children and parents, 241
Married women in labor force, 289
Mass behavior problems, 370
Mass media and social control, 392
Mass society, control of, 35
Measure of time uses, 302
Measurement of leisure satisfaction, 307
Mechanization of agriculture, 129
Medical care, apparent trends, 366
  and imperative, 264–6
  and the poor, 364
  resistance to, 365
Medieval cities, management of, 51
"Melting pots," cities as, 119
Memberships in social groups, 202
Merchants, and medieval guilds, 58
  become nobility, 58
  and urban change, 56–7
Metropolis, statistical areas, 115
  transportation control, 410
  as world city, 3–4
Migrants, rural to urban, 65, 152
Migration, and industry, 118
  knights and merchants, 135
  and labor force, 138–40
  "laws" of, 146
  rural and urban, 45
  by sex, 120, 145

Mining communities, 145
Mining hazards, case of, 185
Mining town, deaths in, 127
Mobility, and cccommodation, 155
  and "circulation," 148
  definitions of, 133
  effects on the city, 120
  generational, 153
  and "innate" urges, 135–6
  and innovation, 141
  and labor supply, 144
  male and female, 146
  in new nations, 144
  occupational, 153
  and roads, 133
  and urbanism, 11–12, 118
Modern city, characteristics, 60
Modern society and elites, 214–7
Modus vivendi of social control, 372
Money economy, 19, 69
Monuments and local pride, 189
Mormons, and church control, 382
  community resettles, 182
Movement and concentration, 94
Moving about in the city, 409
Municipal government, changes in, 250
Municipal models of government, 252

"N Achievement" and risk-taking, 357
National economics and leisure, 312
Needs, changing nature of, 351
  social and individual, 351
Neglect of public services, 254
Neighborhood, ideal of, 30, 220
Networks and the community, 3, 29
Newcomers to cities, 111
New nations, mobility in, 144
News and communication, 3
Noblesse oblige, feudal, 80
Norms and social change, 373

Occupational hierarchy, 209
  mobility, 281
Occupations, and class, 208, 279–81
  and communities, 270
  and divorce rates, 235
  evolution of, 9
  and leisure time, 308
  mobility in, 284–6
  rating of, 280
Old age and the labor market, 290
Oldermand, village council, 81
One-generation family, 232, 241
One-industry towns, 271
Order, in the community, 34, 166
  in government work, 259
  in participation, 218

Organizations, and class, 210
  compulsions of, 16
  definition of, 211
  formal, 213–4
  and memberships, 203
Organized groups in communities, 211
Origin of the village, 84

Parent-child relations, 232
Paris, land-use pattern of, 107
Parks, the evolution of, 255
"Partial views of man," 373
Participation in community, 263
Patterns of urban growth, 106
Peasants, German medieval, 75
  passing of, 73
  self-abasement of, 37
Persistence of poverty, 330
Personal relations and work, 276
Personality of the city, 7
Personality and work, 277
Personification of the community, 179
Philanthropy, views regarding, 351
Philosophers, evaluate cities, 159
"Plainville," neighboring in, 31
Planned American communities, 399
  and the authorities, 402
  and the engineers, 405
  and the environment, 397
  government involvement in, 397
  potential, 412
  and the metropolis, 399
  and slum removal, 400
  and urban beauty, 420
  and urban politics, 419
Plebeians, rise of, 50
Pluralism, and government, 390
  in communities, 215
Police, their social utility, 388
Political change in society, 378
Political groups and classes, 211
Political literacy, rural, 79
Politics and urban planning, 420
Pollution, air and water, 163
  and the cities, 403
Poor, acchievement motivation of, 358
Popular vigilance and citizenship, 263
Population, agricultural, 114
  distribution, urban, 114
  and the human condition, 128
  increase in cities, 110
  and rural change, 85
  selection and control, 130
  uneven distribution, 113
"Possibilism" and geography, 90
Poverty, and ability to save, 338
  and depression, 330
  and industrialization, 347

Poverty *(cont.)*
  numbers included, 358
  and poverty culture, 331
  and poverty line, 331
  relative conception, of, 330
Poverty cycle, as a concept, 333
Pressure groups against welfare, 364
Pride in the community, 188
Primary groups and social control, 376
  in community life, 212
  and urban environment, 375
Private charity in England, 347
Private organizations as government, 389
Problems due to suburban growth, 409
Problems of the aged 241
Problem towns, examples, 245–7
  Factoryville, affluent neglect, 245
  Minersville, chronic decline, 245
  Newtown, deficient suburb, 247
  River City, contended inertia, 246
Production-consumption relations, 341
Progress, the idea of, 47
  material concept, 18
Prospects for rural life, 85
Proximity and transportation, 103
Public administration, Roman, 52
Public bureaucracy, ancient, 53
Public medicine and health, 369
Public services, and expectations, 253
  and priorities, 258
  and reformers, 256–8
  in rural areas, 253
  urban diversity of, 254
Public versus private services, 256
Public welfare, fears about, 352–4
  and private welfare, 353
  professionalization of, 368
  rural and urban, 360
Public and private work, 262–7
  increasing variety of, 249–51
  for rejected jobless, 367
Puritan ethic and saving, 341
  work attitudes, 274

Radiating urban influence, 41
Railroads and canals, 137
Recreation, cult aspects, 295
  "ulterior motives" for, 298
Reform comes to a city, 162
Reformers, and the community, 256-8
  their social utility, 257
Religion, and birth rates, 125
  and class conflict, 381
  rural antecedents of, 381
  social control factor, 382
Religious influence in the family, 234
Remarriage, trends in, 237
Resettling an Indian village, 183

Residential areas, changing, 101, 149
Resource control and planning, 403
Resources and land areas, 112
Revival of medieval cities, 53
Risks, pooling of, 359
Risk-taking and security, 357
Rival town, its utility, 196
Roads, colonial makeshift, 98
  and distances, 97–8
  ecology of, 96–7
  and the frontier, 137
  in history, 137
  and mobility, 133
Role conflict for working women, 239
Role-playing as interaction, 374
Romanticism and migration, 134
Rome and the "barbarians," 53
Routinization and mobility, 150
Rules and social order, 74–5
Rural antiurbanism, 74–5
  economic handicaps, 360
  environment and control, 86
  family and work, 224
  housewife, 225
  indifference to urbanism, 76
  life and prospects, 85
  moral outlook, 77
  neighborhood, 31
  political power, 79
  regional planning, 413
  security, 359
  traits in cities, 45
  values and norms, 22
  village, colonial, 80
  villages, number 70
  way of thinking, 71
  women and work, 71
  work and technology, 224
Ruralism, in Canada, 23
  changes in, 83
  qualities of, 68
Rural-urban changes, 320
  continuum, 6
  interaction, 21–2
  interdependence, 41
  migration, 128
  sex ratios, 120–1

Safety and health services, 256
Sagala, an ancient city, 49
Saracen pirates, raids by, 55
Satellites of the city, 200
Saving, ability differences, 338
  ambiguity of, 340
Scholars, urban bias of, 71
Science-authority confrontation, 48
Scope of modern planning, 396
Secondary community consciousness, 409

Secondary control, urban, 349
Secondary and primary groups, 212
Secondary society, maladies of, 371
Security and risk-taking, 357
Self-sufficient man and charity, 349
Separation of work and nonwork, 277
Settlements and environments, 88
Sex ratios, urban and rural, 119, 122
"Shanty-town" slums, 101
Silk culture, migration of, 136
Skyscrapers and land use, 99
Slum removal in Lagos, 101
Slums, case against them, 171
   challenges of, 169–71
   characteristics of, 170
   definition of, 169
   in developing cities, 172
   ecology of, 172
   as interstitial areas, 406
   location of, 100
Social change and norms, 373
   and ruralism, 84
Social class, characteristics of, 208
   and community, 210
   definition of, 202
   dual nature of, 207
   ecological aspects of, 219
   and the norms, 373
   as people see it, 208
   and social order, 376–9
   and written records, 393
   and work system, 207
Social control, in cities, 370
   definition of, 372
   and mass media, 392
   and the norms, 373
   and organizations, 387
   and social order, 376–9
   and written records, 393
Social determinants in ecology, 93
Social elites, diversity of, 203
Social expectations and conformity, 383
Social groups, membership in, 202
Social implications of spending, 336
Social insurance, origins of, 356
Social mobility, aspects of, 150
   and class, 151, 203
   and occupations, 281–4
Social morphology and ecology, 94
Social networks, urban, 33
Social order, and control, 376
   as culture, 36
   definition, 377
   implications, 371–3
   methods of, 375
Social organization as order, 36
Social participation, and class, 218
   in suburbs, 220

Social persistence and change, 379
Social rating of occupations, 280
Social security and philanthropy, 351
Social status and occupations, 281
Social stratification systems, 203–6
Social values and class, 207
Social welfare, objections to, 355
   and *quid pro quo,* 351
Social work, functions of, 369
Social workers, professional, 369
Society and community, 2
Socio-economic change, 320
Socio-religious movements, 386
Spanish-American village, 77
Special-interest organizations, 389
Special interests of elites, 216
Specialization and interdependence, 261
Specialized urban areas, 103
Spending, and collective saving, 340
   and consumer behavior, 336
Space patterns of communities, 95
Space uses, control of 346
Status in industrial society, 269
Strangers, and citizens, 50
   early merchants as, 56
   in the metropolis, 27, 190
Subcultures in communities, 179
Suburban movement and community, 220
Suburbs, and central city, 408
   growth of, 115
   and social class, 410
Succession, types of, 104
"Superlative urge," 18
Symbols and communication, 181

Techno-economic determinants, 93
Technological change, 41
Technology, and mechanisms, 11
   and public services, 254
   and rural work, 224
   and urban change, 59
   and waste, 161–2
Tennessee Valley Authority, 260, 402
Territoriality, idea of, 25
Theories of urban form, 107
"Threat" of automation, 291
Time, budget for leisure, 308
   clocked by a machine, 300
   conceptions of, 299
   ecology of, 96
   mechanical, 14
   work and nonwork, 303
Tolerant milieu of cities, 36, 38, 374
Topography and ecology, 92
Town building on the frontier, 134
Town and country planning, 406
Trade routes, medieval, 56

Tradition, challenge of, 167
and industrial work, 266
influence of, 255
and planning, 410–12
theory of, 97
Tribalism as social order, 204
Tribes, characteristics of, 50
Turner's frontier theory, 138
Twin cities, rivalry, 198–9

Unemployment, luxury of, 368
and morale, 195
and poverty, 330
Unemployment insurance as saving, 341
Upward mobility, barriers to, 283
Urban and rural change, 320
Urban and suburban rivalries, 410
Urban adaptability, 16
appearance and reality, 251
beauty and planning, 420
change process, 45–6
change and waste, 161
community life, 220
community and region, 401
control of planning, 413
decentralization, 137
dominant role, 86
drabness aspect, 164
entertainment areas, 102
government growth, 64
government work, 249
housing downgraded, 418
ignorance of rural, 414
incongruities, 156–76
influence in welfare, 356
land uses, ecology of, 92
life and control, 394
life and mobility, 118
links with history, 44
man and machines, 11
markets and roads, 98
milieu and family, 255–7
movement, pattern of, 96
neighborhoods, 32
order and change, 166
planning and prediction, 420
population increase, 111
poverty, complexity of, 360
radiating influence, 41
residential areas, 95
social networks, 29, 33
space, competition for, 102
space and congestion, 167
specialized areas, 103
sphere of influence, 251
transportation problems, 411
utilitarian man, 164
water needs and supply, 411

Urban adaptability (cont.)
way of life, 1
work, evolution of, 58
Urbanism, accomplishments of, 6
cosmopolitan life, 21
dimensions of, 7–8
dynamics of, 65
and guidance, 157
and industrialism, 111
mission of, 160
and mobility, 11–12
and "monumentality," 190
old and new, 60
and vacations, 311
Urbanities, and neighboring, 191
Urbanization, world spread of, 116
Urbanized areas defined, 115
Uses of ecological method, 108
Utility of leisure, 317
Utility of secondary groups, 213
Utopian view of cities, 159

Vacations, and leisure budget, 312
and social position, 311
stereotype trends, 311
Value attitudes and work, 273–5
Vejen, a Danish village, 82
Views on urban form, 108, 166
Village, definition of, 5
evolution of, 84
government of, 80
tradition-oriented, 71
Villages, number of, 117

Waldenses, case of, 193
Walded cities and technology, 219
"War on Poverty," views on, 352
Waste of community resources, 162
Waste in problem solving, 163
Water needs of cities, 411
Water transportation problems, 137
Way of life, urban, 1–2
Welfare, attitudes in Old World, 354–7
benefits, distribution of, 263
changing views about, 346
contrasted with charity, 349
and full employment, 366
and the ideologies, 354
in preindustrial society, 352
private and public, 353
a public service, 359
and self-respect, 349
social and general, 350
"Welfare State," fears about, 352
Women, changing position of, 238
changing work roles, 228
as factory workers, 272

Women (*cont.*)
  and job opportunities, 238
  married and working, 289
  status in Britain, 229
  workers in Portugal, 225
Work, and food supply, 318
  and man's identity, 269
  new dimensions of, 266
  and nonwork time, 300–3
  organization and bureaucracy, 261
  and the "permanent poor," 345
  and personal expression, 277
  and puritan attitudes, 274

Work (*cont.*)
  and social class, 207
Work day, the shortening of, 294
Work expectations, rural, urban, 267
Work Projects Administration, 215
Work space in cities, 416
Work system and dependency, 344
Workers as "cogs in a machine," 277
Writing and record keeping, 20
Written records and social control, 393
World food sources, 112
World population, growth of, 110
World urbanization trend, 116